HANDBOOK OF PUBLIC ECONOMICS

VOLUME I

HANDBOOKS IN ECONOMICS

4

Series Editors

KENNETH J. ARROW

MICHAEL D. INTRILIGATOR

NORTH-HOLLAND
AMSTERDAM · NEW YORK · OXFORD

HANDBOOK OF PUBLIC ECONOMICS

VOLUME I

Edited by

ALAN J. AUERBACH
University of Pennsylvania

and

MARTIN FELDSTEIN
Harvard University

1985

NORTH-HOLLAND
AMSTERDAM · NEW YORK · OXFORD

ISBN North-Holland for this volume 0 444 87612 x
ISBN North-Holland for the set 0 444 87667 7

Publishers
ELSEVIER SCIENCE PUBLISHERS B.V.
P.O. BOX 1991
1000 BZ AMSTERDAM
THE NETHERLANDS

Sole distributors for the U.S.A. and Canada
ELSEVIER SCIENCE PUBLISHING COMPANY, INC.
52 VANDERBILT AVENUE
NEW YORK, NY 10017, USA

PRINTED IN THE NETHERLANDS

INTRODUCTION TO THE SERIES

The aim of the *Handbooks in Economics* series is to produce Handbooks for various branches of economics, each of which is a definitive source, reference, and teaching supplement for use by professional researchers and advanced graduate students. Each Handbook provides self-contained surveys of the current state of a branch of economics in the form of chapters prepared by leading specialists on various aspects of this branch of economics. These surveys summarize not only received results but also newer developments, from recent journal articles and discussion papers. Some original material is also included, but the main goal is to provide comprehensive and accessible surveys. The Handbooks are intended to provide not only useful reference volumes for professional collections but also possible supplementary readings for advanced courses for graduate students in economics.

CONTENTS OF THE HANDBOOK

VOLUME I

VOLUME II

CONTENTS OF VOLUME I

Chapter 6

Tax Policy in Open Economies

EDITORS' INTRODUCTION

The field of Public Economics has been changing rapidly in recent years, and the seventeen chapters contained in this Handbook survey many of the new developments. As a field, Public Economics is defined by its objectives rather than its techniques, and much of what is new is the application of modern methods of economic theory and econometrics to problems that have been addressed by economists for over two hundred years. More generally, the discussion of public finance issues also involves elements of political science, finance and philosophy. These connections are evident in several of the chapters that follow.

Public Economics is the positive and normative study of government's effect on the economy. We attempt to explain why government behaves as it does, how its behavior influences the behavior of private firms and households, and what the welfare effects of such changes in behavior are. Following Musgrave (1959) one may imagine three purposes for government intervention in the economy: *allocation*, when market failure causes the private outcome to be Pareto inefficient, *distribution*, when the private market outcome leaves some individuals with unacceptably low shares in the fruits of the economy, and *stabilization*, when the private market outcome leaves some of the economy's resources underutilized. The recent trend in economic research has tended to emphasize the character of stabilization problems as problems of allocation in the labor market. The effects that government intervention can have on the allocation and distribution of an economy's resources are described in terms of efficiency and incidence effects. These are the primary measures used to evaluate the welfare effects of government policy.

The first chapter in this volume, by Richard Musgrave, presents an historical development of these and other concepts in Public Finance, dating from Adam Smith's discussion in *The Wealth of Nations* of the role of government and the principles by which taxes should be set. The remaining chapters in the Handbook examine different areas of current research in Public Economics.

Analyses of the efficiency and incidence of taxation, developed in Musgrave's chapter, are treated separately in Alan Auerbach's chapter in the first volume and Laurence Kotlikoff's and Lawrence Summers' chapter in the second volume, respectively. Auerbach surveys the literature on excess burden and optimal taxation, while Kotlikoff and Summers discuss various theoretical and empirical approaches that have been used to measure the distributional effects of government tax and expenditure policies.

These general analyses of the effects of taxation form a basis for the consideration of tax policies in particular markets or environments, as is contained in the chapters by Jerry Hausman, Agnar Sandmo, Avinash Dixit, Harvey Rosen, John Helliwell and Terry Heaps, Mervyn King and Joseph Stiglitz.

Hausman discusses the effects of taxation on labor supply, including a treatment of how one empirically estimates such effects in the presence of tax and transfer programs. He also considers the incentive effects of social welfare programs such as unemployment compensation and social security. Sandmo focuses on the other major factor in production, capital, dealing with theory and evidence about the effects of taxation on private and social saving and risk-taking. Dixit shows how the basic results about the effects of taxation may be extended to the trade sector of the economy, casting results from the parallel trade literature in terms more familiar to students of Public Finance. Rosen's chapter brings out the characteristics of housing that make it worthy of special consideration. He considers the special econometric problems involved in estimating the response of housing demand and supply to government incentives. Because of its importance in most family budgets and its relatively low income elasticity of demand, housing has been seen as a suitable vehicle for government programs to help the poor, and Rosen discusses the efficiency and incidence effects of such programs. Helliwell and Heaps consider the effects of taxation on output paths and factor mixes in a number of natural resource industries. By comparing their results for different industries, they expose the effects that technological differences have on the impact of government policies. King discusses the impact of taxation on financial and investment decisions of corporations, while Stiglitz treats the literature on income and wealth taxation.

The remaining chapters in the Handbook may be classified as being on the "expenditure" side rather than the "tax" side of Public Finance, though this distinction is probably too sharp to be accurate. In Volume I, Dieter Bös surveys the literature on public sector pricing, which is closely related both to the optimal taxation discussion in Auerbach's chapter and Robert Inman's consideration, in Volume II, of models of voting and government behavior. The question of voting and, more generally, public choice mechanisms, is treated by Jean-Jacques Laffont in his chapter.

The chapters by William Oakland and Daniel Rubinfeld focus on the provision of "public" goods, i.e., goods with sufficiently increasing returns to scale or lack of excludability that government provision is the normal mode. Oakland considers the optimality conditions for the provision of goods that fall between Samuelson's (1954) "pure" public goods and the private goods provided efficiently by private markets. Rubinfeld surveys the literature on a special class of such goods: local public goods. Since the work of Tiebout (1956), much research has been devoted to the question of whether localities can provide efficient levels of public goods.

The other two chapters in Volume II also deal with problems of public expenditures. Anthony Atkinson considers the effects of the range of social welfare programs common in Western societies aimed at improving the economic standing of the poor. Some of these policies are touched on in the chapters by Hausman and Rosen, but the coexistence of many different programs itself leads to effects that cannot be recognized by examining such programs seriatim. Jean Drèze and Nicholas Stern present a unified treatment of the techniques of cost benefit analysis, with applications to the problems of developing countries.

References

Musgrave, R.A., 1959, The theory of public finance (McGraw-Hill, New York).

Samuelson, P.A., 1954, The pure theory of public expenditures, Review of Economics and Statistics 36, 387–389.

Tiebout, C.M., 1956, A pure theory of local expenditures, Journal of Political Economy 94, 416–424.

Chapter 1

A BRIEF HISTORY OF FISCAL DOCTRINE

R.A. MUSGRAVE

Harvard University, Emiritus, Cambridge, MA
University of California, Santa Cruz, CA

1. Introduction

There are many ways in which a history of ideas may be written. One is a strict chronological accounting, moving from year to year and encompassing the entire subject. Another is to proceed on an author by author basis, focussing on what the main contributors had to say. Then there is the option to select major themes and to see how they evolved, thus taking a number of runs down (or up) the time-path of doctrinal development. I have chosen the latter option as most appropriate to accommodate the wide range of issues to be covered in a history of the fiscal theory. They are here arranged in five essays, dealing with the theory of public expenditures (Section 2), equity in taxation (Section 3), efficiency in taxation (Section 4), shifting and incidence (Section 5), and macro aspects of fiscal policy (Section 6). Hopefully, this arrangement will set forth both the internal structure of fiscal doctrine and its historical development. But beyond this, there is no single or correct view of intellectual history. Such a history, in both selection and arrangement, is bound to reflect the perspective of the time in which it was written, as well as that of the author in whose prism past events are collected.

The history of fiscal doctrine, perhaps more than that of any other aspect of economics, carries a particular fascination. On the one hand, it reflects the advance of analytical economics, an enrichment of the tool box, to use Joan Robinson's terms, which may then be applied to the solution of fiscal problems. As we shall see, the key fiscal tools were in fact forged by a line of great general theorists, not fiscal specialists. This line ranges from Smith over Ricardo, Mill, Depuit, Edgeworth, Wicksell, Pigou, and Keynes to Samuelson. The close linkages between general and fiscal theory is most evident for the analysis of tax incidence, which at each stage reflects the prevailing theory of price and distribution. The analysis of tax equity was affected profoundly by the growth of utility theory. The rise of Paretian welfare economics permitted the modern analysis of social goods. The advent of Keynesian economics placed the role of budget policy in a new perspective, and so forth.

Handbook of Public Economics, vol. I, edited by A.J. Auerbach and M. Feldstein

But there is more to a history of fiscal doctrine than the tools of economic analysis. This history also responds to changing economic and social institutions. With the decline of feudalism, the property income of the Crown had to be replaced by taxation; and as the rise of modern legal and financial institutions came to be reflected in the tax structure, the complexity of tax structure analysis increased vastly. The growth of popular democracy, in turn, altered what is viewed as the appropriate range of governmental functions, with budget policy replacing the barricades as the area of struggle among group and class interests.

Changing social philosophies and values, finally, also have their bearing on the development of fiscal doctrine. The displacement of Lockean rules of entitlement by the utilitarian model of Bentham greatly altered the premises of tax justice; and the rise of egalitarian philosophy proved a major factor in the growth and significance of transfer payments. Single-minded economists may find these cross-currents disturbing, but to this observer they add sparkle to what even without them would be an intriguing story.

For reasons of space, but also substance, our analysis begins with Adam Smith and *The Wealth of Nations*. This, to be sure, is not the beginning of fiscal doctrine. The Physiocrats had their theory of taxation and the Cameralists had written explicitly on the administration of public finances. However, Smith offers a convenient point of departure to trace the emergence of modern thought. The major issues are already present and neatly arranged, from the duties of the Prince to provide public services to appropriate ways of raising the necessary revenue. What follows over the next two centuries are variations, if dramatic ones, on his essential theme. At the other end of the scale, we shall carry the story up to the 1960s, leaving off where other chapters in these volumes take over to present the current doctrine. Given our space constraint, our treatment has to be selective, both as to issues and authors. It is hoped, however, that the reader will be encouraged to pursue matters further on his own account.[1]

2. Public goods

The core of fiscal theory addresses the question of what public services should be provided by the public sector, and how much. Our first task, therefore, is to examine how this question has been addressed as fiscal theory developed. Not surprisingly, it is here and in matters of tax equity that approaches have differed most widely, in contrast to the theory of incidence which does, and the newer role of fiscal policy which should, offer a more uniform body of thought.

[1]Among histories of fiscal doctrine, see Seligman (1908, 1909), Myrdal (1929), Mann (1937), and Groves (1974). For selected readings, see Musgrave and Peacock, eds. (1958), and Musgrave and Shoup, eds. (1959).

2.1. The duties of the sovereign

The operation of the public sector, as developed by the classical economists, is seen in the context of a natural order which calls for reliance on and non-interference with the market. Public provision and taxation for its finance is called for only where exceptional circumstances demand it. A definition of these circumstances is attempted, but the tools for precise analysis were still lacking. An essential feature of the classical approach, still widely followed, is that the economics of expenditures and taxation are pursued as separate issues: while benefit taxation was viewed as the ideal, the bulk of tax revenue and hence tax analysis had to be examined in a context of ability to pay, with the required total set from the expenditure side.

2.1.1. Adam Smith

Adam Smith, in concluding his critique of mercantilist policy, sets out the "obvious and simple system of natural liberty that will establish itself of its own accord" once governmental restraints are withdrawn [Smith (1776, vol. II, p. 184)]. The prince, therefore, is "discharged from any duty of superintending the industry of private people". But the system of natural liberty still needs the prince. It requires him to perform three duties, "duties of great importance indeed, but plain and intelligible to common understandings". These duties are, first, to protect society against invasion from abroad; second, to protect every member of society from the injustice of every other member; and third, to provide certain institutions and public works. Having staked out these three functions, Smith examines each in detail. Interesting and cogent observations are offered on how these functions have grown and how they should be conducted, but the core issue of why they must be undertaken by the prince (read public sector) remains unsolved.

The discussion begins with defense. As the art of defense becomes more complex, self-protection becomes impossible and even reliance on a militia inadequate. Efficient defense, based on the division of labor, calls for a professional and standing army. But Smith does not go beyond this to question why this army must be maintained by the prince rather than by private providers. Next, Smith shows how the administration of justice is needed to safeguard life, limb, and property against internal offense. The more property there is, so he argues, the more inequality there will be, and the more costly will the protection of property become. Yet, its provision is essential to the functioning of the market system.

Smith then examines how justice should be administered to assure impartiality, and how its finance may be secured without burdening general revenue. Once more he does not address why the administration of justice must be public rather than private. Perhaps no special explanation seemed needed to justify the public conduct of defense and justice. Though a proponent of the market, Smith was not an unbounded libertarian. He did not believe that civil society could be based on market forces only. Natural liberty requires a framework of security and legal rules, and government is needed to provide it. Smith's view of the world may be read between the lines of the *Wealth of Nations*, but is developed in detail in his earlier work, *The Theory of Moral Sentiments* (1759). It is in this earlier work that Smith the moral philosopher presents an extremely complex and subtle structure of human interaction. Comprising a multiplicity of forces and motivations, individuals guided by the invisible hand are led to interact so as to produce a socially desirable outcome. In this interaction, benevolence as well as self-interest has an important role to play.

Turning to the expense for education, both university and elementary education are considered. The finance of university education is examined in its bearing on the quality of teaching, with scathing comments on how public financing and endowment lead to laziness and abuse once faculty is paid without relation to services rendered to their students [Smith (1776, vol. II, p. 249)]. Major concern, however, is with elementary education. Here public support is needed because division of labor, as it progresses, leads to monotonous and simple tasks, a specialized dexterity which is "acquired at the expense of the intellectual, social, and martial virtues" of the laboring population [Smith (1776, vol. II, p. 267)]. For moral as well as economic and military reasons, government must take some pain to prevent this process, and this calls for public provision of elementary education. Implicit in the argument is that education involves externalities, but once more the criteria of publicness is not addressed in explicit form.

The need to do so arises only when Smith turns to the provision of public works. Here a criteria had to be established to determine just which public works government should undertake. Such a criteria is offered in a preamble to the section on public works [Smith (1776, vol. II, p. 539)]:

> "The third and last duty of the commonwealth is that of erecting and maintaining those public institutions and those public works which, though they may be in the highest degree advantageous to a great society, are, however, of such a nature that the profit could never repay the expense to any individual or small number of individuals, and which it therefore cannot be expected that any individual or small number of individuals should erect or maintain."

As is evident from this passage, Smith recognized that market failure occurs in the provision of certain goods, goods which it does not repay the individual to provide. But we are not told just why this is the case. Nor do we receive an explanation in the more detailed discussion that follows, much of which focuses on how finance can be arranged by fees, so as not to burden general revenue. We thus have to rely largely on the preamble. Much can be read into it, including the key concepts of joint consumption, externalities, and free-rider behavior which enter the modern view of social goods. But none of these are made explicit, so that it would be unduly generous to attribute them to Adam Smith. Nevertheless, his passage is not hostile and indeed amenable to these later developments. It contains the important premise that there exist certain functions which for *objective* (not ideological) reasons need be provided for by the public sector.

Unfortunately, however, Smith appears to have overlooked a strikingly insightful passage in Hume's *Treatise of Human Nature* (1739), a treatise which had appeared over 30 years prior to the *Wealth of Nations*. Hume describes how two neighbors might agree to drain a meadow but how a thousand persons cannot reach such agreement, as each will try to lay the whole burden on others. Political society overcomes this difficulty by reliance on magistrates whose interest it is to reflect the interests of [Hume (1739, p. 539)]:

> "any considerable part of their subjects ... Thus bridges are built ... by the care of the government which tho' compos'd of men subject to all human infirmities, becomes, by one of the finest and most subtle inventions possible, a composition, which is, in some measure, exempted from all these infirmities."

Here, as in other instances, an idea running ahead of its time finds no response until the situation is ripe, and then springs up at once in many places.

2.1.2. David Ricardo

Leaving Adam Smith, it is disappointing to find that nothing is to be said in this context about Ricardo. Although his concern with the affairs of the government was paramount, he dealt with the effects of taxation on the private sector only. There is nothing to be found on public expenditures in his treatise, except his approving quotation of the "golden maxim" of J.B. Say, "that the very best of all plans of finance is to spend little, and the best of all taxes is that which is least in amount" [Ricardo (1817, p. 159)]. The same view appears in his scathing rejection of Owen's proposal for workhouse reform [Ricardo (*Collected Works*, vol. VIII, p. 46)].

2.1.3. John Stuart Mill

John Stuart Mill, our next author, viewed society through a quite different window. Concerned as he was with the works of the early Socialists such as

Fourier, Owen, and Sismondi, he addressed the proper scope of government in detail. Like Smith, he held that "laissez-faire should be the general practice: every departure from it, unless required by some great good, is a certain evil" [Mill (1848, p. 952)]. But also like Smith, he found important instances where a departure is called for. These instances are divided into "ordinary" and "optional" functions. The ordinary functions include above all provision for a legal system which secures life, limb, and property, a security which is prerequisite for the system of laissez-faire. But beyond this, "there is a multitude of cases in which governments, with general approbation, assume powers and execute functions for which no reason can be assigned except the simple one, that they conduce to general convenience". As examples he cites not only coinage and the setting of standard weights, but also paving and lighting of streets, erection of harbors, lighthouses, and dykes. The range of functions seems to be left wide open, limited only by the rule that "interference of government should never be admitted but when the case of expediency is strong" [Mill (1848, p. 800)].

Though sceptical whether a specific principle of demarcation can be developed, he nevertheless tries to set forth the conditions under which the principle of laissez-faire and reliance on individual choice may be interfered with. Three such situations are noted: (1) Individuals may be unable to evaluate the utility of certain products. Thus children may be required to undergo elementary education. (2) Individuals lacking foresight may undertake irrevocable contracts and need to be restrained. (3) Regulations may be needed where individuals delegate decisions to managers, whose interests differ. Regulation of stock companies is thus called for, especially of monopolies in whose profits governments should share.

Coming closer to the economic content of publicness, he addresses "matters in which the interference of law is required, not to overrule the judgment of individuals – but to give effect to that judgment: they being unable to give effect to it except by concert, which concert again cannot be effectual unless it receives validity and sanction from the law" [Mill (1848, p. 963)]. Suppose, so he argues, that it is advantageous to reduce the working day from 10 to 9 hours. The individual worker cannot do so, nor can it be accomplished by agreement among them, as particular individuals will find it convenient to break the agreement. Hence legislation may be required. As a further illustration, he points to colonization. Individual colonies will wish to appropriate as much land as possible, while it would be to the advantage of the colonists to require newcomers initially to work as hired hands (the Wakefield system) so as to permit more intensive cultivation of specific parcels. Mill thus recognizes, implicitly at least, the existence of a prisoner's dilemma and free-rider problem, conditions which require public intervention.

He also notes cases in which "acts done by individuals, though intended solely for their own benefit, involve consequences extending indefinitely beyond them, to interests of the nation or posterity" [Mill (1848, p. 970)]. A case in point is again colonization, which requires regulation in line with the permanent welfare of the nation. The same principle, so he continues, "extends to a variety of cases wherein which important public services are to be performed, while yet there is no individual especially interested in performing them, nor would any adequate remuneration naturally or spontaneously attend their performance". A voyage of exploration might produce benefits of great public value, yet "there is no mode of intercepting the benefit on its way to those who profit by it, in order to levy a toll for the remuneration of its authors". Thus, "no one would build lighthouses from motives of personal interest, unless indemnified and rewarded from a compulsory levy by the state" [Mill (1848, p. 975)]. Mill's explanation why certain goods require public provision thus moves beyond Adam Smith's generalization, but still falls short of precise formulation. Emphasis is on the difficulty of collecting tolls, an argument also advanced subsequently by H. Sidgwick. Indeed, it was not until a hundred years later that the lighthouse problem [Coase (1974)] was placed in its proper perspective, i.e., that fee finance of social goods would be inefficient even if fees could be collected. Nevertheless, both Smith and Mill were aware that the nature of certain goods requires public provision, even though they assigned primacy to the market and flayed the inefficiency of governmental action.

2.2. The public economy

The traditions of British authors, from Adam Smith on, viewed the market as the rule and the public sector as the exception, needed to step in if and where a specific market failure occurs. The tradition of continental and in particular of German authors was to view the economic system in dual terms, with the public sector (Staatswirtschaft) equal in birthright to the private sector (Privatwirtschaft). This difference in emphasis had various roots. British fiscal theory emerged from the background of the Lockean model, a society based on individual entitlements and free exchange, guided by the beneficent rule of an invisible hand. The continental approach emerged from the cameralist teaching which had developed rules for the conduct of public affairs in the enlightened state. Kant's view of the state as limited to its productive function had been superceded by the Hegelian vision of the state as "immaterial capital"; and the Historical School's approach to economics, dominant in the closing decades of the 19th century, invited a view of growing state activity as a natural outcome of the historical process. Moreover, a sympathetic view of the public sector was supported in Germany by the rising concern of academic economists (the so-called pulpit socialists) with matters of social welfare.

Among major contributors to this view of public finances we may note Dietzel, Schäffle, and Wagner. Dietzel (1855) addressed the role of the state as a producer of capital, both fixed and "immaterial", with public credit an important instrument of economic growth. Schäffle (1867) advanced his rule of "proportionate satisfaction" of public and private wants, anticipating Pigou's formulation of the mid-1920s. Wagner (1883), the leading figure of his time, formulated his law of expanding state activity, based on technical factors such as increased density and urbanization, as well as a growing acceptance of social-policy objectives in fiscal affairs. This line of thinking, moreover, exerted considerable influence on American scholars, who at that time tended to do graduate work in continental and particularly German universities. This influence is apparent as one compares the basic American text of Adams (1899) with its British counterpart of Bastable (1892).

2.3. Subjective value and public provision

But though the cameralist tradition of German authors had provided a more open-minded view of the public sector, it did not furnish an economic theory of public goods. Such a theory emerged only after the basis had been laid in the 1880s, when the analysis of subjective utility had grounded value theory on the demand side. This new approach, as developed by Menger and Jevons, was soon to find its application to the budget. Thereby the analysis of public provision was placed into an entirely new perspective. Focus was no longer on the duty of the sovereign, but on the demands of the individual consumer. The public sector appeared no longer as an awkward, albeit necessary, exception to the laws of economics. The same principles of efficient resource use were now to be applied to both the public and the private sphere. Integrated into the general theory of value, public sector economics was legitimized.

2.3.1. Marginal utility

The breakthrough emerged in the late 1880s from the contributions of Austrian and Italian writers, among whom Sax (1883), Panteleoni (1883), Mazzola (1890), and de Viti de Marco (1888) may be noted.[2] While nuances differed, the essence of the new doctrine was this: Given the preferences of individuals, welfare is maximized by having each equate marginal utility with price. This basic efficiency rule applies to both public and private goods. To be sure, there is a difference: In the private good case, goods are sold at a uniform price, with individual consumers equating price and marginal utility by quantity adjustment. In the case

[2] For references to these authors and excerpts translated from their major works, see Musgrave and Peacock, eds. (1958).

of public goods, the critical feature of indivisibility (already vaguely noted by Mill) requires the same quantity to be available to all consumers. Since the marginal utility of the same quantity differs among them, the equating process calls for differential prices to be charged. Thus benefit taxation – greatly broadened from its Hobbesian origin as payment for protection – becomes the "supreme law of the fiscal economy" [Musgrave and Peacock (1958, p. 81)].

With public expenditures linked to consumer evaluation, the basis for the modern theory of public goods was laid. But, not surprisingly, this early formulation had its shortcomings. By framing the efficiency rule in terms of benefit taxation, attention was diverted from specifying just how indivisibility affects efficiency conditions, conditions which may be met with or without benefit finance. It would be over half a century for these conditions to be worked out. Moreover, by focusing on the benefit rule as an analogue to market pricing, attention was diverted from the political, not market, process needed to reach an efficient solution. Not that the Italians were unaware of this problem. Mazzola noted that budgetary decisions are made by agencies, but held that agencies must act so as to satisfy voters, lest political equilibrium be disturbed [Musgrave and Peacock (1958, p. 44)]. De Marco, viewing the income tax as a subscription price, thought it to secure a fair solution. While the analogy to a market solution was central, the concept of a competitive political process was also present.

2.3.2. Knut Wicksell

This was the aspect of the problem which drew Wicksell's attention and solicited his seminal contribution to the theory of public finance [Wicksell (1896), also see Musgrave and Peacock (1958, pp. 72–118)]. Wicksell accepted the new doctrine that provision of public goods should be designed to maximize individual satisfaction, and that the benefit rule would accomplish this. But then two concerns arise.

A first reservation relates to the equity implications of benefit taxation. Justice may be said to be served if consumers pay in line with their marginal evaluation but, so he ads, "it is clear that justice in taxation presupposes justices in the existing distribution of property and income" [Wicksell (1896, p. 143), Musgrave and Peacock (1958. p. 108)]. Wicksell thus views distributive justice as primary but then separates it from justice in taxation as payment for the cost of public services, a separation to which we will return later on.

Notwithstanding this qualified endorsement of the benefit rule, Wicksell did not consider it a realistic option. Indeed, he rejected as "really meaningless" [Musgrave and Peacock (1958, p. 81)] Mazzola's new model. Analogy to the market, so he argued, was inapplicable since individuals would not reveal their preferences without injection of a political process. With large numbers the offer made by any one individual has no significant effect on total supply so that consumers "will pay nothing whatsoever" [Musgrave and Peacock (1958, p. 81)]. Wicksell, as did Hume one hundred and fifty years earlier, thus clearly recognized what later came to be known as the free-rider principle. Impatient with the assumptions of altruistic and omnipotent behavior [Wicksell (1896, p. 90)], the real problem as he saw it was to design a practicable process which will approximate an optimal outcome. Ideally, consumers would be asked to vote on bundles of options combining a complete set of budgets and tax shares, with provision based on that bundle which carries unanimous support [Musgrave and Peacock (1958, p. 92)]. Since this ideal situation is impracticable, Wicksell settles for a rule of approximate unanimity, but stresses the need to protect minority rights. He thus laid the basis for a normative approach to voting models, a problem which has again become a subject of lively discussion in recent years.

2.3.3. The Lindahl price

The story continues with the appearance of Eric Lindahl's doctoral dissertation [Lindahl (1918) written under the auspices of Wicksell].[3] Lindahl visualizes two consumers who must share in the cost of a public good. The more A pays, the less B will have to pay. Given the cost schedule for the product, A's offer curve may thus from B's point of view be translated into a supply curve, and vice versa. The two curves are plotted and their intersection determines the quantity to be supplied. At this solution each pays a tax price (the famous Lindahl price) equal to the value of the marginal utility which he derives, with the sum of the two tax prices adding up to the cost of the product [Musgrave and Peacock (1958, p. 89)].

One wonders how pleased Wicksell was with this formulation of his student. To be sure, the Lindahl price (i.e., benefit taxation) was efficient, but the market analogy inherent in the Lindahl diagram was precisely what Wicksell had objected to most in Mazzola's presentation. While a bargaining solution might be reached in the small number case, it hardly need be the efficient one. More important, the analogy does not extend to the large number case, where preferences are not revealed, reducing the Lindahl schedules to "pseudo demand curves", as referred to later on by Samuelson (1954). Lindahl, of course, was aware of these limitations. He notes that the intersection solution is reached only on the assumption of "equal bargaining power" and, in his later writings, expanded upon the political setting in which the budget determination occurs [Lindahl (1928), Musgrave and Peacock (1958, pp. 214–232)]. Nevertheless, the concept of the Lindahl price and its initial demand–supply presentation has remained his key contribution.

[3] For excerpts, see Musgrave and Peacock (1958).

2.4. Pigouvian externalities

The Austrian and Italian model of fiscal analysis and its Wicksellian interpretation in voting behavior did not enter the purview of English language authors for over half a century. Continuing the classical tradition, an *ad hoc* approach to the delineation of expenditure functions prevailed from Mill to the 1920s. Marshall had little to say on the subject, nor did Jevons apply his marginal analysis to the public sector. Bastable's (1892) *Public Finance*, the major English language treatise, offered little advance over Mill, even in its later edition (1903). Various categories of public expenditures are discussed but little attention is paid to the nature of publicness and its bearing on an efficient solution.

Thus it was not until Pigou's (1920) *Economics of Welfare* that a new perspective was introduced. This perspective emerged from the concept of externalities, central to the Pigouvian distinction between social and private net product [Pigou (1920, ch. 9)]. The private net product measures the internalized costs and benefits which are recorded in market price. The social net product will be larger when further benefits accrue to persons other than those engaged in the sales transaction; and it will be smaller if costs are imposed on third parties, costs which need not be compensated for and hence are not reflected in price. Where social benefits are in excess of private, a bounty need be paid to allow for the addition (external) benefits which are not reflected in market demand. Where social costs exceed private cost, a tax is in order. Thus fiscal instruments become a mechanism of adjusting for externalities, be they of the benefit or cost type.

Where a bounty is appropriate, its magnitude will depend on the spread between private and social product. Thus Pigou notes that a moderate bounty to farming may be suitable if farming yields the "indirect service of developing citizens suitable for military training... A more extreme form of bounty, in which a governmental authority provides *all* the funds required, is given upon such services as the planning of towns, police administration, and, sometimes, the clearing of slum areas." Having advanced this close to providing a criteria for public provision, it is frustrating to find that Pigou does not proceed to do so. Yet the logic of this argument suggests that public provision (i.e., a full bounty based on tax finance) is needed where the private net product is zero and the social net product absorbs the entire value.

Nor did Pigou (1928) offer an explicit linkage between externalities and social goods in his subsequent *Study in Public Finances*. This volume, as we shall see presently, made major contributions on the theory of taxation, but gave only brief attention to the expenditure side of the budget. A distinction is drawn between transfers and exhaustive expenditures leading to a principle of expenditure allocation, similar to Schäffle's (1880) much earlier rule of proportional satisfaction. Within a given budget size, the program mix is to be adjusted so as to balance the marginal benefits derived from various projects; and in determining the size of the budget, the marginal benefits from public outlays are to be equated with those from private outlays. Such would be the simple formula if the community was a unitary being [Pigou (1928, p. 52)]. Since it is not, and since the desire of any one taxpayer to contribute depends on the contribution of others, government, as the agent of its citizens collectively, must exercise coercion upon them individually. This coercion creates indirect costs which must be allowed for. But though the need for coercion is noted, there is no consideration of the mechanism by which it will inform government how individuals value social goods. Pigou, evidently, was still unaware of what had been contributed by the Austrians and Swedes three decades earlier. His contribution, however, was to place the extreme case of "full bounty" into the broader spectrum of externalities, which may differ in degrees and kind, i.e., may range from "mixed" social goods to the polar case of full external benefit.

2.5. *Pareto efficiency with public goods*

It was not until 1939 that the continental discussion of the 1880s and 1890s was brought to the attention of the English (and only English) reading part of the profession [Musgrave (1938)]. Howard Bowen's (1948) vertical addition of demand curves for social goods reinvented Lindahl's earlier formulation, and the breakthrough came with Samuelson's (1954, 1955) two three-page papers on the subject. Carrying a benefit–page ratio without rival, at least in the literature of fiscal theory, these papers met the long-delayed need for a rigorous integration of social goods into the conditions of Pareto efficiency. Thirty years later, his solution may seem evident to the well trained senior, but at the time it offered a giant step forward.

2.5.1. *The Samuelson model*

Addressing the implications of indivisibility and joint consumption for Pareto efficiency, Samuelson assumed that there exists an omniscient referee to whom individual preferences are known. Based on this information, given resources and technology, the referee then determines a set of optimal solutions, each involving a mix of output between private and social goods and a division of the former among consumers. Each solution reflects different positions of welfare for particular consumers with the optimal solution or "bliss point", chosen by application of a social welfare function. The set of efficient solutions meets the condition of equality between the sum of differing marginal rates of substitution in consumption and the rate of transformation in production. It differs from the case of private goods where the marginal rate of substitution is the same for all consumers and equal to the rate of transformation. Social goods are thus amenable to the same (if somewhat altered) principles of efficiency as private goods, to be dealt with as a subcase of the Paretian rule.

How did this formulation relate to the Wicksellian system and its use of benefit taxation as an efficiency rule? The two approaches are similar in that both yield efficient solutions. The Lindahl price, approximated by the Wicksellian voting system, is also among the solutions which meet Samuelson's efficiency conditions. But the approaches differ in dealing with distribution.

For Wicksell, a distribution of money income and charging of tax prices is essential. Preferences must be determined by voting, in line with a pattern of effective demand based on a given distribution of money income. In Samuelson's (1969) model, money income and taxes may be inserted, but they are not needed and only clutter up the problem. Given an omniscent referee whose preferences are known, the referee may proceed directly to the solution. Having determined the set of efficient solutions, he then resolves the distribution problem by applying a social welfare function. Optimal distribution is determined in terms of welfare positions. The Wicksellian model begins as just noted with a distribution of money income; and this distribution must be just to begin with if the voting process is to arrive at tax prices which are "just" as well as efficient. But how can a just distribution of money income be taken as predetermined when the distribution of welfare (which is what matters) depends on relative prices (including those of public goods) as well as on money incomes? The appearance of circular reasoning is resolved, however, once the voting rule is allowed for in determining the distribution of money income, and determination of the voting rule is added as a further equation in the system [Musgrave (1969; 1984, p. 67)]. Multiple policy objectives may then be resolved in an interdependent fashion, including a benefit-tax based allocation branch which provides for social goods, and a tax-transfer based distribution branch which secures the desired distribution of money income [Musgrave (1959, ch. 1)].

2.5.2. Extensions and additions

The modern discussion of budget determination thus involves two traditions, both valid and compatible with each other but addressing different aspects of the problem. The analytical neatness and abstract formulation of Samuelson's model meets the pure spirit of Paretian welfare economics and as such has invited the attention of economic theorists. The greater realism of the Wicksellian approach has offered a more workable stepping stone to the problems of budget policy.

Subsequent work has drawn on both traditions. Among the most important extensions, the following are noted briefly, leaving further discussion to subsequent chapters of this volume where the current state of the art is examined:

(1) Extension of the Samuelson model has focused on examination of non-polar cases, such as benefit spillover and congestion [Oakland (1971, 1972)], as well as on the conditions under which private supply of public goods is feasible [Demsetz (1970)].

(2) The Pigouvian analysis of external effects, and in particular external costs, has become a central aspect of growing concern with pollution and environmental economics [Baumol and Oates (1975)].

(3) Much attention has been given to the analysis of local public goods and the implications of spatial benefit limitation [Tiebout (1956)]. Based on Tiebout's hypothesis of voting by feet, the feasibility of Tiebout equilibria has been examined and tested in empirical work [Oates (1972)]. A theory of fiscal federalism based on a theory of clubs [Buchanan (1965)] was developed.

(4) Empirical research has been directed at estimating expenditure functions for government, based on the hypothesis that the political process approximates the preferences of consumers as expressed by their voting behavior. Utilizing median voter models [Downs (1966)] and cross-section data for state and local government, such research has become a rich area of fiscal analysis [Inman (1978)].

(5) Wicksell's primary concern with the political mechanisms by which fiscal decisions are reached was extended in the context of voting theory [Black (1948)], and a model of democracy viewed in analogy to a political market [Downs (1955)]. Early optimism was dampened by Arrow's demonstration that an unambiguous social welfare function cannot readily be determined [Arrow (1951)], and fiscal issues played a central role in the rapid development of public choice theory [Mueller (1979)].

(6) As distinct from normative considerations, a new direction of fiscal analysis emerged as a positive theory of government behavior [Buchanan and Tullock (1962)]. Critical of public sector growth, the new model centered on the propositions (a) that the voting process is biased towards overexpansion, and (b) that this bias is accentuated by the desire of bureaucrats and politicians to maximize their budgets [Buchanan (1975), Niskanen (1971), Borcherding (1977)]. The role of government is seen not as a servant of majority preferences but as a self-interested actor in its own right. Attention shifted to a theory of "government failure" and resulting need for governmental restraint, countering in Hegelian fashion the earlier concern (underlying Pigouvian externalities and public goods theory) with market failure and the need for remedy by governmental action. This analysis, though very different in content, might be viewed as a resumption of interest in fiscal sociology which, fifty years earlier, had been pursued in the context of Marxist thought [Goldscheid (1917), see also Musgrave and Peacock (1958)].

2.6. *Cost–benefit analysis*

It remains to note a further and more operational approach to the economics of public expenditures. Moving to the forefront of fiscal work in the 1960s cost–benefit analysis was designed to provide a practical basis for evaluating "public works and development projects of a sort for which measures of value can be established empirically" [Eckstein (1961, p. 440)]. This episode thus matched the partial approach of tax theorists who, as we shall see presently, dealt with the tax side of the budget only, while disregarding the expenditure side [Musgrave (1969, p. 103)].

While cost–benefit analysis became the vogue in the 1960s, its beginnings, in important part, date back over a century to the work of Jules Dupuit. Drawn to the problem as an engineer in the Corps des Ponts et Chaussées, he was the first to pursue cost–benefit analysis on a rigorous basis and indeed anticipated the essence of much that was to come later [Dupuit (1844), Vickrey (1968)]. In particular, he developed the concept that benefits are measured by the area under the demand curve, not by what is actually paid. The next major contribution appeared nearly one hundred years later when Hotelling (1938, p. 158) formulated the case for marginal cost pricing: "The efficient way to operate a bridge", so he argued, "is to make it free to the public, so long at least as the use of it does not increase to a state of overcrowding." The common assumption "that every tub must stand on its own bottom" is rejected and the rationale for subsidies to increasing cost industries is given. Beginning in the late thirties, the U.S. government adopted standards for cost–benefit analysis of water projects, and studies of cost effectiveness blossomed in the Department of Defense during World War II.

Beginning with the late fifties, an extensive literature on cost–benefits analysis emerged and became the vogue of the 1960s [Layard (1972)]. Theoretical interest centered on problems such as the choice of an appropriate discount rate, measuring the opportunity cost of capital withdrawal from the private sector and the introduction of shadow prices [Marglin (1963), Harberger (1969), Feldstein (1973)]. By the end of the sixties or early seventies, the major analytical issues had been resolved and cost–benefit analysis had become an important tool of applied fiscal analysis.

3. Equity in taxation

In the preceding section, our focus has been on the development of expenditure theory, a development which in large part proceeded independent of the taxation side of the fiscal process. The classics first examined the obligations of the prince and then turned to tax analysis. With benefit taxation applicable to only a small part of the revenue total, criteria of "good taxation" for most of the revenue had to be developed independent of expenditures. Pigou once more dealt with the expenditure side in terms of externalities, then took up taxation theory as a separate issue. Samuelson's model, to be sure, covered both the uses and sources side of the fiscal picture, but at a level of abstraction which did not involve tax institutions. Thus only the Austrian approach and its Wicksellian extension opted for a simultaneous solution to both sides of the budget equation. Taxation theory similarly developed largely in isolation from the expenditure side. Such was the case with the classics, with the Schanz–Simon approach to income taxation and now replays in the context of optimal taxation theory.

Criteria for "good taxation" found an early statement in Smith's (1776, vol. II, p. 310) famous "maxims". Among them Smith includes equality, certainty, convenience of payment, and economy in collection as most important. Equality or equity in turn was interpreted along two lines, i.e., that contributions should match benefits received, and should also reflect ability to pay. In both camps, there emerged a long debate over whether burden distribution should be proportional or progressive, with the ability doctrine more open to egalitarian interpretation. Moreover, it was necessary to specify an index by which benefit and ability to pay is to be measured.

3.1. The benefit doctrine

The benefit approach to tax equity was congenial to the political philosophers of the enlightenment, such as Hobbes, Grotius, and Locke. With legitimacy vested in the hand of the governed, the contracterian model would call upon them to pay the state for protection received. Under the Lockean concept of entitlement, each person had property in the fruits of his labor [Locke (1690, p. 327)], an entitlement compatible with taxation as payment for services rendered but not with state-taking on other than a quid-pro-quo basis. Smith's (1759) grand design for the human condition, as painted in his earlier work, squarely fitted this pattern.

The first of his famous maxims of taxation states the rule of tax equity as follows [Smith (1776, vol. II, p. 310)]:

> "The subject of every state ought to contribute towards the support of the government, as nearly as possible, in proportion to their respective abilities; that is, in proportion to the revenue which they respectively enjoy under the protection of the state. The expense of government to the individuals of a great nation, is like the expense of management to the joint tenants of a great estate, who are all obliged to contribute in proportion to their respective

interests in the estate. In the observation or neglect of this maxim consists, what is called the equality or inequality of taxation."

While the maxim begins with ability to pay, its thrust is in the direction of a benefit rule. As stated in the bottom line, equality in taxation calls for payment in proportion to one's interest in the public estate. Placing Smith in the benefit camp, while somewhat controversial, also matches his repeated call for fee-finance in the expenditure chapters, including a timely admonition that professors be paid in line with student attendance [Smith (1776, vol. II, p. 249)].

While contribution is to be in proportion to revenue received, Smith then qualifies this in various ways. Most important, he excludes wage income needed for subsistence. A tax on subsistence wages (as we shall see below) would have to be absorbed by higher-income consumers or by landlords. Its imposition would be "absurd and destructive" [Smith (1776, vol. I, p. 350)]. He thus shares the view, frequently held by early advocates of proportional taxation, that a subsistence minimum (then necessarily in the form of wages) should be exempt. A further exemption arises in connection with a tax on house rents. Smith supports such a tax, even though it would in general fall upon the rich, adding "that in this sort of inequality there would perhaps not be anything very unreasonable. It is not very unreasonable that the rich should contribute in proportion to their revenue but something more than in that proportion" [Smith (1776, vol. II, p. 337)]. Smith once more is too wise a man to permit neat classification as an all-out advocate of proportional taxation.

Benefit theorists, however, were far from unanimous in support of any particular pattern of rates. Most of the early contractarians, such as Hobbes and Grotius, supported the proportional view. So did Bentham, subject to the exemption of subsistence wages. Sismondi, Rousseau, and Condorcet, among others, favored progression. Robespierre rejected progression as insulting to the poor, while John Stuart Mill (though rejecting the benefit rule) thought it to call for regression: the poor, so he noted, are most in need of protection and thus would have to pay most [Mill (1921, p. 805)]. The question, who benefits most, it appears, was not easily resolved. [See Seligman (1908, part II, ch. 2).]

In past no less than current controversy, disagreement frequently reflects a difference in the question that is asked; but, unhappily, the question is not readily defined until the problem is resolved. The issue, in the interpretation of the benefit rule, is whether focus is on the cost of the service rendered to a particular person, or whether it is on what a person (given his or her income and preferences) would be willing to pay. In the latter case, the benefit tax as we have seen becomes a Lindahl price; and the issue of progressive taxation then hinges on the income and price elasticities of demand, factors which depend on the particular services in question and cannot be generalized upon for the budget as a whole [Buchanan (1964)]. Others have questioned whether Lindahl pricing meets the spirit of the benefit rule. Thus Myrdal has suggested that benefit taxation should be in line with total (not just marginal) benefit received. Interpreted in this fashion, benefit taxation would still be "efficient" but would yield surplus revenue which would then have to be disposed of in other ways [Myrdal (1953)].

3.2. The ability to pay doctrine

The ability to pay doctrine also claims a long history. As with the benefit doctrine, views on the resulting burden distribution varied. Montesqieu and Say found in favor of progression, while early observers such as Bodin deduced a proportional rate [Seligman (1908, part I, ch. 3)].

The modern doctrine may be said to begin with John Stuart Mill's formulation. Writing in the 1840s, Mill responded to a wholly different philosophical and political setting than had Adam Smith. Representative government had progressed and the accepted functions of the state had broadened. Bentham's utilitarian framework had replaced natural law and the Lockean view of entitlement had given way to a new concept of distributive justice. The case had been made as early as 1802, that welfare from a given income total would be maximized by equal distribution [Bentham (1830)]; and the concept of justice, to quote Mill (1848, p. 805), came to "consist not in limiting but in redressing the inequalities and wrongs of nature". Moreover, "government must be regarded as so preeminently the concern for all, that to determine who is most interested in it is of no real importance". The just pattern of taxation, therefore, is not to be derived from the expenditure side of the budget, but is to be based on a general rule of social justice.

Mill (1948, p. 804) defines equal treatment as follows:

> "For what reason ought equality to be the rule in matters of taxation? For the reason that it ought to be so in all affairs of government. As a government ought to make no distinction of persons or classes in the strength of their claim on it, whatever sacrifices or claims it requires from them should be made to bear as nearly as possible with the same pressure upon all, which it must be observed, is the mode by which least sacrifice is occasioned on the whole ... means equality of sacrifice."

Mill then interpreted equal sacrifice to call for a proportional tax on income above subsistence, in line with Pitt's income tax and its 3 percent rate. Following Bentham, he feared the disincentives of progressive income tax rates but (unlike Bentham) he favored sharp progression in inheritance taxation. While mistaken in equating "equal" with "least total" sacrifice, his concern with the latter anticipated the subsequent shift from equity to efficiency aspects of sacrifice doctrine.

His main contribution was to have posed the problem of equity in terms of equal sacrifice, thus setting the framework for half a century of subsequent discussion.

Nearly fifty years later, the argument was resumed by F.Y. Edgeworth. Edgeworth (1897, p. 101) begins with "the purest, as being the most deductive form of utilitarianism, from which Bentham reasoned down to equality". He then deduces equal marginal or least total sacrifice as the optimal solution, not as a principle of distributive justice but on a game theoretical basis. Edgeworth (1897, p. 103) considers two self-interested parties, contracting in the absence of competition:

> "In this setting, neither party in the long run can expect to obtain the larger share of the total welfare ... Of all principles of distribution which would afford him now a greater now a smaller proportion of the sum-total utility obtainable on each occasion, the principle that the collective utility should be on each occasion a maximum is most likely to afford the greatest utility in the long run to him individually ... The solution to this problem in the abstract is that the richer should be taxed for the benefit of the poorer up to the point at which a complete equality of fortunes is attained."

He does not explain why the individual player should agree to this solution, but intuition might have suggested an argument in line with Hasyani's (1953) maximization of expected utility under the veil of ignorance.

Edgeworth thus not only applied the equal marginal sacrifice rule to distributing the cost of public services but he extended it into a system of transfers resulting in an equal distribution of income. But having thus sighted the "acme of socialism", he finds it "immediately clouded over by doubts and reservations" [Edgeworth (1897, p. 104)]. The detrimental effects of the extreme solution are noted, including reduction in output and, here quoting Mill, threats to personal liberty. Thus "minimum sacrifice, the direct emanation of pure utilitarianism, is the sovereigh principle of taxation; [but] it requires no doubt to be limited in practice" [Edgeworth (1897, p. 106)].

In addition to minimum sacrifice, two other species of the "hedonisti theory of taxation" enter. These are the rules of equal absolute and equal proportional sacrifice, as first explored by the Dutch economist Cohen Stuart [Stuart (1889), Musgrave and Peacock (1958)]. Given Bernoulli's assumption of a unit-elastic marginal utility of income curve, the two rules call for proportional and progressive taxation, respectively. More or less elastic schedules respectively call for progressive and regressive rates for equal absolute sacrifice, with proportional sacrifice not amenable to a simple solution of this sort. Suspecting the decline of utility to be more rapid than Bernoulli suggests, Edgeworth concluded that both rules require progression, but once more we are warned that "other utilities" must be allowed for as well, and that this prohibits rigid application of either sacrifice rule.

Writing as a contemporary of Edgeworth, a generally similar position was taken by Henry Sidgwick. Benefit charges should be applied where possible, but the principle of payment in line with services received is of limited applicability. Where it cannot be applied, the "obviously equitable principle – assuming that the existing distribution of wealth is accepted as just or not unjust – is that equal sacrifice should be imposed on all" [Sidgwick (1883, p. 562)]. He takes this to call for exemption of a minimum income, but hesitates to favor progressive rates as these may become excessive and unduly depress capital formation. But given that concern with capital formation is the reason for limiting progression, a case is made for the exemption of saving and the taxation of luxury goods.

Along with this debate among British economists, the case for progressive taxation was argued by Adolf Wagner, the German fiscal economist noted earlier for his "law of expanding state activity". Also writing toward the close of the nineteenth century, Wagner distinguished between (1) a purely financial and (2) a social welfare principle (sozialpolitisches Prinzip) of taxation. The former calls for proportional taxation in the finance of public services, while leaving the distribution of income unchanged. It is then supplemented by the latter, which calls for progression to reduce income inequality. With the development of modern society, Wagner expected this development to expand and viewed it with less concern than did his English contemporaries [Wagner (1883)].

The discussion of ability to pay then lapsed, but was resumed in Pigou's (1928) *Studies in Public Finance*. Pigou accepted least sacrifice as an absolute principle of taxation, viewing it as counterpart to the general rule that public policy should be directed at maximizing welfare. He explored tax formulae applicable to various equity rules and arrived at conclusions similar to those of Edgeworth. Like Edgeworth, he found no convincing basis on which to choose between equal absolute and equal proportional sacrifice, with preference again given to the equal marginal sacrifice rule.

Conclusions regarding progesssivity, from Edgeworth to Pigou, had been based on the assumptions (1) that utility is comparable across individuals and measurable in cardinal terms, (2) that there exists a known marginal income utility schedule, (3) that this schedule shows marginal utility to decline with income, and (4) is identical for all people. Doubts regarding (3) and (4) had been raised by Edgeworth and Pigou, but the fundamental break with (1) did not come until the 1930s. At that time, the feasibility of inter-personal utility comparison was rejected [Robbins (1932, 1938)], and modern welfare economics was restated in terms of Pareto optimality. A welfare gain could be recorded only if there was an improvement in A's position without worsening that of B or, less demanding, if A's gain was sufficient to permit potential compensation of B. Having thus advanced (or retreated) to the impeccable shores of Pareto efficiency, the rug was pulled out from under the older sacrifice doctrine. The distribution of the tax burden, henceforth, would be a matter of social ethics or politics, but no longer of economics.

But the issue of distribution proved too basic to be excluded from economics forever, and the distribution of the tax burden proved too central a part of Public Finance to be permanently expunged from its books. Distributional considerations soon reentered via a social welfare function [Bergson (1938)]. Assuming the shape of such a function to be agreed upon by society, it was then applied to determine the "bliss point" on the utility frontier [Samuelson (1954)]. It soon reappeared in the use of distributional weights in cost–benefit analysis [Weisbrod (1968)] and more recently in optimal income tax rates. By postulating a welfare function which reflects social value judgment (arrived at by a political process as based on the social preference of individual voters), the disputed premise of cardinal measurement and comparability is avoided. But the heart of the matter, we venture to suggest, was not changed as much as is commonly thought.

In concluding this review of equity doctrines, we note that while the ability to pay view of tax equity does not allow for benefit considerations, ability to pay considerations may enter into the benefit doctrine. They will not do so as long as benefit differentials are viewed in terms of differences in service levels provided to the rich and the poor. Thus, as Adam Smith saw it, the rich should pay more because they have more carriages to protect than the poor. But ability to pay enters onces it is seen that the rich will value the benefit per carriage more highly than do the poor, as reflected in differential Lindahl prices. The later interpretation, and with it a linkage between benefit and ability to pay doctrines, also enters in the Wicksellian context where tax prices are needed for purposes of preference revelation.

3.3. The index of equality

So far we have traced the debate over how taxpayers with differing levels of capacity should be taxed. This leaves open the question of how this capacity should be measured. The answer has to be viewed in historical terms, as it depends on the prevailing economic institutions and objects of taxation which may be taken as representative of ability to pay. The answer also depends on the availability of "tax handles", i.e., objects of taxation which can be reached by fiscal administration. From the Middle Ages to the Elizabethan poor laws, "faculty" had been interpreted as property and this was still the case in early colonial taxation. Specific forms of property, such as cattle, windows, or carriages in turn served as indicies for property at large. There then occurred a gradual shift to a broader view of property; and beyond it, faculty came to be interpreted as income, viewing the tax base in terms of flows rather than stocks. The development of tax bases may thus be seen to reflect the institutional changes which accompanied the rise of modern industrial and financial society. Schumpeter (1918) in particular viewed the rise of the income tax as a corollary to the growth of capitalism and a pecuniary economy. The increasing complexity of economic institutions in turn was reflected in the emerging technical discussion over how the specifics of taxation income should be defined.

3.3.1. The income base

Income, as measure of taxable capacity, dates back to Adam Smith and before. But the concept of the comprehensive income base emerged only slowly. Certain sources of income, it appeared, could not be taxed, even if an attempt were made to do so. Thus the Physiocrats viewed the rent of land as the only feasible tax base, simply because land was considered the only genuine source of income [Quesnay (1760)]. The classics, from Smith to Mill, took a broader view of the income base, but still thought it useless to tax subsistence wages or necessities, as such taxes would have to be passed on to rent or profits. Thus only rent, profits, and income flowing into luxury consumption remained as eligible sources of taxation. With taxation of profits involving undue meddling, causing capital flight [Smith (1776, vol. II, p. 333)], and detrimental to growth [Ricardo (1817, p. 94)], the viable tax sources were reduced to rent and income used for luxury consumption.

The modern idea of a comprehensive and global income tax, as the best index of equality and taxable capacity, only emerged towards the close of the nineteenth century. Intensive discussion of the income concept, especially by German authors, then led to the concept of accretion, first proposed by Georg Schanz (1896) and subsequently introduced into the American literature by Haig (1921). With a person's income defined as the money value of net accretion to his/her economic power, the measurement of taxable income was made tax-specific and distinguished from the concept of income shares in the context of national income accounting. Pioneered by Neumark (1947) in Germany and Simons (1938, 1950) in the United States, the development of a broad-based income tax came to occupy much of the tax literature over the following decades. With accretion as the guiding concept, specific issues of tax base measurement could be dealt with in coherent form, covering such items as the treatment of capital gains independent of realization, the integration of corporate source income into the income tax base, the economic measurement of depreciation, and so forth [Seligman (1914), Vickrey (1947), Pechman (1959), Musgrave (1967), Shoup (1969), Goode (1977)]. The comprehensive income tax base thus became the banner of tax reform in the United States, designed to secure equal treatment of taxpayers with equal income (horizontal equity) as well as to provide a global base on which progressive rates could be assessed in a meaningful fashion (vertical equity). How much impact this movement has had on the actual income tax is a different matter, but it clearly provided the focus of analysis and delight for a generation of tax economists in the United States.

In contrast, British public finance literature was reluctant to embrace the accretion concept. The schedular approach to the income tax was deep-rooted. Ursula Hicks (1947), following J.R. Hicks' analysis in *Value and Capital*, still defined income so as to exclude windfall gains. Similarly, a Royal Commission of the mid-fifties rejected the usefulness of establishing criteria for an income concept, with a minority view in favor of the accretion approach joined by Kaldor (1955). More recently, however, the accretion concept and comprehensive base approach has gained acceptance [Prest (1975), Kay and King (1978)], but with it there emerged an alternative approach to broad-based taxation in the form of consumption.

3.3.2. The consumption base

Though emphasis among tax economists had traditionally been on the income base, the case for consumption as index of equality also claims a long ancestry. Thus, over three centuries ago, Hobbes (1651, p. 386) stated the equity case for the consumption base as follows:

> "Equality of imposition, consisteth rather in the equality of that which is consumed, than of the riches of the person who consumes the same. For what reason is there, that he which laboureth much, and sparing the fruits of his labour, consumeth little should be more charged, than he that living idly, getteth little and spendeth all he gets; seeing the one has no more protection from the Common-wealth, than the other."

Adam Smith, while featuring income in his first maxim, subsequently retreated to rent and luxury consumption as the appropriate bases. Ricardo, bypassing the issue of equity, prevailed against the taxation of income which would be returned to capital. It was thus to left to John Stuart Mill to lay the modern basis for the consumption-base doctrine. Beginning with an income-based view of sacrifice, Mill rejected preferential treatment of temporary as against permanent income, but not all income was to be treated alike. Suppose there are two people with the same income, so he argued. One is a wage earner, has no capital and must save for old age. The other has interest income and need not save as his capital will provide for retirement. The wage earner, so Mill (1848, p. 813) argued, has less left for consumption, and to treat him equally, his savings should be omitted from his tax base:

> "If, indeed, reliance could be placed on the conscience of the contributors, or sufficient security taken for the correctness of their statements by collateral precautions, the proper mode of assessing an income tax would be to tax only that part of income devoted to expenditure, exempting that which is

> saved. For when saved and invested (and all savings, speaking generally, are invested) it thenceforth pays income tax on the interest and profits which it brings, notwithstanding that it has already been taxed on the principal. Unless therefore savings are exempted from income tax, the contributors are twice taxed on what they save, and only once on what they spend... The difference thus created to the disadvantage of prudence and economy is not only impolitic but unjust."

Mill concluded that savings should be exempt if this can be administered without abuse, but was sceptical that this can be done. As a more practical solution, he suggested that "life incomes" be taxed at only three-quarters of the rate applicable to "incomes of inheritance".

While Edgeworth conducted his analysis of sacrifice doctrines in income terms, the case for the consumption base – in theory, if not in practice – was made by distinguished theorists such as Marshall (1927), Fisher (1909), Einaudi (1912), and Pigou (1928). With the exception of Fisher, these authors argued the case in principle, but, like Mill, did not think a personalized tax on consumption to be practicable. The first detailed proposal for practical implementation was made by Fisher (1942) and a second by Kaldor (1955). As the readers of this essay are well aware, the expenditure tax recently moved to the center of the academic tax discussion [Pechman, ed. (1980)]. While its fate in the arena of actual tax policy remains to be seen, the idea of personalized and progressive expenditure tax freed consumption taxation from its previous association with regressive burden distribution, an association which had prevailed as long as consumption taxes were viewed as *in rem* taxes on retail sales.

3.4. Unjust enrichment

Before leaving the topic of tax equity, we briefly return to the income base. This is to note views that certain types of earnings should be singled out for taxation, not because they reflect a higher ability to pay, but because the recipient is not entitled to them. Thus, Aristotle and St. Thomas, while defenders of property, questioned the legitimacy of interest income [Schumpeter (1954, p. 82)]; and though this scruple disappeared later on, there remained a presumption that "earned" income might be given preference over "unearned" income, as indeed has been the case until recently with the earned income exemption under the U.S. income tax.

The main instance of differentiation, however, was with regard to land. This thought goes back to John Locke who, in quoting scripture, distinguished between the fruits of labor to which a worker is entitled and the fruits of land which God gave to man to be held in common [Locke (1698, book 11, ch. 5)]. The same theme was taken up with John Stuart Mill who noted that there were certain exceptions to uniform taxation, "consistent with that equal justice which is the groundwork of the rule" [Mill (1948, p. 817)]. Such is the case with regard to rent from land. The ordinary progress of society increases the income of landlords who have no claim, based on the principle of desert to this accession of riches. Introduction of a penalty tax on prevailing land values, so argued Mill, would do injustice to the present owners; but an extra tax on increments is appropriate, provided they reflect the progress of society rather than the industry of the owner. This discussion was continued by Edgeworth and Marshall who, while agreeing stressed the difficulty of isolating external effects [Edgeworth (1887, p. 216)].

The same theme was continued by Henry George, whose single tax doctrine swept the United States in the 80s and 90s of the last century [George (1880)]. While a staunch defender of private property, George viewed the entitlement to land as held in common. Impressed with rapid gains in land values at his time, he viewed such gains as *the* source of inequality and social injustice. Following Herbert Spencer, his case for a 100 percent tax on the rent of land was more drastic than Mill's as it was to apply to entire land values and not only increments therein. George thus became the founder of the single tax movement, a movement which was subsequently supported by Brown (1918) and still continues in existence. As will be noted below, land as the prime base of taxation was to receive further endorsement on efficiency (as distinct from equity) grounds. As shown in Chapter 8 of this volume, the taxation of natural resources has remained a problem of great interest.

Nor is this the only instance in which selective taxation of certain sources of income has been argued in the name of tax justice. The taxation of wartime profits under an excess profits tax, for instance, has been common practice. While the concepts of accretion and global base have been central to the equity rule, the underlying premise of general entitlement has been subject to certain qualifications. Changing views on tax equity must indeed be understood in the context of philosophical views regarding the nature of property, individual entitlement thereto, and the relationship of the individual to the state. Thus, there is a vast gap between the neo-Lockean view of taxation as "forced labor" [Nozick (1974, p. 169)] and, say, Justice Holmes' view of taxation as the cost of civilization.

4. Efficiency in taxation

But equity is not all there is to the construction of a good tax system: efficiency also matters, and here economic analysis takes over. Adam Smith, in his fourth maxim, counsels that "every tax ought to be so contrived as to take out and to keep out of the pockets of the people as little as possible, over and above what it brings into the public treasury of the state" [Smith (1776, vol. II, p. 311)].

Reference is to the cost of tax administration, obstruction to industry, the burden of penalties, and odious examinations. Taxes should be "as little burdensome to the people" as possible. John Stuart Mill quotes Smith with approval but finds that no elaboration is needed. At one point, Mill (1948, p. 803) almost recognizes that payment of similar amounts under different taxes may impose differential burdens, but then backs away from this conclusion. Edgeworth, as noted before, accepted least total sacrifice as the utilitarian solution, but also warned that the "productional" consequences of taxation may outweigh "distributional" requirements. At some point "the utilitarian must sadly acquiesce in inequality of taxation" [Edgeworth (1897)]. Similar views were expressed by most early contributors to the equal sacrifice debate, although concern with potential loss of output and reduced growth was more serious in some cases [Bastable (1892, p. 311)] than in others [Adams (1899, p. 351)]. However, reference was to loss of output rather than to dead-weight loss.

The modern formulation of efficiency in taxation was anticipated once more by Dupuit (1844). As noted earlier, Dupuit anticipated modern utility theory by exploring the conditions under which a public works project should be undertaken. In the process he developed (or came close to developing) the concept of a demand curve, and measured the net loss from a tax diagrammatically by the triangle which after Marshall became the standard picture of excess burden. Indeed, Dupuit already recognized that the net loss is proportional to the square of the tax base. But Dupuit's insight was far ahead of its time, as was that of Gossen's (1854) early vision of marginal utility analysis.

The concept of consumer surplus reemerged forty years later in the works of the marginal utility theorists such as Wieser, Menger, and Jevons. Jenkin (1871), as noted below, was the first to use demand and supply curves in incidence analysis, and to show how the burden of a tax exceeds the amount of revenue collected. Marshall (1890, book III, ch. 6), during the same period, developed the concept of consumer surplus on his own terms and warned of the underlying assumption of constant marginal utility of income. He then applied the concept to tax analysis. Inquiring whether competitive equilibrium produces maximum welfare, he suggested that welfare may be raised by giving a bounty to decreasing cost industries while taxing those with increasing cost. In a footnote, he added that the "net loss" (now referred to as excess burden, dead-weight loss, or efficiency cost) of a product tax would be larger for the case of a luxury than for a necessity since demand tends to be more elastic [Marshall (1890, p. 467)]. Ever since, the concept of consumer surplus has played a key role in tax economics – first in the evaluation of particular taxes and most recently in the theory of optimal taxation.

Marshall's application of consumer surplus to taxation was by way of illustrating general principles of price theory, as was the case for most of his tax analysis.

The efficiency implications of taxation were given central focus only thirty years later. Pigou (1928, part II, ch. 5), after discussing sacrifice rules as had Edgeworth, proceeded to an explicit analysis of "announcement effects". As a tax is introduced, a taxpayer finds his options changed and adjusts his behavior accordingly. This results in "announcement burdens" or loss of consumer and producer surplus. The announcement burden of the income tax will be larger if a given revenue is drawn from a particular taxpayer under a progressive rate schedule, than if a proportional or regressive schedule applies. But for a given total revenue to be obtained, the use of less progressive rates requires that the taxpayer with lower income be taxed more. It thus remains questionable which schedule has the greater announcement burden for the group. In all, Pigou expects labor supply to be relatively inelastic and concludes that distributional considerations should be given the major weight.

But the principle of least sacrifice calls for the exclusion of saving from the income tax base. Inclusion, so he argued correctly, taxes future consumption at a higher rate than present consumption. This offends the principle of least sacrifice. It does so, so his argument continues somewhat strangely, because saving is the more elastic use of income and should, if anything, be taxed at a lower rate [Pigou (1928, p. 138)]. Efficiency considerations thus call for an expenditure tax. But Pigou holds a progressive expenditure tax unworkable and thus opts for exclusion of investment income as an equivalent solution. To avoid unjust windfalls, this exclusion is limited to earnings from future investment income only, a proviso which anticipates the transition problems in the expenditure tax debate to follow fifty years later [Pechman, ed. (1980)]. Other situations may also arise where announcement considerations call for discrimination against certain sources of income. Thus the unimproved value of land is a prime source of taxation, as there are no announcement effects. And so are unanticipated windfalls. However, once more, care need be taken lest sudden introduction of a high land tax discriminates against old holders.

While allowing for bearing of demand and supply elasticities on announcement effects of product taxes, Pigou (1928, p. 128) was aware of the complexity of the problem and concluded that a "more powerful engine of analysis is needed" to construct an optimal system. This analysis was provided by F.P. Ramsey who, in response to Pigou's inquiry, laid the basis for what has now come to be known as the theory of optimal taxation. Ramsey (1927) demonstrated that "the optimal system of proportionate tax yielding a given revenue will cut down the production of all commodities in equal proportions. Assuming labor supply to be fixed, this will be achieved by uniform proportional taxes; but with labor supply variable, differential *ad valorem* rates will be called for, depending on the elasticities of demand and supply". But differentation between products causes distributional inequities among taxpayers with equal income but different tastes. Given this further conflict between equity (now within the income group) and efficiency, Pigou (1928, p. 132) suggests that progression be applied via the income tax, supported perhaps by some luxury taxation. He thus stresses the importance of taste differentials, a factor destined to be largely neglected by the optimal taxation to follow fifty years later.

While the contributions of Pigou and Ramsey laid the basis for the modern theory of optimal taxation, its current formulation was slow in coming. The first major contribution, following Pigou (but evidently unaware of Pigou's and Ramsey's writing) was that of Hotelling (1938). Departing from Dupuit's work, Hotelling derived the superiority of a lump sum over an excise tax in general equilibrium terms, based on ordinal analysis and without using the concept of consumer surplus. More questionably, he then extended this conclusion to claiming superiority of an income over an excise tax. In subsequent writings, this superiority became accepted doctrine. It remained so until Little (1951) showed that the earlier conclusion had depended crucially on the assumption of fixed labor supply and that, with labor supply variable, no such a priori judgment could be drawn. As recognized later (although not noted by Little), allowance for a variable goods–leisure choice invalidates the a priori case for ranking a general consumption ahead of a general income tax. Focus on the importance of the goods–leisure choice pointed to product complementarity with leisure as key factor in the selection of an efficient tax base [Corlett and Hague (1953)].

With these foundations laid, Harberger (1964) carried the argument beyond theorizing into the empirical measurement of dead-weight losses for particular taxes. Thus the analysis of excess burden was moved to an applied base and has been actively pursued since then. At the theoretical level, it was not until 1971 that the model of optimal taxation, visualized fifty years earlier by Ramsey, was resumed and expanded [Diamond and Merlees (1971)]. As treated in the following chapter, optimal taxation then became the center of tax theoretical work in the 1970s.

5. Shifting and incidence

Economists have for long been aware that there exists a difference between the point at which taxes are imposed (their "statutory" incidence) and the "final" point at which burdens come to rest. The transition or shifting process has been at the center of tax economics from the Physiocrats on. Indeed, the development of incidence theory closely reflects the development of economic theory at large. Developments in the theory of tax incidence have mirrored the advances of price and distribution theory, including both their general and partial equilibrium settings.

5.1. The precursors

The first general equilibrium model was that of the Physiocrats and it also spawned the first well defined incidence theory. But the discussion of incidence dates further back. Hobbes' proposal for a tax on expenses, made in 1651, was based on the premise that such a tax falls on consumers. The growth of excises that was to follow focussed the early debate on such taxes. Leading up to the furor created by Walpole's excise reform of 1733, a wide variety of views emerged. Thomas Mun (1664) argued that taxation of necessities would not only raise their price, but also cause wages to rise accordingly. The final burden would thus fall on the rich. Sir William Petty (1667), in what was the first English treatise on tax theory, held that all excises, even those on necessities, will be borne by consumers. This was the case even for consumers of necessities. For some this was reason to reject such taxes as inequitable; but others (including Petty) thought it to be a virtue. A tax on necessities, so they argued, would reduce laziness, add to output, and in line with the contemporary doctrine favoring low wages, would thus be to the advantage of the British economy. Anticipating Physiocratic doctrine, John Locke (1692) held that all taxes, including excises on necessities, would be borne by the landlord. The landowner cannot shift a tax on land since such a tax does not change the "tenant's bargain and profit". A tax on necessities raises wages and thereby the cost to the farmer who, in turn, is able to pay less rent to the landlord.

There is thus a wide range of early opinion based on diverging views regarding the shape of labor supply, including vertical and backward bending. Moreover, many points featured in later discussion already appear in one or another part of this early debate. These include allowance for how tax revenue is spent, the concept of capitalization, the idea that old taxes are good taxes, and a warning that excessive rates will reduce revenue. However, the views are advanced mostly in ad hoc terms and will not be pursued here. The interested reader is referred to Seligman's (1899, book I) scholarly account.

As noted before, rigorous incidence theory begins with the Physiocratic model of income generation, and its first vision of an equilibrating economic system [Schumpeter (1954, part II, ch. 4)]. According to this model, only land was able to produce a net product [Quesnay (1758)]. Labor could merely produce an output needed to maintain itself; and the capitalist's return, net of compensation for risk, was similarly limited. With land the only factor capable of producing a surplus, it followed that land could be the only lasting source of taxation. Taxation of wages or of products could only lead to economic decline without any lasting revenue gain to the Crown. The sensible way to tax, therefore, was to proceed directly to a tax on land. The Physiocratic model thus led to a warped view of incidence, less realistic indeed than the ad hoc theorizing which had gone before. It is not suprising, therefore, that Turgot, while an ardent proponent of the doctrine, made no attempt to introduce the single tax on land during his tenure in office.

With one extreme leading to its opposite, we may note here the theory of Canard (1801), celebrated at its time, that the search for rents of surplus leads to a diffusion of tax burdens which continues until the burden is shared equally by all participants in the exchange. The burden of taxation, so he held, results from the disturbance caused by this adjustment process and vanishes as the tax comes to rest. Hence, the conclusion that "every old tax is good; every new tax is bad" [Seligman (1899, p. 162)].

5.2. The classics

The system of the classical economists, like that of the Physiocrats, centered on the division of output among factor shares. But the essentially two-factor model of the Physiocrats was now extended to include capital, reflecting the change in perspective from an agricultural to a manufacturing economy. Focus on the return to the three factors not only served as a central analytical tool to explore the laws of value and production, but also dealt with the division of output among the major classes – landlords, capitalists, and workers – which defined the social and economic structure of the times. A view of incidence theory as distribution of the tax burden among these factor shares, therefore, not only fitted the analytical scheme but also provided a political economy of taxation.

In addition to adding the third factor, capital and manufacture, the classical model also broadened the framework of tax analysis by tracing taxation effects through the price adjustment of the market and by drawing a distinction between short- and long-run responses. In this broadened setting, the classics remained true to the Physiocratic tradition of viewing incidence in the context of a truly general equilibrium system. Moreover, the assumption of infinitely elastic labor supply was largely retained, at least in the longer-run context, so that the expanded model still yielded a set of relatively simply solutions.

5.2.1. Adam Smith

The heart of classical incidence analysis is to be found in the work of David Ricardo, but his analysis responded to the pattern developed by Adam Smith. It is thus well to begin with that version as developed in *The Wealth of Nations*

[Smith (1776)]. After presenting his maxims, Smith in a series of chapters offers a detailed discussion of the major taxes, including their incidence.

Not suprisingly, the story begins with a tax on the rent of land. If imposed directly on the landlord, so Smith asserts without further explanation, the tax will be absorbed in rent. The same result obtains if the tax is levied on the tenant. The tenant is charged a rent equal to the amount by which the value of his output exceeds what he needs to maintain himself [Smith (1776, vol. I, p. 145)]. Thus he cannot absorb the tax and deducts it from his rental payment. "The landlord is in all cases the real contributor" [Smith (1776, vol. II, p. 313)]. While arriving at a valid conclusion, the reasoning still rests on a Physiocratic notion of net product, rather than on a view of rent as an intra-marginal return. This is evident when Smith arrives at a faulty result for the tax on agricultural produce. Such taxes, Smith (1776, vol. II, p. 321) asserted, "are in reality taxes upon rent", and like taxes on rent they are eventually paid by the landlord. The essential distinction between a tax on rent and a tax on agricultural produce was not as yet recognized.

A direct tax on the wages on labor, so Smith continues, cannot be borne by the worker. The wage is set by the cost of subsistence and therefore cannot be reduced. If the tax is on the wages of agricultural labor, the farmer (as employer of such labor) must pass it back to the landlord through reduced rent. The outcome is similar to that of a tax on agricultural produce. If the tax is on the wages of manufacturing labor, the manufacturer will add it to price. What happens next depends on whether the taxed labor is engaged in the production of luxury goods or necessities. In the former case, the tax is borne by the consumer. In the latter case, the consumer, already living on a subsistence wage, cannot absorb the tax. Wages must rise and the tax, once more, is passed back to the landlord in the form of reduced rent. Smith (1776, vol. II, p. 357) thus concludes as follows:[4]

> "Taxes upon necessities, so far as they affect the laboring poor, are finally paid, partly by landlords in the diminished rent of their lands, and partly by rich consumers, whether landlords or others, in the advanced price of manufactured goods. [Therefore] the middling and superior ranks of people, if they understand their own interest, ought always to oppose all taxes upon the necessities of life, as well as direct taxes upon the wages of labor."

[4] Smith throughout argues that a tax on wages or products would raise prices "in a higher proportion" than the rate of tax [Smith (1776, vol. II, p. 349)], and thus impose an additional burden on the landlord or rich consumer. One reason is that a tax of 10 percent imposed on the gross wage must raise the gross wage by 11 percent to keep the net wage from falling. True enough, but hardly a reason to conclude that the real burden of the tax is increased. Another reason is that the producer will charge a profit on the funds needed to advance the tax, thus resulting in what is later referred to as "tax spiralling".

Smith notes that the "middling and superior ranks of people" should not only be indifferent between taxes on luxuries and rent, which they pay directly, and taxes upon wages and necessities, which they must absorb indirectly; they should indeed prefer the former. The reason, it appears, is that the latter are taken to raise prices by more than the tax, thereby imposing an additional burden.

The conclusion that wages and necessities cannot be taxed conflicts with Smith's (1776, vol. I, p. 71; vol. II, p. 384) recognition that subsistence may be more or less liberal, depending on whether the demand for labor is increasing, stationary, or declining. Given this range, he might have noted that circumstances may allow for a reduction in the market wage net of tax, on at least a temporary basis. His focus, however, is on the longer run, where the wage returns to its subsistence level. If reduced below that level, population would fall, economic advance would be retarded, and the revenue base would be lost.

Next consider Smith's view of a general tax on profits. Profits or the "return from stock" are divided into compensation for trouble or risk of employing the stock and into interest which belongs to the owner. The former cannot be taxed, as entrepreneurs also seem to have their subsistence wage. The part which reflects interest, however, is likened to rent [Smith (1776, vol. II, p. 331)]. "With the quantity of stock or money in the country, like the quantity of land, being supposed to remain constant, the same after tax as before", Smith (1776, vol. II, p. 352) concludes that interest, like rent, can absorb taxation. The assumption that stock remains constant, however, is qualified by subsequent counsel against its excessive taxation as causing undue inquisition and capital flight.

Taxes which are imposed on profits of particular industries, finally, are passed to the consumer, as capital will be withdrawn until the tax is recovered in higher prices [Smith (1776, vol. II, p. 310)]. Smith thus recognized that returns will be equalized across industries, but he mistakenly interpreted this as burdening the consumer rather than as spreading the tax among all uses of capital.

5.2.2. David Ricardo

We now turn to David Ricardo, the main architect of the classical system of incidence theory.[5] Ricardo's central concern with taxation is evidenced by the very title of his major work, the *Principles of Political Economy and Taxation* (1819). The market, so Ricardo held, does best without interference; but, unhappily, public expenditures are made and taxes are needed to finance them. Thus interference is inevitable: "It is here then that the most perfect knowledge of the science is required." Indeed, "political economy, when the simple principles of it are once understood, is only useful as it directs governments to right measures of taxation" [Ricardo (*Collected Works*, vol. VIII, p. 132)].

[5] For a penetrating discussion of the Ricardian incidence analysis, see Shoup (1960).

All taxes, so Ricardo notes at the outset, are either paid from income or from stock. But government expenditures are "unproductive consumption". They add neither to capital nor provide for advances to labor. Therefore if such expenditures are financed by taxes which fall on revenue, i.e., reduced private consumption, the national capital remains unimpaired; but if such consumption is not reduced, taxes must fall on capital, and eventually distress and ruin follows [Ricardo (*Collected Works*, vol. I, p. 151)]. No neater formulation of the supply side view of the budget could be desired.

Following the pattern laid out by Adam Smith, Ricardo then turns his attention to particular taxes, taking a critical view of earlier doctrine. A *tax on rent*, or a land tax levied in proportion to rent, does not apply to marginal land which yields no rent. Since this is the land on which the price of produce is determined, a tax on rent cannot be reflected in that price and must be borne by the landlord. The conclusion is similar to that of Adam Smith, but the reasoning differs. The Physiocratic view of land as the basic source of income is now replaced by rent as an intra-marginal return which does not affect price.

With this clarification, Ricardo proceeds to correct Adam Smith's conclusion that a *tax on raw produce* is borne by the landlord. By raising the cost of produce at the margin of cultivation, such a tax also raises the price of produce. Hence the tax is not paid by the landlord but by the consumer. Such at least is the case until further adjustments, similar to those of a tax on manufactured products, are allowed for. As noted previously, such a tax, if on necessities, cannot be borne by the consumer.

Ricardo's most intriguing argument applies to a *tax on wages*. As a wages tax is imposed on the worker, nominal wages must rise. This must be the case since labor supply is fixed in the short run and the wage rate is at subsistence. As wages are raised, profits are reduced. Suppose now that as nominal wages rise, the employer comes to recoup his profits by raising prices. This would call for a further rise in wages so as to maintain the real wage at subsistence, generating a further increase in prices, and so forth. Ricardo (*Collected Works*, vol. I, p. 225) rejects this reasoning as "indefensible", as it suggests that the tax is paid by no one. To determine where the tax falls, he views the problem in terms of resource use. If total output is fixed and part thereof is transferred to government, some other use of resources must be cut. But these cuts cannot be in the wages fund. Since government engages in unproductive consumption (consumption which does not add to necessary advances to labor), since labor supply is fixed and since wages are at subsistence, the wages fund (circulating capital) must remain intact.[6] Therefore, the only resource uses that can be cut are consumption by capitalists

[6]Ricardo further notes that the overall demand for labor remains unchanged with the introduction of the tax. While demand based on capitalist consumption and investment falls, increased government demand takes its place. Thus the wage bill net of tax remains constant.

and the stock of fixed capital. Since both are paid for out of profits, this is where the tax must fall.[7] Any attempt to recoup the increase in wages by raising price only requires further wages increases and will not help.

Much the same reasoning applies to a *tax on profits*. Such a tax cannot be recouped in higher prices because this would require an increase in wages, nor can wages be reduced since the wages fund must be kept intact to compensate the fixed labor supply at its subsistence wage. Since "a tax on wages is in fact a tax on profits", so Ricardo (*Collected Works*, vol. I, p. 226) concludes, "I should think it of little importance whether the profits of stock or the wages of labor were taxed." Turning finally to a tax on manufactured products, much depends on whether the product is in the form of necessities or luxuries. A tax on the former must again fall on profits, whereas a tax on the latter can be absorbed in reduced consumption of the well-to-do.

Given the *short-run* context in which labor supply and hence the wage bill in real terms is held fixed, Ricardo thus arrives at these two conclusions: (1) taxes on rent, profits, and luxury products are absorbed by the payee, whereas taxes on wages and necessities are passed on to and borne by profits; and (2) the resource release from the private sector must be either in reduced consumption of landlords and capitalists, or in their reduced contribution to the maintenance or expansion of the fixed capital stock. But the story does not end here. In the *longer-run*, reduced accumulation will result in a decline "in society's demand for labor" [Ricardo (*Collected Works*, vol. I, p. 222)]. As a result, population declines – Ricardo (*Collected Works*, vol. I, p. 218) quotes Malthus with approval – until the wages fund is distributed among fewer workers and the market wage has been returned to its natural level of subsistence. Thus, a new equilibrium is established at a lower level of population. The net real wage rate is restored, rent is reduced, and there is a lower capital stock. Taking the *very long* view, profit taxes hasten the arrival of the stationary state, as the net (after tax) return to capital reaches zero at an earlier point and (returning to the Physiocratic outcome) only rent remains as a taxable income.

[7]Ricardo's argument might be interpreted thusly: Suppose that before tax wages equal \$80 and profits equal \$20. Expenditures on necessities equal \$80 and investment plus capitalists' consumption equal \$20. After a tax of \$10 is introduced, gross wages rise to \$90, net wages remain at \$80, and profits fall to \$10. Expenditures on necessities, equal to net wages, remain at \$80, outlays on capitalists' consumptions and investment fall to \$10, and government outlays rise to \$10. The total remains at \$100 and prices are unchanged.

One wonders what would happen to Ricardo's argument if government outlays were made for "productive consumption". In that case, wages could remain constant, permitting a decline in net wages. There would no longer be a need for the tax to fall on profits! Due to the peculiarity of the Ricardian model (holding the net wage bill fixed in real terms), incidence thus depends directly on how the revenue is used.

This, to be sure, is a simplified version of a highly complex system in which many additional factors are involved. Thus, Ricardo considers how adjustments to a partial tax will differ depending on whether the industry is intensive in fixed or circulating capital, how adjustments to profit and commodity taxes will differ depending on whether the output of precious metals (the monetary standard) is included in the tax base or not, on how the role of trade is affected, and on how government spends the funds. Due to these complications and abundant quarrels with other authors, it is difficult to draw out the core of his argument. Our summary therefore cannot but involve interpolation and interpretation [see also Shoup (1960)].

From the perspective of later analysis, the system is biased by conducting most of the arguments under the assumption of fixed labor supply and subsistence wage, supplemented in the longer run by a Malthusian labor-supply response. Nevertheless, Ricardo offers an impressive structure of micro and macro analysis. Schumpeter (1954, p. 473) may have been uncharitable, therefore, in disposing of the Ricardian model as "an excellent theory that can never be refuted and lacks nothing save sense". Indeed, as we shall see below, it has only been in recent years that incidence analysis on a Ricardian scale has been resumed in the context of neo-classical growth models.

5.3. The marginalists

Adam Smith and Ricardo, of course, were not the only classical economists who wrote on the incidence of taxation. Others to be noted in a more detailed accounting include McCulloch (1845) who stressed the "reproductive effect of taxation", and Mill (1849) who restated the Ricardian position in a more flexible fashion and extended its application to international trade. However, the essential theme has been given with Adam Smith and Ricardo, so that we may proceed directly to the next stage, i.e., the rise of marginalism and the modern view of factor pricing.[8]

The revolution in economic analysis which occurred in the closing decades of the 19th century began with the recognition of utility as a determinant of value. Value was no longer derived from input of labor but from utility in use; and demand, based on relative utilities, was assigned a stragetic role in setting relative product prices. This advance was followed by application of marginal analysis to factor pricing and the theory of distribution. The return to labor was no longer determined by a subsistence wage and the Malthusian mechanism of adjustment was dropped. The rule of capital as a factor of production, dealt with ambigu-

[8] For a review of this development, see Stigler (1941).

ously by the classics, was given specific content. The return to capital and saving was now seen as compensation for contribution to increased productivity via round-aboutness in production. The pricing of all factors in line with their marginal product thus became subject to one and the same principle of compensation. "The theories of the values of labor and of the things made by it", as Marshall (1890) put it in the introduction to his *Principles of Economics*, "cannot be separated: they are parts of one great whole; and what differences there are between them even in matters of details, turn out on inquiry to be, for the most part, differences of degree rather than of kind." The new model was bound to revolutionize incidence doctrine, just as the classical formulation had superceded that of the Physiocrats.

5.3.1. Fleming Jenkin

A first and striking contribution was made by Jenkin (1871); see also Musgrave and Shoup, eds. (1959). Drawing on Jevons' presentation of marginal utility curves to show gains from trade, Jenkin interpreted these as offer curves in relation to price. He was thus the first to have viewed incidence analysis in terms of supply and demand curves, with taxes resulting in shifts therein. He then uses this newly found apparatus to show how the burden of a unit tax is divided between buyers and sellers, and how the injury to each exceeds the tax paid. The total loss for each then depends on the slopes of the demand and supply curves. The terminology, to be sure, was not as yet in terms of consumer and producer "surplus"; and the concept of elasticity remained to be introduced. Nevertheless, the substance of Jenkin's analysis was essentially the same as may be found in textbooks of today.

5.3.2. Leon Walras

While Jenkin was the first to apply marginal analysis to incidence theory in a partial equilibrium setting, it is not suprising that Walras (1874), in his *Elements of Pure Economics*, was the first to apply it in the context of general equilibrium.

Walras concluded his treatise with a chapter on taxation. Incidence is viewed in the context of an interdependent set of factor and product prices. Taxes on the three factors (land, labor, and capital) are examined, as are taxes on products. A distinction is drawn between partial and general taxes. While taxes are not formally entered into the set of Walrasian equations, the general argument and its conclusions are in line with modern doctrine.

The incidence of a tax on capital income (i.e., on interest, as there are no profits in competitive equilibrium) will depend on how saving responds. Since this cannot be predicted, "we may as well assume that the incidence of the tax falls on the capitalist" [Walras (1874), p. 454)]. A tax on wages, similarly, will depend on the response in labor supply, which once more cannot be foreseen. Special attention is given to taxes on capital which apply unequally to various uses. Two effects are distinguished. Suppose that the tax is imposed on rental income from housing. Capital in the housing industry will decline, rentals will rise and tenants will bear the burden. But this is not all and Walras (1874, p. 455) continues as follows:[9]

> "Hence a tax on house rent would work out like a tax on consumption–or at least in part, for, if we look at the matter closely, we observe that a portion of the burden is borne by the capitalist. Since some of the capital goods previously employed in the construction of houses will be transferred to all sorts of other employments, a general decline in the rate of income (from capital goods) will result, and this decline will be to the detriment of all capitalists including home owners and to the advantage of all consumers, including tenants. One could, therefore, inquire into the extent to which the consumers thus recover, through the decline in the prices of other services and products, what they lose by the rise in house rents."

Given a somewhat modern interpretation, Walras thus distinguished neatly between (1) how the depressing effects of the tax on net capital income are generalized among capital in all uses, and (2) how consumers are affected by more or less offsetting "excise effects". The modern theory of property tax incidence [Mieszkowski (1972)] has its antecedent.

The incidence of product (or indirect) taxes, finally, will be borne partly by the consumers of the taxed product and partly by the owners of the productive services which are employed in their manufacture. The outcome, therefore, is extremely complex, depending on the conditions of demand and supply in the particular markets. Walras' discussion, while held in fairly general terms, is unobjectionable, to be improved upon only in its specifics in later analysis.

5.3.3. Knut Wicksell

Wicksell's primary contribution to fiscal theory, as noted earlier, is related to the voting process as a mechanism of preference determination. However, his fiscal treatise begins with an extensive analysis of incidence. Wicksell (1896, p. 5) opens with two methodological observations of importance. First, he rejects the term "shifting" as misleading, because it suggests that A, the initial payee, passes part

[9]It may be noted that this version first appears in the third edition (1889) prior to which the tax was assigned entirely to consumers [Walras (1874, p. 609)].

of the tax to B and so forth until the entire tax (equal to revenue) is distributed among a chain of payees. This is misleading, because the burden at any one stage may exceed the amount of tax paid, so that the total burden may exceed the total tax. Dead-weight loss, in modern language, should be allowed for. Secondly, he notes the confusion encountered in earlier analysis, which combines the expenditure and tax sides of the budget. While the pattern of government demand matters, this should be separated from the analysis of tax incidence. To do so, government expenditures should be held constant and the incidence of alternative taxes (collecting the same revenue) should be compared. That is to say, incidence should be conducted in differential terms [see also Musgrave (1959, p. 212)].

Wicksell then turns to a tax on monopoly profits. Based on Cournot's (1838) much earlier work [see also Musgrave and Shoup, eds. (1959)], he shows that a tax on profits cannot be shifted. For the case of product taxes, he further shows that the increase in price needed to obtain a given revenue will be smaller under an *ad valorem* than under a unit tax. The *ad valorem* approach, therefore, imposes a lesser burden and is to be preferred.

Wicksell's major concern, however, was not with changes in product prices but with the classical problem of incidence among social classes and factor shares. A new formulation was needed, as the Ricardian model of a fixed wages fund, divided among a fixed labor supply, had been discarded by the advances of marginal analysis. Wicksell (1896, p. 35) attempted to fill the void by application of Böhm Bawerk's capital theory. Beginning with the simplest case, he assumes a two-factor model, including labor and capital only, engaged in the production of a single product. Moreover, labor supply and the capital stock are fixed. The only question is how the capital stock is to be used, i.e., how long the "average period of production", t, should be. As t is lengthened, the productivity of labor is increased, and for any given wage the producer will choose that period for which the rate of interest is maximized. But the wage rate, equal to k/t, where k is the capital stock, must fall as t is increased. In combination, these two relationships establish an equilibrium position, determining t as well as the wage and interest rate.

Wicksell then uses this model – with its peculiar mixture of marginal productivity and wage fund setting – to examine incidence. A tax on income, be it on wages or on interest, will have no effect on the optimal period. The wage and interest rate are unchanged and the tax is absorbed by the payee. But a product tax will affect the outcome, as it is equivalent to an increase in the cost of labor and hence leads to a lengthening of t. Both interest and wages are reduced as a result, with the outcome depending on the shape of the production function or relation between t and labor productivity. By assuming a one-product model, Wicksell thus bypasses the issue of how incidence is affected by partial taxes and differing production functions. He does, however, amend his model by introducing land and allowing for variable capital and labor supply.

5.3.4. *Alfred Marshall*

Marshall frequently used the analysis of tax changes to "throw side-lights on the problem of value" [Marshall (1890, p. 412)].[10] In particular, tax illustrations are used to show how the nature of return to capital depends on the length of time under consideration. Returns obtainable from a given stock or machine are in the nature of quasi-rents, and taxes thereon (like taxes on the rent of land) cannot be shifted. The situation differs, however, in the longer run, when supply is variable. The return to capital is no longer a rent and the tax enters as a cost. Emphasis on the distinction between short- and longer-run adjustments may thus be considered one of his major contributions to incidence analysis. Marshall again shows how a tax on monopoly profits cannot be shifted, while a tax on the monopolist's product leads to adjustments. Once more, general and selective taxes are distinguished.

Special attention is given to the incidence of local rates [Marshall (1901)]. A distinction is drawn between "onerous" rates, which leave the property without benefits and "beneficial" rates which are reflected in public improvements. He notes that capital movement in response to local differentials relates to the *net* of the two, but such movement is not considered substantial. Incidence is shown to differ for taxes on sight or building values and once more the adjustment process and the resulting incidence depend on the length of period allowed for.

5.3.5. *F.Y. Edgeworth*

Next in our parade of early neo-classical incidence theorists, Edgeworth's (1897) contribution is to be noted. This contribution is distinguished by its systematic approach. Combining assumptions regarding fixed and variable supply, fixed and mobile uses of factors, and increasing and decreasing cost, the incidence of product taxes under various combinations is explored. Special attention is given to "peculiar cases" which arise under conditions of complementarity among products in consumption and production. He thus presents the famous "Edgeworth's paradox" where it is shown that imposition of a tax on first-class fares may lead to a reduction in both first- and third-class fares [Edgeworth (1897, p. 93), Hotelling (1932)]. Enriched by lovely illustrations of changing slopes drawn from hiking trips in the French Alps, Edgeworth exhibits virtuosity in addressing fine points of incidence.

[10] Page references are to the 9th edition.

5.3.6. *Enrico Barone*

Finally, we note Barone's (1899) ingenious application of marginal utility analysis to determine the effects of a tax on work effort [see also Musgrave and Shoup, eds. (1959)]. Primus, producing for his own use, will work so as to equate the marginal utility of output x with the marginal disutility of work c. Maximum utility is established at the maximum difference between $U(x) - C(x)$, i.e., where $u(x) = c(x)$. After a lump-sum tax is introduced, this becomes $u(x-a) = c(x)$. The marginal utility of x curve shifts to the right and intersects the marginal utility of work curve at a higher level of output. If, however, the tax is proportional to output, the difference to be maximized equals $U(x-tx) - (Cx)$. The optimal value of x is given by $(1-t)u(x-tx) = c(x)$ and x may rise or fall. Barone thus anticipates later results arrived at by the distinction between income and substitution effects. Moreover, he shows that output will increase or decrease, depending on whether the elasticity of the marginal utility schedule at the pre-tax equilibrium exceeds or falls short of $1-t$.

5.4. *Later developments*

These and other contributions to incidence theory during the closing decades of the last century had provided the major breakthrough. Subsequent developments offered improvements built on that base. We shall note very briefly some of the steps in this development, by no means complete but leading up to the current state of the art.

5.4.1. *Imperfect competition*

We have noted repeatedly how innovations in price and value theory came to be reflected in incidence analysis. A prize exhibit is provided by the work on product tax incidence which flourished in the late 1930s, following the birth of imperfect and monopolistic competition [Robinson (1933), Chamberlin (1938)]. Robinson, in developing the principles of imperfect competition, made extensive use of tax analysis, restating and expanding on Cournot's earlier work on monopoly taxation and even designing a tax device by which to correct monopolistic practice. This was followed by a spate of papers, exploring the relation between unit and ad valorem taxes under competition and monopoly, and given varying cost and demand conditions [Fagan and Jastram (1939), von Mering (1942)].

5.4.2. Income and substitution effects

In the earlier discussion, it had become evident that the incidence of factor taxes will differ, depending on how factor supplies respond to a reduction in the net rate of return. The tools for addressing this problem were refined with the distinction between income and substitution effects [Hicks (1938, p. 3l)] and its application to tax analysis. Since the two effects work in opposite directions, it followed that no *a priori* conclusion can be drawn whether factor supplies will fall or rise, a conclusion which had already been reached by Barone. Going further, subsequent analysis pointed to a significant difference between proportional and progressive rates. Since the substitution effect depends on marginal and the income effect depends on average rates of tax, factor supply will tend to be lower under a progressive tax [Hicks (1938)], but not necessarily so since substitution of a progressive for a flat schedule not only raises marginal rates of tax for some but also lowers them for others [Musgrave (1959, ch. 11B)].

5.4.3. Risk

The taxation of capital income, by reducing the net rate of return, may reduce saving and the supply of capital, following reasoning similar to that for a tax on wages. But the return to investment is not certain. Rather, it is the expected value of probable gains and losses. The effect of a tax thus depends on how probable gains and losses are dealt with. If the tax law is such as to assure loss offset (be it by carry-backs, carry-overs, or refunds), government becomes a participant in both possible gains and losses and the outcome is not readily predicted [Simons (1938), Lerner (1943), Domar and Musgrave (1944), also Musgrave and Shoup, eds. (1959)]. Examination of taxation effects thus leads into portfolio analysis and investment choice [Tobin (1958), Feldstein (1969)], a topic examined in Chapter 5 of this volume.

5.4.4. Depreciation

Also relating to the definition of taxable income from capital, much attention has been directed at the treatment of depreciation. The effective rate of tax is shown to depend on the nominal rate and the time pattern at which depreciation is allowed [Brown (1948)]. Depreciation rules, unless carefully designed, may lead to differential effective rates of tax for industries with different assets lives. Thus the analysis of depreciation was directed at both the use of accelerated depreciation as tax incentive and at devising a depreciation rule which would be neutral among investments of differing asset lives. Economic depreciation as the neutral method emerged [Samuelson (1964)] and the topic resurfaced fifteen years later when it was given new currency in the context of neutrality of tax incentives [Harberger (1980)] and of inflation [Auerbach and Jorgenson (1980)].

5.4.5. *General equilibrium*

Recent developments of incidence theory have moved towards a rigorously formulated general equilibrium approach. As we have seen, the classics had such an approach, but the underlying model was incomplete (a lack of capital theory) and unrealistic (the population response). The development of marginal productivity analysis at the close of the last century required a new model. It was recognized that taxes on any one factor may affect returns to other factors, as well as relative product prices; and that taxes on any more product may affect the prices of other products as well as factor returns. Returned to the general equilibrium perspective [Brown (1924)], incidence analysis came to be viewed in differential terms, with any particular tax substitution affecting both the uses and sources' sides of their accounts [Musgrave (1959)].

Mathematical models of general equilibrium incidence made their appearance [Shephard (1944), Meade (1955)] and took hold with Harberger's (1962) model of corporate tax incidence. This was the first model to offer a general yet workable approach. The burden of a profits tax on one industry is shown to be distributed among labor, capital, and consumers, depending on certain characteristics of the taxed industry relative to those of tax-free industries. Assuming the elasticity of substitution of capital for labor to be unity in both industries, factor shares are unaffected and the tax is absorbed by profits, including profits in both taxed and tax-free industries. The analysis is directed at an intermediate period with capital allowed to move, but the total capital stock is held fixed. Moreover, perfect capital mobility and competitive markets are stipulated. Based on this model, a wave of theoretical and empirical work developed and is still in process [Mieszkowski (1969)].

5.4.6. *Growth models*

Appearance of the neo-classical growth model [Solow (1956)] was followed by introduction of tax variables, thus opening a new dimension of incidence analysis [Krzyzanisk (1967), Feldstein (1974)]. Thus incidence theory closed the circle by returning to the long-term perspective of the classics. With focus directed at effects on factor shares under conditions of steady growth, earlier conclusions from comparative statics were changed. Incidence under steady growth is shown to depend on savings propensities as well as on elasticities of factor supply. Thus, substitution of a tax on capital income for an equal yield tax on labor income will (1) leave part of the burden on labor, even if both factor supplies are inelastic, provided that the propensity to save out of capital income is higher; and will (2) leave capital with the entire burden, even if labor supply is elastic, provided that propensities to save are the same.

5.4.7. Empirical studies

Empirical studies of tax incidence began slowly but recently exploded under the impact of newly available computer technology. Among the early work, mostly directed at income tax, we may note the Colwyn Report with its contributions by Coates (1927), as well as studies of income tax effects on labor supply [Break (1957)] and on saving [Harberger and Bailey (1969), Break (1974)]. Current work bearing on these key issues is examined in Chapters 4 and 5 of this volume and effects on housing are taken up in Chapter 7.

At the same time, empirical studies tracing the actual incidence of particular taxes from observed data remained relatively scarce. An early attempt at econometric estimation of corporation tax incidence concluded that there may be substantial shifting [Krzyaniak and Musgrave (1963)], but the outcome of this and subsequent studies remained controversial [Harberger et al. (1967)].

While the concern of classical analysis had been with the distribution of the tax burden by factor shares, this was no longer the relevant consideration for purposes of policy analysis. With the change in social structure, attention had shifted to the distribution of the burden among individuals or households arranged by income brackets. A systematic attempt at assessing the distributional effects of the entire tax system along these lines begins with a study by Colm and Tarasov (1940), continued by Musgrave et al. (1951), and leading up to the comprehensive work by Pechman and Okner (1974). The methodology underlying this family of studies was to test the implications of various shifting hypotheses by estimating the distributional effects which would result. Product taxes are imputed to consumers, income taxes to the suppliers of factors, and alternative assumptions are applied regarding the incidence of the corporation and property tax. Proceeding along similar lines, attempts were made to allocate the distribution of expenditure benefits, thus aiming to arrive at a pattern of "net redistribution" through the budget [Musgrave et al. (1974)].

Among various shortcomings of this methodology, it has been noted that the approach is based on shifting hypotheses rather than on empirical evidence as to actual shifting. Also, the approach has been critiqued for being limited to a partial equilibrium setting [Prest (1955)]. Taxes are assigned to either the uses or sources' side of the taxpayer's account, while neglecting second-round effects. Moreover, dead-weight losses are disregarded. In the defense of this methodology, it has been argued that the distributional impact of first-round effects will dominate and that the implications of alternative shifting assumptions may be tested readily.

In recent years, a new approach to general equilibrium estimation has emerged, based on the tradition of the Harberger model and made possible by the advances of computer technology. Taxation effects are estimated in the context of a general equilibrium system, based on production functions and elasticities as deduced from prevailing output and price relationships [Shoven and Whalley (1984)]. Thus the complete chain of secondary effects is included and dead-weight losses are allowed for. However, the outcome still depends on the quality of the parameters which are built into the model. Moreover, it cannot be claimed that the model estimates the observed outcome of actual tax changes. Rather, it simulates the results which emerge on the assumption that adjustments proceed in a perfectly competitive and flexible economy.

6. Stabilization and debt

Up to the 1930s, fiscal economics, with few exceptions, dealt with the effects of budget policy on alternative uses of resources and the distribution of income. This analysis, as we have seen, was conducted in the context of a full-employment economy. Much attention was given to fiscal effects on the division of output between capital formation and consumption, and thereby on growth; but by the nature of the underlying macro model, effects on the level of employment were outside the confines of analysis. With the "Keynesian revolution" of the 1930s [Klein (1947)], aggregate demand became a major factor in determining the level of employment; and with it budget policy gained a new and strategic role. The stabilization function was added to the more traditional aspects of budget policy, and fiscal policy moved into the center of macro economics. Most of the fiscal literature of the 1930s and 1940s was directed at exploring this new dimension.

6.1. Fiscal policy and stabilization

While this phase of fiscal analysis gained dominance with the rise of Keynesian economics, it also had its antecedents.

6.1.1. Early Keynesians

Aggregate demand was of concern in mercantilist thought, and Sir James Steuart (1767, vol. II, pp. 642, 644), writing a decade before the *Wealth of Nations*, argued that stagnant money "lent to government, is thrown into a new channel of circulation – thereby to augment the prominent income of the country". Then there was that "brave army of heretics, Mandeville, Malthus, Gesell, and Hobbson who, following their intuition, have preferred to see the truth obscurely and imperfectly rather than to maintain error, reached indeed with clearness and consistency and by easy logic, but on hypotheses inappropriate to the fact" [Keynes (1936, p. 371)].

That central hypothesis, of course, was Say's (1821) law, i.e., the proposition that there could be no general glut since, commodities being exchanged against commodities, supply would create it own demand. Malthus (1820, p. 316), the chief heretic among the classics, was critical of "Mr. Say, Mr. Mill, and Mr. Ricardo, the principle authors of these new views". An adequate level of "effectual demand" is needed, so Malthus (1820, p. 326) argued, to sustain output:

> "But if the conversion of revenue into capital pushed beyond a certain point must, by diminishing the effectual demand for produce, throw the laboring classes out of employment, it is obvious that the adoption of parsimonious habits beyond a certain point, may be accompanied by the most distressing effects at first, and by a market depression of wealth and population afterwards."

His primary problem with saving, it appears was not that funds will be withheld from the expenditure stream, as in the Keynesian model. Rather it was that too much is spent on capital formation, leaving consumer demand insufficient to absorb the increase in potential output that results. In consequence, profits will fall and accumulation will decline. Balance may be restored but only after distress has occurred. Malthus thus explains the depression which followed the Napoleonic War by under-consumption. Of particular interest in our context are certain implications which Malthus draws for budget policy. If the problem is one of deficient consumer demand, budget policy can be helpful. Consumer demand might be raised by redistributing income towards "those classes of unproductive consumers who are supported by taxes" [Malthus (1820, p. 410)]. Moreover, budget policy can be harmful if consumer demand is reduced by excessively rapid repayment of public debt. Having noted this much, Malthus (1820, p. 411) hastens to add that property rights must not be violated by redistribution, and assures the reader that he is not "insensible to the great evils of public debt".

Malthus, along with Sismondi, was among the first to advance an underconsumption theory of crisis. Marx offered a related doctrine and underconsumption theories reached high fashion in the writings of the 1920s. [For a discussion, see Hansen (1927), McCord Wright (1942), Keynes (1936, ch. 23).] However, these contributions paid little attention to the role of the public budget, nor did monetary theories of business cycles of that period.

6.1.2. *The Keynesian model*

Analysis of budgetary effects on employment enter the public finance literature only in the mid-1930s, when the stage had been set by Keynes' (1936) *General Theory of Income and Employment*. The impact of Keynesian economics on fiscal theory profoundly changed its focus. Whereas the problem had been to observe resulting shifts in resource use, concern now was with effects on its overall level. With employment seen to depend on aggregate demand and with budget policy a direct contributor thereto, budget policy became a critical determinant of the level of employment. This new function of budget policy was the more important because departure from full employment was seen no longer as a temporary aberation, but a central tendency of the economy. A continuing tendency towards oversaving [Keynes (1936, p. 31)] and stagnation [Hansen (1938, 1941)] was expected to prevail, with expansionary fiscal policy called for on a sustained basis in order to maintain high employment in a mature economy. Moreover, fiscal policy was not only one but *the* policy instrument with which to remedy the problem of underemployment. Monetary policy at least in the earlier depression phase of Keynesian economics was rendered ineffective by the existence of a liquidity trap. Aggregate demand, like a string, could not be pushed up by monetary expansion, but it could be pulled up by government outlays.

The Keynesian case for deficit finance, from the beginning, was doubly controversial. Not only were the underlying analytics questioned, but the model carried political and ideological implications which contributed to the heat of the debate. If fiscal expansion had to be secured via increased government expenditures, it would also add to the size of the public budget. Moreover, the central proposition that private saving may be a public vice offended deeply held values based on Puritan tradition. The notion that different principles of prudence applied to the public and the private sector ran counter to the concept of a society based on the beneficial interplay of individuals in the market.

In the course of time, the extreme view of the early Keynesian model was moderated, and the supreme powers of fiscal policy were turned down. However, its role in stabilization remained a key factor. The field of "Public Finance", traditionally a subject in micro economics, became part of macro teaching and macro issues claimed dominant attention. No attempt can be made here to trace the development of macro theory from the thirties to the sixties, not to speak of entering into the current debate. Rather, we limit ourselves to a brief look at certain macro issues which arose in the context of fiscal policy. Among the major contributors to the development of the fiscal policy concept we may note Alvin Hansen, whose Fiscal Policy Seminar, conducted at Harvard during the late 1930s, was the mainspring of the new approach in the United States [Hansen (1941)] and, in Great Britain, Beveridge's (1945) program for full employment in a free society was to be the blue-print for macro policy in the post-World War II years. In the United States, the Employment Act of 1946 made it the President's responsibility to "promote maximum employment, production, and purchasing power" and, as added in 1953, "a dollar of stable value". It also established the Council of Economic Advisors to pursue these goals.

Multiplier analysis. Central to the role of fiscal variables in the Keynesian model was their treatment in the multiplier formula. Initially this was thought of as the multiplier effect of an increase in "government investment", observed while holding tax revenue constant. By adding government purchases, the level of autonomous expenditures would be raised, thus offsetting a higher level of private sector saving and permitting a higher level of income. The measurement of the fiscal multiplicand was explored [Clark (1935), Currie and Krost (1939), Villard (1940)], based on the assumption of a fixed level of investment. Samuelson's (1939) multiplier–accelerator model then expanded multiplier analysis to include investment effects and to examine the pattern of resulting income fluctuations. While initial emphases had been on increases in government purchases, subsequent analysis admitted tax reduction as a second device, leading to the analysis of alternative packages of tax and expenditure changes which would secure the same overall leverage effect [Beveridge (1945), Hansen (1945), Musgrave (1945), Samuelson (1948)].

In line with the early focus on excess savings as the villain, the creation of a public deficit (public dissaving) was first seen as an essential feature of fiscal leverage. It therefore came as somewhat of a shock when it was demonstrated in the early 1940s that even a balanced-budget increase could exert a leverage, albeit with a multiplier of unity only [Gelting (1941), Salant (1942), Havelmo (1945)]. Within a short time span the "balanced-budget theorem" had been advanced independently in a number of places, a nice illustration of how what was once unthinkable becomes commonplace when the time is ripe [Salant (1975)]. Examination of the multiplier time period [Metzler (1948)] and further exploration of various policy lags followed [Friedman (1948)], and the estimation of multiplier effects became a central part of the newly developed breed of econometric models [Klein and Goldberger (1955)].

Fiscal structure. The newly formed role of fiscal policy also placed the quality of various taxes in a new perspective. Taxes which fell heavily on consumption would carry a larger (negative) multiplicand than those falling on saving and thus do less damage to the leverage of the budget. Thus full-employment policy was linked to progressive taxation. A tax on undistributed profits was enacted briefly in 1937 [Colm (1940)] and the feasibility of a tax on hoarding, linking back to Gesell's idea of stamped money, was considered [McWright (1942)].

Given these new uses of tax and expenditure instruments in the context of macro policy, the question arose how they could be reconciled with the traditional fiscal objectives, i.e., the provision for needed public services and the design of an efficient and equitable tax structure. Keynes (1936, p. 220) was pleased to shock his bourgeois reader by noting that even the construction of pyramids or the digging of holes would increase the national income, without adding that constructing a useful highway may be even better. Lerner (1943), in his "functional finance" doctrine, viewed taxation merely as a means to reduce the purchasing power of the public in contrast to its traditional role of transferring resources to the public sector. This author, concerned with avoiding distortions due to conflicting objectives of various policy functions, proposed a "three-branch model" in which various functions of the budget could be reconciled and be performed in a compatible fashion [Musgrave (1959, ch. 1)]. Changes in fiscal leverage, in that context, would be expedited primarily via changes in tax rates with government purchases set so as to meet the need for public services at a full-employment level of income. These considerations, we may add, are no less relevant in the current setting where macro considerations point in the direction of budgetary restriction.

Built-in flexibility. By the late 1940s, a distinction emerged between the stabilizing effects of the fiscal system which arise as the result of discretionary changes in fiscal parameters and those which arise automatically in response to changes in the level of economic activity. Measures of built-in flexibility were devised and the comparative flexibility of various taxes was explored. Critics of discretionary policy held that changes in fiscal leverage should be limited to those which result automatically, while setting the level of tax rates so as to balance the budget at full employment [Friedman (1948), Committee for Economic Development (1947)]. Others held that discretionary changes cannot be dispensed with.

Over time it appeared that built-in flexibility might not be an unmixed blessing. Whereas the automatic decline in revenue in the course of a recession would be helpful, the automatic increase in the upswing, or a secular increase in response to growth might generate a fiscal drag [*Economic Report of the President* (1962), Heller (1967)].

6.1.3. The neo-classical model

The economic experience of World War II, with its massive growth in the budget and rise in GNP, had demonstrated the powers of expansionary policy under wartime conditions, and during the forties thinking about postwar policy projected a continued need for expansionary fiscal measures. As it turned out, the postwar decades produced a much stronger economy, and with it reinstated monetary policy as an effective policy tool. The approximate mix of fiscal and monetary policy was examined in the context of a "neo-classical" policy model, designed to accommodate both monetary and fiscal policy variables and to allow for the effects of unbalanced budgets (deficit or surplus) on the structure of claims [Samuelson (1951)]. Various degrees of monetary and fiscal tightness (or ease) could be combined to achieve the same level of aggregate demand but they would differ in the resulting mix of consumption and investment with a tight fiscal and easy money mix more favorable to growth. There would also be a difference in balance of payment effects, with the tight money and easy fiscal mix yielding the more favorable results. Adding selective instruments here needed, policy tools would be adequate, if wisely used, to achieve various macro policy goals.

The high point of optimism regarding the New Economics [Heller (1967)] and the powers of stabilization policy was reached in the first *Economic Report* of the Kennedy Administration (1962) and the recovery following the tax cut of 1964. Thereafter, the changing economic scene, with its shift in concern from unemployment to stagflation, produced a setting less favorable to the powers of fiscal policy. With it, changing perspectives on macro theory and the ensuing monetarist–fiscalist debate called for reconsideration of earlier tenets. Thus a new chapter was opened, but one which extends beyond the time span of this essay.

6.2. Public debt

The economics of public debt, the final topic to be considered here, has been among the most controversial parts of fiscal doctrine. In some measure, this reflects its strategic role in fiscal politics. Resort to debt finance is said to facilitate spending, remove public outlays from taxpayer control, and burden the future. The very proposition that the rules of prudence in private debt accumulation may not apply to the public sector offends, as noted before, the image of a natural order based on the rules of the market. But beyond this, subtle problems of economic analysis arise, problems which are still (or better, again) at a debatable stage.

6.2.1. Debt burden and future generations

Central to the debate is the issue whether the burden of the debt is paid for by future generations. The mercantilists thought not. Credit was viewed as a creation of wealth and outstanding debt was no burden. As stated by Melon (1734), an associate of John Law, public debts, if domestically owed, are debts which the "right hand owes to the left". Pintus, Voltaire, and Condorcet took similar positions. The growth of French and British debts in the eighteenth century, however, produced a more critical view. Thus Montesquieu and Hume rejected Melon's proposition as specious [Hume (1742)]. Smith (1776, vol. I, pp. 410, 412) similarly rejected the transfer argument as "sophistry of the mercantile system" as well as the mercantilist view that the national debt is an addition to the nation's capital. Debt finance may be needed in wartime, or on other special occasions, but tax finance is to be the general rule. Tax finance will be drawn largely from funds otherwise used in the employment of unproductive labor, whereas loan finance will divert funds from the maintenance of productive labor, thus impairing the country's capital stock [Smith (1776, vol. II, p. 410)]. Moreover, the burden of tax finance is felt at once, thus creating taxpayer resistance and providing protection against public waste.

Ricardo's contribution to debt theory has regained recent attention as the "Ricardian equivalence theorem". Hidden in a chapter on commodity taxes in the *Principles* [Ricardo (1817, p. 244)] and restated in his essay on the *Funding System* [Ricardo (1820, p. 187)], he offered this intriguing contribution to debt theory: Suppose, so he argues, that £20 million has to be raised to pay for the expenses of a year's war. In the case of tax finance, let a particular individual be called upon to pay £2,000, or 1/10,000 thereof. In the case of loan finance, and with interest of 5 percent, £1 million per annum must be paid in interest to the lenders. Of this, our taxpayer is asked to pay £100. Under tax finance, he could have borrowed from the same lenders to finance his tax of £2,000, being left once more with an annual charge of £100. From the taxpayer's point of view, the two methods are therefore equivalent.

Put in modern terms, Ricardo concludes that the taxpayer in the loan finance case discounts his future tax liability and finds his net worth reduced as it would be under tax finance. "In point of economy", there is no real difference "between the two modes" [Ricardo (1820, p. 186)]. The burden of the war is paid for by the taxpayer during the year in which it is financed, be it in his role of paying £2,000 at once or as assuming a tax obligation of £100 per annum. Future interest payments, therefore, are only transfers among the future generation and impose no burden.

But having posed this argument as holding "in economy" – meaning, we take it, on the assumption of perfect foresight and rational behavior – Ricardo hastens to reject it as unrealistic. Asked to pay the full £2,000 in the case of tax finance, the taxpayer will endeavor at once to "save speedily" that amount from his income. Under loan finance, he has to pay only £100, and will thus "consider that he does enough" by saving this lesser sum "and then deludes himself with the belief that he is as rich as before". In short, "loan finance is a system which tends to make us less thrifty – to blind us to our real situation" [Ricardo (1817, p. 247)].

Tax and loan finance both involve the diversion of resources to wasteful use, but they differ in their effect on capital formation and hence on the position of future generations. Saving and capital formation are reduced as tax finance is replaced by loan finance, and the future generation *is* burdened by having a lower income. Ricardo's rejection of the equivalence theorem could not be more explicit, and it is strange that the equivalence theorem could now be presented under his banner [Shoup (1960), Driscoll (1977)].

The economics of public debt also received lively attention among continental authors. German writers, tending towards a more favorable view of the public sector, saw the growth of public debt with less alarm. Dietzel (1855), impressed with the economic advance of Great Britain, attributed it to the rapid growth of public debt. Equating growth of public debt with public capital formation, he viewed the former as a sign of growing national wealth. Public capital formation, moreover, would include not only the real but also the "immaterial" capital of the state, such as the existence of legal institutions. Notwithstanding his overly enthusiastic view of state outlays, he anticipated future thought by calling for loan finance in the case of capital and tax finance in the case of current outlays. A similar, though more cautious support, of public debt was advanced by Wagner (1883, p. 184), whose views on the growth of public expenditures we previously encountered. The Italian literature of the 1890s, that decade of flourishing fiscal theory, accepted and elaborated upon the Ricardian equivalence theme [de Viti de Marco (1893), and, for a review of the Italian literature, Buchanan (1960)]. The leading French, British, and American texts [Leroy-Beaulieu (1906), Bastable (1892), Adams (1892)], however, adhered to the view that debt finance reduces private capital formation and thus places a burden on future generations by reducing the capital stock which is bequeathed to them.

This view was shaken by the impact of Keynesian economics. Not only would creation of debt be a necessary byproduct of fiscal expansion needed to secure high employment, but outstanding debt would pose no serious subsequent problem. The old doctrine that interest payments constitute a transfer from the right to the left hand now reappeared as "we owe it to ourselves". Public debt, so Lerner (1948) argued, differs from private debt because the latter is owed "to others" whereas the former is owed to citizens of the "same nation". Creation of national debt, therefore, is no subtraction from national wealth, nor do interest payments by members of a future generation reduce the national income of that generation.

To be sure, tax finance of interest payments might induce burdensome disincentives and dead-weight losses. But, so Lerner argued, tax finance of interest charges is not needed, since interest payments may in turn be loan financed. Tax finance becomes necessary only after interest payments become so large, relative to earnings, that further loan finance would become inflationary. At this point, a large national debt might become a serious problem, but he did not think this situation likely to arise. The wealth effect of growing debt reduces the propensity to save and thus terminates the need for further debt expansion, leading to an equilibrium level of public debt at full employment.

Essential to this view of debt and interest burdens is the assumption of an underemployment economy which calls for aggregate demand to be raised by fiscal expansion. Government borrowing activates funds (recall our earlier reference to Sir John Steuart), but does not reduce private investment. Hence there are no depressing effects on future generations by leaving it with a reduced capital stock. Given an extreme Keynesian model with fixed investment and excess saving, this conclusion follows, just as the opposite conclusion (that loan finance burdens future generations) is appropriate for a full-employment model.

While the case for deficit finance (increase in debt) came to be accepted as an appropriate employment policy, concern with the burden of interest service and its effects on future generations continued. This fear was allayed, however, by the proposition that interest burden was a function of the ratio of interest bill to GNP, rather than its absolute level. Given a constant ratio of deficit to GNP and constant yields, the ratio of interest bill to GNP also approaches a constant level [Domar (1944)].

Subsequent discussion returned the argument to a full-employment setting. Attack on the "new orthodoxy" (i.e., the we-owe-it-to-ourselves proposition) was led by Buchanan's (1958) subjective approach. There can be no initial burden, so he argued, since lenders are not called upon to contribute anything. Thus no burden is imposed in the initial period. Future taxpayers, however, are burdened by having to finance interest payments. Thus burden transfer occurs. Others continued to stress reduced capital formation and the burden which it imposes as the future generation as a whole is left with a reduced capital stock [Shoup (1962)]. With future tax payments needed to finance interest service equal to the loss of capital income, the two formulations yield essentially similar results.

The difference between loan and tax finance was thus left to depend on resulting differences in resource withdrawal from consumption and capital formation [for major contributions to this debate, see Ferguson (1964)]. The fact that loan finance may involve burden transfer, however, is not necessarily an argument against it. In the context of public capital formation, transfer of burden via loan finance may serve as an instrument of intergeneration equity and a rationale for a capital budget approach [Musgrave (1959, p. 562)]. A further equity-oriented case for loan finance may arise in the context of war finance, where the use of "refundable taxes" permits a postwar correction of inevitably heavy wartime burdens on low income groups [Keynes (1939)].

6.2.2. *Public debt and liquidity structure*

Apart from the differential implications of tax and loan finance, much attention was given during the 1940s and 1950s to how an outstanding debt should be managed. The two major issues were the choice between marketable and non-marketable bonds, and the maturity structure of the debt. With the former essentially a question of distributional outcome, the latter led into the linkage between fiscal and monetary theory. With issuance of debt viewed as a purchase of liquidity, the Treasury should choose between short- and long-term issues so as to minimize the cost of securing a given reduction in liquidity [Rolph, (1957)]. Short-term debt, being closer in nature to money, would buy less illiquidity than long-term debt and hence be worth more to the Treasury.

The proposition that debt issue reduces liquidity was questioned, however, as debt policy came to be viewed in the context of general portfolio choice [Tobin (1963)]. Moreover, attention was given to the fact that the choice of maturities so as to minimize interest cost involves not only the prevailing term structure of rates, but also anticipation of future changes therein [Smith, (1970)]. Finally, there was the question of how maturity structures of different lengths would affect the stability of the market. Long-term debt would avoid the hassles of refinancing but would result in larger fluctuations in the market value of outstanding bonds, thereby increasing the risk of "disorderly conditions", especially in the case of monetary restrictions. With the drastic shortening of the debt in the postwar decade, these issues which once were lively topics have largely disappeared from the discussion.

7. Conclusion

This closes our account of the evolution of fiscal theory. Over the two centuries here surveyed, the economics of public finance has grown enormously both in breadth and sophistication, moving with and benefitting from the growth of economic analysis at large, but also contributing thereto. This growth, however, has been far from linear, with insights cropping up, dropping out, and reappearing when their time had come. But great progress has been made. Yet, the basic problems have remained the same. The questions of what public services should be provided, how they should be financed, and what role government should play in the macro conduct of economic affairs were visible to Adam Smith, and they still pose the basic problem.

So does the fact that many issues in public finance remain inherently controversial. To establish the economic case for the public sector is to delimit the sphere that can be left to the invisible hand and the rules of the market. The scope of existing externalities, the acceptability of a market-determined income distribution, the shape of the social welfare function, maintaining full resource utilization, the issues of inflation and growth, all these have powerful bearings on the appropriate size and activities of the public sector. So does the capability of public policy to apply appropriate corrections, with the scope of public policy failure matched against that of market failure. Given this array of problems and their linkages, ideological and value issues are never far away. Moreover, the tools of fiscal policy changes with changing fiscal institutions. It is not surprising, therefore, that the history of fiscal doctrine deals with more than the development of economic analysis per se. To this writer at least, that adds to rather than detracts from the fascination of our subject.

References

Adams, H.C., 1899, The science of finance (Henry Holt & Co., New York).

Arrow, K., 1951, Social choice and individual values (Wiley, New York).

Auerbach, A.J. and D.W. Jorgenson, 1980, Inflation-proof depreciation of assets, Harvard Business Review 58.

Barone, E., 1899, About some fundamental theorems on the mathematical theory of taxation, Giornale degli Economisti, Serv. 2, 4.

Bastable, C.F., 1892, Public finance, 3rd ed., 1903 (Macmillan, London).

Baumol, W.J. and W. Oates, 1975, The theory of environmental policy (Prentice Hall, Englewood Cliffs, NJ).

Bentham, J., 1902, Principles of the civil code. Reprinted in: J. Bentham, 1931, The theory of legislation, edited by C.K. Odgen (Kegan Paul, London).

Bergson, A., 1938, A reformulation of certain aspects of welfare economics, Quarterly Journal of Economics 52.

Beveridge, W.H., 1945, Full employment in a free society (W.E. Norton, New York).

Black, D., 1948, On the rationale of group decision-making, Journal of Political Economy 56.

Borcherding, T.E., 1977, Budgets and bureaucrats (Duke University Press, Durham, NC).

Break, G.F., 1957, Income taxes and incentives to work: An empirical study, American Economic Review 47.

Break, G.F., 1974, The incidence and economic effects of taxation, in: The economics of public finance (Brookings Institution, Washington, DC).

Bowen, H., 1948, Toward social economy (Rinehart & Co., New York).

Brown, H.G., 1924, The economics of taxation (Henry Holt & Co., New York).

Brown, H.G., 1929, Economic science and the common welfare (Lucas, Columbia, MT).

Brown, E.C., 1948, Business-income taxation and investment incentives, in: Income, employment, and public policy (W. Norton, New York).

Buchanan, J., 1959, Public principles of public debt (Irwin, Homewood, IL).

Buchanan, J., 1961, Fiscal institution and collective outlay, American Economic Review 51.

Buchanan, J., 1965, An economic theory of clubs, Economica 32.

Buchanan, J., 1975, The limits of liberty (Chicago University Press, Chicago, IL).

Canard, F., 1801, Principles d'économie politique (Paris).

Chamberlin, E.H., 1938, The theory of monopolistic competition, 3rd ed. (Harvard University Press, Cambridge, MA).

Clark, J.M., 1935, Economics of planning public works (National Resources Committee, Washington, DC).

Coase, R.H., 1974, The lighthouse in economics, Journal of Law and Economics 17.

Coates, A.M., 1927, Incidence of the income tax, Appendices to the Report of the Commission on National Debt and Taxation (H.M. Stationary Office, London).

Cohen Stuart, A.J., 1889, Bijdrage tot de theorie der progressive inkomsteuerbelasting (The Hague). Also see Musgrave and Peacock, eds. (1958).

Colm, G., 1940, Full employment through through tax policy, Social Research 7.

Colm, G. and H. Tarasov, 1940, Who pays the taxes? (Temporary National Economic Committee, Washington, DC).

Committee for Economic Development, 1947, Taxes and the budget: A program for prosperity in a free society (New York). Also see Smities and Butters, eds. (1955).

Corlett, W.J. and D.C. Hague, 1953–54, Complementarity and the excess burden of taxation, Review of Economic Studies, Ser. 1, 2, no. 54.

Cournot, A., 1838, Récherches sur les principes mathématiques de la théorie des richesses (L. Hachette, Paris).
Currie, L. and M. Krost, 1939, Explanation of computing net contribution, Mimeo. (Board of Governors of the Federal Reserve System, Washington, DC).
Demsetz, H., 1970, The private production of public goods, Journal of Law and Economics 13.
Diamond, P. and J.A. Mirlees, 1971, Taxation and public production I: Production and efficiency, and II: Tax rules, American Economic Review 61.
Dietzel, C., 1885, Das System der Staatsanleihen im Zusammenhang der Volkwirtschafft betrachtet (Heidelberg).
Domar, E.D., 1954, The burden of the debt and the national income, American Economic Review 34.
Domar, E.D. and R.A. Musgrave, 1944, Proportional income taxation and risk taking, Quarterly Journal of Economics 58.
Downs, A., 1956, An economic theory of democracy (Harper, New York).
Dupuit, J., 1944, De la mesure de l'utilité des traveaux publics. Reprinted in: De l'utilité et de sa mesure: Écrits choisis et republiés par Mario de Bernardi (La Riforma Sociale, Turin). English translation in: 1952, International Economic Review 2.
Eckstein, O., 1961, A survey of the theory of public expenditure criteria, in: J. Buchanan, ed., Public finances: Needs, sources, and utilization (Princeton University Press, Princeton, NJ). Economic Report of the President, 1962 (Government Printing Office, Washington, DC).
Edgeworth, F.Y., 1897, The pure theory of taxation, Economic Journal 7. Reprinted in: Papers relating to political economy, Vol. II (Macmillan, London).
Einaudi, L., 1912, Intorno al concetto di reddito imponible e di un sistema d'imposte sul viddita consummato (Turin).
Fagan, E.D. and R.W. Jastram, 1939, Tax shifting in the short run, Quarterly Journal of Economics 53.
Feldstein, M., 1969, The effects of taxation on risk taking, Journal of Political Economy 77.
Feldstein, M., 1974a, Financing in the evaluation of public expenditures, in: W.L. Smith and J.M. Culbertson, eds., Public finance and stabilization policy: Essays in the honour of Alvin Hansen (North-Holland, Amsterdam).
Feldstein, M., 1974b, Tax incidence in a growing economy with variable factor supply, Quarterly Journal of Economics 88.
Ferguson, J.M., ed., 1964, Public debt and future generations (University of North Carolina Press, Durham, NC).
Fisher, I., 1906, Nature of capital and income (Macmillan, New York).
Fisher, I. and H.W. Fisher, 1942, Constructive income taxation (Harper and Brothers, New York).
Friedman, M., 1948, A monetary and fiscal framework for economic stability, American Economic Review 38.
Gelting, J.H., 1941, Some observations on the financing of public activity. Reprinted in: 1975, History of Political Economy 7.
George, H., 1880, Progress and poverty, 1954 ed. (R. Schalkenbach Foundation, New York).
Goldscheid, R., 1917, Finanzsoziologie (Wien). Also see Musgrave and Peacock, eds. (1958).
Gossen, H., 1854, Entwicklung der Gesetze des menschlichen Verkehrs, 1927 ed. by F. Hayek (Praeger, Berlin).
Groves, H.M., 1974, Tax philosophers, edited by D.J. Curran (University of Wisconsin Press, Madison, WI).
Haavelmo, T., 1945, Effects of a balanced budget, Econometrica 13.
Haig, R.M., 1921, The concept of income, in: The federal income tax (Columbia University Press, New York).
Hansen, A.H., 1927, Business cycle theory (Ginn & Co., Boston, MA).
Hansen, A.H., 1939, Economic progress and declining population growth, American Economic Review 29.
Hansen, A.H., 1941, Fiscal policy and business cycles (W.W. Norton, New York).
Hansen, A.H., 1945, Three modes of expansion through fiscal policy, American Economic Review 35.
Harberger, A.C., 1962, The incidence of the corporation on income tax, Journal of Political Economy 70. Also see A.C. Harberger, Taxation and welfare (Little, Brown & Co., Boston, MA).
Harberger, A.C., 1969, The opportunity cost of public investment financed by borrowing. Reprinted in: R. Layard, ed., Cost benefit analysis (Penguin Books, Baltimore, MD).

Harberger, A.C., 1974, Taxation and welfare (Little, Brown & Co., Boston, MA).
Harberger, A.C., 1980, Tax neutrality in investment incentives, in: H.J. Aaron and M. Boskin, eds., The economics of taxation (Brookings Institution, Washington, DC).
Harberger, A.C., and M.J. Bailey, eds., 1969, The taxation of income from capital (Brookings Institution, Washington, DC).
Hasyanyi, J.C., 1955, Cardinal welfare, individualistic ethics and interpersonal comparison of utilities, Journal of Political Economy 63.
Heller, W., 1967, New dimensions of fiscal policy (W.W. Norton, New York).
Hicks, J.R., 1939, Value and capital (Oxford University Press, Oxford).
Hicks, U., 1947, Public finance (Pitman, New York).
Hobbes, T., 1651, Leviathan (Penguin Classics, Baltimore, MD).
Hotelling, H., 1938, The general welfare in relation to problems of taxation and utility rates, Econometrica 6.
Hume, D., 1739, A treatise of human nature, 1975 ed. by L.A. Selby-Bidge (Clarendon Press, Oxford).
Hume, D., 1758, Of public credit, in: Essays, moral, political and literary, Vol. I, 1882 ed. (London).
Inman, R.P., 1978, The fiscal performance of local governments: An interpretative review, in: P. Mieszkowski and M. Straszhein, eds., Current issues in urban economics (Johns Hopkins University Press, Baltimore, MD).
Jenkin, F., 1871–72, On the principles which regulate the incidence of taxes, in: Proceedings of the Royal Society of Edinburgh. Reprinted in: Musgrave and Shoup, eds. (1959).
Kaldor, N. et al., 1955a, Memorandum of dissent, in: Royal commission on the taxation of profits and income (H.M. Stationary Office, London).
Kaldor, N., 1955b, An expenditure tax (Allen and Unwin, London).
Kay, J.A. and M.A. King, 1978, The British tax system (Oxford University Press, Oxford).
Keynes, J.M., 1936, The general theory of employment, interest, and money (Harcourt, Brace & Co., New York).
Keynes, J.M., 1939, Paying for the war, The Times, 14 & 15 Nov. Reprinted in: D. Muggridge, ed., 1978, The collected writing of J.M. Keynes, Vol. 22 (Cambridge University Press, Cambridge).
Klein, L.R. and A.S. Goldberger 1955, An econometric model of the United States, 1929–1952 (North-Holland, Amsterdam).
Krzyzaniak, M., 1967, The long run burden of a general tax on profits in a neo-classical world, Public Finance, Finance Publiques no. 4.
Layard, R., 1972, Introduction, in: Cost–benefit analysis (Penguin Books, Baltimore, MD).
Lerner, A.P., 1944, The economics of control (Macmillan, New York).
Lerner, A.P., 1948, The burden of the national debt, in: Income, employment, and public policy: Essays in honour of Alvin Hansen (W.W. Norton, New York).
Leroy-Beaulieu, P., 1906, Traité de la science finances, Vol. II, 7th ed. (Paris).
Lindahl, E., 1919, Die Gerechtigkeit der Besteuerung (Gleerupska Universitets Bokhandeln, Lund).
Lindahl, E., 1928, Einige strittige Fragen der Steuertheorie, in: Hans Mayer, ed., Die Wirtschaftstheorie der Gegenwart, Vol. IV (Vienna). Also see Musgrave and Peacock, eds. (1958).
Little, I.M.D., 1951, Direct vs. indirect taxes, Economic Journal 61. Reprinted in: Musgrave and Shoup, eds. (1959).
Locke, J., 1690, Two treatises on government, 1960 ed. by Peter Lasset (Mentor Book, Cambridge University Press, Cambridge).
Mann, F.K., 1937, Steuerpolitische Ideale (G. Fisher, Jena).
Marglin, S., 1963, The opportunity costs of public investment, Quarterly Journal of Economics 77.
Malthus, T.R., 1836, Principles of political economy. Reprinted in: 1964, Reprints of economic classics (A.M. Kelley, New York).
Marshall, A., 1890, Principles of economics, 8th ed. (Macmillan, London).
Marshall, A., 1917, The equitable distribution of taxation. Reprinted in: A.C. Pigou, ed., 1925, Memorials of Alfred Marshall (Macmillan, London).
McCord Wright, D., 1942, The creation of purchasing power (Harvard University Press, Cambridge, MA).
McCulloch, J.R., 1845, A treatise on the principles and practical influence of taxation and the funding system (Longman, Brown & Co., London).
Meade, J.E., 1955, The effects of indirect taxation upon the distribution of income, in: Trade and welfare, Vol. II (Oxford University Press, Oxford).

Mering, O. von, 1942, The shifting and incidence of taxation (Blakiston & Co., Philadelphia, PA).
Metzler, L.A., 1948, Three lags in the circular flow of income, in: Income, employment and public policy: Essays in honour of Alvin Hansen (W.W. Norton, New York).
Mieszkowski, P., 1969, Tax incidence theory: The effects of taxes on the distribution of income, Journal of Economic Literature 7.
Mieszkowski, P., 1972, The property tax: An excise tax or a profits tax?, Journal of Public Economics 2.
Mill, J.S., 1921, Principles of political economy, New ed. by W.J. Ashley (Longman's, Green & Co., London). Also reprinted in: 1965, Reprints of economic classics (A.M. Kelley, New York).
Mueller, D.C., 1979, Public choice (Cambridge University Press, Cambridge).
Musgrave, R.A., 1938, The voluntary exchange theory of public economy, Quarterly Journal of Economics 53.
Musgrave, R.A., 1945, Alternative budgets for full employment, American Economic Review 35.
Musgrave, R.A., 1959, The theory of public finance (McGraw-Hill, New York).
Musgrave, R.A., 1969a, Cost–benefit analysis in the theory of public finance, Journal of Economic Literature 7.
Musgrave, R.A., 1969b, Provision for social goods, in: J. Margolis and A. Guilton, eds., Public economics (Macmillan, London).
Musgrave, R.A. and P.B. Musgrave, 1973, Public finance in theory and practice (McGraw-Hill, New York).
Musgrave, R.A. and A.T. Peacock, eds., 1958, Classics in the theory of public finance (Macmillan, London).
Musgrave, R.A. and C.S. Shoup, eds., 1959, Readings in the economics of taxation (Irwin, Homewood, IL).
Musgrave, R.A. et al., 1951, Distribution of tax payments by income groups: A case study for 1945, National Tax Journal 4.
Musgrave, R.A., K.E. Case and H. Leonard, 1974, The distribution of fiscal burdens and benefits, Public Finance Quarterly 2.
Myrdal, G., 1929, The political element in the development of economic theory, 1953 English translation (Routledge, London).
Neumark, F., 1947, Theorie und Praxis der modernen Einkommensbesteuerung (A. Francke, Bern).
Niskanen, W.A., 1974, Bureaucracy and representative government (Aldine, Chicago, IL).
Nozick, R., 1974, Anarchy, state and utopia (Basic Books, New York).
Oates, W., 1972, Fiscal federalism (Harcourt, Brace & Co., New York).
Oakland, W., 1972, Congestion, public goods, and welfare, Journal of Public Economics 1.
Panteleoni, M., 1883, Contributo alla teoriea del ripurto delli spese pubbliche, Rassegna Italiana. Reprinted in: M. Panteleoni, Scritti varii de economia, Vol. I.
Peacock, A.T. and R.A. Musgrave, eds., 1958, Classics in the theory of public finance (Macmillan, London).
Pechman, J., ed., 1980, What should be taxed: Income or expenditures? (Brookings Institution, Washington, DC).
Pechman, J. and B.A. Okner, 1974, Who bears the tax burden? (Brookings Institution, Washington, DC).
Petty, Sir W., 1662, A treatise of taxes and contributions in: C.H. Hull, ed., 1899, The economic writings of Sir William Petty (The University Press, Cambridge).
Pigou, A.C., 1920, The economics of welfare (Macmillan, London).
Pigou, A.C., 1928, A study in public finance (Macmillan, London).
Prest, A.R., 1955, Statistical calculations of tax burdens, Economica 22.
Prest, A.R., 1975, Public finance in theory and practice (Weidenfeld and Nicholson, London).
Quesnay, F., 1760, 1762, Le tableau économique, and Theorie de l'impôt. See August Oncken, ed., 1888, Oeuvres économiques et philosophiques de Francois Quesnay (J. Bear, Frankfurt).
Ramsey, F., 1927, A contribution to the theory of taxation, Economic Journal 37.
Ricardo, David, 1817, The principles of political economy and taxation, in: Pierro Sraffa, ed., 1962, The works and correspondence of David Ricardo, Vol. I (Cambridge University Press, Cambridge).
Ricardo, David, 1820, Funding system, in: Pierro Sraffa, ed., 1962, The works and correspondence of David Ricardo, Vol. IV (Cambridge University Press, Cambridge).
Robbins, L., 1932, An essay on the nature and significance of economic science (Macmillan, London).

Robbins, L., 1938, Interpersonal comparison of utility, Economic Journal 48.
Robinson, J., 1933, The economics of imperfect competition (Macmillan, London).
Rolph, E.R., 1957, Principles of debt management, American Economic Review 50.
Salant, Walter W., 1975, Introduction to William A. Salant's 'Taxes, the multiplier, and the inflationary gap', History of Political Economy 7.
Salant, William, 1942, Taxes, the multiplier, and the inflationary gap. Reprinted in: 1975, History of Political Economy 7.
Sax, E., 1983, Grundlegung der theoretischen Staatswirtschaft (Wien).
Samuelson, P.A., 1939, Interactions between multiplier analysis and the principle of acceleration, Review of Economics and Statistics 21.
Samuelson, P.A., 1945, Foundations of economic analysis (Harvard University Press, Cambridge, MA).
Samuelson, P.A., 1948, The simple mathematics of income determination, in: Income, employment, and public policy: Essays in honour of Alvin Hansen (W.W. Norton, New York).
Samuelson, P.A., 1954, The pure theory of public expenditures, Review of Economics and Statistics 36.
Samuelson, P.A., 1955a, Principles and rules in modern fiscal policy: A neo-classical reformulation, in: Money, trade, and economic growth: Essays in honour of J.H. Williams (Macmillan, New York).
Samuelson, P.A., 1955b, Diagrammatic exposition of a theory of public expenditure, Review of Economics and Statistics 32.
Samuelson, P.A., 1964, Tax deductability of economic depreciation to insure invariant valuations, Journal of Political Economy 72.
Schäffle, A., 1867, Das gesellschaftliche System der menschlichen Wirschaft (Tübingen).
Schanz, G., 1896, Der Einkommensbegriff und die Einkommensteuergesetze, Finanzarchiv 13.
Schumpeter, J., 1918, Die Krise des Steuerstaates, in: Zeitfragen aus dem Gebiete der Soziologie (Graz). English translation in: 1954, International Economic Papers 5 (London).
Schumpeter, J., 1954, History of economic analysis (Oxford University Press, New York).
Seligman, E.R., 1899, Incidence of taxation, 4th ed., 1921 (Macmillan, New York).
Seligman, E.R., 1908, Progressive taxation in theory and practice, American Economic Association Quarterly (New York).
Seligman, E.R., 1911, The income tax (Macmillan, New York).
Shephard, R.W., 1944, A mathematical theory of the incidence of taxation, Econometrica 12.
Shoup, C.S., 1960, Ricardo on taxation (Columbia University Press, New York).
Shoup, C.S. and R.A. Musgrave, eds., 1959, Readings in the economics of taxation (Irwin, Homewood, IL).
Shoven, J. and J. Whalley, Applied general equilibrium models of taxation and international trade: An introduction and survey, Journal of Economic Literature 22.
Sidgwick, H., 1883, The principles of political economy (Macmillan, London).
Smith, Adam, 1759, The theory of moral sentiments, 1969 ed. by G. West (Liberty Classics, Indianapolis, LA).
Smith, Adam, 1776, An inquiry into the wealth of nations, 1904 ed. by E. Cunnan (Putnam's Sons, New York).
Smith, W.L., 1970, Macroeconomics (Irwin, Homewood, IL).
Smities, A. and J.K. Butters, eds., 1955, Readings in fiscal policy (Irwin, Homewood, IL).
Simons, H., 1948, Economic policy for a free society (University of Chicago Press, Chicago, IL).
Simons, H., 1958, Personal income taxation (University of Chicago Press, Chicago, IL).
Solow, R.M., 1956, A contribution to the theory of economic growth, Quarterly Journal of Economics 70.
Steuart, Sir James, 1776, An inquiry into the principles of political economy, 1966 ed. by A.R. Skinner (University of Chicago Press, Chicago, IL).
Tiebout, W., 1956, A pure theory of local government expenditures, Journal of Political Economy 64.
Tobin, J., 1958, Liquidity preference as behaviour towards risk, Review of Economic Studies 25.
Tobin, J., 1963, An essay in principles of debt management, in: Commission on Money and Credit, ed., Fiscal and debt management policies (Prentice Hall, Englewood Cliffs, NJ).
Vickrey, W., 1947, Agenda for progressive taxation (The Ronald Press, New York).
Vickrey, W., 1968, Dupuit, Jules, in: Encyclopedia of the social sciences, Vol. 4 (Macmillan, London).

Viti de Marco, A. de, 1888, Il carratere teorico dell'economia finanziara (Rome).

Viti de Marco, A. de, 1936, First principles of public finance (Harcourt, Brace & Co., New York).

Walras, L., 1874, Elements of pure economics, 1954 translation by W. Jaffe (Irwin, Homewood, IL).

Wicksell, K., 1896, Finanztheoretische Untersuchungen und das Steuerwesen Schwedens (Fisher, Jena). For translation of exerpts, see Musgrave and Peacock, eds. (1958).

Wagner, A., 1883, Lehr- und Handbuch der politischen Oekonomie, Vierte Hauptabteilung: Finanzwissenschaft (C.F. Winter, Leipzig).

Weisbrod, B., 1968, Income redistribution effects and benefit–cost analysis, in: S.B. Chase, ed., Problems in public expenditure analysis (Brookings Institution, Washington, DC).

Chapter 2

THE THEORY OF EXCESS BURDEN AND OPTIMAL TAXATION

ALAN J. AUERBACH*

University of Pennsylvania, Philadelphia, PA
National Bureau of Economic Research, Cambridge, MA

1. Introduction

The theory of excess burden and optimal commodity taxation is one of the oldest subjects of study in public finance, dating back to Dupuit (1844), and yet is also closely associated with the rapid analytical development of the field which commenced in the early 1970s. Perhaps more than in most areas of economics, there has been a tendency to overlook contributions made in earlier decades. As a result, much of the "new" public economics of the last decade may be viewed, in part, as a restatement and extension, perhaps in less arcane language and terminology, of previously proven propositions.

Probably the most celebrated example of such "rediscovery" is that of Ramsey's (1927) derivation of optimal commodity tax formulae, now referred to as the Ramsey rule. The lapse here is even harder to understand in that Ramsey's results were succinctly described in Pigou's classic public finance text (1947) and rederived by Boiteux (1956). The deadweight loss "triangles" made popular by the work of Harberger (1964) were considered by Hotelling (1938), and appear implicitly in Dupuit (1844):

> "It follows that when the change in consumption brought about by a tax is known, it is possible to find an upper limit to the amount of the utility lost by multiplying the change in consumption by half the tax."[1]

Indeed, the generalization of such excess burden formulae by Boiteux (1951) and Debreu (1951, 1954) has until recently[2] been almost entirely ignored in the subsequent literature. Even the "Laffer curve", popular for a time among non-economists, might more appropriately be called the "Dupuit curve":

*I am grateful to Angus Deaton, Avinash Dixit, Liam Ebrill, Jerry Hausman, Mervyn King, Randy Mariger, Jack Mintz, Harvey Rosen, Efraim Sadka, Jon Skinner, Nick Stern and Lars Svensson for comments on an earlier draft.

[1] Dupuit (1844).

[2] See, for example, Diewert (1981).

Handbook of Public Economics, vol. I, edited by A.J. Auerbach and M. Feldstein

"If a tax is gradually increased from zero up to a point where it becomes prohibitive, its yield is at first nil, then increases by small stages until it reaches a maximum, after which it gradually declines until it becomes zero again. It follows that when the state requires to raise a given sum by means of taxation, there are always two rates of tax which would fulfill the requirement, one above and one below that which would yield the maximum. There may be a very great difference between the amounts of utility lost through these taxes which yield the same revenue."[3]

The purpose of this chapter is to present the chronological development of the concept of excess burden and the related study of optimal tax theory. A main objective is to uncover the interrelationships among various apparently distinct results, so as to bring out the basic structure of the entire problem.

1.1. *Outline of the chapter*

Any discussion of welfare economics inevitably begins with the problem of welfare measurement, which in the present context involves a treatment of Marshall's consumers' surplus and its relationship to Hicks' (1942) notions of compensating and equivalent variations. These are discussed in Section 2, where special attention is paid to the distinction between the measurement of the welfare effects of price changes and the distortionary impact of tax changes. Section 3 develops the various measures of excess burden, focusing on issues of approximation, informational requirements and aggregation over individuals, and the effects of a more general technology than the commonly supposed one with fixed producer prices. Section 4 reviews some of the empirical attempts to estimate various deadweight losses. Section 5 presents and interprets the basic rules for optimal commodity taxation, including a discussion of the role of profits taxation and the desirability of production efficiency. The analysis in Section 6 concerns the relative desirability of direct and indirect taxation and the structure of individual preferences. Section 7 presents some applications of optimal tax theory to questions such as the provision of public goods, correction of externalities, and the allocation of risk. Finally, in Section 8, we explore the issue of tax reform, as distinct from *de novo* tax design. This literature dates back to Corlett and Hague (1953–54), and asks whether specified local movements away from an initial suboptimal equilibrium will improve social welfare. In general, movement of prices in the direction of their optimal levels does not guarantee such an improvement.

[3] Dupuit, *op. cit.*, p. 278. For this particular rediscovery, I am indebted to the historical analysis of Atkinson and Stern (1980).

2. Measures of surplus and excess burden

2.1. Consumers' surplus and the Hicksian variations

We begin with Marshall's (1920, p. 811) diagram, in Figure 2.1, depicting consumers' and producers' surplus. The consumers' surplus is defined, somewhat vaguely, to be the amount that consumers would pay in excess of the amount they are paying, $p_0 x_0$, for the amount they are purchasing, x_0. Interpreting the demand curve as an expression of willingness to pay, we obtain area A as such a measure by integrating the vertical gap between the demand curve and p_0 over x. Similarly, interpreting producers' surplus as the level of profits received in supplying the quantity sold, and assuming that competitive supply causes the marginal social cost to coincide with the supply schedule S, we obtain the area B. The sum $A + B$ is maximized when price equals marginal cost, and changes in each measure following from a price change are easily calculated. For example, if the price rises from p_0 to p_1, the change in consumers' surplus is the area of a

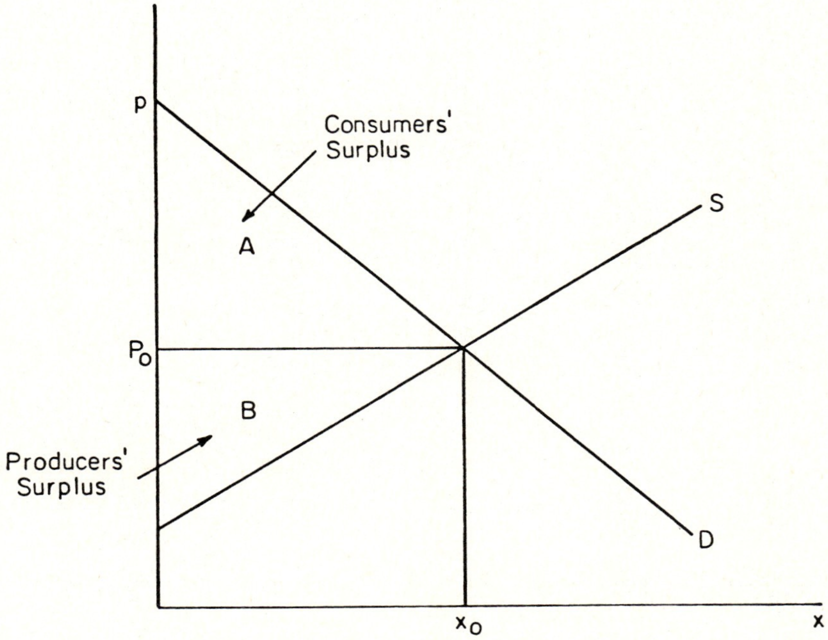

Figure 2.1. Consumers' and producers' surplus.

trapezoid which equals

$$\Delta S = -\int_{p_0}^{p_1} x(p)\,\mathrm{d}p, \tag{2.1}$$

where $x(\cdot)$ is the demand function with respect to the good's own price, holding other prices fixed.[4]

The basic problem with consumers' surplus as a welfare measure is that it does not come directly from underlying consumer preferences. As a result, it has the serious flaw of path-dependence: if more than one price changes, the order in which the trapezoids in (2.1) are calculated matters. That is, if we let x^i and p^i be the quantity demanded and price in the ith market, the sum of individual changes in consumers' surplus, ΔS^i, i.e., the line integral

$$\Delta S = \sum_i \Delta S = -\int_{\boldsymbol{p}_0}^{\boldsymbol{p}_1} \sum_i x^i\,\mathrm{d}p^i, \tag{2.2}$$

takes on different values according to the path of integration from the initial price vector $\boldsymbol{p}_0$ to the ultimate price vector $\boldsymbol{p}_1$. To see this, consider a simple example with two markets. If we change the price in market 1 first, the change in surplus is

$$\Delta S_1 = -\int_{p_0^1}^{p^1} x^1(p^1, p_0^2)\,\mathrm{d}p^1 - \int_{p_0^2}^{p_1^2} x^2(p_1^1, p^2)\,\mathrm{d}p^2, \tag{2.3a}$$

while if we change the price in market 2 first, we obtain

$$\Delta S_2 = -\int_{p_0^1}^{p_1^1} x^1(p^1, p_1^2)\,\mathrm{d}p^1 - \int_{p_0^2}^{p_1^2} x^2(p_0^1, p^2)(\mathrm{d}p^2). \tag{2.3b}$$

Subtracting ΔS_1 from ΔS_2, we obtain

$$\begin{aligned}\Delta S_2 - \Delta S_1 = &-\int_{p_0^1}^{p_1^1} \left[x^1(p^1, p_1^2) - x^1(p^1, p_0^2)\right]\mathrm{d}p^1 \\ &+ \int_{p_0^2}^{p_1^2} \left[x^2(p_1^1, p^2) - x^2(p_0^1, p^2)\right]\mathrm{d}p^2.\end{aligned} \tag{2.4}$$

[4] Note that, by integrating (2.1) by parts, we obtain the formula for ΔS based on the difference between the two levels of surplus themselves, i.e.,

$$\Delta S = \int_{x(p_0)}^{x(p_1)} p(x)\,\mathrm{d}x - [p_1x_1 - p_0x_0] = \int_0^{x(p_1)} p(x)\,\mathrm{d}x - p_1x_1 - \left[\int_0^{x(p_0)} p(x)\,\mathrm{d}x - p_0x_0\right].$$

For this term to equal zero, it must generally be zero over all subintervals between $\boldsymbol{p}_0$ and $\boldsymbol{p}_1$. In particular, for small changes in p^1 and p^2, with $p_1^2 = p_0^2 + \mathrm{d}p_0^2$ and $p_1^1 = p_0^1 + \mathrm{d}p^1$, (2.4) becomes

$$\Delta S_2 - \Delta S_1 = \frac{\partial x^2(p_0^1, p_0^2)}{\partial p^1}\mathrm{d}p^1\mathrm{d}p^2 - \frac{\partial x^1(p_0^1, p_0^2)}{\partial p^2}\mathrm{d}p^1\mathrm{d}p^2, \tag{2.5}$$

which equals zero only if the cross-price derivatives $\partial x^1/\partial p^2$ and $\partial x^2/\partial p^1$ are equal.[5] Such symmetry holds for *compensated* demands: the Slutsky matrix *is* symmetric [Hicks (1946)]. However, ordinary demand derivatives also possess income effects that are not generally equal.

The path-dependence problem does not arise from surplus measures based on compensated commodity demands, for which the symmetry property holds. Here, however, we face a different question: since utility does change with the change in prices, which utility level should be used as a reference level for the compensated demand functions? Two natural candidates are the levels of utility prevailing before and after the price changes. Following Hicks (1942), we define the *compensating* variation of a price change to be that amount of income the consumer must receive to leave utility unaffected by the price change, and the *equivalent* variation as the amount of income the consumer would forego to avoid the price change. By definition, the compensating variation of a price change from $\boldsymbol{p}_0$ to $\boldsymbol{p}_1$ equals the equivalent variation of a change from $\boldsymbol{p}_1$ to $\boldsymbol{p}_0$. Using the expenditure function, defined by the minimization of expenditure at given prices to satisfy a given level of utility:

$$E(\boldsymbol{p}, \bar{U}) = \min(\boldsymbol{p}\cdot\boldsymbol{x}) \quad \text{subject to} \quad U(\boldsymbol{x}) \geq \bar{U}, \tag{2.6a}$$

we may express concisely the equivalent and compensating variations as $E(\boldsymbol{p}, \bar{U}) - E(\boldsymbol{p}_0, \bar{U})$, where $\bar{U}$ is the pre-change utility level in the case of the compensating variation, and the post-change utility level in the case of the equivalent variation. Letting y be the consumer's actual income,[6] we can express these two measures as functions of prices and income alone through use of the indirect utility function, $V(\boldsymbol{p}, y)$, defined by

$$V(\boldsymbol{p}, y) = \max U(\boldsymbol{x}) \quad \text{subject to} \quad \boldsymbol{p}\cdot\boldsymbol{x} \geq y. \tag{2.6b}$$

Substituting (2.6b) into (2.6a), we obtain for the compensating variation of a price

[5] See Hotelling (1938) for the original statement of this result.

[6] y should be thought of as a comprehensive "full income" measure not affected by individual decisions regarding, for example, labor supply. This is discussed further in Section 5 below.

change from $\boldsymbol{p}_0$ to $\boldsymbol{p}_1$,

$$CV(\boldsymbol{p}_0, \boldsymbol{p}_1) = E(\boldsymbol{p}_1, V(\boldsymbol{p}_0, y)) - E(\boldsymbol{p}_0, V(\boldsymbol{p}_0, y))$$

$$= E(\boldsymbol{p}_1, V(\boldsymbol{p}_0, y)) - y, \tag{2.7a}$$

and for the corresponding equivalent variation,

$$EV(\boldsymbol{p}_0, \boldsymbol{p}_1) = E(\boldsymbol{p}_1, V(\boldsymbol{p}_1 y)) - E(\boldsymbol{p}_0, V(\boldsymbol{p}_1, y))$$

$$= y - E(\boldsymbol{p}_0, V(\boldsymbol{p}_1, y)), \tag{2.7b}$$

[where we use the identity $y = E(\boldsymbol{p}, V(\boldsymbol{p}, y))$].

These measures may be depicted graphically. By the envelope theorem, the derivative of the expenditure function with respect to an individual price p^i is

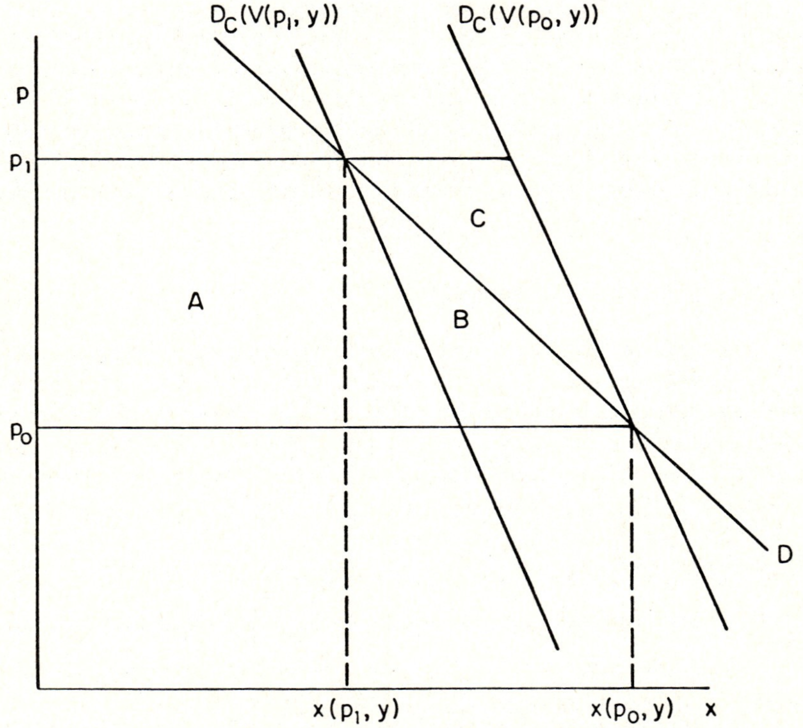

Figure 2.2. Compensating and equivalent variations.

simply the Hicksian or compensated demand $x_C^i(\boldsymbol{p},\bar{U})$. Thus, either of the Hicksian variations may be expressed (for the appropriate value of $\bar{U}$) as

$$E(\boldsymbol{p}_1,\bar{U})-E(\boldsymbol{p}_0,\bar{U})=\int_{\boldsymbol{p}_0}^{\boldsymbol{p}_1}\frac{\mathrm{d}E}{\mathrm{d}\boldsymbol{p}}(\boldsymbol{p},\bar{U})\,\mathrm{d}\boldsymbol{p}=\int_{\boldsymbol{p}^0}^{\boldsymbol{p}_1}\boldsymbol{x}_C(\boldsymbol{p},\bar{U})\,\mathrm{d}\boldsymbol{p}. \tag{2.8}$$

Since the cross-price derivatives are symmetric for compensated demands, these measures are path-independent. For the case of a single price change, they may be easily compared to the simple change in consumers' surplus, which is then well-defined. This is shown in Figure 2.2, where $D_C(\bar{U})$ is the compensated demand curve corresponding to the compensated demands $x_C(\boldsymbol{p},\bar{U})$, drawn more steeply than the ordinary demand curve D under the assumption of normality. The ordinary consumers' surplus changes by the area $A+B$ with an increase in price from p_0 to p_1. The compensating variation of the change equals the area $A+B+C$, while the equivalent variation equals the area A. The bracketing of the Marshallian measure by the two Hicksian measures was emphasized by Hicks (1942) and Willig (1976) in their attempts at rehabilitation of consumers' surplus as a welfare measure. However, their argument becomes weaker when more than one price changes, for then consumers' surplus is not even single-valued. Moreover, for estimating the excess burden of a tax, it is not the entire loss to the consumer in which we are interested but rather the loss in excess of revenue collected. It turns out that in such a case, the felicitous outcome with respect to the relative sizes of the three measures no longer holds.

2.2. *Definitions of excess burden*

The deadweight loss from a tax system is that amount that is lost in excess of what the government collects. Unfortunately, while this definition makes intuitive sense, it is too vague to permit a single interpretation.

We begin again with the simple Marshallian approach, which is adequate for purposes of illustrating the concept of excess burden in a single market. We can see the effects of a tax t in Figure 2.3. By raising the consumer price from p_0 to p_1+t, the tax reduces consumers' surplus by the area $A+B$. Producers' surplus is reduced by $C+D$, by the drop in producer price to p_1, but tax revenues amount only to $A+C$, yielding a social loss of $B+D$, or approximately $\frac{1}{2}t(x_0-x_1)=-\frac{1}{2}t\Delta x$, as suggested by Dupuit.

A key aspect of this measure is that it is greater than zero whether the tax is positive or negative. The case of a subsidy at rate s is depicted in Figure 2.4. Here, there is an increase in consumption to x_1, and consumers' surplus and producers' surplus both rise by the areas $H+I$ and $F+G$, respectively. But the

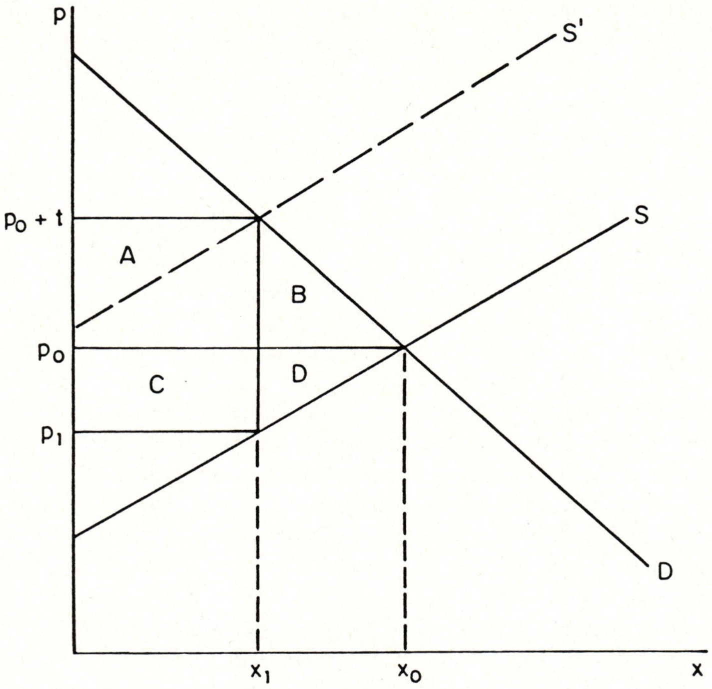

Figure 2.3. Excess burden of a tax.

amount of the subsidy exceeds those gains by the area J, equal to $\frac{1}{2}s\Delta x$ or, again, $-\frac{1}{2}t\Delta x$ for $t=-s$ being the algebraic value of the tax. The loss comes from the distortion of a Pareto optimal allocation, not simply the reduction in output.

For the case where a tax already exists, we may ask what additional excess burden would be caused by a tax increase. In this case, we subtract the *change* in government revenue from the change in producers' and consumers' surplus, since revenue is positive at the initial point. The resulting measure is shown in Figure 2.5.

By raising the consumer price from p_1+t_1 to p_2+t_2, the tax causes a loss in consumers' surplus of $A+B$. Producers' surplus declines by $C+D$, and, as before, the government collects additional revenue on the purchases x_2 equal to $(t_2-t_1)\cdot x_2$, or area $A+C$. However, the government loses the revenue it was collecting on the purchases in excess of x_2, equal to area E. Thus, the welfare loss of the tax increase equals the trapezoidal area $B+E+D$, or approximately $-(t\Delta x+\frac{1}{2}\Delta t\Delta x)$. Thus, even if Δt is very small, the additional excess burden

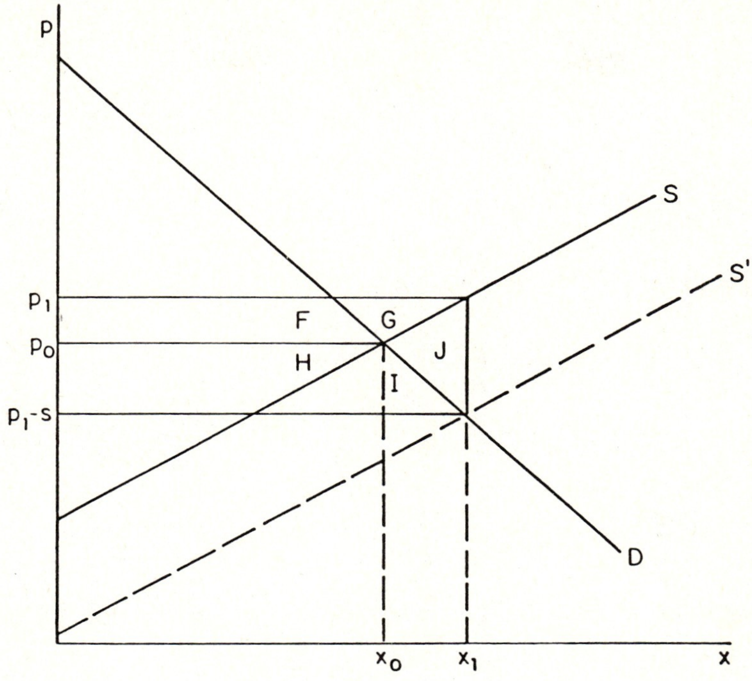

Figure 2.4. Excess burden of a subsidy.

need not be, unlike in the case where no tax exists initially: there is now a first-order welfare loss resulting from marginal tax changes.

If we wish to consider the effects of several taxes at once, we must use more sophisticated measures based on the Hicksian variations. For the remainder of this subsection, we focus on the case of a single consumer facing fixed producer prices. These restrictions are relaxed in Section 3.

Using the equivalent variation, Mohring (1971) suggests that the excess burden of taxation is the amount in excess of taxes being collected that the consumer would give up in exchange for the removal of all taxes; that is, how much more could be collected from the consumer (and thrown away) than is currently being collected, with no loss in utility, if the collection method were lump sum taxation. In the terminology used above, we may write this measure as

$$\begin{aligned} EB_{\mathrm{E}} &= E(\boldsymbol{p}_1, V(\boldsymbol{p}_1, y)) - E(\boldsymbol{p}_0, V(\boldsymbol{p}_1, y)) - R(\boldsymbol{p}_1, y) \\ &= y - E(\boldsymbol{p}_0, V(\boldsymbol{p}_1, y)) - (\boldsymbol{p}_1 - \boldsymbol{p}_0)\cdot \boldsymbol{x}(\boldsymbol{p}_1, y), \end{aligned} \tag{2.9}$$

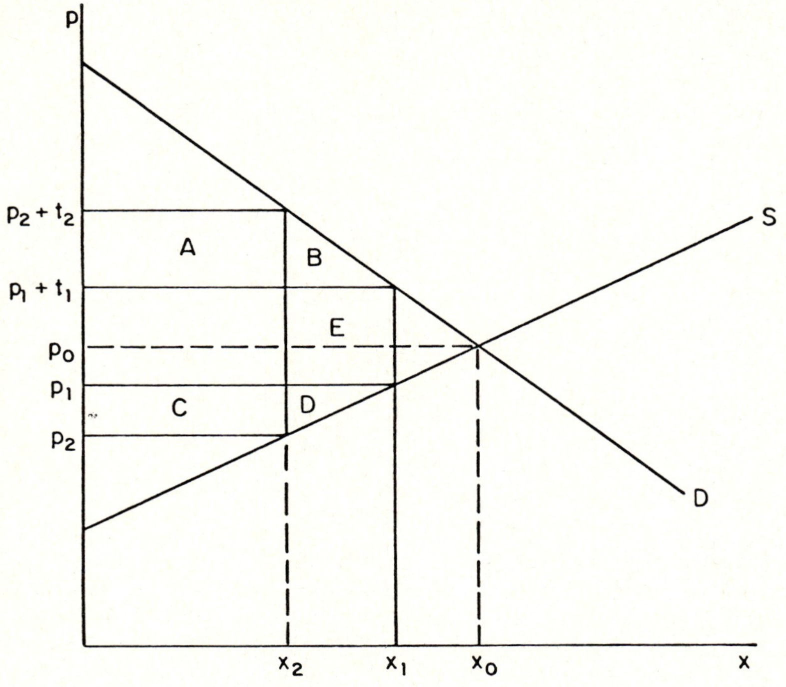

Figure 2.5. Excess burden with a pre-existing tax.

where $R(\mathbf{p}_1, y)$ is the tax revenue collected when prices are at $\mathbf{p}_1$ and the consumer's income equals y.

Alternatively, Diamond and McFadden (1974) suggest the use of the compensating variation by defining excess burden to be that amount, in addition to revenues collected, that the government must supply to the consumer to allow him to maintain the initial utility level. That is, how much must come from "outside" the system to compensate for the tax distortion. To avoid double-counting, we include in the government's revenue the additional amount it collects because the individual is compensated and (for a normal good) demands more of the taxed commodity. Thus, the Diamond–McFadden measure may be written

$$\begin{aligned} EB_C &= E(\mathbf{p}_1, V(\mathbf{p}_0, y)) - E(\mathbf{p}_0, V(\mathbf{p}_0, y)) - R(\mathbf{p}_1, E(\mathbf{p}_1, V(\mathbf{p}_0, y))) \\ &= E(\mathbf{p}_1, V(\mathbf{p}_0, y)) - y - (\mathbf{p}_1 - \mathbf{p}_0) \cdot \mathbf{x}(\mathbf{p}_1, E(\mathbf{p}_1, V(\mathbf{p}_0, y))) \\ &= E(\mathbf{p}_1, V(\mathbf{p}_0, y)) - y - (\mathbf{p}_1 - \mathbf{p}_0) \cdot \mathbf{x}_C(\mathbf{p}_1, V(\mathbf{p}_0, y)), \end{aligned} \tag{2.10}$$

[where the last step uses the identity $\boldsymbol{x}(\boldsymbol{p}, E(\boldsymbol{p}, \bar{U})) = x_{\mathrm{C}}(\boldsymbol{p}, \bar{U})$]. As with EB_{E}, EB_{C} must be non-negative.

For a single price change, these two measures of excess burden may be graphically compared to the Marshallian measure shown in Figure 2.3. The three measures together are shown in Figure 2.6. To obtain the equivalent variation measure or the consumers' surplus measure of excess burden, we subtract the revenue actually collected at $x(\boldsymbol{p}, y)$ from the respective measures shown in Figure 2.2. For the compensating variation measures, we subtract the revenue that would be collected if utility were kept at $V(\boldsymbol{p}_0, y)$. This yields the areas A, $A + B$, and C for the three respective measures. Note that the two Hicksian

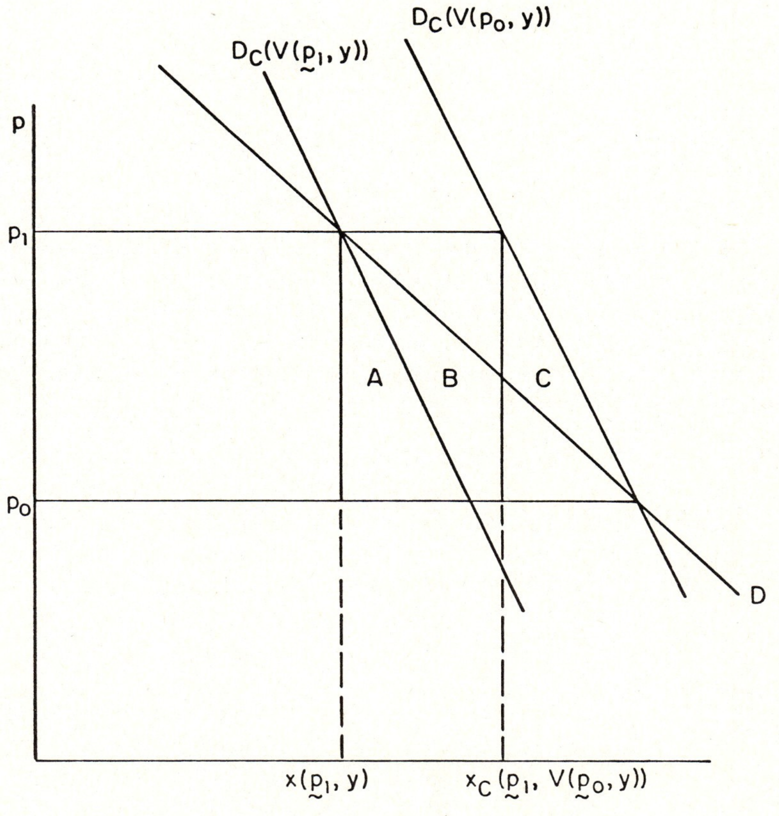

Figure 2.6. A comparison of excess burden measures.

measures no longer bracket the Marshallian one.[7] If the taxed good is normal, the latter is necessarily larger than each of the former, and the discrepancy may be quite large.

Other logical measures of excess burden involving the equivalent and compensating variations may be conceived.[8] In addition, it is easy to adapt the two measures already derived to the case where the initial equilibrium is not Pareto optimal but is already distorted by taxes. The equivalent variation measure of additional excess burden would then be the amount, in excess of additional tax revenues, that the consumer would pay to avoid the latest price increase from $\boldsymbol{p}_1$ to $\boldsymbol{p}_2$,

$$\begin{aligned} EB_{\mathrm{E}} &= E(\boldsymbol{p}_2, V(\boldsymbol{p}_2, y)) - E(\boldsymbol{p}_1, V(\boldsymbol{p}_2, y)) \\ &\quad - [R(\boldsymbol{p}_2, y) - R(\boldsymbol{p}_1, E(\boldsymbol{p}_1, V(\boldsymbol{p}_2, y)))] \\ &= y - E(\boldsymbol{p}_1, V(\boldsymbol{p}_2, y)) - (\boldsymbol{p}_2 - \boldsymbol{p}_0) \cdot \boldsymbol{x}(\boldsymbol{p}_2, y) \\ &\quad + (\boldsymbol{p}_1 - \boldsymbol{p}_0) \cdot \boldsymbol{x}_{\mathrm{C}}(\boldsymbol{p}_1, V(\boldsymbol{p}_2, y)) \\ &= y - E(\boldsymbol{p}_1, V(\boldsymbol{p}_2, y)) - (\boldsymbol{p}_2 - \boldsymbol{p}_1) \cdot \boldsymbol{x}(\boldsymbol{p}_2, y) \\ &\quad + (\boldsymbol{p}_1 - \boldsymbol{p}_0) \cdot (\boldsymbol{x}_{\mathrm{C}}(\boldsymbol{p}_1, V(\boldsymbol{p}_2, y)) - \boldsymbol{x}(\boldsymbol{p}_2, y)). \end{aligned} \tag{2.11}$$

Comparing (2.11) with (2.9), we find that (2.11) contains an additional expression representing the reduction in tax revenues as demand declines with the new rise in price, with utility held constant at $V(\boldsymbol{p}_2, y)$. This additional term corresponds to that found for the basic consumers' surplus measure in Figure 2.6. Likewise, the compensating variation measure would be the amount in excess of the change in revenues that would be required to maintain the initial utility level, or

$$\begin{aligned} EB_{\mathrm{C}} &= E(\boldsymbol{p}_2, V(\boldsymbol{p}_1, y)) - E(\boldsymbol{p}_1, V(\boldsymbol{p}_1, y)) \\ &\quad - [R(\boldsymbol{p}_2, E(\boldsymbol{p}_2, V(\boldsymbol{p}_1, y))) - R(\boldsymbol{p}_1, y)] \\ &= E(\boldsymbol{p}_2, V(\boldsymbol{p}_1, y)) - y - (\boldsymbol{p}_2 - \boldsymbol{p}_0) \cdot \boldsymbol{x}_{\mathrm{C}}(\boldsymbol{p}_2, V(\boldsymbol{p}_1, y)) \\ &\quad + (\boldsymbol{p}_1 - \boldsymbol{p}_0) \cdot \boldsymbol{x}(\boldsymbol{p}_1, y) \\ &= E(\boldsymbol{p}_2, V(\boldsymbol{p}_1, y)) - y - (\boldsymbol{p}_2 - \boldsymbol{p}_1) \cdot \boldsymbol{x}_{\mathrm{C}}(\boldsymbol{p}_2, V(\boldsymbol{p}_1, y)) \\ &\quad + (\boldsymbol{p}_1 - \boldsymbol{p}_0) \cdot (\boldsymbol{x}(\boldsymbol{p}_1, y) - \boldsymbol{x}_{\mathrm{C}}(\boldsymbol{p}_2, V(\boldsymbol{p}_1, y))), \end{aligned} \tag{2.12}$$

[7] This was pointed out by Hausman (1981a), among others.
[8] See Auerbach and Rosen (1980) for further discussion.

where the additional term compared to (2.10) is the revenue lost as demand declines with utility held constant at $V(\boldsymbol{p}_1, y)$.

3. Evaluating the measures of excess burden

3.1. Taylor approximations and informational requirements

For purposes of exposition, it is sometimes easier to express the deadweight loss calculations above in terms of second-order Taylor approximations. For example, if we expand the exact measure EB_C around the initial price vector $\boldsymbol{p}_1$, we obtain

$$EB_C = \left.\frac{\mathrm{d}EB_C}{\mathrm{d}\boldsymbol{p}}\right|_{\boldsymbol{p}_1} \cdot(\boldsymbol{p}_2-\boldsymbol{p}_1)+\tfrac{1}{2}(\boldsymbol{p}_2-\boldsymbol{p}_1)'\left.\frac{\mathrm{d}^2EB_C}{\mathrm{d}\boldsymbol{p}^2}\right|_{\boldsymbol{p}_1}(\boldsymbol{p}_2-\boldsymbol{p}_1)+\cdots, \tag{3.1}$$

which, ignoring all terms beyond the second order, yields

$$EB_C \approx \left[-(\boldsymbol{p}_1-\boldsymbol{p}_0)'\left[\frac{\mathrm{d}\boldsymbol{x}_C}{\mathrm{d}\boldsymbol{p}}\right](\boldsymbol{p}_2-\boldsymbol{p}_1)\right.$$
$$\left. +\tfrac{1}{2}(\boldsymbol{p}_2-\boldsymbol{p}_1)'\left[-\frac{\mathrm{d}\boldsymbol{x}_C}{\mathrm{d}\boldsymbol{p}}-(\boldsymbol{p}_1-\boldsymbol{p}_0)\frac{\mathrm{d}^2\boldsymbol{x}_C}{\mathrm{d}\boldsymbol{p}^2}\right](\boldsymbol{p}_2-\boldsymbol{p}_1)\right], \tag{3.2}$$

where $\boldsymbol{x}_C$ is evaluated at $\boldsymbol{p}_1$ and $V(\boldsymbol{p}_1, y)$. If we make a further approximation by ignoring the curvature terms of the compensated demand function $\mathrm{d}^2\boldsymbol{x}_C/\mathrm{d}\boldsymbol{p}^2$, we obtain

$$EB_C \approx -(\boldsymbol{t}'S\Delta\boldsymbol{t}+\tfrac{1}{2}\Delta\boldsymbol{t}'S\Delta\boldsymbol{t}) = -(\boldsymbol{t}'\Delta\boldsymbol{x}_C+\tfrac{1}{2}\Delta\boldsymbol{t}'\Delta\boldsymbol{x}_C), \tag{3.3}$$

where $\boldsymbol{t}=(\boldsymbol{p}_1-\boldsymbol{p}_0)$, $\Delta\boldsymbol{t}=(\boldsymbol{p}_2-\boldsymbol{p}_1)$, $S=\mathrm{d}\boldsymbol{x}_C/\mathrm{d}\boldsymbol{p}$ is the Slutsky matrix, and $\Delta\boldsymbol{x}_C=S\Delta\boldsymbol{t}$. This is of a form similar to the single-market measure derived above for simple consumers' surplus, but the changes in demand are now compensated changes rather than ordinary ones. The approximation in (3.3) is that originally derived by Harberger (1964), although the procedure used to derive it here is somewhat simpler.[9]

From (3.3), we may observe a number of additional characteristics of tax-induced excess burden. First of all, when there are pre-existing taxes in other

[9]One can also derive higher-order approximations of EB_C. For a comparison of the errors involved in using second- and third-order approximations, see Green and Sheshinski (1979).

markets, the introduction of another tax need not worsen things. We must weigh the strictly positive term $-(\Delta t_i)^2 S_{ii}$ for the new tax in market i against the cross-effects $-t_j S_{ji} \Delta t_i$ in each other market j, which represent the loss in revenue from the tax t_j due to the drop in demand resulting from the price increase in market i. Since S_{ji} may be positive or negative, so may each of those terms. In general, if pre-existing taxes are on goods substitutable for good i ($S_{ji} > 0$), the new tax is more likely to lessen the total excess burden of the tax system.

A second observation to make from (3.3) is that excess burden is a non-linear function of tax rates. Consider, for example, a single tax t_i imposed upon a state without taxes. The excess burden is approximately $-\frac{1}{2}t_i^2 S_{ii}$, so that it increases with the *square* of the tax. This suggests that to raise a certain amount of revenue, we might reduce excess burden by using several small taxes rather than a few large ones, perhaps tilting toward those with smaller own-substitution effects for which the scale of excess burden is lower. However, once several taxes are used, the cross-effects just discussed need also be evaluated. How these aspects fit together will become clearer in Section 5 when we formally consider the optimal tax problem.

Aside from expositional purposes, the use of a Taylor approximation can only be justified on grounds of insufficient information. If we know the consumer's expenditure function, we can calculate either of the exact measures of excess burden explicitly. Even if we know only the consumer's ordinary demand function, we can solve for his indirect utility function and hence his compensated demand function (in principle) using the system of partial differential equations generated by Roy's identity,[10]

$$x(p, y) = -\frac{\mathrm{d}U/\mathrm{d}p}{\mathrm{d}U/\mathrm{d}y}. \tag{3.4}$$

Thus, we must know less than the consumer's demand function if we are to justify the use of an approximation; perhaps only its local properties. However, even in this case, it is probably preferable to construct an exact measure to the extent of one's limited knowledge of demand characteristics away from the initial equilibrium, and use confidence bounds based on the precision of our underlying parameter estimates. Alternatively, one can use revealed preference theory in conjunction with observed data to derive bounds, without ever specifying a particular demand function [Varian (1982)].

A second defense of the use of approximations or even of simple consumers' surplus measures is that the demand function as estimated is not integrable, so that we cannot use the procedure suggested above to derive the associated

[10]See Hausman (1981a). Vartia (1983) presents a numerical algorithm for generating utility functions from demand functions.

compensated demand function. However, lack of integrability is synonomous with the violation of the laws of demand. If such laws are violated, what interpretation can we give *any* measure we use?

3.2. Variations in producer prices

The assumption made thus far in this section that producer prices are fixed is a common one in the literature, but may do violence to our representation of the actual situation prevailing in the economy. For example, we know that a tax on a good in absolutely fixed supply is equivalent to a lump sum tax and therefore non-distortionary, regardless of how elastic the demand for the good is. Our preliminary examination of excess burden using consumers' surplus in Section 2 suggested that the excess burden of a tax is proportional to the reduction in the output of the taxed good, taking account of both demand and supply conditions. It would be useful to extend the Hicksian measures in the same direction.

The complication that arises in doing so is that it is no longer sufficient to posit a certain money value of compensation: since producer prices change, the form of compensation matters. For example, to extend the compensating variation measure of excess burden, we must specify the form in which the compensation from "outside" the system, in excess of collected revenue, will come.

To develop a compensating variation measure of the additional excess burden caused by an increase in taxes, starting at a distorted equilibrium, we let $\boldsymbol{\alpha}$ be the compensation vector of the elements of $\boldsymbol{x}$, and β the scalar that determines how much of the compensation bundle the consumer receives, $\beta\alpha$. If we denote producer prices by $\boldsymbol{q}$ and consumer prices by $\boldsymbol{p}$, then the compensating variation measure of excess burden $\boldsymbol{\beta}$ can be defined implicitly by the equation

$$V(\boldsymbol{p}_2, y_2 + R_2 - R_1 + \boldsymbol{q}_2 \cdot \boldsymbol{\alpha}\beta) = V(\boldsymbol{p}_1, y_1), \tag{3.5}$$

where $\boldsymbol{p}_1$ is the initial consumer price vector, $\boldsymbol{p}_2$ the distorted price vector, $\boldsymbol{q}_1$ and $\boldsymbol{q}_2$ the corresponding producer price vectors, y_1 and y_2 the lump sum income in the two states, and $R_1 = (\boldsymbol{p}_1 - \boldsymbol{q}_1) \cdot \boldsymbol{x}(\boldsymbol{p}_1, y_1)$ and $R_2 = (\boldsymbol{p}_2 - \boldsymbol{q}_2) \cdot x_C(\boldsymbol{p}_2, V(\boldsymbol{p}_1, y_1))$ the revenue in the two states. The values of y are indexed by their respective states because they may vary when producer prices change. For example, if the economy's production function exhibits decreasing returns to scale in the consumer goods $\boldsymbol{x}$, then the pure profits from competitive production are positive and change with the change in producer prices. Letting z be the vector of goods produced (negative for net factor inputs), total profits are $y = \boldsymbol{q} \cdot z$. Note that production and consumption differ by the infusion of additional compensation, $\beta\boldsymbol{\alpha}$.

Expression (3.5) can be transformed into another that is similar to those of the previous section. Using the fact that $U_A = U_B \rightarrow E(\boldsymbol{p}, U_A) = E(\boldsymbol{p}, U_B)$, and that $E(\boldsymbol{p}, U(\boldsymbol{p}, y)) = y$, we obtain

$$\begin{aligned} \boldsymbol{q}_2 \cdot \boldsymbol{\alpha}\beta &= E(\boldsymbol{p}_2, V(\boldsymbol{p}_1, y_1)) - y_2 - (R_2 - R_1) \\ &= [E(\boldsymbol{p}_2, V(\boldsymbol{p}_1, y_1)) - E(\boldsymbol{p}_1, V(\boldsymbol{p}_1, y_1))] + (y_1 - y_2) - (R_2 - R_1). \end{aligned} \tag{3.6}$$

Compared to (2.12), there is a new term, $(y_1 - y_2)$, representing the reduction in profit between states 1 and 2. Thus, there are now three terms in the expression for excess burden, representing the changes in consumers', producers' and government surplus, as in the simple, Marshallian example depicted in Figure 2.3.

This expression for excess burden also differs in that it is not actually a *solution* for β. It will hold regardless of the choice of $\boldsymbol{\alpha}$, though the solution for β depends on this choice. This dependence can be demonstrated by considering the second-order approximation for β,

$$\beta \approx \frac{\mathrm{d}\beta}{\mathrm{d}\boldsymbol{t}} \Delta \boldsymbol{t} + \tfrac{1}{2} \Delta \boldsymbol{t}' \frac{\mathrm{d}^2\beta}{\mathrm{d}\boldsymbol{t}^2} \Delta \boldsymbol{t}, \tag{3.7}$$

evaluated at the initial point 1. Total differentiation of (3.5) yields

$$\frac{\mathrm{d}V}{\mathrm{d}\boldsymbol{p}} \cdot \mathrm{d}\boldsymbol{p} + \frac{\mathrm{d}V}{\mathrm{d}y} \left[\frac{\mathrm{d}y}{\mathrm{d}\boldsymbol{q}} \cdot \mathrm{d}\boldsymbol{q} + \beta\boldsymbol{\alpha} \cdot \mathrm{d}\boldsymbol{q} + \mathrm{d}\beta\,\boldsymbol{\alpha} \cdot \boldsymbol{q} + \boldsymbol{t} \cdot \mathrm{d}\boldsymbol{x} + \boldsymbol{x} \cdot \mathrm{d}\boldsymbol{t} \right] = 0, \tag{3.8}$$

where $\boldsymbol{t} = (\boldsymbol{p} - \boldsymbol{q})$.

Again using the envelope theorem, one can show that $\mathrm{d}y/\mathrm{d}\boldsymbol{q} = \boldsymbol{z}$. Using this and Roy's identity [(3.4) above], we obtain from (3.8)

$$\frac{\mathrm{d}V}{\mathrm{d}y} [-\boldsymbol{x} \cdot \mathrm{d}\boldsymbol{p} + \boldsymbol{z} \cdot \mathrm{d}\boldsymbol{q} + \beta\boldsymbol{\alpha} \cdot \mathrm{d}\boldsymbol{q} + \mathrm{d}\beta\,\boldsymbol{\alpha} \cdot \boldsymbol{q} + \boldsymbol{t} \cdot \mathrm{d}\boldsymbol{x} + \boldsymbol{x} \cdot \mathrm{d}\boldsymbol{t}] = 0. \tag{3.9}$$

But since $\boldsymbol{x} = \boldsymbol{z} + \beta\boldsymbol{\alpha}$ and $\mathrm{d}V/\mathrm{d}y \neq 0$, (3.9) simplifies to

$$\boldsymbol{q}_2 \cdot \boldsymbol{\alpha}\,\mathrm{d}\beta = -\boldsymbol{t} \cdot \mathrm{d}\boldsymbol{x}, \tag{3.10}$$

which is precisely the form of the first-order effect derived above in (3.3).

We derive the second-order term by totally differentiating (3.10). This yields

$$\boldsymbol{q}_2 \cdot \boldsymbol{\alpha}\,\mathrm{d}^2\beta = -\mathrm{d}\boldsymbol{t} \cdot \mathrm{d}\boldsymbol{x} - \mathrm{d}\beta\,\boldsymbol{\alpha} \cdot \mathrm{d}\boldsymbol{q} - \boldsymbol{t} \cdot \mathrm{d}^2\boldsymbol{x}, \tag{3.11}$$

which, even if one ignores the last curvature term, has an additional term compared to the second-order effect in (3.3), caused by the changing value of the compensation bundle. This may be seen by substituting (3.10) and (3.11) into (3.7) to obtain

$$\boldsymbol{q}_2 \cdot \boldsymbol{\alpha}\beta \approx -\left(\boldsymbol{t}'\Delta \boldsymbol{x} + \tfrac{1}{2}\Delta \boldsymbol{t}'\Delta \boldsymbol{x} + \tfrac{1}{2}\beta\boldsymbol{\alpha}\cdot\Delta\boldsymbol{q}\right), \tag{3.12}$$

where the right-hand side of (3.12) includes the first-order approximations $(\mathrm{d}\boldsymbol{x}/\mathrm{d}t)\Delta \boldsymbol{t}$ for Δx, $(\mathrm{d}\boldsymbol{q}/\mathrm{d}t)\Delta t$ for $\Delta \boldsymbol{q}$, and $(\mathrm{d}\beta/\mathrm{d}t)\Delta \boldsymbol{t}$ for β. Only in the case that all compensation is in the form of the numeraire commodity will (3.12) reduce to (3.3).[11]

This extra term may be represented graphically by considering the exact measure (3.6) for the case in which there are two goods, one of which is taxed. This is done in Figure 3.1. Let the untaxed good serve as numeraire, so that its price does not change. The supply curve S shows the increasing relative producer price, q, of the taxed good as its production increases. The ordinary demand curve D represents the consumer's preference, given income y_1. With an initial tax of $(p_1 - q_1)$, the initial equilibrium consumption is at x_1, where the supply curve S_1 is that facing the consumer.

As the tax is increased further, we assume the individual is maintained on the same indifference curve, so that demand for x is described by the compensated demand curve passing through the initial point. The supply curve facing the consumer now depends on the form the compensation takes. If some of the taxed good is included in $\boldsymbol{\alpha}$, then the supply to the consumer is described by curve S_2', rather than S_2, since total supply will exceed production. This leads to consumption at x_2, and production at z_2, rather than the single value in between that would obtain if all compensation were in the form of the numeraire commodity.

Consider now the three terms in expression (3.6). All may be represented in Figure 3.1. The first, as before, is the area to the left of the compensated demand curve between p_1 and p_2. Since $\mathrm{d}y = z\,\mathrm{d}\boldsymbol{q}$, the second term in (3.6) equals the area to the left of the supply curve S between q_1 and q_2. Finally, R_1 and R_2 equal in area the rectangles defined by p_1, q_1 and x_1, and p_2, q_2 and x_2, respectively. The resulting area for $q_2 \cdot \boldsymbol{\alpha}\beta$ is the usual trapezoid defined by the supply curve, the compensated demand curve, x_1 and x_2 (shaded in Figure 3.1), *less* that of the triangle defined by the producers' supply curve S, the social supply curve S', and prices q_1 and q_2 (cross-hatched in Figure 3.1). This new piece has an area approximately equal to $\frac{1}{2}(q_1 - q_2)(x_2 - z_2)$ or, since $\boldsymbol{x} = \boldsymbol{z} + \beta\boldsymbol{\alpha}$ and only this good's price changes, $-\frac{1}{2}\beta\boldsymbol{\alpha}\cdot\Delta\boldsymbol{q}$.

Another familiar expression for the second-order effect may be derived from (3.11). Again ignoring the last curvature term, we use the fact that $\boldsymbol{x} = \beta\boldsymbol{\alpha} + \boldsymbol{z}$ to

[11] In deriving a similar measure, Diamond and McFadden (1974) made this assumption.

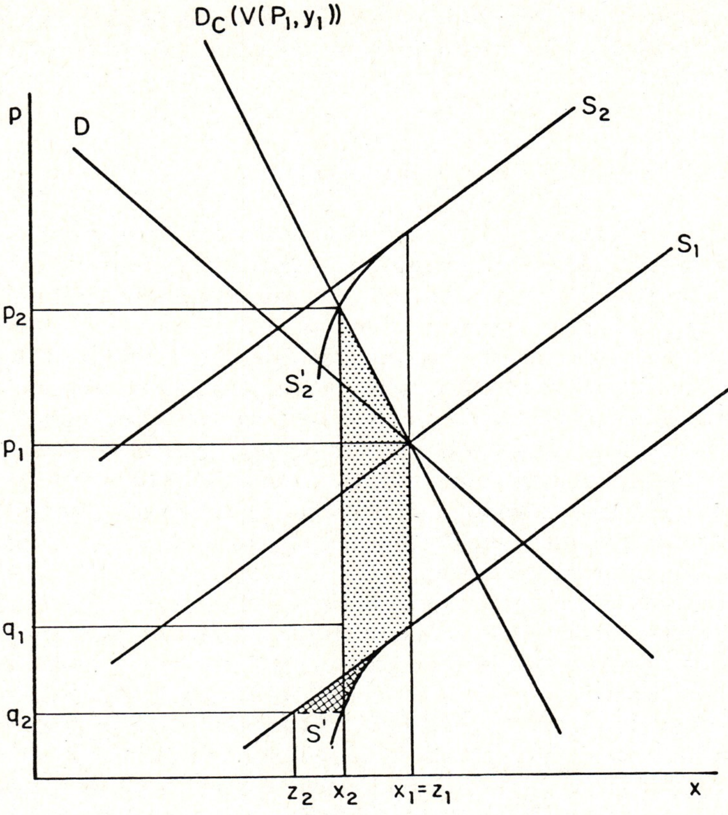

Figure 3.1. Excess burden with changing producer prices.

obtain

$$d^2\beta \approx -d\boldsymbol{p}\cdot d\boldsymbol{x} + d\boldsymbol{q}\cdot dz = -d\boldsymbol{p}'S\,d\boldsymbol{p} + d\boldsymbol{q}'H\,d\boldsymbol{q}, \tag{3.13}$$

where H is the Hessian of the profit function $d^2y/d\boldsymbol{q}^2 = dz/d\boldsymbol{q}$.

This expression for the second-order effect of a change in taxes on welfare was first developed by Boiteux (1951), although his derivation was limited to the case where the initial equilibrium is undistorted and the first-order effect $d\beta$ vanishes.

Using the notion of equivalent variation, we can construct a measure by asking what level of resources can be extracted from the consumer in excess of additional revenue to avoid an additional tax increase. This yields the following implicit definition of β:

$$V(\boldsymbol{p}_2, y_2) = V(\boldsymbol{p}_1, y_1 - (R_2 - R_1) - \boldsymbol{q}_1 \cdot \boldsymbol{\alpha}\beta), \tag{3.14}$$

where, in this case, state 2 is the actual state with taxes at $\boldsymbol{t}_2$, whereas state 1 is the hypothetical state in which taxes do not rise from $\boldsymbol{t}_1$ but income is reduced to yield the same level of utility as prevails in state 2. Here, $(1-\beta)$ is related to Debreu's (1951) *coefficient of resource utilization*, which he defines to be the proportion of society's resources that would be necessary to maintain each individual's current level of utility if all distortions were removed. Our measure differs in that we consider the marginal change, rather than removal of a distortion, and let the vector $\boldsymbol{\alpha}$ be arbitrary. (Of course, Debreu's measure is defined relative to all kinds of distortions leading to an inefficient allocation, not just tax-induced changes in the prices of consumer goods.) As before, we cannot solve for β explicitly, but we can calculate the first-order and second-order effects $\mathrm{d}\beta$ and $\mathrm{d}^2\beta$ at the initial distorted point. We leave further discussion of this measure to the next subsection, which deals with aggregation over consumers.

3.3. Aggregation and welfare comparisons

Thus far, we have defined all our measures of excess burden for the case of a single individual. They are easily generalized to the case of several identical individuals. However, matters become more complicated if we wish to allow for differences in individual tastes, or even differences in income among otherwise identical individuals.

Except under very strict conditions on preferences, any measure of aggregate excess burden will depend on the initial distribution of income. Consider the case of fixed producer prices examined in Section 2, and define a measure of aggregate excess burden, using the compensating variation, as the amount that must come from outside the system to maintain each consumer at his pre-tax level of utility. For two individuals, this measure equals [compare to (2.10)]

$$\begin{aligned} L = {} & E^1(\boldsymbol{p}_1, V^1(\boldsymbol{p}_0, y^1)) + E^2(\boldsymbol{p}_1, V^2(\boldsymbol{p}_0, y^2)) - (y^1 + y^2) \\ & - (\boldsymbol{p}_1 - \boldsymbol{p}_0) \cdot (\boldsymbol{x}_{\mathrm{C}}^1(\boldsymbol{p}_1, V^1(\boldsymbol{p}_0, y^1)) + \boldsymbol{x}_{\mathrm{C}}^2(\boldsymbol{p}_1, V^2(\boldsymbol{p}_0, y^2))), \end{aligned} \tag{3.15}$$

where superscripts index the consumers 1 and 2.

Suppose now that the initial income distribution is changed by a small reduction in y^1 and an equal size increase in y^2. The change in L would be

$$\mathrm{d}L = -\frac{\partial E^1}{\partial U}\cdot\frac{\partial V^1}{\partial y} + 1 + \frac{\partial E^2}{\partial U}\cdot\frac{\partial V^2}{\partial y}$$

$$-1 - (\boldsymbol{p}_1 - \boldsymbol{p}_0)\cdot\left(-\frac{\partial \boldsymbol{x}_C^1}{\partial U}\cdot\frac{\partial V^1}{\partial y} + \frac{\partial \boldsymbol{x}_C^2}{\partial U}\cdot\frac{\partial V^2}{\partial y}\right), \tag{3.16}$$

which, using the fact that $\boldsymbol{x}_C(\boldsymbol{p}_1, V(\boldsymbol{p}_0, y)) = \boldsymbol{x}(\boldsymbol{p}_1, E(\boldsymbol{p}_1, V(\boldsymbol{p}_0, y)))$, can be rewritten as

$$\mathrm{d}L = -\frac{\partial E^1}{\partial U}\cdot\frac{\partial V^1}{\partial y} + \frac{\partial E^2}{\partial U}\cdot\frac{\partial V^2}{\partial y}$$

$$-(\boldsymbol{p}_1 - \boldsymbol{p}_0)\cdot\left(-\frac{\partial \boldsymbol{x}^1}{\partial y}\cdot\frac{\partial E^1}{\partial U}\cdot\frac{\partial V^1}{\partial y} + \frac{\partial \boldsymbol{x}^2}{\partial y}\cdot\frac{\partial E^2}{\partial U}\cdot\frac{\partial V^2}{\partial y}\right). \tag{3.17}$$

Since $E(\boldsymbol{p}_0, V(\boldsymbol{p}_0, y)) = y$, we may rewrite (3.17) as

$$\mathrm{d}L = -\frac{\hat{\mu}^1}{\mu^1}\left(1 - (\boldsymbol{p}_1 - \boldsymbol{p}_0)\cdot\frac{\mathrm{d}\boldsymbol{x}^1}{\mathrm{d}y}\right) + \frac{\hat{\mu}^2}{\mu^2}\left(1 - (\boldsymbol{p}_1 - \boldsymbol{p}_0)\cdot\frac{\mathrm{d}\boldsymbol{x}^2}{\mathrm{d}y}\right), \tag{3.18}$$

where

$$\mu^i = \frac{\partial E^i}{\partial U}(\boldsymbol{p}_0, V^i(\boldsymbol{p}_0, y^i)) \quad \text{and} \quad \hat{\mu}^i = \frac{\partial E^i}{\partial U}(\boldsymbol{p}_1, V^i(\boldsymbol{p}_0, y^i))$$

are the marginal expenditures needed per unit of increased utility at base utility level $V^i(\boldsymbol{p}_0, y^i)$ and price levels $\boldsymbol{p}_0$ and $\boldsymbol{p}_1$, respectively. Thus, $\mathrm{d}L$ will equal zero, in general, only if two conditions are met:

1) $\hat{\mu}^i/\mu^i$ equals some common function of prices alone (not income) for the two individuals; and
2) the vector of income effects $\mathrm{d}\boldsymbol{x}^i/\mathrm{d}y$ equals some common function of prices alone.

Condition 2) implies that ordinary demand functions take the form

$$\boldsymbol{x}^i(\boldsymbol{p}, y^i) = \boldsymbol{\phi}^i(\boldsymbol{p}) + \boldsymbol{\theta}(\boldsymbol{p})y^i, \tag{3.19}$$

for some functions $\boldsymbol{\phi}^i(\cdot)$ and $\boldsymbol{\theta}(\cdot)$, the latter common across individuals. [The laws of consumer demand imply, in turn, that $\phi^i(\cdot)$ is homogeneous of degree 0 in prices and $\theta(\cdot)$ is homogeneous of degree -1 in prices, since a proportional change in p and y cannot affect $x^i(\cdot)$.] The demand function specified in (3.19) corresponds to the well-known Gorman (1953) "polar form", which plays a central role in the theory of exact aggregation.

Condition 1) implies that, for suitable transformation of the utility function, consumer i's expenditure function can be written

$$E^i(p, U^i) = \delta^i(p) + \gamma(p) \cdot U^i, \tag{3.20}$$

[with $\delta^i(\cdot)$ and $\gamma(\cdot)$ homogeneous of degree 1 in prices]. This is the expenditure function corresponding to the Gorman polar form [see Muellbauer (1976)], so that conditions 1) and 2) are each satisfied if and only if preferences satisfy this very restricted pattern that allows variations from identical homothetic preferences only through individual-specific displacements through the "basic needs" function of zero-income consumption, $\phi^i(\cdot)$.

Note that even identical preferences, unless homothetic, will not suffice. For example, suppose individuals have a price-inelastic compensated demand for a commodity at high incomes but an elastic demand at low incomes. Then the excess burden of a tax on this good will be increased if we transfer income to the poorer individual, for this will increase the overall demand elasticity for the taxed good. Thus, any measure of excess burden we envisage is not independent of the income distribution. Similarly, if we required not that each individual's utility be kept constant, but that individual 1 receive one dollar less than would be necessary, this, too, would affect the aggregate measure for the same reason.

Of course, it is still possible to *define* measures of excess burden for the multi-individual case, given the initial resource distribution. For example, we may implicitly define a compensating variation measure analogous to (3.5) by the identities

$$V^i(p_2, \omega^i(y_2 + R_2 - R_1 + q_2 \cdot \alpha\beta)) = V^i(p_1, \bar{\omega}^i y_1), \quad \forall i, \tag{3.21}$$

where i indexes the individual, $\bar{\omega}^i$ is individual i's actual profit share, and ω^i is the share needed to maintain each individual on the same indifference curve as prices rise to p_2 and the extra compensation vector $\alpha \cdot \beta$ "enters" the system. For the equivalent variation, the measure for β corresponding to (3.14) for several individuals is

$$V^i(p_2, \bar{\omega}^i y_2) = V^i(p_1, \omega^i(y_1 - R_2 + R_1 - q_2 \cdot \alpha\beta)). \tag{3.22}$$

Again, it is not generally possible to solve explicitly for β in either case, but we can derive expressions for the first-order and second-order effects $\mathrm{d}\beta$ and $\mathrm{d}^2\beta$ by totally differentiating (3.21) or (3.22) for each i and then adding over i, making use of the adding-up constraint on the profit shares ω. While the resulting expressions for the compensating variation measure are essentially the same as those described in Section 3.2 (with aggregate demands replacing individual ones), an interesting result occurs in the second-order effect derived from the measure defined by (3.22). It contains an additional term reflecting the indirect impact of taxes on excess burden through the change in the income distribution in state 1 [Debreu (1954)]. Since for an equivalent variation measure state 1 is simply a hypothetical state based on the utility levels in state 2, changes in taxes, even starting at a no-tax position, influence the distribution of real income in state 1. Indeed, it should not be surprising that the condition required for this extra term to vanish is the same one required above for excess burden to be independent of the initial income distribution.

There is a temptation to respond to this dependency of excess burden on the distribution of income by conceptually separating questions of allocation and distribution, following Musgrave's (1959) framework for the different "branches" of government: let the distribution branch worry about distribution, and the allocation branch concern itself with minimizing excess burden. However, there are two problems with this approach. First, if the distribution branch is not in operation, we cannot obtain well-behaved social welfare prescriptions by comparing levels of excess burden in different allocations through the device known as the compensation principle: one state being preferred to another if winners *could* compensate losers. Unless such compensation actually occurs, the orderings coming out of such a procedure need not be well-behaved or consistent with any particular social welfare function. This is the essence of the critique of the Hicks (1940)–Kaldor (1939) approach to welfare economics [Samuelson (1947)].

A second response might be that we are only interested in efficiency, not distribution, and so will assign equal distributional weights to individuals, thereby allowing the interpretation of the aggregate measures derived above as "efficiency-only" social welfare measures. Such is the approach suggested by Harberger (1971). Unfortunately, this will not work either. We can certainly imagine a social welfare function of the form

$$w(U^1,\dots,U^H)=\sum_{i=1}^{H}U^i, \tag{3.23}$$

and can even choose a normalization for the individual utility functions so that, in the initial state, the marginal utility of income and hence the social marginal utility of income for each individual is one ("money metric" utility). However, once prices change, as they will when taxes are introduced, the changes in real income, and hence the marginal utility of income, will generally be different.

totally differentiating (3.21) or (3.22) for each i and then adding over i, making use of the adding-up constraint on the profit shares ω. While the resulting expressions for the compensating variation measure are essentially the same as those described in Section 3.2 (with aggregate demands replacing individual ones), an interesting result occurs in the second-order effect derived from the measure defined by (3.22). It contains an additional term reflecting the indirect impact of taxes on excess burden through the change in the income distribution in state 1 [Debreu (1954)]. Since for an equivalent variation measure state 1 is simply a hypothetical state based on the utility levels in state 2, changes in taxes, even starting at a no-tax position, influence the distribution of real income in state 1. Indeed, it should not be surprising that the condition required for this extra term to vanish is the same one required above for excess burden to be independent of the initial income distribution.

There is a temptation to respond to this dependency of excess burden on the distribution of income by conceptually separating questions of allocation and distribution, following Musgrave's (1959) framework for the different "branches" of government: let the distribution branch worry about distribution, and the allocation branch concern itself with minimizing excess burden. However, there are two problems with this approach. First, if the distribution branch is not in operation, we cannot obtain well-behaved social welfare prescriptions by comparing levels of excess burden in different allocations through the device known as the compensation principle: one state being preferred to another if winners *could* compensate losers. Unless such compensation actually occurs, the orderings coming out of such a procedure need not be well-behaved or consistent with any particular social welfare function. This is the essence of the critique of the Hicks (1940)–Kaldor (1939) approach to welfare economics [Samuelson (1947)].

A second response might be that we are only interested in efficiency, not distribution, and so will assign equal distributional weights to individuals, thereby allowing the interpretation of the aggregate measures derived above as "efficiency-only" social welfare measures. Such is the approach suggested by Harberger (1971). Unfortunately, this will not work either. We can certainly imagine a social welfare function of the form

$$w(U^1,\ldots,U^H)=\sum_{i=1}^{H}U^i, \tag{3.23}$$

and can even choose a normalization for the individual utility functions so that, in the initial state, the marginal utility of income and hence the social marginal utility of income for each individual is one ("money metric" utility). However, once prices change, as they will when taxes are introduced, the changes in real income, and hence the marginal utility of income, will generally be different.

Thus, for our measure of excess burden to correspond to a social welfare function, it would require price-dependent individual weights, even if the weights were initially equal. Only when preferences satisfy the Gorman conditions will weights initially set equal remain equal in all cases [Roberts (1980)]. Thus, it will generally not be possible to make welfare comparisons on the basis of aggregate measures of excess burden, no matter what our attitude is about the relative importance of equity and efficiency.

4. The empirical measurement of excess burden

Several recent studies have used exact measures to calculate the excess burden of

The ultimate value of the theory developed in Sections 2 and 3 is in its application to measuring real world distortions. This section offers a brief review of some of the research that has been done in this popular area of investigation. No attempt will be made to provide an exhaustive summary of the empirical literature on the measurement of excess burden.

example, the compensating variation measure (2.10) would become

4.1. *Measurement with Taylor approximations*

The earliest empirical work on the measurement of excess burden was done by Harberger, in a series of papers. In each case, he applied a second-order Taylor approximation of the form (2.31) ... An example of this research may be found in Harberger (1964), which considers the welfare cost of a progressive tax on labor income by individual income classes. Treating capital as a factor supplied by households in static model, Harberger (1966) considered the deadweight loss from the production distortion caused by differential taxation of the return to capital in the corporate and non-corporate

point A, we may pretend that he did so in response to a proportional tax at rate

also be analyzed using standard excess burden formulae [Harberger (1954)]. One

from distortionary and lump sum taxation, and compare the tax revenue. However, the changes in utility take account of switches in regime that may occur in

Feldstein (1978).

frontier, changes in production prices would normally act to lessen the excess

excess burden of capital income taxation.

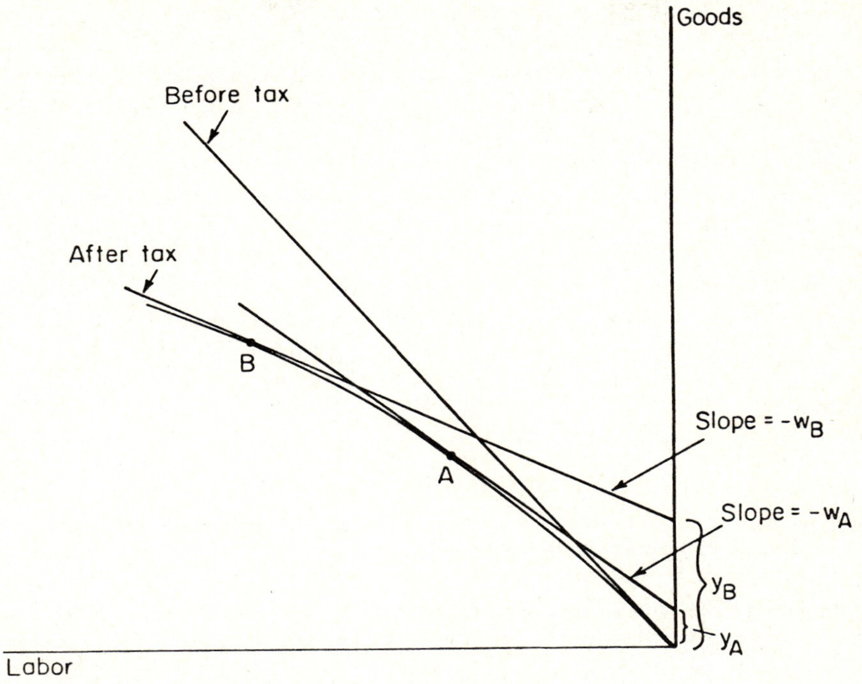

Figure 4.1. Progressive taxes and virtual income.

each case. This is a straightforward calculation when the consumer's indirect utility function is known, for it is simple to identify the regime chosen in any situation. However, if one wishes to use approximation formulae, one must take explicit account of the effect of taxes on the probability of switching regimes. [See Small and Rosen (1981).] An example of excess burden calculations with discrete decision variables is the analysis of housing subsidy programs by Venti and Wise (1984), in which individuals must decide whether to move or stay, and face different budget constraints in the two situations.

4.3. Simulation methods

Ultimately, there are limitations on the extent to which we can obtain closed form solutions for excess burden. This is particularly true of general equilibrium calculations, for we must solve explicitly for the changes in producer prices consistent with changes in consumer behavior. A solution to this problem is the simulation model, in which explicit parameterizations of preferences and technology are made and actual equilibria calculated. It is then straightforward to estimate changes in utility caused by a change in tax regime, or the resources one could extract or must add to compensate for a given change. The latter type of calculation corresponds to the price-varying excess burden measures cited in Section 3. The use of disaggregated, static general equilibrium models to analyze the effects of taxation has now become rather common. An early example of the use of simulation technique is Shoven's (1976) reconsideration of the excess burden caused by the corporate income tax. For other applications, see the contributions in Feldstein (1983). In more recent work, Auerbach, Kotlikoff and Skinner (1983) use a perfect-foresight, overlapping-generations growth model to analyze the effects on different cohorts of individuals of various dynamic tax changes, such as an unannounced switch from income taxation to consumption taxation.

5. The theory of optimal taxation

Taxes distort behavior and cause excess burden. How can this excess burden be kept to a minimum while government simultaneously raises the revenue it requires for public expenditures? This is the optimal tax problem, solved in its basic form by Ramsey (1927).

Of course, there do exist non-distortionary taxes, at least hypothetically. Taxes on pure profits are just one form of such taxation. The optimal tax problem, in a sense, embodies the concession that such ideal taxes may be difficult to institute in practice. One might cite a number of reasons for this, including the political constraints on non-uniform taxation dependent on personal characteristics. For example, we might succeed in having a non-distortionary and progressive tax system by taxing according to genetic characteristics associated with ability, but such schemes are typically proscribed. In addition, it may be impossible to observe such characteristics.

In the next subsection, we present and interpret the basic, single-individual optimal tax results, paying particular attention to the role of the "untaxed" numeraire commodity that is often a confusing part of such analysis. Section 5.2 discusses the relationship of the optimal tax solution to the measures of excess burden described above. In Sections 5.3 and 5.4, we show how the results can be extended to allow for profits and changing producer prices, and interpret the classic results of Diamond and Mirlees (1971) and Stiglitz and Dasgupta (1971) concerning the desirability of production efficiency in the presence of distortionary commodity taxes.

5.1. Basic optimal tax results

We imagine a representative consumer who has exogenous income y, and faces consumer prices $\boldsymbol{p} = (p_0, p_1, \dots, p_N)$ for the commodities 0, 1,..., N, which have fixed producer prices $\boldsymbol{q} = (q_0, q_1, \dots, q_n)$. Without any loss of generality, we may choose good zero as the numeraire and set $q_0 = 1$.

The government may use unit excise taxes $\boldsymbol{t} = (t_0, t_1, \dots, t_N)$ on the goods $0, 1, \dots, N$, to raise a certain amount of required revenue, R. (We will relax this ignorance of the expenditure side below.) Assuming the consumer maximizes utility $U(\boldsymbol{x})$ in the goods $\boldsymbol{x}$, subject to the prices $\boldsymbol{p}$ and income y, we may express the optimal tax problem by

$$\max_{p} \left[\max_{x} U(\boldsymbol{x}) \text{ subject to } \boldsymbol{p} \cdot \boldsymbol{x} = y \right] \quad \text{subject to} \quad (\boldsymbol{p} - \boldsymbol{q}) \cdot \boldsymbol{x} = R, \tag{5.1}$$

or, using the definition of the indirect utility function $V(\cdot)$,

$$\max_{p} V(\boldsymbol{p}, y) \quad \text{subject to} \quad (\boldsymbol{p} - \boldsymbol{q}) \cdot \boldsymbol{x} = R. \tag{5.2}$$

Note that we specify the price vector, $\boldsymbol{p}$, as our control rather than $\boldsymbol{t}$, but this is a trivial distinction when the social cost vector $\boldsymbol{q}$ is fixed since $\mathrm{d}\boldsymbol{t}/\mathrm{d}\boldsymbol{p} = I$, the identity matrix of order $N + 1$.

The first-order conditions for the Lagrangian

$$V(\boldsymbol{p}, y) - \mu[R - (\boldsymbol{p} - \boldsymbol{q}) \cdot \boldsymbol{x}] \tag{5.3}$$

are

$$-\lambda x_i + \mu \left[\sum_j t_j \frac{\partial x_j}{\partial p_i} + x_i \right] = 0, \quad \forall i, \tag{5.4}$$

where $\lambda = \mathrm{d}V/\mathrm{d}y$ is the consumer's marginal utility of income. Condition (5.4) may be rearranged in a number of ways. Perhaps the most useful involves splitting the cross-price effects $\partial x_j/\partial p_i$ using the Slutsky equation, and defining

$$\alpha = \lambda + \mu \sum_j t_j \frac{\partial x_j}{\partial y} \tag{5.5}$$

to be the *marginal social utility* of income [Diamond (1975)], to obtain

$$-\sum S_{ij}t_j = \left(\frac{\mu-\alpha}{\mu}\right)x_i, \quad \forall i, \tag{5.6}$$

where the S_{ij}s are components of the Slutsky matrix S. The term α differs from λ because, in the presence of excise taxes, a dollar given to the individual increases his utility directly by λ *and* indirectly by the increased revenue resulting from additional expenditure. Since we can interpret the Lagrange multiplier of the revenue constraint, μ, as the shadow cost in terms of utility of raising an additional dollar of revenue, the indirect gain of revenue added by increased expenditures out of an additional dollar of income equals $\mu\sum_j t_j(\partial x_j/\partial y)$, the second term in the definition of α.

The term $(\mu-\alpha)$ represents the difference between raising a dollar of revenue at the actual margin and raising it through a direct taking of income from the consumer: the marginal excess burden of the tax. This term is always non-negative [see expression (7.8)] and hence the terms $\sum S_{ij}t_j$ are also non-negative.

There is one potential solution to (5.6) that would be particularly attractive, for it involves no distortion. If we choose equal proportional *ad valorem* taxes, or

$$t_i = \theta p_i, \quad \forall i, \tag{5.7}$$

for some constant θ, we obtain

$$-\theta\sum S_{ij}p_j = \left(\frac{\mu-\alpha}{\mu}\right)x_i, \quad \forall i. \tag{5.8}$$

But $\sum S_{ij}p_j$ equals $(1/\lambda)(\mathrm{d}U/\mathrm{d}p_i)|_u = 0$ for all i. (This is simply a statement of the envelope theorem.) Therefore, the system of equations in (5.8) is satisfied for $\mu=\alpha$ and hence no excess burden. Thus, proportional excise taxes would appear to be the solution.

The reason such taxes are non-distortionary, however, is the key to their limited applicability. Since $\boldsymbol{p}=\boldsymbol{q}+\boldsymbol{t}=\boldsymbol{q}+\theta\boldsymbol{p}$, $\boldsymbol{p}=\boldsymbol{q}/(1-\theta)$. Hence, the consumer's budget constraint becomes

$$\frac{\boldsymbol{q}}{1-\theta}\cdot\boldsymbol{x}=y \quad \text{or} \quad \boldsymbol{q}\cdot\boldsymbol{x}=y(1-\theta), \tag{5.9}$$

where θ is chosen to satisfy $\theta=R/y$. A system of equal excise taxes is nothing more than a tax on the consumer's exogenous income, and hence a lump sum tax.

If $y = 0$, then no finite value of θ will satisfy the revenue constraint, so we must ask when y will be non-zero.

First of all, y will be non-zero in general if there are decreasing returns to scale in production (in a more general model not assuming fixed producer prices). Even in the absence of pure profits, y will be non-zero if we interpret it as "full income" and the $\boldsymbol{x}$ vector as consumption rather than demand. For example, suppose the $\boldsymbol{x}$ vector consists of two commodities, consumption C and leisure l, and that the consumer has a labor endowment L. Without pure profits, the consumer's budget constraint in the absence of taxes may be written either as

$$qC_C + (l - L) = 0, \tag{5.10a}$$

or

$$qC_C + l = L, \tag{5.10b}$$

where labor is the numeraire and C and q_C are the amount and relative price of consumption. Interpreting the labor commodity we can tax as net *purchase* of leisure $(l - L)$, we have no income y to tax through proportional excise taxes. Interpreting the commodity as *consumption* of leisure, l, we can use the proportional tax solution on C and l to tax L indirectly. Hence, the inability to use proportional taxes to raise revenue is equivalent to restriction of taxing only explicit purchases, rather than total consumption. Under this restriction, a proportional tax raises no revenue [Baumol and Bradford (1970)]. Based on examples of this sort, various authors have equated the need to use distortionary taxes with the inability to tax leisure, but this is somewhat misleading on two counts: we *can* tax leisure *purchases* (labor supply), and this restriction applies to any commodity in which the consumer has an endowment.

Once we do restrict our taxes to net purchases, it is easiest to interpret the vector $\boldsymbol{x}$ to be such flows rather than total consumption. In exchange for the loss of non-distortionary tax scheme, we gain an additional free normalization. Since the consumer's indirect utility function is homogeneous in prices and income, and is now simply $V(\boldsymbol{p})$, it is also homogeneous of degree zero in prices. So is the revenue constraint: since $\boldsymbol{p} \cdot \boldsymbol{x} = 0$, it follows that for any constant ϕ,

$$(\phi \boldsymbol{p} - \boldsymbol{q}) \cdot \boldsymbol{x} = (\phi - 1)\boldsymbol{p} \cdot \boldsymbol{x} + (\boldsymbol{p} - \boldsymbol{q}) \cdot \boldsymbol{x} = (\boldsymbol{p} - \boldsymbol{q}) \cdot \boldsymbol{x}. \tag{5.11}$$

Thus, we may choose any scale for $\boldsymbol{p}$. It is customary to set $p_0 = 1$, thereby making the numeraire also the arbitrarily "untaxed" good. Typically, in models where there is a single factor supplied, labor, and several commodities purchased, labor is chosen as this numeraire. While such a normalization is innocuous and in no way affects the real characteristics of the outcome, it can be very confusing:

the untaxed good, labor, just happens to be the only good with an endowment, L, that we cannot tax independently of its consumption, l; hence the loss of distinction between untaxable and untaxed goods. If we chose corn as the untaxed good, labor would still have an untaxable endowment. This distinction is important when one interprets the various rules derived below.

We now have only N first-order conditions, from (5.6), having dropped that corresponding to p_0. Hence, the strategy of equal proportional taxes at rate θ (with a zero tax on good zero, of course) now gives us the terms

$$-\theta \sum_{j\neq 0} S_{ij}p_j = \theta S_{i0}, \tag{5.12}$$

on the left-hand side of (5.6). This will stand in constant proportion to x_i over i, as required for a solution, only if the compensated cross-elasticity of demand for each good i with respect to the price of good 0, $\varepsilon_{i0} = S_{i0} \cdot p_0/x_i = S_{i0}/x_i$, is the same for all $i \neq 0$. Thus, equal proportional taxes on all *taxed* goods satisfy the first-order conditions only if all goods are equally complementary [in the sense of Hicks (1946)] to the *untaxed* good. Naturally, if these conditions are satisfied for a given choice of untaxed good, they will not generally work for another.

Our analysis of (5.6) has now generally ruled out uniform taxation. But how should the taxes diverge from uniformity? Note that the N conditions in (5.6) can be stacked to yield

$$\hat{S}\hat{t} = -\left(\frac{\mu-\alpha}{\mu}\right)x, \tag{5.13}$$

where $\hat{S}$ is the Slutsky matrix excluding good zero and $\hat{t} = (t_1, \ldots, t_N)$. Although there is no independent condition with respect to the tax on good zero (which has been normalized to zero), it is helpful to note that these N conditions imply that (5.6) also holds for good zero. This may be shown as follows. Adding a term multiplied by t_0 to each of the N first-order conditions in (5.6) has no effect, since $t_0 = 0$. Thus,[12]

$$\begin{aligned}\sum_{i=0}^{N} S_{0i}t_i &= \sum_{i=0}^{N}\left(-\sum_{k=1}^{N} p_k S_{ki}\right)t_i = -\sum_{k=1}^{N} p_k \sum_{i=0}^{N} S_{ki}t_i \\ &= -\sum_{k=1}^{N} p_k\left(-\left(\frac{\mu-\alpha}{\mu}\right)x_k\right) = -\left(\frac{\mu-\alpha}{\mu}\right)x_0.\end{aligned} \tag{5.14}$$

[12] This uses the facts that $\sum_{k=0}^{N} p_k S_{ki} = 0$ and $\boldsymbol{p}\cdot\boldsymbol{x} = 0$.

Combined with (5.13), this yields

$$\boldsymbol{St} = -\left(\frac{\mu-\alpha}{\mu}\right)\boldsymbol{x}. \tag{5.15}$$

Suppose that the government is currently raising its revenue through lump sum taxes, and must now shift over some of the revenue collection to distortionary taxes. From above, we know that there is no first-order effect on utility of introducing distortionary taxes from a Pareto optimum, so that the effects on demand of this small change in prices will be compensated effects. Thus, to a first-order Taylor approximation, the reduction in the demand for good i will be

$$-\Delta x_i = -\sum_j S_{ij}\Delta p_j = -\sum_j S_{ij}t_j, \tag{5.16}$$

so that (5.15) calls for an equiproportional reduction in demand for each good. As suggested by Dixit (1970), this makes intuitive sense in light of the excess burden formulae calculated above. From (3.3), the introduction of small taxes $\boldsymbol{t}$ starting from a Pareto optimum induces an excess burden of approximately

$$L = \tfrac{1}{2}\sum_i \Delta t_i \Delta x_i = \tfrac{1}{2}\sum_i t_i \Delta x_i, \tag{5.17}$$

so that each small tax t_i will induce an excess burden proportional to Δx_i. On the other hand, the revenue raised by such a tax is $t_i x_i$. Thus, holding $\Delta x_i / x_i$ constant across goods results in a constant ratio of excess burden to a revenue for each tax. This is precisely the sort of marginal condition one would expect from minimizing total excess burden subject to a revenue constraint.

The actual taxes that lead to the achievement of (5.13) and (5.15) may be obtained by inverting $\hat{S}$ and multiplying both sides of (5.13) by $\hat{S}^{-1}$ to obtain

$$\hat{\boldsymbol{t}} = -\left(\frac{\mu-\alpha}{\mu}\right)\hat{S}^{-1}\boldsymbol{x}. \tag{5.18}$$

This yields no neat general expressions for $\hat{\boldsymbol{t}}$, though for various special cases one can go a little further.

If there are only three goods, two taxed, then (5.18) yields the two equations

$$t_1 = \frac{1}{\Delta}\left(\frac{\mu-\alpha}{\mu}\right)(-S_{22}x_1 + S_{12}x_2), \tag{5.19a}$$

$$t_2 = \frac{1}{\Delta}\left(\frac{\mu-\alpha}{\mu}\right)(S_{21}x_1 - S_{11}x_2), \tag{5.19b}$$

where $\Delta = S_{11}S_{22} - S_{12}S_{21}$, which must be ≥ 0 because S is negative semi-definite. Since $S_{i0} + p_1 S_{i1} + p_2 S_{i2} = 0$ for $i = 1, 2$, we may divide (5.19a) by (5.19b) and substitute to obtain

$$\frac{t_1}{t_2} = \frac{\frac{1}{p_2}(S_{20} + p_1 S_{21})x_1 + S_{12}x_2}{\frac{1}{p_1}(S_{10} + p_2 S_{12})x_2 + S_{21}x_1}, \tag{5.20}$$

or, defining $\theta_i = t_i/p_i$ and dividing the numerator and denominator of the right-hand side of (5.20) by $x_1 x_2$, we obtain [Corlett and Hague (1953–54) and Harberger (1964)]

$$\frac{\theta_1}{\theta_2} = \frac{\varepsilon_{20} + \varepsilon_{21} + \varepsilon_{12}}{\varepsilon_{10} + \varepsilon_{21} + \varepsilon_{12}}, \tag{5.21}$$

where, as before, ε_{ij} is the compensated cross-elasticity $S_{ij}(p_j/x_i)$. As we discovered above, $\theta_1 = \theta_2$ is an optimal solution only if the cross-elasticities ε_{10} and ε_{20} are equal.

Because $\Delta \geq 0$, expression (5.21) calls for a higher tax on the taxed good that is the relative complement to the numeraire (ε_{i0} is smaller). This has generated the somewhat misleading explanation that we "cannot" tax good zero, so we minimize distortions by taxing more heavily its relative complement. Recall that the choice of untaxed good is arbitrary, and that (5.21) applies for any numbering of the three goods.

For a larger number of commodities, a simple result obtains if we assume that the matrix $\hat{S}$ is diagonal: all cross-effects except with respect to good zero are zero. Since $\sum_j S_{ij} p_j = 0$, this implies that, for $i = 1, \ldots, N$,

$$S_{ii} p_i + S_{i0} = 0. \tag{5.22}$$

Thus, this restriction *does* depend on the choice of untaxed commodity. With such a simplification, (5.18) yields the expressions

$$t_i = -\frac{1}{\Delta}\left(\frac{\mu - \alpha}{\mu}\right)\frac{x_i}{S_{ii}} \quad \text{or} \quad \theta_i \sim \frac{1}{\varepsilon_{ii}}. \tag{5.23}$$

This is the celebrated "inverse elasticity" rule that calls for higher proportional taxes on goods with relatively low own-price elasticities. By (5.22), this rule is equivalent to

$$\theta_i \sim \frac{1}{\varepsilon_{i0}}, \tag{5.24}$$

as derived above for the three-good case.

Since the inverse elasticity rule results from a restriction on preferences, the choice of untaxed good becomes relevant in that it may make more sense to assume no cross-effects among taxed goods if labor is numeraire and the other goods are commodities, than to do so if one of the commodities serves as the untaxed good.

The inverse elasticity rule of (5.24) is expressed in terms of compensated elasticities. Yet in various places in the literature [Diamond and Mirrlees (1971) and Bradford and Rosen (1976)], it is expressed in terms of uncompensated elasticities. This is the result neither of a revision of demand theory nor an assumption of zero-income effects. Rather, it comes about because of a different, and equally arbitrary, restriction on preferences. We can express the optimal tax formulae in terms of ordinary uncompensated demands by rearranging (5.4),

$$-\sum_j t_j \frac{\partial x_j}{\partial p_i} = \left(\frac{\mu - \lambda}{\mu}\right) x_i, \tag{5.25}$$

which, assuming $\partial x_j / \partial p_i = 0$ unless $i = 0$ or j, yields

$$\theta_i \sim \frac{1}{\eta_{ii}}, \tag{5.26}$$

where $\eta_{ii} = -(p_i/x_i)(\partial x_i/\partial p_i)$ is the uncompensated own-elasticity of demand for good i. Expressions (5.26) and (5.24) differ because they result from different restrictions on the structure of preferences: different matrices are being assumed diagonal.

5.2. *Minimizing excess burden through optimal taxation*

By its definition, excess burden ought to be minimized when taxes are chosen to maximize utility. However, even for the fixed producer price case, we have at least two candidates for measuring excess burden, and they will generally take on different values. It turns out that only one of these, that based on the equivalent variation, satisfies the desirable duality property of being minimized by optimal taxes [Kay (1980)].

Recall from (2.9) that the equivalent variation measure of the excess burden of tax is

$$EB_{\mathrm{E}} = E(\boldsymbol{p}_1, V(\boldsymbol{p}_1, y)) - E(\boldsymbol{p}_0, V(\boldsymbol{p}_1, y)) - R$$

$$= y - E(\boldsymbol{p}_0, V(\boldsymbol{p}, y)) - R. \tag{5.27}$$

Thus, minimizing this for a given value of R amounts to maximizing $E(\boldsymbol{p}_0, V(\boldsymbol{p}_1, y))$. But, for a given price vector, expenditure increases monotonically with the level of utility. Thus, we are maximizing $V(\boldsymbol{p}_1, y)$, just as in the optimal tax problem. This is easily verified by differentiating the Lagrangian

$$E(\boldsymbol{p}_0, V(\boldsymbol{p}_1, y)) + \pi(R - (\boldsymbol{p}_1 - \boldsymbol{p}_0)\cdot \boldsymbol{x}), \tag{5.28}$$

with respect to $\boldsymbol{p}_1$.

For the compensating variation measure, which [from (2.10)] equals

$$EB_{\mathrm{C}} = E(\boldsymbol{p}_1, V(\boldsymbol{p}_0, y)) - E(\boldsymbol{p}_0, V(\boldsymbol{p}_0, y)) - R$$

$$= E(\boldsymbol{p}_1, V(\boldsymbol{p}_0, y)) - y - R, \tag{5.29}$$

minimizing excess burden amounts to minimizing $E(\boldsymbol{p}_1, V(\boldsymbol{p}_0, y))$: choosing taxes to minimize the expenditure necessary to achieve the pre-tax utility level. This need not be the same price vector as the one dictated by optimal taxation. The appropriate Lagrangian here is

$$E(\boldsymbol{p}_1, V(\boldsymbol{p}_0, y)) - \pi(R - (\boldsymbol{p}_1 - \boldsymbol{p}_0)\cdot \boldsymbol{x}), \tag{5.30}$$

which yields first-order conditions

$$-x_i + \pi\left[\sum_j t_j \frac{\partial x_j}{\partial p_i} + x_i\right] = 0, \tag{5.31}$$

which looks like the one derived from (5.28). However, the value of $\boldsymbol{x}$ here is at the hypothetical point at higher prices but with compensation. In the previous case, it is at the actual optimal tax point.[13]

[13] *A fortiori*, it can be seen that replacing $\boldsymbol{p}_0$ with any arbitrary "reference price vector" $\boldsymbol{p}_0^*$ in the expenditure function in (5.27), to define a different concept of excess burden, i.e.,

$$EB_{\mathrm{E}}^* = E(p_1, V(p_1, y)) - E(p_0^*, V(p_1, y)) - R,$$

would also yield a measure consistent with the optimal tax problem [King (1983b)].

This problem with the compensating variation also means that we cannot compare two hypothetical alternatives to a given tax situation by comparing their marginal excess burden measures. Only if preferences are homothetic [Chipman and Moore (1980)] will this problem dissappear. Of course, for pairwise comparisons, where the "initial" point is not well-defined, the equivalent variation and compensating variation are symmetrically defined, so there can be no *a priori* benefit of using one versus the other.

5.3. Changing producer prices

The simple relaxation of the fixed producer price assumption has, perhaps surprisingly, no effect at all on the optimal tax formulae in (5.18) as long as producer prices result from competitive behavior and any pure profits are taxed away by the government.

In place of the fixed producer price assumption of Section 5.1, we assume that production is governed by the production function

$$f(z)=0, \tag{5.32}$$

where, as in Section 3, z is the production vector in the commodities $0,1,\dots,N$. By the assumption of competitive behavior, we know that the producer prices $\boldsymbol{q}$ are proportional to the vector of derivatives of f, $\mathrm{d}f=(f_0,f_1,\dots,f_N)$. Without any loss of generality, we may set this proportionality constant equal to $1/f_0$ and, as before, choose good zero as numeraire, i.e., $q_0=1$.

The government's revenue requirement must now be specified in terms of individual commodities (as was the case of the compensation vector in Section 3), since relative producer prices can change. We refer to this as the revenue vector, $\boldsymbol{R}$. Thus, $z=\boldsymbol{x}+\boldsymbol{R}$, where $\boldsymbol{x}$ is the household's vector of net purchases.

Once production has been generalized to this stage, the possibility arises of pure profits coming from decreasing returns to scale. We will consider this more general case after first solving the optimal tax problem when $f(\cdot)$ embodies constant returns to scale, i.e., is homogeneous of degree zero in all commodities. By Euler's Theorem, profits are $\boldsymbol{q}\cdot z=0$. Thus, the government's optimization problem becomes

$$\max_{\boldsymbol{p}} V(\boldsymbol{p}) \quad \text{subject to} \quad f(\boldsymbol{x}+\boldsymbol{R})=0, \tag{5.33}$$

where, because pure profits are zero, we can set $p_0=q_0=1$ without any loss of generality, and choose only $p_1,\dots,p_N$. To use $\boldsymbol{p}$ rather than $\boldsymbol{t}$ as the control variables, we must insure that arbitrary changes in $\boldsymbol{p}$ can be brought about by changes in $\boldsymbol{t}$. This is accomplished by noting that

$$\mathrm{d}\boldsymbol{p} = \mathrm{d}\boldsymbol{t} + \mathrm{d}\boldsymbol{q} = \mathrm{d}\boldsymbol{t} + \mathrm{d}(\mathrm{d}f) = \mathrm{d}\boldsymbol{t} + H(\mathrm{d}\boldsymbol{x} + \mathrm{d}\boldsymbol{R}), \tag{5.34}$$

where H is the Hessian $\mathrm{d}^2 f$ of the production function, as before. Since $\mathrm{d}\boldsymbol{R} = 0$ and $\mathrm{d}\boldsymbol{x}$ may be characterized by the Slutsky equation, we have

$$\mathrm{d}\boldsymbol{p} = \mathrm{d}\boldsymbol{t} + H\left(S - \frac{\partial \boldsymbol{x}}{\partial y}\boldsymbol{x}'\right)\mathrm{d}\boldsymbol{p}, \tag{5.35}$$

or

$$\mathrm{d}\boldsymbol{p} = \left[I - H\left(S - \frac{\partial \boldsymbol{x}}{\partial y}\cdot\boldsymbol{x}'\right)\right]^{-1}\mathrm{d}\boldsymbol{t},$$

where S is the Slutsky matrix. Moreover, since the changes in $\boldsymbol{t}$ are constrained to keep revenue constant, and hence, in the neighborhood of the optimum, utility as well, the changes in $\boldsymbol{x}$ are compensated and (5.35) simplifies to

$$\mathrm{d}\boldsymbol{p} = [I - HS]^{-1}\mathrm{d}\boldsymbol{t} = \Omega\,\mathrm{d}\boldsymbol{t}. \tag{5.36}$$

As long as Ω exists (i.e., $[I - HS]$ is of full rank), we may control $\boldsymbol{t}$ indirectly through $\boldsymbol{p}$.

The Lagrangian corresponding to (5.33) yields the first-order conditions

$$-\lambda x_i - \mu \sum_j f_j \frac{\partial x_j}{\partial p_i} = 0, \qquad i = 1, \ldots, N, \tag{5.37}$$

where $\lambda = \mathrm{d}V/\mathrm{d}y$ and μ is the Lagrange multiplier on the production constraint. Since $\boldsymbol{p}\cdot\boldsymbol{x} = 0$,

$$\sum_j p_j \frac{\partial x_j}{\partial p_i} + x_i = 0. \tag{5.38}$$

Using this and the fact that $\boldsymbol{q} = \mathrm{d}f$, we may express (5.37) as

$$-\lambda x_i + \mu\left[\sum_j t_j \frac{\partial x_j}{\partial p_i} + x_i\right] = 0, \tag{5.39}$$

which is precisely condition (5.4). This result is due to Diamond and Mirrlees (1971).

In the more general case where $f(\cdot)$ is not homogeneous of degree zero, there may be pure profits, $y = \boldsymbol{q}\cdot \boldsymbol{z} > 0$. In this case, we know from before, equal taxes on all commodities amount to a profits tax on y, giving us $N+1$ rather than N independent instruments. Hence, if we cannot tax one good, this represents a restriction unless we can tax profits directly. For expositional purposes, it is easiest to let the $N+1$ instruments be the taxes on goods $1,\dots,N$ and the profits tax, keeping $t_0 = 0$. We let τ be the rate of profits tax. The Lagrangian now is

$$V(\boldsymbol{p},(1-\tau)y) - \mu f(\boldsymbol{x}+\boldsymbol{R}). \tag{5.40}$$

Using the fact that $\boldsymbol{p}\cdot\boldsymbol{x} = (1-\tau)y$, we may arrange the N first-order conditions with respect to the taxes $t_1,\dots,t_N$ to be

$$-\lambda x_i + \lambda(1-\tau)\frac{\mathrm{d}y}{\mathrm{d}p_i} + \mu\left[\sum_j t_j \frac{\mathrm{d}x_j}{\mathrm{d}p_i} + x_i - (1-\tau)\frac{\mathrm{d}y}{\mathrm{d}p_i}\right] = 0. \tag{5.41}$$

It is straightforward to show that if τ may be freely varied, then the $N+1$ first-order conditions are solved for $\boldsymbol{t} = 0$ and $\lambda = \mu$: no excess burden, with profits taxes being used to raise all revenue. However, if τ is constrained, we must solve the N conditions (5.41), given τ. Unless profits taxes just happen to equal $\boldsymbol{q}\cdot\boldsymbol{R}$, we again face an optimal tax problem.

If $\tau = 1$, so that all profits are taxed away, then (5.41) reduces to the previous optimal tax program, (5.39). Thus, pure profits do not change the picture unless they accrue at least partially to the household [Stiglitz and Dasgupta (1971)]. If τ is fixed at some value not equal to one, the formulas differ.

Since producer prices, and hence profits, change with p, the derivatives $\mathrm{d}x_j/\mathrm{d}p_i$ in (5.41) include the indirect effect of p_i on profits through changes in production,

$$\frac{\mathrm{d}x_j}{\mathrm{d}p_i} = \frac{\partial x_j}{\partial p_i} + \frac{\partial x_j}{\partial y'}\cdot(1-\pi)\frac{\mathrm{d}y}{\mathrm{d}p_i}, \tag{5.42}$$

where $y' = (1-\tau)y$. Using (5.42), the Slutsky equation, and the definition of α, the social marginal utility of income, from (5.5), we may rewrite (5.41) as

$$\sum_j S_{ij}t_j = -\left(\frac{\mu-\alpha}{\mu}\right)\left(x_i - (1-\tau)\frac{\mathrm{d}y}{\mathrm{d}p_i}\right), \tag{5.43}$$

which differs from (5.6) only through the replacement of x_i with $(x_i - (1-\tau)(\mathrm{d}y/\mathrm{d}p_i))$. One can interpret these terms as the net increase in resources needed to maintain a given level of utility with respect to an increase in p_i in the two respective cases.

If the profits tax $\tau = 0$, and if good zero is the single production factor and the sole good from which revenue is extracted, then one can show that (5.43) yields the result obtained above for fixed producer prices, that to a first-order Taylor approximation, substituting optimal taxes for lump sum taxes causes an equiproportional reduction in the output of all taxed commodities. *A fortiori*, the outcome also holds for the constant returns case just examined. This result is due to Stiglitz and Dasgupta (1971), who in turn attribute it to Ramsey (1927), though the exact equivalence is obscured by differences in methodology.

The key to the single-factor assumption is that, since the production function may be written

$$f(\boldsymbol{x}) = \hat{f}(x_1, \ldots, x_N) - x_0, \tag{5.44}$$

the Hessian $H = \mathrm{d}^2 f$ is block diagonal in the untaxed good and all other goods ($H_{i0} = H_{0i} = 0$ for $i \neq 0$). Thus, the product of H and the substitution matrix S is

$$HS = \left(\begin{array}{c|c} H_{00} & 0 \\ \hline 0 & \hat{H} \end{array}\right)\left(\begin{array}{c|c} S_{00} & \boldsymbol{S}_0' \\ \hline \boldsymbol{S}_0 & \hat{S} \end{array}\right) = \left(\begin{array}{c|c} H_{00}S_{00} & H_{00}\boldsymbol{S}_0' \\ \hline \hat{H}\boldsymbol{S}_0 & \hat{H}\hat{S} \end{array}\right), \tag{5.45}$$

where $\boldsymbol{S}_0' = (S_{01}, \ldots, S_{0N})$ and $\hat{H}$ and $\hat{S}$ are the blocks of H and S for goods 1 through N. This means that the changes in consumer prices of the taxed goods, $\boldsymbol{p} = (p_1, \ldots, p_N)$, can be expressed [using (5.36)] in the neighborhood of the optimum as

$$\mathrm{d}\hat{\boldsymbol{p}} = [I - \hat{H}\hat{S}]^{-1}\mathrm{d}\hat{\boldsymbol{t}} = \hat{\Omega}\,\mathrm{d}\hat{\boldsymbol{t}}, \tag{5.46}$$

where $\hat{\boldsymbol{t}} = (t_1, \ldots, t_N)$. That is, $\mathrm{d}\hat{\boldsymbol{p}}$ does not depend on the demand for x_0. From (5.46), we may express the first-order change around $\hat{\boldsymbol{t}} = 0$ in $\hat{\boldsymbol{x}}$, the vector of taxed goods, as

$$\Delta\hat{\boldsymbol{x}} = \hat{S}\Delta\hat{\boldsymbol{p}} = \hat{S}\hat{\Omega}\Delta\hat{\boldsymbol{t}} = \hat{S}\hat{\Omega}\hat{\boldsymbol{t}} = \hat{S}\hat{\Omega}\hat{S}^{-1}\hat{S}\hat{\boldsymbol{t}}. \tag{5.47}$$

The elements of the vector $\hat{S}\hat{\boldsymbol{t}}$ are described in (5.43). By the envelope theorem and the fact that $q_0 = 1$, we may solve for the term $\mathrm{d}y/\mathrm{d}p_i$,

$$\frac{\mathrm{d}y}{\mathrm{d}p_i} = \sum z_j \frac{\mathrm{d}q_j}{\mathrm{d}p_i} = \sum_{j>0} z_j \sum_k H_{jk}S_{ki} = \sum_{j>0} z_j \sum_{k>0} H_{jk}S_{ki}, \tag{5.48}$$

where the last step relies on the assumption that $H_{j0} = 0$ for $j \neq 0$. Stacking these terms, we obtain

$$\frac{\mathrm{d}y}{\mathrm{d}\hat{\boldsymbol{p}}} = SH\hat{z}, \tag{5.49}$$

where $\hat{z} = (z_1, \ldots, z_N)$. But by assumption, all revenue is spent on good zero, so $\hat{z} = \hat{\boldsymbol{x}}$. Since, also by assumption, $\tau = 0$, it follows from (5.43) that

$$\hat{S}\hat{t} = \left(\frac{\mu - \alpha}{\mu}\right)(I - \hat{S}\hat{H})\hat{\boldsymbol{x}}. \tag{5.50}$$

Substituting (5.50) into (5.47), we obtain

$$\begin{aligned} \Delta\hat{\boldsymbol{x}} &= \left(\frac{\mu - \alpha}{\mu}\right)\hat{S}\hat{\Omega}\hat{S}^{-1}(I - \hat{S}\hat{H})\hat{\boldsymbol{x}} \\ &= -\left(\frac{\mu - \alpha}{\mu}\right)\hat{S}\hat{\Omega}\hat{\Omega}^{-1}\hat{S}^{-1}\hat{\boldsymbol{x}} = \left(\frac{\mu - \alpha}{\mu}\right)\hat{\boldsymbol{x}}, \end{aligned} \tag{5.51}$$

as required.

In the special case where both $\hat{H}$ and $\hat{S}$ are diagonal (i.e., there is no joint production and commodity demands are independent except with relation to the numeraire), the expression (5.49) for $\mathrm{d}y/\mathrm{d}\boldsymbol{p}$ simplifies to

$$\frac{\mathrm{d}y}{\mathrm{d}p_i} = z_i H_{ii} S_{ii}, \tag{5.52}$$

which, if we again assume that all revenue raised is spent on the numeraire ($z_i = x_i$ for $i > 0$), allows us to rewrite (5.43) as

$$-S_{ii}t_i = \left(\frac{\mu - \alpha}{\mu}\right)(1 - (1 - \tau)H_{ii}S_{ii}), \tag{5.53}$$

or

$$\theta_i = -\left(\frac{\mu - \alpha}{\mu}\right)\cdot\frac{\left(\frac{1}{\varepsilon_{ii}} + (1 - \tau)\frac{1}{\sigma_{ii}}\right)}{\left(1 + (1 - \tau)\frac{1}{\sigma_{ii}}\right)},$$

where $\varepsilon_{ii} = -S_{ii}(p_i/x_i)$, $\sigma_{ii} = (1/H_{ii})(q_i/x_i)$ and $\theta_i = t_i/p_i$ are the demand and supply elasticities and *ad valorem* tax for good i. [See Stiglitz and Dasgupta (1971) for a slightly different formulation. Also see Atkinson and Stiglitz (1980).]

5.4. Production efficiency

Thus far, we have assumed production to be efficient, with the only distortions imposed by taxes to be with respect to household decisions. However, government can induce distortions in production, either through differential taxation of factors in different uses or through the use of different shadow prices in public enterprises than those generated by coexisting competitive private markets. Should these extra policy instruments be used? Under certain well-defined conditions, they should not.

To consider the desirability of such distortions, we follow Diamond and Mirrlees (1971) and suppose there to be two production sectors, each efficient in its own production behavior. We shall refer to these as the private and public sectors, though in some cases it may be more useful to think of them both as subsectors of the private sector. The results are easily extended to several sectors.

As before, we let $f(\cdot)$ and $\boldsymbol{z}$ be the production function and output of the private sector, and introduce $g(\cdot)$ and $\boldsymbol{s}$ as the corresponding variables for the public sector. The use of distortions in the allocation of resources between the two sectors may be thought of as the direct choice of public inputs, $\boldsymbol{s}$. Thus, the government's expanded choice problem is

$$\max_{\boldsymbol{p},\boldsymbol{s}} V(\boldsymbol{p},(1-\tau)y) \quad \text{subject to} \quad f(\boldsymbol{x}+R-\boldsymbol{s})=0 \quad \text{and} \quad g(\boldsymbol{s})=0, \tag{5.54}$$

where y is private sector profits. Attaching the Lagrange multipliers μ and ζ to the production constraints, we obtain the same first-order conditions as before with respect to $\boldsymbol{p}$. With respect to $\boldsymbol{s}$, we get

$$\lambda(1-\tau)\frac{\mathrm{d}y}{\mathrm{d}s_i}-\mu\left(\sum_j f_j\frac{\partial x_j}{\partial y'}(1-\tau)\frac{\mathrm{d}y}{\mathrm{d}s_i}-f_i\right)-\zeta g_i=0. \tag{5.55}$$

Using the normalization $\boldsymbol{q}=\mathrm{d}f$ and the consumer's budget constraint, we rewrite this as

$$\lambda(1-\tau)\frac{\mathrm{d}y}{\mathrm{d}s_i}-\mu\left(-\sum_j t_j\frac{\partial x_j}{\partial y'}(1-\tau)\frac{\mathrm{d}y}{\mathrm{d}s_i}+(1-\tau)\frac{\mathrm{d}y}{\mathrm{d}s_i}-f_i\right)-\zeta g_i=0, \tag{5.56}$$

or

$$g_i = \frac{\mu}{\zeta}\left(f_i - \left(\frac{\mu-\alpha}{\mu}\right)(1-\tau)\frac{\mathrm{d}y}{\mathrm{d}s_i}\right),$$

where, as before, $\alpha = \lambda + \mu(\mathrm{d}R/\mathrm{d}y)$ is the social marginal utility of income. Thus, there are two important cases in which efficient overall production ($f_i/f_j = g_i/g_j$) will result: constant returns to scale in the private sector [Diamond and Mirrlees (1971)] and decreasing returns with 100 percent profits taxation [Stiglitz and Dasgupta (1971)]. Otherwise, inefficient production will be part of the optimal solution. The basic intuition is that as long as we can tax all but one of the commodities, we can bring about any possible configuration of relative prices consistent with a given level of revenue. When after-tax profits $(1-\tau)y$ equal zero, these prices are the sole determinants of the consumer's decision. Thus, any attainment of a set of relative prices using a production distortion could also be obtained without one, with the simple result that the consumer could be made better off. Note that this logic only holds if all the taxes t_1 through t_N can be adjusted. With some of these held fixed, production inefficiencies may be helpful in imposing indirect taxes on the goods that cannot be freely taxed directly. We return to this point below in our discussion of tax reform.

For the case where profits are not zero, we may simplify (5.56) for the case of independent production. Considering $\mathrm{d}y/\mathrm{d}s_i$, we have (using the envelope theorem and independence assumption)

$$\frac{\mathrm{d}y}{\mathrm{d}s_i} = \sum_j z_j \frac{\mathrm{d}q_j}{\mathrm{d}z_j}\cdot\frac{\partial x_j}{\partial y'}\cdot(1-\tau)\frac{\mathrm{d}y}{\mathrm{d}s_i} - z_i\frac{\mathrm{d}q_i}{\mathrm{d}z_i}, \tag{5.57}$$

which, using the facts that $\boldsymbol{q} = \mathrm{d}f$ and $\mathrm{d}\boldsymbol{q} = H$, and the assumption that all government expenditures are on the numeraire commodity ($\hat{x} = \hat{z}$), we may solve as

$$\frac{\mathrm{d}y}{\mathrm{d}s_i} = -\frac{x_i H_{ii}}{1-(1-\tau)\sum_j x_j H_{jj}\left(\partial x_j/\partial y'\right)} = -\frac{f_i/\sigma_{ii}}{\Gamma}, \tag{5.58}$$

where σ_{ii} is the supply elasticity for good i, and Γ must be positive for a stable solution. Thus (5.56) yields

$$\frac{g_i}{g_j} = \frac{f_i}{f_j}\cdot\left(\frac{1+k/\sigma_{ii}}{1+k/\sigma_{jj}}\right) \quad \text{where} \quad k>0. \tag{5.59}$$

6. Optimal taxation and the structure for preferences

This section considers the implications of the tax formulae derived above for actual tax rates under different assumptions about the structure of preferences, and for the more general case where there are several individuals and hence distributional objectives to be satisfied. Although the results already presented expressed the optimal taxes in terms of the demands and substitution matrix of the representative consumer, these terms are not generally constant, so we have little insight into the general conditions on consumer preferences required for either uniform taxation or any other specific tax structure to be optimal. In exploring this question, we will also be able to investigate more easily the impact of distributional objectives on the optimal tax structure.

6.1. Optimal taxation from the dual perspective

To consider the role of preferences in determining optimal tax rules, it is helpful to derive such rules using the direct utility function rather than the indirect utility function. Though the derivation is less straightforward, the results are in terms of the characteristics of the utility function and, hence, preferences. This approach is taken by Atkinson and Stiglitz (1972, 1976, 1980). However, a simpler and more elegant way of arriving at their results is by transforming the optimal tax formulae themselves using duality theory. The technique described by Deaton (1979a, 1981a, 1981b) makes use of the "distance" function, sometimes referred to as the "direct" expenditure function [Cooter (1979)]. Our analysis here will generally follow that of Deaton. Because consumer preferences are defined with respect to consumption, rather than purchases, it is useful to separate these concepts by letting the vector of purchases $\boldsymbol{x}$ equal $\tilde{\boldsymbol{x}} - \bar{\boldsymbol{x}}$ where $\tilde{\boldsymbol{x}}$ is the consumption vector and $\bar{\boldsymbol{x}}$ the endowment vector. Thus, we may rewrite the indirect utility function $V(\boldsymbol{p})$, which implicitly holds $\bar{\boldsymbol{x}}$ as fixed, as $V(\boldsymbol{p}, \boldsymbol{p} \cdot \bar{\boldsymbol{x}})$, which does not. This allows us to consider the effects of changes in the consumer's lump sum income.

In words, the distance function is the solution to the following problem: consider a consumption bundle $\tilde{\boldsymbol{x}}$, and also all the combinations of price vector $\boldsymbol{p}$ and total endowment income y such that $V(\boldsymbol{p}, y)$ equals (strictly speaking, at most equals) some constant utility level $\bar{U}$. Choose the vector of prices that minimizes $\boldsymbol{p}^* \cdot \tilde{\boldsymbol{x}}/y$, given $\tilde{\boldsymbol{x}}$. The resulting value is the distance function $D(\tilde{\boldsymbol{x}}, \bar{U})$. Algebraically, the problem is

$$\min_{\boldsymbol{p}} (\boldsymbol{p}^* \cdot \tilde{\boldsymbol{x}})/y \quad \text{subject to} \quad V(\boldsymbol{p}^*, y) \leq \bar{U}. \tag{6.1}$$

It is explained diagrammatically in Figure 6.1, for the case of two goods. For simplicity, we assume that $\tilde{x}$ is on the indifference curve corresponding to the utility level $\bar{U}$, although only the scale of $D(\cdot)$ and not the price vector chosen would be affected by increasing or decreasing $\tilde{x}$ along the ray shown. This is easily verified from inspection of (6.1), since minimizing $(\boldsymbol{p}^*, \tilde{\boldsymbol{x}})/y$ is equivalent to minimizing$(\boldsymbol{p}^* \cdot \lambda\tilde{\boldsymbol{x}})/y$ for any $\lambda > 0$. By choosing $\tilde{x}$ to be just feasible, given $\bar{U}$, we will obtain a value $D(\tilde{x}, \bar{U}) = 1$.

The figure depicts two different combinations of $\boldsymbol{p}^*$ and y, indexed 1 and 2, that satisfy $V(\boldsymbol{p}^*, y) = \bar{U}$. Since the price vector $\boldsymbol{p}_2^*$ results in a tangency away from $\tilde{x}$, purchase of $\tilde{x}$ would require a greater expenditure than y_2. This is not the case with $\boldsymbol{p}_1^*$, since it is tangent to the indifference curve at $\tilde{x}$. (A flatter budget line would again necessitate an increase in expenditure to purchase $\tilde{x}$.) Thus, the price vector chosen, given $\tilde{x}$ and $\bar{U}$, is tangent to the indifference curve corresponding to $\bar{U}$ at point $\tilde{x}$ (or, more generally, if $\tilde{x}$ is not on the indifference curve, at the point on the indifference curve on the ray through $\tilde{x}$ from the

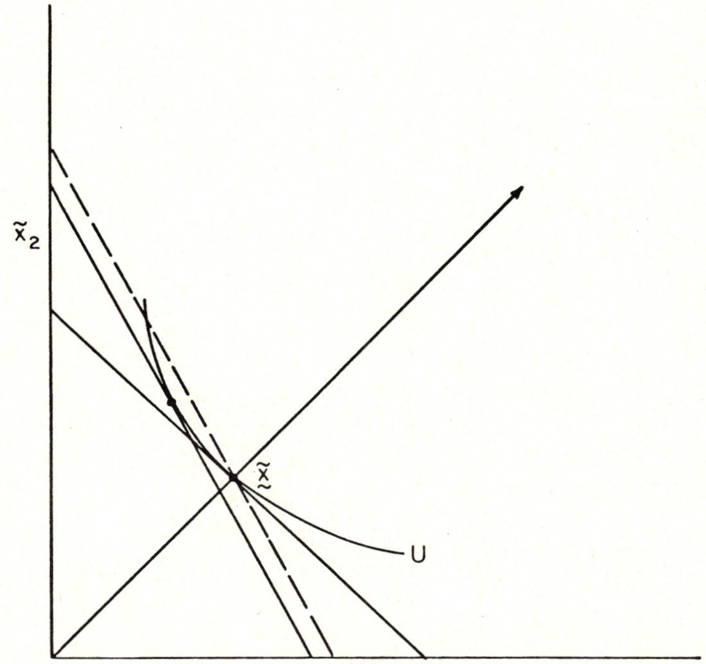

Figure 6.1. The distance function.

origin). Just as the indirect expenditure function chooses consumption, given prices and utility, the distance function chooses normalized prices, given consumption and utility. Since these prices are based on the consumer's indirect utility function, we may interpret them as points on the consumer's inverse compensated demand curve, expressing willingness to pay. By the envelope theorem, the partial derivatives of the distance function with respect to the elements of $\tilde{x}$ are those normalized inverse demands:

$$\frac{\partial D}{\partial \tilde{x}_i} = a_i(\tilde{x}, \bar{U}) = \frac{p_i^*}{y}. \tag{6.2}$$

The Hessian of the distance function is referred to as the Antonelli matrix $A = (a_{ij})$.[14]

Now, consider the actual price vector that prevails, $\boldsymbol{p}$, and choose $\tilde{x}$ such that $\tilde{x} = \tilde{x}_C(\boldsymbol{p}, U)$. Then by construction, $\boldsymbol{p}^* = \boldsymbol{p}$ and $y = E(\boldsymbol{p}, \bar{U})$ solve (6.1), and we have the identity [from (6.2)]

$$a_i(\tilde{x}(\boldsymbol{p}, \bar{U}), \bar{U}) = \frac{p_i}{E(\boldsymbol{p}, \bar{U})}. \tag{6.3}$$

Multiplying (6.3) through by $E(\boldsymbol{p}, \bar{U})$, and differentiating with respect to each price, we obtain conditions which can be stacked to yield

$$E(\boldsymbol{p}, \bar{U})AS = I - \boldsymbol{a}\boldsymbol{x}_C(\boldsymbol{p}, \bar{U}), \tag{6.4}$$

where $\boldsymbol{a} = (a_0, \dots, a_N)$. Evaluating at $\bar{U} = V(\boldsymbol{p}, \boldsymbol{p} \cdot \bar{x})$, this yields

$$(\boldsymbol{p} \cdot \bar{x})AS = I - \boldsymbol{a}\boldsymbol{x}(\boldsymbol{p}, \boldsymbol{p} \cdot \bar{x}). \tag{6.5}$$

Now, let us return to the optimal tax results described in Section 5. Multiplying both sides of (5.15) by $(\boldsymbol{p} \cdot \bar{x})A$, and using the fact that since $\boldsymbol{a}$ is homogeneous of degree zero with respect to $\tilde{x}$, $A\tilde{x} = 0$, we obtain

$$\begin{aligned} \boldsymbol{t} &= \boldsymbol{a}(\boldsymbol{x} + \bar{x})'\boldsymbol{t} - \left(\frac{\mu - \alpha}{\mu}\right)(\boldsymbol{p} \cdot \bar{x})A(\boldsymbol{x} - \bar{x}) \\ &= \boldsymbol{a}(R + \boldsymbol{t} \cdot \bar{x}) + \left(\frac{\mu - \alpha}{\mu}\right)(\boldsymbol{p} \cdot \bar{x})A\bar{x}, \end{aligned} \tag{6.6}$$

[14] See Deaton (1979a) for further discussion of the properties of the function $D(\cdot)$ and the matrix A.

where $R = \boldsymbol{t}\cdot\boldsymbol{x}$ is tax revenue. Using the fact that $t_0 = 0$ to eliminate $(\mu-\alpha)/\mu$, we obtain [Deaton (1981b)]

$$\theta_i = \frac{t_i}{p_i} = \left(\frac{R+\boldsymbol{t}\cdot\bar{\boldsymbol{x}}}{\boldsymbol{p}\cdot\bar{\boldsymbol{x}}}\right)\left(1-\frac{(A\bar{\boldsymbol{x}})_i}{(A\bar{\boldsymbol{x}})_0}\cdot\frac{a_0}{a_i}\right) = \nu\left(1-\frac{\sum_j \bar{x}_j \partial \ln a_i/\partial x_j}{\sum_j \bar{x}_j \partial \ln a_0/\partial \tilde{x}_j}\right), \tag{6.7}$$

which, in turn, implies that, for any i and j,

$$\theta_i - \theta_j = \nu' \sum_k \bar{x}_k \frac{\partial \ln(a_j/a_i)}{\partial \tilde{x}_k}, \tag{6.8}$$

where $\nu' = \nu/\left(\sum \bar{x}_j \,\mathrm{d}\ln a_0/\mathrm{d}\tilde{x}_j\right)$. From (6.8), we see that a sufficient condition for the taxes to be the same is that the ratio of marginal valuations (a_j/a_i) be independent of the consumption of commodities in which the consumer has an endowment. This is equivalent to the distance function being separable, or capable of being expressed as

$$D(\tilde{\boldsymbol{x}},\bar{U}) = f(\tilde{\boldsymbol{x}}_1,\tilde{\boldsymbol{x}}_2,\bar{U},\phi(\tilde{\boldsymbol{x}}_3,\bar{U})), \tag{6.9}$$

where $\tilde{\boldsymbol{x}}_1$ are the commodities in which there is an endowment and $\tilde{\boldsymbol{x}}_3$ are the goods on which taxes are uniform.[15] It also follows that the normal or indirect expenditure function is separable in the corresponding prices [Gorman (1976)]. This separability of the expenditure function is referred to as implicit separability and differs from the separability of the direct and indirect utility functions.[16] Indeed, they are the same only if the utility function is homogeneous in $\tilde{\boldsymbol{x}}_3$ as well [Deaton (1981a)], and it is easy to construct counter-examples for the case where preferences are just weakly separable [Auerbach (1979a)].

In the special case where the consumer's only endowment is in the numeraire commodity, good zero (presumably leisure), the sufficient (and now necessary, as well) condition for uniform taxation of commodities is implicit separability from leisure. It is also possible in this case to say more about which goods will be taxed more heavily if weak separability but not homogenity is satisfied. We begin by

[15] Because $D(\cdot)$ is homogeneous of degree 1 in $\tilde{\boldsymbol{x}}$, f must be homogeneous of degree 1 in $\tilde{\boldsymbol{x}}_1$, $\tilde{\boldsymbol{x}}_2$ and ϕ, and ϕ homogeneous of degree 1 in $\tilde{\boldsymbol{x}}_3$.

[16] (Weak) separability of the direct utility function, for example, would allow the utility function $U(\boldsymbol{x})$ to be written $f(\boldsymbol{x}_1,\boldsymbol{x}_2,\phi(\boldsymbol{x}_3))$, i.e., the marginal rate of substitution between elements of $\boldsymbol{x}_3$ is independent of the levels of $\boldsymbol{x}_1$ and $\boldsymbol{x}_2$.

rewriting (6.8) as

$$\theta_i - \theta_j = \nu' \bar{x}_0 \frac{\partial \ln(a_j/a_i)}{\partial \tilde{x}_0}, \tag{6.10}$$

where $\nu' = \nu/(x_0 a_{00}/a_0)$.

By the convexity of $D(\cdot)$, ν' has the opposite sign of ν and hence is negative. Since $a_j/a_i = p_j/p_i = U_j/U_i$,

$$\frac{\mathrm{d}\ln(U_j/U_i)}{\mathrm{d}\tilde{x}_0} = \frac{\mathrm{d}\ln(a_j/a_i)}{\mathrm{d}\tilde{x}_0} = \frac{\partial \ln(a_j/a_i)}{\partial \tilde{x}_0} + \frac{\partial \ln(a_j/a_i)}{\partial \overline{U}} \cdot \frac{\mathrm{d}U}{\mathrm{d}\tilde{x}_0} \tag{6.11}$$

[Deaton (1981a)]. Thus, when utility is separable into goods and leisure, (6.10) becomes

$$\theta_i - \theta_j = -\nu' \bar{x}_0 \frac{\partial \ln(a_j/a_i)}{\partial \overline{U}} \cdot \frac{\mathrm{d}U}{\mathrm{d}\tilde{x}_0}, \tag{6.12}$$

so that taxes will be higher on those goods that are necessities, if these are defined by those whose valuation by the consumer declines relatively with an increase in real income. This is particularly important if we use empirical demand estimates based on restricted functional forms to estimate optimal taxes. For example, the linear expenditure system

$$\tilde{x}_i(\boldsymbol{p}, p_0\tilde{x}_0) = c_i + \left(\frac{b_i}{\sum_j b_j}\right) \cdot \frac{\left(p_0 x_0 - \sum_j p_j c_j\right)}{p_i}, \tag{6.13}$$

often used in empirical work, comes from the Stone–Geary utility function

$$U(\tilde{\boldsymbol{x}}) = \prod_i (\tilde{x}_i - a_i)^{b_i}, \tag{6.14}$$

which is strongly separable, but not homogeneous unless the terms a_i equal zero (in which case it is simply Cobb–Douglas).

6.2. Distributional objectives

Once we allow for the presence of several individuals with different tastes or income, distributional considerations become an issue.[17] As stressed in Section 3, these considerations must be represented by the specification of an explicit social welfare function based on individual utilities. This cannot normally be achieved by the direct choice of distributional weights on individual income unless the weights are allowed to change with prices in a complicated fashion. There are two problems we consider in this subsection. First, when and how are the previously derived optimal tax rules influenced by equity considerations? Second, if we choose leisure as numeraire and admit lump sum taxes that *cannot* vary across individuals, when will uniform commodity taxes be optimal?

We begin by specifying a social welfare function of the form

$$W = W(U^1, \ldots, U^H), \tag{6.15}$$

which, maximized subject to the usual revenue constraint under the assumption of zero profits in the private sector, yields the following N first-order conditions for optimal commodity taxes $\hat{t} = (t_1, \ldots, t_N)$:

$$-\sum_h W_h \lambda^h x_i^h + \mu\left[\sum_j t_j \sum_h \frac{\partial x_j^h}{\partial p_i} + x_i\right] = 0, \qquad i = 1, \ldots, N, \tag{6.16}$$

where $W_h = \partial W/\partial U^h$, $\lambda^h = \mathrm{d}U^h/\mathrm{d}y^h$ and $x_i = \Sigma_h x_i^h$. Defining α^h, as before, to be the social marginal utility of individual h's income,

$$\alpha^h = W_h \lambda^h + \mu \frac{\mathrm{d}R}{\mathrm{d}y^h}, \tag{6.17}$$

we may express the conditions (6.16) as

$$\sum_j t_j S_{ij} = -\left(\frac{\mu - \tilde{\alpha}_i}{\mu}\right) x_i, \qquad i = 1, \ldots, N, \tag{6.18}$$

where $S_{ij} = \Sigma_h S_{ij}^h$ and

$$\tilde{\alpha}_i = \sum_h \left(\frac{x_i^h}{x_i}\right) \alpha^h \tag{6.19}$$

is the average value of α, weighted by individual consumption shares of good i.

[17] Indeed, even if all individuals are identical, the optimal tax system need not dictate identical treatment. This is discussed in Section 7.

This neat formulation [due to Diamond (1975)] shows that the "equal proportional reduction" rule is amended to call for a greater proportional reduction in the purchase of commodities for which $\tilde{\alpha}_i$ is small. The implication of this result is more clearly seen if we note [following Feldstein (1972)] that

$$\tilde{\alpha}_i = \mathrm{cov}\left(\left(\frac{x_i^h}{x_i}\right), \alpha^h\right) + \frac{1}{H}\sum_h \alpha^h, \tag{6.20}$$

so that $\tilde{\alpha}_i$ exceeds the unweighted mean of α^h if and only if purchases of commodity i are positively correlated with α over individuals. Normally, this would define a necessary good, whose budget shares fall with income and hence rise with α. Note, however, that (6.18) applies to proportional reductions in purchases of different commodities, and does not offer an explicit solution for individual tax rates, unless we assume aggregate commodity demands to be independent ($S_{ij} = 0$ for $i \neq j$). This yields

$$\frac{\theta_i}{\theta_j} = \frac{\varepsilon_{jj}}{\varepsilon_{ii}} \cdot \left(\frac{\mu - \tilde{\alpha}_i}{\mu - \tilde{\alpha}_j}\right), \tag{6.21}$$

which says that the normal inverse elasticity rule is changed by the addition of a second term expressing distributional concerns. Note that as marginal excess burden, and hence the size of μ relative to $\tilde{\alpha}$, increases, efficiency considerations come to dominate these optimal tax rules [Feldstein (1972)].

The addition of the possibility of lump sum taxation increases the generality of the problem without much additional complexity. If individuals have one source of income, then the combination of N commodity taxes and a lump sum tax may be thought of as a linear income tax plus $N-1$ additional commodity taxes. The ability to use lump sum taxation simply adds a constant tax term T to each consumer's indirect utility function and a term HT to the revenue constraint. Differentiating the expanded Lagrangian with respect to T, we obtain the additional first-order condition

$$-\sum_h W_h \lambda^h + \mu\left[\sum_j t_j \sum_h \frac{\partial x_j^h}{\partial y^h} - H\right] = 0, \tag{6.22}$$

to be added to the N conditions in (6.16). This new condition simplifies to

$$\mu = \frac{1}{H}\sum_h \alpha^h = \bar{\alpha}. \tag{6.23}$$

thus, (6.18) becomes

$$\sum_j t_j S_{ij} = \frac{\operatorname{cov}\left(\left(\frac{x_i^h}{x_i}\right), \alpha^h\right)}{\bar{\alpha}} x_i, \qquad i = 1, \ldots, N. \tag{6.24}$$

Now, there should be reductions in commodity purchases only to the extent that the good in question is consumed relatively more by people with low values of α; purchases of some goods will increase. With equal distributional weights, α^h, each of these reductions would be zero, and hence pure lump sum taxation would be optimal.

An interesting question to ask here is under what conditions proportional taxes $\boldsymbol{\theta} = (t_1/p_1, \ldots, t_N/p_N)$ will be equal? In other words, since such uniform taxes are equivalent to a single, proportional tax on the numeraire, labor, when is a linear income tax optimal? A sufficient condition [Deaton (1979b)] is that each individual h have a utility function weakly separable into goods and leisure, with the subfunction in goods possessing linear Engel curves with common slopes across individuals. The intuition behind this result is that the restriction on goods is that preferences obey the Gorman polar form required for exact aggregation of commodity demands. If we can perform such aggregation, then we cannot use differential taxation to distinguish among individuals for purposes of redistribution: a linear income tax exhausts our capacity in this regard.

Note the similarity of this result to that of the case of *non*-linear income taxation [Atkinson and Stiglitz (1976)], where weak separability alone is sufficient for the optimality of income taxation. There is a clear relationship here between the relaxation of the restriction on the linearity of taxes, on the one hand, and that of the linearity of preferences, on the other.

Empirical studies of optimal taxation are not very common, perhaps because the information needed concerning various cross-substitution terms is difficult to obtain without a restriction on preferences that prejudges the result. Two studies, by Atkinson and Stiglitz (1972) and Deaton (1977), utilize the linear expenditure system, which calls for higher taxes on necessities in the single-consumer case (as discussed above) and, in the multi-consumer case with lump sum taxes available, calls for no differential commodity taxes at all, since the Gorman conditions are satisfied. Nevertheless, these calculations are still instructive. Deaton, for example, calculates the optimal taxes on commodities under the assumption that labor is fixed and there are no lump sum taxes. Obviously, with fixed labor supply, uniform taxes on commodities are non-distortionary, but may have undesirable distributional effects. For a demand system estimated for the U.K., he calculated optimal tax rates for eight groups of commodities under various assumptions about the degree of inequality in the social welfare function. Perhaps the most interesting result obtained was that optimal tax rates do not behave monotonically with respect to the degree of inequality aversion implicit in the social welfare function.

A recent application of the optimal tax results in the context of developing countries (India) may be found in Heady and Mitra (1982). Still another approach has been to infer from an existing indirect tax structure what the government's preferences would have to be for the structure to be optimal [Christiansen and Jansen (1978) for Norway, Ahmad and Stern (1981) for India].

7. Further topics in optimal taxation

There are a number of particular problems involving taxation generally to which optimal tax theory has been applied. This section presents some of these.

7.1. Public goods provision

The classic conditions for efficiency in the provision of public goods were derived by Samuelson (1954). Aside from the standard requirement that, for private (rival) goods, each consumer's marginal rate of substitution between two goods should equal the social marginal rate of transformation, there was the new condition that, between a private and a public good, the marginal rate of transformation should equal the *sum* of individual marginal rates of substitution. This is because every consumer partakes of each additional unit of the public good.

Pigou (1947) argued that in considering the benefits of a new public project, the government should recognize that its undertaking may require the introduction of additional deadweight loss through the tax system. The implication that this increases the social cost of public goods has been addressed by a number of authors, including Diamond and Mirrlees (1971), Stiglitz and Dasgupta (1971) and Atkinson and Stern (1974).

Even to examine the question of public goods, we must allow for the presence of several individuals. Since we are not directly interested in distributional issues here, we assume all H individuals to be identical in all respects. If we let G be a public good on which all government revenue is spent and which all consume, then each individual's indirect utility function becomes

$$V(\boldsymbol{p}; G) = \max_{\boldsymbol{x}} U(\boldsymbol{x}; G) \quad \text{subject to} \quad \boldsymbol{p} \cdot \boldsymbol{x} = 0, \tag{7.1}$$

with $\partial V/\partial G = \partial U/\partial G|_{\boldsymbol{x}=\boldsymbol{x}_C(\boldsymbol{p};G)}$. The production function is $\boldsymbol{f}(\boldsymbol{x}; G) = 0$. The government maximizes the welfare of the representative individual by maximizing the sum of individual utilities, since all individuals are the same. This gives rise to the Lagrangian

$$L = HV(\boldsymbol{p}; G) - \mu f(\boldsymbol{x}; G), \tag{7.2}$$

with first-order conditions with respect to each price (except that of the untaxed numeraire)

$$-H\lambda x_i^h - \mu \sum_j f_j \frac{\partial x_j}{\partial p_i} = 0, \qquad i = 1, \ldots, N, \tag{7.3}$$

where λ and μ are defined in the usual way. As in Section 5.3, we use the fact that $\boldsymbol{p} \cdot \boldsymbol{x}^h = 0$ for each individual h to obtain

$$\lambda x_i + \mu \left[\sum t_j \frac{\partial x_j}{\partial p_i} + x_i \right] = 0, \qquad i = 1, \ldots, N, \tag{7.4}$$

where

$$x_i = \sum_h x_i^h = Hx_i^h.$$

As before, this may be rewritten as

$$\boldsymbol{St} = -\left(\frac{\mu - \alpha}{\mu} \right) \boldsymbol{x}, \tag{7.5}$$

where S is the aggregate Slutsky matrix and α is the social marginal utility of each individual's income.

The first-order condition with respect to the choice of public good G is

$$H \frac{\partial U}{\partial G} - \mu \left[\sum_i f_i \frac{\partial x_i}{\partial G} + f_G \right] = 0, \tag{7.6}$$

which yields (since $\lambda \equiv \mathrm{d}U/\mathrm{d}x_0^h$, $q_i \propto f_i$, $q_0 = 1$ and $\boldsymbol{p} \cdot \boldsymbol{x}^h = 0$)

$$\sum_h \frac{\mathrm{d}U^h/\mathrm{d}G}{\mathrm{d}U^h/\mathrm{d}x_0} = \left(\frac{\mu}{\lambda} \right) \left(\frac{f_G}{f_0} - \frac{\mathrm{d}R}{\mathrm{d}G} \right), \tag{7.7}$$

where R is the revenue collected (equal to the public goods purchased, in equilibrium). This result says that the appropriate social cost of the public good G in terms of the numeraire, x_0, to which the sum of marginal rates of substitution should be set equal, differs from the marginal rate of transformation f_G/f_0 for two reasons. First, if public goods are complementary to taxed goods, increasing G may reduce excess burden by increasing consumption of taxed goods, making $\mathrm{d}R/\mathrm{d}G > 0$ [Diamond and Mirrlees (1971)]. The other term μ/λ, equals the ratio of the marginal disutility of raising a dollar of revenue divided by the marginal utility of income, and exceeds one to the extent that an increase in revenue increases excess burden. This corresponds to the point raised by Pigou. However, it need not be the case that μ/λ exceeds one. Again, there is an income effect at work.

This possibility is demonstrated (following Atkinson and Stern) by multiplying both sides of (7.5) by the vector $\boldsymbol{t}$ to obtain

$$\boldsymbol{t}'S\boldsymbol{t} = -\left(\frac{\mu-\alpha}{\mu}\right)R, \tag{7.8}$$

which, by the negative semi-definiteness of S, implies that $\mu > \alpha$ for positive revenue. But $\alpha \geq \lambda$ [see equation (5.5)] only if $\mathrm{d}R/\mathrm{d}y$ is positive. If taxed goods are, on average (weighted by tax rates) inferior, $\mathrm{d}R/\mathrm{d}y < 0$ and $\lambda > \alpha$. Hence, λ may actually exceed μ, meaning that raising an additional dollar to pay for public goods may actually lessen excess burden by causing a shift toward the consumption of taxed goods.

7.2. *Externalities*

Referring again to Pigou, we know that the appropriate response by the government (under conditions of perfect information) to an externality is the imposition of a tax that causes producers of the externality to internalize the additional social cost (or benefit) of their action. Suppose, however, that all commodities, including the one possessing the externality, are subject to distortionary taxation. How is the Pigouvian prescription affected? Following Sandmo (1975), we assume identical individuals, fixed producer prices and let the externality be a symmetric consumption externality related to total consumption of good N. Thus, individual utility for the representative individual h is $U(\boldsymbol{x}^h; x_N)$, where $x_N = Hx_N^h$. The partial derivative of U with respect to x_N may be positive or negative. Assuming for convenience that each individual takes x_N as given (as will be approximately true for H large), we may express the corresponding indirect utility function as $V(\boldsymbol{p}; x_N)$, parallel to the public good example, with $\partial V/\partial x_N = \partial U/\partial x_N|_{\boldsymbol{x}_C(\boldsymbol{p};x_N)}$.

Maximizing the sum of utilities with respect to $\boldsymbol{p}$ subject to the need to raise revenue R through distortionary taxes yields the N first-order conditions

$$-\lambda x_i + H\frac{\partial U}{\partial x_N}\cdot\frac{\partial x_N}{\partial p_i} + \mu\left[x_i + \sum_j t_j \frac{\partial x_j}{\partial p_j}\right] = 0, \quad i = 1,\dots, N, \tag{7.9}$$

or

$$-\lambda x_i + \mu\left[x_i + \sum_j t_j^* \frac{\partial x_j}{\partial p_i}\right] = 0, \quad i = 1,\dots, N, \tag{7.10}$$

where

$$\begin{aligned} t_i &= t_i^*, & i &= 1,\dots, N-1, \\ &= t_i^* - H\frac{\partial U}{\partial x_N}/\mu, & i &= N. \end{aligned}$$

Equation (7.10) is the standard optimal tax result, but it applies to the vector $\boldsymbol{t}^*$ rather than $\boldsymbol{t}$. The difference between them implies that the optimal tax on good N equals that dictated by the standard formula plus the externality imposed by additional consumption of the good: the Pigouvian tax. Thus, the optimal tax and Pigouvian taxes are separable, in a sense; we may imagine choosing the two independently. However, this independence is only present analytically, since the actual level of the externality, and hence the Pigouvian tax, depends on the actual equilibrium and hence the optimal tax rates; the same is true in the other direction.

7.3. Pre-existing distortions

If the government faces pre-existing distortions (of which the preceding example of externalities is a specific kind), it may wish to alter its choice of optimal taxes. Following Green (1961), let us assume that lump sum taxes are available, but certain prices are distorted and cannot be influenced directly. This could be the result of non-competitive behavior, but we shall assume it to be due to some tax that must be maintained, perhaps for political purposes. Assuming that the representative individual's only lump sum income is from the government, we have the problem

$$\max_{\boldsymbol{p}^*, T} V(\boldsymbol{p}, -T) \quad \text{subject to} \quad (\boldsymbol{p}-\boldsymbol{q})\cdot\boldsymbol{x} + T = R, \tag{7.11}$$

where $\boldsymbol{p}^*$ is the subset of $\boldsymbol{p}$ that may be adjusted. Note that unless at least two prices are fixed, equiproportional, non-distortionary taxation is possible.

Differentiating the Lagrangian corresponding to (7.11) with respect to p_i and T yields

$$-\lambda x_i + \mu\left[\sum_j t\frac{\partial x_j}{\partial p_i} + x_i\right] = 0, \qquad \forall p_i \in p^*, \tag{7.12a}$$

$$-\lambda + \mu\left[-\sum_j t_j\frac{\partial x_j}{\partial y} + 1\right] = 0, \tag{7.12b}$$

which may be written as

$$\sum_j S_{ij}t_j = -\left(\frac{\mu-\alpha}{\mu}\right)x_i, \qquad \forall p_i \in p^*, \tag{7.13a}$$

$$\mu = \alpha, \tag{7.13b}$$

for α defined as above. These conditions are quite familiar, and yield the requirement that

$$\sum_j S_{ij}t_j = 0, \qquad \forall p_i \in p^*. \tag{7.14}$$

This does not result in uniform taxes unless at most one tax is fixed (in which case the zero degree homogeneity of S allows us to choose any level of proportional taxes). In particular, suppose all taxes but t_1 are fixed, and $t_0 = t_3 = \cdots = t_N = 0$. Then there is one condition, corresponding to the choice of t_1. Using compensated elasticities $\varepsilon_{ij} = S_{ij}(p_j/x_i)$, we may express this as

$$\theta_1 = -\theta_2\varepsilon_{12}/\varepsilon_{11}, \tag{7.15}$$

where $\theta_i = t_i/p_i$ is the proportional tax on good i. Since $\varepsilon_{11} < 0$, this calls for a tax on good 1 (assuming $\theta_2 > 0$) if $\varepsilon_{12} > 0$, and a subsidy if $\varepsilon_{12} < 0$. If the distorted good is a substitute to good 1, a tax on good 1 will shift consumption into good 2, lessening the original distortion. Taxing a complement, however, would worsen the distortion. (Compare butter and margarine vs. left shoes and right shoes.)

In the wider case in which there are several pre-existing distortions and a single free instrument, t_1, the condition is

$$\theta_1 = -\sum_{j\neq 1} \theta_j \varepsilon_{1j}/\varepsilon_{11}, \tag{7.16}$$

so that the complement–substitute rule now applies to the tax-weighted commodity average. More generally, when several instruments can be set, the results are more complicated.

Several other authors have considered particular restrictions on commodity taxation and profits taxation [for example, Dasgupta and Stiglitz (1972) and Mirrlees (1972)] and the effect of such restrictions on the desirability of production efficiency. Auerbach (1979b) considers the particular production distortion of differential capital income taxation, obtaining a uniform taxation result about separability of factors in production that closely parallels those on the consumption side already discussed in Section 6.

7.4. Taxation and risk

There are many interesting questions that concern the interaction between taxes and risk-bearing. A particular one that fits into the current discussion is the optimal taxation of risky assets. This problem was first examined by Stiglitz (1972) and extended by Auerbach (1981). The basic insight is that the optimal tax results already derived can be applied directly to the case of risky assets by imagining the commodities being taxed to be Arrow–Debreu state-contingent ones. The differences that arise come from the fact that we normally make different assumptions about the structure of utility functions and the completeness of markets when we deal with risk.

The basic model we consider, following Stiglitz (1972), is a two-period model in which the representative individual may consume a certain good (leisure) out of some endowment, and may purchase one of two linearly independent assets yielding returns in two states at date 1. Because the two assets span the states of nature, the consumer may purchase any combination of state-contingent commodities at date 1, and there is a well-defined implicit price for each. A corollary of this is that there is a unique pair of tax rates on commodities in the two states corresponding to each tax regime that applies to the assets themselves. This is helpful, because though our optimal tax results apply to the former, actual tax rules normally apply to the latter. In the more general case without asset spanning, the optimal tax problem becomes more complicated, just as it would if individual commodities in a riskless world could not be purchased independently. Stiglitz (1972) obtained his main result concerning the relative taxation of a risky and a riskless asset from a direct consideration of the effects of taxation on asset demands. It is, perhaps, easier to see the connection with previous results, and the effects of particular assumptions, if we begin with the state-contingent commodities themselves [following Auerbach (1981)].

Letting the good consumed in period 0 be good zero, and the other two commodities be labelled 1 and 2, and taking good 0 to be numeraire, we have the basic optimal tax rule (5.21), which we write here for convenience

$$\frac{\theta_1}{\theta_2} = \frac{\varepsilon_{12} + \varepsilon_{21} + \varepsilon_{20}}{\varepsilon_{12} + \varepsilon_{21} + \varepsilon_{10}}. \tag{7.17}$$

This result can be simplified if we adopt the axioms necessary for the consumer to engage in expected utility maximization. In this case, the consumer's objective function becomes

$$U(x_0, x_1, x_2) = \pi_1 U^1(x_0, x_1) + \pi_2 U^2(x_0, x_2), \tag{7.18}$$

where $U^1(\cdot) = U^2(\cdot)$, π_i is the possibility of state i occurring, and ε_{10} and ε_{20} may be expressed as

$$\varepsilon_{i0} = M\left[-\left(\frac{U^j_{22}x_j}{U^j_2}\right) + p_j x_j \frac{\mathrm{d}\ln(U^j_2/U^i_2)}{\mathrm{d}x_0}\right], \qquad i = 1,2, \quad j = 2,1, \tag{7.19}$$

where M is a positive constant and U_i and U_{ij} are first and second derivatives of utility. The second term in brackets in (7.19) is familiar from Section 6, and equals zero if preferences are weakly separable between periods. If this is so (in which case, utility is also strongly separable, since it is already assumed separable between states), then the tax on good 1 should be higher than that on good 2 if and only if $-(U^1_{22}x_1/U^1_2) > -(U^2_{22}x_2/U^2_2)$, but these are just the Arrow (1965)–Pratt (1964) measures of relative risk-aversion in the two states. Intuitively, as an individual becomes more risk-averse, his behavior becomes less responsive to differences in rates of return. Thus, a tax is less distortionary.

That taxes should be equal when relative risk aversion is constant is not suprising, even without knowledge of the basic optimal tax results. It is for this class of preferences that the basic results of Samuelson (1969) and Merton (1969) concerning the separation of portfolio and savings decision apply. If we cannot influence the amount of savings, and hence leisure consumed, by inducing portfolio shifts, then such a relative distortion has no benefit.

To convert these results to the taxes on the two assets themselves, which we label A and B, we use the fact [see Auerbach (1981)] that

$$\mathrm{sgn}(\theta_A - \theta_B) = \mathrm{sgn}(r^1_A r^2_B - r^2_A r^1_B)\,\mathrm{sgn}(\theta_1 - \theta_2), \tag{7.20}$$

where r_j^i is the return in state i of asset j. Assuming one asset, which we take to be asset A without loss of generality, is risk-free, then the tax should be greater (smaller) on the risky asset B if relative risk-aversion is higher (lower) in the state with the higher (lower) return. In other words, the risky asset should face a higher or lower tax than the safe asset according to whether relative risk-aversion is increasing or decreasing [Stiglitz (1972)]. More generally, if both assets are risky, then one can apply any standard notion of increasing risk [Rothschild and Stiglitz (1970)] to argue that if asset B is riskier than asset A, its return will be more dispersed and hence $(r_A^1 r_B^2 - r_A^2 r_B^1)$ will be positive. This will yield a similar result for taxation of the *riskier* asset.

It is important to recognize that these results assume complete, competitive markets. While a common assumption without risk, it is less acceptable when the commodities concerned are state-contingent. (The same critique also applies to intertemporal problems with date-indexed goods.) In particular, we are implicitly assuming that the government cannot increase the diversification of risk by collecting risky taxes and pooling them. In a real world context where many assets are not traded, this may be a highly questionable restriction to impose.

A second issue of taxation and risk concerns the question of whether the government can increase the welfare of the representative individual by *inducing* risk through the tax system. Normally, risk averse individuals are made worse off by being forced to bear risk. However, the optimal taxation equilibrium is a distorted one, and the famous dictum of Lipsey and Lancaster (1956–57) applies here: once one condition for a Pareto optimum is violated, there is no reason to expect that the violation of others will necessarily worsen matters.

There are two general strands in the literature that deal with the use of induced risk as a policy tool. Weiss (1976) and Stiglitz (1982) show that a random tax system, or one in which there is tax evasion with a probability of detection, may be superior to a certain tax system because, under specified conditions with respect to individual preferences, such risk may lessen the labor supply distortion of the income tax. [Also see Sandmo (1981) on the subject of tax evasion.]

A second issue relates to the case of several individuals, and arises from the possibility that in the presence of indirect taxation, the utility possibility frontier may be non-convex. Even with identical individuals, then, we might wish to tax the consumption of the same good by different individuals at different rates [Atkinson and Stiglitz (1976, 1980), Stiglitz (1982), Balcer and Sadka (1982)]. This is depicted in Figure 7.1. Suppose two individuals, 1 and 2, have identical preferences and consume goods and leisure. If we seek to maximize $(U_1 + U_2)$ by choosing individual-specific excise taxes on consumption, the first-order condition will be zero with equal taxes at $U_1 = U_2 = U^E$, by the symmetry of the problem. But this may represent a local minimum, as shown. Social welfare may be improved by choosing either point A or point B. This represents an unequal treatment of equal individuals and may violate proscriptions of such horizontal inequity. However, suppose the tax system were randomized so that point A were

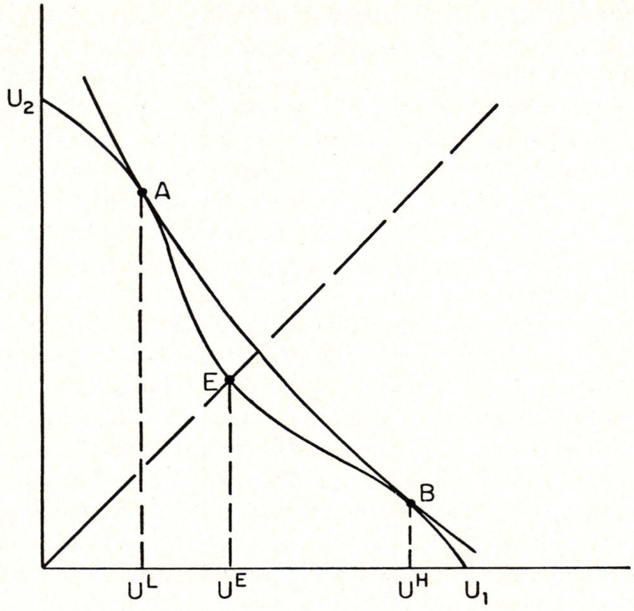

Figure 7.1. Optimal taxation and non-convexities.

chosen half the time, and point B the other half. This would give the same expected utility to each individual. Moreover, it would yield the same value of the social welfare function, defined on individual expected utilities, as before at either A or B,

$$EU_1 + EU_2 = \tfrac{1}{2}[U^L + U^H] + \tfrac{1}{2}[U^H + U^L] = U^H + U^L. \tag{7.21}$$

Thus, randomization may be desirable.

8. Tax reform

All of the optimal tax problems analyzed thus far share in common the fact that global optima are sought. There are a number of new issues arising from a consideration of tax *reform*, rather than tax design.

One problem of tax reform derives from the existence of an initial allocation. Though a new tax system may be more efficient and more equitable than the existing one, the transition from old to new may cause a redistribution of resources to occur than in itself is undesirable. For example, it has often been suggested in the U.S. that the tax subsidy for state and municipal bonds be removed. If this were done unexpectedly, it would cause a capital loss for the holders of such bonds, but not for other, otherwise identical individuals. Such treatment may be thought of as a violation of horizontal equity [Feldstein (1976)] which may be explicitly accounted for in an expanded social welfare function [King (1983a)]. This problem undoubtedly is one of the reasons why tax reform is so difficult to achieve.

A second general problem of tax reform, which shall be the main focus of this section, is that the *direction* in which to move from the current system is not always evident. Even if all distortions can be reduced somewhat, this may not increase economic efficiency. The basic difficulty is that we can only be sure that movement in the direction of a global optimum will improve matters if we are sufficiently close to that optimum initially. A related problem is whether one can increase economic efficiency in a piecemeal fashion, by removing distortions one at a time. In general, such a scheme for tax reform may decrease welfare along the transition path to a global optimum. Restrictions on preferences and production sufficient to prevent this are extremely restrictive [Boadway and Harris (1977)].

8.1. Moving to lump sum taxation

Lump sum taxes are non-distortionary, but it need not follow that partially reducing distortions and replacing them with lump sum taxes will improve efficiency. One case in which it *will* is when the distortionary tax rates are set at each point of the transition at the optimal tax rates for the revenue being collected by non-lump sum taxes. That is, if a certain amount of revenue, R, is collected initially by the distortionary taxes, and a lump sum tax T is introduced, the new taxes should be those optimal for collecting $R-T$. As T increases, this sequence of optimal tax rates insures a monotonic increase in utility. This result is due to Atkinson and Stern (1974), and demonstrated as follows. Consider the optimal tax problem

$$\max_{T,\boldsymbol{p}} V(\boldsymbol{p},-T) \quad \text{subject to} \quad (\boldsymbol{p}-\boldsymbol{q})\cdot\boldsymbol{x}+T\geq R, \tag{8.1}$$

where T is the lump sum tax faced by the individual. Differentiating the corresponding Lagrangian with respect to T yields the effect of an increase in T on utility, given that $\boldsymbol{p}$ is chosen optimally,

$$\frac{\mathrm{d}\mathscr{L}}{\mathrm{d}T}=-\lambda+\mu\left[-\sum t_j\frac{\partial x_j}{\partial y}+1\right]=(\mu-\alpha), \tag{8.2}$$

where λ, α and μ are defined in the usual way to be the marginal utility of income, the social marginal utility of income and the Lagrange multiplier on the revenue constraint. However, we know from expression (7.8) that $\mu > \alpha$, so utility must increase as T does: when the tax vector $\boldsymbol{t}$ is chosen optimally, there is always a positive marginal excess burden to revenue collection.

Unfortunately, this is not a very realistic assumption to make in the current context. The taxes we may wish to reform may cause unnecessarily large distortions, and we may be restricted to a proportional reduction formula, or some other constraint on how they are to be lowered.

Consider the case of an arbitrary change in the levels of excise taxes $\boldsymbol{t}$ and lump sum taxes T for the case of a single individual and fixed producer prices. [This latter assumption can be relaxed; see Dixit (1975).] We have [following Atkinson and Stiglitz (1980)]

$$\mathrm{d}U = \sum_i \frac{\partial V}{\partial p_i}\,\mathrm{d}t_i - \frac{\partial V}{\partial y}\,\mathrm{d}T = -\lambda(\boldsymbol{x}\cdot \mathrm{d}\boldsymbol{t} + \mathrm{d}T), \tag{8.3a}$$

and

$$\mathrm{d}R = \mathrm{d}(\boldsymbol{t}\cdot\boldsymbol{x} + T) = \boldsymbol{x}\cdot\mathrm{d}\boldsymbol{t} + \boldsymbol{t}\cdot\mathrm{d}\boldsymbol{x} + \mathrm{d}T = 0, \tag{8.3b}$$

which yields

$$\mathrm{d}U = \lambda\boldsymbol{t}\cdot\mathrm{d}\boldsymbol{x}. \tag{8.4}$$

Utility is increased by the tax change if consumption changes to increase revenue from the existing taxes, thereby reducing the associated excess burden.

From the Slutsky equation, we have

$$\mathrm{d}\boldsymbol{x} = \frac{\partial\boldsymbol{x}}{\partial\boldsymbol{p}}\,\mathrm{d}\boldsymbol{t} - \frac{\partial\boldsymbol{x}}{\partial y}\,\mathrm{d}T = S\,\mathrm{d}\boldsymbol{t} - \frac{\partial\boldsymbol{x}}{\partial y}(\boldsymbol{x}'\mathrm{d}\boldsymbol{t} + \mathrm{d}T), \tag{8.5}$$

which, combined with (8.3b) and (8.4), yields

$$\mathrm{d}U = \frac{\lambda}{1 - \boldsymbol{t}\cdot\partial\boldsymbol{x}/\partial y}\cdot\boldsymbol{t}'S\,\mathrm{d}\boldsymbol{t}. \tag{8.6}$$

This holds for any change in $\boldsymbol{t}$ and T, and can be useful in analyzing particular kinds of tax reforms. For example, suppose all distortions are reduced proportionally, i.e., $\mathrm{d}\boldsymbol{t} = -b\boldsymbol{t}$. Then because S is negative semi-definite, $\mathrm{d}U \geq 0$ if and only if $(1 - \boldsymbol{t}\cdot\partial\boldsymbol{x}/\partial y) \geq 0$ [Dixit (1975)]. This condition says that a dollar increase in income causes the consumer to pay less than a dollar in additional excise taxes.

Since $\boldsymbol{p} = \boldsymbol{q} + \boldsymbol{t}$, it is equivalent to the requirement that $\boldsymbol{q} \cdot \boldsymbol{x}$ increase with y: as the consumer spends more, the *social* cost of the goods purchased also increases. If this condition is violated, then it is possible that multiple equilibria exist, and the tax reduction may move the economy away from the undistorted optimum [Foster and Sonnenschein (1970)].

This may be demonstrated graphically [following Hatta (1977)] for the simple case in which there are only two goods. Suppose that a certain revenue R (measured in units of commodity 1) must be raised, and that the consumer has an endowment $\bar{x}_1$. The possible equilibria lie along the social production constraint M in Figure 8.1. Superimposed on this constraint are a series of indifference curves, the highest feasible one passing through point A, the undistorted optimum. Normally, we would expect that as we travel along M from point A toward either axis, decreasing the feasible utility level, the marginal rate of substitution between x_1 and x_2 changes monotonically. (This is true, of course, for movements along an indifference curve and, hence, for *local* movements away from A along M, where there is no first-order income effect.) If this is the case, then a

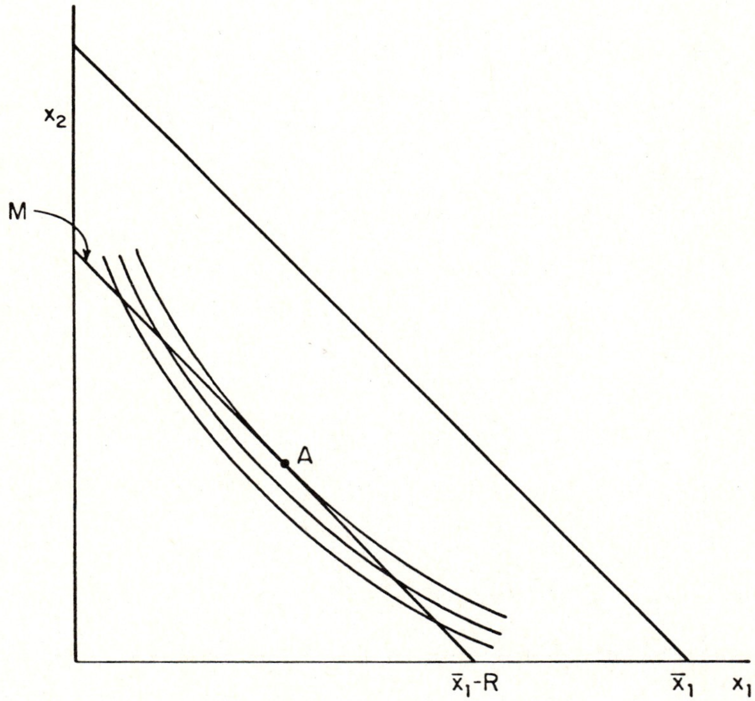

Figure 8.1. Prices and utility.

revenue-preserving reduction in the divergence between the relative price of x_2 and its social cost, in terms of x_1, must increase utility, for it will induce a movement along M toward point A. However, there may be cases in which there is no such monotonicity, and a given slope may occur at an odd number of different points on M, not just one. In this case, reductions in the price distortion may actually move the consumer *away* from point A.

That this possibility is equivalent to the condition derived from (8.6) is demonstrated graphically in Figure 8.2, where an increase in lump sum income above $\bar{x}_1$ causes the consumer to shift from point B to point C, inside the production constraint M. Since the indifference curve slopes at B and C are the same, the slope at D must be flatter than at B. Thus, a steepening of the consumer's budget line resulting from a reduction in the price distortion will cause a movement away from B, along M, toward the x_1 axis rather than toward D and A, thereby lowering the consumer's utility.

A particular application of this result is that when equilibrium is unique, a consumption tax is superior to a wage tax in the presence of pure rents, since the

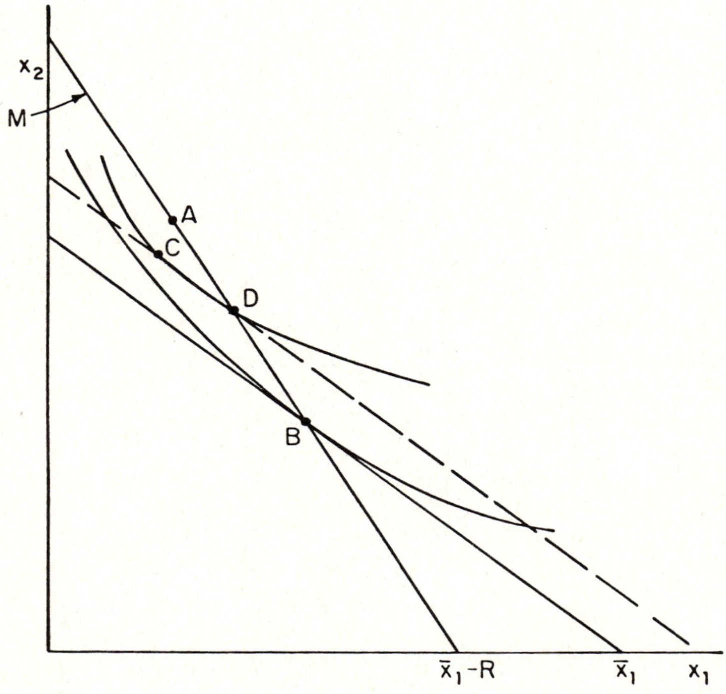

Figure 8.2. Multiple equilibria with taxes.

former tax is equivalent to the latter in conjunction with a lump sum rent tax [Helpman and Sadka (1982)].

Another result that follows from (8.6) is for the case where the tax distortion is zero for one good (arbitrarily, good zero) and equiproportional for other goods. That is, in our previous notation, $\hat{\boldsymbol{t}} = \theta \hat{\boldsymbol{p}}$. Since $\boldsymbol{p}'S = 0$, (8.6) may be rewritten as

$$\mathrm{d}U = -\frac{\lambda}{1 - \boldsymbol{t} \cdot \mathrm{d}\boldsymbol{x}/\mathrm{d}y} \boldsymbol{S}_0 \cdot \mathrm{d}\hat{\boldsymbol{t}}, \tag{8.7}$$

where $\boldsymbol{S}_0 = (S_{01}, S_{02}, \ldots, S_{0N})$. A sufficient condition for this to be positive (assuming $\mathrm{d}R/\mathrm{d}y < 1$) is that taxes be decreased on substitutes for good zero ($S_{0i} > 0$) and increased on complements [Dixit (1975)].

8.2. *Reform without lump sum taxation*

This problem is harder, because there is no obvious "first-best" looming in the distance to guide our movement. General characterization of the direction in which taxes should be changed is a difficult problem, and while progress has been made [Guesnerie (1977), Diewert (1978)], there is little we can say of a concrete nature without further assumptions.

One approach that sidesteps this problem is to characterize observable changes in equilibrium that will result *if* welfare is improved. Following Pazner and Sadka (1981), we can use revealed preference theory to evaluate a balanced budget change in distortionary taxes. Let $\boldsymbol{t}_0 = \boldsymbol{p}_0 - \boldsymbol{q}$ be the initial set of taxes (with producer prices fixed) and $\boldsymbol{t}_1 = \boldsymbol{p}_1 - \boldsymbol{q}$ be the prospective change. If $\boldsymbol{p}_1 \cdot \boldsymbol{x}_1 > \boldsymbol{p}_1 \cdot \boldsymbol{x}_0$ (where $\boldsymbol{x}_0$ and $\boldsymbol{x}_1$ are the purchases in the two situations), then $\boldsymbol{x}_1$ is preferred by the consumer. Hence, utility has increased. However, since $\mathrm{d}(\boldsymbol{t} \cdot \boldsymbol{x}) = 0$, $\boldsymbol{q} \cdot \boldsymbol{x}_1 = \boldsymbol{q} \cdot \boldsymbol{x}_0$, so that $\boldsymbol{t}_1 \cdot \boldsymbol{x}_1 > \boldsymbol{t}_1 \cdot \boldsymbol{x}_0$, or $\boldsymbol{t}_1 \cdot \Delta \boldsymbol{x} > 0$. [Note the similarity of this discrete condition to (8.4).] Likewise, if $\boldsymbol{t}_0 \cdot \Delta \boldsymbol{x} < 0$, the original situation is preferred. Unfortunately, there is an indeterminate range in which neither of these conditions is satisfied.

If we assume producer prices to be fixed (here this restriction is necessary) and that all goods but the numeraire are taxed uniformly, then we can characterize a utility increasing tax change. The three-good case was analyzed by Corlett and Hague (1953–54), with a generalization provided by Dixit (1975), whose analysis we follow. Note that (8.4) still is valid in determining whether a tax change increases utility. However, since lump sum taxes are unavailable, $\boldsymbol{t} \cdot \boldsymbol{x} = 0$. Using (8.5), for $\mathrm{d}T = 0$, we have

$$0 = \mathrm{d}(\boldsymbol{t} \cdot \boldsymbol{x}) = \boldsymbol{x} \cdot \mathrm{d}\boldsymbol{t} + \boldsymbol{t} \cdot \mathrm{d}\boldsymbol{x} = \boldsymbol{x} \cdot \mathrm{d}\boldsymbol{t} + \boldsymbol{t}'\frac{S}{\Delta}\,\mathrm{d}\boldsymbol{t} = \left(\boldsymbol{x}' + \boldsymbol{t}\frac{S}{\Delta}\right)\mathrm{d}\boldsymbol{t}, \tag{8.8}$$

where $\Delta = 1 - \boldsymbol{t} \cdot \partial \boldsymbol{x}/\partial y$. For the case where $t_0 = 0$ and $\hat{\boldsymbol{t}} = \theta \hat{\boldsymbol{p}}$, we use the homogeneity of S to rewrite this as

$$\left(\boldsymbol{x}' - \frac{\theta}{\Delta}\boldsymbol{S}_0'\right)\mathrm{d}\boldsymbol{t} = 0, \tag{8.9}$$

which, using the definition of compensated elasticities $\varepsilon_{ij} = S_{ij}(p_j/x_i)$, may be written

$$\sum_i x_i\left(1 - \frac{\theta}{\Delta}\varepsilon_{i0}\right)\mathrm{d}t_i = 0.$$

From (8.4), we have (for $\mathrm{d}T = 0$)

$$\mathrm{d}U = -\lambda \boldsymbol{x} \cdot \mathrm{d}\boldsymbol{t}. \tag{8.10}$$

If we assume that

$$x_i\left(1 - \frac{\theta}{\Delta}\varepsilon_{i0}\right) = \frac{\mathrm{d}R}{\mathrm{d}t_i}$$

is positive, and make the related assumption that Δ is positive, then [comparing (8.9) and (8.10)], in changing two taxes, we should decrease the one for which

$$\frac{x_i\left(1 - \frac{\theta}{\Delta}\varepsilon_{i0}\right)}{x_i} \tag{8.11}$$

is smaller, or ε_{i0} is larger – increase the tax on the relative complement. This extends in an obvious way if we choose pairs of taxes successively.

References

Ahmad, E. and N. Stern, 1981, On the evaluation of indirect tax systems: An application to India, Feb. (University of Warwick, Coventry).

Arrow, K., 1965, Essays in the theory of risk-bearing (North-Holland, Amsterdam).

Atkinson, A.B. and N.H. Stern, 1974, Pigou, taxation and public goods, Review of Economic Studies 41, 119–128.

Atkinson, A.B. and N.H. Stern, 1980, Taxation and incentives in the UK, Lloyds Bank Review, 43–46.

Atkinson, A.B. and J.E. Stiglitz, 1972, The structure of indirect taxation and economic efficiency, Journal of Public Economics 1, 97–119.

Atkinson, A.B. and J.E. Stiglitz, 1976, The design of tax structure: Direct versus indirect taxation, Journal of Public Economics 6, 55–75.

Atkinson, A.B. and J.E. Stiglitz, 1980, Lectures on public economics (McGraw-Hill, New York).
Auerbach, A.J., 1979a, A brief note on a non-existent theorem about the optimality of uniform taxation, Economics Letters 3, 49–52.
Auerbach, A.J., 1979b, The optimal taxation of heterogeneous capital, Quarterly Journal of Economics 93, 589–612.
Auerbach, A.J., 1981, Evaluating the taxation of risky assets, HIER working paper 857.
Auerbach, A.J. and H. Rosen, 1980, Will the real excess burden please stand up?, HIER working paper 767.
Auerbach, A.J., L.J. Kotlikoff and J. Skinner, 1983, The efficiency gains from dynamic tax reform, International Economic Review 24, 81–100.
Balcer, Y. and E. Sadka, 1982, Horizontal equity, income taxation and self-selection with an application to income tax credits, Journal of Public Economics 19, 291–309.
Baumol, B. and D. Bradford, 1970, Optimal departures from marginal cost pricing, American Economic Review 60, 265–283.
Boadway, R. and R. Harris, 1977, A characterization of piecemeal second best policy, Journal of Public Economics 8, 169–190.
Boiteux, M., 1951, Le "revenue distribuable" et les pertes économiques, Econometrica 19, 112–133.
Boiteux, M., 1956, Sur le gestion des monopoles publics astreints à l'equilibre budgetaire, Econometrica 24, 22–40. Translated and reprinted in 1971, Journal of Economic Theory 3, 219–440.
Bradford, D. and H. Rosen, 1976, The optimal taxation of commodities and income, AEA Papers and Proceedings 66, 94–101.
Chamley, C., 1981, The welfare cost of capital income taxation in a growing economy, Journal of Political Economy 89, 468–496.
Chipman, J.S. and J.C. Moore, 1980, Compensating variation, consumer's surplus, and welfare, American Economic Review 70, 933–949.
Christiansen, V. and E.S. Jansen, 1978, Implicit social preferences in the Norwegian system of indirect taxation, Journal of Public Economics 10, 217–245.
Cooter, 1979, A new expenditure function, Economics Letters 2, 103–110.
Corlett, W.J. and D.C. Hague, 1953–54, Complementarity and the excess burden of taxation, Review of Economic Studies 21, 21–30.
Dasgupta, P.S. and J.E. Stiglitz, 1972, On optimal taxation and public production, Review of Economic Studies 39, 87–103.
Deaton, A.S., 1977, Equity, efficiency and the structure of indirect taxation, Journal of Public Economics 8, 299–312.
Deaton, A.S., 1979a, The distance function in consumer behaviour with applications of index numbers and optimal taxation, Review of Economic Studies 46, 391–406.
Deaton, A.S., 1979b, Optimally uniform commodity taxes, Economics Letters 2, 357–361.
Deaton, A.S., 1981a, Optimal taxes and the structure of preferences, Econometrica 49, 1245–1260.
Deaton, A.S., 1981b, Numeraires and endowments in optimal tax formulae: A note, Discussion paper 81/113, Sept. (University of Bristol).
Debreu, G., 1951, A classical tax-subsidy problem, Econometrica 22, 14–22.
Debreu, G., 1954, The coefficient of resource utilization, Econometrica 19, 273–292.
Diamond, P.A., 1975, A many-person Ramsey rule, Journal of Public Economics 4, 335–342.
Diamond, P.A. and D.L. McFadden, 1974, Some uses of the expenditure function in public finance, Journal of Public Economics 3, 3–21.
Diamond, P.A. and J. Mirrlees, 1971, Optimal taxation and public production I: Production efficiency, and II: Tax rules, American Economic Review 61, 8–27 and 261–278.
Diewert, W.E., 1978, Optimal tax perturbations, Journal of Public Economics 10, 139–177.
Diewert, W.E., 1981, The measurement of deadweight loss revisited, Econometrica 49, 1225–1244.
Dixit, A.K., 1970, On the optimum structure of commodity taxes, American Economic Review 60, 295–301.
Dixit, A.K., 1975, Welfare effects of tax and price changes, Journal of Public Economics 4, 103–123.
Dupuit, J., 1844, De la mesure de l'utilité des travaux publics, Annales des Ponts et Chaussées 8. Translated and reprinted in: K. Arrow and T. Scitovsky, eds., 1969, AEA readings in welfare economics, 255–283.
Feldstein, M.S., 1972, Distributional equity and the optimal structure of public prices, American

Economic Review 62, 32–36.
Feldstein, M.S., 1976, On the theory of tax reform, Journal of Public Economics 6, 77–104.
Feldstein, M.S., 1978, The welfare cost of capital income taxation, Journal of Public Economics 86, 29–51.
Feldstein, M.S., ed., 1983, Behavioral simulation methods in tax policy analysis (University of Chicago Press, Chicago, IL).
Foster, E. and H. Sonnenschein, 1970, Price distortion and economic welfare, Econometrica 38, 281–297.
Gorman, W.M., 1953, Community preference fields, Econometrica 21, 63–80.
Gorman, W.M., 1976, Tricks with utility functions, in: M.J. Artis and A.R. Nobay, eds., Essays in economic analysis (Cambridge University Press, London).
Green, H.A.J., 1961, The social optimum in the presence of monopoly and taxation, Review of Economic Studies 29, 66–78.
Green, J. and E. Sheshinski, 1979, Approximating the gains from welfare reforms, Journal of Public Economics 11, 179–195.
Guesnerie, R., 1977, On the direction of tax reform, Journal of Public Economics 7, 179–202.
Harberger, A., 1954, Monopoly and resource allocation, American Economic Review 42, 77–87.
Harberger, A., 1964, Taxation, resource allocation and welfare, in: The role of direct and indirect taxes in the Federal Reserve system (Princeton University Press, Princeton, NJ, for the NBER and Brookings Institution).
Harberger, A., 1966, Efficiency effects of taxes on income from capital, in: M. Krzyzaniak, ed., Effects of corporation income tax (Wayne State University Press, Detroit, MI) 107–117.
Harberger, A., 1971, Three postulates for applied welfare analysis, Journal of Economic Literature 9, 785–797.
Hatta, T., 1977, A theory of piecemeal policy recommendations, Review of Economic Studies 44, 1–21.
Hausman, J.A., 1981a, Exact consumer's surplus and deadweight loss, American Economic Review 71, 662–676.
Hausman, J.A., 1981b, Labor supply, in: H. Aaron and J. Pechman, eds., How taxes affect economic behavior (Brookings Institution, Washington, DC) 27–84.
Heady, C.J. and P.K. Mitra, 1982, Restricted redistributive taxation, shadow prices and trade policy, Journal of Public Economics 17, 1–22.
Helpman, E. and E. Sadka, 1982, Consumption versus wage taxation, Quarterly Journal of Economics 97, 363–372.
Hicks, J.R., 1940, The valuation of social income, Economica N.S. 7, 105–124.
Hicks, J.R., 1942, Consumer's surplus and index numbers, Review of Economic Studies 9, 126–137.
Hicks, J.R., 1946, Value and capital, 2nd ed. (Oxford University Press, Oxford).
Hotelling, H., 1938, The general welfare in relation to problems of taxation and of railway utility rates, Econometrica 6, 242–269.
Kaldor, N., 1939, Welfare propositions in economics, Economic Journal 49, 549–552.
Kay, J.A., 1980, The deadweight loss from a tax system, Journal of Public Economics 13, 111–120.
King, M.A., 1983a, An index of inequality: With applications to horizontal equity and social mobility, Econometrica 51, 99–115.
King, M.A., 1983b, Welfare analysis of tax reforms using household data, Journal of Public Economics, forthcoming.
Lipsey, R.G. and R.K. Lancaster, 1956–57, The general theory of second best, Review of Economic Studies 24, 11–32.
Marshall, A., 1920, Principles of economics (Macmillan, London).
Merton, R.C., 1969, Lifetime portfolio selection under uncertainty: The continuous-time case, Review of Economic Statistics 51, 247–257.
Mirrlees, J.A., 1972, On producer taxation, Review of Economic Studies 39, 105–111.
Mohring, H., 1971, Alternative welfare gain and loss measures, Western Economic Journal 9, 349–368.
Muellbauer, J.N.J., 1976, Community preferences and the representative consumer, Econometrica 44, 979–999.
Musgrave, R.A., 1959, The theory of public finance (McGraw-Hill, New York).
Pazner, E.A. and E. Sadka, 1981, Welfare criteria for tax reforms: Efficiency aspects, Journal of Public

Economics 16, 113–122.
Pigou, A.C., 1947, A study in public finance, 3rd ed. (Macmillan, London).
Pratt, J.W., 1964, Risk aversion in the small and in the large, Econometrica 32, 122–136.
Ramsey, F.P., 1927, A contribution to the theory of taxation, Economic Journal 37, 47–61.
Roberts, K.W.S., 1980, Price-independent welfare prescriptions, Journal of Public Economics 13, 277–297.
Rosen, H., 1978, The measurement of excess burden with explicit utility functions, Journal of Political Economy 86, S121–136.
Rothschild, M. and J.E. Stiglitz, 1970, Increasing risk I: A definition, Journal of Economic Theory 2, 225–243.
Samuelson, P.A., 1947, Foundations of economic analysis (Harvard University Press, Cambridge, MA).
Samuelson, P.A., 1954, The pure theory of public expenditure, Review of Economics and Statistics 36, 387–389.
Samuelson, P.A., 1969, Lifetime portfolio selection by dynamic stochastic programming, Review of Economic Statistics 51, 239–246.
Sandmo, A., 1975, Optimal taxation in the presence of externalities, Swedish Journal of Economics 77, 86–98.
Sandmo, A., 1981, Income tax evasion, labour supply, and the equity–efficiency tradeoff, Journal of Public Economics 16, 265–288.
Shoven, J.B., 1976, The incidence and efficiency effects of taxes on income from capital, Journal of Political Economy 84, 1261–1284.
Small, K.A. and H.S. Rosen, 1981, Applied welfare economics with discrete choice models, Econometrica, 105–130.
Stiglitz, J., 1972, Taxation, risk taking and the allocation of investment in a competitive economy, in: M. Jensen, ed., Studies in the theory of capital markets (Praeger, New York) 294–361.
Stiglitz, J., 1982, Utilitarianism and horizontal equity: The case for random taxation, Journal of Public Economics 18, 1–33.
Stiglitz, J. and P.S. Dasgupta, 1971, Differential taxation, public goods and economic efficiency, Review of Economic Studies 38, 151–174.
Varian, H.R., 1982, The nonparametric approach to demand analysis, Econometrica 50, 945–973.
Vartia, Y.O., 1983, Efficient methods of measuring welfare change and compensated income in terms of ordinary demand functions, Econometrica 51, 79–98.
Venti, S.F. and D.A. Wise, 1984, Moving and housing expenditure: Transactions costs and equilibrium, Journal of Public Economics 23, 207–243.
Weiss, L., 1976, The desirability of cheating incentives and randomness in the optimal income tax, Journal of Political Economy 84, 1343–1352.
Willig, R.E., 1976, Consumer's surplus without apology, American Economic Review 66, 589–597.

Chapter 3

PUBLIC SECTOR PRICING

DIETER BÖS*

University of Bonn, Bonn

1. Public pricing institutions

1.1. What is priced publicly in different countries?

Prices are an excellent instrument for coordinating supply and demand, provided people who do not pay can be excluded from consumption. Hence, prices are used not only by private entrepreneurs, but also by politicians, bureaucrats, and public utility managers.

Public prices can be found in almost every economic activity. However, looking across countries, there are particular areas where public pricing is more likely to be found than in others. These areas are closely associated with supplying *essential goods and services*, either to industries or directly to consumers. "Essential" means that they cannot be cut off without danger of total or partial collapse of an economy. Starting from an allocative point of view, we stress the importance of these goods and services as being part of the *infrastructure* for producers and consumers. Starting from a distributional point of view, we would have to stress their importance for providing consumers with *necessities of life*.

Essential goods and services are almost the same in all industrialized countries. Hence, it is possible to present a fairly general basic catalogue of candidates for public pricing. How many of these candidates are priced publicly in any one country, depends on the prevailing degree of confidence in the efficiency of the private sector, which differs from country to country. The institutional arrangements which are used to attain the aims mentioned above, vary widely and range from the establishment of public enterprises to the regulation of private enterprises.

*I am grateful to Alan Auerbach, Dieter Elixmann, Kåre Hagen, Kurt Klappholz, Wolfgang Peters, Hans-Dieter Stolper, Georg Tillmann, Ruth Watzke, Robert von Weizsäcker, Wolfgang Wiegard and Hans-Georg Zimmermann for extensive comments on previous drafts of this paper.

Handbook of Public Economics, vol. I, edited by A.J. Auerbach and M. Feldstein

This basic catalogue is as follows:

(1) *Public utilities*, i.e., energy, communication and transportation.
Examples include:
- electricity, gas, water,
- telephone, postal services,
- radio, TV,
- airlines, railroads, urban traffic, toll bridges,
- stockyards, refuse collection.

These industries are publicly priced in most Western countries. In the United States they are either regulated private or public enterprises, in Europe they tend to be public enterprises.

(2) *Basic goods industries*, producing coal, oil, atomic energy and steel. Nationalized enterprises in these branches can be found in any Western European country. The percentages of nationalized enterprises in these branches do, however, vary from country to country, Austria, France, Great Britain, Italy, and Spain being the countries with the highest percentages.

(3) *Finance*. Savings banks are often established as local public enterprises, whence their interest rates are public prices. In most European countries there are at least some publicly owned banks, more extensive nationalization including the large or even all banks (Austria, Italy, France). Private and public insurance companies are extensively regulated in most countries, from rates to terms of policies and the calculation of risks and reserves.

(4) *Agriculture*. Farming in Western Europe is done by regulated enterprises, the EEC regulations on the common agricultural market constituting one of the most intensively planned sectors of these economies. In a lot of U.S. states the milk price is regulated on a "public interest basis".

(5) *Education and health*. Here we may refer to fees of publicly owned schools and universities, pricing of publicly owned hospitals (and also those of regulated ones). In Europe, moreover, there is extended price regulation of physicians' accounts and publicly fixed lump-sum prices for medicines bought on prescriptions by people covered by one of the various kinds of public "insurance" schemes.

After presenting this basic catalogue we must again stress that it is impossible to explain all prevailing instances of public pricing by reference to such an expository scheme. There is almost no good or service which has not been publicly priced at some time in some country. Confining myself to the present, the following are some examples, presented in alphabetic order: ale (State

Hofbräuhaus in Munich), automobiles (British Leyland, Renault), books (government printing offices), china (Royal Prussian china manufacture in Berlin), cigarettes (public monopolies in France and in Austria), etc., etc.

1.2. Why public pricing?

Let us begin with some *historical considerations*. Many European public enterprises were established in the past either to raise revenue or to promote technical progress. Some leftovers of these mercantilistic policies can still be found: the above mentioned example of cigarettes refers to the first case, the china manufacture exemplifies the second. A little later, *liberal ideas* lead to nationalization, where monopolistic market structures could not be avoided. This was the primary reason for the nationalization of railways and local traffic enterprises in the second half of the last century. *Public interest* was another argument for such public activities, mainly with respect to industries providing basic goods. This argument, moreover, received priority in the many public takeovers of private enterprises which were incurring persistent losses.

In *contemporary Western market economies*, public pricing can mainly be justified by different forms of *market failure*.

Most cases of public pricing by public utilities can best be justified by their being *natural monopolies*. Such monopolies are characterized by a subadditive cost function and by sustainability [Baumol (1977)]: It is cheaper to produce goods by a monopoly than by many firms and potential market entrants can be held off without predatory measures. In such cases unregulated enterprises would exploit the market. Regulating private enterprises or establishing public enterprises should ensure economically *or* politically wanted prices and at the same time guarantee the reliability of supply.

The stabilization of *cobweb markets* is another market failure argument for public pricing. Without regulation unwanted sharp fluctuations of prices and quantities would result from low short-run price elasticities of demand and supply. Agricultural pricing provides the best-known examples. But medical care (pricing of hospital and physicians' services) is of equal importance. Note that this justification for public pricing can clearly be separated from distributional reasons. Taxi pricing is regulated all over the world, mainly because of the cobweb problem. But taxi pricing has nothing to do with distribution policy.

Nevertheless, *distributional objectives* must be mentioned as further economic reasons of public pricing. The regulation of necessities like milk is a good example, rent control is another one. (However, there exists a variety of combinations between public and private price regulation in the housing market.) The many differentiations between classes of users, as exemplified by first- and second-class railway fares, etc., are distributionally relevant although they can be primarily interpreted as monopolistic price discrimination.

Closely related to the distribution argument are "*merit wants*" arguments in favor of public pricing. Public zero tariffs for primary and secondary schools are a good example, publicly priced cultural institutions like museums are another.

But beyond all economic considerations it is often *ideological or other political reasoning* that is at the back of public pricing. The extension of the scope of public pricing by the recent French nationalization of 1982 derived from President Mitterand's socialist attitude of mind. In Great Britain, partial denationalization is always discussed or enacted if the political power changes from the Labour Party to the Tories (and vice versa). The great 1946/47 Austrian nationalization acts, on the other hand, were passed unanimously by a parliament with absolute conservative majority (fearing that the occupying powers could confiscate those enterprises that were "German property" from the time of the German occupation of Austria 1938–45).[1]

1.3. Who fixes public prices?

The responsibility for public pricing is shared between government agencies and enterprises' boards.

The appropriate *government agencies* can be appointed by federal, state or local governments, or by other appropriate public authorities.[1a] Whether national banks are part of government or public enterprises, has often been disputed. Whatever the sources of this dispute, it remains the case that they perform some typical governmental functions with respect to which they should be denoted as a part of government. (Their control over interest rates demanded or offered by other monetary institutions has the same character as other controls over prices by government agencies.)

The relevant *boards* represent the management of public or regulated private enterprises. To follow the United Nations' (1968) definition, public enterprises are entirely, or mainly, owned and/or controlled by public authorities. They can be either government's departmental agencies, public corporations or state companies. We denote any price of a public enterprise as a public price. But "public prices" also refer to prices charged by publicly regulated private enterprises. We are interested in all enterprises whose pricing behavior is directly or indirectly

[1] Moreover, public pricing is a general phenomenon in *times of war* and in *collapsing economies*, fixed prices being a means of coping with unwanted results of extreme shortage of resources. As a member of a lucky generation, I will restrict myself to public pricing of the conventional peace time kind.

[1a] For example, social insurance institutions: if such an institution owns a hospital or an outpatients department, the relevant "government agency" of our public pricing models is appointed by this institution.

constrained by some public authority. Within these basic categories there is much additional institutional differentiation as reflected in the many terminological distinctions of the literature on institutions.[2]

This paper, however, aims at presenting the common economic features of public pricing regardless of the details of individual institutional arrangements. For this purpose, we characterize the institutional background as including one "board" and one "government", ignoring any other institutional differences. The board can alternatively be thought of as the management of a single public or regulated enterprise, as the management of some public or regulated branch, or as the composite management of the public sector (excluding or including regulated private enterprises). Typically, our economic models allow for all these institutional interpretations. For convenience, however, we will always speak of the *public* sector, *public* production or *public* supply only. – The government must be interpreted accordingly, as the sponsor department of a single public enterprise, or as the regulatory agency of a single regulated private enterprise, or as some representative government agency of a branch or of the total public sector.

But even in this stylized world there is no unique answer to our question "who fixes public prices?" Consider a principal–agent relationship between the government as principal and the board as agent. Government and board should agree upon guidelines which stimulate the board to maximize government objectives whenever the board wants to maximize its own interests.

The main problem of drafting such regulatory rules may be illustrated with the example of social welfare maximization. In the case of a *public* enterprise one could think of concentrating the rules for maximizing social welfare in the enterprise itself. The board then has to achieve optimal prices, input and output quantities in the light of benefit–cost analytical considerations. But will the board have the necessary incentive to act along this line? This will be the case for a competitive, profit maximizing nationalized enterprise working under decreasing returns to scale where marginal cost pricing is identical to welfare maximization. But this is only a very special type of public enterprise! The board of a *regulated private* enterprise will have even less incentive to maximize social welfare.

Therefore, the aim of maximizing social welfare is often entrusted to the government, which in turn will try to implement "incentive-compatible" regulatory rules to induce the board to act according to the usual managerial targets of a firm under certain constraints formulated by government. Typically the firm is assumed to maximize profits and the government to fix pricing rules. Special incentive schemes can be introduced if necessary, e.g., linking manager incomes negatively with the deviation from welfare-optimal prices [Gravelle (1982)].

[2]For a good survey of the literature on the institutional aspects of U.S. regulated industries, see Kahn (1970, 1971); of European public enterprises, see C.E.E.P. (1984) and Keyser and Windle (1978); of Japan, see Yoshitake (1970).

Whereas the above approach indicates the institutional distribution of responsibility for public pricing is a complex phenomenon of decision sharing between government and board, it will be convenient in our theoretic models to *concentrate the decision on public pricing at the board* which is assumed to be adequately constrained by government.

1.4. What price schedule should be chosen?

Pricing can follow very different institutional patterns. The uniform price per unit of quantity is only one, very usual, extreme case. Natural monopolies whose products cannot be resold, will typically tend to some sort of price discrimination. Uncertainty and administration costs prevent such firms from fixing different prices for individual customers. But some standardized forms of price discrimination can be found everywhere in public utility pricing, the best-known being two-part tariffs and block tariffs.

In the case of *two-part tariffs* the customer pays a basic fee for the right to buy any desired amount of the goods at given unit prices. Such tariffs have often been proposed as a means of break-even pricing for decreasing cost industries: The running charge should equal marginal costs, and the deficit be financed by the fixed charge, ideally a perfectly discriminating lump-sum tax. Such a pricing procedure is welfare-optimal unless we explicitly regard the number of customers as endogenous [Oi (1971), Ng and Weisser (1974), Spremann (1978)].

Block tariffs define a sequence of prices for successive intervals of quantity demanded. Increasing the number of blocks increases the number of fiscal instruments and will therefore never decrease the maximal welfare attainable [Leland and Meyer (1976)].

A theoretically and practically interesting price structure gives the individual customer the right to choose between two different two-part tariffs (usually low basic fee and higher unit prices, or vice versa). The theory of this price structure has been investigated by Faulhaber and Panzar (1977). Practical applications can be exemplified by the U.S. telephone pricing system for local services or by the West German electricity and gas pricing – household tariffs I and II.

All these problems of institutional practice lead to the theoretical question of how to relate in an optimal manner the quantities bought to the customer's expenditure. Consider any customer's expenditures on the consumption of publicly priced goods. These expenditures depend on the quantities bought and on public prices, following a functional relationship that must be uniquely defined over all quantities and prices, respectively, but that is not necessarily fixed a priori. We call this a *price schedule*. Now consider an enterprise's board which wants to choose the functional form of this price schedule in a welfare maximizing way. This welfare-optimal price schedule will not necessarily be linear in quantities. Hence, we speak of "*non-linear pricing*" [Spence (1977), Roberts (1979)]. Formally this problem is the same as finding a welfare maximizing direct-tax function.

Despite this theoretical challenge I have restricted this exposition to *linear* (*uniform*) *pricing* because the basic ideas of public pricing can be best elaborated for the simplest possible functional form of a price schedule.

2. Public pricing policies for welfare maximization

2.1. Theoretical foundation

2.1.1. Optimum policy

(*a*) *Introduction*

When M. Boiteux published in 1956 his seminal paper on the management of public monopolies subject to budgetary constraints he was not only a qualified economic theorist, but at the same time manager at the nationalized French electricity industry. Therefore he did not visualize his approach as a purely theoretical exercise in welfare economics. Rather he speculated on the actual applicability of his results and offered some rules of thumb for an approximative numerical solution. But his original model could not be implemented in an empirically sensible way because of the assumption of perfect competition or equivalent behavior in the non-nationalized sector [Boiteux (1971, pp. 233–234)]. Meanwhile, however, his model has been extended and the version to be presented below allows for a monopolistic private economy as well. (As we shall see in one of the sections below, the model can even be extended to integrate quantity rationing of labor supply!) Moreover, Boiteux's restriction to compensated demand can be given up to include income effects and to deal with public pricing with distributional objectives. For all these reasons I have chosen an extended version of the Boiteux model as the best approach to tackle public sector pricing, from the theoretical point of view as well as from the empirical one.

Before presenting many technical details I would like to sketch the institutional (and ideological) background of the Boiteux model. Its central figure is an *enterprise's board*, acting in a democracy of the U.S. or Western European type. Hence the approach is basically individualistic. The aim of welfare optimization, as imputed to the board, starts from individual consumers' utilities, although the board may attach different weights to individual utilities.

This board has to take account of the market economy on the one hand and the government on the other hand.

To take account of the *market economy* implies taking account of demand, be it demand from consumers or private or public producers. The board must be aware of the existence of many private firms, mostly operating under some sort of monopolistic competition. Moreover, the board must have regard for market clearing conditions.

There exists, in addition, some superior authority outside of the model, call it *government*. This authority has decided that some parts of the economy's production are to be publicly run – by public utilities, nationalized enterprises, etc. And it has fixed those enterprises' minimal profits or maximal deficits. Public production possibilities and financial limitations are therefore constraints which the board has to take into account.

Considering all these constraints from the market and from the government leads to a realistic second-best model. The basic features of this model follow.

(b) The actors of the model

(i) The consumers. We consider an economy with $n+1$ private goods. They are sold at prices p_i, $i \in I$, $I = \{0,1,\ldots,n\}$. Labor is used as numeraire. Its price p_0 equals 1.

There are H *consumers*, $h = 1,\ldots,H$. Their consumption plans are $x^h = (x_0^h,\ldots,x_n^h)$, where positive quantities denote net demand, negative quantities net supply.[3] The individual consumption plans result from maximizing the strictly increasing and quasi-concave utility functions $u^h(x^h)$ subject to the individual's budget constraint, given lump-sum incomes $r^h \gtreqless 0$:

$$v^h(p,r^h) := \max_{x^h} u^h(x^h) \quad \text{s.t.} \quad \sum_{i=0}^{n} p_i x_i^h = r^h, \qquad h = 1,\ldots,H, \tag{2.1}$$

where v^h are the indirect utility functions.

(ii) The producers. The production side is characterized by one aggregate public sector and J private enterprises, $j = 1,\ldots,J$. Their production plans are $z = (z_0,\ldots,z_n)$ and $y^j = (y_0^j,\ldots,y_n^j)$, respectively. Positive quantities denote net output, negative quantities net input. This "netput" concept is an improvement upon the usual consumer surplus approach that deals with final goods only.

[3] We use the following definitions: A good is a private good if $\Sigma_h x_i^h = x_i$, where x_i is total demand; it is a public good if $x_i^h = x_i$, $\forall h$. Both types of goods can be provided publicly or privately. An extension of the Boiteux model to public goods is given by Drèze and Marchand (1976) and Hagen (1979).

Products of the public sector are very often intermediate goods. Transport services, gas, electricity and the products of many (other) nationalized enterprises provide good examples.

The public sector is assumed to produce efficiently[4] according to a *production function*

$$g(z) = 0. \tag{2.2}$$

The technology of the private firms is not explicitly modelled. We assume, however, that the board in the public sector has a priori information on the net supply functions $y_i^j(p)$ of the private firms. This does not imply any particular knowledge on the private firms' decision rules. In our model the private sector is exogenous and the public sector has to accept that and to accommodate to it, as is typical for a second-best approach.

The public sector, moreover, is restricted by a *revenue–cost constraint*,

$$\sum_{i=0}^{n} p_i z_i = \Pi, \qquad \Pi \gtreqless 0. \tag{2.3}$$

$\Pi = 0$ implies break-even pricing; $\Pi < 0$ determines a deficit; $\Pi > 0$ demands public sector profits. Of course, there exist lower and upper bounds for Π. The lowest Π that can be found in practice will correspond to zero tariffs of the publicly supplied goods. The highest possible Π corresponds to the profit maximizing behavior of the public sector.

Π may be an exogenously fixed value,

$$\Pi = \Pi^0. \tag{2.4a}$$

It may, also, depend on particular prices, public sector netputs and exogenously given regulated variables, denoted by the vector ρ,

$$\Pi = \Pi(p, z, \rho). \tag{2.4b}$$

For a description of empirical reality, however, we do not need such a general formulation. In considering profit limitations that result from fixing a fair return on investment, a fair mark-up on cost or a fair profit per unit of output, it is sufficient to deal with

$$\Pi = \Pi(z, \rho), \tag{2.4c}$$

[4]To produce efficiently in second-best economies is welfare optimal under comparatively weak assumptions.

assuming factor prices for labor and capital to be given and other prices not to enter the profit constraint.

The values of Π^0 or ρ are exogenously given and the public sector has to accommodate to them. (Once again: this is typical of a second-best approach.) The fixing of Π^0 or ρ may be due to ideological motives regarding the desired size of the public sector, or political fears of losing votes because of high public sector deficits or economic motives, i.e., opportunity costs of public sector deficits as compared with alternative use of resources in the private sector.

Assuming a *binding constraint* for all cases of Π implies a particular view of the objectives of public pricing that, perhaps, may be unfamiliar to the American reader. Let us distinguish two cases:

– Π exceeds or equals the unconstrained welfare-optimal revenue–cost difference. Then an inequality constraint $\sum p_i z_i \geqq \Pi$ would be binding and without loss of generality we can assume a priori an equality constraint as is done in (2.3).
– Π falls below this critical value. In this case, an inequality constraint is not binding. But it may well be possible that, for distributional or other reasons, the politician wants some institutions to follow a policy that leads to such a low Π. Museums or universities or schools provide examples where it makes sense not to follow a zero-tariff policy, but to fix a Π that is below the unconstrained welfare optimal value. If, because of their budgetary constraints the German states (Länder) had to introduce school fees or university fees, they would certainly choose fees below the unconstrained welfare-optimal ones! And these cases can be treated nicely by assuming an equality constraint as in (2.3).

(iii) The market. Any firm's output is either used for consumption or as an input for its own or other firms' production. Consumers supply labor to the private and to the public sector; they buy commodities from private firms and from the public sector. Assume the existence of an equilibrium. Then we have the following *market clearing conditions*:

$$\sum_h x_i^h(p, r^h) - z_i - \sum_j y_i^j(p) = 0, \qquad i = 0, \ldots, n. \tag{2.5}$$

The net profits of private firms and of the public sector are equal to the sum of lump-sum payments as can be seen easily by multiplying (2.5) by p_i for every i and adding up to obtain

$$\sum_i \sum_h p_i x_i^h - \sum_i p_i z_i - \sum_i \sum_j p_i y_i^j = 0, \tag{2.6}$$

which leads to

$$\sum_h r^h - \Pi - \sum_j \pi_j = 0, \tag{2.7}$$

where π_j is the profit of firm j. Thus our model implies a total redistribution of private profits to consumers and the public sector. If, however, private and public "profits" lead to an aggregate deficit, consumers are forced to finance it by lump-sum taxes.

(iv) The board. Now consider a board which maximizes its *social welfare function W*,

$$\max W(v^1,\ldots,v^H), \qquad \partial W/\partial v^h \geqq 0, \qquad h=1,\ldots,H, \tag{2.8}$$

subject to the market clearing conditions, public sector's technology and revenue–cost constraint. W is non-decreasing in the individual utility levels v^h (strictly increasing in at least one utility level). This is a very general description of the board's welfare judgments. It includes both the utilitarian welfare function, as a simple sum of individual utilities, and the consideration of the utility of the worst-off individual only (Rawls) as limiting cases.

Let the board control some prices p_e and the net production plans z_i.

The *controlled prices* $\{p_e, e \in E \subset I\}$ are a subset of all prices. We assume prices of goods that are only supplied or demanded by the public sector are controlled in any case. But there may exist also regulated prices of privately supplied or demanded goods and non-regulated prices of publicly supplied or demanded goods. We exclude regulation of wages, p_0.[5] – The *uncontrolled prices* $p_i, i \notin E$, are exogenously given which is a sensible assumption for a model aimed at showing the accommodation of public pricing to given pricing structures of the private economy.

The *controlled net production plans* $\{z_i\}$ are, of course, a subset of all net production plans of the economy $\{z_i, y_i^j\}$. Thus control of prices *and* control of production refer to parts of the economy only. These parts do not necessarily coincide.

(c) Solving the model

(i) The optimization approach.[6] The welfare maximizing controlled prices and net production plans can be obtained from maximizing the following Lagrangian

[5] Except in Section 3.3.3 where the influence of trade unions is explicitly considered.

[6] As usual in public economics literature we leave open the questions whether: the second-order conditions for a maximum are fulfilled; there is a unique optimum; the achieved optimum is a local one only; the optimum derived can actually be achieved by decentralized decisions of economic agents. Explicit answers to any of the above questions can only be given if very restrictive assumptions are fulfilled. As the restrictive assumptions cannot be justified by usual microeconomic theory, it is not sensible to treat the above questions in general theoretical analyses. In any empirical case, however, the restrictive assumptions are either fulfilled or not, whence the investigation of the above questions in empirical case studies is always appropriate.

function:[7]

$$\max_{p_e, z_i} \mathscr{L} = W(\cdot) - \sum_{i=0}^{n} \alpha_i \left[\sum_h x_i^h(p, r^h) - z_i - \sum_j y_i^j(p) \right] - \beta g(z)$$

$$- \bar{\gamma}\left(\Pi(\cdot) - \sum_{i=0}^{n} p_i z_i \right). \qquad (2.9)$$

The necessary maximum conditions are as follows:

$$\sum_h \frac{\partial W}{\partial v^h} \frac{\partial v^h}{\partial p_e} - \sum_i \alpha_i \left(\sum_h \frac{\partial x_i^h}{\partial p_e} - \sum_j \frac{\partial y_i^j}{\partial p_e} \right) + \bar{\gamma} z_e = 0, \qquad e \in E, \qquad (2.10)$$

$$\alpha_i - \beta \frac{\partial g}{\partial z_i} - \bar{\gamma}\left(\frac{\partial \Pi}{\partial z_i} - p_i \right) = 0, \qquad i = 0, \ldots, n. \qquad (2.11)$$

Inserting (2.11) into (2.10) we obtain

$$\sum_h \frac{\partial W}{\partial v^h} \frac{\partial v^h}{\partial p_e} - \sum_i \left[\beta \frac{\partial g}{\partial z_i} + \bar{\gamma}\left(\frac{\partial \Pi}{\partial z_i} - p_i \right) \right] \left[\sum_h \frac{\partial x_i^h}{\partial p_e} - \sum_j \frac{\partial y_i^j}{\partial p_e} \right] + \bar{\gamma} z_e = 0. \qquad (2.12)$$

We divide these equations by $\beta_0 := \beta(\partial g/\partial z_0) > 0$,[8] and define $\lambda^h := (\partial W/\partial v^h)/\beta_0$, $\gamma := \bar{\gamma}/\beta_0$, $c_i := (\partial g/\partial z_i)/(\partial g/\partial z_0)$.

$\lambda^h \geqq 0$ is the "normalized" social marginal welfare of individual utility. An equality-conscious government will choose those λ^h that increase with decreasing individual utility.

γ is a "normalized" measure of the welfare effects of the size of the public sector. The higher γ, the higher these welfare effects. If the revenue–cost constraint Π exceeds the unconstrained welfare-optimal profit, then $0 < \gamma < 1$.[9]

c_i is a shadow price which measures the marginal *labor* costs of publicly producing good i (for $z_i > 0$; otherwise it is a partial marginal rate of transformation). However, as most recent papers on the topic denote c_i as marginal costs, we will adhere to this convention in the following.[10]

[7] The politician must control at least three prices to avoid degeneration of the optimization approach because of insufficient degrees of freedom. Corner solutions are always excluded.

[8] Differentiate the Lagrangian function $\mathscr{L}$ with respect to initial endowments of labor z_0 and y_0, respectively. $\alpha_0 > 0$ and $\beta_0 > 0$ follow with economic plausibility. See Drèze and Marchand (1976, p. 67).

[9] This is explicitly proved for a fixed revenue–cost constraint in Section 2.2.2 and for rate of return regulation in Section 2.2.3 below.

[10] The reader should be aware of the difference between the shadow prices c_i, as used here, and the marginal costs C_i, as derived from a cost function and very often used in the public pricing literature. An explicit treatment of this difference is given in Boiteux (1971, pp. 234–239). c_i and C_i will of course coincide if labor is the only input.

Using these new symbols the marginal conditions (2.12) can be rewritten as follows:

$$\sum_h \lambda^h \frac{\partial v^h}{\partial p_e} - \sum_i \left[c_i - \gamma p_i + \gamma \frac{\partial \Pi}{\partial z_i}\right]\left[\sum_h \frac{\partial x_i^h}{\partial p_e} - \sum_j \frac{\partial y_i^j}{\partial p_e}\right] + \gamma z_e = 0. \tag{2.13}$$

For a better economic interpretation we want to proceed to price–cost differences $(p_i - c_i)$ instead of using $(\gamma p_i - c_i)$. Hence we add $(1-\gamma)\sum_i p_i[\sum_h(\partial x_i^h/\partial p_e) - \sum_j(\partial y_i^j/\partial p_e)]$ on both sides of the marginal conditions (2.13) to obtain

$$\sum_h \lambda^h \frac{\partial v^h}{\partial p_e} - (1-\gamma)\sum_i \sum_h p_i \frac{\partial x_i^h}{\partial p_e} - \sum_i \left[c_i - p_i + \gamma \frac{\partial \Pi}{\partial z_i}\right]\left[\sum_h \frac{\partial x_i^h}{\partial p_e} - \sum_j \frac{\partial y_i^j}{\partial p_e}\right]$$

$$= -\gamma z_e - (1-\gamma)\sum_i \sum_j p_i \frac{\partial y_i^j}{\partial p_e}, \qquad e \in E. \tag{2.14}$$

This equation consists of five terms which we shall consider, reading from left to right.

(ii) Distributional objectives. The first two terms reflect *distributional considerations*.

The first term describes the social valuation of price changes $\sum_h \lambda^h(\partial v^h/\partial p_e)$. This term refers to the *price structure*, its absolute value being high for necessities and low for non-necessities. This can be seen most easily after applying Roy's identity

$$\sum_h \lambda^h \frac{\partial v^h}{\partial p_e} = -\sum_h \lambda^h x_e^h \frac{\partial v^h}{\partial r^h}, \qquad e \in E. \tag{2.15}$$

In the following it will be convenient to define a "distributional characteristic" of any good $e \in E$ as a distributionally weighted sum of individual consumption shares:

$$F_e := \sum_h b^h \frac{x_e^h}{x_e} \quad \text{where} \quad b^h := \lambda^h \frac{\partial v^h}{\partial r^h}. \tag{2.16}$$

According to the usual economic assumptions b^h will be a decreasing function of individual income, thereby bringing about the above mentioned distributional weighting. A similar notation can be found in Feldstein (1972a, b, c) and Atkinson and Stiglitz (1980, pp. 387, 469).

The second term refers to the *price level*. It does not include any particular distributional differentiation between necessities and non-necessities. Its absolute value is the larger, the smaller γ. Smaller γ, in turn, will typically result from lower Π. But the lower Π, the lower the level of prices:[11] to take a simple example, the level of prices of a welfare maximizing deficit enterprise will be lower than that of a perfect monopolist.

Formally, we apply the Slutsky equation to this second term

$$(1-\gamma)\sum_i \sum_h p_i \frac{\partial x_i^h}{\partial p_e} = (1-\gamma)\left[\sum_i \sum_h p_i \frac{\partial \hat{x}_i^h}{\partial p_e} - \sum_i \sum_h p_i x_e^h \frac{\partial x_i^h}{\partial r^h}\right]$$

$$= -(1-\gamma)\sum_h x_e^h,^{12} \tag{2.17}$$

where $\hat{x}_i^h$ denotes compensated demand. The reader should recall that for any individual h the compensated expenditures for all goods do not react to price changes ($\sum_i p_i(\partial \hat{x}_i^h/\partial p_e) = 0$). Moreover, differentiating the individual budget constraint always yields $\sum_i p_i(\partial x_i^h/\partial r^h) = 1$.

Hence the first two terms can be rewritten as follows:

$$-F_e x_e + (1-\gamma)x_e, \tag{2.18}$$

the first term referring to the price structure, the second one to the price level.

(iii) Allocation in the public sector. The third and the fourth term of (2.14) reflect the problems of the *allocation in the public sector*. They are centered on the question whether and how far prices should deviate from marginal costs, as expressed by $(p_i - c_i)$. The theoretical interest of the last decades has shifted from marginal cost prices to second-best prices which deviate from marginal costs. The Boiteux model itself is an important step in that direction, with its stress on the revenue–cost constraints of the public sector. In our extended version of Boiteux's model these constraints are represented by γz_e and by $\gamma(\partial \Pi/\partial z_i)$, the latter term reflecting possible distortions caused by choosing revenue–cost constraints which are asymmetric with respect to different kinds of inputs (or outputs). As these distortions mostly refer to inputs, it is often convenient to define "modified" marginal costs as

$$\tilde{C}_i = c_i + \gamma \frac{\partial \Pi}{\partial z_i}. \tag{2.19}$$

[11] "Level of prices" may be interpreted as referring to some adequately defined price index. It does not necessarily imply $\partial p_e/\partial \Pi > 0$ for all $e \in E$.

[12] Low prices will typically imply high demand x_e which reinforces the tendencies mentioned in the text.

But the allocation in the public sector does not only depend on the supply side, but on the price sensitivity of demand for publicly supplied goods as well. This can be clarified by defining $z_i^D(p)$[13] as "demand for public supply" which implies

$$\frac{\partial z_i^D}{\partial p_e} := \sum_h \frac{\partial x_i^h}{\partial p_e} - \sum_j \frac{\partial y_i^j}{\partial p_e}. \tag{2.20}$$

Note that z_i^D is a normal, "Marshallian" demand function and not a "Hicksian" compensated one.

(iv) The public and the private sector. The fifth term in (2.14) reflects the *accommodation of public sector pricing to monopolistic structures in the private economy.* We assume that prices p_i, $i \notin E$, are exogenously fixed by the private sector. Likewise exogenously fixed are $c_i^j := -\mathrm{d}y_0^j/\mathrm{d}y_i^j$, the marginal costs of producing good i in firm j in the optimum (for $y_i^j > 0$; otherwise c_i^j is a partial marginal rate of transformation). c_i^j can be interpreted as "producer prices". Hence we know that in case of efficient production,

$$\sum_i \sum_j c_i^j \frac{\partial y_i^j}{\partial p_e} = 0. \tag{2.21}$$

Hence the following extension is valid [Hagen (1979)]:

$$(1-\gamma)\sum_i \sum_j p_i \frac{\partial y_i^j}{\partial p_e} = (1-\gamma)\sum_i \sum_j (p_i - c_i^j)\frac{\partial y_i^j}{\partial p_e}, \qquad e \in E, \tag{2.22}$$

which clearly shows that monopolistic structures of the private economy influence public sector pricing.

Reconsidering all the above new definitions and transformations, we can rewrite our basic marginal conditions as follows:

$$F_e x_e - (1-\gamma)x_e + \sum_i (\tilde{C}_i - p_i)\frac{\partial z_i^D}{\partial p_e}$$

$$= \gamma z_e - (1-\gamma)\sum_i \sum_j (c_i^j - p_i)\frac{\partial y_i^j}{\partial p_e}, \qquad e \in E. \tag{2.23}$$

[13] The net supply z_i in the market clearing condition (2.5) does not directly depend on any other variable of the model because z_i is an instrument variable. After determining the optimal z_i from the optimization approach (2.9), we can define consumer net demand z_i^D as depending on prices.

It seems natural to think of public sector pricing within the general framework given by (2.23). This means that we
- look at the interaction between public and private supply;
- include distributional welfare judgments;
- start from the usual, non-compensated demand for public supply and consider the possibility of regulatory distortions.

Hence, it is surprising that the conventional literature did not follow this framework which naturally suggests itself. It was not until 1956–57 that Lipsey and Lancaster stressed the interaction between the public and private sectors. And it was not until 1972 that Martin Feldstein stressed the distributional component of the problem. Moreover, the allocative "center" of our framework had been truncated also by the exclusive concentration on compensated demand functions. The basic philosophy behind this latter restriction is a "concentration on allocation" as public sector pricing does not seem to be the best possible instrument for redistribution. However, in dealing with compensated demand only, incomes are redistributed optimally by some sort of compensating lump-sum payments the empirical feasibility of which is at least questionable. Moreover, the consumer surplus approaches, which are often employed, do not make this basic redistributional procedure explicit, thereby hiding the implied value judgements.

Not only the importance but also the conceptual weakness of this traditional procedure can be revealed by considering explicitly the redistributions required to obtain compensated demand functions in the Boiteux model.

(d) Compensating for income effects

Let us suppose that the board can *control the distribution of lump-sum incomes* $\{r^h\}$. Hence it maximizes our Lagrangian function (2.9) not only with respect to prices and quantities, but also with respect to r^h.[14]

The resulting marginal conditions

$$\frac{\partial W}{\partial v^h}\frac{\partial v^h}{\partial r^h} - \sum_i \alpha_i \frac{\partial x_i^h}{\partial r^h} = 0, \qquad h = 1, \ldots, H, \tag{2.24a}$$

can be transformed by inserting Roy's identity. We obtain

$$\frac{\partial W}{\partial v^h}\frac{\partial v^h}{\partial p_e} = -\sum_i \alpha_i x_e^h \frac{\partial x_i^h}{\partial r^h}, \qquad h = 1, \ldots, H, \quad e \in E. \tag{2.24b}$$

[14] The number of controlled prices plus the number of consumers must exceed 2 as to avoid degeneration of the optimization approach because of insufficient degrees of freedom.

The incomes are redistributed in such a way that for each consumer the weighted sum of all income effects that result from changing price p_e is just equalized with the board's evaluation of this individual's utility change because of the change in the price p_e. Hence, in this optimum the distributional evaluations and all income effects cancel. This implies the elimination of all distributional consideration in the pricing structure, the optimal income distribution being guaranteed by the optimal choice of lump-sum incomes r^h, leaving only allocational tasks for the public pricing structure. At the same time all income effects are eliminated from the pricing structure, leading to a concentration on substitution effects, i.e., on compensated demand only.

Formally we insert (2.24b) into (2.10) and denote

$$\frac{\partial \hat{z}_i}{\partial p_e} = \left[\sum_h \left(\frac{\partial x_i^h}{\partial p_e} + x_e^h \frac{\partial x_i^h}{\partial r^h}\right) - \sum_j \frac{\partial y_i^j}{\partial p_e}\right], \qquad i=0,\dots,n, \quad e \in E, \tag{2.25}$$

where $\hat{z}_i(p)$ is the "compensated aggregate demand" for public supply of good i.[15]

The resulting equations

$$-\sum_i \alpha_i \frac{\partial \hat{z}_i}{\partial p_e} + \bar{\gamma} z_e = 0, \qquad e \in E, \tag{2.26}$$

can then be transformed analogously to the above "non-compensated" case[16] to obtain

$$\sum_i (\tilde{C}_i - p_i) \frac{\partial \hat{z}_i}{\partial p_e} = \gamma z_e - (1-\gamma) \sum_i \sum_j (c_i^j - p_i) \frac{\partial y_i^j}{\partial p_e}, \qquad e \in E. \tag{2.27}$$

2.1.2. Piecemeal policy

Political and institutional obstacles may prevent a total rearrangement of public prices and the realization of an optimum. The optimum being unknown, and

[15] The reader should be aware that the integrability conditions are not necessarily fulfilled for the demand $\hat{z}_i$. $\partial \hat{z}_i / \partial p_e$ equals $\partial \hat{z}_e / \partial p_i$ only if $(\sum_j (\partial y_i^j / \partial p_e)) = (\sum_j (\partial y_e^j / \partial p_i))$ which is the case for perfect competition in the private economy only (Hotelling's lemma). However, our model explicitly takes into account the possibility of private monopolistic pricing.

[16] During this transformation it is necessary to add $(1-\gamma)\sum_i p_i (\partial \hat{z}_i / \partial p_e)$ on both sides of the marginal conditions. For the further transformation of the right-hand side the reader may note that $\sum_i p_i (\partial \hat{z}_i / \partial p_e) = -\sum_i \sum_j p_i (\partial y_i^j / \partial p_e)$, because $\sum_i \sum_h p_i (\partial \hat{x}_i^h / \partial p_e) = 0$ in case of compensated demand.

possibly far away, the board starts from given prices and lump-sum incomes, the level and structure of which will usually not be optimal, and searches for small price changes which increase welfare. If lump-sum incomes are available as instruments, their changes can also be integrated in such a piecemeal policy. The welfare increasing piecemeal policy in a Boiteux world has to be market clearing, technologically and financially feasible. Any small step has to consider the usual constraints, as treated above.

A theory of piecemeal policy yields *sufficient* conditions for welfare improvement, contrary to an optimum theory which yields *necessary* conditions which are fulfilled in the optimum. Let us give a simple example. The optimum Ramsey pricing policy tells us that it is a necessary condition for an optimum that price–cost margins are fixed according to an inverse elasticity rule. A piecemeal Ramsey policy tells us that, given some public prices, near the optimum, but still non-optimal, an increase of the price–cost margin of a price-inelastic good is a sufficient condition for welfare improvement.[17]

The above exposition should not mislead the reader into expecting too much from piecemeal policy. If the present situation is far from the welfare optimum, there are so many different ways to increase welfare that clear-cut rules, comparable to our optimum rules, usually will *not* result. Therefore the general results of a *theory* of piecemeal policy are disappointing. This does not mean that a theory of piecemeal policy is unimportant. After specifying all relevant functions, it may well serve as the basis of the board's decisions on how to proceed gradually.

As the general results are disappointing, it is not necessary to deal with all different possible cases of changing prices and lump-sum incomes in full detail. We might, however, present one well-known special case of piecemeal policy. Consider a board which intends to increase welfare ($\mathrm{d}W > 0$) by price changes $\mathrm{d}p_i$ in the presence of the constraints of the Boiteux model. We assume quantities and lump-sum incomes to be optimally accommodated to any price changes. If in such a case the budget constraint of the public sector is not binding, it is only the accommodation to price distortions in the private economy that requires public prices to deviate from marginal costs. Now assume the price, marginal cost differences for any good are equal in the public sector and in any private firm. In this case welfare will be increased by changing prices according to the sufficient condition

$$\sum_{k=1}^{n} \sum_{i=1}^{n} (\tilde{C}_i - p_i) \frac{\partial \hat{x}_i}{\partial p_k} \mathrm{d}p_k < 0. \tag{2.28}$$

[17] But this property need not always hold for all welfare increasing price changes along a path from non-optimal prices to optimal prices.

If all prices change in proportion to the existing distortions ($\mathrm{d}p_k = (\tilde{C}_k - p_k)\mathrm{d}s$), the above mentioned inequality reads as follows:

$$\sum_{k=1}^{n} \sum_{i=1}^{n} (\tilde{C}_i - p_i) \frac{\partial \hat{x}_i}{\partial p_k} (\tilde{C}_k - p_k)\,\mathrm{d}s < 0, \tag{2.29}$$

which is fulfilled only if $\mathrm{d}s > 0$:[18] An equal relative reduction of all price, marginal cost differences increases welfare. If all prices move towards marginal costs in proportion to the existing distortions, welfare increases. Even more puzzling than this result is its corollary that piecemeal movements of single prices towards marginal costs need not necessarily increase welfare! It is possible to find examples where *in*creasing price–cost margins of some goods increase welfare. [For further details on this approach, see Dixit (1975), Hatta (1977), Hagen (1979), Wiegard (1980).]

2.2. *Basic rules*

2.2.1. *Marginal cost pricing*

(a) Theoretical basis and practical examples

We begin with the most conventional case. Let us assume that:

(i) only prices of publicly produced goods are controlled, these goods being neither supplied nor demanded by private firms;
(ii) all uncontrolled prices equal marginal costs in any firm, including the public sector;
(iii) distribution of lump-sum incomes is optimally chosen, hence we deal with compensated demand;
(iv) there is no revenue–cost constraint on the public sector.

Then the marginal conditions (2.27) reduce to

$$\sum_{i \in E} (c_i - p_i) \frac{\partial \hat{z}_i}{\partial p_e} = 0, \qquad e \in E. \tag{2.30}$$

This can be interpreted as a homogeneous system of equations in the unknown variables $(c_i - p_i)$. If we assume the matrix $\partial \hat{z}_i / \partial p_e$ to be regular,[19] we obtain the

[18] We assume that at least one price does not equal marginal costs.
[19] We postulate that $\partial \hat{x}_i / \partial p_k$, $i, k = 1, \ldots, n$, being a submatrix of the Slutsky substitution matrix, is negative definite and has full rank.

well-known marginal cost pricing rule

$$p_i = c_i(z), \qquad i \in E. \tag{2.31}$$

This rule is normatively valid for any kind of public enterprise: for competitive public enterprises (nationalized steel industry, communal breweries, ...) as well as for monopolistic ones (telephone, broadcasting, television, ...).

With this in mind it is not surprising to find a wide range of proposals for the practical application of marginal cost pricing:

- nationalized enterprises in general [White paper (1967) for the U.K.;[20] the project failed – see N.E.D.O. (1976); the new White Paper (1978) avoided any explicit pricing rule];
- electricity [papers by Boiteux and his team are collected in Nelson (1964); for Electricité de France, see furthermore Quoilin (1976); for the U.K., Turvey (1968, 1971)];
- railways [frequently suggested since Hotelling's (1938) seminal paper];
- television [Samuelson (1964) opposing Minasian (1964) under the assumption of zero marginal costs for TV];
- telephone, theater, airports, etc.

(b) Deficits under marginal cost pricing

Marginal cost pricing is a challenge for economists, regarding both theory and practice, because it provides a theoretical justification for public supply with permanent deficits. This consequence of marginal cost pricing results if there exist strict local scale economies (as defined below). This is of considerable importance since according to empirical studies, a lot of public enterprises' production takes place under scale economies.

Let us consider more closely the conditions required for such a welfare-optimal deficit. It can be shown that strict *local* increasing returns to scale are a sufficient *and* necessary condition for a marginal cost pricing deficit. The proof is comparatively simple although we deal with a multiproduct enterprise. The reason for this simplicity lies in the particular definition of marginal costs in our extended Boiteux model which allows a straightforward definition of local increasing returns to scale which directly depends on the marginal costs.[21]

[20] According to this White Paper nationalized enterprises should normally follow long-run marginal cost pricing. There were, however, some further recommendations, including break-even strategies by two-part tariffs or prices proportional to marginal costs.

[21] For the multiproduct case the general proof is more complicated as shown by Baumol (1976, 1977) and Panzar and Willig (1977a).

For this purpose we solve the production function $g(z)=0$ as to obtain $z_0 = z_0(z_1,\dots,z_n) = z_0(z.)$ which implies $\partial z_0/\partial z_i = -(\partial g/\partial z_i)/(\partial g/\partial z_0) = -c_i$. We define local economies of scale by means of an adequately chosen elasticity of production,[22]

$$\varepsilon(z) = \lim_{s\to 1} \frac{s}{z_0(sz.)} \sum_{i=1}^{n} \frac{\partial z_0(sz.)}{\partial s}$$

$$= \frac{1}{z_0} \sum_{i=1}^{n} \frac{\partial z_0(z.)}{\partial z_i} z_i$$

$$= -\frac{1}{z_0} \sum_{i=1}^{n} c_i z_i. \tag{2.32}$$

This is an elasticity of the labor input with respect to the scale parameter s. The production function exhibits strict local increasing returns to scale if labor input increases by a smaller proportion than all netputs $z_1,\dots,z_n$, whence $\varepsilon(z) < 1$.

Strict local increasing returns to scale are therefore given if

$$z_0 + \sum_{i=1}^{n} c_i z_i < 0.$$

Now consider a marginal cost pricing deficit

$$\sum_{i=0}^{n} p_i z_i = \sum_{i=0}^{n} c_i z_i = z_0 + \sum_{i=1}^{n} c_i z_i < 0,$$

to see that $\varepsilon(z) < 1$ is equivalent to the case of a marginal cost pricing deficit.

Strict *global* increasing returns, on the other hand, are only a sufficient, but not a necessary condition for deficits under marginal cost pricing in multiproduct enterprises. Deficits can arise also if returns to scale are decreasing in some parts and increasing in others.

(c) Marginal cost pricing and general equilibria

Recently there has been a revival of interest in the theory of marginal cost pricing under economies of scale. The main points of this discussion will be mentioned shortly although in the Boiteux framework existence problems are not handled at

[22] For a similar procedure, see Intriligator (1971, pp. 181–182).

all. Mentioning those recent papers enables us, however, to stress some shortcomings of the Boiteux approach.

First, the *existence* of marginal cost pricing equilibria is challenged [Beato (1982), Cornet (1982)]: How can such an optimum be achieved by decentralized decisions of economic agents? Will marginal cost pricing firms go bankrupt because of losses? Will consumers go bankrupt who are liable as shareholders of public enterprises? In the Boiteux approach this problem is solved by assuming (optimal) lump-sum taxes which finance possible deficits. But although this is a satisfactory way to deal with an allocative optimum, it is not a satisfactory way to deal with decentralization because there are no a priori arrangements that assure positive individual incomes given any distributions of profits and endowments. To overcome this problem, we must consider special distributions [Beato (1982)]. Further research should concentrate on the existence of marginal cost pricing equilibria if public deficits are financed by taxes on goods and factors in inelastic supply (the old Hotelling proposal) or by two-part tariffs, where the sum of the fixed parts covers the deficit from the marginal cost variable prices.

Second, the *optimality* of marginal cost pricing is challenged [Guesnerie (1975), Brown and Heal (1979, 1980a, 1980b), Tillmann (1981)]. If the production possibilities are non-convex, marginal cost equilibria may fail to be Pareto-optimal. The literature tries to find conditions under which at least one equilibrium is Pareto-efficient. However, there exist examples showing that even in very simple cases such conditions cannot be found. The best exemplification can be given by using Brown and Heal's (1979) figure for a two-consumer, one-producer economy (Figure 2.1).

Let the production possibility frontier of the non-convex economy be as shown in the figure. The Scitovsky social indifference curve through A is denoted I_A. If endowments and relative prices change, the social indifference curve also changes, say from I_A to I_B. This implies a new equilibrium of B. Both A and B are equilibria (they fulfill the first-order conditions), but are not Pareto-optimal.

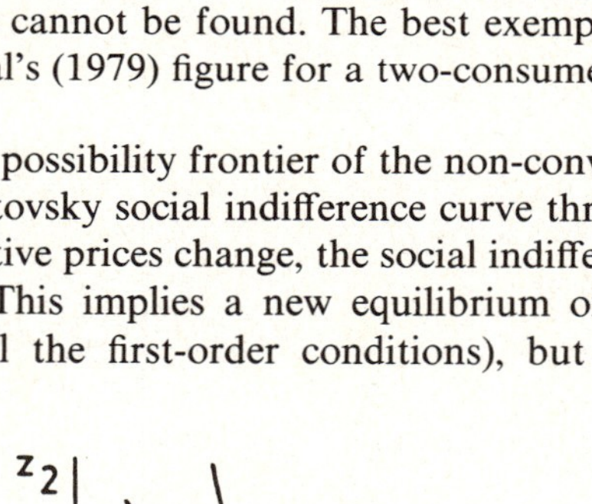

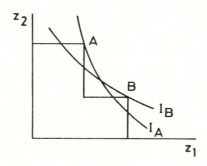

Figure 2.1

Whether such problems arise, depends on the endowments of the consumers because they affect the social indifference curves and their possible intersection.

2.2.2. *Ramsey pricing*

(a) Optimum Ramsey policy

Let us now consider the case where (i) only prices of publicly produced goods are controlled, these goods being neither supplied nor demanded by private firms; (ii) all uncontrolled prices equal marginal costs in any firm, including the public sector; and (iii) we deal with compensated demand. In contrast to the last subsection the public sector is restricted by an exogenously fixed deficit or profit Π^0.

Then the marginal conditions (2.27) reduce to

$$\sum_{i\in E} (c_i - p_i)\frac{\partial \hat{z}_i}{\partial p_e} = \gamma z_e, \qquad e \in E, \tag{2.33}$$

where $\gamma \neq 0$. For the most relevant case where Π^0 exceeds the unconstrained, welfare optimal profit, $0 < \gamma < 1$.[23]

It is quite common to find the following transformations of this Ramsey condition in the public economics literature:[24]

$$\text{(i)} \quad \sum_{i\in E} t_i S_{ie} = -\gamma \hat{z}_e, \qquad e \in E, \tag{2.33a}$$

where $t_i = p_i - c_i$ and $S_{ie} = \partial \hat{z}_i/\partial p_e$ is the Slutsky substitution effect. This transformation is well-known from the theory of optimal indirect taxation. Also

$$\text{(ii)} \quad \sum_{i\in E} \Theta_i \eta_{ei} = -\gamma, \qquad e \in E, \tag{2.33b}$$

where $\Theta_i = (p_i - c_i)/p_i$ is the price–cost margin and $\eta_{ei} = (\partial \hat{z}_e/\partial p_i)(p_i/\hat{z}_e)$ is the

[23] Remember from the general presentation of the Boiteux model that $\alpha_0 > 0$ and $\beta_0 > 0$. Now assume a fixed profit constraint Π^0 which exceeds unconstrained, welfare optimizing profit. Differentiate $\mathscr{L}$ [in (2.9)] with respect to Π^0. $\partial\mathscr{L}/\partial\Pi^0 = -\bar{\gamma} < 0$ follows from economic plausibility (and from the appropriate Kuhn–Tucker formulation of the problem). Therefore $\gamma > 0$. Moreover, (2.11) yields $\alpha_0/\beta_0 = 1 - \gamma$, because $\partial\Pi/\partial z_0 = 0$ in our case. Hence $1 - \gamma > 0$ and $\gamma < 1$. If, on the other hand, Π^0 falls below the unconstrained, welfare optimizing profit, $\gamma < 0$.

[24] For these transformations it is important to remember that:
(i) $z_e(p, r^h(p, u^{h*})) = \hat{z}_e(p, r^h)$, hence in the optimum the right-hand side of equations (2.33) equals $\hat{z}_e$.
(ii) $\hat{z}_i = \hat{x}_i$ because of assumption (i), and therefore $\partial \hat{z}_e/\partial p_i = \partial \hat{z}_i/\partial p_e$.

compensated price elasticity of demand. This transformation is mostly used for public two-product enterprises where γ can be simply eliminated to obtain the condition

$$\frac{\Theta_1}{\Theta_2} = \frac{\eta_{22} - \eta_{12}}{\eta_{11} - \eta_{21}}. \tag{2.33c}$$

Ramsey pricing is characterized by a particular trade-off between the level of prices and the structure of prices.

The *level of prices* is primarily influenced by the value of Π^0 chosen. Ramsey pricing therefore can stand for low pricing as well as for high pricing policies, for deficit enterprises, cost covering ones, or for profit making enterprises. All or some prices can fall below marginal costs to bring about a deficit Π^0. The lower and the upper bound for Π^0, as mentioned above, are far away from each other. Hence, Ramsey prices range from zero tariffs to unconstrained profit maximizing prices. The economic consequences of pricing under revenue–cost constraints depend on the concrete choice of Π^0. The usual exclusive concentration on the structure of prices prevents many economists from realizing that! Low Π^0 will imply a low pricing level and, if demands react normally, a comparatively large public sector. Low Π^0 may imply cheaper prices of publicly provided goods in order to help low income people. (This argument is mainly relevant if Π^0 refers to a single public enterprise the goods of which are mainly demanded by low income people.)

What about the *structure of prices*? Recall that the public sector has to observe a revenue–cost constraint and to serve all demand. Hence the board must consider the price elasticities of demand for the different goods. The less price elastic a good, the easier can its price be increased in order to achieve Π^0 because the public sector need not be too afraid of loosing its customers. If, on the other hand, a good is comparatively price elastic, the customers will leave the market if the price is increased. The board will therefore abstain from too intensive price increases of very price elastic goods.

Of course, cross-price elasticities may destroy this basic pattern. However, the above considerations suggest a similarity between the Ramsey price structure and the price structure of a profit maximizing monopolist, which can be easily shown. Assume a monopolist who calculates his profit maximizing prices p_e, $e \in E$, considering production possibilities $g(z)=0$ and acting along compensated demand functions $\hat{z}_e(p)$. He will arrive at the following price structure:[25]

$$\sum_{i \in E} (c_i - p_i) \frac{\partial \hat{z}_i}{\partial p_e} = \hat{z}_e, \qquad e \in E. \tag{2.34}$$

[25] For an explicit derivation, see Drèze (1964, p. 31). Remember that we always assume $p_i = c_i$, $\forall i \notin E$.

Therefore Ramsey pricing converges to monopoly pricing if $\gamma \to 1$ and if the monopolist takes account of compensated demand functions.

Hence a board which chooses Ramsey pricing behaves as if it were an unconstrained, profit maximizing monopolist who inflates all compensated price elasticities by a factor $1/\gamma$.[26]

If Π^0 exceeds the unconstrained, welfare optimal revenue–cost difference, the inflating factor $1/\gamma > 1$. The board has to overestimate all price elasticities and thus to react more carefully than a monopolist would, being more anxious to loose customers, which implies a lower level of prices than for a profit maximizing monopolist.

For the sake of completeness we must deal also with the case of Π^0 below the unconstrained, welfare optimal revenue–cost difference. In this case the inflating factor $1/\gamma$ is negative. The board behaves like a monopolist who changes the signs of all price elasticities.

It may be noted in passing that I do not believe that the above mentioned properties of Ramsey pricing can directly serve as a basis for *regulating* public pricing. If a public enterprise is directed by a public authority to inflate all price elasticities and then behave monopolistically, I usually would expect the public enterprise to switch to the correct elasticities and to give wrong information to the public authority. I do not believe in incentive structures that imply strategies by which the public sector cheats itself by computing profits under elasticities which the actors know to be wrong.

This section must not be concluded without mentioning a very special, but particularly well-known, case of Ramsey pricing. If we totally neglect all cross-price elasticities of demand ($\partial \hat{z}_i / \partial p_e = 0$, $i, e \in E$, $i \neq e$), the Ramsey price structure reduces to the famous "*inverse elasticity rule*",

$$\frac{p_e - c_e}{p_e} = -\frac{\gamma}{\eta_{ee}}, \qquad e \in E, \tag{2.35}$$

where η_{ee} is the own compensated price elasticity of demand. In this special case any price–cost margin is proportional to its inverse price elasticity.

The price–cost margin of a good is the larger, the smaller the absolute value of its price elasticity. As the compensated elasticities are always negative, all prices lie either above or below marginal costs. The case of positive price–cost margins may, for instance, be achieved by a break-even constraint for a public enterprise working under increasing returns to scale. The case of negative price–cost

[26] Divide (2.34) by γ and set $(\partial \hat{z}_i / \partial p_e)/\gamma = (\partial \hat{z}_i / \partial p_e)^{\text{infl}}$, $\forall i, e$. The compensated price elasticities are then easily obtained by multiplying each partial derivative by the corresponding price/compensated quantity ratio. $\eta_{ie}^{\text{infl}} = (1/\gamma)\eta_{ie}$ immediately follows.

margins is plausible for public enterprises that have to follow "low pricing procedures".[27]

The economic consequences of the inverse elasticity rule are different for positive and for negative price–cost margins respectively. The case of positive price–cost margins leads to relatively higher prices of price inelastic goods and to relatively cheaper prices of price elastic goods. The case of negative price–cost margins leads to the contrary. Now assume that goods mainly bought by lower-income consumers are comparatively price inelastic [which must empirically be computed in any case – Timmer (1981)]. Then lower-income consumers are burdened in the case of positive price–cost margins, favored in the case of negative ones.

(b) A piecemeal policy interpretation of the Ramsey optimum

Some of the best-known interpretations of Ramsey pricing follow a piecemeal approach. Consider a situation where the controlled prices change by $\mathrm{d}p_i$ and the uncontrolled prices remain constant. Then the total differentials of the demand functions $\hat{z}_e = \hat{z}_e(p)$ are as follows:

$$\mathrm{d}\hat{z}_e(p) = \sum_{i\in E} \frac{\partial \hat{z}_e}{\partial p_i} \mathrm{d}p_i, \qquad e \in E. \tag{2.36}$$

Let all price changes be proportional to the price, marginal cost difference,

$$\mathrm{d}p_i = (c_i - p_i)\,\mathrm{d}s, \qquad i = 1,\dots,n. \tag{2.37}$$

$\mathrm{d}s > 0$ implies that prices move towards marginal costs (and decrease if price exceeds marginal costs); for $\mathrm{d}s < 0$ the contrary holds.

Inserting into (2.33) yields

$$\gamma\hat{z}_e = \sum_{i\in E} (c_i - p_i)\frac{\partial \hat{z}_i}{\partial p_e} = \frac{1}{\mathrm{d}s}\sum_{i\in E} \frac{\partial \hat{z}_i}{\partial p_e}\mathrm{d}p_i$$

$$= \frac{1}{\mathrm{d}s}\sum_{i\in E} \frac{\partial \hat{z}_e}{\partial p_i}\mathrm{d}p_i = \frac{1}{\mathrm{d}s}\mathrm{d}\hat{z}_e(p), \tag{2.38}$$

[27] Equations (2.35) clearly reveal that, for prices above marginal costs $\gamma > 0$, and for prices below marginal costs $\gamma < 0$. But, of course, this does not hold generally if all cross-price elasticities are taken into account as in equations (2.33).

and by rearranging we obtain

$$d\hat{z}_e = \gamma \hat{z}_e ds, \qquad e \in E. \tag{2.39}$$

This is one of Boiteux's main results for a second-best optimum: The price, marginal cost deviations are proportionate to those infinitesimal variations in price that entail a proportionate change in the demands for all publicly provided goods. This proportionate change in demand may, however, imply that for some goods demand decreases, although the own price decreases or vice versa.[28] Consider the following example: Π^0 exceeds the unconstrained revenue–cost difference. Hence, $\gamma \in (0,1)$. Assume $ds < 0$. Recall that, for a given Π^0, some prices may exceed marginal costs, some others may fall short of them. The proportionate price changes then imply increasing as well as decreasing prices. But the quantities change in the same direction: demand decreases, even for those goods whose prices decrease. The reason for such an inverse reaction of demand is straightforward. If the relevant good k does not react too intensively to its own price, but quite intensively to prices of other goods that are complements of it, its second-best price may fall below marginal costs even if other prices exceed marginal costs. But in such a case the proportionate price change implies increasing prices of the complements which may imply decreasing quantity of good k, although its own price decreases.

A very common alternative interpretation going back to Ramsey (1927) concerns the case of the transition from second-best to marginal cost pricing:[29] in a second-best optimum the relative deviations of second-best quantities from those quantities that would have been demanded if the goods were sold at marginal cost prices are equal for all goods. Usually the authors add some remarks on the empirical applicability of such a result: if the public enterprise sells every good, not at the present price but at a price given by the marginal cost of the present production, it will not be in a state of second-best optimum if the relative shifts of demand for the various goods turn out to be different.

However, the reader should always be aware that these results are approximations only (contrary to our interpretations of second-best prices given in the previous subsection). The reason is that by use of the total differential (2.36) all results are strictly valid only for infinitesimal deviations from marginal cost pricing or for demand functions that are linear in prices. Therefore I have never understood why this approach and its extensions play such a prominent role in many recent papers, for instance, in papers on optimal commodity taxation [Diamond (1975), Mirrlees (1975)].

[28] Of course $\partial \hat{z}_e / \partial p_e$ is always negative. However, as we are considering simultaneous changes of all prices, the cross-price effects may overcompensate this direct effect.

[29] This is a special case of (2.39), where we start from Ramsey prices and integrate over ds from 0 to 1. Then $[\hat{z}_i(p^{\mathrm{MC}}) - \hat{z}_i(p^{\mathrm{Ramsey}})]/\hat{z}_i(p^{\mathrm{Ramsey}}) = \gamma, \forall i$.

2.2.3. *Rate of return regulation*

(a) An intuitive introduction

A fixed profit constraint Π^0 suffers from being totally exogenous and therefore too inflexible for every-day-life regulation. It involves frequently recurring regulatory review processes, especially in inflationary times. But asking government for changing constraints is always a tedious procedure, leading to regulatory lags and unwanted intensive bureaucratic engagement of the enterprises' boards.

Hence, it seems to be a more elegant and flexible procedure to restrain profits by fixing the maximum return on investment (in real terms).[29a] This procedure can often be found in regulatory practice, e.g., in the United States and in different proposals of the British White Papers on Nationalised Industries (1967, 1978). Moreover, this kind of regulation has been the object of an intensive scientific discussion, from the paper of Averch and Johnson (1962) up to the book of Mrs. Bailey (1973).

The above examples show the rate of return regulation to be relevant for public as well as for regulated private enterprises. Public enterprises may consider the rate of return limitation as a constraint on welfare maximization in the framework of our Boiteux model. Regulated private enterprises will typically treat it as a constraint on profit maximization. Then the results of both approaches can be compared with each other.

Let government fix a maximum rate on investment (for short "rate of return"). The definition of this rate of return discloses a capitalistic bias as it implicitly assumes all profits to be earned by the capital inputs only: the rate of return equals profit plus capital costs per unit of capital inputs. Thus implicitly capital is assumed to earn its own costs and the whole profit:

$$\text{Rate of return} = \frac{\text{Profit} + \text{Capital costs}}{\text{Capital inputs}}. \tag{2.40}$$

By fixing a maximum rate of return government restricts the enterprise's profit. And from (2.40) we easily learn that the maximum allowed profit, given a maximum allowed rate of return, equals

$$\text{Profit} = (\text{Rate of return} - \text{Interest rate}) \times \text{Capital inputs}. \tag{2.41}$$

Such a profit constraint evidently differs from a "neutral" constraint Π^0 because of its asymmetric treatment of the inputs. Compared with the neutral

[29a] Other profit constraints which are partly endogenous include fixing a "fair" mark-up on cost or fixing a "fair" profit per unit of output. See Bailey and Malone (1970) for the resulting allocation inefficiencies.

constraint, rate of return regulation will typically distort the capital–labor input ratio. And the output prices of the multiproduct public sector or regulated private enterprise will be distorted as well.

Proceeding to a more concise notation we separate outputs $z_e \geqq 0$ from inputs which we aggregate into labor inputs $l > 0 (= -z_0)$ and capital inputs $\kappa > 0$. The respective prices are p_e, $e \in E$, p_0 and p_κ, the input prices being fixed.

Capital and labor being perfectly divisible in production, the necessary inputs depend on the produced output quantities as follows:

$$l = l(z, \kappa), \qquad \kappa = \kappa(z, l), \qquad \left(\frac{\partial l}{\partial z_e}, \frac{\partial \kappa}{\partial z_e}\right) \gg 0, \tag{2.42}$$

where $z = (z_e)$ is the vector of the outputs.

Fixing a rate of return, d, restricts profit in the following way:

$$\sum_{e \in E} p_e z_e - p_0 l - p_\kappa \kappa \leqq (d - p_\kappa)\kappa. \tag{2.43}$$

As in the case of a fixed constraint above we will always choose a binding profit limitation. Most interesting, once again, is the case of a profit that exceeds the unconstrained, welfare maximizing one. However, even this case may well imply a deficit. Hence we cannot a priori conclude whether $(d - p_\kappa) \gtreqless 0$.

(b) *A more rigorous treatment*

Pricing under rate of return regulation can be seen as a special case of our Boiteux model solution (2.27). We assume again that (i) only prices of publicly produced goods are controlled, these goods being neither supplied nor demanded by private firms; (ii) all uncontrolled prices are equal to marginal costs in any firm, including the public sector; and (iii) demand is compensated. The welfare optimization is, however, restricted by the rate of return constraint (2.43).

Then the marginal conditions (2.27) reduce to

$$\sum_{i \in E} (\tilde{C}_i - p_i) \frac{\partial \hat{z}_i}{\partial p_e} = \gamma z_e, \qquad e \in E, \tag{2.44}$$

where the modified marginal costs $\tilde{C}_i$ equal

$$\tilde{C}_i = c_i + \gamma(d - p_\kappa)\frac{\partial \kappa}{\partial z_i} = p_0 \frac{\partial l}{\partial z_i} + \gamma(d - p_\kappa)\frac{\partial \kappa}{\partial z_i}, \tag{2.45}$$

after inserting for $\partial \Pi / \partial z_i$ and for c_i, respectively.

If the regulated profit exceeds the unconstrained, welfare maximizing one, $0 < \gamma < 1$.[30] The limiting cases refer to marginal cost pricing ($\gamma = 0$) and to a rate of return regulated profit maximizing monopolist ($\gamma = 1$).

The pricing structure (2.44) resembles the Ramsey result, replacing c_i with $\tilde{C}_i$. Hence, the enterprise's board will once again behave like a profit maximizing monopolist who inflates all compensated price elasticities by a factor $1/\gamma$. However, the board does not only take account of the shadow prices c_i, but also of the marginal capital inputs, weighted by the difference between the rate of return and the interest rate. This asymmetric treatment of labor and capital is due to the asymmetric profit constraint.

The welfare maximizing board will always fix prices in such a way that it *undercapitalizes* compared with the efficient capital–labor ratio. This implies too low prices for labor-intensive goods and vice versa.

The reason is that the board is interested not in profit, but in welfare. And the best strategy to maximize welfare is to keep the profit $(d - p_\kappa)\kappa$ low by low capital inputs. Then the "level of prices" can be kept lower and welfare increases.

The totally exogenous profit constraint Π^0, on the other hand, always leads to an efficient capital–labor ratio because it treats inputs symmetrically. This is an important theoretical advantage of Ramsey regulation as compared with rate of return regulation. This theoretical advantage has, however, to be balanced against the practical disadvantages mentioned above. And these disadvantages may be more important for practical application as we do not know the exact empirical relevance of the theoretically inefficient input choices.

(c) Welfare versus profit maximization: The Averch–Johnson effect

The analysis and practice of U.S. rate of return regulation concerns profit maximization rather than welfare maximization. Hence we should compare this approach with the above mentioned Boiteux case.

For this purpose we consider a profit maximizing *board* of a public or private enterprise, fixing prices p_e and output quantities z_e, $e \in E$. The board considers the market equilibria for all goods ($x_e = z_e$). In our partial approach, however, there is no necessity for the firm to consider the equilibrium of the labor and capital markets. We exclude lump-sum transfers. This exclusion can be justified ideologically: we do not want to give the profit maximizing enterprise the right to control the income distribution in order to maximize its profit. It can also be interpreted technologically: the enterprise is restricted to one-part tariffs and not

[30] $\gamma > 0$ can be shown as follows: Differentiate $\mathscr{L}$ in the presentation of the Boiteux model [equation (2.9)]: $\partial\mathscr{L}/\partial d = -\bar{\gamma} < 0$. Because of $\beta(\partial g/\partial z_0) > 0$, this implies $\gamma > 0$.

allowed to fix individually different income deductions and transfers as fixed parts of a two-part tariff.

The maximum profit the board is allowed to make depends on the rate of return, as fixed by the *government*. To deal with the most relevant case, we assume this rate of return to exceed the interest rate, since otherwise the enterprise would have to achieve a deficit (and a private enterprise would leave the market). On the other hand, the rate of return must be chosen in such a way that the allowed profit falls below the unconstrained monopoly profit. Under these conditions the profit constraint will always be binding.

Hence, we impute to the enterprise the following optimization approach:

$$\max_{p_e, z_e} \mathscr{L} = \sum_{e \in E} p_e z_e - p_0 l - p_\kappa \kappa - \sum_{e \in E} \alpha_e [x_e(p) - z_e]$$

$$-\delta\left[(d - p_\kappa)\kappa - \left(\sum_e p_e z_e - p_0 l - p_\kappa \kappa\right)\right], \tag{2.46}$$

which, after some transformations, leads to the following first-order conditions:

$$\sum_i (\tilde{C}_i - p_i)\frac{\partial x_i}{\partial p_e} = x_e, \qquad i, e \in E, \tag{2.47}$$

where the modified marginal costs $\tilde{C}_i$ equal

$$\tilde{C}_i = p_0 \frac{\partial l}{\partial z_i} + \left[p_\kappa + \frac{\delta}{1+\delta}(d - p_\kappa)\right]\frac{\partial \kappa}{\partial z_i}. \tag{2.48}$$

The Lagrangian multiplier in this case is $-1 \leqq \delta \leqq 0$, the limiting cases being

- zero profits ($\delta = -1$, $d = p_\kappa$), and
- monopoly profits ($\delta = 0$).[32]

Note that for the monopolist $\tilde{C}_i$ reduces to $C_i = p_0\ (\partial l/\partial z_i) + p_\kappa(\partial \kappa/\partial z_i)$ as can easily be seen by inserting $\delta = 0$ into (2.48). In C_i both inputs are treated symmetrically, in $\tilde{C}_i$ the price of capital is reduced by the factor $[\delta/(1+\delta)] \times (d - p_\kappa) < 0$.

Hence, the rate of return regulated profit maximizer behaves as if he were an unconstrained monopolist who underestimates the price of capital. This property of our pricing formula corresponds to the well-known Averch–Johnson effect of overcapitalization as resulting from this kind of regulation.

[31] Sign and range of this Lagrangian multiplier is an intensively discussed topic of the Averch–Johnson literature. For details, proofs and references, see Bailey (1973, pp. 25–28, 73–74, 80). It should be mentioned that this restriction of the range of δ does not necessarily imply $\partial\delta/\partial(d - p_\kappa) > 0$, although the above mentioned interpretation may suggest that.

The resulting price structure cheapens the prices of capital-intensive goods. The price of any good, p_e, will be the lower, the higher ceteris paribus its marginal capital intensity of production.[32] The rate of return regulation, therefore, does not only imply a suboptimal structure of inputs, but also a suboptimal structure of outputs because of a distortion of output prices resulting from regulation.

This effect vanishes only if the constraint is non-binding as then the enterprise will follow the usual perfect monopoly price structure which does not imply any misestimation of the price of capital. (If $\delta = 0$, $\tilde{C}_i$ reduces to C_i.) This reveals a puzzling feature of the rate of return regulation: if the enterprise is restricted in its profit maximizing abilities, it will misallocate inputs and outputs. If it is not restricted, it will allocate inputs and outputs correctly, albeit monopolistically.

Thus the misallocation does *not* decrease if a regulated enterprise is confronted with a lower difference between the rate of return and the interest rate. [This has been a decisive counterargument against Klevorick's (1966) proposal of a "graduated rate of return" that diminished with increasing capital input.] In our case it cannot be shown whether the misestimation of the price of capital inputs increases or decreases when the difference between the rate of return and the interest rate decreases.

The production technology, as introduced by the simple assumptions (2.42), influences the misestimation of the price of capital. Whereas no further comments are necessary as far as neoclassical technologies are concerned, we should say more about the case of fixed coefficients of production. Consider a firm which, because of its profit target, moves along expansion paths of Leontief technologies for every good e,

$$\frac{\partial l}{\partial z_e} = k_e \frac{\partial \kappa}{\partial z_e}. \tag{2.49}$$

Then $\tilde{C}_e$ is as follows:

$$\tilde{C}_e = p_0 k_e \frac{\partial \kappa}{\partial z_e} + \left[p_\kappa + \frac{\delta}{1+\delta}(d - p_\kappa) \right] \frac{\partial \kappa}{\partial z_e}, \tag{2.50}$$

and there will still be a distorting effect influencing the output price structure. The profit maximizing rate of return regulated firm will still behave like a monopolist who underestimates the price of capital inputs and thus the price structure will differ from that of an unconstrained monopolist.

Of course, this misestimation will not imply suboptimal *input* combinations in the production of any single good as the enterprise follows the expansion paths

[32] For a proof insert (2.48) into (2.47) and solve explicitly for p_e. Differentiating p_e with respect to the marginal capital intensity of production leads to the above mentioned result.

(2.49), regardless of the structure of input prices. However, the prices of *outputs* are still distorted in favor of capital-intensive goods. The firm that is confronted with Leontief technologies of any good can maximize its profit by changing the composition of produced goods towards higher capital intensity of its total production. This is the Averch–Johnson effect of a multiproduct enterprise under Leontief technology.

We should mention once again that all these inefficiencies vanish if an exogenous profit constraint Π^0 is fixed. But a definite answer whether Ramsey or rate of return regulation is superior is as impossible as it was in the case of welfare maximization. There is no clear-cut empirical evidence that the Averch–Johnson effect actually matters. [See Joskow and Noll (1980) for further references.]

2.2.4. Pricing for distributional aims

(a) Prices versus taxes

In many European countries public pricing is not only considered as an instrument of allocation policy, but also as an instrument of distribution policy. The most favorable conditions for this approach prevail if different classes of goods can be identified which typically are demanded by consumers with different incomes: first- and second-class railway or hospital accommodation provide good examples. But we could think also of a nationalized enterprise producing minis for low-income consumers and maxis for high-income consumers and deviating from allocatively optimal pricing by cheapening minis at the expense of maxis.

Such a pricing policy favors poor people, but it avoids the compromising need for a means test and reduces the administrative costs of implementing a system of distributional pricing. Moreover, people are still given the freedom to choose the good they prefer. A rich man who likes to chat with less rich people is not prohibited from using second-class railway.

However, we must examine the following two main objections against the use of public pricing as means of income redistribution:

(i) First, *liberal economists* often oppose distributionally modified public pricing. They view progressive income taxation or subsidization as the most effective instruments of income redistribution and wish to restrict public sector pricing to the allocational objectives only. ("Why do you want to favor poor people simply because they go by railway? If you regard them as poor give them money" as A.A. Walters formulated it in a personal discussion with the author some years ago.)

The traditional liberals argue that income taxation distorts the labor–leisure decision only, whereas distributional public prices distort a lot of price relations in the economy. This classical argument has to be rejected from the usual second-best point: if distortions are unavoidable, there is no proof that "one distortion only" is better than "many distortions".

Despite this second-best argument there is a more recent formulation of the case against distributional public prices which is theoretically better substantiated [Ng (1984)]. Consider individuals who do not suffer from any fiscal illusion. A rich man, reflecting upon his labor–leisure choice, does not only consider the marginal income tax rate on additional income, but also that he has to pay more for goods he wants to buy than a poor man. By whatever means he is deprived of a dollar, the disincentives for his labor effort will be the same. Hence, public pricing is the inferior instrument of redistribution. For the same degree of redistribution it leads to the same welfare losses from distorted labor–leisure relations as an income tax. But it leads to additional welfare losses because of distorted price relations.

However, it can be shown that this conclusion is not generally valid:

- While this argument presupposes a total absence of fiscal illusion, the degree of fiscal illusion may be positive and may vary with the kind of public revenue (taxes, prices, etc.).
- The postulated absence of fiscal illusion is particularly questionable where price differences are associated with quality differences and where the absence of fiscal illusion would require the purchaser to distinguish between the part of the higher price due to quality and the part due to redistribution.
- The disincentive effects of means tested public pricing may differ totally from those of progressive income taxation. If one is given the right to buy good e at a lower price if one's income falls below a threshold r^{h0}, there will be particular disincentive effects in the neighborhood of r^{h0} only! And rich people will be unaffected from such disincentives.

(ii) *Social democrats*, on the other hand, oppose distributional public prices because they do not depend on personal means unlike, for example, the payment of income taxes. The rich man in the second-class railway offers a good example. Moreover, this kind of price differentiation typically implies some quality differentiation which has often been criticized from ideological reasons, stressing the merits of uniform public supply of schooling, health, etc. As a remedy means tested public prices have been proposed, for qualitatively unified public supply.

But the arguments for means tested public pricing are not totally convincing. Non means tested tariffs for differentiated products imply more freedom of choice for the consumer. The implied quality differentiation enriches public supply. Different types of schools are perhaps the best example.

For all these reasons I do not believe in the unambiguous superiority of progressive income taxation as an instrument of redistribution. Moreover, if we start from a social welfare function that includes distributional weighting of individual incomes and choose income taxation *and* public pricing as instruments, we expect social welfare to increase, or at least not to decrease compared with a case where the income tax is the only instrument. And this will remain valid as well if the disincentive effects of both progressive income taxation and distributional pricing are taken into account.[33]

In the following subsection we will consider non means tested public pricing. As the public sector usually sells many different goods, some of them primarily bought by lower-income earners, some by higher-income earners, distribution policy will concentrate on the *structure of prices*. (If a public enterprise sells a single good only, bought mainly by lower-income earners, it is sufficient to concentrate on the level of prices.)

(b) A model for distributional pricing

We must first make sure that public prices are the actual instruments of distribution policy. Therefore we have to exclude those lump-sum transfers which are the distributional instruments in the earlier subsections on marginal cost pricing, Ramsey pricing, and rate of return pricing. Public pricing with distributional objectives must be located in a world of Marshallian demand functions, not in a world of compensated demand functions.

Next we have to consider the financial difficulties the enterprise's board will encounter if it applies distributional pricing: revenue will tend to fall, perhaps below costs, because any internal subsidization of the poor is limited by the possibility that the rich leave the market totally or switch to the consumption of lower priced goods. Redistribution effects of a considerable extent will thus lead to a marked increase in the demand for low priced goods and a marked decrease in the demand for high priced goods, implying a tendency towards a deficit. Hence we must always include a profit constraint for the public sector, be it total profit or the rate of return.

To concentrate on distribution the following analysis will neglect the interdependencies with the private sector: (i) Only prices of publicly produced goods are controlled. These goods are neither supplied nor demanded by private firms. (ii) All uncontrolled prices equal marginal costs in any firm, including the public sector. Needless to say these restrictions can be easily relaxed.

Under these special assumptions the marginal conditions (2.23) reduce to

$$\sum_{i \in E} (\tilde{C}_i - p_i) \frac{\partial z_i^D}{\partial p_e} = (1 - F_e) z_e, \qquad e \in E. \tag{2.51}$$

[33] For a detailed analysis of such an approach, see Bös (1984).

The reader should recall that z_i^D represents *non*-compensated demand and F_e the distributional characteristics

$$F_e = \sum_h \frac{x_e^h}{x_e} b^h = \sum_h \frac{x_e^h}{x_e} \lambda^h \frac{\partial v^h}{\partial r^h}, \qquad e \in E. \tag{2.52}$$

The distributional characteristic of any good is the higher, the larger is its share of consumption by lower-income people: quantities x_e^h of a necessity are given higher weights λ^h; moreover, $\partial v^h/\partial r^h$ will be higher for lower income. Hence F_e of a necessity will usually be higher than F_e of a non-necessity.

The most general interpretation of the distributional price structure (2.51) can be given once again by comparing this price structure with that of the perfect monopolist. The distributionally oriented board behaves as if it were a monopolist who inflates each price elasticity of demand η_{ie} by $1/(1-F_e)$.[34] This implies a much more complicated behavior by the board than in the Ramsey case as there will typically exist as many different inflating factors as publicly priced goods.

How this procedure of inflating works can be illustrated most easily if we neglect cross-price effects. Then the pricing rule is as follows:

$$(\tilde{C}_e - p_e)\frac{\partial z_e^D}{\partial p_e} = (1 - F_e) z_e, \qquad e \in E. \tag{2.53}$$

Let us exclude inverse reactions of demand by assuming $\partial z_e^D/\partial p_e < 0$. Then the price of good e will exceed the modified marginal costs $\tilde{C}_e$ if $1 > F_e \geqq 0$ and fall below $\tilde{C}_e$ if $F_e > 1$.

For the economically most interesting case of a good priced above marginal cost the inflating factor $1/(1-F_e)$ will be positive and will increase with increasing F_e. The demand sensitivity must therefore be overestimated and the degree of overestimation increases with increasing social evaluation of individual consumption as reflected in F_e. This means particular overestimation of the sensitivity of demand for necessities because monopolistic pricing always implies greater care in the pricing of goods with higher demand elasticities.

If, on the other hand, a good is priced below marginal costs, the inflating factor $1/(1-F_e)$ will be negative and will again increase with increasing F_e. This implies once again a tendency to cheapen necessities.

[34] For any $e \in E$ we can divide (2.51) by $(1-F_e)$ and define $(\partial z_i^D/\partial p_e)/(1-F_e) = (\partial z_i^D/\partial p_e)^{\text{infl.}}$. Elasticities can then be obtained easily by multiplying each partial derivative with the corresponding price/quantity ratio p_e/z_i^D.

2.3. Disequilibrium setting

2.3.1. Accommodation to monopolistic pricing in the private sector

(a) The second-best paradigm: Accommodation to versus interference in the private sector of the economy

Let some prices in the private economy deviate from marginal costs because of the monopoly power of some entrepreneurs, or because of the application of rules of thumb (mark-up pricing), or because of administrative actions, or because of commodity taxation. Any of these cases will be called "monopolistic pricing", the degree of monopoly being measured by the positive price–cost margin,

$$\Theta_i^j := (p_i - c_i^j)/p_i > 0, \qquad i = 1,\dots,n, \quad j = 1,\dots,J. \tag{2.54}$$

If these prices cannot or are not brought down to marginal costs, then the second-best philosophy tells us that in general the prices of the other goods will also deviate from marginal costs in order to obtain maximal welfare. The rationale is that the attainable welfare in an economy is maximized if the price structure corresponds to the relative scarcity of goods. And such a correspondence will in general be better approximated if unavoidable distortions are compensated by other distortions than if the rest of the economy does not react to these distortions.

Lipsey and Lancaster (1956–57) and Green (1961) were the first to articulate some challenging hypotheses on public pricing in a monopolistic environment. This second-best approach to public pricing was then strongly attacked because it took as unalterable the fact that prices in the private economy cannot be brought down to marginal costs and therefore required that public prices adjust to the private degrees of monopoly, thus implying a public pricing policy that did everything to enable private monopolists to make profits. If privately and publicly priced goods are substitutes, public prices must be increased to mitigate the competition with the monopoly. If they are complements, public prices must be reduced to make the joint purchase of both goods cheaper, which again helps the private enterprise. Opponents argued that this meant "abdication of economic policy".

In my opinion these objections are not totally fair. The criticism may be valid if a public enterprise actually adjusts its price structure to a perfect private monopolist. But monopolistic pricing in the private sector, as defined above, refers to all enterprises whose prices exceed marginal costs. And usually there will exist many cases of politically acceptable positive price–cost margins. Then the chosen structure of public prices only implies the best possible way to restore price relations that indicate the relative scarcity of goods. Therefore, publicly priced substitutes have to be more expensive to restore at least partly the price relations that would have prevailed in the absence of private monopolistic pricing. On the other hand, publicly priced complements have to be cheapened: if public prices remained at marginal costs, the "composite" price for both complements would be farther from the price relations that would have prevailed in the absence of private monopolistic pricing.

Objections against an accommodation of public to private pricing can be criticized for yet another reason. It is correct that this approach assumes private price–cost margins to be exogenously given and public ones to be endogenously adjusted. However, this does not exclude the entire influence of the public sector on the private economy. Assume the public price–cost margins to be lower than those in a private industry producing substitutes. This will decrease the demand for the privately supplied goods although the public sector does not follow marginal cost pricing. One should always consider the accommodation of the private economy to public pricing which is also included in our approach. The importance of this feedback will, of course, depend on the relative size of the public sector and the private economy.

The adjustment of public pricing to typical private pricing can be treated in partial and in general microeconomic models.

(i) Typical partial analyses consider duopolistic or oligopolistic market structures where one of the participants is the public sector [Bös (1981, ch. 5), Beato and Mas-Colell (1984)]. Such analyses show public and private pricing to depend on the different possible strategies of the economic agents involved. The simplest *duopoly* approach confronts a profit maximizing private enterprise and a welfare maximizing public sector, each selling one good only. If the private price is given, the public price follows a marginal cost pricing rule (which constitutes the reaction function of the public sector). If the public price is given, the private enterprise's reaction function is given by an inverse elasticity rule. The outcome of the duopoly game depends on the behavior of the players. *Cournot-type behavior* assumes that both duopolists always adhere to their reaction functions and never learn how the opponent changes his behavior in reaction to their own behavior. The asymmetric *Stackelberg-type behavior*, on the other hand, assumes one player is active, maximizing profit or welfare respectively, whereas the other player passively accommodates to this policy by staying on its reaction function. Of particular interest is the *Pareto-efficient set* where increasing welfare is only possible by decreasing profit and vice versa. This implies a welfare maximizing public sector which has somehow restricted the private monopoly to a maximum permitted profit. It can be shown that this approach leads to all the usual results of the general analysis to be dealt with below [Bös (1981, pp. 78–82)].

(ii) The predominant theoretical approach, however, is concerned with public and private pricing in a *general microeconomic model*, in our case in the extended Boiteux model presented in Section 2.1.1 above.

(b) A model for public prices in an imperfect market economy

Let us consider an economy with private monopolistic pricing. We restrict ourselves to compensated demand.

Then the marginal conditions (2.27) of the extended Boiteux model hold:

$$\sum_i (\tilde{C}_i - p_i)\frac{\partial \hat{z}_i}{\partial p_e} = \gamma z_e - (1-\gamma)\sum_i \sum_j (c_i^j - p_i)\frac{\partial y_i^j}{\partial p_e}, \qquad e \in E. \tag{2.55}$$

For the economic interpretation of this pricing structure we *first* assume a revenue–cost constraint which exceeds unconstrained profits ($\gamma > 0$). If p_e, one of the controlled prices, refers to a good that is publicly supplied ($\hat{z}_e > 0$), we learn from (2.55) that

$$p_e = \tilde{C}_e - \frac{\gamma z_e}{\partial \hat{z}_e/\partial p_e} + \sum_{i \neq e} (\tilde{C}_i - p_i)\frac{\partial \hat{z}_i/\partial p_e}{\partial \hat{z}_e/\partial p_e}$$
$$+ (1-\gamma)\sum_i \sum_j (c_i^j - p_i)\frac{\partial y_i^j/\partial p_e}{\partial \hat{z}_e/\partial p_e}, \qquad e \in E. \tag{2.56}$$

Hence, the controlled price p_e will usually differ from marginal costs. The second term on the right-hand side of (2.56), measuring the effects of the revenue–cost constraint, implies the expected tendency for the price p_e to exceed the marginal costs of producing good e in the public sector (because of $\gamma > 0$, $\partial \hat{z}_e/\partial p_e < 0$). The last two terms on the right-hand side, the "reallocation effects" [Hagen (1979)] imply a unique tendency for price p_e to exceed $\tilde{C}_e$ if all prices exceed the respective marginal costs *and* if good e is a net substitute for all other goods ($\partial \hat{z}_i/\partial p_e > 0$, $\partial y_i^j/\partial p_e > 0$, $\forall i \neq e$). Complementarities between good e and (some) other goods point in the opposite direction; there is no general answer in this case.

If, on the other hand, a controlled price p_e refers to a good that is produced only privately, we obtain [35]

$$p_e = \sum_j c_e^j \frac{\partial y_e^j/\partial p_e}{\sum_j \partial y_e^j/\partial p_e} + \sum_{i \neq e} \sum_j (c_i^j - p_i)\frac{\partial y_i^j/\partial p_e}{\sum_j \partial y_e^j/\partial p_e}, \qquad e \in E. \tag{2.57}$$

[35] These equations are easily derived from (2.55) by setting $z_e = 0$ and $\partial \hat{z}_e/\partial p_e = 0$. For simplicity we assume $\partial \hat{z}_i/\partial p_e = 0$. The extension for $\partial \hat{z}_i/\partial p_e \neq 0$ is straightforward.

The optimal regulated price p_e depends on a weighted mean of the marginal costs c_e^j, the weights depending on differences in the supply elasticities of good e by different firms. It depends, moreover, on the mark-ups in the private supply of all other goods (regulated or not regulated): the regulated price p_e has to exceed the (weighted) marginal costs if good e is a net substitute for all other goods and the private prices exceed marginal costs. Net complementarities between good e and (some) other goods imply a tendency towards lower prices.

Let us *second* consider public pricing without a binding budget constraint, but with given price distortions in the private economy. The general interpretation of this case is straightforward and can be left to the reader. [Set $\gamma = 0$ in (2.56).] One special interpretation, however, must be treated more extensively. Assume the mark-up for any good i to be identical for all private firms and for the public sector,

$$\Theta_i = (p_i - c_i)/p_i = (p_i - c_i^j)/p_i, \qquad i = 1, \dots, n, \quad j = 1, \dots, J,$$

$$\Theta_0 = 0. \tag{2.58}$$

The theoretical literature on the topic usually tries to motivate such parallel behavior by some hints to identical commodity taxation.

Then (2.55) can be written as follows:

$$\Theta_e p_e \frac{\partial \hat{x}_e}{\partial p_e} = - \sum_{i \neq e} \Theta_i p_i \frac{\partial \hat{x}_i}{\partial p_e}, \qquad e \in E. \tag{2.59}$$

But as the compensated expenditures for all goods do not react to price changes $(\sum_k p_k(\partial \hat{x}_k/\partial p_e) = 0)$, we obtain

$$\Theta_e = \sum_{i \neq e} \Theta_i w_{ie}, \qquad e \in E, \tag{2.60}$$

where

$$w_{ie} = p_i \frac{\partial \hat{x}_i}{\partial p_e} \Bigg/ \sum_{k \neq e} p_k \frac{\partial \hat{x}_k}{\partial p_e}, \qquad \sum_{i \neq e} w_{ie} = 1. \tag{2.61}$$

The price–cost margin Θ_e is a weighted average of all other Θ_i. This implies that the optimal price–cost margin lies somewhere between the minimum and the maximum price–cost margin if good e is a net substitute for all other goods. With some modifications this result can be found in Green (1961), Bergson (1972), Hatta (1977), Kawamata (1977), Wiegard (1978, 1979), Hagen (1979).

However, for the following two reasons I do not believe that this celebrated result is of great importance:

(i) Exogenously fixing $\Theta_i = \Theta_i^j$ for all i and j implies the exogenous determination of variables that are endogenously determined in the model: the optimal values of Θ are the result of the optimization approach! An equality of Θ_i and Θ_i^j can only result by chance or from particular theoretical assumptions regarding the private sector that we have intentionally avoided in this section. Moreover, there is no economic justification for introducing this identity of mark-ups as additional constraints in our optimization approach.

(ii) The result is only valid if good e is a net substitute for all other goods, which is empirically not very plausible. There exist many net complementarity relations between regulated and non-regulated goods. Take, e.g., the situation of demand for different goods that are relevant for producing transportation services. Publicly priced railway services are substitutes for private motor-car traffic, publicly priced toll roads or petrol are complements to private motor-car traffic. The demand for regulated airline tickets is complementary to the demand for hotel services, as often there is a joint demand for both.

2.3.2. Accommodation to the rationed labor markets

(a) Public pricing in a situation of general underemployment

Most European governments' utterances on the recent situation of public enterprises rank employment problems first. What is the role of public pricing in such a situation? In which way should public pricing cheapen labor-intensive goods, accepting the resulting welfare losses, as compared with first-best pricing? We have already mentioned that rate of return regulation for welfare maximizing public enterprises implies such a result. But, as such a policy starts from an exogenously given rate of return, the problem at issue here is dealt with there only implicitly.

Therefore, we must explicitly consider employment as an instrument variable. Does this imply that we have to give up our microeconomic approach to public pricing? This is by no means the case. We assume the public sector to be large enough so as to warrant considering as an instrument a macro-variable, namely total employment L.

For a realistic model of the recent economic situation, however, we should give up the assumption of the usual equilibria in the labor and private commodity markets and instead deal with equilibria under rationing [Malinvaud (1977)].

Following Drèze (1984) we assume the supply of labor of any consumer to be constrained as follows:[36]

$$x_0^h \geqq \bar{x}_0^h(L), \qquad h = 1, \ldots, H, \quad \sum_h \bar{x}_0^h = L, \tag{2.62}$$

where $L < 0$ is total labor demand by private and public firms. $\bar{x}_0^h(L)$ is an exogenously given rationing function that may even set consumer's labor supply equal to zero. In the following we always assume this constraint to be binding. The excess supply of labor is assumed to result from fixed prices of privately supplied goods, and a fixed wage rate,[37] respectively. Excess supply on commodity markets may lead to prices in the private sector which exceed marginal costs ($p_i \geqq c_i^j$, $i \notin E$).

(b) A microeconomic model with macro-features

Let us consider our usual Boiteux model for the case of constrained labor supply. Because of the rationing function (2.62), individual demand for all goods, and individual utilities, depend on L, as does the private supply of any good. Moreover, we explicitly consider the rationed labor-market equilibrium

$$L = z_0 + \sum_j y_0^j(p, L). \tag{2.63}$$

The board chooses optimal public prices p_e, optimal input and output quantities z_i (including public labor input z_0 and all netputs z_e), optimal lump-sum transfers r^h and optimal total employment L. Private and public sector supply are assumed to be disjoint sets of consumption goods. The board considers the usual constraints, taking into account the rationing of labor. Hence, it has to solve the following problem:

$$\max_{p_e, r^h, z_i, L} \mathscr{L} = W(v^h(p, r^h, L)) - \alpha_0\left[L - z_0 - \sum_j y_0^j(p, L)\right]$$
$$- \sum_{i=1}^{n} \alpha_i \left[\sum_h x_i^h(p, r^h, L) - z_i - \sum_j y_i^j(p, L)\right]$$
$$- \beta g(z) - \bar{\gamma}\left[\Pi(\cdot) - \sum_{i=0}^{n} p_i z_i\right]. \tag{2.64}$$

[36] For the following inequality remember $x_0^h < 0$.
[37] Which in our model is achieved by choosing labor as numeraire ($p_0 = 1$).

Applying the usual derivations and transformations leads to the following structure of public pricing:[38]

$$\sum_{i=1}^{n} (\tilde{C}_i - p_i) \frac{\partial \hat{z}_i}{\partial p_e} = \gamma z_e + (1-\gamma) \frac{\partial \hat{L}}{\partial p_e}$$

$$- (1-\gamma) \sum_{i=0}^{n} \sum_{j} (c_i^j - p_i) \frac{\partial y_i^j}{\partial p_e}, \qquad e \in E, \tag{2.65}$$

where the compensated sensitivity of total employment with respect to price changes is defined as follows:

$$-p_0 \frac{\partial \hat{L}}{\partial p_e} := \sum_{i=1}^{n} p_i \frac{\partial \hat{x}_i}{\partial p_e}, \qquad e \in E. \tag{2.66}$$

Equation (2.65) is identical to equation (2.55), except for the term $(1-\gamma)(\partial \hat{L}/\partial p_e)$.

This result reflects the accommodation of public pricing to disequilibria in the private commodity markets (utmost right term) *and* the influence of employment policy on public sector pricing:[39] a tendency to cheapen good e results if increasing p_e decreases total employment $(\partial \hat{L}/\partial p_e > 0)$ and vice versa. This tendency is the more pronounced, the more sensitively employment reacts to changes of p_e. Usually labor-intensively produced goods will be characterized by such a high sensitivity. Hence, as we expected, labor-intensive goods will be sold at cheaper prices.

The above effects depend, moreover, on the public profit allowed $[(1-\gamma)!]$. The lower this profit, the more relevant becomes the influence of employment policy on the pricing structure. This implies an interesting rule of thumb for considering employment factors in public sector pricing: If a public or regulated enterprise comes near to monopolistic pricing, there is almost no case for taking into account employment effects in pricing decisions. It is only the public deficit or cost covering enterprises that should be obliged to do so.

2.4. *Time dependent pricing*

2.4.1. *Pricing through time, adjustment clauses*

The rapid inflation of the Seventies has increased the interest in pricing rules through time. The more rapidly input prices increase, the more quickly must

[38] We neglect the term $\gamma(\partial \Pi/\partial z_0)\Sigma_j(\partial y_0^j/\partial p_e)$, because it is equal to zero for the empirically relevant cases of a fixed revenue–cost constraint and for a rate of return regulation.

[39] The reader may explicitly solve (2.65) for a particular price p_e as we have done in (2.56). Then the following economic interpretation follows immediately.

output prices be adjusted, the more important are profit losses because of regulatory lags. This challenge of the Seventies has brought about theoretical as well as practical responses.

The *theoretical response* consists in the dynamic analysis of public pricing: what is the ideal path of prices through time which optimizes an appropriately defined integral over the welfare function at the different points of time, given some relevant constraints. Using discrete or continuous control theory, such an ideal path of prices $p_e(t)$, t being the index of time, can be found. A nice and easy example for such an analysis is given by Crew and Kleindorfer (1979, ch. 7).

The basic idea of such a theory is the instantaneous optimal adjustment of prices over the whole horizon. This constitutes the difference between these dynamic models and a static analysis, applying the Boiteux model period by period. This theoretical difference has a characteristic institutional counterpart. A static analysis is the correct theory to describe the common system of fixing public prices by discretionary actions, by rate hearings. A dynamic theory describes an ideal adjustment path. Hence this dynamic theory of public pricing can be regarded as the basis of automatic adjustment clauses.

Sophisticated adjustment clauses are of stochastic nature: neither government nor the board of the public sector know whether some or all input prices will change at time t; there is uncertainty about future factor prices. The problems which arise from this uncertainty have been investigated explicitly for fuel adjustment clauses that provide for automatic adjustment in output prices in response to changes in the factor prices of fuel and gas, but not in response to other factor prices. Assume a technology where the fuel and capital inputs can be substituted ex ante, but where their ratio is fixed ex post. The fuel price development is uncertain at the time of the fuel–capital ratio is chosen. Then a fuel adjustment clause implies a risk sharing between firm and regulator [Baron and DeBondt (1981)]. The fuel adjustment clause can lead the firm to an inefficient fuel–capital ratio. Moreover, the incentives for the choice of the least-cost fuel supply can be dampened. These problems are relevant primarily in cases of decreasing returns to scale. Both problems can be mitigated by extending the "collection lag" if the firm is not permitted to collect the adjusted price until after some time [Baron and DeBondt (1979)].

The *practical response* has consisted in actually applied or proposed adjustment clauses for different electricity utilities and Bell telephone companies. They are either fuel adjustment clauses, or general factor-price adjustment clauses, permitting the firm to adjust automatically to increases in all factor prices. The first type of adjustment clauses weakens the incentives for efficient choice of inputs, whereas the latter avoids this bias. However, both types weaken the incentives for the regulated firm to increase its productivity. Hence, some proposals permit automatic output price increases only as far as the weighted input price increases exceed a rate of increase of productivity [Kendrick (1975), Sudit (1979)]. The price increase of any input is weighted by the respective share of that input in total costs. Productivity is measured either by man-hour per output (Kendrick) or by a Divisia index of total factor productivity change[40] (Sudit). To avoid controversies between firm and regulator over the accuracy and reliability of actual company specific data, Sudit proposes to base the adjustment clause on market reference input prices and industry productivity trends.

In a multiproduct enterprise, moreover, the *many* adjustment paths of the different prices have to be compatible with the *overall* productivity incentives of the firm. Sudit therefore suggests (i) individual price changes which are determined by minimizing a quadratic loss function, postulating automatically adjusted price increases to be as close as possible to certain desirable levels of price changes, as defined by the regulator, *and* (ii) an overall adjustment formula which restricts the weighted sum of individual price changes to the weighted sums of input price changes minus factor productivity changes, the weights being the respective revenue and cost shares.

Pros and cons of the practical application of adjustment clauses have intensively been discussed recently. Proponents argue that damages to firms from regulatory lags are decreased and competitiveness between regulated and non-regulated industries is restored. Opponents, on the other hand, stress the implied abandonment of regulatory control, the resulting inefficiencies, the reduction of built-in stabilizing effects of regulatory lags and the possible manipulations by utilities. They argue that problems like profit squeeze of regulated firms could equally well be diminished by granting them interim relief.

2.4.2. Peak load pricing

(a) Setting the problem

Consider goods the *demand* for which fluctuates cyclically over time, both daily and seasonally. Electricity or gas demand peaks in the morning, at noon and in the evening, and is highest in winter times. Local bus and underground services are used most intensively between 7 to 9 a.m. and 4 to 7 p.m. Air and railway traffic have a holiday demand peak; telecommunication a business demand peak. In all these cases it is impossible to use off-peak production to serve peak demand as the produced goods are not storable, at least not at reasonable costs.

The *supply* side of such goods also has certain particularities. Production is typically characterized by high fixed costs and low variable costs; there exist

[40] This is the difference between the sum of the percentage changes in physical outputs weighted by their respective shares in total revenue and the sum of the percentage changes in physical inputs weighted by their respective share in total costs [Sudit (1979, p. 60)].

many cases of increasing returns to scale. In other words, the characteristics of "natural monopolies" are often present: enterprises producing those goods could keep others out of the market by their pricing policy and still make profits. For all these reasons they are typically either nationalized or regulated public utilities.

In practice such public utilities are usually required to serve all demand, however high it may be. (There are some theoretical arguments to justify this requirement.) A public utility which charges only one price for its good will therefore face a trade-off between capacity costs and price. Profit maximizing as well as welfare maximizing monopolies have developed price differentiation to cope with this trade-off.

The *simplest rule of thumb* in our peak load case adapts the distinction between operating and capacity costs: only consumers who are responsible for the capacity costs should pay for them. Hence peak demand has to pay operating plus capacity costs whereas off-peak demand is priced at the low operating costs only. This should increase the off-peak demand, lead to a more uniform utilization of capacity and increase welfare, including welfare gains by not driving people out of the market.

The welfare optimality of this rule of thumb has been shown by Steiner (1957) and Williamson (1966), albeit under very restrictive assumptions: there are at least two periods of fixed length, each being characterized by a given demand function $x_e(p_e)$. For a given price demand within any period is assumed to be constant ("time independent demand"). The chosen cost function is of the simplest possible type, namely a fixed proportions technology, leading to constant operating costs and constant capacity costs.

But already at this earliest stage an interesting counterexample could be found in the literature. Assume that peak and off-peak demand do not differ too much and that capacity costs are very high. At a single price there may be an undesired peak/off-peak structure of demand. The public utility introduces peak load pricing and follows the above mentioned rule of thumb. The off-peak price falls drastically because the capacity costs are assumed to be very high. The peak price increases drastically. This may imply a *shifting peak* where the former off-peak demand becomes the new peak demand and vice versa. An empirical example is the German "Moonlight-tariff" for phoning after 10 p.m. It was abolished in 1981 because it lead to an intensive demand peak between 10 and 11 p.m. Under the restrictive assumptions on cost functions mentioned above, welfare optimal pricing requires a price discrimination which equalizes peak and off-peak demand. Off-peak demand has to pay a share of capacity costs.

The plausibility of the above mentioned rules should not prevent us from recognizing that their validity rests on their very restrictive assumptions. They do not remain valid if we work with the usual neoclassical cost functions [Panzar (1975)], or allow for time dependent demand.

Therefore a more general model of the peak load problem is needed. A priori we could think of applying the usual Boiteux model of public pricing. Classify, e.g., electricity demand into so many periods (= goods) so as to make sure that demand is time independent within each period. Then the Boiteux model can be directly applied. We obtain peak load, marginal cost pricing rules; peak load, Ramsey pricing rules, etc. The peak load problem turns out to be a special case of joint production and by always considering the optimal input choice we can find an optimal mix between operating and capacity costs.

If there are too many periods that must be distinguished, some empirical problems might arise, but the above mentioned way seems at least to be a straightforward theoretical solution of the peak load problem [Bös (1981, pp. 31–33)]. This position is, however, a little superficial. If it were totally correct, one could not understand the immense interest in the peak load problem in the last five to ten years [as surveyed in Crew and Kleindorfer (1979), Mitchell, Manning and Acton (1977), and Turvey and Anderson (1977), to mention only a few outstanding recent books].

What, then, is the reason for developing a special theory of peak load pricing? It is the following peak load trilemma:

- First, government does not want too many different prices because this leads to high information costs, administrative costs or uncertainty for consumers.[41] Hence the chosen periods are too long to neglect that demand does not depend on prices alone, but fluctuates within the periods as well, either stochastically,[42] or deterministically depending on an index of time ("time dependent demand").
- Second, government wants to avoid high peak prices, mostly because of distributional arguments. High peak prices for local transport may hit the lower-income working population most and not the better-off car owner.
- Third, government wants to serve all demand as reliability is an important quality characteristic of public supply.

The direct application of the Boiteux model does not come to grips with time dependent demand. It copes with points two and three above. Hence we have to extend our usual Boiteux approach to the case of time dependent demand. Moreover, recent peak load theory gives up condition three of the trilemma and accepts excess demand and rationing, arguing that it may be welfare optimal to accept excess demand instead of spending too much money for public utilities' capacity costs or applying too high peak prices.

[41] With microprocessing, the technical possibilities of adequate metering would allow for many more periods than previously the case.

[42] Electricity demand, for instance, depends heavily on weather.

(b) A model with excess demand and rationing

We treat the peak load problem in a particular version of the Boiteux model. The public sector consists of one firm producing one good, say electricity. The market demand for this good is different in different periods of the day. These periods are labelled $e \in E$. The number of periods and their respective length, $L(e)$, are exogenously fixed. The board uses the instruments p_e and z_i to maximize welfare under some relevant constraints.

What we want to show is the trade-off between rationing by price and rationing by quantity. This trade-off would be distorted if the board were allowed to apply lump-sum transfers $\{r^h\}$ or $\{r_e^h\}$, as such transfers would introduce a further means of rationing: rationing by redistribution, shifting purchasing power from peak demand to off-peak. Despite this exclusion of lump-sum transfers we want to concentrate on allocation. Hence the board is assumed to evaluate the individual marginal utilities of income in such a way that in the optimum the social marginal utility of individual incomes is constant. Needless to say our model could be extended to include further controlled prices, lump-sum redistribution or different types of social marginal utilities of individual incomes. These refinements would add additional complicated terms to the basic price structure on which we want to concentrate in this subsection.

To deal with the peak problem we define all demand and supply quantities x_e and z_e per unit of time in a period (say, the demand in one second). This way of definition enables us to come to grips with fluctuations of demand within a given period $e \in E$. Quantities of all other goods $i \notin E$ are defined as usual.

The *quantity demanded per unit of time*, x_e, depends on the period price and on time in an additively separable way[43] [Dansby (1975)]

$$x_e(p_e, t_e) = x_e(p_e) + \tau(t_e), \qquad e \in E. \tag{2.67}$$

The demand depends on the price p_e which is the same for all units of time (moments) of period e. It does not depend on prices in other periods: no cross-price elasticities enter our formulae.[44] On the other hand, demand is allowed to fluctuate within the period, depending on t_e, the index of units of time (moments) of period e, $t_e \in e$. The price sensitivity of demand is invariant with respect to time and the time sensitivity is invariant with respect to the period price.

[43] The derivations of our model can analogously be applied to the case of stochastic demand $x_e = x_e(p_e, u)$, where u is a random variable. Our specification corresponds to the additive stochastic demand function $x_e = x_e(p_e) + u$. For further discussion of these problems, see Brown and Johnson (1969), Visscher (1973), and Carlton (1977).

[44] They can be easily introduced into our derivations. However, the interpretation of the resulting price structure (2.79) becomes far more complicated. Hence we follow the usual tradition of the stochastic pricing literature and suppress them.

The minimal demand in any period is denoted as

$$x_e^m(p_e) = \min_{t_e} x_e(p_e, t_e) = x_e(p_e) + \min_{t_e} \tau(t_e), \qquad e \in E, \tag{2.68}$$

which may be given at one, or more than one, moment of time in the interval t_e.

The *quantity supplied per unit of time*, z_e, is assumed to be time independent. It is constant within a period, but may differ between the periods. Typically, we expect to deal with cases of $z_e \geqq 0$. A change of z_e influences the production possibilities $g(z)$ in every single moment of period e. Hence our usual definition of marginal costs refers to costs per unit of time:

$$\tilde{C}_e = \gamma \frac{\partial \Pi}{\partial z_e} + \frac{\partial g / \partial z_e}{\partial g / \partial z_0} > 0, \qquad e \in E. \tag{2.69}$$

With respect to the other quantities z_i, $i \notin E$, all our conventions hold, be it the convention of denoting $z_0 < 0$ as public labor input or the usual definition of marginal costs $\tilde{C}_i$.

The market may be *in equilibrium or in disequilibrium*. Therefore, at any point of time the public sector will sell the following quantity:

$$S(e, t_e) = \min\{x_e(p_e, t_e), z_e\}, \qquad e \in E, \tag{2.70}$$

whence its revenue–cost constraint is

$$\sum_{e \in E} \int_{t_e \in e} p_e S(e, t)\, \mathrm{d}t + \sum_{i \notin E} p_i z_i = \Pi. \tag{2.71}$$

Let us define:

$$E(e, t_e) := E((p_e, z_e), t_e) = \max(x_e(p_e, t_e) - z_e, 0), \qquad e \in E. \tag{2.72}$$

We denote ψ_e as the set of all moments of period e where excess demand exists $(E > 0)$ and ψ_e^c as its complement $(E = 0)$.

If excess demand exists, the consumers must be rationed. The usual peak load literature deals with different *theoretical* alternatives to rationing: consumers are either excluded randomly or with respect to their willingness to pay, usually measured by the individual consumer surplus or by the compensating variation. In the latter case rationing may exclude people in order of lowest or highest willingness to pay until capacity is exhausted.

These are theoretical solutions of the rationing problem and can be handled nicely in the peak load calculus. Practical rationing, for instance of telephone

The minimal demand in any period is denoted as

$$x_e^m(p_e) = \min_{t_e} x_e(p_e, t_e) = x_e(p_e) + \min_{t_e} \tau(t_e), \qquad e \in E, \tag{2.68}$$

which may be given at one, or more than one, moment of time in the interval t_e.

The *quantity supplied per unit of time*, z_e, is assumed to be time independent. It is constant within a period, but may differ between the periods. Typically, we expect to deal with cases of $z_e \geqq 0$. A change of z_e influences the production possibilities $g(z)$ in every single moment of period e. Hence our usual definition of marginal costs refers to costs per unit of time:

$$\tilde{C}_e = \gamma \frac{\partial \Pi}{\partial z_e} + \frac{\partial g/\partial z_e}{\partial g/\partial z_0} > 0, \qquad e \in E. \tag{2.69}$$

With respect to the other quantities z_i, $i \notin E$, all our conventions hold, be it the convention of denoting $z_0 < 0$ as public labor input or the usual definition of marginal costs $\tilde{C}_i$.

The market may be *in equilibrium or in disequilibrium*. Therefore, at any point of time the public sector will sell the following quantity:

$$S(e, t_e) = \min\{x_e(p_e, t_e), z_e\}, \qquad e \in E, \tag{2.70}$$

whence its revenue–cost constraint is

$$\sum_{e \in E} \int_{t_e \in e} p_e S(e, t)\, \mathrm{d}t + \sum_{i \notin E} p_i z_i = \Pi. \tag{2.71}$$

Let us define:

$$E(e, t_e) := E((p_e, z_e), t_e) = \max(x_e(p_e, t_e) - z_e, 0), \qquad e \in E. \tag{2.72}$$

We denote ψ_e as the set of all moments of period e where excess demand exists ($E > 0$) and ψ_e^c as its complement ($E = 0$).

If excess demand exists, the consumers must be rationed. The usual peak load literature deals with different *theoretical* alternatives to rationing: consumers are either excluded randomly or with respect to their willingness to pay, usually measured by the individual consumer surplus or by the compensating variation. In the latter case rationing may exclude people in order of lowest or highest willingness to pay until capacity is exhausted.

These are theoretical solutions of the rationing problem and can be handled nicely in the peak load calculus. Practical rationing, for instance of telephone calls, etc., follows other criteria. Hence I will not follow one of these concepts, but use a more general concept to formulate the welfare losses of rationing.

We start from a *social welfare function per unit of time* $W(p, t_e)$, depending on both controlled and uncontrolled prices. According to the usual definition, this [illegible]

$$[illegible]$$

[illegible] $\Gamma(E(e,t_e)) \cdot W(p,t_e)$ where $\Gamma(E)$ can take values between 0 and 1. This is a fairly general formulation of welfare losses from rationing. The function $\Gamma(E)$ may represent individual consumers' actually accrueing welfare losses as well as the board's evaluation of such losses. By normalization $\Gamma(E)=1$ if there is no excess demand. But the board may decide to set $\Gamma(E)=1$ even if $E>0$, thus totally ignoring welfare losses from rationing. On the other hand, the board may decide to value welfare losses from rationing [illegible] more than the individual consumer losses; in the limiting case assuming $\Gamma(E)=0$ as soon as $E>0$. Usually, the board will follow some middle course, in particular it may follow the actual individual losses.[45]

Aggregating over all moments of time and over all periods we obtain the board's total welfare measure

$$\tilde{W}(p,z)=\sum_{e\in E}\int_{t_e\in e}\Gamma(E(e,t))\cdot W(p,t)\,\mathrm{d}t. \tag{2.73}$$

The larger the extent of rationing, the lower the *reliability of supply*. The welfare optimal choice of output may well imply that during some periods there is no equilibrium moment at all. But people would not be willing to accept a telecommunication system which is rationed all day long and unrationed between 0 and 5 a.m. only. As a matter of fact, very low reliability of electricity [illegible] supplies in single periods is unwanted and usually leads to adverse reactions from customers. The quality structure of public utilities' supply obviously includes political facets. Government will be afraid of losing votes, of campaigns because of electricity blackouts, etc. Hence it requests the enterprise's board explicitly to consider reliability constraints as follows:[46]

$$z_e - x_e^m(p_e) \geqq 0,^{47} \qquad e \in E. \tag{2.74}$$

For all other goods $i \notin E$ the market equilibria are assumed to hold as usual [illegible]

[45] Some particular cases of rationing cannot be directly expressed by $\Gamma(E)$ if the planning board takes the actual individual losses as a measure of the socially relevant welfare losses. Random rationing, for instance, can only be expressed by a function $\Gamma(E,x)=(1-E/x)$. The extension of our derivations to such a case is straightforward, albeit a little tedious.

[46] As these constraints will reduce the extent of rationing, they can be thought of as a surrogate for explicitly regarding administrative rationing costs [Crew and Kleindorfer (1979, p. 91)].

[47] In stochastic models of peak load pricing such constraints have been dealt with since Meyer (1975) by saying that the probability of excess demand at any moment e must not exceed a level ε_e.

What is the economic meaning of those marginal conditions? First they reveal that it is *welfare optimal to have excess demand* as soon as there are any fluctuations of demand during a period e. (This shows that the very usual assumption of time independent demand in each and every period is crucial.)

This can be proved as follows. We start from the weakest possible condition for fluctuating demand: there exists at least one moment t_0 where $x_e(p_e, t_0) > x_e^m(p_e)$. Now *assume* that at the optimum there is no moment of excess demand ($\psi_e = \emptyset$), which for any moment e implies $z_e - x_e(p_e, t_e) \geqq 0$, $\forall t_e \in e$. This is also valid for moment "0": $z_e - x_e(p_e, t_0) \geqq 0$, and because of $x_e(p_e, t_0) > x_e^m(p_e)$ this implies $z_e - x_e^m(p_e) > z_e - x_e(p_e, t_0) \geqq 0$. But this inequality implies $\bar{\alpha}_e = 0$. Considering equation (2.77) for this case of $\psi_e = \emptyset$ and of $\bar{\alpha}_e = 0$, we obtain $\tilde{C}_e = 0$, which contradicts our assumption $\tilde{C}_e > 0$. Therefore there must exist excess demand at the welfare optimum.

We now examine the *pricing implications* of peak load effects. Inserting (2.77) into (2.76) leads, after some easy steps, to the pricing rule

$$(\tilde{C}_e - p_e)\frac{\partial x_e}{\partial p_e}L(e) + \sum_{i \notin E}(\tilde{C}_i - p_i)\frac{\partial z_i^D}{\partial p_e}$$
$$= \int_{t_e}\left[\gamma S(e,t) - \frac{\Gamma(E)}{\beta_0}x_e\right]\mathrm{d}t - (1-\gamma)\left[p_e\frac{\partial x_e}{\partial p_e}L(e) + \sum_{i \notin E}p_i\frac{\partial z_i^D}{\partial p_e}\right], \quad e \in E. \tag{2.79}$$

The particular properties of peak load pricing can be seen more easily if we follow the usual peak load literature and suppress the relations to other public outputs or inputs. Our interpretation therefore focuses on the price structure

$$(\tilde{C}_e - p_e)\frac{\partial x_e}{\partial p_e}L(e) = \int_{t_e}\left[\gamma S(e,t) - \frac{\Gamma(E)}{\beta_0}x_e\right]\mathrm{d}t - (1-\gamma)p_e\frac{\partial x_e}{\partial p_e}L(e), \quad e \in E. \tag{2.80}$$

The main economic meaning of this formula will be indicated for the limiting case $\gamma = 1$. (It is left to the reader to consider further limiting cases.) If in such a case the board is as sensitive as to set $\Gamma(E) = 0$ if $E > 0$,[48a] the pricing rule reduces to

$$(\tilde{C}_e - p_e)\frac{\partial x_e}{\partial p_e} = \frac{L(\Psi_e)}{L(e)}z_e + \frac{\beta_0 - 1}{\beta_0}\frac{L(\Psi_e^c)}{L(e)}\bar{x}_e^c, \quad e \in E, \tag{2.81}$$

[48a] Differentiability, in that case, can be achieved by replacing the discontinuous function $\Gamma(E)$ by a sequence Γ_k of differentiable functions converging to $\Gamma(E)$. Under the assumption that the sequence of prices and quantities is convergent, the limit system of prices and quantities can be characterized by (2.81).

where $\bar{x}_e^c$ is the average demand per unit of time in period Ψ_e^c. The right-hand side of (2.81) is a weighted average of $S(e, t_e)$. A profit-maximizing monopolist who faces the reliability constraints follows similar conditions, but uses the arithmetic mean of $S(e, t_e)$. For $\beta_0 \to \infty$ therefore welfare maximization and profit maximization lead to the same result. Hence, for large β_0 the board concentrates on rationing by high prices, reducing the extent of rationing by quantity.

If, on the other hand, the board is totally insensitive with respect to rationing $[\Gamma(E) = 1$ if $E > 0]$, the pricing formula becomes

$$(\tilde{C}_e - p_e)\frac{\partial x_e}{\partial p_e} = \frac{L(\Psi_e)}{L(e)}(z_e - \bar{x}_e/\beta_0) + \frac{\beta_0 - 1}{\beta_0}\frac{L(\Psi_e^c)}{L(e)}\bar{x}_e^c$$

$$= \frac{\beta_0 - 1}{\beta_0}\bar{x}_e^{\text{act}} - \bar{E}(e), \quad e \in E, \tag{2.82}$$

where $\bar{x}_e^{\text{act}}$ is actual demand per unit of time, $\bar{x}_e^{\text{act}} = \int_{t_e} x_e(t)\,\mathrm{d}t/L(e)$; $\bar{E}(e)$ is average excess demand per unit of time, $\bar{E}(e) = \int_{t_e} E(e, t)\,\mathrm{d}t/L(e)$. For small β_0 ($\beta_0 < 1$) prices fall below marginal costs. We obtain low prices: the board concentrates on rationing by quantity, reducing the extent of rationing by prices. Prices above marginal costs are obtained if $\beta_0 > 1$ and if the excess demand is not too large.

One central question remains: will peak prices exceed off-peak prices in our model? There is no general answer to this question, but we can show the conditions for such a result to occur.

Consider two periods only, e(peak) and e(off-peak), and assume the following relations to hold:

$$z_e(\text{peak}) \geqq x_e^m(\text{peak}) > z_e(\text{off-peak}) \geqq x_e^m(\text{off-peak}). \tag{2.83}$$

Now consider the right-hand side of our pricing rule (2.80). z_e increases if we switch from off-peak to peak. This means a *tendency* for the difference quotient,

$$\Delta\left\{\int_{t_e}\left[\gamma S(e, t) - \frac{\Gamma(E)}{\beta_0}x_e\right]\mathrm{d}t - (1-\gamma)p_e\frac{\partial x_e}{\partial p_e}L(e)\right\}\Big/\Delta x_e^m, \tag{2.84}$$

to be positive. And there always exist values of γ that are large enough and of $\Gamma(E)$ that are small enough to ensure that this tendency becomes effective for the whole difference quotient (2.84). But then the following must also hold:

$$\Delta\left\{(\tilde{C}_e - p_e)\frac{\partial x_e}{\partial p_e}L(e)\right\}\Big/\Delta x_e^m > 0. \tag{2.85}$$

This implies a higher price, marginal cost difference in the peak period *if* the price sensitivity of demand $\partial x_e/\partial p_e$ is unchanged in spite of the change from off-peak to peak or does not change too sharply. And if, additionally, marginal peak costs exceed marginal off-peak costs, higher peak prices are obtained.

The following conditions are sufficient for higher peak than off-peak prices:

- Government fixes a sufficiently high budget requirement.
- The enterprise's board is sufficiently sensitive to excess demand and rationing.
- The price sensitivity of peak demand does not differ too much from that of off-peak demand.
- Marginal peak costs do not fall below marginal off-peak costs.

This result shows clearly the crucial importance of the particular assumptions of those older theories on peak load pricing that *always* obtained higher peak than off-peak prices.

Let us deal briefly with one special case of particular interest that has for a long time dominated the literature in the field: the case of *time independent demand* $x_e(p_e)$. In this case supply always equals demand. The proof is simple. We have postulated reliability constraints $[z_e \geqq x_e^m(p_e)]$. But time independence implies $x_e^m(p_e) = x_e(p_e)$ and therefore $z_e \geqq x_e(p_e)$. But then $\psi_e = \emptyset$ and no excess demand occurs. Moreover, if $z_e > x_e$, then $\bar{\alpha}_e = 0$ and equation (2.77) reduces to $\tilde{C}_e = 0$ which contradicts our assumption $\tilde{C}_e > 0$. Therefore, $z_e = x_e(p_e)$ is the only feasible solution. Supply always exactly meets demand.

3. Public pricing policies to achieve politicians' and managers' aims

3.1. *Theoretical foundation*

The theory and application of welfare optimal public pricing have been criticized because of the normative character of the welfare function W, because of the excessive information requirements, and because of the implied lack of incentives for efficiency.

It is often urged that the Bergsonian welfare function be abandoned because it is a purely normative concept and that public pricing theory be based on the actual objectives of the relevant economic agents. For example, politicians may be interested in winning votes, bureaucrats in maximizing their budgets. Managers of public enterprises may try to maximize output or revenue instead of welfare. Labor unions may try to induce public enterprises to follow a policy that increases as far as possible labor inputs or wages.

If we postulate such possible actual objectives, the information requirements will be lower than those of the normative approach as there is no need to go back to the social valuation of individual utilities.

Moreover, we can also ignore lump-sum transfers which, if they were actually made, would raise insurmountable difficulties of getting data. In contrast, if revenue or output is maximized, or if a Laspeyres price index is minimized (given some revenue–cost constraint), the required data are readily available. This implies that it is possible to ascertain whether the above mentioned objectives of, e.g., politicians and managers have been achieved. In contrast, "maximal welfare" is an abstract concept. Enterprises' boards might find it both unattractive and unfeasible to follow such an abstract guideline. In pleading managerial success the board would prefer to be able to rely on some high output or revenue figures of the preceding year, or the number of employees in public production. A management which only pleads that it worked for the public welfare might give the impression of being less dynamic and of using "welfare" as an excuse behind which to hide its poor economic performance.

For all these reasons boards in practice will tend to apply the objectives usually postulated in the economics of political choice and in managerial economics. This section deals with the theoretical analysis of public pricing under such objectives. It should be stressed that there are many similarities between our present approach and that of welfare maximization. Although the objectives differ and we exclude lump-sum transfers, the remaining environment can be treated in the same way as in the Boiteux model (Section 2.1 above). There is an economy with H utility maximizing consumers, J private enterprises and a public sector. A board once again chooses prices $\{p_e\}$ and production plans $\{z_i\}$, given the production technology, market clearing constraints and a revenue–cost constraint. Many objectives of political and managerial economics require explicit differentiation between inputs and outputs. Hence we have to include such differentiation in our model. $z_i \leqq 0$, $i = 0, \ldots, m$, denote public inputs and $z_i \geqq 0$, $i = m+1, \ldots, n$, denote public outputs.

Using $\Phi(p, z)$ as a general notation for an objective function, we impute to the enterprise's board an optimization approach characterized by the following Lagrangian:

$$\max_{p_e, z_i} \mathscr{L} = \Phi(p, z) + \sum_{i=0}^{n} \alpha_i \left[\sum_h x_i^h(p, r^h) - z_i - \sum_j y_i^j(p) \right] - \beta g(z) - \gamma\left(\Pi(\cdot) - \sum p_i z_i\right). \tag{3.1}$$

Differentiating $\mathscr{L}$ with respect to prices and quantities leads to a system of necessary conditions for an optimum. These marginal conditions can be transformed in the usual Boiteux way. To get to the very bottom of the particular economic consequences of optimizing the different objectives $\Phi(p, z)$, we neglect all interdependencies between the public and private sector: (i) Only prices of publicly supplied goods are controlled.[49] These goods are neither supplied nor demanded by private firms. (ii) All uncontrolled prices equal marginal costs in any firm, including the public sector. Needless to say these restrictions can be given up easily, extending all relevant marginal conditions by particular terms on the accommodation of public pricing to private pricing (to be interpreted similarly to Section 2.3.1 above).

Given the above assumptions (i) and (ii) we obtain

$$\sum_{i \in E} \left[\tilde{C}_i - p_i - \frac{1}{\beta_0} \frac{\partial \Phi}{\partial z_i} \right] \frac{\partial z_i^D}{\partial p_e} = z_e + \frac{1}{\beta_0} \cdot \frac{\partial \Phi}{\partial p_e}, \qquad e \in E, \tag{3.2}$$

where $\beta_0 = \beta(\partial g / \partial z_0)$. This structure of public pricing will be the basis of our following analyses. For this purpose we will always define the chosen objective function $\Phi(p, z)$ in such a way that $\beta_0 > 0$. γ which enters (3.2) as part of $\tilde{C}_i$ will be positive if the objectives are defined as above and if the prescribed profit exceeds the unconstrained, Φ optimizing profit. $\gamma < 1$ can be deduced as usual as long as the objective function does not depend directly on labor inputs.

3.2. *Politicians and bureaucrats*

3.2.1. *Winning votes*

Pricing of public utilities tends to be one of the major determinants of the political climate in local communities. Local politicians try to postpone until after the next election any price increases for local public transportation, for gas and electricity. Moreover, the popularity of any local politician seems to be at stake if local public utilities work inefficiently or if price increases are in the offing.

Consider a politician who chooses public prices so as to maximize votes. We expect such a policy to favor the interests of lower-income groups as in any economy the incomes of more than 50% of the population fall short of the average income. However, there are different ways of favoring lower-income consumers by public pricing. Examples range from cheaper railway or local bus fares for retired people, school children and students, to lower basic rates for the telephones of

[49] We always implicitly assume that politicians use sufficiently many instruments as to avoid degeneration of the optimization approach because of a lack of degrees of freedom.

lower-income people; from different first- and second-class railway fares or hospital fees to lower school fees for lower-income people.

Which kind of price differentiation should such a politician pursue? There are at least the following three possibilities:

- Direct differentiation between *lower-income* and *higher-income* people (e.g., if the recipient has to prove that his income falls below a particular threshold value in order to be eligible to pay a lower price).
- Differentiation between different *classes* or *groups* of people who differ statistically with respect to their income although not in every case (e.g., retired and non-retired, students and non-students, etc.).
- Differentiation between *goods* which statistically are demanded more by lower-income than by higher-income people (although, again, not necessarily in every case as, e.g., with the distinctions between first- and second-class railway or hospital services).

All these different cases can be treated in a uniform framework after adequate definition of outputs. Consider a simple example: to deal with differentiation between social groups, we define students' demand for local traffic as x_1, the old-age pensioners' demand as x_2, other people's demand as x_3. We should note that this differentiation among groups (and goods, respectively) is one of the instruments of the politician who is in search for political support. However, after this differentiation of goods has taken place we can always find prices for them which maximize votes.

Political choice in a democratic context is only well-defined if there are at least two alternatives. Consider therefore *two price systems*, p and p^*, both market clearing, technologically feasible, and subject to the same profit constraint Π. Because of these identical constraints, vote maximization will have to consider the trade-off frontier where some prices p_i are lower than p_i^*, and some others are higher, thus excluding the trivial cases of $p \ll p^*$ or $p \gg p^*$.

Assume $\{p_e\}$ to be the instruments of a politician who wants to maximize votes and $\{p_e^*\}$ to be a given reference price system. Various institutional stories can be told to rationalize this reference price system, for example, we have at least the following two possibilities: according to one we treat public pricing in a two-party competition model, according to the other we treat it in the context of a monopoly approach of public choice. In the first, p^* would be the price system offered to the voter by the other political party.[50] In the second, p^* would be a sort of "reversion policy" that will apply if the price system p is not supported by a majority, similar to Romer and Rosenthal's (1979) agenda setter model.

[50] This implies a Cournot solution of the political duopoly. Note that we do not deal with a voting equilibrium where both parties react to each other. Only under very restrictive assumptions will such equilibria exist, e.g., under a generalized single-peakedness concept for voting decisions on multidimensional issues.

Last but not least p^* can simply mean the present system of prices. In that case we describe a referendum on public pricing or a demoscopic opinion poll.

Regardless of which of the above versions we adopt, any politician will always be interested in finding that platform p which the greatest possible number of people prefers to p^*.[51]

Voters, however, do not decide on economic criteria alone. Therefore, we assume an individual h to vote for a price system p if

$$\omega^h + s^h \geqq 0. \tag{3.3}$$

ω^h measures the "economic" component of the voter's decision, the utility gain or loss from price system p,

$$\omega^h(p, r^h) := v^h(p, r^h) - v^h(p^*, r^h). \tag{3.4}$$

s^h, on the other hand, measures the "sympathy" or "antipathy" component of his decision. Some individual might not be willing to vote for platform p which increases his utility because he "does not like" the politician who proposes price system p. On the contrary, somebody may be willing to vote for platform p which diminishes his utility because the proposal comes from "his party".

Now turn to the *vote maximizing politician*. Every "yes" counts one vote; every "no" does not count, as measured by the function $\mu(\cdot)$,

$$\begin{aligned} \mu(\omega^h + s^h) &= 1 \quad \text{if} \quad \omega^h + s^h \geqq 0, \\ &= 0 \quad \text{if} \quad \omega^h + s^h < 0. \end{aligned} \tag{3.5}$$

Every voter, of course, knows the exact values of his ω^h, and s^h, respectively. The politician, however, is only incompletely informed on the individual voters' behavior. Let us assume, he exactly knows the economic consequences of his pricing policy, as expressed by the utility differences ω^h. But he does not exactly know whether some particular person likes or dislikes him. He only knows, there is some distribution of sympathy and antipathy among the voters. The politician therefore starts from a random variable, $\tilde{s}^h$. Let him assume, without limitation of generality, $\tilde{s}^h$ is normally distributed with density function $\psi(s^h)$, expectation of zero and variance σ^2,

$$\psi(s^h) = \frac{1}{\sigma\sqrt{2\pi}} \exp\left[-\frac{1}{2}\left(\frac{s^h}{\sigma}\right)^2\right]. \tag{3.6}$$

[51]If p^* happens to be the vote maximizing price system, the politician will apply $p = p^*$. This case of indifference is excluded in the text.

For any single individual, then, the incompletely informed politician assumes sympathy $\tilde{s}^h$ to be distributed with $\psi(s^h)$.

Only knowing $\tilde{s}^h$ is a normally distributed random variable, the politician can rely upon the expectation of any single vote. Replacing $\omega^h + \tilde{s}^h =: \tilde{t}^h$, we obtain

$$\Phi_h(\omega^h) = \int_{-\infty}^{+\infty} \mu(\omega^h + s^h)\psi(s^h)\,\mathrm{d}s^h = \int_{-\infty}^{+\infty} \mu(t^h)\psi(t^h - \omega^h)\,\mathrm{d}t^h, \qquad (3.7)$$

as shown in Figure 3.1.

Figure 3.1 shows how an individual with utility difference ω^h can be expected to vote. For $\sigma^2 \to 0$ the voters would be expected to be pure homines oeconomici, deciding according to their utility difference only,

$$\begin{aligned} \Phi_h(\omega^h) = \mu(\omega^h) &= 1 \quad \text{if} \quad \omega^h \geqq 0, \\ &= 0 \quad \text{if} \quad \omega^h < 0. \end{aligned} \qquad (3.8)$$

The higher σ^2, on the other hand, the more sympathy and antipathy will count, as shown in Figure 3.1 for $\sigma = 0.2$ and $\sigma = 1$, respectively.

The objective function of the vote maximizing politician results from aggregating the expectation of votes, wherefore we obtain

$$\Phi(p) = \sum_{h=1}^{H} \Lambda(r^h)\Phi_h(\omega^h(p, r^h)), \qquad (3.9)$$

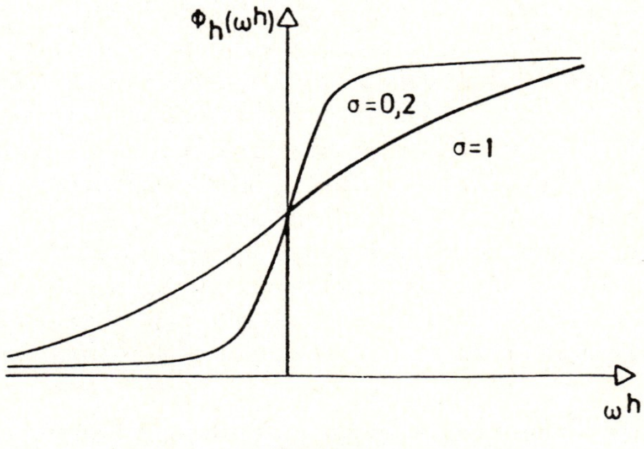

Figure 3.1

where $\Lambda(r^h)$ measures the relative frequency of the expectation ϕ_h in the population, the population being subdivided into $h=1,\ldots,H$ groups of identical people, $\sum_h \Lambda(r^h)=1$.[52]

Differentiating this objective function leads to

$$\frac{\partial \Phi}{\partial p_e}=\sum_{h=1}^{H} \Lambda(r^h)\int_{-\infty}^{+\infty} \mu(t^h)\frac{\partial}{\partial p_e}\psi(t^h-\omega^h)\,\mathrm{d}t^h.$$

Excluding all ranges where $\mu(t^h)=0$ we obtain

$$\frac{\partial \Phi}{\partial p_e}=\sum_{h=1}^{H} \Lambda(r^h)\int_{0}^{\infty} \frac{\partial}{\partial p_e}\psi(t^h-\omega^h)\,\mathrm{d}t^h$$

$$=-\sum_{h=1}^{H} \Lambda(r^h)\frac{\partial v^h}{\partial p_e}\int_{0}^{\infty} \psi'(t^h-\omega^h)\,\mathrm{d}t^h.$$

But the inner integral can easily be computed, wherefore

$$\frac{\partial \Phi}{\partial p_e}=-\sum_{h=1}^{H} \Lambda(r^h)\frac{\partial v^h}{\partial p_e}\left[\psi(t^h-\omega^h)\right]_0^{\infty}$$

$$=\sum_{h=1}^{H} \Lambda(r^h)\frac{\partial v^h}{\partial p_e}\psi(\omega^h). \qquad (3.10)$$

For voters who follow economic reasoning only, $\sigma^2=0$, the above differentiation (3.10) will degenerate. All $\omega^h \neq 0$ do not contribute to the sum. $\partial\Phi/\partial p_e \neq 0$ can therefore only occur if there happen to be people whose income r^* leads to $\omega^h(r^*)=0$. Then the whole weight of $\psi(\omega^h)$ is attached to those people whence $\partial\Phi/\partial p_e=\infty$. Hence $\partial\Phi/\partial p_e$ varies erratically between 0 and ∞, depending not only on the incomes, but also on the price vector p. For $\sigma^2=0$, it is therefore impossible to employ the usual optimization approach. Only if we assume a continuum of consumers, everything works nicely [Bös and Zimmermann (1983)]. Assuming this continuum to be an approximation to $n\to\infty$, we can treat the case of $\sigma^2=0$ as equally important as the case of $\sigma^2>0$ in the following pricing rules.

[52]Any bracket $\Lambda(r^h)$ consists of many people, which allows to concentrate on the expectation alone, ignoring the variance.

The influence of changing price p_e on the objective function, according to (3.10), depends on the individual utility sensitivities $\partial v^h/\partial p_e$ weighted by the number of people with the respective utility and the politician's attention paid to the individual utility difference, $\psi(\omega^h)$, as shown in Figure 3.2. Note that originally we introduced $\psi(s^h)$ as the density function of the individual "sympathy" variable s^h. In the course of the above differentiation we obtained $\psi(\omega^h)$ which can best be interpreted as politician's attention.

For any pair of p and p^* the politician must pay most attention to utility differences in a close neighborhood of $\omega^h = 0$. This includes the "sympathizers" with small negative ω^h and the "just converted" with small positive ω^h. The sympathy of the first group may represent the votes of tomorrow; the votes of the second can be lost easily. Both groups may be floating voters at the next election. Less attention is paid to the "political opponents" with large negative ω^h and the "permanent followers" with large positive ω^h. The sympathy of the first can be won only at disproportionate effort; the votes of the second seem almost certain.

Which price structure will a politician employ who follows the political strategy of maximizing $\Phi(p)$? As a special case of our general rule (3.2) we obtain

$$\sum_{i\in E} (\tilde{C}_i - p_i)\frac{\partial z_i^D}{\partial p_e} = (1 - D_e)z_e, \qquad e \in E, \tag{3.11}$$

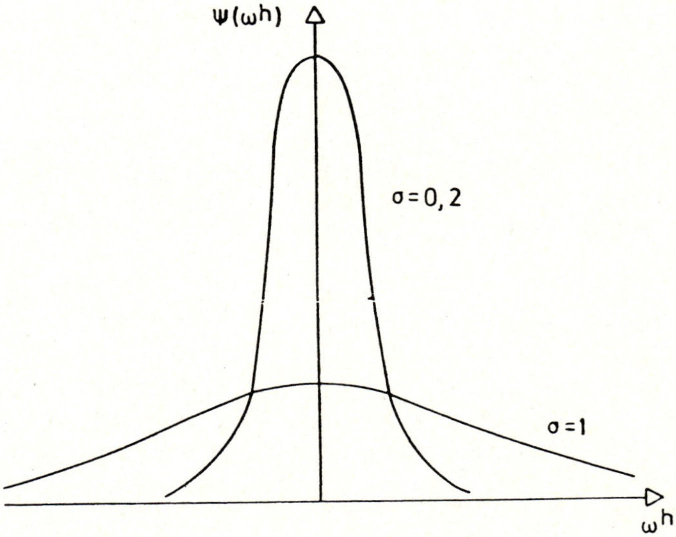

Figure 3.2

where (after inserting Roy's identity) D_e equals

$$D_e = \frac{1}{\beta_0} \sum_{h=1}^{H} \Lambda(r^h)\psi(\omega^h(p, r^h)) \frac{\partial v^h}{\partial r^h} \cdot \frac{x_e^h}{x_e}, \qquad e \in E. \tag{3.12}$$

There is a striking formal similarity between distributionally oriented pricing (2.51) and politicial pricing (3.11). Is democratic maximization of votes actually a good vehicle towards distributionally wanted results? Yes and no.

Remember first that F_e in (2.51) weighted the individual consumption shares by $\lambda^h(\partial v^h/\partial r^h)$, which is always assumed to be a decreasing function of individual incomes. Weighting by such a decreasing function can be found also in D_e. But here only the individual marginal utilities $(\partial v^h/\partial r^h)$ are of relevance, which excludes many of the typical features of distribution policy as represented by λ^h, for instance Rawlsian policy.

Can we argue that $\Lambda(\cdot)\psi$ replace the social valuation λ^h? $\Lambda(r^h)$ is an approximation to a density function of the income distribution. From empirical estimations we know that such a function increases for lower and decreases for higher incomes. Hence weighting with $\Lambda(r^h)$ will typically not imply a particular stressing of *poor* people. However, as usually there are more lower-income than higher-income people, the $\Lambda(r^h)$ values accentuate policies in favor of lower-income people.

Last but not least we have to emphasize the role of ψ. It stresses the importance of fishing for political sympathy and of being afraid of losing "uncertain" voters. In other words, it stresses the interests of floating voters. Needless to say, this criterion has nothing to do with distribution policy. Moreover, in our general model we lack specific information as to which income earners are the floating voters and which publicly priced goods are primarily bought by floating voters.

Thus, there are some plausible arguments which suggest that distributionally "desirable" results may follow from political pricing. However, no such general conclusion can be established.[53]

3.2.2. *Maximizing budgets*

Political determination of public prices must not be restricted to maximizing votes. It may be even more realistic to assume a principal–agent relationship where the majority seeking politician does not fix the prices himself, but delegates

[53] If we assume a continuum of consumers we can perform the transition $\sigma^2 \to 0$ in our results. Then D_e depends only on those individuals whose utility difference is just equal to zero. The vote maximizing politician will therefore cheapen those goods that are intensively demanded by the floating voters. No particular distributional components remain in D_e.

this function to the bureaucracy (of a ministry or of a public utility). The government becomes the "sponsor", the price fixing board becomes the "bureaucracy".

If a bureaucrat wants to maximize his influence, his prestige, his income, he can do so most successfully by maximizing the number of his subordinates, the amount of money he can decide upon, in short: by maximizing his budget [Niskanen (1971)]. However, the sponsor who has to grant the bureaucrat's budget will not appropriate any amount the bureaucrat applies for. The budget B the sponsor is willing to grant will rather depend on the output the bureau is offering,

$$B = B(z_{m+1},\dots,z_n), \qquad B_e = \frac{\partial B}{\partial z_e} > 0, \qquad \frac{\partial^2 B}{\partial z_e^2} < 0, \tag{3.13}$$

where $z_e \geqq 0$ are the outputs of the bureau. For the one-service bureau with which he deals almost exclusively, Niskanen specifies B as a quadratic function of output, thus assuming a linearly decreasing marginal valuation of the bureau's service. This political valuation may be rooted in arguments about political sustainability. Needless to say, there exist many other possible explanations we do not need to consider as in this section we are interested mainly in bureaucrat's behavior.

Consider a bureaucrat whose budget comes from two sources: from the revenue of selling his services to his customers and from a grant B. This is Niskanen's (1971, pp. 87–105) "*mixed bureau*", where the bureaucrat faces "two separate demands" for any particular good: a market demand $x_e(p)$ and a "sponsor demand" B_e. However, there is a great difference between these "demand" functions: the sponsor does not consume any quantity of good z_e, but only pays for it. Hence we shall characterize B_e as a political valuation function rather than as a demand function.

This mixed bureau can be nicely interpreted as a public enterprise selling its goods or services at prices which do not cover costs, and expecting some ministry to cover its deficit.

The most interesting economic feature of such a bureau is the particular demand–cost balance. In extreme situations the mixed bureau may be constrained by demand only: customers and sponsor are willing to grant a budget that altogether exceeds the costs. (Assume that a unique optimum exists in such a case because of the satiation properties of customers' and sponsor's demand.) Usually, however, we expect the mixed bureau to be constrained by the budget, by the deficit limit (or profit prescription) Π:

$$\sum_{i=0}^{n} p_i z_i + B(z_{m+1},\dots,z_n) = \Pi(z,\rho). \tag{3.14}$$

This budget restriction implies an interesting twofold political influence on the bureau. On the one hand, government (the sponsor) is willing to appropriate grants B, depending on the quantities produced. On the other hand, the bureau is expected to break even, or to avoid too high deficits or to achieve a profit ($\Pi \gtreqless 0$ respectively).

Given this revenue–cost constraint, the market equilibrium conditions and its technology, the mixed bureau will maximize its budget, consisting of revenue plus grant,

$$\Phi(p, z) = \sum_{i=m+1}^{n} p_i z_i + B(z_{m+1}, \ldots, z_n). \tag{3.15}$$

Note that in applying (3.2) we have not only to consider $\partial\Phi/\partial z_i$ and $\partial\Phi/\partial p_e$, but also to replace $\tilde{C}_i$ with $\tilde{C}_i - \gamma B_i$ because of the unusual revenue–cost constraint (3.14). The resulting price structure can be written as follows:

$$\sum_{i\in E} \left[\left(\frac{\beta_0}{1+\beta_0} \right) \tilde{C}_i - \left(\frac{1+\beta_0\gamma}{1+\beta_0} \right) B_i - p_i \right] \frac{\partial z_i^D}{\partial p_e} = z_e, \qquad e \in E. \tag{3.16}$$

The mixed bureau behaves as if it were a perfect monopolist who acts on a modified marginal cost function,

$$C_i = \delta_1 \tilde{C}_i - \delta_2 B_i, \qquad i \in E, \qquad 0 < \delta_1, \delta_2 < 1, \tag{3.17}$$

instead of the usual marginal cost function $\tilde{C}_i$ [the exact meaning of δ_1 and δ_2 can be seen in (3.16)].

This "social cost function" shows that the bureaucrat adopts a cost–benefit attitude, integrating the politicial marginal valuation as a sort of external social benefit which reduces the marginal production costs. This may even imply negative social costs C_i!

How production economics and political economics are integrated depends on the percentages δ_1 and δ_2. *Production costs* consideration is determined by production side problems only, as we could well expect. (δ_1 depends on β_0 only.) The more sensitively the achievable budget reacts to additional endowments of labor, the larger the influence of production costs on public pricing. (δ_1 is increasing in β_0.) The *political considerations*, on the other hand, depend on the demand–cost balance of the bureau. Heuristically speaking the percentage δ_2 is the lower, the more the bureaucrat's position converges to the demand constrained case ($\gamma \to 0$). The more customers and sponsor are willing to pay, given a particular situation, the less the necessity for the bureaucrat to concentrate on the political valuation. How far the political valuation is taken into account in the limiting, demand constrained, case depends on production side arguments only. If, on the other hand, political valuation has to be considered increasingly the bureaucrat's position is increasingly determined by the deficit limit ($\gamma \to 1$), the maximum political influence being given for the limiting case $\gamma = 1$. This structure of public pricing reveals the sponsor's political dilemma: he looses influence on public pricing the more money he is willing to pay for it.

3.3. *Managers of public enterprises and unions*[54]

3.3.1. *Maximizing output or revenue, minimizing energy inputs*

Proving managerial success with reference to output or revenue data is of particular interest for public enterprises. The latter are often prevented from seeking maximum profits, and therefore their managers' success cannot be appraised with reference to profit data. An interesting example of the practical application of *output maximization* by a public enterprise is the maximization of passenger miles pursued by London Transport some years ago [Glaister and Collings (1978), Bös (1978b)].

Although economists would argue that adding quantities of different goods does not make any sense, in practice such targets can often be found. For example, consider patients of hospitals who receive first-class (z_1) and second-class (z_2) treatment, respectively, or rail passengers travelling first-class (z_1) or second-class (z_2). It can be seen that, under certain circumstances, the maximization of a sum of different quantities makes sense.

The board's objective function is therefore as follows:

$$\Phi(z) = \sum_{i=m+1}^{n} z_i, \tag{3.18}$$

which leads to a pricing structure

$$\sum_{i \in E} \left(\tilde{C}_i - p_i - \frac{1}{\beta_0} \right) \frac{\partial z_i^D}{\partial p_e} = z_e, \qquad e \in E. \tag{3.19}$$

The board behaves as if it were a monopolist but underestimates marginal costs ($\tilde{C}_i - 1/\beta_0$ instead of $\tilde{C}_i$). As each marginal cost term is reduced by the same

[54] In most of this section we use linear objective functions. Thus, there may arise particular problems in the case of constant returns to scale and with respect to corner solutions, but these will be ignored.

absolute amount, high-cost goods will be favored relatively less than low-cost goods with the expected result of increasing the sales of the latter. The maximum output will therefore consist of too much low-cost output as compared with the welfare optimal mix.

Let us now turn to *revenue maximization*. Revenue is a somewhat superficial indicator of economic success. Management is often inclined to use such an objective mainly because in the recent past of rapid growth these figures were growing impressively. Attempting to show managerial success with reference to revenue data is also of interest in private enterprises. Baumol (1959, pp. 47–48) has pointed out that in practical business any "program which explicitly proposes any cut in sales volume, whatever the profit considerations, is likely to meet a cold reception". Let us now investigate the economic consequences of revenue maximization as another possible objective of our board,

$$\Phi(p,z) = \sum_{i=m+1}^{n} p_i z_i. \tag{3.20}$$

After some transformations we obtain the following pricing structure:

$$\sum_{i\in E}\left[\frac{\beta_0}{1+\beta_0}\tilde{C}_i - p_i\right]\frac{\partial z_i^D}{\partial p_e} = z_e, \qquad e\in E, \tag{3.21}$$

which, as might be expected, equals the budget maximizing result, except for the sponsor demand B_e. The board behaves as if it were a monopolist, but underestimates marginal costs $[\beta_0/(1+\beta_0)<1]$. As every marginal cost term is reduced by the same relative amount, there is no inherent tendency to mass production of low-cost goods, in contrast to the case of output maximization.

Another simple managerial objective is *energy saving*. Let good k be energy, supplied by private firms, $j\in K$.[55] The board is interested in minimizing energy inputs, wherefore it maximizes

$$\Phi = z_k - \sum_h x_k^h(\cdot) + \sum_{j\notin K} y_k^j(\cdot), \qquad k\in\{1,\dots,m\}. \tag{3.22a}$$

[55] Analogous results can be obtained if the only supplier of energy is the public sector. The objective of minimizing energy inputs, then, reads as follows:

$$\Phi = -\sum_h x_k^h(\cdot) + \sum_j y_k^j(\cdot), \qquad k=\{1,\dots,m\}, \tag{3.22b}$$

yielding a price structure

$$\sum_{i\in F}(\tilde{C}_i - p_i)\frac{\partial z_i^D}{\partial p_e} + \frac{1}{\beta_0}\cdot\frac{\partial z_k^D}{\partial p_e} = z_e, \qquad e\in F=\{k,m+1,\dots,n\}. \tag{3.23b}$$

The energy saving pricing structure reads as follows:

$$\sum_{i \in E} (\tilde{C}_i - p_i) \frac{\partial z_i^D}{\partial p_e} + \frac{1}{\beta_0} \sum_{j \in K} \frac{\partial y_k^j}{\partial p_e} = z_e, \qquad e \in E = \{m+1, \ldots, n\}. \quad (3.23a)$$

The economic meaning of this pricing structure can be seen best if we neglect cross-price elasticities among outputs and transform the above condition as follows:

$$\left[\left(\tilde{C}_e + \frac{1}{\beta_0} \frac{\sum_{j \in K} \partial y_k^j / \partial p_e}{\partial z_e^D / \partial p_e} \right) - p_e \right] \frac{\partial z_e^D}{\partial p_e} = z_e, \qquad e \in E. \quad (3.24)$$

Assume normal reaction of demand for publicly supplied goods, $\partial z_e^D / \partial p_e < 0$, and complementarity of energy and other goods, $\partial y_k^j / \partial p_e < 0$, $j \in K$. The more energy intensive the production of some good, the higher in absolute value $\sum_{j \in K} \partial y_k^j / \partial p_e$.

Therefore a board that follows pricing rule (3.24) behaves as if it adhered to monopolistic pricing but overestimates the marginal costs. The more energy intensive the production, the more the respective marginal costs must be overestimated, resulting in higher prices of energy intensive goods.

3.3.2. Minimizing price indices

In countries with large public enterprise sectors attempts are sometimes made to reduce the rate of inflation through the pricing policies of those enterprises [Bös (1978a)]. Great Britain or Austria provide appropriate examples. In other countries public pricing is more likely to be aimed at the target of index minimization the higher the inflation rate and the larger the sector of "indexation" in an economy.

The simplest attempt to reduce a price index drastically is by setting public prices of zero. However, such a policy is usually excluded in our general approach, since we explicitly consider a revenue–cost constraint. In our case the board will consider one of the statistical price indices, as computed and published by some statistical office. Such indices compare quantities of money that can purchase a constant basket of commodities at changed prices. Thus substitution by consumers is ignored in this analysis (which therefore leads to an overestimation of effective price changes when Laspeyres indices are used and an underestimation when Paasche indices are used). The most common index follows Laspeyres and takes as fixed some base period's basket of consumer goods. We denote variables of this base period by the superscript "o" and define the board's objective function as follows:

$$\Phi(p) = -\sum_{i=m+1}^{n} p_i x_i^{\circ} \Big/ \sum_{i=m+1}^{n} p_i^{\circ} x_i^{\circ}. \tag{3.25}$$

The resulting price structure equals

$$\sum_{i \in E} (\tilde{C}_i - p_i) \frac{\partial z_i^D}{\partial p_e} = (1 - L_e) z_e, \qquad e \in E, \tag{3.26}$$

where

$$L_e = \frac{x_e^{\circ}}{x_e} \cdot \frac{1}{\Sigma p_i^{\circ} x_i^{\circ}} \cdot \frac{1}{\beta_o}, \qquad e \in E. \tag{3.27}$$

But, according to the common practice of statistical offices x_e° is always of the size of order of individual demand, whereas $z_e(=x_e)$ is total supply. This problem can be taken into account by simply transforming (3.24) into

$$L_e = \frac{x_e^{\circ}}{\bar{z}_e} \cdot \frac{1}{H \Sigma p_i^{\circ} x_i^{\circ}} \cdot \frac{1}{\beta_o}, \qquad e \in E, \tag{3.28}$$

where $\bar{z}_e = z_e/H$, H being the number of consumers.

The periodical index revisions for developed countries have shown a shifting of consumption from necessities towards non-necessities. Hence L_e is high for such goods where lower income groups account for a large share of total consumption.

Therefore, the economic interpretation of equation (3.26) is analogous to the interpretation of equation (2.51). Qualitatively, minimizing a Laspeyres price index has the same distributional effects as maximizing a welfare function which explicitly considers distributional aims! This result is due to the fact that, in minimizing a Laspeyres index account is taken of the weights of the base period in which necessities bought by lower-income groups get higher weights than those which would correspond to present consumption. This is a "desirable" distributional consequence of the "politician's error", i.e., of acting on the basis of past consumption patterns, which ought, perhaps, to induce second thoughts regarding the frequent "a priori" rejection of an index minimization strategy for public pricing.

Furthermore, we have to bear in mind that, with a constant basket of commodities, the distributionally "desirable" effects increase quantitatively with the passage of time, because deviations of actual consumption from the corresponding proportions of the basket of the base period increase with time. Therefore, after some years minimizing a Laspeyres index may not only imply qualitatively equal, but also quantitatively similar, results as maximizing a distributionally weighted welfare function.[56]

3.3.3. *The influence of unions*

The influence of employees' pressure groups on the management of nationalized enterprises or public utilities differs widely from country to country.

A first extreme are labor managed firms, like in Yugoslavia, the pressure groups being the workers' councils. They typically try to maximize value added per employee and the disincentive effects of such a policy are well-known from both practice and theory. Labor unions, starting from a wider horizon, will oppose the job restrictions that do often result from such a firm's policy.

The other extreme are nationalized firms which behave in the same way as private firms without any special influence of labor unions. Hence, in these cases there is no particular difference between the objectives of the managers of nationalized and of private firms.

Typically, however, nationalized enterprises or public utilities will follow a middle course, their objectives being some compromise between those of management and the union. Such a result need not only follow from close contacts between managers of public enterprises and unionists although such contacts will often be found. Unions will strongly be interested in public firms in any case, as they are usually large firms whose management policy has great influence on the whole economy.

Let us formulate the compromise between the management of a public enterprise and the representatives of some labor union in the following simple way. Management may be thought of as aiming to maximize output, while the union's utility may be assumed to depend on the number of working hours and on the real wage rate [Gravelle (1984), Rees (1982)].

Hence, we impute to the public sector the following objective:

$$\Phi(p, z) = \sum_{i=m+1}^{n} z_i + \rho U(p_0, z_0), \tag{3.29}$$

where the first part describes managers' interest in output, the second part

[56] For details, see Bös (1978a). Minimizing a true cost of living index under revenue–cost constraint leads to welfare optimal, i.e., Ramsey pricing.

describes the union's interest in wage rate and working hours, the partial derivatives of the union's utility function being $U_p > 0$ and $U_z < 0$ (additional plausible assumptions are that $U_{pp} < 0$ and $U_{zz} > 0$). $\rho > 0$ is a parameter measuring the strength of the union's influence, which depends on its bargaining power [Rees (1982)].

As usual, we treat public inputs and outputs $\{z_i\}$, and public prices $\{p_e\}$ as instruments. Additionally, the board has to fix the wage rate p_0.[57] This instrument choice makes it necessary to differentiate between different kinds of labor, p_0 referring to the labor force used in the public sector only, whereas some other kind of labor is used in the private sector only, its wage rate being determined by demand and supply in that sector.[58]

We apply (3.2) to obtain the following price structure:

$$\sum_{i=0}^{n}\left(\tilde{C}_i - p_i - \frac{1}{\beta_0}\frac{\partial \Phi}{\partial z_i}\right)\frac{\partial z_i^D}{\partial p_e} = z_e + \frac{1}{\beta_0}\frac{\partial \Phi}{\partial p_e}, \qquad e = 0, m+1, \ldots, n, \tag{3.30}$$

where

$$\begin{aligned}
\frac{\partial \Phi}{\partial z_i} &= \rho U_z \quad &&\text{for} \quad i = 0,\\
&= 0 &&\text{for} \quad i = 1, \ldots, m,\\
&= 1 &&\text{for} \quad i = m+1, \ldots, n,\\
\frac{\partial \Phi}{\partial p_e} &= \rho U_p &&\text{for} \quad e = 0,\\
&= 0 &&\text{otherwise.}
\end{aligned}$$

The economic interpretation of this pricing structure is a little complicated. How regulated prices deviate from marginal costs can best be seen if (3.30) is transformed as follows:

$$\begin{aligned}
p_e - \tilde{C}_e = &- \frac{z_e}{\partial z_e^D/\partial p_e} + \sum_{\substack{i=0\\ i\neq e}}^{n} (\tilde{C}_i - p_i)\frac{\partial z_i^D/\partial p_e}{\partial z_e^D/\partial p_e}\\
&- \sum_{i=m+1}^{n} \frac{1}{\beta_0}\cdot\frac{\partial z_i^D/\partial p_e}{\partial z_e^D/\partial p_e} - \frac{\rho U_z}{\beta_0}\cdot\frac{\partial z_0^D/\partial p_e}{\partial z_e^D/\partial p_e} - \frac{1}{\beta_0}, \qquad e = m+1, \ldots, n.
\end{aligned} \tag{3.31}$$

[57]As p_0 is an instrument variable, some other price must be taken as numeraire.
[58]If z_0 and only z_0 were labor, assumption (i) presented in Section 3.1 would exclude labor inputs of private firms.

The first two terms on the right-hand side can be interpreted similarly to the corresponding terms in equation (2.56) above. There is, first, a *monopolistic tendency* for p_e to exceed $\tilde{C}_e$ if demand reacts normally ($\partial z_e^D/\partial p_e < 0$). There is, second, a *reallocation effect* towards p_e above $\tilde{C}_e$ if all prices exceed the respective marginal costs and if good e is a "substitute" for all other goods in the sense $\partial z_i^D/\partial p_e > 0$, $\forall i \neq e$.

The third term reflects the managers' *interest in output maximization*, again implying a tendency for p_e to be above $\tilde{C}_e$ if good e is a "substitute" for all other goods in the sense mentioned above.

The fourth term reflects the *union's interests*. It implies a tendency for lower p_e if decreasing p_e increases total public labor input ($\partial z_0^D/\partial p_e > 0$). This, in turn, implies a tendency towards lower prices of relatively labor intensive goods. The economic plausibility for these effects is as follows: let e be a labor intensive good and let its price decrease. If demand reacts normally, z_e^D increases. Hence the input pattern of the public sector will be shifted to a higher percentage of labor inputs. This tendency will be intensified if we think of the demand for other goods which will also be influenced by changing p_e.

The typical influence of a union's policy, summarized in the fourth term, will be stronger the greater the union's bargaining power (ρ) and the more interested the union is in securing jobs (U_z). The influence will be counterbalanced by production side effects of labor inputs (β_0).[59]

3.4. *A set of axioms for prices to achieve a fair allocation of costs*

This subsection is devoted to a recent approach to public pricing that differs conceptually from all the other approaches outlined in this paper. The approach to be outlined now does not rest on the principles of optimizing some objective function subject to production feasibility and a revenue–cost constraint, and the

[59] It may be noted that one cannot deduce unambiguously whether the union's influence leads to wage increases or decreases. Transforming (3.30) for $e = 0$ in a similar way as (3.31) shows that the influence of the union on the wage level p_0 is reflected by

$$\frac{\rho}{\beta_0} \cdot \frac{1}{\partial z_0^D/\partial p_0} \cdot \left[\frac{\partial U}{\partial z_0} \cdot \frac{\partial z_0^D}{\partial p_0} + \frac{\partial U}{\partial p_0} \right],$$

which can be rewritten simply as

$$\frac{\rho}{\beta_0 \partial z_0^D/\partial p_0} \frac{\partial U^*}{\partial p_0},$$

taking into account that our definition of $z_0^D(p_0)$ together with $z_0 = z_0^D$ implies $U^* = U^*(z_0^D(p_0), p_0)$ at the optimum. But $\partial U^*/\partial p_0$ can, of course, be either positive or negative.

conditions for market equilibria. Rather it proceeds by formulating some basic axioms to which prices should correspond and seeks those pricing rules that are uniquely determined by these axioms. The (game) theoretical background is rather advanced, yet the basic ideas of the approach as presented below, are nevertheless easily understandable. Moreover, the approach is not purely theoretical exercise of l'art pour l'art, but has actually been applied in practice.

Some economists at Cornell University were asked to compute fair internal telephone billing rates for their university [Billera, Heath and Raanan (1978)]. Problems arose because costs for long distance calls follow different schedules, consisting of different basic fees and variable charges the university has to pay to the telephone company (direct distance dialing – DDD, foreign exchange lines – FX, wide area telecommunications services – WATS). Thus two people calling Chicago at the same time may cause different costs for the university, if one uses the FX line, the other DDD, because the computer routes the first call to the cheaper FX line and the second, which comes in some seconds later, to DDD, as FX and all WATS lines are occupied. Is it fair to charge different internal billing rates in such a case?

The authors solved the problem by applying the Shapley value of non-atomic games [Aumann and Shapley (1974)]. Billera and Heath (1979), Mirman and Tauman (1982), and Samet and Tauman (1982) then redefined the game theoretic axioms as axioms on the relation between prices and cost functions. They succeeded in finding a nice set of axioms that is understandable on its own even by readers who are not familiar with sophisticated game theory. Thus they created a new, generally applicable, theory of pricing which meanwhile has been further developed in Mirman, Samet and Tauman (1983), Bös and Tillmann (1983), and Samet, Tauman and Zang (1981).

The most striking feature of such cost axiomatic pricing is that it starts from axioms on the relation between prices and cost functions and hence needs no information on consumer tastes. However, there is not a priori guaranteed that the application of such price schedules will always imply a general equilibrium. And if such an equilibrium under cost axiomatic prices is to obtain, the estimation of private tastes enters again.

Consider a producer who has to produce particular quantities of consumption goods $\zeta = (\zeta_1, \ldots, \zeta_n)$, $\zeta_i > 0$. Total costs of producing ζ are given by $C(\zeta)$, a continuously differentiable long-run cost function [all fixed inputs are treated as variable: $C(0) = 0$]. Input prices are fixed. Of course, increasing returns to scale are included. The quantities ζ shall be sold at prices $p = (p_1(C, \zeta), \ldots, p_n(C, \zeta))$ that fulfill the following four axioms [Samet and Tauman (1982)]:

Axiom 1 (Rescaling): The price should be independent of the unit's measurement. Let G and C be two cost functions, and

$$G(z_1, \ldots, z_n) = C(s_1 z_1, \ldots, s_n z_n), \qquad s_i > 0, \quad \forall i. \tag{3.32}$$

Then for each ζ and each $i = 1, \ldots, n$,

$$p_i(G, \zeta) = s_i p_i(C, (s_1\zeta_1, \ldots, s_n\zeta_n)). \tag{3.33}$$

The rationale for this axiom is trivial: the price of ζ_i if measured in tons, has to be 1000 times the price of ζ_i if measured in kilos.

Axiom 2 (Consistency): The same price shall be charged for goods which have the same influence on costs in the following sense: if G is a one variable cost function and if, for every z,

$$C(z_1, \ldots, z_n) = G\left(\sum_i z_i\right), \tag{3.34}$$

then, for every i and every ζ,

$$p_i(C, \zeta) = p\left(G, \sum_i \zeta_i\right). \tag{3.35}$$

Typical examples are red and blue cars which should be sold at the same price. Objections against this axiom stress different situations of demand: if, at the same prices, red cars can and blue cars cannot be sold, it makes sense to sell blue cars at a lower price.

Axiom 3 (Additivity): If the cost function can be broken into subcosts, the prices can be found by adding the prices determined by the subcosts.

If C, G^1 and G^2 are cost functions and, for each z,

$$C(z_1, \ldots, z_n) = G^1(z_1, \ldots, z_n) + G^2(z_1, \ldots, z_n), \tag{3.36}$$

then, for each ζ,

$$p(C, \zeta) = p(G^1, \zeta) + p(G^2, \zeta). \tag{3.37}$$

Axiom 3 refers only to cases where the cost function is separable. Then there are no interdependencies between subcosts and the additivity of pricing makes sense.

Axiom 4 (Positivity): The price of a commodity the production of which requires investment, is not negative.

Let ζ be given. If C is not decreasing at any $z \leqq \zeta$, then

$$p(C, \zeta) \geqq 0. \tag{3.38}$$

The reasoning is straightforward.

Samet and Tauman (1982) prove that prices which correspond to these four axioms are of the form

$$p_i(C,\zeta)=\int_0^1 C_i(s\zeta)\,\mathrm{d}\mu(s), \qquad i=1,\dots,n, \qquad \zeta\neq 0. \tag{3.39}$$

This rather complicated mathematical formulation can be grasped most easily if one interprets the prices p as "some average" of the marginal costs C_i where the measure $\mu(s)$ denotes how "the average" is to be computed. We can clarify this further if we show how, by changing μ, we can generate, as polar cases of the same pricing formula, the "pure" marginal cost prices as well as the "Aumann–Shapley" break-even prices:

(a) Marginal cost pricing. Axiom 4 is strengthened in order to obtain Axiom 4*:

*Axiom 4** (Positivity). Let ζ be given. If C is non-decreasing in a neighborhood of ζ, then

$$p(C,\zeta)\geqq 0. \tag{3.40}$$

This requires that prices be non-negative at ζ even if C is non-decreasing in a neighborhood of ζ only.

If Axioms 1 to 3 and 4* are fulfilled,[60] the price mechanism reduces to

$$p_i(C,\zeta)=C_i(\zeta), \tag{3.41}$$

which is the marginal cost pricing rule as a special case of the above general pricing rule.

(b) Aumann–Shapley pricing. We add a break-even axiom:

Axiom 5 (Break-even).

$$\sum_i p_i(C,\zeta)\zeta_i=C(\zeta) \quad \text{for each} \quad \zeta>0. \tag{3.42}$$

If Axioms 1 to 5 (including 4, not 4*) are fulfilled, the pricing rule is as follows:

$$p_i(C,\zeta)=\int_0^1 C_i(s\zeta)\,\mathrm{d}s. \tag{3.43}$$

[60] Some additional normalization is necessary as shown in Samet and Tauman (1982 p. 905).

The reader should be aware that (3.43) does not mean the usual kind of average cost pricing. As we are dealing with a more-than-one-good approach the average is found by proportionate variations s of all quantities ζ along a ray going from 0 to ζ.

Thus cost axiomatic prices include marginal cost prices and cost covering prices as special cases. We recall that welfare maximizing prices also include marginal cost and cost covering prices as special cases. What, then, is the *difference between pricing according to these two approaches*?

First, *marginal costs* enter the pricing rules in different ways. All kinds of welfare maximizing pricing, following our general rules (2.23) or (2.27) depend on the marginal costs $\tilde{C}_i$ at the optimum – and only at the optimum. Cost axiomatic pricing, following (3.39), also depends on alternative production possibilities, on the values of the respective marginal costs for any quantity along a ray between 0 and ζ. This difference is interesting with respect to the whole philosophy of the meaning of pricing rules. Perhaps one should think of pricing rules as depending also on further alternative production possibilities, e.g., the production of higher quantities $[C_i(s\zeta)$ for $s > 1]$.

Only in the case of pure marginal cost pricing does this particular difference between the welfare approach and the cost axiomatic approach disappear.

Second, the *demand side* is treated differently. The welfare approach typically assumes an equilibrium between demand and supply. No such constraint enters the cost axiomatic approach. But will prices that are determined only by cost axioms always be "demand compatible"? Or will demand at given prices exceed or fall short of supply? Mirman and Tauman (1982) have already shown that Aumann–Shapley prices are demand compatible, and Bös and Tillmann (1983) have shown that *all* cost axiomatic prices are demand compatible if the financing of deficits of public utilities is explicitly included in an equilibrium approach.

The proof has, of course, extended the applicability of cost axiomatic pricing to a considerable extent. Only after this general proof of the demand compatibility of cost axiomatic pricing can these price schedules be treated as an equivalent and perhaps superior alternative to welfare maximizing price schedules.

Generally, it will be complicated to decide which approach is superior. Compare, for example, Ramsey and Aumann–Shapley prices. Both are cost covering. But one cannot expect these prices to coincide. If there are different price elasticities of demand for two goods that have the same influence on costs (in the sense of Axiom 2 above), Ramsey prices of these two goods will differ, Aumann–Shapley prices will be equal. In such a case, somebody who adheres to the welfare approach will stress the welfare losses caused by Aumann–Shapley prices. Somebody who adheres to the above axioms on costs will stress the weaknesses of the social welfare function. There is no generally accepted result concerning the superiority of one of these two approaches.

4. Conclusion

The theory of public pricing which I endorse rests on a certain ideological background. It is appropriate to remind the reader that this paper is written:

(i) in a neo-classical tradition. It deals with a world where people maximize utility under given constraints. The public sector is characterized primarily as a producer whose activities should not be determined by profit maximization but by maximization of welfare, or some other objectives, given certain constraints.

(ii) in the tradition which regards public prices as the main device to embed the public sector into the surrounding private economy where enterprises do not necessarily behave competitively.

(iii) in the tradition which holds that public pricing should concentrate primarily on optimal allocation, and not on redistribution of real incomes.

Accordingly, this paper starts from welfare maximization, welfare being defined over public and private prices and individual incomes. The maximization has to take into account the constraints regarding market equilibrium, production feasibility and different revenue–cost limitations of public or regulated private firms. This extended version of the Boiteux model unifies many different models as presented in Section 2. Moreover, given the Boiteux environment, different alternative objectives of public pricing can be treated in a way which lends itself immediately to a comparison with welfare maximization. These models are presented in Section 3.

The resulting theory of public prices characterizes them as a separate category, clearly differing from private prices on the one hand and commodity taxation on the other hand. Prices as instruments of economic policy are designed to achieve other objectives than *prices which result from market processes*. That is why we have analysed public pricing as an instrument of welfare maximization, or, in political models, as an instrument for maximizing budgets and votes. In contrast, we have analysed private pricing as a means of maximizing profits. Moreover, public pricing is constrained differently from private pricing. The fixed profit constraint and the rate of return constraint in public pricing have no counterparts in perfect or imperfect competition models. Public pricing also differs from *commodity taxation or subsidization*. The well-known similarity between the Ramsey formulas for public pricing and commodity taxation is purely formal. The institutional setting of public pricing, with different kinds of principal–agent relations, finds no counterpart in commodity taxation. This point applies mainly to pricing with particular reference to the production side, like pricing resulting from rate of return regulation (which leads to input inefficiencies), peak load pricing (which attempts to solve capacity problems), and cost axiomatic pricing (which concentrates on costs only). Moreover, the revenue from selling publicly priced goods accrues to the selling enterprise, while taxes go to the state. Hence, with public pricing, there are neither problems of shifting, as in the case of commodity taxation, nor problems of the economic consequences of public spending from revenues. This implies an important difference between public pricing and commodity taxation, both in partial models and in general equilibrium models.

Let me conclude these remarks with some hints on promising directions for further research:

- We still lack economic and political theories of *(de)nationalization and (de)regulation*. Comparing the efficiency of private and public sector (including regulated enterprises) may indeed give some hints about the reasons for such decisions. Ideological arguments may also be presented. Yet all this is far from being a theory which integrates property right problems, lack of competition, different objectives of public authorities, and further relevant economic and political determinants in some model of sufficient generality.
- We need more theoretical structuring of the *institutional setting of public sector pricing*. Here we have in mind the different principal–agent relations between consumers, government, board(s) of public or regulated private firms, unions and employees of the firms. This structuring would require further endogenization of the political and bureaucratic determinants of public pricing, further research on informational and incentive problems at different institutional stages, from appropriate incentives to avoid bureaucratic red tape to incentives to avoid X-inefficiency in public or regulated private firms.
- The usual models are typically restricted to static analysis. *Stabilization* models are underrepresented. We require more scientific concentration on dynamic structures of public pricing, and on decisions under uncertainty. How will or should a firm fix public prices in times of uncertain economic prospects? What is to be done if there is some probability that the political leadership will change in the next year and introduce a fundamental change in basic pricing rules? Moreover, what is to be done if this probability is not exactly known? In our world of disequilibria, we should concentrate also on disequilibrium analysis of public pricing. Two first steps were presented above (public pricing in the case of rationed labor markets, rationing demand by peak load pricing). Many others remain to be taken.

5. Bibliographical note

This brief guide to further reading includes only some of the more important papers on the different topics.

The basic *Boiteux model* has been applied to public good pricing by Drèze and Marchand (1976) and Hagen (1979), and to optimal discount rates for public enterprises by Marchand, Pestieau and Weymark (1982). In the absence of lump-sum transfers consumers can be assumed to own shares in the private enterprises from where their incomes arise [Drèze and Marchand (1976)]. Public deficits can be covered also by indirect taxes [Wiegard (1978, pp. 56–74)]. – For the alternative model which derives public pricing rules from maximizing consumer plus producer surplus, see Bös (1981).

Further literature on *Ramsey pricing* deals with different revenue–cost constraints of different firms [Boiteux (1956, 1971)]. Opportunity costs of public deficits can be considered explicitly [Feldstein (1974)]. Interesting recent discussions refer to cross-subsidization [Faulhaber (1975), Faulhaber and Levinson (1981)], and adjustment processes that lead to Ramsey prices [Vogelsang and Finsinger (1979)].

The *rate of return* regulation can explicitly consider an optimal fair rate of return [Klevorick (1971), Sheshinski (1971)], include regulatory lags [Bailey and Coleman (1971), Klevorick (1973)]. A classic paper on rate of return, peak load pricing is Wellisz (1963).

Recent papers on *peak load pricing* consider variable price switching points [Dansby (1975)], and give up the additive structure of demand [Watzke (1982)]. Moreover, one can consider the influence of peak load pricing on congestion [Glaister (1974)] and on energy conservation [Crew and Kleindorfer (1979, pp. 179–193)]. A particular new development is spot pricing [Vickrey (1971), Bohn, Caramanis and Schweppe (1981)].

Straightforward extensions of the *vote maximizing approach* refer to opinion polls in which different price schedules are compared [Bös (1983)]; the *bureaucracy* model has been discussed further by Niskanen (1975), Fiorina and Noll (1978), and Bös, Tillmann and Zimmermann (1984).

Further reading on *cost axiomatic pricing* should include Mirman, Samet and Tauman (1981) and Samet, Tauman and Zang (1981). The reader should also consult other game theoretic approaches towards public pricing. An approach that takes consumers and producers as players of pricing games instead of quantities produced, has been used by Faulhaber (1975), Sorensen, Tschirhart and Whinston (1978), Guesnerie and Oddou (1979), and Faulhaber and Levinson (1980). The nucleolus instead of the Shapley value has been applied to airport pricing [see Littlechild (1974), Littlechild and Owen (1976), and Littlechild and Thompson (1977)].

References

Atkinson, A.B. and J.E. Stiglitz, 1980, Lectures on public economics (McGraw-Hill, London).

Aumann, R.J. and L.S. Shapley, 1974, Values of non-atomic games (Princeton University Press, Princeton, NJ).

Averch, H. and L.L. Johnson, 1962, Behavior of the firm under regulatory constraint, American Economic Review 52, 1053–1069.

Bailey, E.E., 1973, Economic theory of regulatory constraint (Heath, Lexington, MA).

Bailey, E.E. and R.D. Coleman, 1971, The effect of lagged regulation in an Averch–Johnson model, Bell Journal of Economics and Management Science 2, 278–292.

Bailey, E.E. and J.C. Malone, 1970, Resource allocation and the regulated firm, Bell Journal of Economics and Management Science 1, 129–142.

Baron, D.P. and R.R. DeBondt, 1979, Fuel adjustment mechanisms and economic efficiency, Journal of Industrial Economics 27, 243–261.

Baron, D.P. and R.R. DeBondt, 1981, On the design of regulatory price adjustment mechanisms, Journal of Economic Theory 24, 70–94.

Baumol, W.J., 1959, Business behavior, value and growth (Harcourt, Brace & World, New York).

Baumol, W.J., 1976, Scale economies, average cost, and the profitability of marginal cost pricing, in: R.E. Grieson, ed., Public and urban economics: Essays in honor of William S. Vickrey (Heath, Lexington, MA) 43–57.

Baumol, W.J., 1977, On the proper cost tests for natural monopoly in a multiproduct industry, American Economic Review 67, 809–822.

Baumol, W.J. and D.F. Bradford, 1970, Optimal departures from marginal cost pricing, American Economic Review 60, 265–283.

Beato, P., 1982, The existence of marginal cost pricing equilibria with increasing returns, Quarterly Journal of Economics 97, 669–688.

Beato, P. and A. Mas-Colell, 1984, The marginal cost pricing rule as a regulation mechanism in mixed markets, in: M. Marchand, P. Pestieau and H. Tulkens, eds., The performance of public enterprises (North–Holland, Amsterdam) 81–100.

Bergson, A., 1972, Optimal pricing for a public enterprise, Quarterly Journal of Economics 86, 519–544.

Billera, L.J. and D.C. Heath, 1979, Allocation of shared costs: A set of axioms yielding a unique procedure, Technical report (Cornell University, Ithaca, NY).

Billera, L.J., D.C. Heath and J. Raanan, 1978, Internal telephone billing rates: A novel application of non-atomic game theory, Operations Research 26, 956–965.

Bohn, R.E., M.C. Caramanis and F.C. Schweppe, 1981, Optimal spot pricing of electricity: Theory, MIT Energy Laboratory working paper MIT-EL 81-008 WP (Massachusetts Institute of Technology, Cambridge, MA).

Boiteux, M., 1956/1971, Sur la gestion des monopoles publics astreints à l'équilibre budgétaire, Econometrica 24, 22–40. English edition: On the management of public monopolies subject to budgetary constraints, Journal of Economic Theory 3, 219–240.

Bös, D., 1978a, Cost of living indices and public pricing, Economica 45, 59–69.

Bös, D., 1978b, Distributional effects of maximisation of passenger miles, Journal of Transport Economics and Policy 12, 322–329.

Bös, D., 1981, Economic theory of public enterprise, Lecture notes in economics and mathematical systems 188 (Springer, Berlin).

Bös, D., 1983, Public pricing with distributional objectives, in: J. Finsinger, ed., Public sector economics (Macmillan, London) 171–188.

Bös, D., 1984, Income taxation, public sector pricing and redistribution, Scandinavian Journal of Economics 86, 166–183.

Bös, D. and G. Tillmann, 1983, Cost-axiomatic regulatory pricing, Journal of Public Economics 22, 243–256.

Bös, D. and H.-G. Zimmermann, 1983, Winning votes and political sympathy, Mimeo. (Institute of Economics, University of Bonn, Bonn).

Bös, D., G. Tillmann and H.-G. Zimmermann, 1984, Bureaucratic public enterprises, in: D. Bös, A. Bergson and J.R. Meyer, eds., Entrepreneurship, Zeitschrift für Nationalökonomie, Suppl. 4, 127–176.

Brown, D.J. and G. Heal, 1979, Equity, efficiency and increasing returns, Review of Economic Studies 46, 571–585.

Brown, D.J. and G. Heal, 1980a, Two-part tariffs, marginal cost pricing and increasing returns in a general equilibrium model, Journal of Public Economics 13, 25–49.

Brown, D.J. and G. Heal, 1980b, Marginal cost pricing revisited, Mimeo., Econometric Society world congress, Aix-en-Provence.

Brown, G., Jr. and M.B. Johnson, 1969, Public utility pricing and output under risk, American Economic Review 59. 119–128.

Carlton, D.W., 1977, Peak load pricing with stochastic demand, American Economic Review 67, 1006–1010.

C.E.E.P. (Centre Europeen de l'Entreprise Publique), 1984, Public enterprise in the European Economic Community, English version of the C.E.E.P. review 1984 (C.E.E.P., Brussels).

Cornet, B., 1982, Existence of equilibria in economies with increasing returns, Working paper (University of California, Berkeley, CA).

Crew, M.A. and P.R. Kleindorfer, 1979, Public utility economics (Macmillan, London).

Dansby, R.E., 1975, Welfare optimal peak-load pricing and capacity decisions with intraperiod time varying demand, Economic discussion paper no. 39 (Bell Laboratories, Holmdel, NJ).

Diamond, P.A., 1975, The many-person Ramsey tax rule, Journal of Public Economics 4, 335–342.

Dixit, A., 1975, Welfare effects of tax and price changes, Journal of Public Economics 4, 103–123.

Drèze, J.H., 1964, Some postwar contributions of French economists to theory and public policy, American Economic Review 54, no. 4, part 2 (suppl.), 1–64.

Drèze, J.H., 1984, Second-best analysis with markets in disequilibrium: Public sector pricing in a Keynesian regime, in: M. Marchand, P. Pestieau and H. Tulkens, eds., The performance of public enterprises (North-Holland, Amsterdam) 45–79.

Drèze, J.H. and M. Marchand, 1976, Pricing, spending, and gambling rules for non-profit organizations, in: R.E. Grieson, ed., Public and urban economics: Essays in honor of William S. Vickrey (Heath, Lexington, MA) 59–89.

Faulhaber, G.R., 1975, Cross-subsidization: Pricing in public enterprises, American Economic Review 65, 966–977.

Faulhaber, G.R. and S.B. Levinson, 1981, Subsidy-free prices and anonymous equity, American Economic Review 71. 1083–1091.

Faulhaber, G.R. and J.C. Panzar, 1977, Optimal two-part tariffs with self-selection, Economic discussion paper no. 74 (Bell Laboratories, Holmdel, NJ).

Feldstein, M.S., 1972a, Distributional equity and the optimal structure of public prices, American Economic Review 62, 32–36. (Corrected version of p. 33, footnote 7: American Economic Review 62, 763.)

Feldstein, M.S., 1972b, Equity and efficiency in public sector pricing: The optimal two-part tariff, Quarterly Journal of Economics 86, 175–187.

Feldstein, M.S., 1972c, The pricing of public intermediate goods, Journal of Public Economics 1, 45–72.

Feldstein, M.S., 1974, Financing in the evaluation of public expenditure, in: W.L. Smith and J.M. Culbertson, eds., Public finance and stabilization policy: Essays in honor of Richard A. Musgrave (North-Holland, Amsterdam) 13–36.

Fiorina, M.P. and R.G. Noll, 1978, Voters, bureaucrats and legislators: A rational choice perspective on the growth of bureaucracy, Journal of Public Economics 9, 239–254.

Glaister, S., 1974, Generalised consumer surplus and public transport pricing, Economic Journal 84, 849–867.

Glaister, S. and J.J. Collings, 1978, Maximisation of passenger miles in theory and practice, Journal of Transport Economics and Policy 12, 304–321.

Gravelle, H.S.E., 1982, Incentives, efficiency and control in public firms, in: D. Bös, R.A. Musgrave and J. Wiseman, eds., Public production, Zeitschrift für Nationalökonomie, Suppl. 2 (Springer, Vienna) 79–104.

Gravelle, H.S.E., 1984, Bargaining and efficiency in public and private sector firms, in: M. Marchand, P. Pestieau and H. Tulkens, eds., The performance of public enterprises (North-Holland, Amsterdam) 193–220.

Green, H.A.J., 1961, The social optimum in the presence of monopoly and taxation, Review of Economic Studies 28, 66–78.

Guesnerie, R., 1975, Pareto optimality in non-convex economies, Econometrica 43, 1–29.

Guesnerie, R., 1980, Second-best pricing rules in the Boiteux tradition: Derivation, review and discussion, Journal of Public Economics 13, 51–80.

Guesnerie, R. and C. Oddou, 1979, On economic games which are not necessarily superadditive: Solution concepts and application to a local public good problem with few agents, Economics Letters 3, 301–306.

Hagen, K.P., 1979, Optimal pricing in public firms in an imperfect market economy, Scandinavian Journal of Economics 81, 475–493.

Hatta, T., 1977, A theory of piecemeal policy recommendations, Review of Economic Studies 44, 1–21.

Hotelling, H., 1938, The general welfare in relation to problems of taxation and of railway and utility rates, Econometrica 6, 242–269.

Intriligator, M.D., 1971, Mathematical optimization and economic theory (Prentice-Hall, Englewood Cliffs, NJ).

Joskow, P. and R. Noll, 1980, Theory and practice in public regulation: A current overview, Conference paper no. 64 (National Bureau of Economic Research, Cambridge, MA).

Kahn, A.E., 1970/1971, The economics of regulation: Principles and institutions, 2 vols. (Wiley, New York).

Kawamata, K., 1977, Price distortion and the second best optimum, Review of Economic Studies 44, 23–29.

Kendrick, J.W., 1975, Efficiency incentives and cost factors in public utility automatic revenue adjustment clauses, Bell Journal of Economics 6, 299–313.

Keyser, W. and R. Windle, eds., 1978, Public enterprise in the EEC, 7 vols. (Sijthoff & Noordhoff, Alphen aan den Rijn).

Klevorick, A.K., 1966, The graduated fair return: A regulatory proposal, American Economic Review 56, 477–484.

Klevorick, A.K., 1971, The 'optimal' fair rate of return, Bell Journal of Economics and Management Science 2, 122–153.

Klevorick, A.K., 1973, The behavior of a firm subject to stochastic regulatory review, Bell Journal of Economics and Management Science 4, 57–88.

Leland, H.E. and R.A. Meyer, 1976, Monopoly pricing structures with imperfect discrimination, Bell Journal of Economics 7, 449–462.

Lipsey, R.G. and K. Lancaster, 1956–57, The general theory of second-best, Review of Economic Studies 24, 11–32.

Littlechild, S.C., 1974, A simple expression for the nucleolus in a special case, International Journal of Game Theory 3, 21–29.

Littlechild, S.C. and G. Owen, 1976, A further note on the nucleolus of the 'airport' game, International Journal of Game Theory 5, 91–95.

Littlechild, S.C. and G.F. Thompson, 1977, Aircraft landing fees: A game theory approach, Bell Journal of Economics 8, 186–204.

Malinvaud, E., 1977, The theory of unemployment reconsidered (Basil Blackwell, Oxford).

Marchand, M., P. Pestieau and J.A. Weymark, 1982, Discount rates for public enterprises in the presence of alternative financial constraints, in: D. Bös, R.A. Musgrave and J. Wiseman, eds., Public production, Zeitschrift für Nationalökonomie, Suppl. 2 (Springer, Vienna) 27–50. Correction, 1984, Zeitschrift für Nationalökonomie 44, 289–291.

Meyer, R.A., 1975, Monopoly pricing and capacity choice under uncertainty, American Economic Review 65, 326–337.

Minasian, J.R., 1964, Television pricing and the theory of public goods, Journal of Law and Economics 7, 71–80.

Mirman, L.J. and Y. Tauman, 1982, Demand compatible equitable cost sharing prices, Mathematics of Operations Research 7, 40–56.

Mirman, L.J., D. Samet and Y. Tauman, 1983, An axiomatic approach to the allocation of a fixed cost through prices, Bell Journal of Economics 14, 139–151.

Mirrlees, J.A., 1975, Optimal commodity taxation in a two-class economy, Journal of Public Economics 4, 27–33.

Mitchell, B.M., W.G. Manning, Jr., and J.P. Acton, 1977, Electricity pricing and load management: Foreign experience and California opportunities, Rand study R-2106 CERCDC (Rand Corporation, Santa Monica, CA).

N.E.D.O. (National Economic Development Office), 1976, A study of U.K. nationalised industries, Report, appendix volume and several background papers (Her Majesty's Stationery Office, London).

Nelson, J.R., ed., 1964, Marginal cost pricing in practice (Prentice-Hall, Englewood Cliffs, NJ).

Ng, Y.-K., 1984, Quasi-Pareto social improvements, American Economic Review 74, 1033–1050.

Ng, Y.-K. and M. Weisser, 1974, Optimal pricing with a budget constraint: The case of the two-part tariff, Review of Economic Studies 41, 337–345.

Niskanen, W.A., 1971, Bureaucracy and representative government (Aldine, Chicago, IL).

Niskanen, W.A., 1975, Bureaucrats and politicians, Journal of Law and Economics 18, 617–643.
Oi, W.Y., 1971, A Disneyland dilemma: Two-part tariffs for a Mickey Mouse monopoly, Quarterly Journal of Economics 85, 77–96.
Panzar, J.C., 1975, A neoclassical approach to peak load pricing, Bell Journal of Economics 6, 521–530.
Panzar, J.C. and R.D. Willig, 1977, Economies of scale in multi-output production, Quarterly Journal of Economics 91, 481–493.
Quoilin, J., 1976, Marginal cost selling in Électricité de France, Annals of Public and Co-operative Economy 47, 115–141.
Ramsey, F., 1927, A contribution to the theory of taxation, Economic Journal 37, 47–61.
Rees, R., 1982, Principal–agent theory and public enterprise control, Mimeo., CIRIEC conference on the concept and measurement of the performance of public enterprise, Liège.
Roberts, K.W.S., 1979, Welfare considerations of nonlinear pricing, Economic Journal 89, 66–83.
Romer, T. and H. Rosenthal, 1979, Bureaucrats versus voters: On the political economy of resource allocation by direct democracy, Quarterly Journal of Economics 93, 563–587.
Samet, D. and Y. Tauman, 1982, The determination of marginal-cost prices under a set of axioms, Econometrica 50, 895–909.
Samet, D., Y. Tauman and I. Zang, 1981, An application of the Aumann–Shapley prices for cost allocation in transportation problems, Working paper no. 803 (Faculty of Commerce and Business Administration, University of British Columbia, Vancouver).
Samuelson, P.A., 1964, Public goods and subscription TV: Correction of the record, Journal of Law and Economics 7, 81–83.
Sherman, R. and A. George, 1979, Second-best pricing for the U.S. postal service, Southern Economic Journal 45, 685–695.
Sheshinski, E., 1971, Welfare aspects of a regulatory ocnstraint: Note, American Economic Review 61, 175–178.
Sorenson, J., J. Tschirhart and A. Whinston, 1978, A theory of pricing under decreasing costs, American Economic Review 68, 614–624.
Spence, M., 1977, Nonlinear prices and welfare, Journal of Public Economics 8, 1–18.
Spremann, K., 1978, On welfare implications and efficiency of entrance fee pricing, Zeitschrift für Nationalökonomie 38, 231–252.
Steiner, P.O., 1957, Peak loads and efficient pricing, Quarterly Journal of Economics 71, 585–610.
Sudit, E.F., 1979, Automatic rate adjustments based on total factor productivity performance in public utility regulation, in: M.A. Crew, ed., Problems in public utility economics and regulation (Heath, Lexington, MA) 55–71.
Tillmann, G., 1981, Efficiency in economies with increasing returns, Mimeo. (Institute of Economics, University of Bonn, Bonn).
Timmer, C.P., 1981, Is there 'curvature' in the Slutsky matrix?, Review of Economics and Statistics 63, 395–402.
Turvey, R., 1968, Optimal pricing and investment in electricity supply (Allen & Unwin, London).
Turvey, R., 1971, Economic analysis and public enterprises (Allen & Unwin, London).
Turvey, R. and D. Anderson, 1977, Electricity economics (John Hopkins University Press, Baltimore, MD).
United Nations, 1968, A system of national accounts (United Nations, New York).
Vickrey, W., 1971, Responsive pricing of public utility services, Bell Journal of Economics and Management Science 2, 346–373.
Visscher, M.L., 1973, Welfare-maximizing price and output with stochastic demand: Comment, American Economic Review 63, 224–229.
Vogelsang, I. and J. Finsinger, 1979, A regulatory adjustment process for optimal pricing by multiproduct monopoly firms, Bell Journal of Economics 10, 157–171.
Watzke, R., 1982, The peak-load problem, Mimeo. (Institute of Economics, University of Bonn, Bonn).
Wellisz, S.H., 1963, Regulation of natural gas pipeline companies: An economic analysis, Journal of Political Economy 71, 30–43.
White Paper, 1967, Nationalised industries: A review of economic and financial objectives, Cmnd. 3437 (Her Majesty's Stationery Office, London).

White Paper, 1978, The nationalised industries, Cmnd. 7131 (Her Majesty's Stationery Office, London).
Wiegard, W., 1978, Optimale Schattenpreise und Produktionsprogramme für öffentliche Unternehmen (Lang, Bern).
Wiegard, W., 1979, Optimale Preise für öffentliche Güter bei gegebenen Preisstrukturen in der privaten Wirtschaft, Finanzarchiv N.F. 37, 270–292.
Wiegard, W., 1980, Theoretische Überlegungen zu einer schrittweisen Reform der indirekten Steuern, Jahrbuch für Sozialwissenschaft 31, 1–20.
Williamson, O.E., 1966, Peak load pricing and optimal capacity under indivisibility constraints, American Economic Review 56, 810–827.
Yoshitake, K., 1973, An introduction to public enterprise in Japan (Sage, Beverly Hills, CA).

Chapter 4

TAXES AND LABOR SUPPLY*

JERRY A. HAUSMAN

National Bureau of Economic Research and
Massachusetts Institute of Technology, Cambridge, MA

1. Introduction

The effect of taxes on labor supply introduces interesting questions in economic theory, econometrics, and public finance. Since the greatest share of federal tax revenue, approximately 50% in 1980, is raised by the individual income tax, we are certainly interested in its effects on economic activity. The federal income tax is based on the notion of "ability to pay"; and its progressive structure has received wide acceptance. The income tax has not been thought to induce large economic distortions so that it has been generally accepted as probably the best way to raise revenue where an unequal distribution of income exists. At the same time we finance social security by FICA (Federal Insurance Contributions Act) taxes which is a proportional tax with an upper limit. As both the tax rate and limit have grown rapidly in recent years, FICA taxes have become the subject of much controversy. In 1980, FICA taxes represented 28% of total federal tax revenue. In Table 1.1 the income tax and payroll tax revenues are given for the period 1960–1980. It is interesting to note over that same period while the marginal income tax rate of the median taxpayer remained constant, the FICA tax rate more than doubled. At the same time the earnings limit rose about 220% in constant dollars. Over the same 20-year period the corporate income tax has decreased from 24% to 13% of federal tax revenues. Likewise, excise taxes have decreased from 13% to 5%. Thus, taxes on labor supply currently amount to about 75% of federal taxes raised.[1] Their potential effects on labor supply and welfare are important because of the large and increasing reliance on direct taxation.

To measure empirically the effect of taxes on labor supply, problems in economic theory and econometrics need to be treated. First, the effect of

*The NSF and NBER provided research support; and A. Auerbach, S. Blomquist and J. Poterba made helpful comments on an earlier draft of this chapter.

[1] Of course, not all income tax revenue is a tax on labor supply because of the taxation of capital income which was about 12% of adjusted gross income in 1980. Also, a portion of the incidence of FICA taxes fall on the employer although the amount is likely to be small.

Handbook of Public Economics, vol. I, edited by A.J. Auerbach and M. Feldstein

Table 1.1
Revenues from income and payroll taxes (billions).

Year	Income tax revenues	Payroll tax[a] revenues	Income tax % of federal revenues	Payroll tax % of federal revenues	Median marginal tax rate[b]	Tax rate for payroll tax	Earnings limit for payroll tax
1960	$40.7	$11.3	45%	12%	20%	3.0%	$ 4800
1965	48.8	17.6	43	15	20	3.626	4800
1970	90.4	39.5	47	21	20	4.8	7800
1975	122.4	75.6	45	28	20	5.85	14100
1980	244.1	139.3	49	28	20	6.05	25900

[a] Includes old-age, survivors, disability, hospital insurance, and railroad retirement taxes.
[b] From Steverle and Hartzmark (1981) with interpolation to have years match up.

progressive taxation is to create a convex, non-linear budget set where the net, after-tax wage depends on hours worked. Since most of consumer theory is based on constant market prices which are independent of quantity purchased, theoretical notions such as the Slutsky equation need to be modified to assess the effect of a change in the tax rate. Theoretical problems increase in complexity when we realize that other provisions of the tax code such as the earned income credit, the standard deduction, and FICA together with transfer programs such as AFDC create important non-convexities in the budget set. Then certain portions of the budget set cannot correspond to utility-maximizing points. Little definite knowledge can be gained by a theoretical analysis of the effect of taxation. In fact, we cannot usually tell whether an increase in tax rates will increase or decrease hours worked. Nor can we decide how an increase in exemptions or other similar changes will affect hours worked. Thus, only empirical investigation can determine the sign and magnitude of the effect of taxation.

Appropriate econometric techniques to measure the effect of taxation also need to treat the non-linearity of the budget sets which taxation creates. Other problems such as components of the stochastic specification, limited dependent variables, and unobserved wages for non-workers arise. Econometric procedures to handle these problems, many of which have only recently been developed, have been used to estimate labor supply functions. We review these results and discuss the possible effects on labor supply of various tax reform proposals which have been enacted or have been discussed in the U.S.

The other important aspect of the taxation of labor supply is the effect on economic welfare. If Hicksian deadweight loss (excess burden) is accepted as the appropriate efficiency measure of the distortion created by taxation, we know that the deadweight loss is proportional to the square of the tax rate.[2] The ratio of deadweight loss to tax revenue raised rises approximately with the tax rate. In

[2] See Auerbach (this volume) for a discussion of appropriate welfare measures in the presence of taxation.

Table 1.1 it can be seen that the marginal tax rate for the median taxpayer is 26%, while the top marginal tax rate on labor supply is 50%. If compensated labor supply elasticities are non-zero, even though small, the deadweight loss from the income tax is likely to be substantial. The important redistributive aspect of the income tax must not be lost sight of, but the cost of the current means of doing so is an important consideration. Again, we will consider various tax reform proposals and their possible effect on economic welfare.

The plan of the paper is as follows. Section 2 considers the theory of labor supply with taxes. The effect of the non-linearity of the budget sets complicates the analysis so few definite conclusions can be reached. In Section 3 we develop an econometric model of labor supply so that the problems created by convex and non-convex budget sets can be solved. Section 4 discusses the various tax systems in the United States. The federal income tax, FICA tax, and state income taxes all are used to develop the appropriate budget sets. We also discuss AFDC, social security benefits, and a negative income tax to determine how they affect labor supply budget sets. In Section 5 we present empirical estimates for husbands and wives labor supply functions. We also calculate the economic cost of the tax system for certain individuals. Because of small numbers in cross-section samples, and measurement problems, high-income individuals are difficult to treat within the context of a labor supply model. Thus, in Section 6 we review the individual questionnaire data for high-income people. It is interesting to note that it agrees broadly with the econometric evidence. In Section 7 we review the evidence from the negative income tax experiments and from samples of social security beneficiaries. These individuals face extremely high marginal tax rates so that interesting evidence of the effect of taxes is produced in these situations. The purpose of this chapter is to concentrate on the effects of taxes. A vast empirical literature in labor economics exists which considers labor supply without explicit consideration of taxes. A recent survey of this literature is given by Killingsworth (1983).

2. The theory of labor supply with taxes

In a world without taxes, the theory of labor supply is characterized by the same conditions which characterize the theory of consumer demand. That is, the Slutsky conditions completely exhaust the theoretical restrictions on consumer response to a price change. Thus, in most previous work on the effect of taxation on labor supply, the authors consider taxes as lowering the net, after-tax wage. Using the Slutsky equation

$$\frac{\mathrm{d}h}{\mathrm{d}w} = \left.\frac{\partial h}{\partial w}\right|_{u=\bar{u}} + h\frac{\partial h}{\partial y}, \tag{2.1}$$

we decompose the change in hours into the substitution effect and the income effect. Since labor is supplied while leisure is demanded, the sign of the substitution effect is positive, while the sign of the income effect is negative if leisure is a normal good. We can conclude that the sign of the sum of the effects is indeterminate. It might then be considered the goal of empirical analysis to determine the sign and magnitude of the effect of taxation.

However, this approach is seriously misleading in all cases except one. Consider the two-good diagram of Figure 2.1. The composite good is used as numeraire, so consumption is measured on the vertical axis with hours supplied on the horizontal axis. Non-labor is denoted by y. The original pre-tax market wage is w and preferred hours of labor are h^*. The effect of a proportional tax is then to lower the net, after-tax wage to $w_t = w(1-t)$. Depending on the individual's preferences, the desired hours of work h^* can either increase or decrease according to equation (2.1). Thus, in the case of proportional taxation, the traditional analysis is correct. But, only for proportional taxes is the analysis so simple. What makes the proportional tax case so special is that non-labor income y is unaffected by the tax which is implicitly assumed to be only a tax on labor income. If y were also subject to taxation at rate t, we would have to take account of another income effect which would cause h^* to rise. Equation (2.1) would then need to be modified to account for taxation of y to

$$\frac{\mathrm{d}h}{\mathrm{d}t} = \left.\frac{\partial h}{\partial w}\right|_{u=\bar{u}} \frac{\mathrm{d}w}{\mathrm{d}t} + h\frac{\partial h}{\partial y} + \frac{\partial h}{\partial y}\frac{\mathrm{d}y}{\mathrm{d}t}. \tag{2.2}$$

When we consider the effect of taxation, the income and substitution effect of a change in the wage as well as the change in non-labor income must be accounted

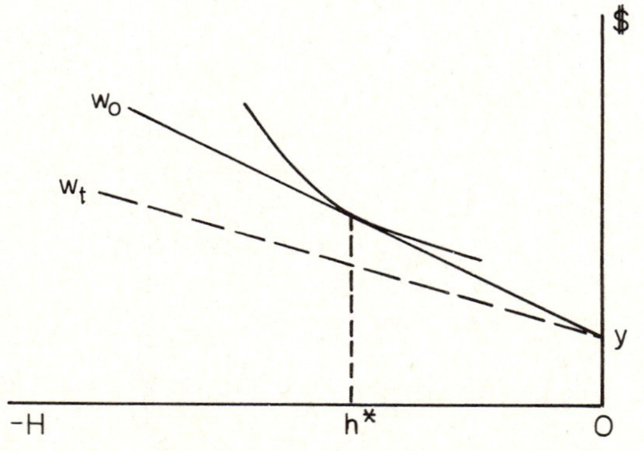

Figure 2.1

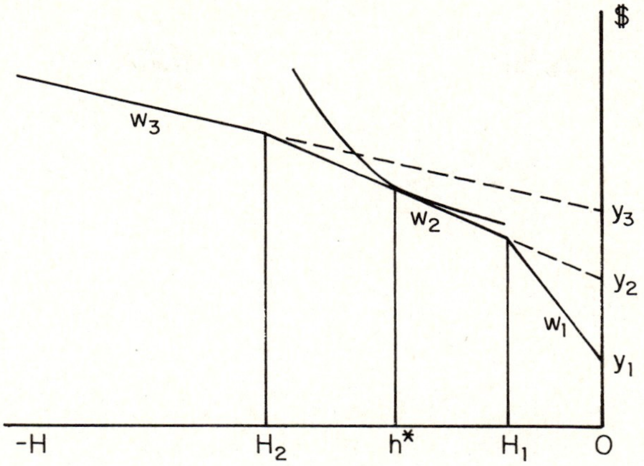

Figure 2.2

for. This equation becomes the key device in analyzing the effect of taxation on desired hours of work. The total effect of taxation is still indeterminate but a complication has been added since changes in both w and y must be considered. In cases of progressive taxation or government tax and transfer programs, both w and y are affected. The traditional analysis has neglected to account for the effect on y of the tax system. We now consider how the analysis changes when non-proportional tax systems are considered.

Let us first analyze the simplest case, that of a progressive tax on labor income so that the marginal tax rate is non-decreasing. In Figure 2.2 three marginal tax rates are considered, t_1, t_2 and t_3, which lead to three after-tax net wages, w_1, w_2 and w_3, where $w_i = w(1 - t_i)$. H_1 and H_2 correspond to kink point hours which occur at the intersection of two tax brackets. But an important addition to the diagram are the "virtual" incomes y_2 and y_3, which follow from extension of a given budget segment to the vertical axis. They are denoted as virtual income because if the individual faced the linear budget set $B_2 = (w_2, y_2)$, he would still choose hours of work h^* as in Figure 2.2. In assessing the effect of taxation on labor supply, two questions arise. How does h^* in Figure 2.2 differ from the no-tax situation of Figure 2.1? And how is h^* in Figure 2.2 affected by a change in the market wage w or the tax rates t_i?

To consider the first question we combine Figures 2.1 and 2.2 in Figure 2.3. We see that no general effect can be identified. If the individual's h^* falls on the first budget segment $B_1 = (w_1, y_1)$ we are back in the case of Figure 2.1 with offsetting income and substitution effects. Alternatively, if h^* falls on either B_2 or B_3, then the net wage is lower than w which leads to an income and substitution effect, which virtual income y_2 or y_3 exceeds y_1 and a further income effect from

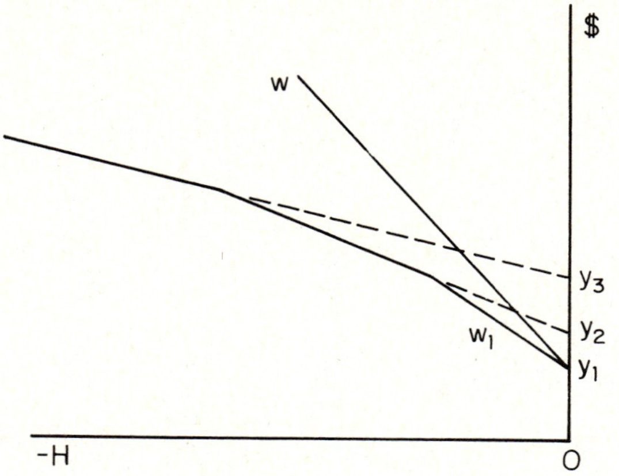

Figure 2.3

equation (2.1) is created which would reduce labor supply.[3] One result which does follow is that on the budget segment B_2 or B_3 labor supply is *less* than it would be if the analysis were based on (w_2, y_1) or (w_3, y_1); that is, if the effect of the virtual income were ignored.

To answer the second question we initially consider an increase in the market wage from w to w'. In Figure 2.4 we see that this wage change leads to a clockwise rotation of the budget set. The effect of the rotation is to raise the w_i, but it also leaves the virtual incomes unchanged. For instance, the virtual income y_2 is

$$y_2 = E_1\left(\frac{t_2 - t_1}{1 - t_1}\right) - y_1\left(\frac{1 - t_2}{1 - t_1}\right),$$

where E_1 is the earnings limit for the first tax bracket, i.e., $E_1 = y_1 + w_1 H_1$. Thus, the virtual incomes depend only on the tax system and non-labor income y_1. Therefore, so long as the individual's preferred hours of work h^* remain on the same budget segment B_i, the effect of a wage change can be analyzed using the traditional local analysis which is contained in the Slutsky equation (2.2)

The effect of a change in a tax rate t_i depends on which t_i changes. To take the simplest case, suppose t_3 rises so that in Figure 2.2 the w_3 segment rotates counterclockwise. The virtual income y_3 also rises. We have the same effect as

[3]It may well be this latter income effect, which creates the appearance of a backward bending labor supply curve which has been found in many empirical studies. The important point here is that not only do we have a income effect from the change in wage, but virtual income also rises due to the effect of the tax system.

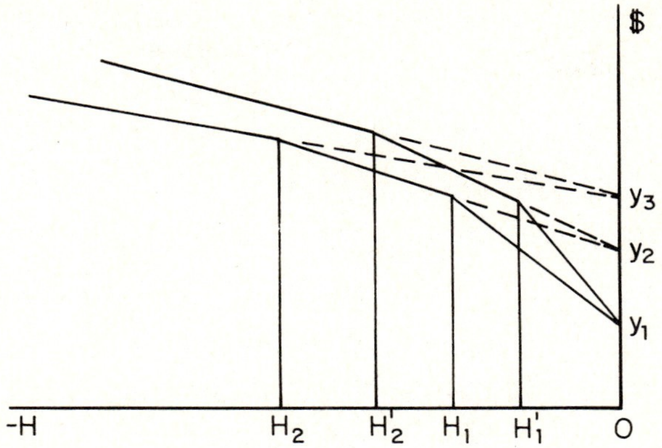

Figure 2.4

before where the change in wage alone induces both an income and substitution effect and the change in virtual income induces more labor supply from equation (2.2). It is important to note that a person, whose preferred hours were previously on the third budget segment B_3 so that $h^* > H_2$, may now decrease his preferred hours to H_2 if the substitution effect is large enough, but will not decrease the preferred hours down to the second budget segment. Individuals, whose preferred hours were less than H_2 before the change, will not be affected. However, if the tax rate were to decrease, we could again have people shifting from the second segment to the third segment because of the substitution effect. For these cases, we need "global" information on the individual's preferences, since the local information in the Slutsky equation is not sufficient to analyze the possible changes. Now if either t_1 or t_2 were to change, the situation is more complicated since all later budget segments are also affected. However, the later budget segments are affected only by a change in their virtual income since the net wage remains the same. Thus, if t_1 rises, for those individuals with $h^* > H_1$, the effect of the tax change is to cause their preferred hours to rise. For people whose initial $h^* \leq H_1$, only w_1 changes (although y_1 may change also) so that the Slutsky equation can be used. Lastly suppose one of the tax bracket limits E_i changes. If E_i is lowered, all virtual incomes on later budget segments fall. Therefore if initially $h^* > H_1$, we have a similar qualitative effect to a rise in t_1. Preferred hours of work will rise. For an individual whose initial $h^* \leq H_1$ but the E_1' have $H' < h^*$, the analysis is more complicated. They may switch to B_2 with its lower net wage and higher virtual income, or they may decrease their desired hours of work so that $h^* < H_1'$ and they remain on the first segment.

From the analysis of the progressive tax case we see that very few general propositions can be deduced about the effect of taxes on labor supply. The

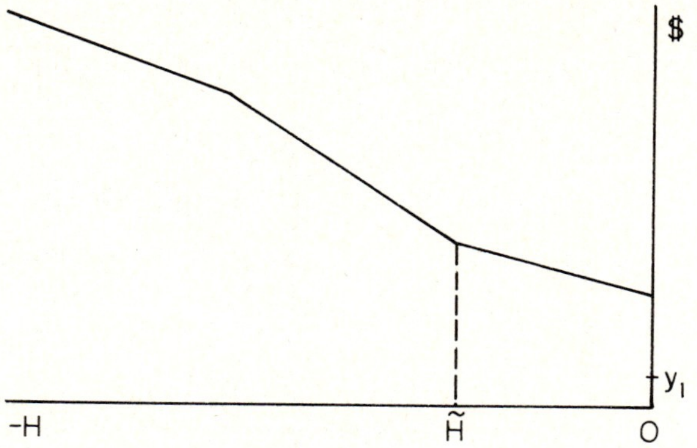

Figure 2.5

piecewise linear progressive tax system is defined by a sequence of budget segments $B_i = (w_i, y_i)$ of net wages and virtual incomes for the individual over a set of hours (H_i, H_{i+1}). Some limited results are possible for changes in t_i and E_i for individuals whose initial hours of work are on a subsequent budget segment B_{i+j}, $j > 0$. But to assess the effect of taxation adequately we really need to know the individual's preferences or, equivalently, his utility function. We will show how knowledge of his utility function arises in the process of estimating his labor supply function so that numerical computations of the effect of taxation can be carried out.

When we do not have a progressive tax system, matters become more complex since the budget set is no longer convex.[4] Non-convex budget sets arise from the presence of government transfer programs. The three most important programs of this type are AFDC, social security, and a negative income tax (NIT) program. In Figures 2.5 and 2.6 we show the two most common types of non-convex budget sets.[5] In the first type of budget set used in the NIT experiments, and in the majority of AFDC programs, non-labor income is raised by the amount of the government transfer. The individual then faces a high marginal tax rate, usually 0.4 or higher, until he reaches H, the breakeven point at which all benefits have been taxed away. Beyond the breakeven point, the individual rejoins the federal tax system, here taken to be convex. Figure 2.6 has one additional complication which arises as an earnings disregard in social security benefits or as a maximum

[4]As we will discuss subsequently, even the federal tax system is not truly convex because of the effect of social security payments, the earned income credit, and the standard deduction. However, it may well be the case that treating taxes in a convex budget set is a sufficiently good approximation for empirical work.

[5]A non-convexity may also arise, not from the tax system, but due to fixed costs to working; e.g., Hausman (1980). We will discuss fixed costs in the next section.

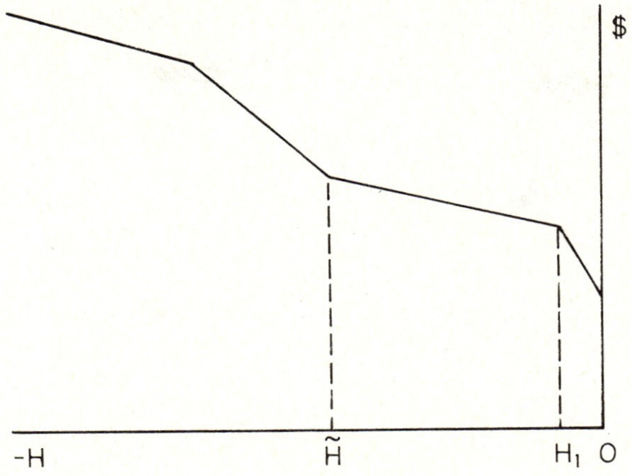

Figure 2.6

payment amount in some AFDC programs.[6] Hours up to H_1 are taxed only at FICA rates where H_1 is determined by E_1. Thus earnings up to a set amount are "disregarded" or not taxed by the program which is giving the transfer. Beyond this point, the individual faces the high marginal rates until breakeven hours are again reached. On *a priori* grounds, almost nothing can be said about the effect of taxation in the non-convex budget case. The added complication arises from the possibility of multiple tangencies between indifference curves at the budget set.

Figures 2.7 and 2.8 demonstrate two cases of multiple tangencies although actual cases may be even more complex due to the possibility of skipping entire budget segments. The possibility of having multiple optima as in Figure 2.7 because $w_1 < w_3$ while $y_2 < y_3$. In the convex case this possibility does not arise because as w_i falls y_i is rising. To determine the global optimum we need to have knowledge of the utility function. Figure 2.8 demonstrates the case of a joint tangency, the possibility of which arises with each non-convex segment. Small changes in the wage or any parameter of the tax system can then lead to large changes in desired hours of work.

In the convex budget case, we must always have a tangency which is unique and which represents the global optimum if desired hours are positive. For if we had two tangencies we could connect the two points, and the connecting lines which would lie inside the original budget set would represent preferred points by the assumed concavity of preferences.[7] Furthermore, the effect on h^* of a change in the market wage, taxes, or the earnings limits is "smooth" in an appropriate

[6]See Hanoch and Honig (1978) for a theoretical analysis of the social security case. Burtless and Moffitt (1982) discuss the social security budget set within a model of labor supply and retirement. See also Blinder, Gordon and Wise (1980) for a treatment of intertemporal considerations.

[7]See Hausman (1979) for further analysis and implications of this case.

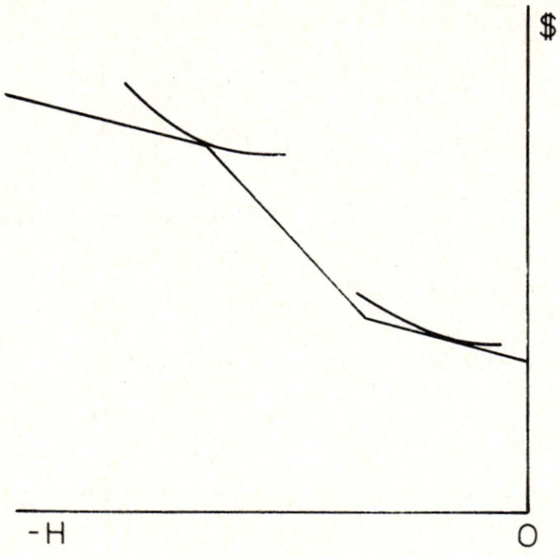

Figure 2.7

mathematical sense that the change is continuous and differentiable. For the non-convex case, this reasoning no longer follows since the line connecting the multiple tangencies no longer lies within the budget set. Thus, multiple tangencies may occur. Likewise, the effect of changes in the budget set are no longer smooth since a small change may cause a jump in desired hours from an initial tangency to the neighborhood of another initial tangency. Thus, it seems that no general propositions hold. The extended Slutsky equation (2.2) is not usable since the possibility of a jump from one budget segment to another is always present.

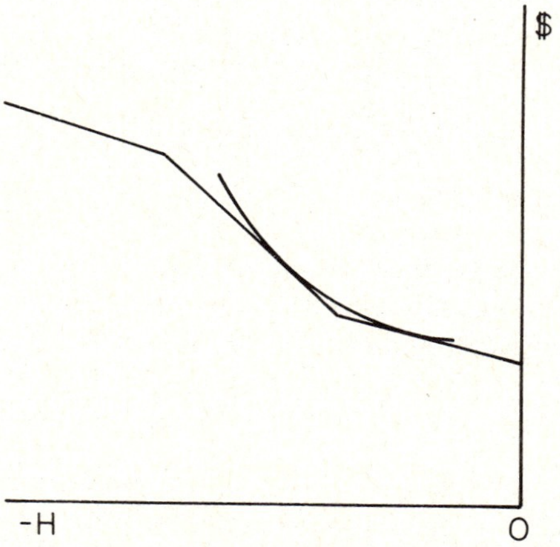

Figure 2.8

We briefly consider the cases where we could say something definite in the convex case: a rise in t_1 or a drop in E_1 for individuals not on the first segment. For individuals who remain on the convex budget segments like w_2 and w_3 in Figure 2.7, virtual incomes again fall while w_i remains constant so that the local effect is again a rise in desired hours of work. But one cannot rule out the possibility of a non-local jump down to the first segment or even withdrawal from the labor force entirely. Similar possibilities exist if E_1 is decreased. Thus, the analysis of the non-convex case cannot proceed without knowledge about the form of the individual's utility function.

Important potential shortcomings exist in this theory of labor supply which we now discuss briefly. Future work on econometric models will need to incorporate these problems into the theory and estimation.[8] First, individuals may face quantity restrictions in labor supply. That is, h^* may not be possible for systematic reasons. Certainly "involuntary" unemployment falls into this category. In principle, even if quantity restrictions exist, we can estimate the underlying demand function or preference structure and analyze the effect of taxes. But a more difficult problem is to ascertain if individuals are actually constrained. Endless debates on the possibility of involuntary unemployment highlight this problem. Furthermore, survey questions on the ability of a person to work more hours are very untrustworthy. To date, only limited progress has been made on this problem.[9] Better data seems to be required to put quantity constraints into an empirical model in a totally satisfactory manner.

This type of labor supply theory also does not adequately treat the type of jobs people take or their intensity of work while on the job.[10] An effect of taxes is to make non-pecuniary rewards more attractive so that a measure of earnings may seriously misrepresent the preference comparisons being made among jobs. Academics need hardly be reminded of this fact in the present world of falling real academic wages. Yet it is doubtful that this problem will ever be completely solved. "Perks" from a job could be evaluated monetarily and included in earnings. But we cannot hope to measure adequately certain types of non-monetary rewards to jobs.

A last consideration is intertemporal aspects of the model. We have considered a static world devoid of human capital considerations and intertemporal factors

[8] Considerable research is currently undertaken in these areas.

[9] Ham (1982) has introduced quantity constraints into a labor supply model without taxes. See Deaton (1981) and Deaton and Muellbauer (1981) for further research on quantity restrictions. Brown et al. (1982) have attempted to incorporate quantity restrictions in a short-term labor supply model which does incorporate taxation.

[10] To the extent that wages reflect intensity of work, this problem may not be too serious. However, for many jobs wages may be only loosely related to current effort with longer-run goals important. We discuss this issue subsequently. See Rosen (1980) for a discussion of these problems.

such as savings. But intertemporal issues may be quite important for new entrants into the labor market and for individuals close to retirement. The eighty-hour weeks put in by young lawyers will be rewarded in the not-too-distant future so that current compensation in an inadequate measure of earnings. Furthermore, issues of on-the-job training may be important. To date, research on issues of intertemporal labor supply have indicated only limited empirical importance of this problem. But further empirical research based on less restrictive models may find a more important role for intertemporal considerations.

Another potentially important intertemporal consideration is that the models that we have specified are static labor supply models. Intertemporal considerations may render the static approach inapplicable except under very strong separability assumptions. How would our approach change if life cycle considerations are accounted for? Blundell and Walker (1984) have demonstrated that only a minor change is required. Under the assumption which is typically made in life cycle models, a two-stage budgeting approach makes the labor supply decision conditional on planned life cycle asset accumulation.[11] At the first stage the lifetime budget is allocated to equalize the marginal utility of money in each period. At the second stage the labor supply decision is made conditional on this allocation. The second-stage decision is therefore analogous to our static approach except that non-labor income must be replaced by net dissaving in the period. MaCurdy (1981) discusses the interpretation of the estimated coefficients from the labor supply model in a life cycle context. However, note that the tax system still only taxes the income component of this dissaving. The static specification then becomes correct only if assets remain constant over the life cycle.

The specification of a static labor supply model may thus lead to biased estimates because the incorrect measure of virtual income is being used in the labor supply equation. Note, however, that most of the variation in virtual income, which enters the labor supply equation occurs because of the tax system. The variation in net dissavings compared to the variations caused by the tax system may be small. More research is required here. What is primarily needed is a cross-section data set which contains both labor supply information and also carefully constructed information on net dissavings over the period of observation.

MaCurdy (1983) takes a different approach to the problem of incorporating life cycle considerations. He estimates the marginal rate of substitution function between consumption and hours of work. Thus, data on both labor supply and consumption is needed. Unfortunately, it is not straightforward to see how constraints such as zero hours of work can be applied in the MaCurdy formulation. Further econometric problems exist with respect to errors-in-variables problems in representing the tax system. In its initial application to the Denver

[11] Deaton and Muellbauer (1980) discuss two-stage budgetary approaches.

Income Maintenance Experiment, MaCurdy estimates labor supply elasticities which are extreme outliers with respect to previous results which will be discussed subsequently. Further research will hopefully determine whether MaCurdy's results arise because of the life cycle considerations which previous studies have ignored or because of the econometric specifications which he uses.

In this section we have considered from a theoretical point of view the effect of taxes on labor supply. The Slutsky equation, which has been traditionally used to analyze the problem, is inadequate except for the case of a proportional tax. Progressive taxation results in a convex budget constraint which leads to a multiplicity of net wages and virtual incomes. We see that except for a few cases the effect of a change in the tax rate cannot be determined on *a priori* grounds even if reasonable assumptions are made such as leisure being a normal good. Government tax and transfer programs result in non-convex budget sets which are even more difficult to analyze theoretically. Thus, we now turn to the econometrics of the problem so that models can be estimated. From the estimated models we can assess the effect of taxation. However, as with all models, we discuss certain aspects of the problem which have not been included. The results should be interpreted with these limitations in mind.

3. Tax systems

In the previous section we have discussed the theory of labor supply with taxes. We will now describe the type of tax systems which exist in the United States. To give a historical perspective on the problem, we will outline the evolution of the income tax rate over the century. We will also provide data on actual marginal tax rates since 1960 when the data become available. We shall discuss federal and state income taxes first. It turns out that, even though the basic federal income tax is progressive, the resulting budget set that an individual faces is not convex. FICA payments, the standard deduction and the earned income credit all introduce non-convexities. These additions to the basic progressive tax system will be explained. Next we discuss AFDC tax systems for each state. Lastly we briefly discuss tax systems for social security beneficiaries and negative income tax (NIT) recipients. All of these tax systems have very large non-convexities together with quite high marginal tax rates.

We first outline the basic federal income tax system in 1980 by twelve brackets.[12] The first bracket is $1,000 wide with succeeding brackets falling at intervals of $4,000. Since we are interested in the effect of taxes on labor supply, we consider only taxes on earned income. Table 3.1 lists the brackets along with

[12] Here we discuss our procedure for joint returns. We follow similar procedures for single persons and heads of households, but do not report the details here.

Table 3.1
Basic federal tax rates for 1980 on earned income for married couples.

Taxable income	Marginal rate	Average rate at midpoint
0–2,000	0.14	0.140
2,000–4,000	0.16	0.147
4,000–8,000	0.18	0.160
8,000–12,000	0.21	0.174
12,000–16,000	0.24	0.189
16,000–20,000	0.28	0.204
20,000–24,000	0.32	0.222
24,000–32,000	0.37	0.250
32,000–42,000	0.43	0.287
42,000–56,000	0.49	0.331
56,000 +	0.50	—

the marginal tax rates and average tax rates at the midpoint of the bracket. It is interesting to note that the average tax rate remains significantly below the marginal tax rate until quite high levels of earned income are reached. Thus a theory which stated that individuals react to average after-tax income when making marginal decisions, might come up with rather different results. However, the theory of individual behavior with respect to progressive taxation contains both the marginal net wage and the appropriate virtual income which reflects average tax rates up to the current tax bracket. In a certain sense, the entire characteristics of the tax system are accounted for in this way.

In determining taxable income, personal exemptions need to be accounted for. An exemption of $1,000 per person was allowed in 1980. The standard deduction, or zero bracket amount, was $3,400 for married couples in 1980.[13] Itemized deductions in excess of $3,400 could also be subtracted from gross income. They were approximately 9% of adjusted gross income in 1980. The standard deduction, i.e., no itemized deductions, was used on approximately 70% of all tax returns in 1980. Next, the earned income credit grants of 10% below $5,000 of gross income. From $6,000 to $10,000 the credit is reduced by 12.5%, so that the breakeven point is reached at $10,000 when the credit has been completely exhausted. A non-convexity is created at $10,000 because the tax rate falls by the 12.5% payment when the breakeven point is reached. Lastly FICA contributions were 6.05% up to a limit of $25,900 in 1980. Thus, in the appropriate bracket when the FICA limit is reached, the marginal tax rate falls from about 0.38 to about 0.32, which also creates a non-convexity.[14] We provide some historical data

[13]Tables exclude the zero bracket amount for the standard deduction.

[14]However, empirical work by Hausman (1981a) did not indicate that the non-convexities created by the earned income credit and FICA had an important influence on the econometric estimates.

Table 3.2
Federal income tax: Selected marginal rates.

Taxable income (1000's)	1950 (1.0, 3.3)[c]	1969 (1.23, 5.6)	1970[a] (1.61, 9.8)	1980 (3.42, 21.0)	1984[b]
2–4	22	22	19	16	12
6–8	30	30	26	21	16
10–12	38	38	33	26	20
16–18	50	50	43	40	30
20–22	56	56	49	43	23
26–32	62	62	54	50[d]	38
38–44	69	69	59	50	42
50–60	75	75	64	50	46
60–70	78	78	66	50	48
70–80	81	81	68	50	48
80–90	84	84	70	50	49
90–100	87	87	71	50	50
100–150	89	89	72	50	50
150–200	90	90	72	50	50

[a] Includes 2.5% surtax.
[b] The 1984 rates reflect the entire 25% tax reduction pased by Congress in 1981. The tax will then be indexed.
[c] First entry is CPI in 1950 dollars and second entry is median family income in thousands of current dollars.
[d] Maximum tax on earned (labor) income was 50% beginning in 1972 under the Tax Reform Act of 1969.

on tax rates and actual marginal rates to provide a historical perspective on the income tax system.[15]

In Table 3.2 we provide a summary of marginal tax rates for the period 1950–1984, according to current legislation.[16] These rates are for single taxpayers, with no exemptions or deductions accounted for. We also give the CPI and median family income, so that valid comparisons across different years can be made. First, note that the tax system between 1950 and 1980 was only imperfectly indexed for inflation. The median income faced a marginal tax rate of 22% in 1950, but multiplied by the change in the CPI, this amount faced a marginal rate of 26% in 1980. Similarly, $10,000 of earned income in 1950 had a marginal tax rate of 38% in 1950, but adjusted for inflation, this marginal tax rate increased to 43% in 1980. Similar increases in marginal tax rates occurred over the periods 1960–1980 and 1970–1980. Of course, this imperfect indexation corresponds to greater progressivity which may have been the intent of Congress over the period. However, note that under the tax reform of 1981, marginal rates will drop

[15] Tax law changes in 1981 provide for exclusion from taxation of 10% of the secondary worker's earnings up to $30,000 beginning in 1983. This change greatly increased the neutrality of the tax system towards married persons.

[16] The tax rates are taken from Tax Foundation (1981).

substantially by 1984 due to the 25% tax reduction, with the exact amount depending on inflation over the 1982–1984 period. Much of the "bracket creep" of the past decade will be eliminated. Under current legislation, the tax system will then be indexed after 1984. Another interesting finding which emerges from Table 3.2 is the significantly higher marginal tax rates faced by the median earned over the period. Besides the effect of inflation and imperfect indexation, real wage growth also led to higher marginal taxes. Lastly, note the remarkable decline in maximum taxes on earned income which arose with the Tax Reform Act of 1969. To determine the effect of these tax changes we now consider the actual marginal rates faced by given segments of the population.

We present marginal tax rates from a sample of returns in Table 3.3, calculated by Steverle and Hartzmark (1981) in a very useful paper. Of course, the tax rates correspond to total income rather than just labor income which was considered in Table 3.2. The significant rise in the progressivity of the income tax in the 1960–1980 period is evident in Table 3.3. Note that for those households which paid tax, the marginal rate was between 0.18 and 0.26 up through the 95% percentile. In fact, 59% of all taxpayers who had a non-zero marginal rate had a rate of 18%. While the marginal rate for the median return increased by 10% between 1961 and 1979, the difference in rates on the interquantile range increased by 33%. This considerable increase in the progressivity of the marginal tax rates will be decreased by the tax legislation changes of 1981.

Another historical comparison of marginal tax rates is provided by Seater (1982) who based his estimates on the *Statistics of Income* rather than a sample of individual returns. Except for the years 1964–1967 when the Kennedy tax cut

Table 3.3
Marginal rates of taxation on personal income.

Percentile of returns	Marginal rates				Average marginal tax rates[b]		
	1961	1969[a]	1974	1979	Year	Rate	Payroll tax included
1%	0.00	0.00	0.00	0.00	1950	15.2	—
5%	0.00	0.00	0.00	0.00	1955	16.3	—
10%	0.00	0.00	0.00	0.00	1960	16.4	19.4
25%	0.18	0.15	0.15	0.14	1965	14.0	17.6
50%	0.18	0.23	0.20	0.20	1970	17.2	22.0
75%	0.22	0.25	0.22	0.24	1975	17.4	23.3
90%	0.22	0.28	0.28	0.32			
95%	0.26	0.32	0.32	0.38			
99%	0.38	0.47	0.47	0.50			

[a] Includes an approximation for surtax changed in 1969.
[b] From Seater (1982).

lowered tax rates, the average marginal tax rate increased over the period 1950–1980. When the effects of the payroll tax are included, the increase is from an average marginal tax rate of about 15% in 1950 to an average rate of over 23% in 1975, which is an increase of 43% in the 25-year period. Therefore, the increases in the payroll tax over the period have a large effect on the marginal tax rates.

State income taxes (including the District of Columbia) should also be briefly mentioned. In 1980, nine states did not tax earned income, but the other forty-two states had either progressive of proportional tax systems. Sixteen states permitted deduction of federal income taxes. Among the states with progressive tax systems Delaware had the highest overall marginal tax rate of 19.8%. However, at $15,000 after personal exemptions, the marginal rate in California was 10%, in Hawaii 10%, in Minnesota 14%, and in New York state 10%. In Oregon the marginal tax rate was 10% above $15,000, and in Wisconsin the marginal rate was 11.4% at $15,000. Nebraska, Rhode Island and Vermont were the only states which took a constant percentage from the federal taxes paid. Rhode Island took the highest proportion, 17%. Among states with proportional rates after personal exemptions, Illinois had a rate of 2.5%, Massachusetts a rate of 5.4%, and Indiana and Pennsylvania rates of 2%. State governments increasingly turned to direct taxation as a source of revenue over the past 20 years.

Beside the operation of the Federal tax system, another potentially more important influence on labor supply of female heads of household is the AFDC, Aid for Dependent Children, tax and transfer system. It has often been contended that AFDC presents a significant disincentive to labor supply, and its replacement by NIT, Negative Income Tax, could significantly decrease the work disincentive. The basic design of AFDC programs is a transfer payment which depends on family size, accompanied by a tax rate of 67% until the breakeven point is reached and the person returns to the federal tax system. A sizeable non-convexity is created because at the breakeven point the marginal tax rate decreases from 0.67 to approximately 0.16. Thus, the potential disincentive effect is quite large.[17] States differ in the size of the transfer payment and also in the exact operation of the AFDC tax system. The majority of the states permit $30 of earned income per month before starting to levy the 0.67 tax. Thus, in Figure 3.1 we show the basic outline of the AFDC budget set. Breakeven hours $\tilde{H}$ may not be reached even by women who work full time at the level of wages which AFDC recipients typically receive.

The workings of NIT tax systems resemble AFDC as in Figure 3.1, although no earnings disregard exists. Major differences are eligibility, since all families would qualify, and benefit and tax parameters. The NIT guarantee is a function of the

[17]Under current legislation, in certain cases the tax rate is 100%. An important distinction exists between the statutory tax rate and the effective tax rate because of various allowable deductions. Moffitt (1981) estimates the effective AFDC tax rates over a sample of recipients.

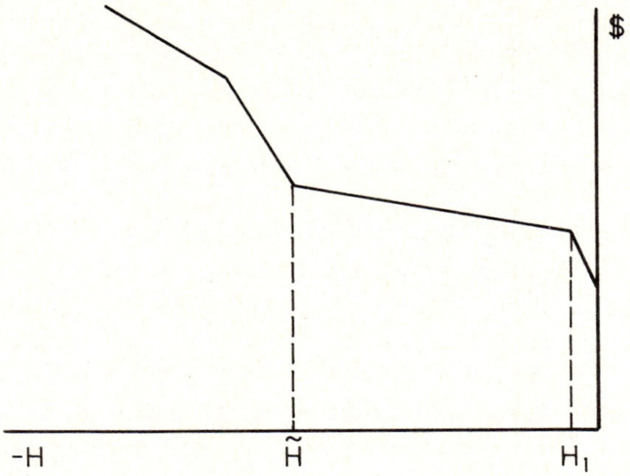

Figure 3.1

poverty limit which depends on family size and the local cost of living. The guarantee has been set at between 0.75 and 1.25 times the poverty limit in the NIT experiments. For instance, in Indiana 0.75 times the poverty limit was 28% higher than the AFDC payment for non-labor force participation for a family of four. Thus the NIT guarantee is typically more generous than the AFDC payment. The marginal tax rate up to breakeven hours is also lowered from 0.67 to a value between 0.4 and 0.6. The budget set has the non-convex form of Figure 3.2, where beyond breakeven hours, $\tilde{H}$, the individual returns to the federal tax system. At breakeven hours, the marginal tax rate falls from 0.4 and 0.7 to around 0.25 when federal taxes and FICA are accounted for. For male heads of households with good jobs on the less generous plans of a low guarantee and high tax rate, breakeven hours will be reached at about 120 hours per month of work. For males on very generous plans or those with low wages, breakeven costs will not be reached even for high hours of work. Likewise, for female heads of household the majority will not reach breakeven hours because of their relatively low wages. Thus the position of the first tax segment and the non-convexity created at $\tilde{H}$ hours may have a significant influence on labor supply decisions.

The last tax system we consider is the operation of the social security earnings test for individuals between 62 and 70 years old who are receiving social security benefits. The budget set has exactly the same form as the operation of AFDC in Figure 3.1. A level of benefits is determined by the earnings history covered by social security and by family composition. An "earnings disregard" then exists up to an amount which determines H_1 hours. Beyond H_1 hours earnings are taxed at a rate of 0.5 until breakeven hours $\tilde{H}$ are reached. Thus, we again seem to have a

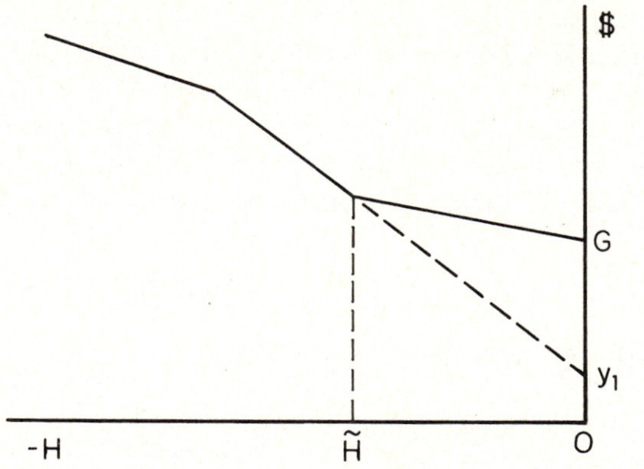

Figure 3.2

possibly large disincentive to working.[18] But this diagram leaves out a potentially important effect which Blinder, Gordon and Wise (1980) point out. The effect is that current earnings will replace lower previous earnings, which are used to compute average monthly earnings which the benefit level is partly based on. Especially with the low levels of previous FICA amounts, current earnings could replace the $3,600 level in force in 1951–1954 and for about 20% of near-retirement workers replace previous zero FICA earnings years. Thus, if individuals understand the admittedly extremely complex social security benefit formulas, the work disincentives can be greatly diminished. Blinder, Gordon and Wise actually give an example where the earnings test is more than compensated for as a work *incentive* exists. Thus, empirical studies which use historical data may have great difficulty in adequately representing the correct budget set. The indexing provision of the 1977 Social Security Amendments greatly lowers the quantitative significance of earnings replacement. However, the disincentive effect of the earnings test is still diminished. The intertemporal aspects of the interaction of social security and the retirement decision probably require a more complex model than our essentially one-period representation of the budget set. While the problem is quite difficult to represent in a model, social security may have a significant effect on retirement.[19]

In this section we have discussed the effect of federal and state tax systems on the budget set. While federal tax rates are uniformly progressive, non-convexities

[18] If the individual is eligible to receive benefits but continues working without receiving benefits, his future benefits are increased by an approximately actuarily fair amount between the ages of 62 and 65. The adjustment for ages 65–70 is considerably less.

[19] The Blinder et al. conclusions have been challenged by Burkhauser and Turner (1981); a reply is given by Blinder et al. (1981). For empirical estimates of the effect of social security on retirement, see Gordon and Blinder (1980), Boskin and Hurd (1982), Burtless and Moffitt (1982) and Diamond and Hausman (1982). These results are reviewed in the last section of this paper.

still exist in the budget set due to the presence of the standard deduction, earned income credit, and FICA contributions. State income tax and AFDC programs are also discussed. Next the NIT tax system and its relation to AFDC is considered. Lastly, the budget set for the social security earnings test and the complex intertemporal aspects of retirement are outlined. In this last area further work seems required to extend the labor supply model to account for intertemporal decisions.

4. The econometrics of labor supply with taxes

The essential feature which distinguishes econometric models of labor supply with taxes from traditional demand models is the non-constancy of the net, after-tax wage.[20] Except for the case of a proportional tax system, the net wage depends on hours worked because of the operation of the tax system. Also the marginal net wage depends on the specific budget segment that the individual's indifference curve is tangent to. Thus, econometric techniques need to be devised which can treat the non-linearity of the budget set. However, it is important to note at the outset that a simultaneous equation problem does not really exist, even though the net wage received depends on hours worked.[21] Given a market wage which is constant over hours worked and a tax system which is given exogenously by the government, the non-linear budget set faced by the individual in deciding on his preferred hours of work is determined exogenously to his choice.[22] An econometric model needs to take the exogenous non-linear budget set and to explain the individual choice of desired hours. We first describe such a model for convex and non-convex budget sets. As expected, the convex case is simpler to deal with. We then consider other issues of model specification, such as variation in tastes, fixed costs to working, and quantity constraints on available labor supply.

Econometric estimation is quite straightforward in the case of a convex budget set. Since a unique tangency or a corner solution at zero hours will determine desired hours of work, we need only determine where the tangency occurs. To do

[20] Non-constant prices do exist in the demand for other goods, e.g., electricity with a declining block rate. A general treatment of econometric techniques for non-linear budget sets is given by Hausman (1982a).

[21] In initial work on introducing taxes into labor supply models, Hall (1973) used the observed after-tax wage which creates simultaneous equation bias in the estimated coefficients. Wales (1973), Hausman and Wise (1976), and Rosen (1976) introduced instrumental variable techniques to take account of this problem.

[22] If the market wage depends on hours worked, the same reasoning holds since the budget set is still exogenous. A more fundamental problem exists over the question of whether labor supply models, with or without taxes, are identified. Unobserved individual effects may exist in both the wage equation and hours equation. If these individual effects also influence variables such as education which appear in the wage equation but not in the hours equation and thus serve to identify the hours equation, we would lose identification.

so we begin with a slight generalization of the usual type of labor supply specification,

$$h = \tilde{g}(w, y, z, \beta) + \varepsilon = h^* + \varepsilon, \tag{4.1}$$

where w is a vector of net wages, y is a vector of virtual income, z are individual socioeconomic variables, β is the unknown vector of coefficients assumed fixed over the population, and ε is a stochastic term which represents the divergence between desired hours h^* and actual hours. The typical specification that has been used in $\tilde{g}(\;)$ is linear or log-linear and scalar w and y corresponding to the market wage and non-labor income. The stochastic term is assumed to have classical properties so that no quantity constraints on hours worked exist. However, $0 \le h \le \overline{H}$, where H is a physical maximum to hours worked. We also assume that, when the β's are estimated, the Slutsky conditions are satisfied so that $\tilde{g}(\;)$ arises from concave preferences.

The problem to be solved is to find h^* when the individual is faced with the convex budget set, B_i for $i = 1, \dots, m$.[23] To find h^* we take the specification of desired hours on a given budget segment B_i,

$$h_i^* = g(w_i, y_i, z, \beta). \tag{4.2}$$

Calculate h_i^* and if $0 \le h_i^* \le H_i$ where the H_i's are kink point hours in Figure 2.2, then h_i^* is feasible and represents the unique tangency of the indifference curves and the budget set. However, if h_i^* lies outside the interval $(0, H_i)$ it is not feasible, so we move on to try the next budget segment. If $H_1 \le h_2^* \le H_2$, we again would have the unique optimum. If we have bracketed the kink point so that $h_1^* > H_1$ and $h_2^* < H_1$, then $h^* = H_1$ so that desired hours fall at the kink point. Otherwise we go on and calculate h_3^*. By trying out all the segments we will either find a tangency or find that $h_i^* < H_{i-1}$ for all i in which case $h^* = 0$, or $h_i^* > H_i^*$ for all i in which case $h^* = \overline{H}$. Then a non-linear least squares procedure or Tobit procedure to take account of minimum hours at zero should be used to compute the unknown β parameters. The statistical procedure would basically minimize the sum of $\sum_{j=1}^{N}(h_j - h_j^*)^2$, where j represents individuals in the sample.[24] Perhaps a better technique would be to use Tobit, which enforces the constraint that $h_j \ge 0$.

The case of the non-convex budget set as in Figure 2.5 or Figure 2.6 is more complicated because equation (4.2) can lead to more than one feasible tangency which leads to many potential h_i^*'s. How can we decide which of these feasible

[23] The technique used here is more fully explained in Hausman (1979b). See also Hausman (1981a, 1982a).

[24] A potential problem exists in the asymptotic expansions used to compute the standard errors of the coefficients.

h_i^*'s is the global optimum? Burtless and Hausman (1978) initially demonstrated the technique of working backwards from the labor supply specification of equation (4.2) to the underlying preferences which can be represented by a utility function.[25] The basic idea is to make use of Roy's identity which generated the labor supply function from the indirect utility function $v(w_i, y_i)$,

$$\frac{\partial v(w_i, y_i)}{\partial w_i} \Big/ \frac{\partial v(w_i, y_i)}{\partial y_i} = h_i^* = g(w_i, y_i, z, \beta), \tag{4.3}$$

along a given budget segment. As long as the Slutsky condition holds $v(w_i, y_i)$ can always be recovered by solving the differential equation (4.3). In fact, $v(\ )$ often has a quite simple closed form for commonly used labor supply specifications. For the linear supply specification

$$h_i^* = \alpha w_i + \beta y_i + z\gamma, \tag{4.4}$$

Hausman (1980) solved for the indirect utility function

$$v(w_i, y_i) = e^{\beta w_i}\left(y_i + \frac{\alpha}{\beta} w_i - \frac{\alpha}{\beta^2} + \frac{z\gamma}{\beta}\right). \tag{4.5}$$

Given the indirect utility function, all of the feasible tangencies can be compared, and the tangency with highest utility is chosen as the preferred hours of work h^*.[26] Then, as with the convex budget set case, we can use either non-linear least squares or a Tobit procedure to estimate the unknown coefficients. While using a specific parameterization of the utility function seems upsetting to some people, it should be realized that writing down a labor supply function as in equation (4.2) is equivalent to writing down a utility function under the assumption of utility maximization. To the extent that the labor supply specification yields a robust approximation to the data, the associated utility function will also provide a good approximation to the underlying preferences. The utility function allows us to make the global comparisons to determine the preferred hours of labor supply. The convex case needs only local comparisons, but the non-convex case requires global comparisons because of the possibility of multiple tangencies of indifference curves with the budget set.

[25] Their work was done in the framework of labor supply and a composite consumption good. The technique can also be used in the many-good case, although it is more difficult to apply. Alternatively, one can begin with a utility function specification and derive the labor supply function as Wales and Woodland (1979), Ashworth and Ulph (1981a), and Ruffell (1981) did.

[26] The indirect utility function can be used to evaluate tangencies on both budget segments and at kink points so that the direct utility function is unnecessary. See Hausman (1980) or Deaton and Muellbauer (1981) for techniques to be used here. As Figure 2.8 shows, a tangency will not occur at a non-convex kink point, but it may occur later on a convex portion of the budget set.

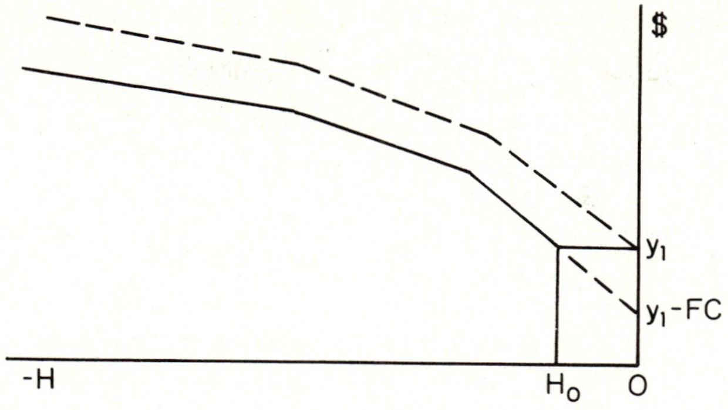

Figure 4.1

We next introduce the possibility of variation in tastes.[27] In the labor supply specification of equation (4.1), all individuals are assumed to have identical β's so that the variation of observationally equivalent individuals must arise solely from ε. However, empirical studies seemed to do an inadequate job of explaining observed hours of work under the assumption of the representative individual. Burtless and Hausman (1978) allowed for variation in preferences by permitting β to be randomly distributed in the population. Their results indicated that variation in β seemed more important than variation in α.[28] They also found that variation in β represented approximately eight times as much of the unexplained variance as did variation in ε. Hausman (1981) also found parameter variation to be an important part of his econometric specification. Blomquist (1983) tests and rejects the constant preference (no parameter variation) model. However, his results in terms of policy interest are quite similar whether or not preference variation is specified. An even more satisfactory procedure would be to allow all the taste coefficients to vary in the population. At present the requirement of evaluating multiple integrals over non-rectangular regions for the more general specification has led to the use of the simple case of one or two taste coefficients varying. Further research is needed to determine whether this more complex specification would be an important improvement over current models.

Another consideration which can have an important effect on the budget set for women's labor force participation is fixed costs to working. Transportation costs,

[27]For many linear regression specifications where the effect of taxes are not accounted for, variation in preferences leads only to an efficiency issue for the econometric estimator. However, taxes create an essential non-linearity in the problem so that variation in preferences can be quite important. A similar issue arises in the specification of discrete choice models; e.g., Hausman and Wise (1978). Greenberg and Kosters (1973) seemed to be the first paper that allowed for a dispersion of preferences to affect their model in an important way.

[28]It is interesting to note that Greenberg and Kosters had a similar type of variation in preferences. However, they did not allow for the effect of taxes so that the results cannot be compared.

the presence of young children, and search costs of finding a job, all can lead to a fixed cost element in the labor supply decision. The basic effect of fixed costs is to introduce a non-convexity in the budget set at the origin. Thus, even if the original budget set is convex as in Figure 2.2, the presence of fixed costs leads to a minimum number of hours H_0, which depends on the wage below which an individual will not choose to work. In Figure 4.1 non-labor income is y_1 with the original convex budget set drawn by the dotted line. However, presence of fixed costs lowers the effective budget set to the point $y_1 - FC$. The individual would not choose to work less than H_0 hours because she would be better off at zero hours. This non-convexity invalidates the simple reservation wage theory of labor force participation since hours also need to be accounted for. Hausman (1980, 1981a) has found average fixed costs to be on the order of $100 per month. The importance of fixed costs could explain the often noted empirical fact that very few individuals are observed working less than ten or fifteen hours per week.[29]

We now turn to the question of quantity constraints which seems to enter labor supply models in two possible ways. The first type of quantity constraint might arise if an individual has the choice of working either full time, say forty hours per week, or not working at all. We can still estimate the parameters of his labor supply function by discrete choice models which allow a distribution of preferences; e.g., Hausman and Wise (1978), Zabalza et al. (1980). For example, suppose we begin with the linear labor supply specification $h_i^* = \alpha w_i + \beta y_i - z\gamma$, along with the associated indirect utility function of equation (4.5). To compare indirect utility at zero and forty hours we need to specify w_i and y_i that would lead to the appropriate number of hours being chosen in an unconstrained setting.[30] But w_i and y_i can be solved for by using the desired hours supply equation and the linear equation through the point that gives net, after-tax earnings for that number of hours of work. For forty hours, the equation is $E_{40} = w_i \cdot 40 + y_i$, where E_{40} arises from the budget set, w_i is the net wage at forty hours, and y_i is the corresponding virtual income. We can solve the two equations in two unknowns for w_i and y_i and use the values for the required comparison so that α, β, and γ can be estimated. It turns out that this procedure is equivalent to solving for the direct utility function, where only quantities appear so that quantity constraints enter in a straightforward manner. For instance, the direct utility function for our example is

$$u(h,x) = \frac{1}{\beta}\left(h - \frac{\alpha}{\beta}\right)\exp\left[\left(1 - \beta\left(x + \frac{z\gamma}{\beta} - \frac{\alpha}{\beta^2}\right)\right)\Big/\left(\frac{\alpha}{\beta} - h\right)\right], \tag{4.6}$$

[29]Similar results in a model without taxes were found by Cogan (1981). Hanoch (1980) and Nakamura and Nakamura (1981) have also included fixed costs in models of female labor supply.

[30]Neary and Roberts (1980) and Deaton and Muellbauer (1980) discuss this technique in a general demand setting. However, they do not consider the effect of taxes.

where x is consumption of the composite commodity. However, the direct utility function need not exist in closed form, in which case the previous solution procedure can be used with the indirect utility function. Of course, specification of a direct utility function could be done ab initio, but it might not be easily combined with the labor supply functions of unconstrained individuals.

The other type of quantity constraints which people seem to have in mind is the choice among jobs, each of which comes with a distinct market wage and hours of work combination. However, if the individual takes a given job he is constrained to work the given number of hours which come with the job. Again a discrete choice framework seems appropriate to model this situation. Use of either the indirect or direct utility function would allow the appropriate utility comparisons to be made. We would need to know the range of choices which a given individual faces. But the choice set might be either established by survey questions or estimated from a data set of choices of similar individuals. At this point we have strayed rather far from our original theory of flexible hours of work. In our empirical estimation we have not accounted for the possibility of quantity constraints. It seems unclear how important an empirical problem quantity constraints are. As we discuss later, even conditional on working in a given week, the standard deviation of hours worked for prime age males is around fourteen hours. Thus, the model of flexible labor supply with fixed costs may provide a reasonably good approximation, especially in the long run.[31]

A question of some interest might be: what are the directions of biases in estimated labor supply models which do not account for taxes? Given the complexity of a model which incorporates taxes, the answer is not straightforward although a partial solution is possible. Consider the linear labor supply specification of equation (4.4). The net wage for individual i on budget segment j, w_{ij}, and the corresponding virtual income, y_{ij}, are determined simultaneously with the unknown coefficients α, β, and γ. Suppose that market wage w_i and observed non-labor income x_i are used instead. If x_i is measured subject to error, which it almost surely is in any survey, then the estimated coefficient for β will be subject to errors in variables bias towards zero. As an approximation assume that the contribution of virtual income, βy_{ij}, is omitted so that it enters the stochastic disturbance. Since the net wage w_{ij} and virtual income y_{ij} are positively correlated due to progressive taxes and $\beta < 0$ if leisure is a normal good, the estimate of the wage coefficient will have a negative bias. The positive correlation between the net wage and income arises under progressive taxes because higher wages put the taxpayer into higher brackets which will have higher virtual incomes. In fact, empirical studies of males which do not account for taxes typically estimate α to

[31] Ham (1981), in a model without taxes, attempts to provide evidence on quantity constraints by considering the response to a survey question on the possibility of additional work. Deaton (1981) considers quantity constraints by a rationing model of the consumption function.

be negative and substantial.[32] On the other hand, estimates which account for taxes [e.g., Burtless and Hausman (1978), Wales and Woodland (1979), Hausman (1981), Ashworth and Ulph (1981), Blomquist (1983), and Hausman (1982)] estimate α to be much nearer to zero. These latter studies also find considerably more evidence in support of economic theory than do studies which ignore taxes and often find compensated demand curves which slope in the wrong direction.

For labor supply estimates for wives, the husband's before-tax income is often used for y_i in equation (4.4). Then two counteracting biases are present in estimates of the wage parameter α. If the wife's wage is positively correlated with husband's income, then a negative bias of the estimate of α is created. However, the bias from the income term turns out to be positive so that the net effect cannot be determined. To the extent that husband's before-tax income is fairly close to the wife's virtual income, the effect of the bias should not be as important as in the husband's case. The empirical evidence to date supports this tentative conclusion.

In this section we have demonstrated how the non-linearity of the budget set which taxes create can be accounted for in an econometric model. The labor supply (leisure demand) curves are still the focus of model specification. For the convex budget set case the only new complication is to search for the budget segment on which h^* falls. When the budget set is non-convex, we need to solve for the indirect utility function which is associated with the labor supply specification. Then the multiple tangencies of the budget set and indifference curves can be compared to find the h^* which corresponds to maximum utility. We also emphasized the potential importance of allowing for variation in preferences and fixed costs to working. Previous empirical studies indicate the potential importance of both considerations. Lastly, we discuss techniques to handle quantity constraints within the context of our approach. However, unless on a priori grounds we know who in the sample is quantity constrained, it is not clear that these procedures can be applied in a given sample.

5. Results

In this section we summarize the results of studies of labor supply which take account of taxes. The effect of taxes on both labor supply and economic welfare is considered. However, difficulties arise in providing convenient summary measures for the effect of taxes. Elasticity measures for labor supply, which are most often

[32] Heckman and Borjes (1979) present a range of estimates. Despite its title this paper should not be used for policy purposes since the studies reviewed ignore taxes in their models of labor supply.

used as summary measures in demand studies, are not fully adequate to assess the effect of taxation for the following reasons: (1) Non-linearity of the budget sets can lead to large changes in labor supply with small changes in taxes. The non-convexity of many of the budget sets leads to this result. (2) About 50% of all women are not labor force participants. Because of the non-tangency of their utility functions with the budget sets at zero hours, small changes in taxes will not affect most non-workers. (3) When taxes are changed, both the change in the net, after-tax wages and the virtual incomes must be taken account of. Equation (2.2) demonstrates the correct relationship. (4) If variations in preferences are specified [e.g., Burtless and Hausman (1978), Hausman (1981a, 1982a), and Blomquist (1983)], behavior of the "mean" individual may differ from the mean population response.[33] This difference arises from the non-linearity of the budget set. To some extent problems which arise with the first and last reason are decreased by aggregation from individual responses to the population. However, the middle two problems remain.

5.1. *Prime-age males*

These individuals are usually taken to be from 25 to either 55 or 60 years old. Labor force participation among this group is nearly 100%, especially when disabled individuals are not considered. Unemployment is typically low among this group in a non-recession year. Most studies therefore do not account specifically for unemployment or constraints on labor market activity.[34] An integration of behavior when unemployed and hours of work should be a goal of future research, but theoretical advances as well as better data would be required.[35] Another needed advance is an integrated model of family labor supply with taxes to take account of wives labor market activity and its possible effect on husband's labor market behavior. Hausman and Ruud (1984) present results from a family model of labor supply. Significant interaction among the husband's and wife's labor supply behavior is found to be present.[36]

The most natural interpretation of the labor supply results estimated on cross-section data is an equilibrium model where actual hours differ from desired hours because of stochastic reasons. One should not maintain the incorrect image of the prime-age male labor uniformly at work for 40 hours per week and 2,000

[33] Hausman (1983) investigates this issue.

[34] Hausman (1981a) does account for zero hours considerations. Ham (1981) considers constraints on further work at the given wage.

[35] Moffitt and Nicholson (1982) consider this problem for a special sample of individuals for which data are available.

[36] Ashworth and Ulph (1981b) also estimate household models of labor supply.

hours per year. On the contrary, significant variation exists in both normal hours per week and weeks worked per year. Hours per week of work, conditional on being employed, typically have a mean of about 42 hours with a standard deviation of 10–15 hours in typical cross-section data.[37] Men presumably choose jobs which have the number of hours which most closely correspond to their desired hours taking account of overtime and possible layoffs. However, for a significant proportion of the prime-age male population, changes between employers is fairly rare, see Hall (1982). How much of the year-to-year variation in labor supply for this group arises from fluctuations in their market wage is problematical. Therefore, the models of labor supply and empirical results presented here are probably less relevant for short-term labor supply response to business cycle conditions.

We consider from sets of results for prime-age males: Wales and Woodland (1979), Ashworth and Ulph (1981), Hausman (1981a), Blomquist (1983), and Hausman and Ruud (1984).[38] The results are given in Table 5.1. First, note that the uncompensated labor supply elasticity is much closer to zero than is typically found in labor supply studies which ignore taxes. This result concurs with the econometric bias arguments given in the last section. The next difference is that the income elasticities vary from -0.04 to -0.17 which imply that leisure is a normal good in contrast to many studies which ignore taxes and find the opposite sign. Given the magnitude of virtual income with progressive taxation, the clear implication is that taxes will affect the labor supply decision. The combination of these two results leads to the last result, which is perhaps the most satisfying. All five studies imply a positive compensated wage elasticity so that the compensated labor supply curve is upward sloping. These results are in stark contrast to models which ignore taxation, and very often estimate a compensated elasticity of the wrong sign. This finding is difficult, if not impossible, to justify even when more general models of labor supply are considered. Since a non-negative compensated elasticity is the only implication of economic theory for models of labor supply, it is satisfying to find that the results become acceptable to the theory when the effect of taxes is taken into account.

We now turn to the effect of taxes on labor supply. As equations (2.1) and (2.2) demonstrate, the theoretical effect is indeterminate. Most models for prime-age males which ignore taxes estimate a backward-bending labor supply curve.[39] Therefore, a reduction in tax rates which has recently occurred in the U.S. and U.K. would lead to a reduction in hours of work. A contrary view has been put forward by "supply side" advocates in the U.S. who have argued that a reduction

[37] This variation is calculated after the self-employed and farmers have been eliminated from the sample.

[38] We do not use the earlier result of Hall (1973), Wales (1973), and Brown, Levin and Ulph (1976) because of difficulties of interpretation and econometric technique.

[39] Some models find a backward-bending curve only for medium- and high-wage males.

Table 5.1
Prime-age male labor supply results.

Authors	Data	Model	Wage elasticity	Income elasticity
Wales–Woodland	PSID[a]	CES	0.09[b]	−0.11[b]
Ashworth–Ulph	U.K.	Generalized CES	−0.13	−0.05
Hausman[c]	PSID	Linear	0.00	−0.17
Blomquist[c]	Sweden	Linear	0.08	−0.04
Hausman–Ruud[d]	PSID	Generalized linear	−0.03	−0.10

[a] Panel Study of Income Dynamics.
[b] Results are approximate since means of data were not given.
[c] Specification permits variation in preferences. Mean results are given.
[d] Estimated from a model of family labor supply.

in tax rates will lead to such a large increase in labor supply that government revenue would actually increase.

We first present some results of Hausman (1981a, 1981c) for the U.S. He found, using 1975 data that compared to a no-tax situation, desired labor supply was 8.2% lower because of the U.S. tax system, including FICA taxes and state income taxes. In Table 5.2 the results are given by wage quintiles from the PSID sample. In the second row the change from the no-tax situation is given. Note that the effect of the progressiveness of the tax system is to cause high-wage individuals to reduce their labor supply more from the no-tax situation than do low-tax individuals. The higher marginal tax rates lead to higher virtual income and a greater reduction in desired labor supply. Of course, this pattern of labor supply has an adverse effect on tax revenues because of the higher tax rates that high-income individuals pay tax at. In the second and third rows of Table 5.2 we present the expected change in labor supply for tax cuts of 10% and 30%. Note that desired labor supply *increases* with a tax reduction. We find the expected pattern that the effect on high-wage individuals is greatest since the linear labor supply model used has an increasing elasticity with virtual income. The effect of a 30% tax cut is roughly three times as large as a 10% cut, but the ratios are not

Table 5.2
The effect of taxes on prime-age male labor supply in the U.S.

	Market wage				
	$3.15	$4.72	$5.87	$7.06	$10.01
Change in labor supply	−4.5%	−6.5%	−8.5%	−10.1%	−12.8%
10% tax cut	+0.4%	+0.5%	+0.9%	+1.7%	+1.47%
30% tax cut	+1.3%	+1.6%	+2.7%	+3.1%	+4.6%

Table 5.3
The effect of tax rate changes on prime-age male labor supply in the U.K.

	Quintiles					
	1	2	3	4	5	Total
15% tax cut	−0.3%	+0.7%	+0.8%	+1.6%	+2.1%	+1.8%
7% tax cut	−0.1%	+0.3%	+0.3%	+0.9%	+0.9%	+0.8%
7% tax rise	+0.1%	−0.5%	−1.0%	−0.9%	−0.8%	−1.2%
15% tax rise	+0.3%	−1.1%	−2.3%	−2.6%	−2.1%	−2.9%

exact. However, neither of the two tax cuts is nearly self-financing as Hausman's (1981c) results indicate.

Lastly, we consider two types of radical tax reform. We consider a progressive linear income tax with all current deductions removed, e.g., interest deductability. Therefore, we have broadened the tax base considerably and then determined the tax rate which would raise the same amount of tax revenue as the current U.S. tax system using 1975 data. With a zero exemption level so that a flat tax results, the required tax rate is 14.6%. Desired labor supply for the prime-age males rises about 8.1%. For a progressive tax with an exemption level of $4,000 (1975 dollars), the required tax rate rises to 20%. Desired labor supply increases by about 7.7%. Therefore, a decrease in marginal tax rates does lead to an increase in desired labor supply of significant amounts although much of the progressivity of the tax system is lost with such a proposed tax reform.

Ashworth and Ulph (1981a) also considered the effect of tax changes on labor supply. They considered changing the standard rate of tax in the U.K. from its present value of 30% to four other rates representing changes of plus or minus 7% and 15%. The standard rate of tax is the marginal tax rate for almost 90% of prime-age males in the U.K. In Table 5.3 the percentage change in labor supply is given for the entire sample as well as for each quintile of the income (not wage) distribution.[40]

Note the qualitative similarity between the Ashworth–Ulph results and the Hausman results. A much larger change in labor supply is forecast from the higher-income quintiles. The magnitude of the predicted changes also do not differ too much, although Ashworth and Ulph find that the income effect dominates in the lowest quintile, leading to a small decrease in labor supply when taxes are lowered. The labor supply changes given in Table 5.3 are not sufficient to make a tax cut self-financing. The rise in labor supply would offset about 10% of the fall in revenues from the tax cut which is again fairly close to what Hausman (1981c) found.

[40] Note that a distribution ordered by wages is probably better, since labor supply choice enters the income measure.

Table 5.4
The effect of taxes on prime-age males in Sweden.

	Market wage			
	10.0 Skr	20.03 Skr	40.0 Skr	Total
Change in labor supply	−4.7%	−13.6%	−27.1%	−13.1%
Proportional tax	−1.9%	+6.2%	+11.4%	+6.9%

The last set of results which we consider are Blomquist's (1983) estimates for Sweden. Using 1973 data, he calculates the effect of taxes on labor supply for the mean individual at wage rates of 10.0 Skr, 20.3 Skr, and 40.0 Skr which correspond to a low wage, the average wage rate in the sample, and a higher wage rate, respectively. In Table 5.4 the first row estimates the change in labor supply from the no-tax situation. Note that the results are almost twice as large as the estimates for the U.S. in Table 5.2. Much of this difference arises from the considerably higher level of taxation in Sweden. In the second row of Table 5.4 an equal yield proportional tax is considered for each of the "representative" males. The corresponding tax rates are 27.8%, 39.1%, and 47.8%, respectively. For the entire sample the equal yield proportional tax is 34% with desired labor supply increasing 6.9% from its current level. Blomquist's estimates indicate a substantial effect of taxes on labor supply in Sweden.

5.2. *Economic welfare*

The welfare cost of the distortion created by the imposition of a tax is measured by use of deadweight loss (excess burden). We briefly sketch the theory of the deadweight loss measure, and then we present estimates which arise from labor supply studies.[41] The first component of a welfare measure is the effect of the tax on individual utility. Here the measure long used by economists has been some form of consumers' surplus. Consumers' surplus corresponds to the concept of how much money each individual would need to be given, after imposition of the tax, to be made as well off as he was in the no tax situation. Measurement of consumers' surplus often is done by the size of a trapezoid under the individual's demand curve or here it would be the labor supply curve. But Hausman (1981b) has demonstrated that in the case of labor supply this method can be very inaccurate. Instead the theoretically correct notion of either the compensating variation or equivalent variation should be used.[42] These measures, set forth by

[41]Auerbach (this volume) contains a more detailed discussion of deadweight loss.

[42]These measures correspond to the area under the compensated demand curve, which is determined by the substitution effect in the Slutsky equation. For further discussion, see Hausman (1981b) or Diewert (1982).

Sir John Hicks, are probably best defined in terms of the expenditure function. The expenditure function determines the minimum amount of money an individual needs to attain a given level of utility at given levels of wages and prices.[43] Its form is determined by either the direct utility function $U(H, Y)$ or the labor supply function. Consider the simple example of the wage tax for which the compensating variation equals

$$CV(w, w', U) = e(w', U) - e(w, U). \tag{5.1}$$

Equation (5.1) states that the welfare loss to the individual, measured in dollars of the consumption good, equals the minimum amount of non-labor income needed to keep the individual at his original utility level U minus his non-labor income in the no-tax situation y. Since utility is kept at the pre-tax level U, the compensating variation arises solely from the substitution effect in the Slutsky equation (2.1). The income effect is eliminated because the individual is kept on his initial indifference curve. In the more complicated case of progressive taxes, the only difference is that we use virtual non-labor incomes in equation (5.1) rather than actual non-labor income.[44]

We need one more ingredient to complete the measure of the welfare loss from taxation. The government has raised tax revenue, and we need to measure the contribution to individual welfare which arises from the government spending the tax revenue. The assumption commonly used is that the government returns the tax revenue to the individual via an income transfer. Here it would correspond to increasing the individual's non-labor income by the amount of tax revenue raised. Then the total economic cost of the tax is given by the deadweight loss (or excess burden) as

$$\begin{aligned} DWL(w, w', U) &= CV(w, w', U) - T(w, w', U) \\ &= e(w', U) - e(w, U) - T(w, w', U). \end{aligned} \tag{5.2}$$

Equation (5.2) states that the deadweight loss of a tax equals the amount the individual needs to be given to be as well off after the tax as he was before the tax minus the tax revenue raised $T(w, w', U)$.[45] Deadweight loss is greater than or equal to zero, which makes sense given that we expect taxation always to have an economic cost. Of course, if no tax revenue is returned, the compensating

[43] For a more formal treatment, see Varian (1978) or Diewert (1982).

[44] The alternative measure of the equivalent variation uses post-tax utility U' as the basis for measuring welfare loss. For labor supply in the two-good set-up, the equivalent variation typically gives a higher measure of welfare loss than does the compensating variation.

[45] Here we follow Diamond and McFadden (1974) and use taxes raised at the compensated point. Kay (1980) has recently argued in favor of using the uncompensated point. As with CV and EV measures the problem is essentially one of which is the better index number basis.

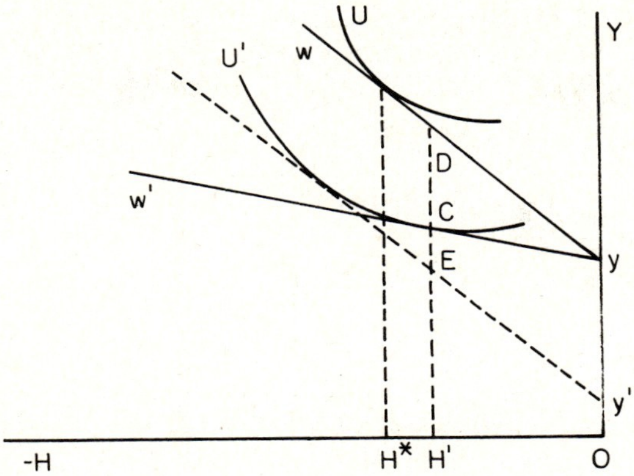

Figure 5.1

variation gives the welfare loss to the individual. In Figure 5.1 the compensating variation and deadweight loss are shown in terms of our simple wage tax example of Figure 2.2. Here the effect of the tax is to reduce labor supply from H^* to H'. The compensating variation is measured by the line segment yy'. We then decompose the compensating variation into its two parts. The line segment CD measures tax revenue collected, while the line CE measures the deadweight loss of the tax. Since the taxpayer has been made worse off but no one has benefited from the amount of the deadweight loss, it represents the economic cost of raising the tax revenue.

In Table 5.5 we present Hausman's results from deadweight loss of taxation of labor supply in the U.S. The first row gives the deadweight loss in each of the wage quintiles. Note that the deadweight loss to tax revenue ratio rises sharply because of the progressivity of the income tax. The "triangle formula" for deadweight loss demonstrates that the loss is proportional to the square of the tax rate so that higher-wage individuals face a higher economic distortion. Overall, Hausman estimates the mean ratio of deadweight loss to tax revenue to be 22.1%, which has important implications given the large proportion of the U.S. tax revenues which are raised via the income tax.[46] The next two rows of Table 5.5 calculate the deadweight loss under two tax cut proposals to give an indication of the size of the marginal change. Lastly, we consider the deadweight loss under an equal yield proportional tax. With no exemption and a tax rate of 14.6%, the

[46]As a historical note it is interesting to point out that Harberger's (1964) seminal calculation of the deadweight loss from the income tax used an income elasticity quite close to the estimate of Hausman (1981). However, he took the uncompensated wage elasticity to be large and negative. Therefore, the Slutsky equation led to a near-zero compensated wage elasticity so that Harberger's estimate of the deadweight loss was very small. On the contrary, Hausman (1981a) finds the uncompensated wage elasticity to be near zero.

Table 5.5
Deadweight loss estimates for prime-age male in the U.S.

	Market wage					
	$3.15	$4.72	$5.87	$7.06	$10.02	Total
DWL/tax revenue	9.4%	14.4%	19.0%	23.7%	39.5%	22.1%
10% tax cut	8.5%	13.3%	17.4%	21.8%	36.1%	19.0%
30% tax cut	6.8%	10.9%	14.5%	17.9%	29.5%	15.4%

deadweight loss to tax revenue ratio declines to 7.1%. A progressive linear income tax of 20.7% with an exemption level of $4,000 leads to a ratio of 14.5%. Both sets of calculations indicate the size of the welfare cost which arises from the progressivity of the U.S. tax system.

Blomquist (1983) does similar deadweight loss calculations for Sweden. For the average individual in his sample who earns 20.3 Skr, he calculates the deadweight loss to tax ratio to be 14%. The marginal tax rate faced by this individual is 62%. An equal yield proportional tax would be 39%, and the deadweight loss to tax ratio would decline to 5.5%. Over the entire sample Blomquist calculates that the deadweight loss ratio is 19%. An equal yield proportional tax of 33.7% would lower the ratio to 4%.

Increased attention in the U.S. and European nations has focused on the incentive effects of the tax systems. Most of the attention has been on output effects. The labor supply results for prime-age males reviewed here do demonstrate that income taxes reduce desired labor supply. The answer to the question of whether taxes increase or decrease desired labor supply is what most policymakers worry about. Yet, the deadweight loss effects may be more important from an economist's viewpoint. Since deadweight loss is a measure of the economic cost or efficiency effect of the income tax, it provides the appropriate measure within which to frame questions about the "optimal" progressivity of the tax system or the cost of marginal government expenditure.[47] Also, deadweight loss calculations are central to proposals for tax reform measures. And the deadweight loss question stands apart from labor supply effects since large deadweight loss exists even when counteracting income and substitution effects lead to small labor supply changes. The size of the deadweight loss associated with the income tax is perhaps the most important finding of the recent labor supply literature which considers the effect of taxes. Deadweight loss calculations are likely to influence future discussions on tax changes among economists and perhaps policymakers as well.

[47]Of course problems still exist due to the necessity of interpersonal comparisons; cf., Atkinson and Stiglitz (1976) and Stiglitz (1982). The optimal income tax literature begins with Mirrlees (1971). For surveys of the literature, see Mirrlees (1982) and Atkinson and Stiglitz (1980).

Table 5.6
Wives labor supply results.

Authors	Data	Model	Wage elasticity	Income elasticity
Ashworth–Ulph	U.K.	Generalized CES	0.19	−0.14
Hausman	PSID	Linear	0.91	−0.50[a]
Nakamura–Nakamura	U.S. Census	Linear	−0.16[b]	−0.05[b]
Nakamura–Nakamura	Canada Census	Linear	−0.30[b]	−0.19[b]
Rosen	Parnes (NLS)	Linear	2.30	−0.42[c]
Hausman–Ruud	PSID	Generalized linear	0.76	−0.36

[a]Evaluated for mean woman who works full time at virtual income which includes husband's earnings.
[b]For the age group 35–39; younger age groups have larger elasticities, while older age groups have smaller elasticities.
[c]Estimated from results given in the paper.

5.3. *Wives*

Income taxation is generally thought to have important effects on wives labor force behavior. Wives labor force participation in the U.S. is approximately 50%. When the labor force participation decision is made by a woman whose husband is employed, the tax rate which enters her decision is calculated from the husband's earnings.[48] Since this marginal tax rate is around 25% on average, taxes should be expected to be important in wives labor supply decisions.[49] Since relatively large uncompensated wages elasticities are often estimated for wives, the effect of various tax reform proposals may have important effects. However, it is important to remember that since 50% of wives do not work, their reaction to marginal changes in taxes will be zero to a great extent. Wives already at work will change their desired hours and some wives will decide to enter the labor force in response to a tax cut, but most non-participants will remain so. Therefore, elasticity estimates should be used with caution in considering tax changes.

We consider five sets of estimates for wives labor supply behavior which consider the effect of taxation: Ashworth and Ulph (1981a) for Great Britain, Hausman (1981a) for the U.S., Nakamura and Nakamura (1981) for Canada and the U.S., Rosen (1976) for the U.S., and Hausman and Ruud (1984) who use a model of family labor supply for the U.S. The results are given in Table 5.6. The estimates vary widely with the Ashworth–Ulph and Hausman results in the range

[48]The child care credit reduces the tax rate, but its effect on the participation decision is decreased because of fixed costs. Also note that beginning in 1983 the appropriate marginal tax rate will decrease because of a credit included in the 1981 tax reform legislation.

[49]Given these facts it is surprising that labor economists who work on female labor supply have largely ignored taxes. The recent book edited by Smith (1980) has only one mention of taxes in all of the papers. This omission is even more surprising in light of the substantial estimated labor supply elasticities.

Table 5.7
The effect of taxes on wives labor supply in the U.S.

	Market wage					
	\$2.11	\$2.50	\$3.03	\$3.63	\$5.79	Total
Change in labor supply	+31.2%	−14.2%	20.3%	−23.8%	−22.9%	−18.2%
DWL/tax revenue	4.6%	15.3%	15.9%	16.5%	35.7%	18.4%

of studies which do not account for taxes. Rosen's estimated wage elasticity of 2.3 seems quite high. Econometric problems which include incorrect treatment of virtual income and an inconsistent estimation technique may explain the divergence. In subsequent analysis Feenberg and Rosen (1983) have used wage elasticity estimates of 1.0. The most surprising result is that of Nakamura and Nakamura (1981) who find significant *negative* uncompensated wage elasticities which range from -0.39 for the 25–29 age group to -0.06 for the 50–54 age group.[50] Almost no other econometric study of wives labor supply, whether or not taxes are considered, estimates a negative wage elasticity. The Nakamura–Nakamura paper has an incorrect treatment of virtual income together with other econometric problems. Yet their finding that higher wages lead to lower labor supply for wives, together with the implication that the effect of income taxation is to increase wives labor supply, is so at odds with previous studies that it should perhaps be disregarded unless further studies provide additional confirmation. The estimated income elasticities are all negative so that taxation has two counteracting effects: by decreasing husbands net earnings it increases wives labor supply, but by its effect on virtual income it decreases labor supply. The overall effect of the income tax seems quite clearly (apart from the Nakamura–Nakamura results) to decrease wives labor supply because of the sizeable uncompensated wage elasticity which is typically found.

In Table 5.7 we present results of Hausman (1981a) for a sample of wives by quintiles.[51] Note that the effect of taxation is to increase labor supply for the lowest-wage quintile but to decrease labor supply for the other quintiles. The overall effect compared to the no-tax case is a reduction in labor supply by 18%. Hausman also found substantial deadweight loss to tax revenues with the ratio about 18%. Given the magnitude of the estimated elasticities the deadweight loss estimate might seem small. However, when the fact that non-participants in the absence of taxation will generally remain non-participants when taxes are levied

[50] The large negative elasticity estimates are incompatible with economic theory because they imply a downward-sloping compensated labor supply curve.

[51] These estimates take into account the labor supply response of husbands and their change in net, after-tax income.

and remain at the same utility level is taken into account, the finding is reasonable. The deadweight loss ratio would more than double, i.e., exceed 40%, for labor force participants. Hausman (1981c) considers a 10% tax cut and estimates that wives labor supply would increase by 4.1%. For a 30% tax cut he estimates the increase in labor supply to be 9.4%. Deadweight loss is decreased significantly. Hausman's results demonstrate an important influence of taxes on wives labor force behavior together with a substantial economic cost of the current tax system.

Feenberg and Rosen (1983) simulate the effects of numerous proposed changes in the tax law on wives labor force behavior. We consider two cases: a tax credit of 10% on the first $10,000 of earnings and taxation of wives as single individuals. For the tax credit case they find only a very small effect on hours of work. The impact of the lower marginal tax rate on some individual is just about cancelled by the income effect it has on other workers. However, the effect of the tax change on current non-participants is not treated altogether correctly. Income splitting leads to a predicted increase in labor supply of about 5.5% for wives. Thus, the effect of lower marginal tax rates leads to increased labor supply, although some of the progressivity of the income tax is lost when it is judged at the family level.

The results for wives demonstrate that income taxation has an important effect on wives labor supply decisions. The economic cost of the tax system is also substantial. Because of the joint treatment of family income, wives typically face substantial marginal tax rates on their earnings. No consensus has been reached on the proper tax treatment of the family in the presence of progressive taxation. Further econometric work will focus on more of a joint decision framework for husband and wives, yet it is unlikely that the major findings of an important effect of taxes will change drastically. Various tax reform proposals such as tax credits reduce the effect of progressivity on wives. However, important issues will remain unless a tax system with constant marginal tax rates is adopted.

6. High-income groups

Considerable interest has arisen over potentially large work disincentive effects on two economic groups: very-low-income and very-high-income groups. Both groups face high marginal tax rates on earned income; usually the marginal rate is 0.5 or higher. Our knowledge of the effect of the high marginal tax rates on low-income groups have been increased considerably by government-constructed cross-section data sets and most importantly by the four negative income tax experiments. The results of these NIT experiments will be considered in the next section. Yet very little reform of the tax system and its treatment of low-income individuals has been accomplished. On the other hand, our knowledge of the effect of high marginal tax rates on high-income groups has advanced little in the past decade.[52] Yet significant changes in the tax systems as they affect earned income for high-income groups have taken place. The United States lowered the maximum marginal tax rate on earned income from 0.7 to 0.5 in 1969, and the Thatcher government in England has also significantly reduced the highest marginal rates in 1979. Furthermore, earnings at which the maximum tax level is reached have increased dramatically in the U.S. under the tax reform legislation of 1981. In 1983, the 50% rate will be reached at $109,000 on a joint return; in 1984, the maximum rate will be reached at $162,000. The change in rates from Table 3.2 is remarkable. While high-income groups certainly complain loudly about taxes, none of the surveys which we will summarize have found a significant disincentive effect of the high tax rates. Thus we might conclude that a convincing efficiency argument does not exist for lowering the marginal rates of high-income groups, but vertical equity considerations have probably been foremost in legislators' deliberations.[53]

Almost all of our empirical knowledge of the effect of taxation on the labor supply of high-income groups arises from interview surveys. An important sample selection problem exists which has remained almost unnoticed [Holland (1976)]. Since we would expect on average high-income groups work more, those individuals who are led to work less by the disincentive effect of the tax system are less likely to be surveyed. Thus, a sample selection bias exists for the finding of a small disincentive effect. And a small disincentive effect has been the overwhelming finding of the interview surveys. Yet the empirical results have been so striking, that it is probably safe to conclude that the sample bias is not giving a spurious result. For instance, it does not appear that within the surveys that the highest-income groups are affected to a lesser extent than lower-income groups. Thus, the primary finding of the survey literature is that, while a disincentive does exist, its likely magnitude is not especially large.

The classic study in disincentive effects on high-income groups is Break's (1957) survey of lawyers and accountants in Great Britain. Break conducted 306 interviews on a group of individuals both familiar with and having the ability to react to the disincentive effect of the high marginal tax rates, which existed in Great Britain at that time. Break found that the majority of the respondents were not significantly affected by the tax system on their work effort. Of the 49% who reported an effect, only 18% cited disincentive effects, while 31% cited an

[52] The last significant survey is Holland (1969). Also, the most recent extensive survey of the literature is Holland (1976).

[53] Certainly large amounts of economic resources are used to lessen the burden of taxation by using the capital gains provisions and other tax preference provisions of the tax laws. But this observation has little bearing on the work effort of the high-income groups themselves.

incentive effect from the tax system. Thus, the overall income effect dominated the substitution effect for these individuals.[54] Using a much more stringent criterion, where the interpretation of the sample responses was clearest, Break concluded that 14% of the sample were significantly affected by taxation. The tax incentive effect still predominated, with 8% of the original sample working harder because of the tax effect. Still, Break concluded that a small net disincentive effect might exist, because the 6% who reported a significant disincentive effect had higher earnings than the 8% who reported an incentive effect.

Break's original study has been repeated by Fields and Stanbury (1970, 1971). Fields and Stanbury find a significantly higher percentage of respondents report a disincentive effect than did Break. They concluded that the disincentive effects had become more important over time as individuals had adjusted their labor supply slowly to the continued high marginal tax rates. But, on the other hand, the 6% who showed significant disincentive effects in Break's survey had fallen to only 2%, while those individuals with significant incentive effects had also declined markedly. Both studies do find that disincentive effects increase with income, yet we might well conclude that this finding primarily arises from an income effect, not a substitution effect. The single important quantitative finding in the Fields and Stanbury survey is that no significant difference exists between average number of hours worked among groups of individuals who reported disincentive effects, incentive effects, or no significant tax effects. Thus, whatever net effect may exist, its likely empirical magnitude is small.

Similar interview surveys of American business executives have been conducted by Sanders (1951) and by Holland (1969). From his interviews of 135 business executives and 25 professional men, Sanders found the effects of taxation to be quite small. Sanders concluded that important non-financial incentives more than outweigh the change in financial incentives that taxation creates. Probably the most important effect of taxation that Sanders found was the amount of time used in creating responses to taxation through investment and tax avoidance programs. The economic cost of this type of response is probably substantial and has undoubtedly increased in magnitude since Sanders' survey.[55]

[54] From a social welfare analysis point of view, little comfort arises from these findings. It is important to remember that only the substitution effect creates deadweight loss. Thus, even if the income effect is large enough to outweigh the substitution effect, considerable deadweight loss may still exist.

[55] Executive compensation through stock options and other non-wage compensation become an effective and important method to partly avoid the high marginal rates. But the combined effect of the 0.5 tax limit on earned income in the 1969 Tax Reform Act and the 1976 Tax Reform Act provision for stock option plans decrease the importance of non-wage compensation. The tax legislation of 1981 increased the attractiveness of stock options to their pre-1976 status.

Holland (1969) conducted interviews of 125 business executives, in which he attempted to isolate the substitution effect by considering a hypothetical tax on potential income. The amount of the tax would be about the same as the tax paid currently. However, it appears to me that the effort is not totally successful because of the non-linearity of the budget set discussed in Section 2. There we pointed out that the Slutsky equation does not adequately describe the tax response because of the presence of virtual incomes different from non-labor income. Thus, Holland's technique would seem to be exactly correct only in the case of a proportional tax system. Holland's findings are much in line with previous results. The hypothetical change in the tax system would have no effect on 80% of the sample. Fifteen percent of the sample indicated they would work harder, while one individual claimed he would work less hard. Holland seems to conclude that on average a tax incentive effect exists, at least in the substitution effect. But he concludes also that the magnitude is likely to be small. Thus, his results accord well with the Break results and Sanders results.

The last sample interview we consider is Barlow, Brazer and Morgan (1966). They conducted 957 interviews with individuals who had incomes exceeding \$10,000 in 1961. They also attempted to include a disproportionately large number of very-high-income people in the sample. Their results are again very similar to previous findings. Approximately 88% of the sample individuals responded that the income tax did not affect their work effort. Among the 1/8 of the sample which reported disincentive effects, Barlow et al. concluded that the actual magnitude of the disincentive is likely to be very small. In fact, they estimated the total effect on the economy to be of the order of 0.3% in 1963. Given the rather different sample coverage, the Barlow results seem quite similar to the results found in the other studies.

From these results we should not reach the too sanguine conclusion that high marginal tax rates may not have a significant economic cost. We have already mentioned the large amount of effort that goes into shifting ordinary income into capital gains which are taxed at a much lower rate. Evidence of considerable economic waste appears periodically from these schemes. But, the important point to note here is that these machinations seem to have very little effect on work effort. Presumably, for most people it is very difficult, if not impossible, to shift compensation from working directly into capital gains. Furthermore, the sensitivity of their work response is low to a given marginal tax rate. Perhaps these results are not too surprising. For low-income individuals, the (uncompensated) work disincentive effect is found to be small in econometric studies. Previous findings that, if anything, the income effect predominates, are in accordance with Break's findings. Recent econometric studies have found the income effect to be the most important determinant in behavior toward taxation. Thus, in terms of work response it does not appear that the rich are different than the rest of us. But, they do have more money.

7. Evidence from NIT's and social security effects

Four negative income tax (NIT) experiments have been conducted by the government to produce information about the likely effects on labor supply of replacing the current welfare system by an NIT. Three urban experiments took place in New Jersey, Gary, Indiana, and Seattle–Denver. A rural experiment also took place in Iowa and North Carolina. We review only the urban experiments, since we have excluded farmers from our previous analysis.[56] In principle, the NIT experiments might seem to be an ideal laboratory in which to determine the effect of taxes on the labor supply response of low-income workers.[57] Observations were recorded on individuals before the experiment began, and during the three-year period of the experiments two groups were observed. The experimental group was subject to an NIT plan, while a control group received nominal payments to participate in the experiments. Yet the initial results were not clear cut. Analysts found the results disappointing. A. Rees, in his summary of the New Jersey results, concluded that "the differences in work behavior between experimentals and controls for male heads... were, as we expected, very small. Contrary to our expectations, all do not show a clear and significant pattern; indeed they show a discernable pattern only after a great deal of refined analysis."[58] Unforeseen problems did arise which, in retrospect, is not surprising since the New Jersey NIT experiment was the first social experiment ever conducted. Statistical problems which arise in conducting experiments with human subjects over time had not been accounted for.[59] For instance, the attrition problem in the New Jersey experiment almost certainly accounts for the anomalous results found for black and hispanic males. Subsequent analysis of the New Jersey and the other two urban NIT experiments has led to more definite conclusions about the labor supply response. We will give a brief review of the evidence.

We first consider the evidence for male heads of households. Two important differences from the non-NIT framework arise for the analysis. Contrary to the usual case of analyzing the effect of taxes on labor supply where the substitution effect is considered to be much more important than the income effect, both the income and substitution effects are important for an NIT. The expected ad-

[56] A further problem exists since the results from the rural experiment seem extremely difficult to interpret. Problems with the rural experiment are discussed in Palmer and Pechman (1978).

[57] All the experiments were designed basically to measure labor supply elasticities. However, other interesting areas of research, such as family consumption patterns and family stability, have been studied. A possible problem with the interpretation of the NIT results is the distinction between transitory and permanent responses. The Seattle–Denver experiment was designed to allow investigation of this potential problem. Hausman (1982b) discusses the issue and finds evidence that it may well affect the estimated responses.

[58] For a series of papers on the New Jersey experiment, see the Spring 1974 volume of *The Journal of Human Resources*.

[59] These problems are discussed in Hausman (1982b).

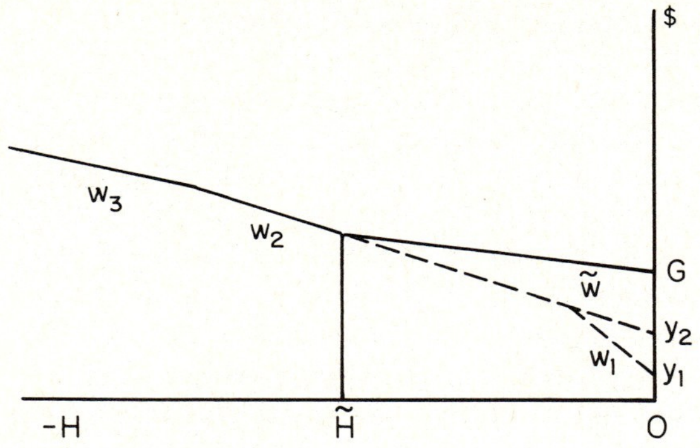

Figure 7.1

ditional cost of an NIT program over the existing welfare program is a crucial consideration. Thus, we are very interested in the overall labor supply response, rather than just the distortion created by taxation. The second difference is that for males both the income and substitution effects work to reduce labor supply. In Figure 7.1 we show how the NIT alters the budget set. Non-labor income y is replaced by the NIT guarantee G, which will have the effect of reducing labor supply for an individual who was initially on the first budget segment so long as leisure is a normal good. At the same time the net wage w_1, which was subject only to FICA contributions, now is lowered to $\tilde{w}$, which is subject to approximately a 0.5 tax rate. Thus, labor supply will be reduced since the NIT budget segment lies uniformly above the first non-NIT budget segment.[60] For individuals initially on the second segment, but below breakeven $\tilde{H}$, the same reasoning holds. Non-labor income has risen from $\tilde{y}_2$, to G, and $\tilde{w}$ is less than w_2. Lastly, many individuals above breakeven hours $\tilde{H}$ will not change their labor supply at all, but others will shift down below $\tilde{H}$ because of the income effect of the guarantee.

In fact, the findings agree with this economic theory. The labor supply reduction in hours worked for white males in New Jersey was about 4% uncorrected for attrition. In Gary for black males it was about 6% uncorrected for attrition and 10% when corrected for attrition, and in Seattle–Denver the response was 5% uncorrected for attrition. While these overall results are of interest, they are not sufficient for policy purposes. They are an average response

[60]So long as the NIT segment lies uniformly above the previous budget segment, the net change in income must be positive. Thus, the income effect will reinforce the substitution effect and cause a reduction in labor supply. Thus, the level of the guarantee removes the usual interdeterminancy of the effect of a change in the net wage.

over the many NIT plans used in each experiment.[61] To obtain reliable cost estimates, it is necessary to construct a model which permits determination of income and substitution effects. Then the cost of different plans can be forecast from the estimated parameters.[62]

Hausman and Wise (1976) was the first paper which took explicit account of the form of the NIT budget set in constructing an empirical model. They used an instrumental variable procedure to predict the net wage and virtual income along with a budget segment, and estimated a log-linear labor supply specification for white males in the New Jersey experiment. They found an uncompensated wage elasticity of 0.14 and an income elasticity of -0.023. Thus both effects in Figure 7.1 have significant effects in reducing labor supply. The poverty level for a four-person family in New Jersey was \$3,300. Thus, for an individual who received the poverty limit as the guarantee and faced a 50% marginal tax rate, the uncompensated wage effect would lead to an expected labor supply reduction of about 8%, while the income response would lead to an expected reduction of between 10–16% if the person had initially been on the first budget segment. Taking midpoints we would have an overall expected response of 21% in labor supply. An individual initially on the second segment might have no response to an NIT at all. For those initially below breakeven hours $\tilde{H}$ on the second segment, the wage effect is 6% with the income effect leading to a reduction of 1%, so that the overall response is about 7%. Taking weighted averages of the two responses leads to an expected labor supply reduction for those individuals *below* breakeven hours of 16.5%. It is very important to note that the model predicts only 17.6% of the population will fall below breakeven, so that the overall population response is about 4%.[63] Some confusion has arisen over the response conditioned on being below breakeven hours and the overall population response. The latter response is appropriate for cost estimates of an NIT.

Burtless and Hausman (1978) analyze the labor supply response among black males in the Gary NIT experiment. They use a procedure to treat taxes very similar to the technique used in Section 5 except for the choice of a log-linear labor supply function. In particular, they treat the budget set as exogenous rather

[61] Unfortunately, insufficient subjects were included in each cell of the experiment to use classical analysis of variance techniques to compute an accurate estimate of the response to each NIT plan. Statistical problems which arose during the design and duration of the experiment may preclude use of these techniques anyway. See Hausman and Wise (1977, 1979, 1981).

[62] Two potential problems arise in using the experimental results to produce cost estimates. First, the demand side of the market could change significantly for a nationwide NIT. In particular, individuals could choose work patterns to convexify their budget sets by working and not working in alternative accounting periods. Also, the limited duration of the experiment may miss important long-range effects on both the supply and demand sides of the labor market.

[63] The low proportion below breakeven is due to the study of white males who were relatively well off in New Jersey and Pennsylvania. Ashenfelter (1983) estimates a probit model which focuses on the probability of an individual being below the breakeven point.

Table 7.1
Location of fifteen budget lines in the Gary experiment.

Financial plan and gross wage/hr ($)	w_1 ($)	w_2 ($)	y_1 ($)	y_2 ($)	Hours at kink point	Expected hours	Change from control (%)	95% confidence range of expected hours	Probability of below break-even point
Control:									
2.25	2.07	1.67	2.72	27.82	43.16	43.55	—	36.8, 45.38	—
4.25	3.92	3.15	2.72	27.82	22.85	40.37	—	36.8, 45.38	—
6.25	5.76	4.63	2.72	27.82	27.82	40.34	—	36.8, 45.38	—
40% tax/low guarantee:									
2.25	1.35	1.67	78.63	27.82	159.59	38.68	−11.8	34.15, 44.95	1.00
4.25	2.53	3.15	78.63	27.82	81.77	38.68	− 4.3	34.15, 44.95	1.00
6.25	3.75	4.63	78.63	27.82	57.45	38.68	4.2	34.15, 44.95	1.00
60% tax/low guarantee:									
2.25	0.90	1.67	78.09	27.82	65.42	38.69	−11.8	34.17, 44.96	1.00
4.25	1.70	3.15	78.09	27.82	34.63	39.62	− 1.9	34.16, 43.48	0.21
6.25	2.50	4.63	78.09	27.82	23.55	40.23	− 0.3	34.16, 45.38	0.02
40% tax/high guarantee:									
2.25	1.35	1.67	102.63	27.82	234.97	38.27	−12.9	33.50, 44.85	1.00
4.25	2.53	3.15	102.63	27.82	120.39	38.27	− 5.3	33.50, 44.85	1.00
6.25	3.75	4.63	102.63	27.82	84.59	38.27	− 5.3	33.50, 44.85	1.00
60% tax/high guarantee:									
2.25	0.90	1.67	101.09	27.82	96.66	38.29	−12.9	33.50, 44.84	1.00
4.25	1.70	3.15	102.09	27.82	51.17	38.29	− 5.3	33.50, 44.84	1.00
6.25	2.50	4.63	102.09	27.82	34.86	39.38	− 2.4	33.50, 45.38	0.23

than using an ad hoc instrumental variable procedure, and they also allow for a distribution of tastes in the population. Here in Table 7.1 we present their results for both control individuals and for experimental individuals on a weekly basis for the mean individual in the sample. We first note that breakeven hours are quite high for some of the plans, so that the individual will almost certainly be below breakeven. Also note that a significant dispersion exists in the expected response – it is about 13% for low-wage groups. Perhaps even more importantly the distribution of tastes parameter indicated that most of the response takes place via the income effect for a small number of individuals. The great majority of individuals do not significantly alter their work response, so that the effect of the NIT leads to a very skewed response in the population. On the other hand, the uncompensated wage change has very little effect. We can see the income and substitution effects by comparing the rows which correspond to a $2.25 wage since the individuals will always be on the first budget segment. No difference in response at all is found for the 0.4 or 0.6 tax rate, while the high guarantee leads to a 9% greater response than does the low guarantee. At higher wage rates the amount of the tax does play a role, but only because it changes the amount of breakeven hours and thus the probability of being above breakeven. The finding that the income effect is the major determinant of labor supply reduction among males was also found by Moffitt (1978), who used a quite different probit type of model. The results differ markedly from the Hausman–Wise findings for New Jersey, where the income effect explained about 68% of the change in hours. It would be interesting to determine if this result occurs because of different model specification or because of a fundamentally different response pattern among the two populations.[64]

Other labor supply results for males that we briefly review are the findings of Keeley et al. (1978) for the Seattle–Denver experiment. While the Seattle–Denver experiment is superior in certain respects to the other urban experiments, the ad hoc method used by the authors to treat the budget set is not entirely satisfactory. They use a first difference specification, where the change in income is done at pre-experimental hours of work for the individual as is the change in the net wage rate. Since pre-experimental hours are an endogenous variable, an important simultaneous equation bias may be introduced.[65] However, the magnitude of the bias is difficult to estimate. At the mean of the sample, Keeley et al. found the income effect to explain 46% of the reduction in hours, while the change in the wage explained the other 54%. These results differ markedly from the results in the New Jersey and Gary sample, where the change in non-labor income is the more important determinant of the reduction in labor supply. Again, it would be interesting to ascertain whether the different results arise because of the model used.

The last study of male labor supply response in the NIT experiments that we review is MaCurdy (1983), who estimates a marginal rate of substitution function between consumption and labor supply from the Denver NIT. As we discussed previously, MaCurdy estimates his model within a life cycle context. MaCurdy's results are extreme in relation to other research on labor supply response. His estimated compensated substitution elasticity lies in the range of 0.74 to 1.43, which is on the order of 10–20 times higher than other estimates. Similarly, his estimated income elasticities range from -0.74 to -0.43, which are much greater in magnitude than other studies. It is possible that these results arise from the incorporation of the previously neglected life cycle considerations; but it seems more likely that they arise because of econometric problems associated with his marginal rate of substitution specification.

[64] The finding that it is the income effect which creates almost the entire labor supply response, is corroborated further by the results of Hausman and Wise (1979) who consider a model which corrects for attrition.

[65] A further problem exists since people initially above breakeven hours will not have their net wage or income affected by the experiment. The authors attempt to treat this problem by including a dummy variable which again would create simultaneous equation bias.

The other group whose labor supply might be markedly affected by introduction of an NIT, is working wives. Neither the New Jersey nor the Gary experiments had sufficient numbers of working wives to allow model estimation. Keeley et al. found an average response elasticity about four times as large for wives as for husbands. The mean labor force reduction is 22%. Here the change in income accounted for 75% of the total effect. Since most of these women presumably had working husbands, such a large-scale withdrawal from the labor force could be an important effect of an NIT.

The last group to be considered is female headed households. Most of the affected population qualifies for AFDC, so that introduction of an NIT leads to a substantially higher guarantee and somewhat lower tax rate under most NIT plans. Keeley et al. found the female heads response to be about twice as large as the male response. The mean labor force reduction is 11%. Here they found the income effect to explain about 66% of the total response. Hausman (1980), in a study of labor force participation among black females who headed households in Gary, again found the level of the guarantee to be much more important than the NIT tax rate. For instance he finds that the change from 0.4 to 0.6 NIT tax rate reduces the probability of participation by about 2.5%, while a change in the NIT guarantee from 0.75 of the poverty limit to the poverty limit reduces the probability of participation by 6.5%. In terms of comparing the expected effort to that of AFDC, it seems likely that a reduction in labor supply would result. Even if the marginal tax rate fell from the AFDC level of 0.67 to an NIT level of 0.4, the accompanying higher benefits would create a net disincentive effect. The net result would be a significant increase in the cost of family support for female headed households. At the same time the extra income, which would go to the lowest-income group in the economy, might well lead to a net gain in social welfare.

The other literature which we review considers the effect of the social security earnings test on retirement behavior and labor supply. We discussed the social security beneficiary budget set in Section 4, where we emphasized the intertemporal aspects of the model. An important empirical fact does appear with respect to social security. Labor force participation has decreased among the elderly over the post-war period in the United States. From 1960 to 1975, labor force participation for males over 65 fell from 33% to 22%. Over the same period for men aged 62–64, it fell from 81% to 60%. 1961 is the year in which social security eligibility for men 62–64 was introduced. An important policy question is whether the decline in male labor force participation is almost wholly a result of the early retirement provision of social security and the rising real benefit level. Rising real income for potential retirees during the period offers an alternative explanation for part of the observed behavior. Given recent policy proposals to extend the age of early retirement from 62 to 65 years of age, the causes of early retirement assume an important role in financial projections for the social security

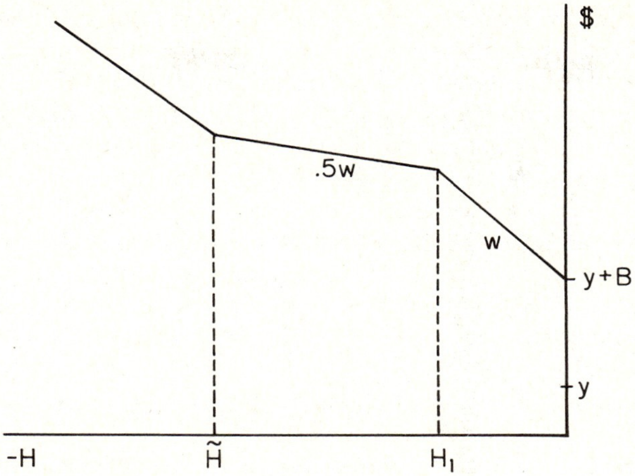

Figure 7.2

system. Three recent papers consider the causes of retirement over the 1965–1975 period. Boskin and Hurd (1982) ascribe almost all the decrease in labor force participation to social security. Diamond and Hausman (1984a, 1984b) find that social security is the most important factor, yet if early retirement between ages 62–65 were stopped, the retirement probability would decrease by about 50%, so that a significant number of men would still retire during that age period.[66] Further research is required here because of the complex interaction of non-retirement labor supply and its effect on future social security benefits; cf. Blinder et al. (1980).

The other dimension of the effect of social security is the earnings test for social security recipients. In 1982 earnings beyond $6,000 are subject to a 50% tax rate until all social security benefits are recovered, i.e., the breakeven point $\tilde{H}$ is reached in Figure 7.2. Burtless and Moffitt (1982) in a recent study find that the earnings test has a major effect on retired males labor supply decisions.[67] Among retired men who are working the frequency distribution of hours worked has a pronounced spike at the kink point H_1 in Figure 7.2 which provides strong evidence of the incentive effect of the earnings test. This effect is to be expected

[66] These studies are in stark contrast to Gordon and Blinder (1980) who in their study of retirement decisions "*assume*(s) that social security is irrelevant to retirement decisions". No empirical study, to the best of my knowledge, has come close to verifying this assumption.

[67] Burtless and Moffitt go a long way towards a complete model of the lifetime budget set. However, since their model is basically cross-sectional, they do not account for increases in future social security benefits from extra years of work in an entirely satisfactory manner.

given the pronounced kink at H_1 hours, where the net wage is reduced from w to $0.5w$. About 50% of working males were located at the kink point and 90% worked hours either at or below the kink point H_1. However, to analyze the overall effect of the earnings test, non-participation must be accounted for since upwards of 80% of the men in the Burtless–Moffitt sample worked zero hours. Thus, overall the earnings test leads to a reduction in expected hours of about 50 hours per year. However, for those men who are working, the removal of the earnings test would increase expected labor supply by about 400 hours per year. Thus, the situation is very similar to the case of wives discussed in Section 5, where tax changes have only a small expected effect on non-labor force participants. But considering the problem in this context, Burtless and Moffitt may have overestimated the wage elasticity by their neglect of fixed costs to working.[68] Still, they have provided strong evidence of the effect of the earnings test on the labor supply behavior of social security recipients.

In this section we have considered the empirical evidence from the NIT experiments. Although numerous statistical and econometric problems arise, I feel we have learned much about labor supply behavior of low-income workers. We now return to our question of the last section. There, we decided that labor supply behavior of high-income persons was not too different from that of middle-income individuals. What about low-income people? From the experimental results, I conclude that the income effect is probably larger than we previously had thought. Especially for male heads of households I feel that introduction of an NIT would lead to a significant labor force supply reduction by a small proportion of the population. I doubt that the NIT tax rate is nearly as important as the level of the NIT guarantee. Thus, low-income males do have low wage elasticities as does the rest of the population; but their income elasticities may have an important effect on labor supply behavior given the size of the NIT guarantee. Similar results were found for female headed households, although they presently have AFDC so that the change might not be as large. Lastly, the NIT results for wives seem quite different than the usual results. Their wages elasticities are much lower and their income elasticities are much higher than had been found for middle-income wives. But, the evidence on wives is based on only one sample and one estimation technique. More research needs to be done on wives behavior under an NIT before we can be confident about the results.

Research of the effects of social security is still in an early stage of development. Little doubt would seem to exist that social security benefits are an important determinant of retirement decisions. Furthermore, the earnings test does have an important effect on labor supply behavior of retirees. Further research that accounts for the intertemporal aspects of the problem and the form of the lifetime budget set is still needed.

[68]Hausman (1981a) found a lower wage elasticity for wives when fixed costs to working here accounted for. Cogan (1981) made a similar finding in a model without taxes.

References

Ashenfelter, O., 1983, Discrete choice in labor supply: The determinants of participation in the Seattle–Denver income maintenance experiment, Journal of the American Statistical Association.

Ashenfelter, O. and J. Heckman, 1974, The estimation of income and substitution effects in a model of family labor supply, Econometrica 42.

Ashworth, J.A. and D.T. Ulph, 1981a, Estimating labour supply with piecewise linear budget constraints, in: C. Brown, ed., Taxation and labor supply (London).

Ashworth, J.A. and D.T. Ulph, 1981b, Household models, in: C. Brown, ed., Taxation and labour supply (London).

Atkinson, A. and N. Stern, 1980, On labour supply and commodity demand, Journal of Public Economics 14.

Atkinson, A. and J. Stiglitz, 1976, The design of tax structure: Direct versus indirect taxation, Journal of Public Economics 6.

Atkinson, A. and J. Stiglitz, 1980, Lectures on public finance (New York).

Atkinson, A. et al., 1980, On the switch from direct to indirect taxation, Journal of Public Economics 14.

Auerbach, A., 1984, Measurement of excess burden and optimal taxation, this volume.

Barlow, R., H. Brazer and J. Morgan, 1966, Economic behavior of the affluent (Washington, DC).

Blinder, A. et al., 1980, Reconsidering the work disincentive effects of social security, National Tax Journal 33.

Blomquist, S., 1983, The effect of income taxation on male labor supply in Sweden, Journal of Public Economics 22.

Blundell, R. and C. Walker, 1982, Modelling the joint determination of household labor supply and commodity demands, Economic Journal 92.

Blundell, R. and C. Walker, 1984, A life cycle consistent empirical model of family labor supply using cross section data, Mimeo.

Borjas, G. and J. Heckman, 1978, Labor supply estimates for public policy evaluation, Proceedings of the IRRA.

Boskin, M. and M. Hurd, 1982, The effect of social security on retirement in the early 1970's, Mimeo.

Break, G., 1957, Taxes and incentives to work: An empirical study, American Economic Review 48.

Brown, C. et al., 1976, Estimate of labour hours supplied by married male workers in Great Britain, Scottish Journal of Political Economy 23.

Brown, C. et al., 1982, Preliminary family labour supply estimates, Mimeo.

Burtless, G. and J. Hausman, 1978, The effect of taxes on labor supply: Evaluating the Gary NIT experiment, Journal of Political Economy 86.

Burtless, G. and R. Moffitt, 1982, The effect of social security on labor supply of the aged, Mimeo.

Cain, G. and H. Watts, 1973, Income maintenance and labor supply (Chicago, IL).

Cogan, J., 1980, Married women's labour supply, in: J. Smith, ed., Female labor supply (Princeton, NJ).

Cogan, J., 1981, Fixed costs and labor supply, Econometrica 49.

Deaton, A., 1981, Theoretical and empirical approaches to consumer demand under rationing, in: A. Deaton, ed., Essays in the theory and measurement of consumer behavior (Cambridge, MA).

Deaton, A. and J. Muellbauer, 1980, Economics and consumer behavior (Cambridge, MA).

Deaton, A. and J. Muellbauer, 1981, Functional forms for labor supply and commodity demand with and without quantity rationing, Econometrica 49.

Diamond, P. and J. Hausman, 1984a, Individual retirement and savings behavior, Journal of Public Economics 23.

Diamond, P. and J. Hausman, 1984b, Retirement and unemployment behavior of older men, in: H. Aaron and G. Burtless, eds., Retirement and economic behavior (Washington, DC).

Diamond, P. and D. McFadden, 1974, Some uses of the expenditure function in public finance, Journal of Public Economics 3.

Diewert, E., 1971, Choice on labor markets and the theory of the allocation of time, Mimeo.

Diewert, E., 1982, Duality approaches to consumer theory, in: K. Arrow and M. Intriligator, eds., Handbook of mathematical economics (Amsterdam).

Feenberg, D. and H. Rosen, 1983, Alternative tax treatment of the family: Simulation methodology and results, in: M. Feldstein, ed., Behavioral simulation methods in tax policy analysis (Chicago, IL).

Fields, D. and W. Stanbury, 1970, Disincentives and the income tax: Further empirical evidence, Public Finance 25.

Fields, D. and W. Stanbury, 1971, Income taxes and incentives to work: Some additional empirical evidence, American Economic Review 60.

Gordon, R. and A. Blinder, 1980, Market wages, reservation wages, and retirement decisions, Journal of Public Economics 14.

Greenburg, D. and M. Kosters, 1973, Income guarantees and the working poor, in: G. Cain and H. Watts, eds., Income maintenance and labor supply (Chicago, IL).

Hall, R., 1973, Wages, income and hours of work in the U.S. labor force, in: G. Cain and H. Watts, eds., Income maintenance and labor supply (Chicago, IL).

Hall, R., 1982, The importance of lifetime jobs in the U.S. economy, American Economic Review 72.

Ham, J., 1982, Estimation of a labour supply model with censoring due to unemployment and underemployment, Review of Economic Studies 49.

Hanoch, G., 1980, A multivariate model of labor supply, in: J. Smith, ed., Female labor supply (Princeton, NJ).

Hanoch, G. and M. Honig, 1978, The labor supply curve under income maintenance programs, Journal of Public Economics 9.

Harberger, A., 1964, Taxation, resource allocation and welfare, in: The role of direct and indirect taxes in the Federal Revenue System (NBER).

Hausman, J., 1979, The econometrics of labor supply on convex budget sets, Economics Letters 3.

Hausman, J., 1980, The effect of wages, taxes, and fixed costs on women's labor force participation, Journal of Public Economics 14.

Hausman, J., 1981a, Labor supply, in: H. Aaron and J. Pechman, eds., How taxes effect economic activity (Washington, DC).

Hausman, J., 1981b, Exact consumers' surplus and deadweight loss, American Economic Review 71.

Hausman, J., 1981c, Income and payroll tax policy and labor supply, in: L.H. Meyer, ed., The supply-side effects of economics policy (St. Louis, MO).

Hausman, J., 1982a, The econometrics of non-linear budget sets, Mimeo.

Hausman, J., 1982b, The effect of time in economic experiments, in: W. Hildenbrand, ed., Advances in econometrics (Cambridge).

Hausman, J., 1983, Stochastic problems in the simulation of labor supply, in: M. Feldstein, ed., Behavioral simulation methods in tax policy analysis (Chicago, IL).

Hausman, J. and P. Ruud, 1984, Family labor supply with taxes, American Economic Review 74.

Hausman, J. and D. Wise, 1976, The evaluation of results from truncated samples, Annals of Economic and Social Measurement 5.

Hausman, J. and D. Wise, 1977, Social experimentation, truncated distributions, and efficient estimation, Econometrica 45.

Hausman, J. and D. Wise, 1978, A conditional probit model for qualitative choice, Econometrica 46.

Hausman, J. and D. Wise, 1979, Attrition bias in experimental and panel data, Econometrica 47.

Hausman, J. and D. Wise, 1981, Stratification on endogenous variables and estimation, in: C. Manski and D. McFadden, eds., The econometrics of discrete data (Cambridge, MA).

Holland, D., 1969, The effect of taxation on effort: The results for business executives, in: S.J. Bowers, ed., Proceedings of National Tax Association.

Holland, D., 1976, The effect of taxation on incentives of higher income groups, in: IFS, Fiscal policy and labour supply, No. 4.

Kay, J., 1980, The deadweight loss from tax system, Journal of Public Economics 10.

Keeley, M. et al., 1978, The estimation of labor supply models using experimental data, American Economic Review 68.

Killingsworth, M., 1983, Labor supply (Cambridge).

Kosters, M., 1969, Effects of an income tax on labor supply, in: A. Harberger and M. Bailey, eds., The taxation of income capital (Washington, DC).

Lewis, G., 1956, Hours of work and hours of leisure, IRRA Proceedings 9.

MaCurdy, T., 1981, An empirical model of labor supply in a life-cycle setting, Journal of Political Economy 89.

MaCurdy, T., 1983, A simple scheme for estimating an intertemporal model of labor supply and consumption in the presence of taxes and uncertainty, International Economic Review 24.

Mirrlees, J., 1971, An exploration in the theory of optimal income taxation, Review of Economic Studies 38.

Mirrlees, J., 1982, The theory of optimal taxation, in: K. Arrow and M. Intriligator, eds., Handbook of mathematical economics (Amsterdam).

Moffitt, R., 1979, A note on the effect of taxes and transfers on labor supply, Southern Economic Journal.

Moffitt, R. and W. Nicholson, 1982, The effect of unemployment insurance on unemployment, Review of Economics and Statistics 64.

Nakamura, A. and M. Nakamura, 1981, A comparison of the labor force behavior of married women in the U.S. and Canada, with special attention to the impact of income taxes, Econometrica 49.

Neary, J. and K. Roberts, 1980, The theory of household behavior under rationing, European Economic Review 13.

Palmer, J. and J. Pechman, 1978, Welfare in rural areas: The North Carolina–Iowa income maintenance experiment (Washington, DC).

Pechman, J., 1976, Federal tax policy, 3rd ed. (Washington, DC).

Rosen, H., 1976, Taxes in a labor supply model with joint wage-hours determination, Econometrica 44.

Ruffell, R.J., 1981, Direct estimation of labor supply functions with piecewise linear budget constraints, in: C. Brown, ed., Taxation and labor supply (London).

Sanders, T., 1951, Effects of taxation on executives (Boston, MA).

Seater, J., 1982, Marginal federal personal and corporate income tax rates in the U.S., 1909–1975, Journal of Monetary Economics 10.

Smith, J., 1980, Female labor supply (Princeton, NJ).

Steverle, E. and M. Hartzmark, 1981, Individual income taxation, 1947–79, National Tax Journal 34.

Stiglitz, J., 1982, Utilitarianism and horizontal equity, Journal of Public Economics 18.

Tax Foundation, 1981, Facts and figures on government finance (Washington, DC).

Varian, H., 1978, Microeconomic theory (New York).

Wales, T., 1973, Estimation of a labor supply curve for self-employed business proprietors, International Economic Review 14.

Wales, T. and A. Woodland, 1979, Labor supply and progressive taxes, Review of Economic Studies 46.

Zabalza, A., 1983, The CES utility function, nonlinear budget constraints, and labor supply, Economic Journal.

Zabalza, A. et al., 1980, Social security and the choice between full-time work, part-time work and retirement, Journal of Public Economics 14.

Chapter 5

THE EFFECTS OF TAXATION ON SAVINGS AND RISK TAKING

AGNAR SANDMO*

The Norwegian School of Economics and Business Administration, Bergen

1. Introduction

The effects of taxation on the volume and composition of private saving has traditionally been considered one of the central questions in public finance. This is hardly surprising. From a policy point of view one can point to a series of arguments for the importance of the problem. If alternative tax systems can lead to different rates of private saving, then the choice between them should take into account the short-run effects on employment and inflation, the medium-term effects on the rate of growth, and the long-term effect on the capital intensity of the economy. These are basically issues of the efficiency of resource allocation, but distributional policy is also involved. A tax policy designed to encourage saving may transfer income from "workers" to "capitalists" and from the present to future generations. Evidently, there are all sorts of tradeoffs to consider in policy design.

Although it is clear that much of the interest in this particular question is derived from a concern with policy problems, it is important to emphasize the conceptual distinction between positive and normative issues. Thus the question of whether an expenditure tax will lead to a higher or lower level of private saving than an equivalent income tax is a positive one. Whether the answer is one or the other does not in itself have any implications for tax policy. It is only when we introduce criteria for social welfare or efficiency that we can begin to consider the normative question of the desirability of an expenditure tax.

In principle, savings decisions can be made by consumers, firms and governments. The tradition in the literature has been to concentrate on consumer decisions and to take the personal saving rate as being the main determinant of the overall rate of saving. This approach is reflected in the emphasis given to consumer decision making in the present paper; however, there is also a need to consider the role of private corporations and government. At the level of private firms the tradition has been to see their saving and investment decisions as reflections of the preferences and market opportunities of the owners, so that

*I am grateful to Alan Auerbach, Mervyn King, Hans-Werner Sinn and Jon Vislie for helpful comments.

Handbook of Public Economics, vol. I, edited by A.J. Auerbach and M. Feldstein

these remain the basic explanatory factors. But behind this view lie a number of assumptions about market structure, incentives, etc., which need both theoretical justification and empirical verification. As far as the government is concerned it does of course intervene directly in private saving decisions through public pension plans and social security provision, and the interaction between private and public saving decisions has recently become a very active area of research.

The tradition in the public finance literature has been to study the effects of taxation on savings as a whole more or less in isolation from the problem of the tax effects on portfolio composition, particularly with regard to its risk characteristics. This tradition is followed in the present survey, which first considers a series of models in which savings take the form of holdings of a single financial asset. Within this framework we then consider successively the tax effects on the saving decisions of an individual consumer (including their connections with corporate saving and social security), the question of the incidence of taxation, and the problem of the optimum tax treatment of savings. Tax effects on portfolio composition and risk taking are then analyzed with reference to the same set of questions; on some of these the literature is not very extensive, so that this part of the survey occupies less space than that which is concerned with pure savings models.

2. Taxation and saving: Models of individual choice

2.1. *The two-period model: Perfect markets*

The simplest context in which one can analyze the intertemporal consumption decisions of a single individual, is the two-period model which was first introduced by Irving Fisher (1930). The simplest version of this model takes labour income to be exogenous and concentrates on the allocation of consumption between the two periods via the saving decision. This has proved to be a fruitful model for many purposes and has been extensively used in public finance; see, e.g., Hansen (1955) and Musgrave (1959).

We imagine a consumer whose preferences are defined over the amounts of consumption enjoyed in the two periods of his life. His preference ordering can be represented by the utility function

$$U = U(C_1, C_2), \tag{2.1}$$

which is assumed to be increasing, strictly quasi-concave and differentiable. Incomes in the two periods are given as y_1 and y_2. The consumer can borrow or lend in a perfect capital market at a rate of interest equal to r. The budget constraint for the first period is

$$C_1 + S = y_1, \tag{2.2}$$

where S is saving, which can be either positive or negative. In the second period, consumption is limited by income in that period plus the amount of saving with interest added, i.e.,

$$C_2 = y_2 + S(1+r). \tag{2.3}$$

Combining (2.2) and (2.3) we have that

$$C_1 + \frac{C_2}{1+r} = y_1 + \frac{y_2}{1+r}, \tag{2.4}$$

which simply states that the present value of consumption must be equal to the present value of income.

To find the maximum of (2.1) subject to (2.4) we form the Lagrangian

$$\mathscr{L} = U(C_1, C_2) - \lambda\left(C_1 + \frac{C_2}{1+r} - y_1 - \frac{y_2}{1+r}\right).$$

Setting the partial derivatives equal to zero we obtain (with subscripts denoting partial derivatives)

$$U_1 - \lambda = 0, \tag{2.5}$$

$$U_2 - \lambda\frac{1}{1+r} = 0, \tag{2.6}$$

which can be combined to give

$$\frac{U_2}{U_1} = \frac{1}{1+r} \quad \text{or} \quad \frac{U_1}{U_2} - 1 = r. \tag{2.7}$$

The first version says that the marginal rate of substitution should be equal to the price of future in terms of present consumption, which is the discount factor. The second version is the famous "rule" that the marginal rate of time preference should be equal to the rate of interest.

So far we have not introduced taxation into the model. It is in fact quite useful to study the properties of the model as it stands; the implications of alternative tax systems can then be inferred fairly directly.

From equations (2.4)–(2.6) we can derive demand functions for consumption in the two periods; of particular interest is the demand for first-period consumption, which can be written as

$$C_1 = C_1(r, y_1, y_2) \quad \text{or} \quad C_1 = C_1(r, y), \tag{2.8}$$

where $y = y_1 + (1+r)^{-1} y_2$. The latter formulation reflects the fact that consumption depends on income only via its present value; a shift of income between periods such that y were unchanged would leave consumption unaffected.

As usual in demand theory there are no *a priori* restrictions on the income effects; consumption could be normal or inferior. However, in view of the aggregate interpretation of consumption in this model it is natural to assume that it is a normal good.

The effect of a change in the rate of interest can be characterized by means of the Slutsky equation. This is easily derived as follows. Taking the differential of the demand function with y_1 constant we have that

$$dC_1 = \frac{\partial C_1}{\partial r} dr + \frac{\partial C_1}{\partial y_2} dy_2. \tag{2.9}$$

For a *compensated* change in the rate of interest it must be the case that

$$dU = U_1 dC_1 + U_2 dC_2 = 0,$$

or, substituting from the first-order conditions (2.5)–(2.6),

$$\lambda\left(dC_1 + \frac{1}{1+r} dC_2\right) = 0.$$

From the budget constraint we have that

$$dC_1 + \frac{1}{1+r} dC_2 = -\frac{y_2 - C_2}{(1+r)^2} dr + \frac{1}{1+r} dy_2.$$

Constant utility therefore requires that

$$dy_2 = \frac{y_2 - C_2}{1+r} dr = -(y_1 - C_1) dr,$$

where the last equality follows from (2.4). Substituting for dy_2 in (2.9) and dividing through by dr, we obtain

$$\left(\frac{dC_1}{dr}\right)_{U=\text{const.}} = \frac{\partial C_1}{\partial r} - (y_1 - C_1)\frac{\partial C_1}{\partial y_2},$$

or, rearranging terms,

$$\frac{\partial C_1}{\partial r} = (y_1 - C_1)\frac{\partial C_1}{\partial y_2} + \left(\frac{\partial C_1}{\partial r}\right)_U. \tag{2.10}$$

The last term is the substitution effect which can be shown to be negative using the second-order maximum conditions. The first term is the income effect which is positive for a lender ($C_1 < y_1$) and negative for a borrower ($C_1 > y_1$). Thus, for a borrower it is clear that an increase in the interest rate implies reduced consumption, while for a lender the outcome depends on the relative magnitudes of the income and substitution effects. These results are demonstrated graphically in Figure 2.1a for the case of a borrower and in Figure 2.1b for the case of a lender. In both diagrams the original budget constraint is the line AA and the consumer's optimum is at a. With an increase in the rate of interest the budget line swings around the income point (y_1, y_2) to the new position CC with the corresponding optimum at c. If a lump sum payment were made to bring the consumer back to his original indifference curve, his optimum would be at b. The substitution effect on present consumption is therefore the horizontal distance between a and b, while the income effect corresponds to the horizontal distance between b and c.

What about the effect on saving itself? From the first-period budget constraint (2.2) it must be the case that $\partial S/\partial r = -\partial C_1/\partial r$, so that our interpretation of the comparative statics results can simply be applied to saving by changing the algebraic sign of the effects. However, Feldstein (1978) has pointed out that if

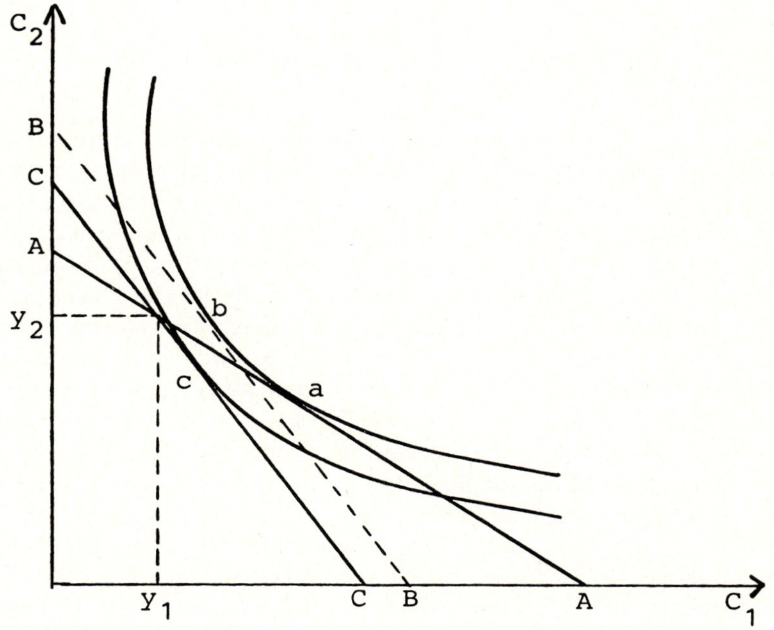

Figure 2.1a. Substitution and income effects of a change in the interest rate: the borrower.

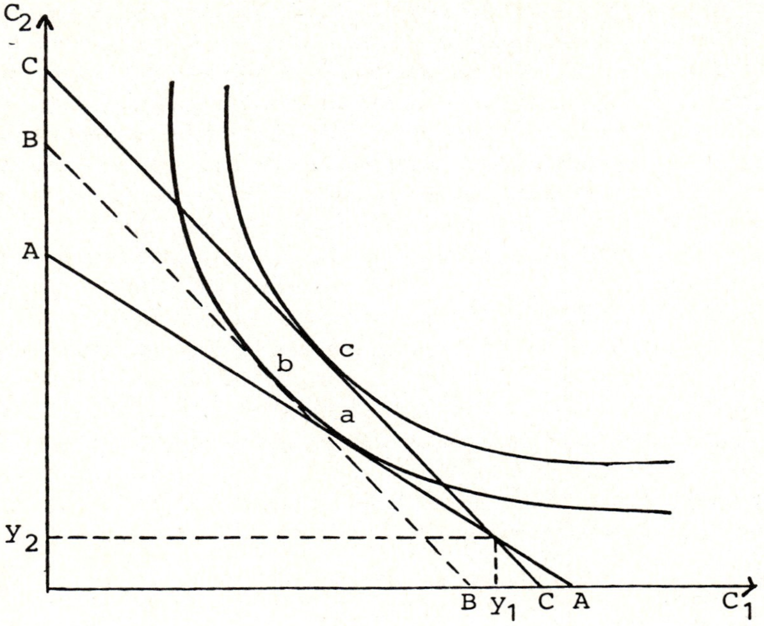

Figure 2.1b. Substitution and income effects of a change in the interest rate: the lender.

saving instead is defined by means of the second-period budget constraint (2.3), an unexpected ambiguity arises. It is easy to show that the compensated interest effect on future consumption is positive, i.e., $(\partial C_2/\partial r)_U > 0$. But since the rate of interest enters into the expression which links saving to future consumption, the compensated effect on saving is ambiguous, while the conventional view is certainly that it is positive. As argued in Sandmo (1981a), rather than proving the conventional view to be wrong, Feldstein has presented a case for paying more attention to the definition of saving than has typically been the case. In the analysis above it was assumed that the compensated demand functions for consumption and saving were established through variations in second-period income; it is easy to see that Feldstein's definition of saving implies that compensation is made in terms of first-period income. In the latter case the income point on the compensated budget line BB in Figure 2.1 lies to the right of y_2, and it is then obvious that the compensated effect on saving becomes ambiguous. However, ambiguity can be avoided by stating all comparative static results in terms of consumption, which is the basic choice variable over which preferences are defined. In other words, "the effects of the rate of interest on saving" should be interpreted as simply a short-hand expression for "the effects of the rate of interest on the intertemporal allocation of consumption".

We finally come to the effects of taxation. Four types of taxes will be considered: lump sum tax, income tax, expenditure tax and indirect taxation. For simplicity, in the last three cases we limit the discussion to proportional taxes, i.e., taxes for which the rates do not vary with the size of the tax base.

A lump sum tax is one whose magnitude cannot be influenced by any decision taken by the consumer. If a is the amount of the tax payment, it would enter the budget constraint (2.4) simply as a deduction from the right-hand side,

$$C_1 + \frac{C_2}{1+r} = y_1 + \frac{y_2}{1+r} - a. \tag{2.11}$$

The lump sum payment could be interpreted as a tax which is paid in the first period only, or as the present value of such taxes paid in the future period only or in both. In any case the lump sum tax has pure income effects on consumption; it does not affect the relative price between present and future consumption. Although it is of limited practical importance, the lump sum tax is of interest as a useful benchmark case when we come to discuss the efficiency of alternative tax systems with respect to savings decisions.

We now consider a tax on all income, i.e., both on exogenous labour income (y_1 and y_2) and on income from capital (rS). If the tax rate is assumed to be constant over time and equal to t, the budget constraint becomes

$$C_1 + \frac{C_2}{1+r(1-t)} = y_1(1-t) + \frac{y_2(1-t)}{1+r(1-t)}. \tag{2.12}$$

An income tax thus works like a combination of a lump sum tax and a special tax on interest income. Since it reduces the rate of interest, it clearly has a substitution effect in favour of present and against future consumption. If the tax rate were allowed to vary between the two periods, the conclusions would be unaffected; interest income would be taxed at the rate t_2, and even though other income would be taxed at rates t_1 and t_2, respectively, the difference in rates would not in itself have any incentive effects for the consumer's adjustment of his consumption decisions.

Indirect taxation at the rate s would raise the price of consumption from 1 to $1+s$. Consequently, the budget constraint in this case would have to be written as

$$(1+s)C_1 + \frac{(1+s)C_2}{1+r} = y_1 + \frac{y_2}{1+r}, \tag{2.13a}$$

or, equivalently,

$$C_1 + \frac{C_2}{1+r} = \frac{y_1}{1+s} + \frac{y_2}{(1+s)(1+r)}. \tag{2.13b}$$

From (2.13b) it is clear that the case of a general indirect tax at a rate which is constant over time is equivalent to a tax on labour income alone, leaving the relative price of present and future consumption unaffected. In terms of the present model, indirect taxation is accordingly also equivalent to a lump sum tax being levied on all consumers in proportion to their labour income. An expenditure tax at the rate s would of course have to be modelled in exactly the same way, and the same conclusion holds.

This line of reasoning is sensitive, however, to the assumption that the tax rate is constant over time. If s_i $(i=1,2)$ is the tax rate in period i, it is immediate from (2.13a) that the tax system will indeed influence the relative price of present and future consumption; if, e.g., $s_2 > s_1$, the effect, as compared with a lump sum tax, is similar to a reduction in the rate of interest. This point becomes important if one considers, e.g., the gradual substitution of an expenditure tax for an income tax. Although the former system is neutral with respect to the rate of interest facing the consumer, during a reform process where the tax rate was gradually increased to its permanent level, the system would have a distortion similar to that implied by the general income tax. The same complication would arise if marginal tax rates were increasing under an expenditure tax system. The basic point is that neutrality with respect to the intertemporal consumption decision can only be achieved by a system which leaves the price of future in terms of today's consumption unaffected by the tax rates.

2.2. *The two-period model: Imperfect markets*

The perfect markets assumption is an idealization which has eventually to be judged against its empirical usefulness. Two features of the model stand out as being particularly strong abstractions from real world conditions. The first is the assumption that the borrowing and lending rates are the same, the second that there is no credit rationing. In considering the implications of relaxing these assumptions one should keep in mind that inequality of borrowing and lending rates and the existence of some form of credit rationing do not necessarily constitute "imperfections" in a real sense; the former clearly arises because of the transactions costs of credit institutions, while the latter can be justified by the asymmetric information possessed by agents in the credit markets. For an interesting early discussion of the notion of perfect capital markets, see Stigler (1967), and for a modern analysis, Stiglitz and Weiss (1981).

Let the lending and borrowing rates be r_L and r_B with $r_L < r_B$. The second-period budget constraint (2.3) now becomes

$$\begin{aligned} C_2 &= y_2 + S(1+r_L) \quad \text{if} \quad S>0, \\ &= y_2 + S(1+r_B) \quad \text{if} \quad S<0. \end{aligned} \tag{2.14}$$

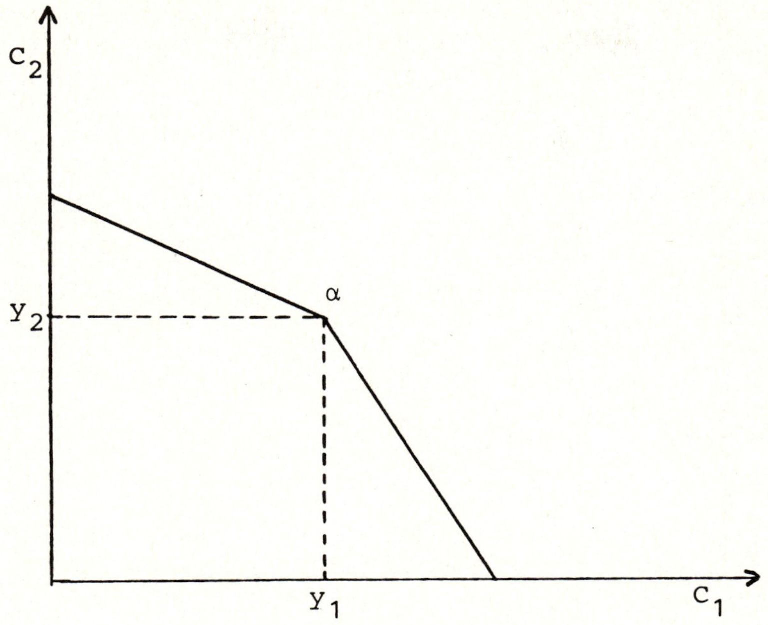

Figure 2.2. Different lending and borrowing rates.

The graphical picture of this situation is shown in Figure 2.2. If, in addition, there is a quantity constraint on the amount that can be borrowed, we must have

$$S > \underline{S}, \tag{2.15}$$

where $\underline{S}$ is some negative number which could possibly depend upon y_1. When both (2.14) and (2.15) hold we have the situation shown in Figure 2.3. It is clear that the effects of the imperfections are to introduce kinks in the budget constraints, and it is likely that the kink points will in fact be the optimum choices for many consumers. The implication of this for the effects of taxation is that taxes which would otherwise be non-neutral with respect to the rate of interest, will in fact not have any substitution effects for the consumers who have chosen their optima at the kink points. To the extent that this is true it diminishes the importance of the substitution effects for the overall results of tax policy.[1]

[1] It should be observed that a kink of the type depicted in Figure 2.2 could also emerge – or become more pronounced – by a tax system in which interest income is taxed but where no deduction is allowed for interest payments.

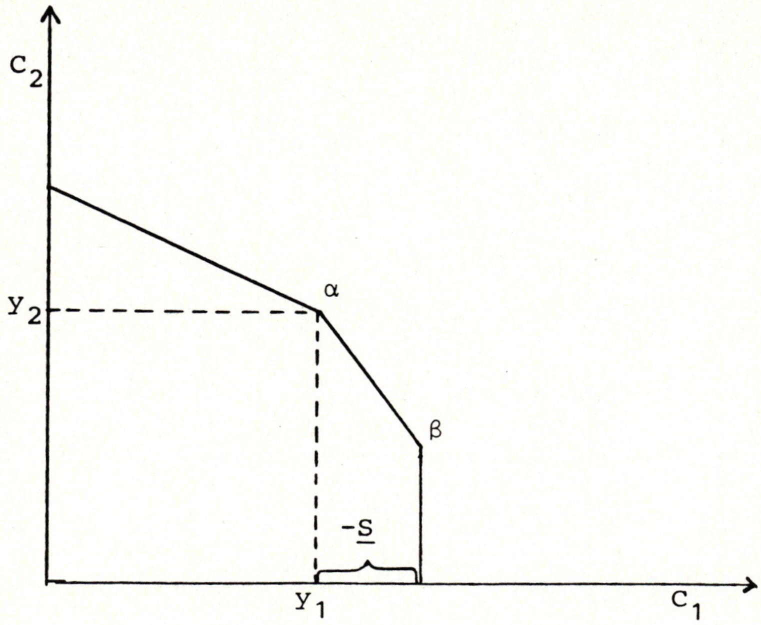

Figure 2.3. Different borrowing and lending rates with a quantity constraint on borrowing.

2.3. *Multi-period models and the bequest motive*

In principle the extension of the analysis to the multi-period case is straightforward. If the consumer's horizon extends over T periods, his problem in the perfect markets case without taxation can be formulated as that of maximizing

$$U = U(C_1, \ldots, C_T), \tag{2.16}$$

subject to

$$\sum_{t=1}^{T} (1+r)^{t-1} C_t = \sum_{t=1}^{T} (1+r)^{t-1} y_t. \tag{2.17}$$

When taxation is introduced, one can as before study its effects as equivalent combinations of income and interest rate changes. From the point of view of descriptive analysis, one is of course particularly interested in the demand for present consumption (C_1), since this is the decision which is actually binding for the consumer; the optimum choices of $C_2, \ldots, C_T$ constitute an optimal plan which can be revised as the future gradually becomes the present.

There is one respect in which the multi-period model significantly modifies a result of the two-period analysis. In the two-period model, the substitution effect of an interest rate change on future consumption is positive; this is the own-substitution effect. Because there are only two goods, these are necessarily substitutes in the Hicksian sense, so that the compensated interest effect on present consumption is necessarily negative; this is essentially the result demonstrated in Figure 2.1 above. However, with more than two periods, consumption in any one future period can be either a complement or a substitute with respect to first-period consumption. Since a change in the rate of interest changes the relative prices of future consumption in all periods, it cannot be ruled out that the compensated interest effect on present consumption is positive. It is worth noting that in the most popular version of (2.16), where U is additive and strictly concave, all goods are necessarily substitutes, and this result is ruled out. However, from a theoretical point of view, there is nothing paradoxical in the possibility of present and future consumption being complements rather than substitutes.

So far we have concentrated on versions of the pure consumption model which explain saving as arising from the adjustment of the life cycle pattern of consumption to the exogenously given time profile of income. This leaves out the bequest motive as a determinant of saving. Formally this is easy to incorporate: one could, e.g., interpret consumption in the final period C_T as bequests and allow for the possibility that this could be taxed at a special bequest tax. Given that bequests is a normal good, both the income and substitution effects of such a tax would lead to a lower level of bequests. Whether it would also lead to increased consumption and less saving in the initial period is a question which involves cross-substitution effects in the same way which was discussed above, and little can be said on an *a priori* basis. For a fuller discussion of the bequest motive, inheritance taxation and its long-run effects on income distribution, the reader is referred to Stiglitz (1978).

2.4. Uncertainty

The precautionary motive for saving comes from the fact that future income, the rate of return on saving, etc. are not known with certainty in the present. Consequently, saving may be influenced by the extent to which it can act as a protection against unfavourable realizations of current expectations. This leads immediately to a consideration of problems of portfolio choice, the demand for insurance, etc., which will be postponed to the section on taxation and risk taking. At the present stage we should note, however, that the re-interpretation of the parameters in terms of expected values is not an adequate way to handle uncertainty. When the rate of interest and/or future income are uncertain, taxation changes not only the expected value, but also the variance and higher moments of the probability distribution. Taking account of uncertainty therefore leads not only to a new set of questions which can be asked; it may also lead to revisions of the qualitative implications of certainty models. As an example of this we may consider the substitution effect on present consumption of a tax on interest income. On the basis of the two-period certainty model we would conclude that the effect is positive, since it is equivalent to a fall in the rate of interest. But, if the rate of interest is uncertain, an increase in the tax rate not only reduces its expected value but also its variance. As shown in Sandmo (1970) the substitution effect of reduced riskiness is likely to be negative, so that the overall tax substitution effect is ambiguous.

2.5. The role of labour supply

The pure consumption model with exogenously given income has played an important role in the literature and has formed the theoretical foundation for much empirical work. However, when the model is used to analyse tax policy it is important to be aware of the problems that cannot be adequately handled by the model. Of the implicit assumptions contained in the model probably the most serious of all is that labour income is exogenous. This implies, e.g., that the choice between direct and indirect taxation can be considered without reference to the effect on labour supply. This is clearly unsatisfactory and leads us to consider a model which gives an integrated treatment of saving and labour supply decisions.

We again postulate a two-period model in which the consumer now works in the first period and is retired in the second. His utility function is

$$U = U(C_1, C_2, L), \tag{2.18}$$

where L is leisure enjoyed in the first period. The time available in the first period is equal to T, so that we have $L + H = T$, where H is working time. According to the specific use that one wants to make of the model, H could be interpreted as the number of hours worked per day or per week, days per year, etc. If a is lump sum income, possibly adjusted for lump sum taxation, the budget constraint in the absence of distortionary taxation is

$$C_1 + \frac{C_2}{1+r} = w(T - L) + a. \tag{2.19}$$

The first-order maximum conditions can be written as

$$\frac{U_2}{U_1} = \frac{1}{1+r}, \tag{2.20}$$

$$\frac{U_L}{U_1} = w. \tag{2.21}$$

We now have a model with three commodities and two prices, and we wish to consider its comparative statics properties. As far as income effects are concerned, it is again the case that these are typically assumed to be positive; such an assumption is of course an implicit restriction on the indifference map. As far as substitution effects are concerned, the direct or "own"-effects are negative, implying that

$$\left(\frac{\partial C_2}{\partial r}\right)_U > 0, \quad \left(\frac{\partial L}{\partial w}\right)_U < 0. \tag{2.22}$$

For a constant level of utility the interest rate effects must clearly satisfy

$$U_1\left(\frac{\partial C_1}{\partial r}\right)_U + U_2\left(\frac{\partial C_2}{\partial r}\right)_U + U_L\left(\frac{\partial L}{\partial r}\right)_U = 0,$$

or, substituting from (2.20) and (2.21),

$$\left(\frac{\partial C_1}{\partial r}\right)_U + \frac{1}{1+r}\left(\frac{\partial C_2}{\partial r}\right)_U + w\left(\frac{\partial L}{\partial r}\right)_U = 0. \tag{2.23}$$

From (2.22) and (2.23) it is clear that we cannot deduce the sign of the substitution effect of the rate of interest on present consumption. In the pure consumption model this was necessarily negative, since leisure was assumed to be fixed. But since we cannot in general exclude the case where leisure and future consumption are Hicksian substitutes, present and future consumption could well be complements. In other words, the compensated demand function for present consumption could depend positively on the rate of interest. In some of the literature one gets the impression that a negative relationship between present consumption and the rate of interest is a very robust implication of economic theory. But as the discussion here and in previous sections has shown, this is not the case. A negative relationship can be established only if restrictive assumptions are made about the consumer's choice set or his utility function or both. This should be kept in mind when we turn to the tax policy implications of the analysis.

Similar remarks apply of course to models of labour supply which implicitly take the saving decision to be exogenous or at least separable from the labour–leisure choice. The narrow framework may lead both to misspecification of theoretical and empirical descriptive models and to misleading conclusions in normative models of taxation.

Table (2.1) summarizes the comparative statics properties of the integrated model and compares the implications with those of the two "pure" models. In each part of the table the first row of signs follows from the assumption that

Table 2.1
Comparative statics properties of alternative models.

1. *Pure consumption model*

$$U = U(C_1, C_2), \quad C_1 + C_2/(1+r) = y_1 + y_2/(1+r) + a$$

Parameter changing	Decision variable C_1	C_2
a	+	+
r (comp.)	−	+

2. *Pure labour supply model*

$$U = U(C, L), \quad C = w(T - L) + a$$

Parameter changing	Decision variable C	L
a	+	+
w (comp.)	+	−

3. *Integrated model*

$$U = U(C_1, C_2, L), \quad C_1 + C_2/(1+r) = w(T - L) + a$$

Parameter changing	Decision variable C_1	C_2	L
a	+	+	+
r (comp.)	?	+	?
w (comp.)	?	?	−

consumption and leisure are normal goods. The signs related to the compensated effects of changes in the wage and interest rates are those which follow from the hypothesis of utility maximization. In the integrated model two of the latter sign restrictions are survivors from the pure models: Future consumption is positively related to the rate of interest, and leisure depends negatively on the wage rate. Non-survivors are the positive relationship between present consumption and the rate of interest as well as that between the wage rate and consumption. The general theoretical point is that models with only two goods are very special in that these have to be substitutes; some of the implications of two-good models will therefore not hold when the models are extended to three or more goods.

Having examined the properties of the model in the absence of taxation, it is now a straightforward task to examine the effects of alternative systems. A lump sum tax increase is equivalent to a decrease of the parameter a. As for the other equivalence results, they are more complex than in the pure consumption model.

Take first the income tax at a constant rate t, which, however, does not apply to the lump sum element a. This could be interpreted to mean either that a is simply tax exempt, or it could be seen as implying a linear but non-proportional tax schedule which is progressive or regressive according to whether $a \gtrless 0$. The budget constraint is

$$C_1 + \frac{C_2}{1 + r(1 - t)} = w(1 - t)(T - L) + a. \tag{2.24}$$

Clearly, a change in the tax rate t will have both income and substitution effects, the former being analogous to the effects of a decrease in a. As far as the substitution effects are concerned, the tax rate changes both the net interest and wage rates, and the total effects of these on present and future consumption cannot be assessed without empirical evidence about the magnitudes of the various effects involved. Thus, whereas in the pure consumption model it was fairly straightforward to conclude that the income tax "discriminated against saving" – in the sense that the substitution effects were in favour of present consumption – this is no longer obvious in the present model. Whereas in the previous model it was clear that a lump sum tax which left the consumer at the same level of utility as the income tax would induce less present consumption, in the present model the overall pattern of substitution effects is too complex for any such conclusion to be drawn.

With the linear expenditure tax or a general indirect tax at rate s, we have the budget constraint

$$(1 + s)C_1 + \frac{(1 + s)C_2}{1 + r} = w(T - L) + a, \tag{2.25a}$$

or, dividing by $(1 + s)$,

$$C_1 + \frac{C_2}{1 + r} = \frac{w}{1 + s}(T - L) + \frac{a}{1 + s}. \tag{2.25b}$$

From (2.25b) it is clear that the imposition of either of these forms of taxation have effects equivalent to a simultaneous reduction of the wage rate and lump sum income, leaving the net rate of interest unchanged. Thus, it is no longer true that these forms of taxation are essentially lump sum in nature, since they do lower the price of leisure in terms of consumption. It might be tempting to compare these taxes with the income tax and conclude that the latter is more discriminatory with respect to saving, since it lowers the net rate of interest. But the argument is clearly unfounded. First, it is not clear what the basis of the comparison ought to be. Suppose, however, that it is constant utility. It is true that the net interest rate is higher under, e.g., indirect taxation, but constant utility must then imply a lower net wage rate. Thus, what is involved is a comparison of two cross-substitution effects on present consumption, and the outcome of this cannot be decided on *a priori* grounds.

The most immediate interpretation of labour supply in this type of model is in terms of hours supplied in a given occupation, and most empirical studies are in fact based on this interpretation; the reader is referred to the survey of this area in Chapter 4. An alternative interpretation is in terms of occupational choice, where the budget constraint can be seen as a market opportunity locus with each point on it representing an occupation offering a fixed income–leisure package. This interpretation suggests that the cross-substitution effects emphasized above may be especially relevant when one thinks of saving as being partly determined by the pattern of occupational choice. E.g., if the tax system were to discriminate in favour of occupations with much leisure relative to income, and if such occupations were also believed to be characterized by relatively stable patterns of annual income over time, one would also believe that the amount of life cycle saving would tend to diminish. In the public finance context, these problems have so far received little attention.

The present discussion has been focussed on the derivation of empirical hypotheses concerning the effects of alternative tax systems. However, it is clear that the issues raised easily lead into normative questions. Is neutrality of the tax system with respect to the interest rate a property which it is particularly desirable to achieve? What determines the relative rates of tax on income from labour and capital in an "optimal" tax system? These and related questions are postponed to Section 7.

3. Taxation and saving: Aggregation and empirical estimation

It is well known from the general theory of consumer behaviour that the conditions for perfect aggregation of demand relationships are extremely restrictive.[2] Perfect aggregation requires that the aggregate consumption function, i.e., the market demand function for present consumption, is such that it could have resulted from the maximization of a single utility function subject to a single budget constraint. A condition ensuring that this is the case is that all consumers have identical homothetic utility functions. This condition implies that any redistribution of income between consumers leaves aggregate consumption unaffected. Although the condition is in itself strong, it is important to keep in mind that it is derived on the assumption that consumers face the same prices. This

[2] See Deaton and Muellbauer (1980, ch. 6) for a good modern treatment of the theory of aggregation.

may not be an unreasonable assumption for ordinary non-durable household goods, but for intertemporal decisions involving the expectations of future prices and interest rates it becomes far from trivial. Where labour supply is involved it clearly becomes untenable. Moreover, taxation itself is important for the possibility of aggregation. E.g., if the income tax has an increasing marginal tax rate, high-income individuals will be faced with a lower rate of interest than low-income individuals. Moreover, if different individuals face different kinds of constraints in the labour and credit markets, we have another set of difficulties preventing the aggregation of individual into market relationships.

In spite of all these difficulties, the estimation of aggregate consumption functions has been one of the most active areas of econometric research. It is also one of the areas where most attention is paid to the theoretical foundations. The transition from the theory of the individual consumer to the estimation of aggregate relationships, however, is usually made on the basis of a number of aggregation problems being assumed away. One would have to be a purist to call this procedure an illegitimate one. But it is still necessary to bear in mind that, e.g., attempts at the aggregate level to estimate the income and substitution effects of interest rate changes may be subject to serious errors of aggregation.

The influential early work of Wright (1969),[3] while neglecting the aggregation problem, provided evidence of a significant negative substitution effect of the rate of interest on present consumption, the compensated elasticity being in the neighbourhood of -0.03. This would mean that an increase in the rate of interest by one percentage point from 4 to 5 percent – brought about by, e.g., a reduction in the rates of tax on interest income – would decrease present consumption by approximately 0.75 percent. Wright emphasized the significance of this result both for the traditional Keynesian view of the effectiveness of monetary policy and for the assessment of the deadweight loss associated with capital income taxation. Blinder (1975) in a later study, which explicitly took the distribution of income into account, found a substitution effect of an order of magnitude of only one tenth of that found by Wright. However, Blinder unlike Wright did not explicitly take account of the effects of taxation on the net rate of interest. Blinder also found that contrary to the usual Keynesian belief, an equalisation of incomes tends to lower aggregate consumption, at least as judged from the evidence of post-war American data. These results may serve as a reminder that the equivalence between changes in tax rates on the one hand and of income and interest rate changes on the other must be interpreted with a great deal of caution. In particular, the distribution of the income effects across the population may be very different for changes in the rate of interest and for changes in taxation.

More recent work by Boskin (1978) and Boskin and Lau (1978) seems to indicate that the interest elasticity of consumption could easily be considerably

[3] Wright claims (1969, p. 284) that prior to his own work only two published attempts had been made to estimate the interest elasticity of consumption or saving.

higher than was previously thought. The authors' preferred value of the savings elasticity is 0.4, which would correspond to a consumption elasticity of -0.30, which is ten times the magnitude of Wright's estimate; indeed, since this estimate is of the uncompensated elasticity, the increase in the estimate of the compensated elasticity should be even higher. Boskin (1978), like Wright and Blinder, estimated a version of the pure consumption model. The later work of Boskin and Lau is particularly notable for the extension of the theoretical framework to an integrated model of consumption and labour supply, where they found significant cross-effects of interest and wage changes on labour supply and consumption, respectively.

Much of the evidence for tax substitution effects on consumption and saving is indirect, in the sense that tax effects are inferred from the estimated interest rate effects using the equivalence results of the theoretical model, while ideally one would like to see direct tests of the tax effects. Another difficulty with using evidence related to the rate of interest is the measurement problem involved in the use of this variable. While earlier studies used nominal before-tax rates of interest, the increases in both the rate of inflation and marginal tax rates have made it important to use some measure of real after-tax rate of return; see the discussion of this in Feldstein (1982). This is done, e.g., by Boskin (1978), while Blinder (1975) does not correct for the effects of taxation; this discrepancy could conceivably account for the difference in the estimated magnitude of the interest elasticity.

Another measurement problem is the choice of the appropriate nominal interest rate. Since in reality we observe different borrowing and lending rates, a varying degree of access to capital markets and increasing marginal tax rates, it is clear that the relevant interest variable should differ between socioeconomic groups of consumers. However, in practice one has had to compromise by choosing some "representative" interest rate, and it therefore becomes to some extent a judgement of the individual researcher to choose such a rate. While Blinder chooses a weighted average of rates paid on time deposits by financial institutions, Boskin relies on the estimates of Christensen and Jorgenson (1973) of rates of return to the household sector, computed as income from assets divided by asset value. Both of these studies, on the other hand, use data for rates of return on an annual basis. It is not clear that annual rates are the relevant ones if the underlying model is that of life cycle saving, for which some long-run measure would seen more appropriate. When the results are used to consider the relative merits of income and expenditure taxation, they are in fact used to predict the effect of a long-run shift in the real after-tax rate of return.

It is not easy to give a summary characterization of the empirical work which has been done in this area. It certainly seems to indicate that the relative price effects could be rather substantial and that the consequence of taxation for saving incentives clearly go beyond those of a pure reduction of real disposable income.

These conclusions have important implications both for the positive assessment of the effects of taxation and for the normative issues of tax design. However, it should be kept in mind that there are as yet relatively few studies in this area, and that these differ both in terms of model specification and in the nature of the data used. With the gradual accumulation of empirical results one will hopefully achieve a firmer basis both for prediction and for policy advice.

4. Corporate savings

In accounting for total private saving it might seem obvious that close attention should be paid to saying by corporations in the form of retained earnings. In theory, there are at least two views of the relationship between corporate and personal saving. The first view is that dividends but not retained earnings should be included in the disposable income which enters the consumption function; Feldstein (1973) refers to this as the Keynesian view, although not necessarily that of Keynes himself. The second point of view is to start from the assumption that the value of corporate assets is reflected in individual wealth; therefore, whether corporate earnings are retained or distributed makes no difference for personal consumption behaviour. This approach goes back to Irving Fisher (1930) and is continued in modern life cycle theories. According to this view, consumers always see through "the corporate veil"; on the other hand the *flow* of capital income has no effect on personal saving.

The empirical results of Feldstein (1973) on U.S. data and of Feldstein and Fane (1973) on British data give qualified support to the Fisher view. Consumers do see through the corporate veil by adjusting personal saving so as to offset changes in corporate saving. On the other hand the flow of capital income, whether dividends or retained earnings, has an effect on personal consumption and saving. It should be noted that later work by Bhatia (1979) on a different data set for the U.S. concluded that retained earnings did not have any independent effect on consumer spending.

5. Social security, pensions and saving

Both social security and public and private pension schemes can be regarded as a kind of compulsory saving. In return for social security taxes and pension contributions in the present the individual is promised payments to provide for his old age. Suppose now that a social security scheme is introduced into an environment where consumers have already drawn up optimal consumption–saving plans covering their entire lifetimes. Since retirement consumption is now to be provided for from public funds, an optimal response on the part of individuals is to reduce their personal saving. How will this affect total saving in the economy? The answer obviously depends on the use which the government makes of the contributions which it collects. If these are used for public consumption and transfers, the overall rate of saving will fall. If, on the other hand, the contributions are left to accumulate in a fund, the rate of saving will be upheld and may even increase. In view of the very large amounts involved, the growth of social security and pension schemes could easily have a powerful effect on the rate of saving.[4]

To see the theoretical issues more precisely, let us go back to our basic two-period consumption model of Section 2. Let b be social security benefits received in period 2 (the retirement period), and let c be the contribution paid in period 1. If we begin by assuming that the contribution is paid in a lump sum manner, the consumer's budget constraint is

$$C_1 + \frac{C_2}{1+r} = y_1 + \frac{y_2}{1+r} - c + \frac{b}{1+r}. \tag{5.1}$$

Let us assume that b is calculated as a multiple of some reference contribution $\bar{c}$ which may but need not be equal to c. If the multiplicative factor is $(1+g)$ we can write $b = (1+g)\bar{c}$ and (5.1) as

$$C_1 + \frac{C_2}{1+r} = y_1 + \frac{y_2}{1+r} - c\left(1 - \frac{1+g}{1+r}\frac{\bar{c}}{c}\right). \tag{5.2}$$

From this formulation several conclusions follow immediately:

(1) If $c = \bar{c}$ and $g = r$, the social security scheme has no effect on present or future private consumption. This implies that personal saving will fall by an amount equal to the amount of the contribution. This is the case where there is no redistribution involved in the scheme, and where the rate of return available to the individual saver equals that available to the government.

(2) If $c = \bar{c}$ and $g \neq r$, there is an income effect on consumption in both periods which is positive or negative according to whether $g \gtrless r$. If marginal propensities to consume are positive and less than one, saving will change in the same direction as consumption. The case $g > r$ may be of particular interest as that in which the government is able to offer a higher rate of return on social security contributions than savers can get in the private capital market.

(3) If $g = r$ and $c \neq \bar{c}$, there are income effects of the same kind dependent on whether $c \gtrless c$. In many countries benefits increase less than proportionately with contributions, so that there might be positive income effects for low-income

[4] The effects of social security and pension schemes on saving are, of course, only one aspect of the growth of these types of saving. The effects on retirement behaviour have been studied by Diamond and Hausman (1984) and others. A survey of the social security reform debate in the United States has been provided by Thompson (1983).

groups, while the effects could be negative for individuals in high-income brackets. There might then be a redistributive effect on aggregate personal saving, the sign of which cannot be determined on *a priori* grounds.

The assumptions on which this model is based are extremely restrictive; of these, a fixed retirement period, complete certainty and the absence of a bequest motive and of distortionary taxes are potentially important as leading to further deviations from conclusion (1).

(4) It has been argued by, e.g., Feldstein (1976a) that retirement age is a decision variable which should not be taken as fixed. The introduction of social security induces individuals to retire earlier and to save more during their working years to provide for a longer period of retirement. This effect comes in addition to the "replacement effect" outlined under (1), and makes the total effect indeterminate.

(5) The implicit yield on social security contributions might be more certain than the rate of return in the capital market, e.g., because the public sector has a risk diversification advantage over private individuals. This would probably lead to a further reduction in private saving, over and above the displacement effect. On the other hand, the yield on social security contributions is based on political guarantees which may not be considered particularly trustworthy; in that case the risk effect could go the other way.

(6) Suppose that the present generation cares not only about its own utility but also about that of its descendants; more precisely, each generation has a welfare function over its own utility and that of its heirs. Because the same is true of the next generation, each generation acts as an individual with an infinite life. Barro (1974) has then argued as follows. Suppose that an unfunded pension scheme were introduced with the immediate effect of reducing private saving. This in itself would lead to a lower capital stock in the future and hence impose a burden on future generations. However, the present generation would realize this and therefore increase their bequests. This would exactly offset the replacement effect and so leave personal saving unaffected.

(7) The formulation (5.2) assumes that social security payments are financed by lump sum taxes. In reality the financing typically takes place through distortionary income taxes which may have further effects on saving via changes in after-tax interest and wage rates; see the discussion in Section 2.

Empirical evidence in this area has been accumulating rather rapidly in recent years. Feldstein (1974c) found that for the United States during the period 1929–71, social security reduced private saving by about 40 percent; however, the picture is much less clear when attention is restricted to the post-war period 1947–71. Feldstein (1977) has also used international cross-section data to study the relationship between private saving and social security. This study confirms the time series evidence of a negative relationship. Feldstein interprets this as evidence that the replacement effect outweighs the induced retirement effect.

The conclusions in Feldstein's pioneering work do not receive unequivocal support from later studies.[5] For the case of private pensions, which have important similarities with social security, Munnell (1976) found a negative effect on saving, while Kotlikoff (1979) found mixed support for the Feldstein position. Both of these papers use cross-section data for men aged 45–59 in the United States. A recent paper by Kurz (1981), using a much more representative sample of households, concludes that there is no effect of social security wealth on the private rate of savings. On the other hand, he finds that private pension plans do have effects on saving, but these are rather complex; there are, e.g., significant differences between the responses of men and women to the availability of pensions.

Barro and MacDonald (1979) have re-examined the international evidence on a basis of mixed cross-section and time series data for sixteen Western countries over the period 1951–60. The conclusions, in contrast to the Feldstein (1977) study, are rather indecisive. The data do not support the conclusion of a pronounced displacement effect, but neither is there evidence of a positive effect on saving.[6]

Detailed studies of data from other countries are also becoming available. Dicks-Mireaux and King (1984) have studied cross-section data for Canadian households for 1977. They conclude that there is a small but significant displacement effect. Using time series data for the United Kingdom, Browning (1982) finds that public pensions tend to increase consumption, but that the effect is very small and hardly significant. The effects of occupational pension schemes in the U.K. have been studied by Green (1981) and Hemming and Harvey (1983).

From a theoretical point of view the influence of social security and pensions on consumer saving is a complex one. Few single hypotheses emerge once we move beyond the framework of the simplest life cycle model. It is therefore not surprising that the econometric evidence should also be conflicting.

6. The incidence of taxation

Tax incidence will be dealt with separately and in more detail in a separate chapter. Here we shall limit the survey to a brief consideration of the main issues, and a few references to the literature on incidence which deals especially with the taxation of savings.

[5] Williamson and Jones (1983) have argued that the conflicting evidence from empirical studies is due to insufficiently detailed theoretical specification of the econometric models.

[6] A later study by Feldstein (1980), using new international cross-section data developed by the U.S. Social Security Administration, confirms his earlier results of a substantial negative impact of social security on private saving. An appendix to this paper by C.Y. Horioka discusses the reasons for the differences between the Feldstein and Barro–MacDonald results.

A simple partial equilibrium analysis of the incidence of an income tax on the rate of interest would focus on the interest rate as an equilibrator of saving and investment. If there were no tax distortions on the investment side, the equilibrium condition would be simply

$$S(r(1-t)) = I(r). \tag{6.1}$$

If either saving or investment were totally inelastic, this would of course require that both sides of the market face a net rate of interest which is independent of the tax. Thus, if investment is inelastic, a change in the tax rate must imply a reverse change in the rate of interest to keep $r(1-t)$ constant; in this case the "cost" of taxation is borne by investors. If saving is inelastic, it is savers who pay the cost through a reduction in their after-tax rate of interest. In general, the effect of the tax rate on the equilibrium rate of interest would depend on the relative magnitudes of the two elasticities.

However, this analysis is unsatisfactory for at least two reasons. First, it is a partial and not a general equilibrium formulation. Second, it is a static theory, while it seems obvious that the equilibrium effects of taxes on saving and investment require a dynamic equilibrium formulation. The first objection could be overcome by incorporating the analysis in a model of tax incidence of the Harberger (1962) type.[7] However, this suffers from the weakness of assuming fixed factor supplies and is not suited for the purpose. Clearly what is required is a model of economic growth which takes account of the long-run consequences for the capital stock of the tax effects on the equilibrium level of saving and investment.

Such an extension of the model was first achieved by Diamond (1970). His point of departure is the integrated consumption–labour model which was discussed above but with labour being supplied inelastically. Population grows exponentially with generations overlapping in the manner of the famous Samuelson (1958) model. There are constant returns to scale in production and competitive behaviour in all markets. Diamond then studies the incidence effects of a tax on interest income as compared to a situation with only lump sum taxation. He finds that the differential incidence of an interest income tax raises the before-tax rate of interest and lowers the wage rate. The effects of this on the functional distribution of income depend of course on the elasticity of substitution.

A similar framework of analysis was used by Feldstein (1974a, 1974b). The latter of these articles comes close to Diamond's analysis in assuming an exogenous labour supply. On the savings side the explicit optimization framework of the overlapping generations model is dropped in favour of a two-class model with different savings propensities. Feldstein shows that a tax on capital income in this

[7] For a detailed discussion of Harberger type models, see Atkinson and Stiglitz (1980, ch. 6).

model is in general borne both by labour and capital, the division of the burden depending on the difference in propensities to save between the two groups and on the sensitivity of these propensities to changes in the rate of interest. One might think that the results would be crucially dependent on the exogeneity of labour supply; however, Feldstein (1974a) showed that in the case of a tax on labour income, the asymptotic incidence of the tax in long-run steady state equilibrium was independent of the elasticity of labour supply. In the short run, the results are different and come closer to those of comparative statics analysis. These results thus demonstrate very clearly how careful one must be in the analysis of tax incidence where saving decisions are involved.[8]

The models which we have been discussing all treat the savings decision as being concerned with a single financial asset with a well defined rate of interest. This is certainly a legitimate simplification for many purposes, but it also abstracts from problems which in practice may be serious ones. Taxable income from capital is usually defined in nominal terms, and when inflation is present this may lead to an effective tax rate which is much higher than the nominal rate. This is clearly a problem even in one-asset models, but with many assets the tax rules typically lead to a system whereby different types of capital income are taxed at very different effective rates of tax. A particularly interesting discussion of the problems raised by this in the U.K. context is in Kay and King (1978). Tax effects on the composition of saving are taken up in more detail in Sections 8–12 below.

7. The optimum tax treatment of savings

The optimum tax treatment of saving – like the optimum tax treatment of anything else – must involve a tradeoff between distributional objectives on the one hand and economic efficiency on the other. To the extent that saving can somehow be treated just like another commodity in the context of general equilibrium analysis, the results of optimum tax theory could be applied fairly directly to this problem.[9] However, there are a number of special issues related to the taxation of saving which are not easily captured in a general framework. One of these is the old argument about the "double taxation of savings". It has been claimed by many writers that a general income tax with the same rates applying to income from labour and capital would involve a discrimination against saving because the income from which asset purchases are made has already been subjected to taxation. Another argument, which can be associated with the names of Böhm-Bawerk and Pigou, is that economic agents are myopic and have a

[8] Other contributions to tax incidence in a growing economy include Friedlaender and Vandendorpe (1978), Kotlikoff and Summers (1979) and Summers (1981).

[9] For surveys of the theory of optimum commodity taxation, see Chapter 2 or Sandmo (1976).

tendency to save too little and thus not provide a sufficiently large capital stock for the future. These and related issues have recently been examined in a series of papers written in an optimum taxation framework; e.g., Ordover (1976), Ordover and Phelps (1979), Atkinson and Sandmo (1980) and King (1980). The analysis which we shall present here is a simplified version of the Atkinson–Sandmo analysis; it is also similar to that of King.

The analytical model is one of steady state growth in which population is increasing at the rate n. Each consumer lives for two periods, working in the first and being retired in the second as in the integrated model described earlier. The government has an exogenously given revenue requirement which has to be financed through distortionary taxes on income from labour and capital; lump sum taxation is ruled out. Within each generation all individuals are identical, and the problem of the representative consumer is to maximize his utility $U(C_1, C_2, L)$ as in (2.18), subject to the budget constraint

$$C_1 + p_2 C_2 = w(1 - t_w)(T - L) + a. \tag{7.1}$$

Here $p_2 = (1 + r(1 - t_r))^{-1}$ is the price of future consumption. Compared to our earlier formulation (2.24), allowance has now been made for the possibility of taxing income from capital and labour at different rates. A lump sum term a has been included although, as already explained, this is in fact constrained to be zero; however, it serves a useful analytical purpose for the derivation of the Slutsky equations.

The consumer's optimum can now be characterized by the first-order conditions

$$U_1 - \lambda = 0, \tag{7.2}$$

$$U_2 - \lambda p_2 = 0, \tag{7.3}$$

$$U_L - \lambda w(1 - t_w) = 0. \tag{7.4}$$

From (7.1)–(7.4) we can solve for the demand functions, and substituting these back into the utility function, we have the indirect utility function

$$V = V(p_2, w(1 - t_w), a), \tag{7.5}$$

which has the partial derivatives

$$\frac{\partial V}{\partial a} = \lambda, \tag{7.6a}$$

$$\frac{\partial V}{\partial t_r} = \frac{\partial V}{\partial p_2} \cdot \frac{\partial p_2}{\partial t_r} = -\lambda C_2 r p_2^2, \tag{7.6b}$$

$$\frac{\partial V}{\partial t_w} = -\lambda w(T - L). \tag{7.6c}$$

The government's problem can now be posed as that of choosing t_r and t_w so as to maximize V[10], subject to the government's budget constraint

$$t_w w(T-L) + t_r \frac{rp_2C_2}{1+n} = R, \tag{7.7}$$

where R is given. The second term on the left is the government's revenue from capital income taxation. The savings of the older generation living now is p_2C_2 and the income from this is accordingly rp_2C_2. In order to make the tax revenue from this comparable with the revenue from labour income taxation we must divide by $(1+n)$ to take account of the smaller number of people in the older generation.

We solve this problem by taking the derivatives with respect to t_r and t_w of the Lagrange function

$$\mathscr{L} = V(P_2, w(1-t_w), a) + \mu\left(t_w w(T-L) + t_r \frac{rp_2C_2}{1+n} - R\right), \tag{7.8}$$

and equating them to zero. This yields

$$-\lambda C_2 r p_2^2 + \mu\left(-t_w w\frac{\partial L}{\partial t_r} + t_r\frac{rp_2}{1+n}\frac{\partial C_2}{\partial t_r} + \frac{rp_2C_2}{1+n} + t_r\frac{r^2p_2^2C_2}{1+n}\right) = 0, \tag{7.9}$$

$$-\lambda w(T-L) + \mu\left(w(T-L) - t_w w\frac{\partial L}{\partial t_w} + t_r\frac{rp_2}{1+n}\frac{\partial C_2}{\partial t_w}\right) = 0. \tag{7.10}$$

Dividing (7.9) by (7.10), we obtain

$$\frac{C_2rp_2^2}{w(T-L)} = \frac{-t_w w\dfrac{\partial L}{\partial t_r} + t_r\dfrac{rp_2}{1+n}\dfrac{\partial C_2}{\partial t_r} + \dfrac{rp_2C_2}{1+n}(1+t_r r p_2)}{w(T-L) - t_w w\dfrac{\partial L}{\partial t_w} + t_r\dfrac{rp_2}{1+n}\dfrac{\partial C_2}{\partial t_w}}.$$

[10] I.e., the government maximizes the utility of a representative generation. For a discussion of the dynamic optimization problem, see Atkinson and Sandmo (1980). We also assume here that w and r are given from the production side; the full analysis is presented in Atkinson and Sandmo and in King (1980).

The expression can be considerably simplified if we substitute from the Slutsky equations.[11] The income effects then cancel out and we are left with

$$\frac{n-r}{1+n}C_2(T-L)+wt_wC_2S_{LL}-\frac{t_r rp_2}{1+n}C_2S_{2L}$$

$$=t_w w(T-L)S_{L2}+\frac{t_r rp_2}{1+n}(T-L)S_{22}.$$

It is convenient to rewrite this in terms of the compensated effects on labour supply rather than on leisure. Defining the former as $S_{HH}=-S_{LL}$ and $S_{H2}=-S_{L2}$, and dividing the equation by $C_2(T-L)$, we finally obtain

$$\frac{t_r r}{1+n}(-\sigma_{22}+\sigma_{H2})=\frac{t_w}{1-t_w}(\sigma_{HH}-\sigma_{2H})+\frac{r-n}{1+n}, \tag{7.11}$$

where the σ's are the compensated elasticities.[12] This equation characterizes the relative levels of the tax rates on income from labour and capital, with the absolute levels being determined by the government's revenue requirement.

We note first that the characterization depends on compensated and not on gross elasticities. The absence of income effects is explained by the fact that the income effects are analogous to the effects of lump sum taxation and therefore irrelevant for an assessment of the relative merits of different kinds of distortionary taxation.

Assume for simplicity of interpretation that $r=n$ and that the cross-elasticities are zero. Then we have that

$$\frac{t_r r}{1+r}\bigg/\frac{t_w}{1-t_w}=\frac{\sigma_{HH}}{-\sigma_{22}}. \tag{7.12}$$

If labour supply is completely inelastic (along the compensated supply curve), the optimal tax on interest income is zero, while the tax on labour income is

[11] These are

$$\frac{\partial L}{\partial t_w}=\left[(T-L)\frac{\partial L}{\partial a}+S_{LL}\right](-w),\qquad \frac{\partial C_2}{\partial t_w}=\left[(T-L)\frac{\partial C_2}{\partial a}+S_{2L}\right](-w),$$

$$\frac{\partial L}{\partial t_r}=\left[-C_2\frac{\partial L}{\partial a}+S_{L2}\right]rp_2^2,\qquad \frac{\partial C_2}{\partial t_r}=\left[-C_2\frac{\partial C_2}{\partial a}+S_{22}\right]rp_2^2.$$

In each case the bracketed expression is the Slutsky equation with respect to the net price, and the last factor is the derivative of the net price with respect to the tax rate.

[12] For a more detailed derivation of this equation, see King (1980).

equivalent to a lump sum tax and could be set arbitrarily high. If, on the other hand, the demand for future consumption is inelastic, the argument is reversed, and interest income is the ideal tax base from an efficiency point of view. In general, the relative rates of tax depend on the relative magnitudes of the two elasticities, and there is no particular reason to believe that the optimal rates should be the same for the two sources of income. This interpretation carries over, with appropriate modifications, to the case of non-zero cross-elasticities. The importance of these is explained by the fact that, for any given rate of tax on labour income, the case for an interest income tax is strengthened if it leads to changes in demand and supply which counteract those associated with the wage tax.

The final term in (7.11) has the sign of the difference between the rate of interest and the rate of growth; it is accordingly zero when the economy is on the golden rule growth path.[13] If we take the case where the coefficients of the tax rates are positive, i.e., where the direct substitution effects dominate, to be the normal one, we see immediately that on an inefficient growth path with $r < n$, the case for an interest income tax would be weakened.[14] Since the rate of interest equals the marginal productivity of capital, this case is where the capital intensity of the economy is too high and where, consequently, one would expect that saving ought to be discouraged. This apparent paradox is resolved by noting that a lower tax on interest income means that the tax on wage income must be increased in order to keep tax revenue constant. This reduces labour supply (in a compensated sense) and hence the income from which saving is generated. With the assumptions which have been made about the elasticities, the overall effect of the switch in taxation is precisely to discourage saving, as one's economic intuition would have it.

This is as close as we come in this model to capturing the arguments of Böhm-Bawerk and Pigou. There is a kind of pecuniary externality from population growth if the growth rate is not equal to the rate of return. This social myopia does not, however, capture the idea of individual myopia which was central to their arguments. If individuals underestimate their "true" willingness to pay for future consumption, there is a merit good argument for the subsidization or public provision of saving. There can be no doubt that in practice this type of paternalistic argument has been seen by many as being of decisive importance for the public provision of social security and pension schemes.

The conclusions of optimum taxation models are sensitive to the assumptions made concerning the range of instruments available to the government. In the present case the importance of the externality corrective last term in (7.11)

[13] For a discussion of this concept and its optimality properties, see Dixit (1976).

[14] This line of reasoning presupposes that the compensated elasticities, which are in general functions of r and, therefore, of the capital intensity of the economy, remain constant over the range in which the comparisons are made.

provides a good illustration of this point. As shown by Atkinson and Sandmo (1980), if the government can transfer income between generations in a lump sum fashion, or if it can pursue an independent debt policy, it can always attain the golden rule growth path with $r = n$. In that case, the results of the analysis are in complete accordance with standard optimum tax theory.

What about the argument of the double taxation of saving? First of all, it should be clear that what finally counts for the evaluation of efficiency is not the number of taxes to which a commodity is subjected, but the final effective rate. Apart from this we see that on purely theoretical grounds there is no strong reason to suspect that efficiency considerations should imply a tax rate on capital income either below or above that on wages. The case has to rest on an empirical assessment of the demand and supply elasticities involved.

Many studies of the welfare loss of capital income taxation start from the pure consumption model in which labour income is given exogeneously while saving is interest elastic. It is obvious that this implies that taxation of interest income involves a deadweight loss and that efficiency calls for a zero rate. King (1980) has considered the empirical evidence very carefully, drawing in particular on the results reported by Boskin and Lau (1978), who use the overlapping generations model with variable labour supply. He finds that the evidence tends to support a negative rate of tax on capital income. The implications of the theory and of the empirical evidence for the choice of the tax base is examined in more detail in another chapter of the Handbook and will not be pursued here. Although it is clear that the choice of tax base has to rest on many more considerations than the efficiency arguments which have been examined here, we have at least indicated the importance of both theoretical arguments and empirical evidence for a rational approach to the tax treatment of savings.

8. Taxation and risk taking: Portfolio choice

In looking at the saving decision as if it takes the form of purchases of a single homogeneous asset we have obviously made a drastic simplification. Although such simplifications are clearly necessary in order to focus attention on the strategically important issues, they may also be misleading. Thus, it may well be that the tax effects on the total volume of saving are less important than their effects on the composition of saving.

Of course, tax effects on portfolio composition may be of many kinds, not all of which may be expected to have any systematic bias in favour of assets with particular characteristics. The classic argument for a systematic effect of taxation on portfolio choice runs in terms of risk-taking behaviour. The popular view has traditionally been that the taxation of income from assets discriminates *against* risk taking through its lowering of the expected rates of return. However, at least since the seminal article by Domar and Musgrave (1944) it has been common among economists to emphasize a different point of view. In addition to taking a share in the expected return, the government also shares in the risk. If there are perfect loss offset provisions, so that losses can be written off against other taxable income, the government will in fact carry the same share of a possible loss as it takes in a gain. If individuals ascribed a sufficiently large weight to the loss sharing property of the tax, the direction of the tax discrimination could possibly go in the opposite direction.

The modern version of this argument, using the expected utility framework of von Neumann and Morgenstern, is due to Mossin (1968) and Stiglitz (1969), and it is useful to start by examining the simplest possible model. This is one in which individuals have preferences for the probability distribution of their wealth (Y) at the end of the investment period, and they evaluate this according to a strictly concave utility function $U(Y)$. Initial wealth can be invested in two assets, money (m) bearing a certain return of zero and a risky asset (a) having a stochastic rate of return of x. The return is taxed at the rate t. The budget constraint is

$$m + a = A, \tag{8.1}$$

where A is initial wealth, and final wealth is

$$\begin{aligned} Y &= a[1 + x(1-t)] + m \\ &= A + ax(1-t), \end{aligned} \tag{8.2}$$

where the last equality is obtained after substitution from (8.1). Expected utility, assuming that x is continuously distributed on the interval $[-1,\infty)$, is

$$\mathrm{E}[U] = \int_{-1}^{\infty} U(A + ax(1-t)) f(x)\,\mathrm{d}x. \tag{8.3}$$

The first-order condition for an interior solution can be written as

$$\mathrm{E}[U'(Y)x(1-t)] = 0. \tag{8.4}$$

The second-order maximum condition is satisfied by the assumption of concavity. It is easy to show [15] that the optimal holding of the risky asset is positive if and only if $\mathrm{E}[x] > 0$. We shall assume that this is the case.

Differentiating (8.4) with respect to t we can write

$$\mathrm{E}\left[U''(Y)\left(\frac{\partial a}{\partial t}x(1-t) - ax\right)x(1-t) - U'(Y)x\right] = 0.$$

[15] See, e.g., the analysis in Arrow (1970).

The last term vanishes because of (8.4) and since t itself is non-stochastic.[16] It is then easy to see that we must have

$$\frac{\partial a}{\partial t}=\frac{a}{1-t} \quad \text{or} \quad \frac{\partial a}{\partial t}\frac{t}{a}=\frac{t}{1-t}. \tag{8.5}$$

This result is striking in its simplicity. The investor's response to taxation can be predicted without knowledge of his risk preferences. The only information required is his holding of the risky asset and his rate of tax.

The result must necessarily have a simple interpretation. By adjusting his portfolio according to the "rule" (8.5), the investor is in fact able to keep the probability distribution *of final wealth* constant.[17] Since this was the distribution chosen as the optimal one in the first place, it is not surprising that the investor should continue to choose it, given that it is still available. Thus, the investor responds to the higher tax rate by *increasing* his holding of the risky asset. The risk subsidization involved outweighs the taxation of expected return.

This is of course a very simple model. Its most obvious shortcoming is that it takes no account of other types of decisions made by the individual, so that, e.g., the total size of the savings portfolio is unaffected by the tax rate. We shall return to this problem later. However, even in the context of the pure portfolio framework the model is based on a number of restrictive assumptions, which will be discussed in turn.

8.1. A non-zero rate of interest

Let r be the rate of return on the safe asset. It can then be shown that positive holding of the risky asset is optimal if and only if its expected return exceeds r. This will be assumed in the following.

Suppose first that the tax is levied only on the excess return to the risky asset, so that the tax base is $a(x-r)$. The budget constraint (8.2) then becomes

$$\begin{aligned} Y &= a(1+x)+m(1+r)-a(x-r)t \\ &= A(1+r)+a(x-r)(1-t). \end{aligned} \tag{8.6}$$

The first-order condition is now

$$\mathrm{E}\left[U'(Y)(x-r)(1-t)\right]=0, \tag{8.7}$$

[16] For an analysis of the case where t is stochastic due to "political risk", see Ekern (1971). Of course the marginal tax rate could also be stochastic if it depended on Y.

[17] From (8.2) we can compute the mean and variance of final wealth as $\mathrm{E}[Y]=A+a\mu(1-t)$ and $\mathrm{var}[Y]=a^2(1-t)^2\sigma^2$, where μ and σ^2 are the mean and variance of the rate of return. The reader may easily convince himself that portfolio adjustment according to (8.5) keeps the mean and variance of final wealth constant, and that the same is true of higher moments of the probability distribution.

and it is easy to see that the analysis goes through as before with the result (8.5) still holding. We shall refer to this as the *net* taxation case.

An alternative assumption is that the returns from both assets are taxed at the rate t; this is the *gross* taxation case, where final wealth becomes

$$\begin{aligned} Y &= a[1+x(1-t)]+m[1+r(1-t)] \\ &= A[1+r(1-t)]+a(x-r)(1-t). \end{aligned} \tag{8.8}$$

The condition that at the optimum the expected marginal utility of a further increase in a must be zero, has exactly the same form as (8.7). But since Y is now defined differently, the comparative statics of this case differs from the previous one. Taking the derivative with respect to t we obtain

$$\frac{\partial a}{\partial t}=\frac{\mathrm{E}[U''(Y)(x-r)]}{\mathrm{E}[U''(Y)(x-r)^2]}\cdot\frac{Ar}{1-t}+\frac{a}{1-t}.$$

It is also straightforward to compute

$$\frac{\partial a}{\partial A}=-\frac{1+r(1-t)}{1-t}\,\frac{\mathrm{E}[U''(Y)(x-r)]}{\mathrm{E}[U''(Y)(x-r)^2]},$$

and substituting into the previous expression we can write

$$\frac{\partial a}{\partial t}=-\frac{Ar}{1+r(1-t)}\,\frac{\partial a}{\partial A}+\frac{a}{1-t},$$

or, in elasticity form,

$$\frac{\partial a}{\partial t}\cdot\frac{t}{a}=-\frac{tr}{1+r(1-t)}\left(\frac{\partial a}{\partial A}\,\frac{A}{a}\right)+\frac{t}{1-t}. \tag{8.9}$$

The last term is the same as in (8.5), while in addition we now have an income effect which is proportional to the wealth elasticity of the risky asset. If this is positive, which is a reasonable assumption, it tends to reduce the demand for the risky asset. We thus have conflicting wealth and substitution effects, and no firm conclusion can be drawn about the relationship between taxation and risk taking.

However, it may be tempting to argue that the substitution effect is likely to dominate the income effect. For "reasonable" parameter values like $t=0.5$ and $r=0.05$, the wealth elasticity must be in excess of 41 in order for the whole expression (8.9) to become negative. But this argument overlooks the fact that the choice of a reasonable value for r depends crucially on the length of the time period. If the holding period is one month instead of one year, $r = 0.004$ would roughly correspond to an annual rate of 5 percent, while if the period were 23 years, one would as an approximation have $r = 2$. In the first case the crucial value of the wealth elasticity is 501, in the second case it is 2. The model does not explain the length of the holding period, and a realistic assumption about it should reflect the application that one has in mind. Perhaps in most cases of interest it would not be realistic to assume holding periods much in excess of one year. If so, there may indeed be reason to suspect the substitution effect of the simple model to be the dominating one.

8.2. Several risky assets

The two-asset model is attractive because it provides a well-defined measure of the degree of risk taking, which is simply measured by the share of the total portfolio going into the risky asset. The assumption that there exists an asset which has a certain return is of course an idealization which is meant to capture the point that some assets are less risky than others. Perhaps more serious is the assumption that there is only one risky asset. Suppose there are two assets whose returns are correlated in some way. The intuitive argument about the tax being a risk subsidy is hardly convincing any longer because one has to take into account the covariances of the returns. Thus, it is no longer clear that one can use the total amount invested in all risky assets as a meaningful measure of the degree of risk taking.

The extension of the analysis to the case of an arbitrary number of risky assets has been considered by Sandmo (1977). It is shown that in the net taxation case the results of the two-asset model carry over without modification, and that no assumption about the joint probability distribution of the rates of return is required. Thus, if the tax rate on the excess return of the jth risky asset is t_j, then (8.5) becomes simply

$$\frac{\partial a_j}{\partial t_j} = \frac{a_j}{1 - t_j} \quad \text{and} \quad \frac{\partial a_i}{\partial t_j} = 0 \quad \text{for} \quad i \neq j. \tag{8.10}$$

A partial increase in the rate of tax on asset j increases the demand for that asset, while leaving the demand for all other assets unchanged. The result for the total share of risky assets when there is a single tax rate follows trivially by summing over j and taking $t_j = t$ for all j.

For the gross taxation case the analysis is more complicated. For a partial tax on the returns from the jth risky asset, it can be shown that the tax effect is a linear combination of the effect of a decrease in expected return and a decrease in riskiness. Although suggestive, this result is somewhat inconclusive, since the theory does not predict how these two opposing effects are to be weighed together. In the case of a general tax which applies to all asset returns with the same rate, it turns out – perhaps surprisingly – that the result (8.9) holds for all assets, and the above comments on that result apply also to the case of many risky assets.

8.3. Imperfect loss offset

The assumption that there are perfect loss offset provisions is clearly a very strong one, and one might indeed suspect that the conclusions are very heavily dependent on this. For if it is true that the government does not take any part in a possible loss, the economic intuition behind the previous results can no longer be upheld. The tax reduces the expected rate of return as before. However, the government now shares in the risk only by taking part in the expected gain, while leaving the losses to be carried by the individual. One might conjecture on this basis that an increase in the tax rate would most likely lead to a reduction of the amount invested in the risky asset.

It was shown by Mossin (1968) and Stiglitz (1969) that the theoretical conclusions that can be drawn with respect to this question are ambiguous. With no loss offset, if the tax rate is sufficiently high, the demand for the risky asset must fall. More surprising is the insight that in general the tax effect on risk taking cannot be determined without fairly restrictive assumptions about the properties of the utility function. On reflection it is clear that even a pure reduction in the expected rate of return – with no further effects on the probability distribution – would have both substitution and income effects on the demand for the risky asset, and these could easily pull in opposite directions. A tax increase with partial or no loss offset would imply a similar ambiguity, to which we have to add the effect of the partial risk reduction associated with the distribution of the positive values of the rate of return. Thus, the ambiguity is not really surprising.[18]

8.4. Other tax forms in the pure portfolio model

The tax on returns from investment is only one of many taxes which could be considered from the viewpoint of its effects on risk taking. Following Stiglitz (1969) we could, e.g., imagine a wealth tax whose base is final wealth. We would

[18] Recently, Eeckhoudt and Hansen (1982) have argued that a tightening of the opportunity to write off losses does not necessarily lead to less risk taking.

then have

$$Y = (A(1+r) + a(x-r))(1-\tau), \tag{8.11}$$

where τ is the tax rate. The first-order condition for expected utility maximization is

$$\mathrm{E}[U'(Y)(x-r)(1-\tau)] = 0. \tag{8.12}$$

Differentiating with respect to τ we obtain

$$\frac{\partial a}{\partial \tau} = \frac{1}{1-\tau} \frac{\mathrm{E}[U''(Y)Y(x-r)]}{\mathrm{E}[U''(Y)(x-r)^2(1-\tau)]}. \tag{8.13}$$

The denominator of this expression is negative from the assumption of risk aversion. Suppose that the utility function has the property of constant elasticity of the marginal utility of wealth or constant relative risk aversion in the Arrow–Pratt sense. We then have that

$$-\frac{U''(Y)Y}{U'(Y)} = \alpha \quad \text{or} \quad U''(Y)Y = -\alpha U'(Y),$$

where α is a positive constant. Substituting into (8.13) we can write

$$\frac{\partial a}{\partial \tau} = \frac{1}{1-\tau} \cdot \frac{-\alpha \mathrm{E}[U'(Y)(x-r)]}{\mathrm{E}[U''(Y)(x-r)^2(1-\tau)]} = 0, \tag{8.14}$$

where the last equality follows from the first-order condition (8.12). Thus, in an interesting special case, the wealth tax has no effect on portfolio composition. In a more general analysis, it turns out that constant relative risk aversion is the borderline case, so that an increase in the tax rate will increase or decrease the amount of the risky asset held according to whether relative risk aversion is increasing or decreasing. It is difficult to say which of these possibilities is the empirically most relevant.

A purely lump sum tax is equivalent to a reduction of initial wealth, A. This too has ambiguous effects unless further assumptions are made; it can be shown that the wealth effect on the demand for the risky asset is positive if and only if the Arrow–Pratt measure of absolute risk aversion is decreasing. However, this result does not carry over to the case of many risky assets.

8.5. Interaction with saving and labour supply decisions

So far we have postulated a decision maker who is solely concerned with the level of his final wealth. This opens for a number of interpretations of the theory. The decision maker could, e.g., be a firm which undertakes investments to maximize the expected utility of its wealth, and this interpretation has been used by a number of writers; see, e.g., Mintz (1981). However, in the present context it is most natural to look at the decision maker who is concerned with the composition of his savings portfolio. But then we must take account of the fact that taxation affects not only the relative degrees of attractiveness of different assets, but also the relative price of present and future consumption. In other words, there is a need for an integrated model of saving and portfolio decisions. As shown in Drèze and Modigliani (1972), there exists a class of utility functions for which saving and portfolio decisions are separable in the sense that, loosely speaking, each can be analyzed taking the other as given. The combined effects of taxation on saving and portfolio decisions can then be studied by "adding up" the results. However, this class is fairly restrictive, and in any case it is not always easy to see how the adding up ought to be done.

It was shown in Sandmo (1969) that when the simple two-asset model with a zero rate of return was extended to account for consumption decisions, the simple result (8.5) carries over without change. The model has two periods, labour supply is fixed, and the consumer maximizes expected utility $\mathrm{E}[U(C_1, C_2]$. The budget constraint can be written as

$$C_2 = A - C_1 + ax(1-t), \tag{8.15}$$

where A is again initial wealth. Working through the comparative statics it is easy to see that

$$\frac{\partial a}{\partial t} = \frac{a}{1-t} \quad \text{and} \quad \frac{\partial C_1}{\partial t} = 0. \tag{8.16}$$

The first part of this result is just (8.5), and the interpretation is the same. The interpretation of the second part follows as a corollary: If the consumer can achieve the same probability distribution of future consumption as before by a simple rearrangement of his portfolio, there is no reason why he should change his level of saving and thereby his present consumption. Of course, the result holds also for the net taxation case in which the tax base is $a(x-r)$.

The gross taxation case is more complicated, and the result (8.9) no longer holds; this is essentially because of the intertemporal substitution effect which changes the size of the savings portfolio. The problem has been analyzed by Ahsan (1976), who considers the class of additive utility functions in a two-period model. Within this framework he considers a number of special cases both with respect to utility functions and with respect to the type of tax in existence. While his results are clearly interesting, they are also quite complex and difficult to summarize in general terms. The only general conclusion one can draw from his analysis seems to be that there is hardly any good reason to believe that income or consumption taxes have any clearcut effect on the degree of risk taking in the framework of intertemporal consumption decisions.[19]

Given the lack of general results in the two-period model, it is hardly to be expected that multi-period models would have more to offer in this regard. Perhaps the most interesting insight that multi-period consumption portfolio models have to offer,[20] is that there exist cases where the effects of taxation on portfolio composition are of exactly the same nature as in the one-period pure portfolio model which was discussed above. Hagen (1970) demonstrated this in a model where there is an infinite horizon utility function of the form

$$U(C_1, C_2, C_3, \ldots) = \sum_{t=1}^{\infty} \alpha^{t-1} c^{\nu},$$

where α is a parameter expressing the consumer's "impatience" ($0 < \alpha < 1$), and the instantaneous utility function has the property that the elasticity of marginal utility or the coefficient of relative risk aversion is constant and equal to $1 - \nu$. In this case the effects on portfolio allocation of investment income and consumption taxes are of exactly the same form as in the one-period model [a similar result is also in Atkinson and Stiglitz (1980, pp. 121–123)]. Hagen shows how tax effects in this model can be neatly separated into saving and portfolio effects. Even in this very special case, however, the combined income and substitution effects on investment in the risky asset are quite complex and do not allow of any unambiguous conclusion as to the total effect on risk taking. To some extent this may be a matter of interpretation, however. One could take the view that the problem of tax effects on risk taking should be seen as one which is conceptually separate from that of the effects on saving and thereby on the size of the portfolio. Seen from this angle one could then argue that Hagen's results confirm those of the pure portfolio models.

With the exception of the work of Drèze and Modigliani (1972), studies of consumption and portfolio behaviour usually ignore problems related to labour supply, occupational choice, etc. An extension to include labour supply in the manner of the models of Section 2 might be particularly interesting if the wage

[19]Ahsan's paper considers both proportional and progressive taxes; the effect of progression on risk taking is explicitly considered in Ahsan (1974) and Cowell (1975).

[20]For a few examples of a large number of contributions to this general topic, see Hakansson (1970) and Merton (1969).

rate were also assumed to be uncertain. The optimum degree of portfolio risk would then clearly be related to labour supply, and the individual would have to consider the riskiness of his portfolio with regard to the riskiness of his occupation. At the level of general equilibrium and welfare economics one could then study the overall effects of taxes on the allocation of resources, not only as a problem related to capital markets but to labour markets as well.

9. Empirical studies of taxation and portfolio choice

When one turns from the theory of the tax effects on risk taking via portfolio adjustment to the empirical study of portfolio composition, it is important to be aware of the fact that taxation may affect portfolio choices from a number of causes which have little or nothing to do with risk taking. In many countries it is, e.g., the case that income from investment in housing gets a more favourable tax treatment than income from common stock. With a progressive tax system we then have a complicated picture of a world in which the rate of tax on asset yield varies not only between assets but also among individuals. This fact emerges clearly from the pioneering econometric study of Feldstein (1976b) of the effects of taxes on the portfolio composition of private investors. His work is based on survey data for the U.S. from 1962, and the results reflect the special provisions of American tax laws and financial market structure; nevertheless, they are of considerable general interest. Feldstein concludes that the effect of the personal income tax on portfolio composition is very powerful. Within each income class the pattern of asset holdings depends on relative net yields. The fact that tax rates, and therefore net yields, vary across income classes explains the pattern of ownership for each particular class.

Higher-income individuals hold a larger proportion of their wealth in common stock; this appears to be largely due to the special treatment of capital gains. The total mean yield on the portfolio is increasing with income, while the variance is increasing in nominal terms and approximately constant in real terms. Due to the complexities of the tax system it is difficult to say whether the results of Feldstein can be said to support the (admittedly weak) theoretical presumption that taxation encourages risk taking; certainly they do not contradict it. It should be noted, however, that Feldstein's study covers only investment in financial assets, excluding in particular investment in residential housing.

A recent article by Shorrocks (1982), using United Kingdom data for 1975–76 reports patterns of asset ownership which are in some ways similar to those found by Feldstein, in particular regarding the high wealth elasticity of common stock. However, Shorrocks makes no attempt to account explicitly for the influence of taxation, so that his results can at most be considered as suggestive of a similar effect of the tax system on portfolio composition.

The study of the effects of taxation on portfolio composition is complicated, chiefly because of the many special provisions made in the tax laws of most countries. This makes it difficult to compare effective rates of tax on different assets. Moreover, since one of the most interesting sets of questions relates to the tax wedge between the real rate of return in production and the corresponding rate received by the saver, one has to study both the personal and corporate tax systems in order to arrive at meaningful conclusions. King and Fullerton (1984) report on an ambitious international comparative study, where they estimate effective rates of tax on investment in three alternative real assets (machinery, buildings, inventories), in three different industries (manufacturing, other industry, commerce), financed by three alternative sources (debt, new share issues, retained earnings), and three ownership categories (households, tax-exempt institutions, insurance companies). The general results of the study, which compares data for the United States, the United Kingdom, Sweden and West Germany, are that effective tax rates vary widely, both within each country (with respect to asset type, industry, source of finance and ownership category) and between countries. It is hardly possible to draw any conclusions from this study as to a possible bias in the tax system with respect to the encouragement of risk taking. It does suggest, however, that for the purpose of empirical application of the theory of taxation and risk taking, it is the model where tax rates are differentiated among assets which is the most relevant one.

Social security and pension wealth, the effects of which on saving behaviour were discussed above, could also be thought to have important effects on the composition of savings. To the extent, e.g., that pension wealth is seen as a close substitute for relatively safe assets, the growth of pension wealth could reasonably be thought to encourage the holding of more risky private portfolios. A recent study by Dicks-Mireaux and King (1982b) on Canadian cross-section data did not, however, find any significant effects of this kind.

10. Other dimensions of risk taking

Individuals' willingness to bear risk reveals itself not only in their choice of portfolio composition but also in other areas of economic decision making. Of such areas, some – like insurance – can easily be interpreted as coming under the portfolio choice framework, for an insurance policy can always be interpreted as an asset with a particular pattern of returns. But there are other areas where the analogy is less obvious and which call for separate analysis.

One of these is *occupational choice*, and the effects of taxation on the choice between safe and risky occupations have been explored by Kanbur (1981). His analysis provides some interesting contrasts with the portfolio choice framework. First, occupational choice is treated as one between mutually exclusive alternatives; the individual is not allowed to choose a portfolio of occupations. Second, because of this assumption, an equilibrium distribution of agents among occupations cannot be defined in partial equilibrium marginal utility terms, but must be defined in terms of equality between *total* expected utilities of alternative occupations. Therefore, unlike in the portfolio choice framework, one cannot ask questions about the individual behavioural response to changes in the level of taxation; the effect has to be evaluated in terms of the equilibrium distribution of the population between occupations.

More specifically, Kanbur's model assumes a population consisting of identical individuals who can choose between two occupations: They can either become labourers, earning a certain wage rate, or they can become entrepreneurs, in which case they hire labourers and produce according to a production function which depends on a random variable, reflecting uncertainty about their entrepreneurial ability. Kanbur's main interest lies not in the positive problems of the effects on occupational distribution of changes in taxation but rather in the normative question of the optimal tax system according to some social welfare function. He finds, e.g., that an optimal linear tax should be a progressive one, but he is unable to derive any firm conclusion as to whether this tax system implies a reduction of the fraction of the population engaged in the risky activity.

A different framework for the study of occupational choice problems in this context has been chosen by Eaton and Rosen (1980a). In their model the individual's demand for leisure is constant. However, in the first period of their lives workers can use some of their time to acquire human capital; this means less income in the first period, but more in the second when the wage rate increases as a result of education. If the rate of return to human capital is uncertain, Eaton and Rosen show that the effect of a proportional income tax may be either to increase or decrease the investment in human capital. On the one hand there is a kind of risk substitution effect which tends to increase investment in human capital; the government bears some of the risk associated with uncertain future wages. But, on the other hand, taxation reduces overall income, and this effect depends on attitudes to risk in a way which makes it difficult to predict the total effect except in very special cases.

Another area in which taxation has an effect on risk taking behaviour is *tax evasion*. As first explored in the articles by Allingham and Sandmo (1972) and Srinivasan (1973), models of tax evasion have several features in common with analyses of portfolio choice. The taxpayer is supposed to have a given income, and he is deciding on the fraction of it to report to the tax authorities. On this fraction he will pay tax at the regular rate, while on the amount evaded he pays either nothing or, in case he is detected, at a penalty rate which is higher than the regular tax rate. The taxpayer is assumed to maximize expected utility (according to Allingham and Sandmo) or expected net income (according to Srinivasan). One can then derive comparative statics results for the effects of changes in the tax parameters and the probability of detection. Even in these simple models it turns out that a number of the results are ambiguous and that the basic simplicity of the portfolio choice results is lost. When the model is extended to take account of variable labour supply, as in Sandmo (1981b) and Cowell (1985), this tendency naturally becomes more pronounced. So far, however, there has hardly been any theoretical work done on the interrelationship between tax evasion and saving decisions (including portfolio choice), although applied work in this area typically emphasizes the importance of the link between income tax evasion and the choice of more or less observable asset holdings.

11. General equilibrium and tax incidence

Returning to the portfolio choice framework for the analysis of risk taking, it should be observed that the partial equilibrium framework for the analysis of taxation is incomplete in several respects. A complete analysis of the effects of taxation on the degree of risk taking in the economy should take into account the supply of alternative investment opportunities and not only the demand. It should also model the link between financial and real investment decisions and provide a description of the connection between public expenditure and tax revenue.

Of course, even the simple model of Section 8 could be given a general equilibrium interpretation. One would then have to assume an economy with only one consumption good, identical individuals, one safe and one risky industry operating under constant (stochastic) returns to scale and a "neutral" disbursement of the tax revenue. But these are very special assumptions which it would be desirable to relax.

The first paper to tackle this set of problems in a systematic fashion was Stiglitz (1972). He postulated an economy with constant stochastic returns to scale,[21] in which firms issue bonds (bearing a safe rate of return) and stocks and choose a policy of investment and financing so as to maximize their market value.[22] Consumers are assumed to invest their wealth in bonds and stocks according to the portfolio model of Section 8 above.[23] Among the results of the analysis is that, if tax revenue simply disappears from the economy, the results of the partial equilibrium analysis focusing on the demand side retain their validity. In general,

[21] If output (X) is taken to depend on the input of some factor of production (I) and on a stochastic parameter (θ), the production function is $F(I,\theta)$. Under constant stochastic returns to scale we have that $X=G(\theta)I$.

[22] This type of model and the limitations of the market value maximization hypothesis are discussed in a separate chapter of the Handbook.

[23] Stiglitz actually formulates his model in a mean–variance framework, but this is not an essential feature of his analysis.

however, the results are sensitive to the particular assumption made about the tax system and the distribution of the tax revenue. This is of course what we should expect. The tax on investment income which has received so much attention in partial equilibrium theory leads to strong conclusions only in a very special case. There is little reason to believe that the result will continue to hold in general equilibrium, or that similar results can be derived for a more general class of tax systems.[24]

12. The optimum taxation of risky assets

The question of the appropriate tax treatment of assets of varying degree of riskiness has been a controversial one both in the debate on practical tax policy and in the theory of public finance. It has commonly been maintained that a market economy requires some stimulus to risk-taking activities either because individuals are too risk-averse from a social point of view or because of some market imperfection. On the other hand, it has also been argued that economic efficiency requires that taxation of assets be non-distortionary or at least "neutral" in the sense of taxing all assets at the same rate. It is evidently necessary to consider carefully both the criterion of welfare or efficiency and the modelling of market structure.

It may be useful to approach the study of this problem by means of a rather extreme case which has recently been studied by Auerbach (1981). He assumes an economy with a full set of Arrow–Debreu markets. In the context of the two-period consumption model this means that assets are state-contingent in the sense that each asset provides a claim to future consumption if and only if state s occurs. Assume that there are two states and that consumer preferences can be represented by the single utility function

$$\begin{aligned} U &= U(C_1, C_{21}, C_{22}) \\ &= \pi_1 U(C_1, C_{21}) + (1-\pi_1) U(C_1, C_{22}), \end{aligned} \tag{12.1}$$

where it has been assumed that the expected utility theorem holds with π_1 being the probability of state 1 and C_{2s} the amount of consumption in state s $(s = 1, 2)$. Assume further that there is a constant coefficient technology such that produc-

[24] Gordon (1981) shows that, where the taxation of corporate profits is on a net basis (in the sense of Section 8), the tax is basically neutral when tax revenue is distributed among investors as lump sum payments. Recent work in the general equilibrium framework by Kihlstrom and Laffont (1983) can be seen as combining elements from the work of Stiglitz (1972) and Kanbur (1981). From the point of view of the firm and its investment and financing decisions, there is now a large literature on the effects of taxation. This is surveyed in a separate chapter in the Handbook.

tion opportunities are given by

$$C_1 + p_{21}C_{21} + p_{22}C_{22} = I. \tag{12.2}$$

Assume now that the government wishes to raise a given amount of tax revenue by levying taxes on the claims to future consumption, raising their consumer prices to $P_{2s} = p_{2s} + t_{2s}$. From a formal point of view, this is a standard problem of optimum tax theory of the form first studied by Corlett and Hague (1953–54), and in this case there exists an appealing characterization of the relative tax rates in terms of the compensated elasticities (see Chapter 2). By utilizing the special structure of perferences implied by the expected utility hypothesis, Auerbach is able to transform the Corlett–Hague characterization into one involving ordinal (the elasticity of substitution) and cardinal (relative risk aversion) properties of the utility function. Although interesting, this result does not in itself tell us much about the taxation of *assets*, since these do not in reality take the form of state-contingent claims. However, the analysis is easily extended to the more general case of asset markets where the number of assets equals the number of states; in the language of capital market theory we then have complete "spanning". For this case Auerbach's analysis leads him to conclude that differential taxation of asset returns is in general desirable, and further that apparently reasonable restrictions on preferences implies a heavier taxation of the more risky asset.

These results should be interpreted with care, particularly since the assumption of a complete set of asset markets is probably a crucial one. One of the complications which arises when this assumption is abandoned concerns the formulation of the government revenue constraint: Should there be one constraint for each state of nature, or should there be one constraint in terms of expected tax revenue? (The latter alternative clearly implies risk neutrality on the part of the government.) The importance of these considerations were one of the points brought out in the pioneering contribution of Stiglitz (1972), who studied the optimal taxation of assets in the context of the model described in the previous section.[25] He shows, e.g., that if the government is risk-neutral while individuals are not, there is a case for taxing the safe asset (or industry) at a higher rate than the risky one.

It seems reasonable to conclude that the few studies which have been made of the optimum taxation of risky assets cannot provide any *a priori* foundation for a recommendation that risky assets be taxed at either higher or lower rates than safe ones. From a practical point of view, tax policy with regard to income from assets should take into account the specific structure of risk markets as well as administrative and political concerns.

[25] For a summary and simplified account of Stiglitz' model, see Allingham (1972).

One important case where the structure of risk markets is such that the conditions for optimum risk sharing are clearly violated, is uncertainty with respect to future wage rates and labour income. Insurance markets are absent here, primarily because of moral hazard problems. Varian (1980) and Eaton and Rosen (1980b) have pointed out that under these conditions lump sum taxation is in general not optimal. Even if lump sum taxes were available, it would be desirable to have a positive marginal tax rate on labour income in order to decrease riskiness. If work effort were given exogenously, the optimum solution in a world of risk-averse individuals would be to have a marginal tax rate of 100% combined with some lump sum redistribution of the tax revenue; what prevents this solution is the effect of high marginal tax rates on labour supply. Thus, the optimal tax scheme represents a compromise between the concern for labour supply incentives on the one hand and the desire for risk diversification on the other. This type of reasoning would of course also be applicable to the case of imperfect capital markets with limited possibilities for portfolio diversification.

13. Concluding remarks

The amount of work done on the theory and econometrics of tax effects on saving and risk taking is impressive. No doubt this reflects the practical importance of the issues as well as the intellectual challenges in the area, and it is pleasant to think that in this area of economics at least the two sets of motivations for research have reinforced each other.

Are there any general lessons for economic policy which can be extracted from the work surveyed here? As far as positive economics is concerned perhaps the most important general lesson is that empirical work of high quality can be done on problems of central concern to policy makers. To some extent there is also valuable information in the numerical estimates which have been made; certainly this is true for the countries which have been studied intensively in empirical work. For other countries there may also be valuable information to be had from empirical results derived, e.g., from the U.S. data. On the other hand, there is hardly any strong reason to believe that empirical results are valid for all countries and periods. The institutions, market structure and tax system of each country must be expected to influence behaviour with respect to saving and portfolio choice.

On the normative side perhaps the most important insight derived from recent work is that there are no easy options in tax policy with respect to saving and risk taking. Feasible tax systems all involve distortions of the decisions made by consumers and firms, and one faces the now familiar second-best problem of designing tax systems which are welfare-maximizing subject to the constraints on the choice of tax instruments. Recent work has also emphasized that tax policy towards saving and risk taking cannot be studied in isolation from the effects on other areas of the economy; thus, one is led to a general equilibrium approach to the issues. To paraphrase a remark by Robert Solow, this makes work in the area more difficult, but also more fun.

References

Ahsan, S.M., 1974, Progression and risk-taking, Oxford Economic Papers 26, 318–328.

Ahsan, S.M., 1976, Taxation in a two-period temporal model of consumption and portfolio allocation, Journal of Public Economics 5, 337–352.

Allingham, M.G., 1972, Risk-taking and taxation, Zeitschrift für Nationalökonomie 32, 203–224.

Allingham, M.G. and A. Sandmo, 1972, Income tax evasion: A theoretical analysis, Journal of Public Economics 1, 323–338.

Arrow, K.J., 1970, Essays in the theory of risk-bearing (North-Holland, Amsterdam).

Atkinson, A.B. and A. Sandmo, 1980, Welfare implications of the taxation of savings, Economic Journal 90, 529–549.

Atkinson, A.B. and J.E. Stiglitz, 1980, Lectures on public economics (McGraw-Hill, London).

Auerbach, A.J., 1981, Evaluating the taxation of risky assets, Unpublished paper (Harvard University and National Bureau of Economic Research, Cambridge, MA).

Barro, R.J., 1974, Are government bonds net wealth?, Journal of Political Economy 82, 1095–1117.

Barro, R.J. and G.M. MacDonald, 1979, Social security and consumer spending in an international cross section, Journal of Public Economics 11, 275–290.

Bhatia, K.B., 1979, Corporate taxation, retained earnings and capital formation, Journal of Public Economics 11, 123–134.

Blinder, A.S., 1975, Distribution effects and the aggregate consumption function, Journal of Political Economy 83, 447–475.

Boskin, M.J., 1978, Taxation, saving, and the rate of interest, Journal of Political Economy 86, S3–S27.

Boskin, M.J. and L.J. Lau, 1978, Taxation, social security and aggregate factor supply in the United States, Unpublished paper (Stanford University, Stanford, CA).

Browning, M.J., 1982, Savings and pensions: Some UK evidence, Economic Journal 92, 954–963.

Christensen, L.R. and D.W. Jorgenson, 1973, U.S. income, saving and wealth, 1929–1969, Review of Income and Wealth 19, 329–362.

Corlett, W.J. and D.C. Hague, 1953–54, Complementarity and the excess burden of taxation, Review of Economic Studies 21, 21–30.

Cowell, F.A., 1975, Some notes on progression and risk-taking, Economica 42, 313–318.

Cowell, F.A., 1985, Tax evasion with labour income, Journal of Public Economics, forthcoming.

Deaton, A. and J. Muellbauer, 1980, Economics and consumer behaviour (Cambridge University Press, Cambridge).

Diamond, P.A., 1970, Incidence of an interest income tax, Journal of Economic Theory 2, 211–224.

Diamond, P.A. and J.A. Hausman, 1984, Individual retirement and savings behaviour, Journal of Public Economics 23, 81–114.

Dicks-Mireaux, L. and M.A. King, 1982, Portfolio composition and pension wealth: An econometric study, National Bureau of Economic Research working paper no. 903.

Dicks-Mireaux, L. and M.A. King, 1984, Pension wealth and household savings: Tests of robustness, Journal of Public Economics 23, 115–139.

Dixit, A.K., 1976, The theory of equilibrium growth (Oxford University Press, Oxford).

Domar, E.D. and R.A. Musgrave, 1944, Proportional income taxation and risk-taking, Quarterly Journal of Economics 58, 388–422.

Drèze, J.H. and F. Modigliani, 1972, Consumption decisions under uncertainty, Journal of Economic Theory 5, 308–335.

Eaton, J. and H.S. Rosen, 1980a, Taxation, human capital, and uncertainty, American Economic Review 70, 705–715.
Eaton, J. and H.S. Rosen, 1980b, Labour supply, uncertainty, and efficient taxation, Journal of Public Economics 14, 365–374.
Eeckhoudt, L. and P. Hansen, 1982, Uncertainty and the partial loss offset provision, Economics Letters 9, 31–35.
Ekern, S., 1971, Taxation, political risk and portfolio selection, Economica 38, 421–430.
Feldstein, M.S., 1973, Tax incentives, corporate saving, and capital accumulation in the United States, Journal of Public Economics 2, 159–171.
Feldstein, M.S., 1974a, Tax incidence in a growing economy with variable factor supply, Quarterly Journal of Economics 88, 551–573.
Feldstein, M.S., 1974b, Incidence of a capital income tax in a growing economy with variable savings rates, Review of Economic Studies 41, 505–513.
Feldstein, M.S., 1974c, Social security, induced retirement, and aggregate capital accumulation, Journal of Political Economy 82, 905–926.
Feldstein, M.S., 1976a, Social security and saving: The extended life cycle theory, American Economic Review 66 (Papers and Proceedings), 77–86.
Feldstein, M.S., 1976b, Personal taxation and portfolio composition: An econometric analysis, Econometrica 44, 631–650.
Feldstein, M.S., 1977, Social security and private savings: International evidence in an extended life-cycle model, in: M.S. Feldstein and R.P. Inman, eds., The economics of public services (MacMillan, London).
Feldstein, M.S., 1978, The rate of return, taxation and personal savings, Economic Journal 88, 482–487.
Feldstein, M.S., 1980, International differences in social security and saving, Journal of Public Economics 14, 225–244.
Feldstein, M.S., 1982, Inflation, tax rates and investment: Some econometric evidence, Econometrica 50, 825–862.
Feldstein, M.S. and G. Fane, 1973, Taxes, corporate dividend policy and personal saving: The British postwar experience, Review of Economics and Statistics 55, 399–411.
Fisher, I., 1930, The theory of interest (MacMillan, New York).
Friedlaender, A.F. and A.F. Vandendorpe, 1978, Capital taxation in a dynamic general equilibrium setting, Journal of Public Economics 10, 1–24.
Gordon, R.H., 1981, Taxation of corporate capital income: Tax revenues vs. tax distortions, Unpublished paper (Bell Laboratories, Murray Hill, NJ).
Green, G.F., 1981, The effect of occupational saving schemes on saving in the United Kingdom: A test of the life cycle hypothesis, Economic Journal 91, 136–144.
Hagen, K.P., 1970, Taxation and investment behaviour under uncertainty: A multiperiod portfolio analysis, Theory and Decision 1, 269–295.
Hakansson, N.H., 1970, Optimal investment and consumption strategies under risk for a class of utility functions, Econometrica 38, 587–607.
Hansen, B., 1955, Finanspolitikens ekonomiska teori (Almqvist & Wicksell, Uppsala). English translation, 1958, The economic theory of fiscal policy (Allen & Unwin, London).
Harberger, A.C., 1962, The incidence of the corporate income tax, Journal of Political Economy 70, 215–240.
Hemming, R. and R. Harvey, 1983, Occupational pension scheme membership and retirement saving, Economic Journal 93, 128–144.
Kanbur, S.M., 1981, Risk taking and taxation: An alternative perspective, Journal of Public Economics 15, 163–184.
Kay, J.A. and M.A. King, 1978, The British tax system (Oxford University Press, Oxford).
Kihlstrom, R.E. and J.-J. Laffont, 1983, Taxation and risk taking in general equilibrium models with free entry, Journal of Public Economics 21, 159–181.
King, M.A., 1980, Savings and taxation, in: G.A. Hughes and G.M. Heal, eds., Public policy and the tax system (Allen & Unwin, London).
King, M.A. and D. Fullerton, eds., 1984, The taxation of income from capital: A comparative study of the U.S., U.K., Sweden, and West Germany (National Bureau of Economic Research, and University of Chicago Press, Chicago, IL).

Kotlikoff, L.J., 1979, Testing the theory of social security and life cycle accumulation, American Economic Review 69, 396–410.

Kotlikoff, L.J. and L.H. Summers, 1979, Tax incidence in a life cycle model with variable labour supply, Quarterly Journal of Economics 93, 705–718.

Kurz, M., 1981, The life-cycle hypothesis and the effects of social security and private pensions on family saving, Technical report no. 335 (Institute for Mathematical Studies in the Social Sciences, Stanford University, Stanford, CA).

Merton, R.C., 1969, Lifetime portfolio selection under uncertainty: The continuous time case, Review of Economics and Statistics 51, 247–257.

Mintz, J.M., 1981, Some additional results on investment, risk taking and full loss offset corporate taxation with interest deductibility, Quarterly Journal of Economics 95, 631–642.

Mossin, J., 1968, Taxation and risk-taking: An expected utility approach, Economica 35, 74–82.

Munnell, A.H., 1976, Private pensions and saving: New evidence, Journal of Political Economy 84, 1013–1032.

Musgrave, R., 1959, The theory of public finance (McGraw-Hill, New York).

Ordover, J.A., 1976, Distributive justice and optimal taxation of wage and interest in a growing economy, Journal of Public Economics 5, 139–160.

Ordover, J.A. and E.S. Phelps, 1979, The concept of optimal capital taxation in the overlapping generations model of capital and wealth, Journal of Public Economics 12, 1–26.

Samuelson, P.A., 1958, An exact consumption–loan model of interest with or without the social contrivance of money, Journal of Political Economy 66, 467–482.

Sandmo, A., 1969, Capital risk, consumption, and portfolio choice, Econometrica 37, 586–599.

Sandmo, A., 1970, The effect of uncertainty on saving decisions, Review of Economic Studies 37, 353–360.

Sandmo, A., 1976, Optimal taxation: An introduction to the literature, Journal of Public Economics 6, 37–54.

Sandmo, A., 1977, Portfolio theory, asset demand and taxation: Comparative statics with many assets, Review of Economic Studies 44, 369–379.

Sandmo, A., 1981a, The rate of return and personal savings, Economic Journal 91, 536–540.

Sandmo, A., 1981b, Income tax evasion, labour supply and the equity–efficiency tradeoff, Journal of Public Economics 16, 265–288.

Shorrocks, A., 1982, The portfolio composition of asset holdings in the United Kingdom, Economic Journal 92, 268–284.

Srinivasan, T.N., 1973, Tax evasion: A model, Journal of Public Economics 2, 339–346.

Stigler, G.J., 1967, Imperfections in the capital market, Journal of Political Economy 75, 287–292.

Stiglitz, J.E., 1969, The effects of income, wealth and capital gains taxation on risk-taking, Quarterly Journal of Economics 83, 262–283.

Stiglitz, J.E., 1972, Taxation, risk taking, and the allocation of investment in a competitive economy, in: M.C. Jensen, ed., Studies in the theory of capital markets (Praeger, New York).

Stiglitz, J.E., 1978, Equality, taxation, and inheritance, in: W. Krelle and A.F. Shorrocks, eds., Personal income distribution (North-Holland, Amsterdam).

Stiglitz, J.E. and A. Weiss, 1981, Credit rationing in markets with imperfect information, American Economic Review 71, 393–410.

Summers, L.H., 1981, Capital taxation and accumulation in a life cycle growth model, American Economic Review 71, 533–544.

Thompson, L.H., 1983, The social security reform debate, Journal of Economic Literature 21, 1425–1467.

Varian, H.R., 1980, Redistributive taxation as social insurance, Journal of Public Economics 14, 49–68.

Williamson, S.H. and W.L. Jones, 1983, Computing the impact of social security using the life cycle consumption function, American Economic Review 73, 1036–1052.

Wright, C., 1969, Saving and the rate of interest, in: A.C. Harberger and M.J. Bailey, eds., The taxation of income from capital (Brookings Institution, Washington, DC).

Chapter 6

TAX POLICY IN OPEN ECONOMIES

AVINASH DIXIT*

Woodrow Wilson School, Princeton University, Princeton, NJ

1. Introduction

The main subject of this paper is the theory of optimum taxation in an economy open to international trade. This is not a topic that lacks surveys. Bhagwati (1964, sec. VI; 1971) and Corden (1974, 1982) are particularly noteworthy. The distinctive feature of this review will be its perspective. I shall approach the subject as a branch of public economics, with the concerns and techniques of modern public finance theory as exemplified by Atkinson and Stiglitz (1980), or earlier chapters of this volume, rather than neoclassical trade theory as recently surveyed by Jones and Neary (1983) and used in the Bhagwati and Corden surveys cited above. Both approaches ultimately derive from the Walrasian general equilibrium model, and therefore have large overlaps, but the apparatus of special production technologies that underlies much of conventional trade theory will be largely unnecessary for my present purpose.

Most formal models of optimum taxation assume away international trade. Its presence does not alter any basic issues or methods. The economic objectives of the policy remain the same, and can be broadly classified as (i) correcting externalities and distortions, (ii) raising revenue for government expenditure, and (iii) redistributing income. There may also be other "non-economic" objectives or constraints. The policy instruments to pursue these aims are taxes or subsidies on the activities and transactions in the economy, within limitations imposed by observability of the actions and enforceability of the policies. International trade introduces a new set of possible externalities and distortions, and a new set of transactions to tax or subsidize.

There are some potentially new features. The objective function of policy in one country normally excludes the welfare of consumers in other countries. Formally this presents no difficulty so long as we are analyzing policy-making in one country only. We can then regard its net trade with the rest of the world as just

*I am very grateful to Alasdair Smith and Alan Deardorff for their detailed reading of the first draft and numerous suggestions for improvement. I also thank Alan Auerbach, Max Corden, Lars Svensson, Wolfgang Mayer, James Anderson, Anne Krueger and John Whalley for their comments on earlier drafts, and Wilfred Ethier and Gene Grossman for useful discussions.

Handbook of Public Economics, vol. I, edited by A.J. Auerbach and M. Feldstein

another transformation possibility, without explicitly accounting for consumption or production in other countries. However, when policies are being made simultaneously in several countries, their mutual interaction presents more complex considerations than are familiar from closed-economy public finance. Some aspects of international interaction of policies are considered in Section 5. Elsewhere, the focus is on policy-making in one country, called the home country.

The most important point to remember is that the general equilibrium interdependence of the system, typical in public economics, applies equally to an open economy. Tariffs, which are taxes levied on transactions with the rest of the world, affect the domestic resource allocation and income distribution, while taxes on domestic transactions affect the trade pattern. Any compartmentalization of activities and policies must be proved, not assumed. Two such separation results are in fact available, and deserve special mention at the outset. One is the Bhagwati–Johnson principle of targeting, which states that a distortion is best countered, or conversely, deliberately introduced if desired as a non-economic objective, by a tax instrument that acts directly on the relevant margin. Thus the first-best policy response to an external economy in production is an appropriate Pigovian subsidy; it is only if this is impossible that the indirect effect of a tariff to stimulate domestic production can be useful as a second-best (or worse) policy. The second result is that income distribution policy is better pursued by use of domestic goods and factor taxes or subsidies than through tariffs. This has important implications for policies to compensate groups that are hurt by trade.

One other result worth highlighting is an application of the Diamond–Mirrlees aggregate production efficiency theorem (see the chapter in this volume by Auerbach, Section 5.3). In this context, it says that marginal rates of transformation should be equalized between domestic production activities and foreign trade. The former equal domestic producer prices, but the latter can differ from the world prices, i.e., the average rates of transformation through trade, if this country has any monopoly power in trade. The optimum policy from this country's point of view will involve trade taxes to achieve the desired equality. This is just the classical optimum tariff. Another implication of production efficiency is that there should be no producer taxation of intermediate goods, i.e., outputs purchased as inputs for other production activities. This has a bearing on the subject of effective protection.

1.1. Outline of the chapter

In the rest of this section, I shall discuss the merits and limits of the approach, and set up the notation. The following three sections take up different aspects of tax and tariff policies. The techniques most suited to the analysis of each also differ, although there are some overlaps. Section 2 considers discrete comparisons of two equilibria, with the object of designing policies that yield a Pareto improvement over the status quo. This deals with the classic questions of gains from trade, optimality of free trade, etc. In Section 3 the optimum tax and tariff policies are characterized for a variety of contexts; in particular, the issues of income distribution and distortion mentioned above are analyzed and the targeting results are derived. Section 4 considers the effects of a small policy change from an arbitrary initial position. This yields some rules for partial reform, including the second-best use of policies when the optimum targeting is not possible.

In Section 5 some aspects of international coordination and competition in trade policy are considered. Section 6 takes up some further topics including effective protection, quotas, and the emerging positive theory of trade policy. Section 7 gives a brief review of some empirical work on the welfare effects of trade policies.

1.2. Scope and limitations

The strengths as well as the weaknesses of the approach followed here stem from its use of the Walrasian equilibrium model. On the plus side, the commodities can be given a wide interpretation, thus giving a unified treatment of disparate topics. There is no need to analyze goods trade and factor trade separately. The basic distinction is between tradeable and non-tradeable commodities; there is no need to begin with the conventional trade model where this coincides with the goods – factors split and then generalize gradually. Similarly, by distinguishing commodities according to the date of availability, the model can be interpreted as treating international borrowing and lending, and taxes thereon. I shall make specific mention of such interpretations only in passing.

One other restriction I shall impose is that of constant returns to scale in all production activities. The Walrasian setting of course rules out increasing returns. Any diminishing returns can be accommodated by defining an artificial factor called "ownership" which receives the pure profit of that activity, and then there will be constant returns to scale when all factors (including the artificial one) are considered. This is a standard trick dating back to McKenzie (1955). The only demand it imposes on the normative theory being considered here is that of the range of tax instruments. The full set of commodity taxes will involve separate taxes on each commodity including the artificial factors. This requires the ability to tax each firm's pure profit at a different rate; a single profits tax will not suffice. However, constant returns to scale are commonly assumed in trade theory, and no special apology is necessary here.

More serious limitations arise from the competitive equilibrium setting. Trade policy in relation to involuntary unemployment or inflation cannot be considered.

That is the province of quite a different branch of public economics, in conjunction with monetary economics. For surveys, see Mundell (1968, ch. 14–18) and Dornbusch (1980, ch. 4, 10, 11). Secondly, trade in imperfectly competitive markets is not considered. Governments may recognize national monopoly power in trade and levy optimum tariffs, but all individual consumers and producers are assumed to be price-takers. Research in recent years has belatedly recognized the practical importance of trade under scale economies and monopolistic competition, and Helpman (1983) has surveyed this work. But the public finance aspects are yet to be developed systematically. Trade policy under monopolistic competition is examined by Venables (1982). Some recent work on oligopoly is reviewed in Dixit (1984). Several contributions in Kierzkowski (1984) consider issues arising from trade with imperfect competition.

Non-linear tariff schedules, sometimes called tariff-quotas, are beginning to receive proper attention; see Saidi and Srinagesh (1981) and Anderson and Young (1982). But a more thorough public finance treatment and survey must wait.

Finally, I should mention a minor omission in the literature, which my survey will share. The government's expenditure on goods and services is taken to be constant and exogenous. However, it is not clear whether any interesting additions to the theory on the expenditure side arise from the openness of an economy per se.

1.3. Model structure and notation

The underlying model is the standard Walrasian or competitive, flex-price equilibrium involving consumption, production and international trade in commodities. These have the usual wide interpretation; in particular, factors supplied by consumers appear as components of the general commodity vector which happen to be consumed in amounts less than the endowments. Distinction by the location and date of availability, and states of the world, can also be made as appropriate.

For our purpose, it is useful to highlight another distinction, namely tradeable and non-tradeable commodities. In principle, one should specify a technology of trade, e.g., transport costs, and determine endogenously which goods will be traded in equilibrium. However, such a model quickly becomes too complex to yield useful results, and it is customary to suppose as an extreme case that transport costs are zero for one set of commodities and infinite for another.

I shall now set out the notation that will be employed throughout this survey. The vector of aggregate home-country consumption quantities will be denoted by c. Its component corresponding to commodity k will be the subscripted scalar c_k. When commodities need to be classified into tradeables and non-tradeables, the vector will be partitioned, with the superscript t for tradeables and n for non-tradeables, i.e., $c = (c^{t}, c^{n})$. When different consumers are distinguished, they will be denoted by the superscript i; thus c^i is the consumption vector for consumer i. The vector of consumer prices will be p, and the vector of commodity endowments held by consumers will be e, with the superscripts, partitions, subscripts, etc. as above and when necessary.

If commodity k is labor, e_k is the total time available, c_k is the consumption of leisure, and $(e_k - c_k)$ the labor supply. Some, even most, components of e will be zero in practice. Some components of c may also be zero, e.g., for pure intermediate goods, and for resources that do not affect consumer utility directly, but only through the income generated when they are inelastically supplied to the limit of the endowment. Consumer prices of produced pure intermediate goods are of course irrelevant, and may be set at any arbitrary level, e.g., zero, without harm.

The budget constraint of consumer i can be written as $p \cdot (c^i - e^i) \leq b_i$, where b_i is transfer income, if any. Consumption taxes can only be levied on net trades $(c^i - e^i)$ with the rest of the economy.

Production quantities in the home country will be denoted by x (inputs appearing as components with negative signs) and the prices facing home producers by q. The set of technologically feasible production vectors can be described in various ways. It can be written as X, a closed convex cone with vertex at the origin, or by means of an inequality $F(x) \leq 0$, where the function F is convex and homogeneous of degree 1. The technical assumptions reflect the properties of constant returns to scale and diminishing marginal rates of transformation. Where different firms or production activities are distinguished, the superscript j will be employed; thus x^j is in the set X^j, or $F^j(x^j) \leq 0$. Other labels or partitions will be as for consumption.

The vector of net imports from the rest of the world will be m. Of course its partitioning gives $(m^{t}, 0)$. Commodities that are exported appear as components with negative signs. The vector r will denote trading prices just outside the home country's borders, namely c.i.f. (inclusive of cost, insurance and freight) before tariffs or subsidies for imports, and f.o.b. (free on board) after any taxes or subsidies for exports are applied. The sub-vector r^{n} is irrelevant. When forming the value $r \cdot m$, the only contribution comes from tradeables since $m^{n} \equiv 0$. Therefore r^{n} can be set at any arbitrary level, e.g., zero, without harm.

The set of feasible net trades is governed by behavior in the rest of the world. For our purpose, this can be summarized in a set M. With just two tradeable goods, its typical appearance is as shown in Figure 1.1. The origin lies on its boundary to the north-east, reflecting the absence of unrequited transfers. Over the range that will concern us most, the boundary is negatively sloped and convex, reflecting a diminishing marginal rate of transformation through trade. In the usual language of trade theory, the boundary is the rest of the world's *offer surface*. At extreme relative prices, income effects in the rest of world may cause the offer surface to bend backwards. Further exports of one good from the home country will then yield negative marginal returns in terms of imports of the other good. Of course a country pursuing an optimal trade policy will not choose such a point, and for simplicity of exposition I shall ignore the problem. But for an arbitrary trade policy, and even in free trade, such an outcome cannot be ruled out, and is the source of many fond paradoxes in the "positive" theory of international trade.

An alternative description of the set M is by means of an inequality $G(m^t) \leq 0$, for a function G satisfying $G(0) = 0$. We can also describe the offer surface by a supply function $m^t = S(r^t)$, which is homogeneous of degree zero. Or, after choosing some normalization for prices in the rest of the world, we can use an inverse supply function $r^t = R(m^t)$, and then let $G(m^t) = R(m^t) \cdot m^t$. If the country is small in world markets, it will face a constant trade price vector r^t (within normalization), and then the offer surface will be a hyperplane $r^t \cdot m^t = 0$.

The home-country government will be assumed to consume a vector g of commodities, and levy a variety of taxes or subsidies. These could be lump sum transfers to consumers, denoted by b, or commodity taxes expressed in specific rates.

Begin with the vector of trade taxes, τ^t. Since r^t is the vector of prices of tradeables just outside our borders, $\pi^t \equiv r^t + \tau^t$ is that just inside, and will be

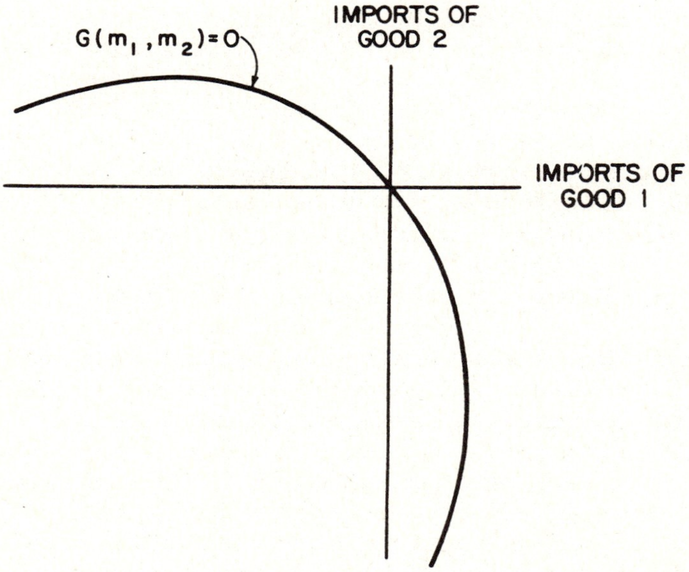

Figure 1.1

called the vector of domestic prices of tradeables. Note that whether a particular commodity k is taxed or subsidized depends on whether it is imported or exported, i.e., $\tau_k > 0$ corresponds to a tax if $m_k > 0$ and a subsidy if $m_k < 0$, and the other way around for $\tau_k < 0$. Thus the sign of the product $\tau_k m_k$ tells us whether we have a tax or a subsidy.

The vector π^t will be supplemented by π^n for non-tradeables to form the complete domestic price vector $\pi \equiv (\pi^t, \pi^n)$. Then there may be taxes or subsidies on domestic consumption and production activities. Writing α for the vector of consumption taxes, $p \equiv \pi + \alpha$ will be the vector of home consumer prices, applicable to their net trades. Writing β for the vector of production subsidies, $q \equiv \pi + \beta$ will be the vector of home producer prices. These are sign conventions similar to those for tariffs, e.g., $\alpha_k > 0$ corresponds to a tax if commodity k is bought by consumers, but a subsidy if it is sold by them as is the case with labor.

The prices facing various agents can differ on account of market distortions as well as taxes. Where there is no risk of confusion, I shall use the same symbols, τ, α, and β, to indicate such price wedges no matter how they arise.

It will be noted that, for the present, the domestic price vector π is something of a fiction. No trader actually pays or receives π. Correspondingly, there is a degree of arbitrariness in defining the various taxes. If k is a non-tradeable good, only the overall tax $(\alpha_k - \beta_k)$ matters. If k is tradeable, only $(\tau_k + \alpha_k)$ and $(\tau_k + \beta_k)$ matter; thus a tariff can be thought of as a combination of a consumption tax and a production subsidy at equal rates.

However, it turns out to be very useful to introduce a separate domestic price vector. When the optimum tax policy is considered, we obtain Lagrange multipliers that are shadow prices of commodities, and it is economically most transparent to express the optimum tax formulae as the differences between various other prices and these shadow prices. Then π can play the part of the shadow prices.

There is further indeterminacy arising from normalization. With constant returns in private production, the consumers have lump sum incomes of zero, or else optimally controlled by a government that can choose lump-sum transfers. In either case, p and q can be normalized independently (see Auerbach's chapter in this volume, Section 5.1). Next, with no cross-country transfers, r can be normalized independently of either. As an example, consider the special case where there is no taxation of domestic activities, and write $p = q = \pi$. Suppose there are just two traded commodities, 1 and 2, the former being imported and the latter exported. We can set $r_2 = \pi_2$ and $r_1 < \pi_1$ (an import tax), or $r_1 = \pi_1$ and $r_2 > \pi_2$ (an export tax). So long as r_1/r_2 and π_1/π_2 are unchanged, the two policies are fully equivalent. This is the famous symmetry theorem of Lerner (1936).

To conclude the construction of the model, let us check the government's budget balance. We know $q \cdot x = 0$ because of constant returns to scale in production, and $r \cdot m = 0$ in absence of international transfers. Next, $p \cdot (c-e) = b$, the net lump sum transfer, if any, from the government. Finally, $c+g=x+m+e$ for equilibrium. Then the government's revenue T is given by

$$\begin{aligned} T &= \alpha \cdot (c-e) - \beta \cdot x + \tau \cdot m - b \\ &= (p-\pi)\cdot(c-e) - (q-\pi)\cdot x + (\pi - r)\cdot m - b \\ &= p \cdot (c-e) - b - q \cdot x - r \cdot m + \pi \cdot (x+m+e-c) \\ &= \pi \cdot g. \end{aligned}$$

This is the usual result: so long as the government's tax and expenditure policies are compatible with general equilibrium, its budget must be balanced. This calculation was done at shadow prices. Any other tax treatment of g, e.g., transaction at consumer prices, with the purchase branch paying the consumption tax to the treasury, will yield balance at the appropriate prices.

2. Discrete comparisons of alternative equilibria

The earliest discussions of normative aspects of international trade, such as Samuelson (1939, 1962) and Kemp (1962), focussed on two questions: is trade better than autarky? and is free trade better than restricted trade? Each was answered by comparing two equilibria under the alternative policies, and finding conditions under which one was revealed preferred. Subsequently, the method was used for comparisons of equilibria involving distortions with the attendant problems of the second best; Bhagwati (1971) and Ohyama (1972) are the most notable syntheses. Comparisons involving the distribution of gains to all consumers were made by Dixit and Norman (1980a). The treatment of this section will broadly follow the development of the subject.

2.1. Potential gains from trade

The basic reason for gains from trade is very simple: trade enlarges the set of consumption possibilities. For a country in autarky, its aggregate consumption vector net of the endowments ($c+g-e$ in our context) must lie in its own aggregate production possibility set (X). When the rest of the world offers net trades from a set M, this set of aggregate net consumption possibilities is the sum of X and M, i.e., the set of vectors $x+m$ as x ranges over X and m over M. The efficient frontier of consumption possibilities can be traced by taking an x on the production possibility frontier, adding on the rest of world's offer surface with the origin at x, and taking the outer envelope as x varies. For a small economy, this is simply the tangent to the production possibility curve corresponding to the world prices. For an economy with monopoly power in trade, this is the Baldwin Envelope. Figure 2.1 shows these cases schematically in two dimensions.

Therefore the consumption possibility frontier (CPF) lies wholly outside the production possibility frontier (PPF), touching the latter where the marginal rates

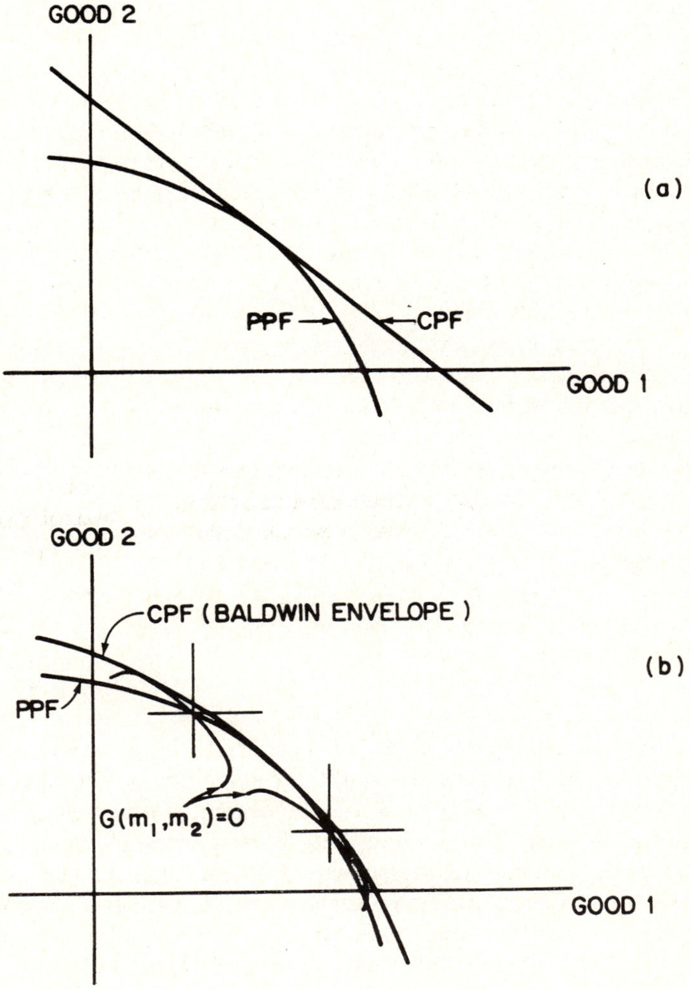

Figure 2.1

of transformation in domestic production happen to equal those attainable by means of a small amount of trade. Thus any feasible autarkic consumption vector can be dominated by a suitable combination of domestic production and foreign trade. Moreover, the sense of domination is strong, i.e., with strictly greater consumption of every good, except where the CPF touches the PPF. On the other hand, no efficient trading outcome can be dominated, even the weak sense of having more consumption of at least one good and no less of any, by an autarkic one.

These gains are still only potential ones, since it does not automatically follow that they can always be realized in equilibria of decentralized markets. The obstacles are familiar ones. First, consider distortions. These can be market failures (externalities, monopolies, etc.) or policy failures (regulation or taxes other than ones that are optimum responses to market failures), and they may affect domestic activities or international trade. If these are present, a laissez-faire equilibrium with trade may be Pareto-inefficient. The general problem of the second-best suggests that adding another distortion or restriction, such as prohibition or taxation of trade, may be beneficial in some such cases. Secondly, the existence of aggregate gains does not guarantee that all consumers will share them. In fact, in the well known two-good two-factor Heckscher–Ohlin model that served as the paradigm of trade theory for many years, it is necessarily the case that any change in the relative product price is unambiguously beneficial to owners of one factor and harmful to those owning the other; see Jones (1965).

For the rest of this section and the next two, we will examine these problems in detail. The findings generally dissipate any pessimism concerning realization of gains from trade. The optimum policies to tackle most of these problems are taxes or subsidies on domestic transactions; no interference with international trade is required except when the distortions arise in trade itself.

2.2. Aggregate gains and revealed preference

To begin in a relatively simple way, I shall set aside issues that require explicit recognition of consumer heterogeneity, namely consumption externalities and income distribution, and examine how aggregate gains can be achieved. Inter-consumer externalities are simply assumed to be absent. Neglect of distributional considerations is allowed in any one of the following circumstances. (1) There is only one aggregate consumer. (2) Lump sum transfers are employed to maximize a Bergson–Samuelson social welfare function, as in Samuelson (1956). This is formally just like a one-consumer case, with the social indifference map representing his preferences. (3) All individuals have identical homothetic preferences, and fixed shares in total income, as in Chipman and Moore (1980). Again we can formally regard the economy as having one consumer with the same homothetic preferences and all the income.

In all of these cases, we have a utility function defined over aggregate consumption, and it serves both to generate demands and to measure welfare. Therefore we can use revealed preference tests to compare two equilibria. If these are labelled A and B, we can say that B is revealed preferred if the actual budget in B would suffice to purchase the A quantities at B prices. Using the notation developed in Section 1.3, the criterion is

$$p^{\mathrm{B}} \cdot c^{\mathrm{B}} \geq p^{\mathrm{B}} \cdot c^{\mathrm{A}}. \tag{2.1a}$$

This is sufficient, but not necessary, for B to be at least as good as A. Likewise, a strict inequality is sufficient for B to be strictly better so long as there is no satiation. The rest consists of applying this criterion in specific contexts.

Let us begin with the classical comparisons of alternative trade regimes. Here we fix the endowments and production possibilities. We also assume that domestic distortions (market failures or tax wedges) are absent. The fixed vector of government purchases (if any) is financed by lump sum taxes.

With $c = e + x + m - g$ in each of A, B, and $e^{\mathrm{A}} = e^{\mathrm{B}}$, $g^{\mathrm{A}} = g^{\mathrm{B}}$, (2.1a) becomes

$$p^{\mathrm{B}} \cdot (x^{\mathrm{B}} - x^{\mathrm{A}}) + p^{\mathrm{B}} \cdot (m^{\mathrm{B}} - m^{\mathrm{A}}) \geq 0. \tag{2.1b}$$

Next note that, with no domestic distortions, $p^{\mathrm{B}} = q^{\mathrm{B}}$. The set X of production possibilities is unchanged, so x^{A} remains feasible when x^{B} is chosen. Therefore $(0 =) q^{\mathrm{B}} \cdot x^{\mathrm{B}} \geq q^{\mathrm{B}} \cdot x^{\mathrm{A}}$. This is the familiar production effect of better adaption to the B prices. We cannot assert a strict inequality in general, since there may be no possibility of substitution among outputs in the relevant range along the transformation surface. However, there is gain in a weak sense, and it works towards (2.1b) being satisfied.

Thus a sufficient condition for (2.1b), and hence in turn for the B equilibrium being at least as good as A, is

$$p^{\mathrm{B}} \cdot (m^{\mathrm{B}} - m^{\mathrm{A}}) \geq 0. \tag{2.2}$$

This can formally be thought of as revealed preference between the two import vectors.

When B is identified with the free-trade regime and A with autarky, we have $p^{\mathrm{B}} = r^{\mathrm{B}}$ and $r^{\mathrm{B}} \cdot m^{\mathrm{B}} = 0$, while $m^{\mathrm{A}} = 0$. Thus (2.2) is satisfied, and free trade is revealed superior to autarky for this economy. This result was long in the folklore of the subject, but was rigorously established by Samuelson (1962) and Kemp (1962).

A simple generalization is due to Ohyama (1972). Let A be autarky, and B a regime with trade taxes or subsidies. Then $p^{\mathrm{B}} = r^{\mathrm{B}} + \tau^{\mathrm{B}}$, with $r^{\mathrm{B}} \cdot m^{\mathrm{B}} = 0$, so (2.2) becomes

$$\tau^{\mathrm{B}} \cdot m^{\mathrm{B}} \geq 0.$$

Provided the trade taxes or subsidies are net self-financing, such trade is not worse than autarky. If the trade taxes make a loss (met by lump sum taxation), this is a kind of subsidy to the rest of the world that could leave the home country worse off.

Next consider the other classical question of whether free trade is the best policy. Here is helps to interpret (2.2) in a different way. If B is free trade, and A is any other feasible regime, $p^{\mathrm{B}} = r^{\mathrm{B}}$ and $r^{\mathrm{B}} \cdot m^{\mathrm{B}} = 0$, so (2.2) becomes $0 \geq r^{\mathrm{B}} \cdot m^{\mathrm{A}}$. Using $r^{\mathrm{A}} \cdot m^{\mathrm{A}} = 0$, this can be written

$$(r^{\mathrm{B}} - r^{\mathrm{A}}) \cdot m^{\mathrm{A}} \leq 0. \tag{2.3}$$

This says that the move to free trade will be beneficial if "on the average" the prices of imported commodities ($m_k^{\mathrm{A}} > 0$) fall ($r_k^{\mathrm{B}} < r_k^{\mathrm{A}}$). More precisely, the A-quantity weighted index of world prices should fall. This is an improvement in the home country's terms of trade.

Conversely, a move to free trade can fail to be beneficial only if the terms of trade worsen. This is the monopoly argument for interfering with trade. Like any monopolist who can affect his terms of trade, a country can benefit by doing so to some extent. Beyond a point, the contraction of volume of trade becomes too serious, and a marginal condition defines the optimum restriction, or the Mill–Bickerdike optimum tariff. Like any monopoly pricing, this is desirable only from the home country's selfish point of view, and not for Pareto efficiency in the world as a whole.

This discussion has two immediate corollaries. For a country too small to affect its terms of trade, $r^{\mathrm{A}} = r^{\mathrm{B}}$, to within an arbitrary normalization, and (2.3) holds. So free trade is optimum for a small country. Next we consider the optimum regime in general. If B is such that

$$m^{\mathrm{B}} \text{ maximizes } p^{\mathrm{B}} \cdot m \text{ over } M, \tag{2.4}$$

then (2.2) holds for any comparison A. This property implicitly defines the optimum tariffs. A simpler interpretation comes from the first-order condition for the maximization: $p^{\mathrm{B}} \cdot \mathrm{d}m = 0$ for any feasible deviation $\mathrm{d}m$ along the rest of the world's offer surface. Thus the domestic price vector is normal to this surface, and the marginal rates of transformation in domestic production and international trade are equalized. With two goods this is just the familiar tangency between the home country's trade indifference curve and the rest of the world's offer curve. In Sections 3 and 4 we shall consider the optimum tariff problem in more general settings where domestic distortions and distributional considerations are present, and obtain generalizations of this rule.

We can use the same method to pose questions of gain from a general increase in trade possibilities. Let A and B be free-trade equilibria, differing only in that more commodities become tradeable in B. The revealed preference sufficient condition for B to be superior to A is formally identical to (2.3). Of course m^A has fewer non-zero components, corresponding to the smaller set of tradeables in A, and only these contribute to the inner product.

Thus an enlargement of the set of tradeables can be welfare-worsening only if it leads to a worsening of the terms of trade of the previously tradeable commodities. Even then, some worsening may be tolerable since (2.3) is only sufficient for B to be better.

For a small country, this is not an issue, and any relaxation of trade is beneficial. A large country that is imposing optimum tariffs in the B regime is also assured of gain. It does not matter whether there are any tariffs in A, optimum or otherwise.

As an example, consider Grossman's (1984) model of gains from factor trade. Starting from complete autarky, the opening of free trade (or even suitably restricted trade) in goods yields gains in the usual way. Does the introduction of factor trade yield further gain? Our sufficient conditions for free trade in goods and factors to be superior to free trade in goods alone apply in either of the following cases: (1) The economy is small. (2) The opening of factor trade does not worsen the terms of trade for goods. A special case is where free trade in goods equalizes factor prices, when the introduction of free trade in factors makes no difference; see Dixit and Norman (1980, pp. 106–125) for a recent statement.

The issue of gains from trade under uncertainty is examined by Helpman and Razin (1978). They find that trade in goods in each state of the world is better than total autarky, and a small country is assured of further gain through the opening up of trade "across states of the world", i.e., trade in securities. Similarly, Smith (1979) considers intertemporal trade, and shows that trade in goods with balance at each date is superior to complete autarky; a small country gains further when international borrowing and lending is introduced so that trade need only be balanced over time in discounted present values.

2.3. *Distortions and growth*

The next step is to extend comparisons based on (2.1a) to a wider class of equilibria, in the manner of Ohyama (1972) and Smith (1982). Here we allow distortions, whether from market failure or taxes, which drive wedges between prices faced by different categories of agents: consumers, producers and foreigners. For expositional simplicity, distortions within each such sector are not recognized, but their introduction is only a matter of algebra. The wedges are most conveniently expressed as departures from the domestic shadow price vector π. The appropriate interpretation of this shadow price vector depends on the specific context, in particular the range of policy instruments available. Some cases will be considered in detail in Section 3 and 4, but the discussion here will be couched in general terms.

Using the notation introduced in Section 1.3, we write

$$\begin{aligned} p^{\mathrm{B}}\cdot(c^{\mathrm{B}}-c^{\mathrm{A}}) &= (\pi^{\mathrm{B}}+\alpha^{\mathrm{B}})\cdot(c^{\mathrm{B}}-c^{\mathrm{A}}) \\ &= \alpha^{\mathrm{B}}\cdot(c^{\mathrm{B}}-c^{\mathrm{A}})+\pi^{\mathrm{B}}\cdot(e^{\mathrm{B}}-e^{\mathrm{A}})-\pi^{\mathrm{B}}\cdot(g^{\mathrm{B}}-g^{\mathrm{A}}) \\ &\quad +(q^{\mathrm{B}}-\beta^{\mathrm{B}})\cdot(x^{\mathrm{B}}-x^{\mathrm{A}})+(r^{\mathrm{B}}+\tau^{\mathrm{B}})\cdot(m^{\mathrm{B}}-m^{\mathrm{A}}). \end{aligned}$$

Hence condition (2.1a) becomes

$$\begin{aligned} &\pi^{\mathrm{B}}\cdot(e^{\mathrm{B}}-e^{\mathrm{A}})-\pi^{\mathrm{B}}\cdot(g^{\mathrm{B}}-g^{\mathrm{A}}) \\ &+q^{\mathrm{B}}\cdot(x^{\mathrm{B}}-x^{\mathrm{A}})+r^{\mathrm{B}}\cdot(m^{\mathrm{B}}-m^{\mathrm{A}}) \\ &+\alpha^{\mathrm{B}}\cdot(c^{\mathrm{B}}-c^{\mathrm{A}})-\beta^{\mathrm{B}}\cdot(x^{\mathrm{B}}-x^{\mathrm{A}})+\tau^{\mathrm{B}}\cdot(m^{\mathrm{B}}-m^{\mathrm{A}})\geq 0. \end{aligned} \tag{2.5}$$

Using the fact that $r^{\mathrm{B}}\cdot m^{\mathrm{B}}=0=r^{\mathrm{A}}\cdot m^{\mathrm{A}}$, we could also write the term $r^{\mathrm{B}}\cdot(m^{\mathrm{B}}-m^{\mathrm{A}})$ as $-(r^{\mathrm{B}}-r^{\mathrm{A}})\cdot m^{\mathrm{A}}$.

As the first application, let us consider the effect of a change in the trade policy pursued by a given distorted small economy. Now $e^{\mathrm{B}}=e^{\mathrm{A}}$, $g^{\mathrm{B}}=g^{\mathrm{A}}$, $r^{\mathrm{B}}=r^{\mathrm{A}}$, and producer behavior ensures $q^{\mathrm{B}}\cdot(x^{\mathrm{B}}-x^{\mathrm{A}})\geq 0$. Therefore our sufficient condition for the B equilibrium to be better is

$$\alpha^{\mathrm{B}}\cdot(c^{\mathrm{B}}-c^{\mathrm{A}})-\beta^{\mathrm{B}}\cdot(x^{\mathrm{B}}-x^{\mathrm{A}})+\tau^{\mathrm{B}}\cdot(m^{\mathrm{B}}-m^{\mathrm{A}})\geq 0. \tag{2.6}$$

This can be interpreted as follows. Suppose for commodity k the distortion α_k^{B} is positive. Then the consumer price, reflecting its marginal value in consumption, is above the shadow price, and there is some net benefit to increasing its consumption. If $(c_k^{\mathrm{B}}-c_k^{\mathrm{A}})$ is positive, this is what happens in B relative to A. The overall benefit criterion is simply the sum of such components over all commodities and distortions. Thus $\beta_k^{\mathrm{B}}>0$ indicates the producer price, i.e., marginal cost, above the shadow price, and therefore the desirability of reducing production, while $\tau_k^{\mathrm{B}}>0$ indicates a domestic shadow price in excess of the world price, and therefore the desirability of expanding imports or reducing exports.

How the various quantities change in the course of the move from A to B depends on the full general equilibrium comparative statics of the system. This is much better done using calculus methods, and Section 4 will examine some cases of this kind. However, no restrictions can be placed on the changes without making specific assumptions about the functional forms of the preferences and technologies. Therefore it is always possible to find cases where the criterion fails to hold. The condition is only sufficient for B to be superior, but it is equally easy to construct examples where B is worse than A. In particular, it is possible to find models of distorted small economies for which free trade is not optimum, and even autarky may be preferable to free trade. This is just an instance of the general problem of the second best.

This discussion assumes that the distortions are unavoidable. If they can be eliminated, it is always better to do so. For example, a consumption externality distortion α_k should be offset by a Pigovian tax of $-\alpha_k$. Where the distortion results from a policy itself, it should be reversed. Call the resulting equilibrium B, with $\alpha^B = \beta^B = \tau^B = 0$. Let A be the equilibrium which accepts the distortions and arranges other policies optimally around them. The comparison of equation (2.6) immediately shows B to be superior. In other words, interference with trade may be a desirable second-best policy for a distorted small economy, but the first-best is to get rid of the distortion and keep trade free. This will be elaborated upon in Sections 3 and 4; see Bhagwati (1971) for a survey.

Next consider an undistorted economy that experiences growth, either in the sense of an endowment increase or an enlargement of the production possibility set X. By (2.5), the new equilibrium is better if

$$\pi^B \cdot (e^B - e^A) + q^B \cdot (x^B - x^A) - (r^B - r^A) \cdot m^A \geq 0. \tag{2.7}$$

The first two terms are the direct effects of the change, and are bound to be non-negative. With non-negative shadow prices π^B, and no decrease in any endowment, the first term is non-negative. Even when some endowments increase and others decrease, it is natural to take an increase in the value of the physical change as our definition of a net increase. As for the second term, the enlargement of X leaves x^A feasible, while x^B maximizes profit at the B producer prices, so $q^B \cdot x^B \geq q^B \cdot x^A$.

The third term is the induced change in the terms of trade, and can be of either sign. In particular, the terms of trade can worsen sufficiently to violate (2.7), and then growth may be welfare-worsening. This possibility was called "economic damnification" by Edgeworth (1894) and "immiserizing growth" by Bhagwati (1958). This is once again a second-best possibility. A country that can affect its terms of trade can levy an optimum tariff τ^B. With $p^B = r^B + \tau^B$, and $p^B \cdot (m^B - m^A) \geq 0$ from (2.4), condition (2.5) is satisfied, and immiserizing growth cannot occur.

Recall that our concept of a commodity encompasses factors as well as goods. Therefore the result can be applied to trade in factors. For example, consider the model of Brecher and Bhagwati (1981), where foreigners own some of the factors of production in the home country. Here the optimum tariff vector must be computed simultaneously for goods trade and foreign factor income. Otherwise immiserizing growth and similar paradoxes can arise.

Finally, similar analysis applies to a small economy with distortions. Growth can be immiserizing if in the new equilibrium the distortions are worse in the sense that the last three terms in (2.5) are affected adversely; see Johnson (1967). Again, the first-best remedy is to act directly on the distortions.

The general conceptual framework has been applied to many kinds of distortions, growth and other comparative static changes. These are too numerous to list here; see Bhagwati and Srinivasan (1983, ch. 16–25) for an exhaustive account. Their formal methods are somewhat different (revealed preference is studied in two-dimensional diagrams, and comparative statics is carried out using production functions), but readers can easily relate them to the approach used here.

2.4. Distributions for Pareto superiority

Finally, I shall consider binary comparisons of equilibria when there are several consumers. It was emphasized earlier that any change in relative prices of traded goods typically favors some factors and harms others. The question is whether tax or subsidy policies can be used to achieve a desirable distribution of aggregate gains. Thus we start with an equilibrium A, and attempt, by a simultaneous change of the trade regime and distributive policies, to produce a superior equilibrium B.

The test of superiority will be relatively stringent, namely a Pareto improvement. Note that we require an actually superior outcome B, not a mere potential improvement through hypothetical compensations. Note also that Pareto superiority is sufficient, but not necessary, for an increase in the value of any Bergson–Samuelson welfare function.

The achievable outcomes depend, of course, on the policy instruments that are available. Lump-sum transfers are the most powerful redistributive tools; in effect they reduce the problem to the one-consumer case already analysed. But such transfers are thought to be impractical for several reasons. Perhaps the most important is the problem of incentive compatibility, discussed by Hammond (1979). To calculate the optimal lump sum transfers, the policy-maker needs information about the characteristics (endowments and preferences) of individuals. When such information must be inferred from observed behavior, each individual has the incentive to alter the behavior so as to secure a larger net transfer receipt. Hammond's conclusion is that incentive compatibility requires that the same set of net trades be available to each individual. The calculation of the optimal set requires information only about the distribution of individuals' characteristics in the population, which is not susceptible to manipulation by any one of them. In our context, commodity taxes or subsidies, and a uniform poll tax or subsidy, satisfy this requirement. These tools, especially the former, are the ones considered below.

The method of analysis comes from Dixit and Norman (1980a, 1980b). The idea is as follows. Let the initial equilibrium A, with its trade regime and any other taxes or subsidies, be specified. Suppose that some move away from it yields aggregate production or terms-of-trade gains. Construct an intermediate equilibrium B where such gains are realised, but all consumers are kept at their A utility levels. This equilibrium involves some slack or waste. We then move to the final position C by disposing of the slack in such a way as to raise some consumers' utilities without lowering any.

Let us examine the process in more detail. Commodity taxation allows us to de-link the prices consumers face, both for commodities they buy (typically goods) and those they sell (typically factors), from the corresponding prices for producers. Thus we can ensure that consumers face the same prices in B as in A; $p^{\mathrm{B}} = p^{\mathrm{A}}$. Uniform poll subsidies (if any) are also unchanged; $b^{\mathrm{B}} = b^{\mathrm{A}}$. Thus each consumer i faces an unchanged budget set $p^{\mathrm{A}} \cdot (c - e^i) \le b^{\mathrm{A}}$. Therefore his choice is unchanged, i.e., $c^{\mathrm{B}i} = c^{\mathrm{A}i}$, and so is his utility.

The producer prices change to q^{B}, and the trade prices to r^{B}, to achieve equilibrium. This implicitly defines the tariff rates $(q^{\mathrm{B}} - r^{\mathrm{B}})$, and domestic commodity tax rates $(p^{\mathrm{B}} - q^{\mathrm{B}})$, with producer prices q^{B} playing the role of shadow prices π^{B}.

In this process the government's tax revenue T will change, and so must its purchases. For expository simplicity, suppose they change according to the rule $g^{\mathrm{B}} = g^{\mathrm{A}} + \lambda g^0$, where g^0 is a strictly positive vector, and the scalar λ accomodates to achieve equilibrium. For budget balance, we need

$$T^{\mathrm{B}} = q^{\mathrm{B}} \cdot g^{\mathrm{B}} = q^{\mathrm{B}} \cdot g^{\mathrm{A}} + \lambda q^{\mathrm{B}} \cdot g^0 .$$

On the revenue side, writing n for the number of consumers, we have

$$T^{\mathrm{B}} = (p^{\mathrm{B}} - q^{\mathrm{B}}) \cdot (c^{\mathrm{B}} - e) + (q^{\mathrm{B}} - r^{\mathrm{B}}) \cdot m^{\mathrm{B}} - nb^{\mathrm{B}} .$$

But $p^{\mathrm{B}} \cdot (c^{\mathrm{B}} - e) = nb^{\mathrm{B}}$ on adding the consumers budgets, and $r^{\mathrm{B}} \cdot m^{\mathrm{B}} = 0$ for trade balance. Finally, substituting for $c^{\mathrm{B}} = c^{\mathrm{A}}$, we have

$$\begin{aligned} T^{\mathrm{B}} &= -q^{\mathrm{B}} \cdot (x^{\mathrm{A}} + m^{\mathrm{A}} - g^{\mathrm{A}}) + q^{\mathrm{B}} \cdot m^{\mathrm{B}} \\ &= q^{\mathrm{B}} \cdot g^{\mathrm{A}} + q^{\mathrm{B}} \cdot (x^{\mathrm{B}} - x^{\mathrm{A}}) + q^{\mathrm{B}} \cdot (m^{\mathrm{B}} - m^{\mathrm{A}}), \end{aligned}$$

where we have used $q^{\mathrm{B}} \cdot x^{\mathrm{B}} = 0$. Comparing the two expressions for T^{B}, we have

$$q^{\mathrm{B}} \cdot (x^{\mathrm{B}} - x^{\mathrm{A}}) + q^{\mathrm{B}} \cdot (m^{\mathrm{B}} - m^{\mathrm{A}}) = \lambda q^{\mathrm{B}} \cdot g^0 . \tag{2.8}$$

The left-hand side of (2.8) is the same as that of (2.1b). In the one-consumer case, we had no commodity taxes, i.e., $p^B = q^B$. Here we see that it is the producer price vector which is relevant with such taxation. But the sources of aggregate gains are the same in the two cases, and are captured in the values of the physical changes in production and imports.

As before, profit-maximization ensures that the production effect is non-negative. The trade effect can be verified to be non-negative for the same comparisons and in the same way as in the one-consumer case: (i) where A is autarky and B is either free trade or self-financing restricted trade, (ii) where B is optimally restricted trade, defined as maximizing the value of net imports at domestic producer prices, and (iii) where B is free trade for a small economy.

If the left-hand side of (2.8) is strictly positive, we have $\lambda > 0$. Since the government's use of goods is not explicitly valued, the excess λg^0 over the requirement g^A is a slack that occurs solely to dispose of the revenue. It would be better to change the policies and use this slack in a way that benefits the consumers. Let us see when and how this can be done. If consumers' demands are continuous functions of the policy instruments, then a sufficiently small change will not increase the total demand by more than λg^0 in any component, and can be absorbed by a reduction in the waste. So the change will be feasible. If the instruments can be adjusted in a direction that benefits some consumers without harming any, the change will be a Pareto improvement. This will be the final position C that we adopt in preference to A.

A uniform poll subsidy clearly does the job. More interestingly, so can commodity taxation on its own, provided there is a commodity, single as in Diamond and Mirrlees (1971) or composite as in Weymark (1979), in the market for which no two consumers are on opposite sides. Thus if some consumers are net buyers and none are net sellers of this commodity, we lower its consumer price; in the opposite case we raise it. The condition invoked is a familiar and basic one in much of public finance; for example, it lies behind the production efficiency property of a commodity tax optimum. Therefore the result seems a robust one: aggregate gains in production or trade can be distributed so as to achieve a Pareto improvement using commodity taxation, and arguments about the distribution of gains do not provide a case for intervention in trade. This point will receive further support when jointly optimal tax and tariff policies are considered in the next section.

Extension of the results of Section 2.3 to many-consumer contexts can be problematic if we want Pareto improvement using commodity taxation alone. The case of endowment growth is considered by Smith (1982). If some consumers experience an endowment increase and none a decrease, the above method applies. But an aggregate increase can occur while some suffer a decrease; in such a case transfers are typically required if a Pareto improvement is to result.

Other problems can arise if gains from the removal of distortions are to be distributed. For example, if there are consumption externalities, the appropriate policy response is an adjustment of consumer prices. This may be incompatible with the approach used above, where all consumers were given unchanged prices at the intermediate step, and more favorable ones at the final equilibrium. However, we shall soon see that if Pareto superiority is not required and interpersonal comparisons are made using a welfare function, commodity taxation has a useful role for tackling such situations.

3. Optimum taxation and tariffs

Here I shall characterize the optimum mix of tax policies with regard to domestic production and consumption activities and international trade. In contrast to the previous section, the focus is on the best deployment of the available instruments, and not on improvement relative to some status quo. Interpersonal comparisons are made by means of a given Bergson–Samuelson welfare function. Therefore the optimum may not be Pareto-superior to some alternative; there may be uncompensated losers if the value judgements so dictate.

This approach comes closest to the modern theory of public finance. In fact, if we regard international trade as just another transformation activity, the model is a special case of the Ramsey–Diamond–Mirrlees framework, and the resulting tax formulae can be obtained from those in Auerbach's chapter in this volume, Sections 5 and 6. Alternatively, we can regard the rest of the world's net supply as that coming from an uncontrolled firm, and obtain optimum tax and price rules as in Guesnerie (1975).

3.1. The first-best optimum

To set the stage, consider the case of a fully controlled economy, i.e., let the vectors of consumption, production and trade be objects of direct choice, subject only to the constraints of technical feasibility and resource availability. The shadow prices associated with such an optimum tell us how it might be decentralized through tax and price policies, and provide a basis for comparison with later cases where policy instruments are more restricted.

First consider a case without external economies or diseconomies. Let $u_i = U^i(c^i)$ be the utility of consumer i, and $W(u_1, u_2, \dots)$ the social welfare function. Let $F^j(x^j) \leq 0$ be the set of feasible net outputs of production activity j, and $G(m^t) \leq 0$ the set of feasible net imports. Then we are to maximize

$$W(U^1(c^1), U^2(c^2), \dots),$$

subject to

$$\sum_i c^i \leq \sum_i e^i + \sum_j x^j + m - g, \tag{3.1}$$

$$F^j(x^j) \leq 0 \quad \text{for} \quad j = 1, 2, \ldots, \tag{3.2}$$

$$G(m^t) \leq 0. \tag{3.3}$$

Let π be the non-negative vector of multipliers for the material balance constraint (3.1), and ϕ_j ($j = 1, 2, \ldots$) and γ the non-negative scalar multipliers for (3.2) and (3.3). Formulate the Lagrangean

$$L = W(U^1(c^1), U^2(c^2), \ldots) + \pi \cdot \left(\sum_i e^i + \sum_j x^j + m - g - \sum_i c^i \right)$$

$$- \sum_j \phi_j F^j(x^j) - \gamma G(m^t). \tag{3.4}$$

For expositional simplicity I shall leave out corner solutions; interested readers can easily extend the method to allow them. Then the first-order conditions are

$$(\partial W/\partial u_i)(\partial U^i/\partial c^i_k) - \pi_k = 0, \tag{3.5}$$

$$\pi_k - \phi_j(\partial F^j/\partial x^j_k) = 0, \tag{3.6}$$

$$\pi_k - \gamma(\partial G/\partial m_k) = 0, \tag{3.7}$$

for all consumers i, all firms j, and all commodities k [only tradeables in (3.7)]. In vector notation, these become (with the numbers preserved)

$$W_i U^i_c - \pi = 0, \tag{3.5}$$

$$\pi - \phi_j F^j_x = 0, \tag{3.6}$$

$$\pi^t - \gamma G_m = 0, \tag{3.7}$$

where $W_i \equiv \partial W/\partial u_i$, U^i_c is the vector with components $\partial U^i/\partial c^i_k$ corresponding to all commodities k, etc.

The interpretation is familiar and straightforward. The proportions in U^i_c give the marginal rates of substitution in consumption for consumer i. Similarly, F^j_x yields the marginal rates of transformation in the jth production activity, and G_m

those achieved through trade. The Lagrange multipliers π yield the increments in social welfare that could be achieved if the material balance constraints could be relaxed, i.e., the shadow prices of commodities. If the government acquired a new production technology (project) that had a small net output vector dx^0, this should be implemented if and only if $\pi \cdot dx^0 > 0$.[1] Now (3.5)–(3.7) say that, within scalar multiples, U_c^i, F_x^j and G_m should all equal π.

The equalities of various marginal rates of substitution are the usual Pareto efficiency conditions. Bhagwati (1971) expresses these as $DRS = DRT = FRT$, where DRS is the marginal rate of substitution in consumption in the home (domestic) economy, DRT is the domestic marginal rate of transformation in production, and FRT is the marginal rate of transformation achievable through foreign trade. This full Pareto efficiency subsumes production efficiency, i.e., the equality of marginal rates of transformation in all production activities and trade.

Further, (3.5) embodies the considerations of interpersonal distribution. For each commodity k, the marginal welfare effect $(\partial W/\partial u_i)\cdot(\partial U^i/\partial c_k^i)$ is equalized across all consumers i.

Decentralized implementation of such an optimum is equally familiar. We set $p = q = \pi$. Consumer i, maximizing $U^i(c^i)$ subject to $p \cdot c^i \le b_i$ sets $U_c^i = \lambda_i p$, and then b_i is adjusted to make the marginal utility of money $\lambda_i = 1/W_i$. Firm j operating activity j maximizes $q \cdot x^j$ subject to $F^j(x^j) \le 0$, for which $q = \phi_j F_x^j$. The only new feature concerns trade. In fact, implicit in (3.7) is just the optimal tariff to exploit monopoly in trade. We can convert it to a familiar form when there are just two tradeables. The foreign offer curve $m_2 = m_2(m_1)$ is defined as the solution of $G(m_1, m_2) = 0$, so along it,

$$\frac{dm_2}{dm_1} = -\frac{\partial G/\partial m_1}{\partial G/\partial m_2}.$$

Using (3.7), therefore

$$\frac{\pi_1}{\pi_2} = \frac{\partial G/\partial m_1}{\partial G/\partial m_2} = -\frac{dm_2}{dm_1},$$

and

$$\frac{\pi_1/r_1}{\pi_2/r_2} = -\frac{r_2}{r_1}\frac{dm_2}{dm_1} = \frac{m_1}{m_2}\frac{dm_2}{dm_1},$$

where the trade balance condition $r_1 m_1 + r_2 m_2 = 0$ has been used. Choosing good

[1] See Dreze (1982) for a discussion of project evaluation.

2 to have zero tariff ($\pi_2 = r_2$), we have the ad valorem tariff on good 1 as

$$\pi_1/r_1 - 1 = \frac{m_1}{m_2}\frac{\mathrm{d}m_2}{\mathrm{d}m_1} - 1.$$

This is the well-known formula involving the elasticity of the foreign offer curve.

An expression with foreign supply derivatives is available for the general case. As in Section 1.3, write $r^{\mathrm{t}} = R(m^{\mathrm{t}})$ and $G(m^{\mathrm{t}}) = R(m^{\mathrm{t}}) \cdot m^{\mathrm{t}}$. Then $G_m = R + R'_m m^{\mathrm{t}}$, where R_m is the matrix of derivatives $\partial r_k / \partial m_l$ for k, l tradeables, and R'_m is its transpose. Choose the scale of prices to make $\gamma = 1$ for algebraic simplicity. Then (3.7) becomes the formula for optimum tariffs,

$$\tau^{\mathrm{t}} \equiv \pi^{\mathrm{t}} - r^{\mathrm{t}} = R'_m(m^{\mathrm{t}}) m^{\mathrm{t}}. \tag{3.8}$$

We can also relate this discussion to that in Section 2.2. For any movement $\mathrm{d}m$ from the optimum along the foreign offer surface $G(m) = 0$, we have $\pi \cdot \mathrm{d}m = G_m \cdot \mathrm{d}m = 0$ by (3.7). This is just the first-order condition for the maximization of (2.4), but now carried out at shadow prices.

As usual, commodities have a wide interpretation, and the formula applies to the case of jointly optimum tariffs on goods and factors when there is international capital mobility, e.g., Jones (1967).

For a small country, with constant r^{t}, the optimum tariffs are zero, i.e., free trade is optimal. Redistribution is better carried out using first-best lump sum transfers.

Next consider externalities, to see how they interact with trade. The principle can be explained with a minimum of algebra by considering a special case. Suppose the total output of commodity 1, written X_1, affects the production possibilities of each firm. Thus (3.2) is replaced by

$$F^j(x^j, X_1) \le 0.$$

If $\partial F^j / \partial X_1 > 0$, we have an external diseconomy. Now the first-order condition (3.6) remains unchanged for $k \neq 1$, but that for $k = 1$ is replaced by

$$\pi_1 - \phi_j(\partial F / \partial x_1^j) - \sum_J \phi_J(\partial F^J / \partial X_1) = 0.$$

This can be implemented in a market economy by altering the price of good 1 as seen by firms. We make the usual assumption that each firm is too small to recognize the effect of its contribution x_1^j on X_1. Then, facing prices q, it will set $q = \phi_j F_x^j$ as before. To make this consistent with the first-order conditions, we need

$$q_1 = \pi_1 - \sum_J \phi_J(\partial F^J / \partial X_1).$$

The second term on the right-hand side is the Pigovian correction, consisting of the external effect on all firms' technological feasibility constraints valued at the respective shadow prices. For the case of a diseconomy, we have $q_1 < \pi_1$, i.e., a tax to discourage production of this commodity.

The same tax rate applies to all firms because they have identical symmetric roles in generating externalities. If there are firm-specific external effects, the corrective policies will have to be firm-specific, too.

No other first-order conditions are affected. In particular, there is no call for interference in trade on account of the production externality. Similar conclusions follow from a general model allowing all kinds of externalities in production and consumption. This is the Bhagwati–Johnson principle of targeting, which was stated in the Introduction, and discussed by revealed preference methods in Section 2.3. A corresponding result for a closed economy is proved by Sandmo (1975, sec. 2).

The earlier statement had a mirror-image counterpart, namely the deliberate introduction of a distortion for non-economic reasons. Just as an undesired distortion is best eliminated by a tax or subsidy policy that acts directly on the relevant margin, a required distortion is best introduced (i.e., attained at least welfare cost) by a similar most direct policy. Again an example suffices to explain the point. Suppose it is desired, for reasons of national security or otherwise, that the production of commodity 1 should not fall below a stipulated level, say $x_1 \geq \bar{x}_1$. Letting ξ be the Lagrange multiplier for this constraint, the corresponding component of the first-order condition (3.6) becomes

$$\pi_1 + \xi - \phi_j\left(\partial F^j / \partial x_1^j\right) = 0 \quad \text{for all } j.$$

This can be decentralized by means of a production subsidy ξ for commodity 1. No other first-order conditions are affected.

It is customary in this branch of theory to accept unspecified non-economic reasons for such constraints. However, they are often merely convenient short-cuts for the introduction of considerations that have an underlying economic rationale, when a full-fledged treatment would be too cumbersome. For example, the floor on production levels may be motivated by problems of disequilibrium dynamics (adjustment) or uncertainty (trade disruption). This is not to deny that there are genuinely non-economic principles that constrain economic policy.

The question of achievement of a certain proportion of self-sufficiency often arises in public policy discussions. We can use the above method to find the optimum way of doing so. Suppose that for commodity 1 it is desired that domestic production should cover at least 75% of consumption, i.e., $x_1 \geq 0.75 c_1$. If ξ is the multiplier, the optimum policy is a production subsidy at rate ξ and a consumption tax at rate 0.75ξ. A tariff alone, in the normal case at some rate between these two values, could achieve the same objective, but it would discourage consumption too much and encourage production too little, relative to the optimum.

We saw in Section 1.3 that there is a degree of arbitrariness in the designation of tax and tariff instruments to implement a given policy. In this case there is one particularly simple method, namely a proportionally distributed quota, as discussed by McCulloch and Johnson (1973). The right to import is awarded to domestic producers, in proportion of one unit of imports for every three units produced domestically. Each unit sold to home consumers can be thought of as 25% imported and 75% home-produced. Free entry eliminates pure profit, so the consumer price p_1, the domestic marginal cost (producer price) q_1, and the world price r_1 must stand in the relation $p_1 = 0.25r_1 + 0.75q_1$ in equilibrium. Writing this as $p_1 - r_1 = 0.75(q_1 - r_1)$, we see that the policy implicitly enforces just the right combination of a consumption tax and a production subsidy.

3.2. *Optimum without lump sum transfers*

Now suppose lump sum transfers across consumers are not possible. In fact, rule out even uniform poll taxes and subsidies. Then we have the standard Ramsey–Diamond–Mirrlees problem of finding the second-best optimal commodity taxation. This is a short-cut just like the use of non-economic constraints; it would be too difficult to carry along the full model that endogenizes the informational costs of lump sum transfers.

The consumers' transfer incomes b_i are zero for all i, and consumer prices p are the only instrument for controlling consumption quantities. Let the demand functions be $c^i(p, b)$, and the indirect utilities $V^i(p, b) = U^i(c^i(p, b))$. Roy's Identity gives

$$V_p^i(p, b) = -\lambda_i\left[c^i(p, b) - e^i\right], \qquad \lambda_i = V_b^i(p, b), \tag{3.9}$$

where V_p^i is the vector with components $\partial V^i / \partial p_k$.

This is the only change from the optimization problem of the previous subsection. The maximand is

$$W(V^1(p,0), V^2(p,0), \ldots).$$

The material balance constraint becomes

$$\sum_i c^i(p,0) \le \sum_i e^i + \sum_j x^j + m - g, \tag{3.10}$$

replacing (3.1). The corresponding first-order conditions replacing (3.5) are

$$-\sum_i W_i\lambda_i\left[c_k^i(p,0)-e_k^i\right]-\sum_i\sum_l \pi_l\left(\partial c_l^i/\partial p_k\right)=0. \tag{3.11}$$

In vector and matrix form, letting primes denote the transposes of (column) vectors, this becomes

$$-\sum_i W_i\lambda_i\left[c^i(p,0)-e^i\right]'-\pi'\sum_i c_p^i(p,0)=0.$$

The other constraints (3.2) and (3.3), and the corresponding conditions (3.6) and (3.7) remain unchanged.

This, too, is mostly familiar. The new condition (3.11) is just the Diamond–Mirrlees optimum tax formula, in the form (66) of Diamond and Mirrlees (1971), or a minor variation of equation (6.18) in the chapter in this volume by Auerbach. Production efficiency is still required, although the second-best nature of commodity taxation precludes full Pareto efficiency. The shadow prices π still equal producer prices q, as in Mirrlees (1969), but differ from consumer prices p, i.e., $DRT \neq DRS$.

The optimal trade policy entails efficiency, i.e., $DRT = FRT$. The monopoly argument is still the only one justifying tariffs; consumption taxes are superior for the redistribution role. A corollary is that the shadow prices of tradeables equal the marginal rates of transformation through trade, or marginal border prices. Note that since factors are included in the list of commodities, we are speaking of taxes or subsidies as required on all goods and factors, and on any ownership rents.

To relate this to results in the previous subsection, let us for a moment re-introduce lump sum transfers b_i. The first-order conditions for them are

$$W_i\lambda_i-\sum_l \pi_l\left(\partial c_l^i/\partial b_i\right)=0.$$

Rewriting (3.11) with b_i as appropriate, and combining with the above, we have

$$\sum_i\sum_l \pi_l\left\{\partial c_l^i/\partial p_k+\left(c_k^i-e_k^i\right)\left(\partial c_l^i/\partial b_i\right)\right\}=0,$$

or

$$\pi'\sum_i\left\{c_p^i+c_b^i\left(c^i-e^i\right)'\right\}=0.$$

The bracketed terms are Slutsky–Hicks substitution matrices. By their singularity property, $\pi = p$ gives a solution. (If the sum of the matrices has the maximal permissible rank, i.e., one less than the number of commodities, it is the only solution to within scale.) Thus the model is reconciled with the earlier one. We can also consider an "intermediate" model of poll taxes or subsidies, where $b_i = b$ for all i but the common value can be optimally chosen. This gives formulae like Diamond (1975); the implications for trade policy are unaffected.

Next consider distortions and constraints when lump sum taxation is impossible. So long as the externalities or non-economic objectives pertain to domestic production or consumption, the condition (3.7) for optimum tariffs is unaffected, and the marginal "border prices" reflect the shadow prices of tradeable commodities. The distortions and constraints are best tackled by the appropriately targeted Pigovian policies even when lump sum transfers are not available. More precisely, what we have is the *additivity property* obtained by Sandmo (1975, sec. 3, 4); "the marginal social damage of commodity m enters the tax formula for that commodity additively, and does not enter the tax formulas for other commodities."

A different problem might arise. These corrective taxes must in general be different for different consumers or firms. This may face the same computational or incentive-compatibility problems as led us to doubt the practicality of lump sum transfers. For externalities or constraints that involve only aggregates over consumers or firms, as in Sandmo's model, the Pigovian policies are uniform across agents and there is no problem. Otherwise we may have to use a restricted optimum as in Diamond (1973). But this still leaves trade policy unaffected, at least in the analytical sense that (3.7) is valid, although the actual values of the various entities may change. For a small country, free trade remains optimum.

This discussion confirms, and extends to the case of commodity taxation, the principle of targeting. One particular facet is worth emphasis. When it is desirable to encourage domestic production, policy calls for subsidies to these producers, instead of tariff protection from imports. This is criticised by laymen on the grounds that import tariffs raise revenue, while production subsidies cost money and put additional strain on other uses of the government's budget. We see this argument to be fallacious. The size of the government's budget has no *direct* welfare relevance. The optimality conditions show that, on considering the overall effects, it is desirable to provide those production subsidies and adjust other taxes appropriately. This is so even when the latter are not of the first-best non-distorting lump sum variety, but commodity taxes involving some distortion between consumer and producer prices, i.e., making $DRS \neq DRT$. One way to explain the point is by observing that a tariff acts like a combination of a production subsidy and a consumption tax at equal rates. So it is just one particular way of financing (in fact overfinancing) the subsidy. The optimum way can do no worse; in fact we expect to have a smaller deadweight loss by levying taxes at lower rates on a broader base of all commodities.

It is worth re-iteration that, although the formulae for optimum tariffs and correction of domestic distortions remain the same whether lump sum transfers or commodity taxation are used in the background, the actual quantities and prices that emerge in the general equilibrium solution will differ. The presumption would be that a subsidy or tax will be set at a lower level if the raising or disbursal of the revenues has to be done through other distortionary taxes or subsidies than it would if lump sum transfers were available. However, general equilibrium interactions can produce counterintuitive outcomes; Atkinson and Stern (1974) provide a case in point for the provision of public goods.

3.3. Optimum tariffs for revenue

We have seen that the revenue argument for tariffs is invalid if domestic commodity taxation can be used. But the administrative apparatus of some less developed countries may be too limited, leaving the taxation of transactions that cross international borders as their only effective source of revenue. Many countries faced this situation in the past. Here I consider a third-best policy problem of this kind. As usual, I do not endogenize the reasons for ruling out lump sum transfers and commodity taxes. Previous literature on the question includes Dasgupta and Stiglitz (1974, sec. 4) in the small-country case, and Boadway, Maital and Prachowny (1973) for a country with monopoly power in trade. My treatment is a continuation of the approach of the previous subsection.

For algebraic simplicity, I shall suppose the domestic economy has an aggregate consumer and an aggregate price-taking firm. The more general case can easily be reconstructed by interested readers. Lump sum transfers are also ruled out, so the consumer's demands are given by $c(p,0)$ and his indirect utility by $V(p,0)$. The latter is also the measure of social welfare. Producer prices must equal p, but under constant returns to scale we cannot use a supply function. Instead we introduce the output vector x separately, then require it to be compatible with producer behavior by imposing a constraint $p = F_x(x)$. Setting the factor of proportionality equal to one is a permissable normalization of prices. Now the policy problem is to choose p, x and m to maximize $V(p,0)$ subject to

$$c(p,0) \leq e + x + m - g, \tag{3.12}$$

$$F(x) \leq 0, \tag{3.13}$$

$$G(m^{\mathrm{t}}) \leq 0, \tag{3.14}$$

$$p = F_x(x). \tag{3.15}$$

Using $p \cdot (c - e) = 0$, the material balance constraint (3.12) becomes $p \cdot g \leq p \cdot m$. If we also use $r \cdot m = 0$, this is $p \cdot g \leq (p - r) \cdot m$, which captures the requirement that the government's expenditure must be financed using trade taxes alone.

Let θ be the vector of Lagrange multipliers for (3.15), and the other multipliers as before. Then the first-order conditions are

$$-\lambda [c(p,0) - e]' - \pi' c_p(p,0) + \theta' = 0, \tag{3.16}$$

$$\pi - \phi F_x - F_{xx}\theta = 0, \tag{3.17}$$

$$\pi^{t} - \gamma G_m = 0. \tag{3.18}$$

The first thing to notice is that the structure of the relationship between the shadow prices and border prices of tradeables is unchanged: (3.18) and (3.7) are identical. Thus we can interpret the "optimal tariff" formula as before, and marginal border prices serve as shadow prices of tradeables.

But the shadow prices π no longer equal domestic producer prices p. It is no longer desirable to keep $DRT = FRT$. This is a "third-best" response to the constraints on other tax instruments. The first-best would use lump sum transfers and keep $DRS = DRT = FRT$; the second-best would use consumption taxes and have $DRS \neq DRT = FRT$.

The differences between p and π can be thought of as the domestic tax component of the policy. It takes the form of a consumption tax and a production subsidy at equal rates. Operationally, the outcome is equivalent to a tariff. The difference between π and r is the foreign component of the policy, and is itself a tariff. Then the shadow prices can be forgotten, and the policy implemented in one piece as a trade tax vector $(p - r)$. This is how the result is usually derived, and it then appears significantly different from earlier tax formulae. But the introduction of the economically meaningful shadow price vector allows us to display the policy package in constituent parts each of which has a clear economic rationale.

Readers might wonder what happens if the optimum tariff that exploits monopoly power in trade raises more than enough revenue. The answer is that we do not achieve the first-best in this way. Government expenditure is fixed, and it becomes necessary to give away some of the revenue by the distortionary means available, namely by reducing tariffs to suboptimal levels.

Finally, we should note a property of the solution. Since F is homogeneous of degree 1, the optimum has $F_x x = F = 0$ and $F_{xx} x = 0$. Then (3.17) gives $\pi \cdot x = 0$, i.e., private production breaks even at shadow prices. This implication of constant returns to scale was discussed in a general model by Diamond and Mirrlees (1976).

4. Gradual reform of policies

The welfare effects of small changes in tax and expenditure policies starting from an arbitrary distorted initial equilibrium have received much attention in public economics. This work is surveyed in Section 8 of Auerbach's chapter in this volume. Similar issues have also been a long-standing concern in trade theory. Haberler (1950) showed how some interference with trade could be beneficial in the presence of domestic distortions. The subject was further developed by Meade (1955), and led to the theory of optimal second-best policies discussed earlier. The design of welfare-improving tariff reforms was studied by Betrand and Vanek (1971), Bruno (1972), Lloyd (1974) and others. Smith (1980) provides a synthesis of much of this literature. The implications for shadow prices in distorted economies have also been extensively studied, and are discussed by Corden (1982).

4.1. Equilibrium and comparative statics

In this section I shall briefly review the basic principles and issues in the framework of a simple comparative-static model. For ease of exposition I shall begin by assuming the country to be small, i.e., take parametric world prices. The case of a large country will be examined in Section 4.4. For the same reason I shall begin with the case where all commodities are tradeable, and extend the analysis to include non-tradeables in Section 4.5. Finally, and in conformity with most of the literature on this subject, I shall ignore distributional issues and assume a one-consumer economy.

Since the allocative effects depend on the *relative* price changes caused by policy reforms or changes in distortions, it helps to specify a numeraire explicitly. I shall modify the notation of Section 1.3 slightly by letting this be commodity 0. Its quantities will be indicated by the subscript 0, and vectors c, x, etc. will comprise all other commodities. Thus the full consumption vector will be (c_0, c), and that of consumer prices $(1, p)$. The consumer's expenditure function will be $E(1, p, u)$, and the compensated demands $E_0(1, p, u)$ and $E_p(1, p, u)$. Subscripts denote partial derivatives; in particular, $E_0(1, p, u)$ is $\partial E(p_0, p, u)/\partial p_0$ evaluated at $p_0 = 1$.

A more important change will be made in the model of production. The assumption of constant returns to scale is useful when studying optimum taxation, but not for comparative statics. Supplies are correspondences, and a small open economy is likely to specialize its production pattern greatly. The literature on gradual reform has avoided these difficulties by assuming a strictly convex technology and single-valued supply functions; I shall follow this practice. The basic construct will be a profit function $\Pi(1, q)$, yielding supply functions

$x_0 = \Pi_0(1, q)$ and $x = \Pi_q(1, q)$. To preserve the independence of consumer and producer price normalizations, this profit will be assumed to be taxed at 100%.

Equilibrium is now easy to describe. The various commodity markets clear, so

$$E_0(1, p, u) = \Pi_0(1, q) + m_0 + e_0 - g_0, \tag{4.1}$$

$$E_p(1, p, u) = \Pi_q(1, q) + m + e - g. \tag{4.2}$$

Trade is balanced, i.e.,

$$m_0 + r \cdot m = 0. \tag{4.3}$$

Finally, the various relative prices differ from one another on account of market failures and taxes. In the notation established in Section 1.3, $p = r + \tau + \alpha$ and $q = r + \tau + \beta$. Recall that there is one degree of freedom in writing this. For algebraic simplicity, I shall utilize it by absorbing τ into each of α and β, or in effect relabelling $(\tau + \alpha)$ as α and $(\tau + \beta)$ as β. Economically, a trade tax or distortion is being separated into the equivalent form of a consumption tax *cum* production subsidy. Thus

$$p = r + \alpha, \qquad q = r + \beta. \tag{4.4}$$

It is readily verified that, in equilibrium, the consumer's net expenditure must equal the net revenues associated with the distortions and taxes, i.e.,

$$E - (e_0 + p \cdot e) = \Pi + (p - q) \cdot c + (q - r) \cdot m - (g_0 + q \cdot g), \tag{4.5}$$

where the arguments of E and Π have been omitted for brevity. But different mechanisms can bring about this balance. Market failures give rise to rents which accrue as lump sums to consumers or profits to producers. The government's budget from commodity and profit taxes and expenditures may be balanced by lump sum transfers to or from consumers. In such cases there is no separate constraint arising from budget balance. Any given set of r, α, β, e_0, e, g_0 and g is compatible with general equilibrium, when lump sum transfers take an appropriate value in the background. Of course, public consumption must not be so high that the private consumers are driven outside the consumption sets that represent their biological survival requirements, but this is not commonly thought to be an issue requiring serious qualification of the theory.

However, if lump sum transfers are not available, the consumer's net expenditure must be zero and the government's budget must balance without transfers, i.e., the two sides of (4.5) must separately equal zero. Then

$$E - (e_0 + p \cdot e) = 0, \tag{4.6}$$

or equivalently,

$$\Pi + (p - q) \cdot c + (q - r) \cdot m - (g_0 + q \cdot g) = 0. \tag{4.7}$$

Such constraints on permissable tax and expenditure policies have corresponding implications for comparative statics. Any change in these policies must preserve general equilibrium. Thus a proposed change in just one component of α or β, or in g_0 or g by itself, will not be feasible. There will have to be an accompanying change, either in the lump sum transfers to preserve (4.5), or in another tax rate to keep each side of (4.5) separately equal to zero. Different offsetting changes of this kind will have different comparative static effects. It is common to assume all such adjustments to be made by means of lump sum transfers, but that is somewhat odd in an area of research founded on the premise of limited possibilities for tax reform.

The comparative static formulae can also differ according to the nature of the distortion or the policy. For example, a consumption tax on commodity k in specific form gives a constant wedge $(p_k - q_k)$, while one in ad valorem form makes the wedge proportional to q_k. Changes in the tax rates will affect the economy differently, especially when the commodity is non-tradeable. If the wedges are due to externalities, the components of α and β will usually depend on various consumption and production quantities, and cannot be treated as exogenous parameters. I shall use wedges in specific form for illustrative purposes because the resulting formulae look simpler, but other applications of the methods may require a different treatment.

The equilibrium conditions can now be simplified. Substituting from (4.1) and (4.2) into (4.3), we have

$$(E_0 - \Pi_0 - e_0 + g_0) + r \cdot (E_p - \Pi_q - e + g) = 0. \tag{4.8}$$

Given the world prices r and the distortions α and β, the consumer prices p and producer prices q are fixed by (4.4). Then, knowing e_0, e, g_0 and g, we can solve (4.8) for u. By totally differentiating this, we can find the welfare effects of changes in any of the exogenous magnitudes. For market failures, or when lump sum transfers are the sole accommodating adjustment, this is all. Otherwise, the changes must preserve the budget balances, i.e., satisfy one of (4.6) and (4.7) as well.

To carry out this program, begin with the total differential of (4.8),[2]

$$\begin{aligned}&\left(E_{0p}' \mathrm{d}p + E_{0u} \mathrm{d}u - \Pi_{0p}' \mathrm{d}q - \mathrm{d}e_0 + \mathrm{d}g_0\right) + m \cdot \mathrm{d}r \\ &+ r'\left(E_{pp} \mathrm{d}p + E_{pu} \mathrm{d}u - \Pi_{qq} \mathrm{d}q - \mathrm{d}e + \mathrm{d}g\right) = 0.\end{aligned}$$

[2] Observe that for two vectors a, b of the same dimension, the inner product $a \cdot b$ equals the matrix product $a' b$.

by homogeneity of E_p and Π_q, we have $E'_{0p} + p'E_{pp} = 0 = \Pi'_{0q} + q'\pi_{qq}$. Therefore the equation simplifies to

$$(E_{0u} + r \cdot E_{pu})\,\mathrm{d}u = (\mathrm{d}e_0 + r \cdot \mathrm{d}e) - (\mathrm{d}g_0 + r \cdot \mathrm{d}g)$$

$$+ (p - r)'E_{pp}\,\mathrm{d}p - (q - r')\Pi_{qq}\,\mathrm{d}q - m \cdot \mathrm{d}r. \tag{4.9}$$

The coefficient on the left-hand side is the sum of the income effects on all commodities weighted by world prices. Dixit (1975) and Hatta (1977) examined this in detail, and argued from considerations of uniqueness and stability that it should be positive; see also Section 8.1 of Auerbach's chapter in this volume. Then the sign of $\mathrm{d}u$ is the same as that of the right-hand side. There, the terms of trade effect and the values of physical changes in endowments and government expenditures are readily interpreted. Noting that $E_{pp}\mathrm{d}p$ and $\Pi_{qq}\mathrm{d}q$ are the substitution effects in consumption and production respectively, the remaining terms reflect the social worth of changing the consumption and production levels when they are non-optimal due to the distortions or taxes. Thus (4.9) is a close analogue of (2.5). The only differences are that the changes are small, and substitution effects in consumption are separated from income effects. In the present context of a small economy, the change $\mathrm{d}r$ in world prices r must be an exogenous shift. In the large-country case of Section 4.4 it will be endogenized. Now we proceed to apply (4.9) to specific contexts.

4.2. Directions of desirable reforms

Here we consider the effects on u of changes in α and β. With r, e_0, e, g_0 and g held constant, (4.9) becomes

$$(E_{0u} + r \cdot E_{pu})\,\mathrm{d}u = \alpha'E_{pp}\,\mathrm{d}\alpha - \beta'\Pi_{qq}\,\mathrm{d}\beta. \tag{4.10}$$

The most immediate result is that an equiproportionate reduction in all distortions, with a balancing lump sum transfer, increases welfare. If $\mathrm{d}\alpha = -\alpha\,\mathrm{d}z$ and $\mathrm{d}\beta = -\beta\,\mathrm{d}z$ for a small positive scalar $\mathrm{d}z$, then the right-hand side of (4.10) is $\{-\alpha'E_{pp}\alpha + \beta'\Pi_{qq}\beta\}\,\mathrm{d}z$. Since E_{pp} is negative semi-definite and Π_{qq} is positive semi-definite, this is non-negative. In fact the matrices omit the numeraire commodity, and are therefore definite so long as there is *some* substitution between that commodity and others. Therefore in practice we can rely on the welfare effect of such a "radial" reform being positive.

A special case is where there is only one distortion, i.e., all others are zero. Then any reduction in this distortion will be an improvement. (This is not self-evident, since the relevant indirect utility function need not be concave in distortion levels.) These results are due to Bruno (1972) and Hatta (1977).

Next consider a reform that changes only one distortion, say by changing the consumer price of the kth commodity. A lump sum transfer again balances the budget. Then $(E_{0u}+r\cdot E_{pu})\,\mathrm{d}u=\sum_l(p_l-r_l)E_{lk}\,\mathrm{d}p_k$, where the sum extends over all commodities l, and the numeraire can be included since $p_0=r_0=1$. Now $\sum_l p_l E_{lk}=0$, i.e., $E_{kk}=-\sum_{l\neq k}p_l E_{lk}/p_k$. Therefore the right-hand side becomes

$$\sum_{l\neq k} p_l E_{lk}\left\{\frac{p_l-r_l}{p_l}-\frac{p_k-r_k}{p_k}\right\}\mathrm{d}p_k.$$

Suppose k is the commodity with the largest proportional distortion, and we lower its consumer price slightly. Then all the terms in brackets above are negative, as is $\mathrm{d}p_k$. Therefore a welfare improvement will result if all the E_{lk} are positive, i.e., this commodity is a substitute to all others. This result was proved by Bertrand and Vanek (1971).

Finally, consider second-best reforms involving the introduction of a new distortion in response to an existing and irreversible one. As an example, consider a consumption subsidy on commodity k, i.e., $\alpha_k<0$. Consider the introduction of a small trade tax $\mathrm{d}\tau_l$ on commodity l, which increases each of α_l and β_l by this amount. Then

$$(E_{0u}+r\cdot E_{pu})\,\mathrm{d}u=\alpha_k E_{kl}\,\mathrm{d}\tau_l,$$

i.e., a welfare improvement emerges from a tariff ($\mathrm{d}\tau_l>0$) if commodities k and l are complements ($E_{kl}<0$), and from an import subsidy if they are substitutes. Of course balancing lump sum transfers are assumed to occur in the background. As we move to finite values of τ_l, a by-product distortion in the trade of commodity l is introduced, and

$$(E_{0u}+r\cdot E_{pu})\,\mathrm{d}u=\{\alpha_k E_{kl}+\tau_l(E_{ll}-\Pi_{ll})\}\,\mathrm{d}\tau_l.$$

The second-best optimum response τ_l is where the bracketed expression on the right-hand side becomes zero, i.e.,

$$\tau_l=-\alpha_k E_{kl}/(E_{ll}-\Pi_{ll}).$$

In particular, if $l=k$, the trade tax offsets the initial distortion, but only partially. Many second-best exercises of this kind can be found in Corden (1974).

In our example, observe that the tariff partly "defeats" the consumption subsidy and raises the consumer price. If the subsidy is a historical accident, or merely implicit in an external diseconomy that leaves consumers facing a price below the social opportunity costs, there may be no problem. But if the subsidy has been achieved by an organized consumer group who can see through the effect of the tariff, they can use their political power to prevent its implementation. Thus second-best remedies may not always be available.

A second critical assumption in all the above results was the presence of balancing lump sum transfers. If we do without them, the proposed reforms must preserve (4.6), i.e.,

$$E_p \cdot \mathrm{d}p + E_u \mathrm{d}u - e \cdot \mathrm{d}p = 0.$$

Combining this with (4.10), we have the constraint on the reform:

$$\{(E_{0u} + r \cdot E_{pu})/E_u\}(e - E_p)'\mathrm{d}\alpha = \alpha' E_{pp}\mathrm{d}\alpha - \beta' \Pi_{qq}\mathrm{d}\beta. \tag{4.11}$$

The welfare effect of any primary reform, e.g., the introduction or reduction of a tariff, will depend crucially on the other elements of the whole reform package. A general theoretical treatment would soon degenerate into a catalogue and a collection of apparent paradoxes. Some special cases such as the Corlett–Hague model are well known (see Section 8.2 of Auerbach's chapter in the volume), but in practice each application must be examined on its own.

We can also use (4.10) and (4.11), with an added Lagrange multiplier, to obtain first-order conditions for optimality of certain packages of policy instruments. In particular, for revenue-raising tariffs to be optimal, we need

$$\mu(e - E_p) = (E_{pp} - \Pi_{qq})\tau,$$

where μ is a scalar multiplier. The same formula can be derived from (3.16) and (3.17).

4.3. *Shadow prices of commodities and projects*

Welfare effects of changes in the consumer's endowments or the government's expenditure on commodities can also be studied using the above methods. In fact we can interpret a change $(\mathrm{d}g_0, \mathrm{d}g)$, not as a change in public consumption, but as the result of the government implementing a small project with net outputs $(-\mathrm{d}g_0, -\mathrm{d}g)$. This allows us to use the analysis for derivation of shadow prices appropriate to project selection.

When lump sum transfers are the balancing policy to preserve equilibrium, (4.9) gives

$$(E_{0u} + r \cdot E_{pu})\,\mathrm{d}u = (\mathrm{d}e_0 + r \cdot \mathrm{d}e) - (\mathrm{d}g_0 + r \cdot \mathrm{d}g). \tag{4.12}$$

In particular, the project $(-\mathrm{d}g_0, -\mathrm{d}g)$ is desirable if and only if its value at the prices $(1, r)$ is positive. In the sense used in Section 3, these prices are the shadow prices that should be used in the cost–benefit tests of small public projects. Dreze (1982) calls them "welfare prices", since they are proportional to the marginal welfare effects of amounts of the commodities.

This is the basic case for the use of world prices as shadow prices even when domestic market prices differ on account of distortions or taxes. The argument goes back to Little and Mirrlees (1969), and the debate that ensued is surveyed by Corden (1982). I shall therefore confine my discussion to some brief remarks.

Several assumptions were made in establishing the result. That of constant world prices will be removed in the next subsection; marginal border prices become the appropriate shadow prices, provided the actual tariff levels are optimum. All commodities were assumed tradeable. This will be generalized in Section 4.5, and we will see that the presence of non-tradeables does not affect the rules for shadow prices of tradeables. However, there is the question of the appropriate definition of a tradeable. The distortions in trade that were allowed took the form of price wedges. If there are quantitative restrictions such as import quotas that are binding, then at the relevant margin those commodities are not tradeable, and their shadow prices must be determined by the methods similar to those used for non-tradeables.

Perhaps the most important assumption is that the marginal adjustment in budgetary balances is carried out using lump sum transfers. If some distortionary taxes must be changed instead, the new equilibrium is described by

$$(E_{0u} + r \cdot E_{pu})\,\mathrm{d}u = (\mathrm{d}e_0 + r \cdot \mathrm{d}e) - (\mathrm{d}g_0 + r \cdot \mathrm{d}g) + \alpha' E_{pp}\mathrm{d}\alpha - \beta' \Pi_{qq}\mathrm{d}\beta,$$

and

$$E_u \mathrm{d}u = (e - E_p) \cdot \mathrm{d}\alpha.$$

Eliminating $\mathrm{d}u$, we have the constraint linking the joint changes in endowments or project outputs, and taxes. Again, it is clear that by restricting the permissible changes suitably, we can create all sorts of paradoxical results. However, we know from the work of Section 3 that if commodity taxes can be chosen optimally, then we will set $\beta = 0$, and $q = r$ will serve as the shadow price vector.

4.4. Endogenous world prices

When the home country is sufficiently large in international trade to affect the equilibrium world prices, we have to use (4.9) remembering that r depends on m through the relation $r = R(m)$, or substituting for m,

$$r = R(E_p - \Pi_q - e + g). \tag{4.13}$$

Differentiating this,

$$\mathrm{d}r = R_m(E_{pp}\mathrm{d}p + E_{pu}\mathrm{d}u - \Pi_{qq}\mathrm{d}q - \mathrm{d}e + \mathrm{d}g).$$

Using $\mathrm{d}p = \mathrm{d}r + \mathrm{d}\alpha$ and $\mathrm{d}q = \mathrm{d}r + \mathrm{d}\beta$, we have

$$\left[I - R_m(E_{pp} - \Pi_{qq})\right]\mathrm{d}r = R_m\left[E_{pu}\mathrm{d}u - \mathrm{d}e + \mathrm{d}g + E_{pp}\mathrm{d}\alpha - \Pi_{qq}\mathrm{d}\beta\right],$$

where I is the identity matrix. Assuming the matrix on the left-hand side is non-singular,

$$\mathrm{d}r = \left[I - R_m(E_{pp} - \Pi_{qq})\right]^{-1}R_m\left[E_{pu}\mathrm{d}u - \mathrm{d}e + \mathrm{d}g + E_{pp}\mathrm{d}\alpha - \Pi_{qq}\mathrm{d}\beta\right].$$

Define the vector ρ by

$$\rho' = \left[m' - \alpha'E_{pp} + \beta'\Pi_{qq}\right]\left[I - R_m(E_{pp} - \Pi_{qq})\right]^{-1}R_m. \tag{4.14}$$

Now collect terms in (4.9), and use the definition (4.14) to write

$$\begin{aligned}(E_{0u} + r\cdot E_{pu})\,\mathrm{d}u = {} & (\mathrm{d}e_0 + r\cdot \mathrm{d}e) - (\mathrm{d}g_o + r\cdot \mathrm{d}g) \\ & + \left(\alpha'E_{pp} - \beta'\Pi_{qq} - m'\right)\mathrm{d}r \\ & + \alpha'E_{pp}\mathrm{d}\alpha - \beta'\Pi_{qq}\mathrm{d}\beta,\end{aligned}$$

or

$$\begin{aligned}\left[E_{0u} + (r+\rho)\cdot E_{pu}\right]\mathrm{d}u = {} & \left[\mathrm{d}e_0 + (r+\rho)\cdot \mathrm{d}e\right] - \left[\mathrm{d}g_0 + (r+\rho)\cdot \mathrm{d}g\right] \\ & + (\alpha-\rho)'E_{pp}\mathrm{d}\alpha - (\beta-\rho)\Pi_{qq}\mathrm{d}\beta. \end{aligned} \tag{4.15}$$

This is the large-country equivalent of (4.9), since it expresses the welfare effects of exogenous changes in distortions, endowments and projects, with the necessary adjustments in lump sum taxation in each case.

Corresponding results follow. First observe that the first-order conditions for the optimum choice of α and β are $\alpha - \rho = 0 = \beta - \rho$. Substituting in (4.14),

$$\rho' = \left[m' - \rho'(E_{pp} - \Pi_{qq})\right]\left[I - R_m(E_{pp} - \Pi_{qq})\right]^{-1} R_m.$$

This is satisfied by $\rho' = m'R_m$ or $\rho = R'_m m$, which is just the optimum tariff formula (3.8). If R_m is non-singular, we have

$$\rho' R_m^{-1} - \rho'(E_{pp} - \Pi_{qq}) = m' - \rho'(E_{pp} - \Pi_{qq}),$$

and the solution is unique.

In view of the optimum, an equiproportionate reduction in all distortions should be defined as a move $\mathrm{d}\alpha = -(\alpha - \rho)\mathrm{d}z$ and $\mathrm{d}\beta = -(\beta - \rho)\mathrm{d}z$, where $\mathrm{d}z$ is a small positive scalar. Using this in (4.15), we see at once that such a move will increase welfare. The asymptotic outcome of successive reforms of this kind will be the optimum.

Now consider the effects of endowments or projects at given distortions. We have

$$\left[E_{0u} + (r+\rho)\cdot E_{pu}\right]\mathrm{d}u = \left[\mathrm{d}e_0 + (r+\rho)\cdot \mathrm{d}e\right] - \left[\mathrm{d}g_0 + (r+\rho)\cdot \mathrm{d}g\right]. \tag{4.16}$$

This looks a lot like (4.12), and using the same arguments as there, we have the shadow prices $(1, r+\rho)$. However, this is an important difference. By analogy with the small-country case, one would have thought that the shadow prices would be the world marginal rates of transformation $G_m = r + R'_m m$, whether or not actual tariffs were optimum. This is not so; the correction term ρ is more complicated. Social cost–benefit analysis in a large economy with suboptimal tax policies is therefore considerably more difficult. For further discussion of this issue, see Smith (1980).

It should be noted again that the above calculation assumes constant tax rates or distortions in specific form (α and β). Under other assumptions, e.g., constant ad valorem tax rates, the principles governing the calculation would be the same but the actual formula for ρ would be different.

Lump sum finance of the project, assumed here, is not the crucial feature; the optimality of indirect taxation is. We saw in Section 3 that the marginal border prices are the appropriate shadow prices for tradeables under optimum commodity taxation (3.7), or when optimum tariffs for revenue are used, (3.18). For a more detailed discussion of the role of optimum taxation for the characterization of shadow prices, see Roberts (1978).

4.5. Non-tradeable commodities

Prices of non-tradeables must be determined endogenously, and change in response to any changes in distortions, taxes or projects. This makes the analysis more complicated, even for a small country. Many of the results on gradual reform, e.g., the benefit from a radial reduction in all distortions, remain valid. Therefore I shall consider only the essentially new aspect of shadow prices, generalizing the model of Warr (1982). The small-country assumption is re-introduced.

Since there must be at least two tradeable commodities, take one of them as the numeraire and write the price vector for consumers as $(1, p^{\mathrm{t}}, p^{\mathrm{n}})$. Then the expenditure function will be $E(1, p^{\mathrm{t}}, p^{\mathrm{n}}, u)$ and E_{t} will denote the vector of compensated demands for tradeables, i.e., the vector of partial derivaitives of E with respect to the components of p^{t}. Similar notation will apply to production and trade. Then the equilibrium conditions are

$$E_0(1, p^{\mathrm{t}}, p^{\mathrm{n}}, u) = \Pi_0(1, q^{\mathrm{t}}, q^{\mathrm{n}}) + m_0 + e_0 - g_0, \tag{4.17}$$

$$E_{\mathrm{t}}(1, p^{\mathrm{t}}, p^{\mathrm{n}}, u) = \Pi_{\mathrm{t}}(1, q^{\mathrm{t}}, q^{\mathrm{n}}) + m^{\mathrm{t}} + e^{\mathrm{t}} - g^{\mathrm{t}}, \tag{4.18}$$

$$E_{\mathrm{n}}(1, p^{\mathrm{t}}, p^{\mathrm{n}}, u) = \Pi_{\mathrm{n}}(1, q^{\mathrm{t}}, q^{\mathrm{n}}) + e^{\mathrm{n}} - g^{\mathrm{n}}. \tag{4.19}$$

Trade balance requires

$$m_0 + r^{\mathrm{t}} \cdot m^{\mathrm{t}} = 0. \tag{4.20}$$

We are assuming constant world prices of tradeables, r^{t}, and constant price wedges $p^{\mathrm{t}} - r^{\mathrm{t}} = \alpha^{\mathrm{t}}$, $q^{\mathrm{t}} - r^{\mathrm{t}} = \beta^{\mathrm{t}}$ (thus fixing $p^{\mathrm{t}}, q^{\mathrm{t}}$), and $p^{\mathrm{n}} - q^{\mathrm{n}} = \alpha^{\mathrm{n}} - \beta^{\mathrm{n}}$. Balancing lump sum transfers are also assumed.

As before, we can combine (4.17), (4.18) and (4.20) into one equation,

$$(E_0 - \Pi_0 - e_0 + g_0) + r^{\mathrm{t}} \cdot (E_{\mathrm{t}} - \Pi_{\mathrm{t}} - e^{\mathrm{t}} + g^{\mathrm{t}}) = 0. \tag{4.21}$$

This, together with (4.19), determines u and q^{n}. If the government undertakes a small public project $(\mathrm{d}g_0, \mathrm{d}g)$, we have

$$(E_{0\mathrm{n}} \mathrm{d}p^{\mathrm{n}} + E_{0u} \mathrm{d}u - \Pi_{0\mathrm{n}} \mathrm{d}q^{\mathrm{n}} + \mathrm{d}g_0)$$

$$+ r^{\mathrm{t}} \cdot (E_{\mathrm{tn}} \mathrm{d}p^{\mathrm{n}} + E_{\mathrm{t}u} \mathrm{d}u - \Pi_{\mathrm{tn}} \mathrm{d}q^{\mathrm{n}} + \mathrm{d}g^{\mathrm{t}}) = 0,$$

and

$$E_{nn} \mathrm{d} p^{n} + E_{nu} \mathrm{d} u = \Pi_{nn} \mathrm{d} q^{n} - \mathrm{d} g^{n}.$$

Since $\mathrm{d} p^{n} = \mathrm{d} q^{n}$, these become

$$(E_{0u} + r^{t} \cdot E_{tu}) \mathrm{d} u + \left[E_{0n} - \Pi_{0n} + r^{t'}(E_{tn} - \Pi_{tn}) \right] \mathrm{d} q^{n} = -(\mathrm{d} g_{0} + r^{t} \cdot \mathrm{d} g^{t}),$$

and

$$E_{nu} \mathrm{d} u + (E_{nn} - \Pi_{nn}) \mathrm{d} q^{n} = -\mathrm{d} g^{n}.$$

So long as there is some substitution between tradeables and non-tradeables, the substitution matrix corresponding to the latter alone will be negative definite. Then we can solve the second equation for $\mathrm{d}q^{n}$, substitute in the first, and obtain $\mathrm{d}u$. To write the result more simply, define π^{n} by

$$\pi^{n'} = -\left[E'_{0n} - \Pi'_{0n} + r^{t'}(E_{tn} - \Pi_{tn}) \right] (E_{nn} - \Pi_{nn})^{-1}. \tag{4.22}$$

Thus we have

$$(E_{0u} + r^{t} \cdot E_{tu} + \pi^{n} \cdot E_{nu}) \mathrm{d} u = -(\mathrm{d} g_{0} + r^{t} \cdot \mathrm{d} t^{t} + \pi^{n} \cdot \mathrm{d} g^{n}). \tag{4.23}$$

Comparison with (4.12) enables us to interpret this at once. The shadow prices of the tradeables are still the world prices r^{t}, while π^{n} gives the shadow prices of the non-tradeables. The coefficient of $\mathrm{d}u$ on the left-hand side is the Hatta term, which should be positive for stability.

In a distortion-free economy, we have $p^{t} = q^{t} = r^{t}$, $p^{n} = q^{n}$, and by homogeneity

$$E_{0n} + p^{t'} E_{tn} + p^{n'} E_{nn} = 0 = \Pi_{0n} + q^{t'} \Pi_{tn} + q^{n'} \Pi_{nn}.$$

Then (4.22) becomes $\pi^{n} = p^{n} = q^{n}$, i.e., the shadow prices of non-tradeables equal their domestic market prices. With distortions, the two can diverge. In fact there is no general guarantee that shadow prices will remain non-negative; this is pointed out by Bhagwati, Srinivasan and Wan (1978). The issue is discussed further by Smith (1980), to pinpoint the source of the difficulties. When the non-tradeable in question is a factor that is inelastically supplied by consumers and does not affect their utilities, any consumption distortions do not matter. Production distortions ($p^{t} \neq r^{t}$) are what gives rise to gaps between the shadow prices of factors and the values of their marginal products at market prices. In fact (4.22) becomes

$$\pi^{\mathrm{n}} = -\left(\Pi_{0\mathrm{n}} + r^{\mathrm{t}\prime}\Pi_{\mathrm{tn}}\right)\Pi_{\mathrm{nn}}^{-1},$$

which in Smith's context can be seen as the value of the marginal product at world prices.

Further complications arise from monopoly power in trade, and absence of lump sum transfers; the issues should now be familiar and need not be discussed again.

5. Multi-country trade policy problems

The last three sections dealt with various aspects of trade and tax policies in one country, under the assumption that the rest of the world followed passive policies. The foreign net supply functions were fixed. They could embody any fixed policies in other countries, but did not shift in response to active changes in those policies.

In fact, several countries make policy decisions simultaneously. Each country's welfare can be affected by the policies of all, and each country is aware of this interdependence and of similar awareness or part of others. In this section I shall consider three issues that arise in this context. The first is a game-theoretical analysis of conflict and cooperation in tariff setting, the second is the possibility of a group of countries coordinating their policies for mutual benefit by forming a customs union, and the third concerns harmonization of different countries' tax systems.

5.1. Tariff setting with retaliation

We saw in Sections 2 and 3 how a country could gain by exploiting its monopoly power in trade against a passive world, and derived a formula for first-best optimum tariffs. The question of whether such gains over free trade for one country could exist even when others retaliate with their own tariffs was studied by Johnson (1953–54). His analysis has been extended by Mayer (1981), and that is the approach I adopt.

For expository simplicity, consider a model with two countries and two tradeable goods. The countries are called home and foreign, with all variables pertaining to the latter distinguished by an asterisk superscript. Let t, t^* be the two countries' *ad valorem* tariff rates on their respective import goods. Determine the equilibrium, and write $W(t, t^*)$ and $W^*(t, t^*)$ for the resulting welfare levels.

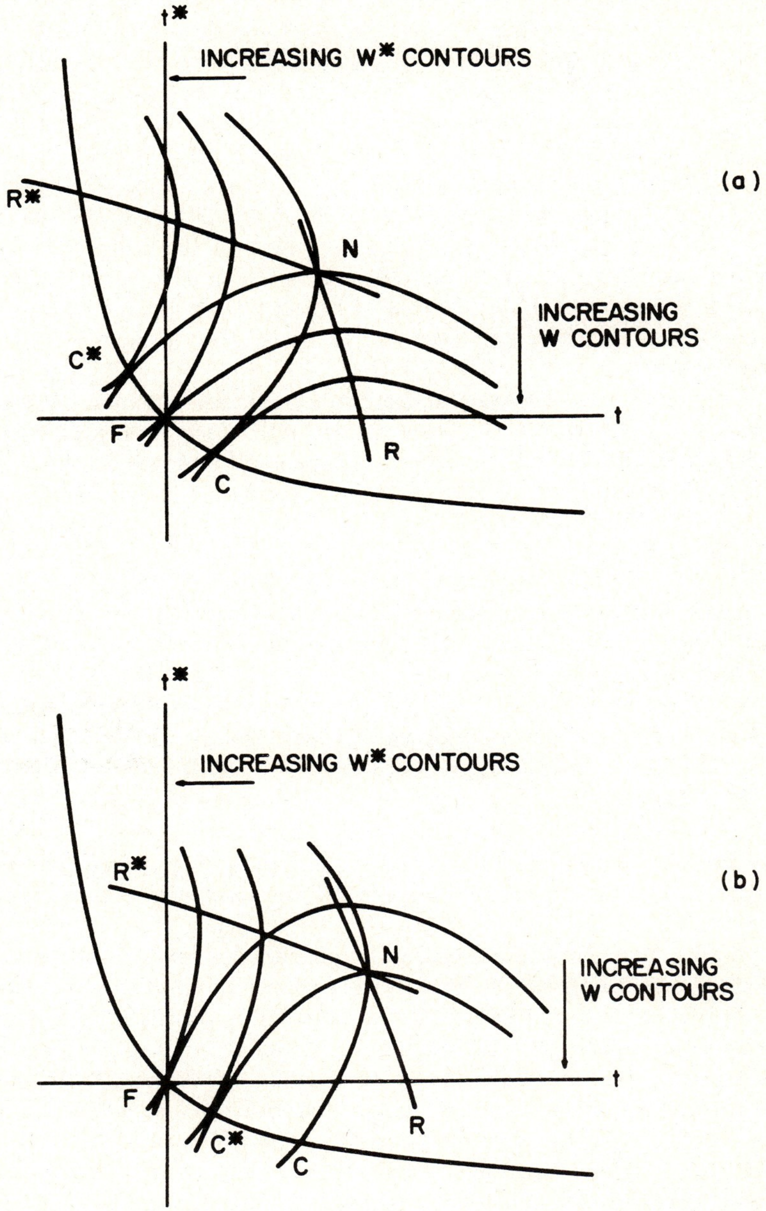
t*
INCREASING W* CONTOURS
(a)
R*
N
INCREASING
W CONTOURS
C*
t
F
R
C
t*
INCREASING W* CONTOURS
(b)
R*
N
INCREASING
W CONTOURS
t
F
R
C*
C

Figure 5.1

In the "normal" case to which I shall confine attention here, the contours of W and W^* are as shown in Figure 5.1. The countries' reaction functions R and R^*, i.e., the loci giving the home and foreign optimum choices of t and t^* corresponding to various given levels of the other country's tariff, are also shown. Detailed discussions of the slopes of these curves can be found in the references given above.

If the tariff game is played non-cooperatively, the usual notion for the outcome is the Nash equilibrium, i.e., the point N where R and R^* meet. Of course this can never be Pareto-superior to the free-trade point F; the latter is Pareto-efficient for the world. But it is possible that one of the countries prefers N to F. Such a case is in Figure (5.1b). In the case of Figure 5.1a, both countries lose from the non-cooperative tariff war relative to free trade. The problem is a standard Prisoner's Dilemma.

Now let the countries cooperate and attain an efficient outcome. Suppose the home country imports good 1, i.e., $p_1 = p_1^*(1+t)$. Similarly $p_2^* = p_2(1+t^*)$. The condition for efficiency is that the relative prices should be equal across countries, so $p_1/p_2 = p_1^*/p_2^*$, or

$$(1+t)(1+t^*) = 1.$$

This locus of Pareto-efficient outcomes is a hyperbola, and is shown in Figure 5.1. The home country prefers points to the south-east along it; the foreign country, to the north-west.

The limits of attainable points along this locus are defined by the outcome that would result if coordination broke down. Suppose this is the Nash equilibrium. Then a negotiated outcome must give each country at least as much welfare as it has at N. This defines the bargaining frontier CC^* of the negotiation game. It is interesting to observe that an outcome on this locus can never involve positive tariffs in both countries. Except at the free-trade point, which lies on the bargaining frontier in the case of Figure 5.1, at least one country must be subsidizing trade.

Economic theory has its usual difficulties in singling out a point on the frontier, or even ruling out a breakdown. Relative bargaining strengths of the countries can vary, depending on their abilities to make credible threats or promises, and their patience and incentives to maintain a reputation if the game is repeated over time. These issues are discussed at length in Schelling (1960, chs. 2, 3, 5), and have implications for tariff negotiations, but not in the form of clear predictions of the outcome.

We can also pose questions similar to those of Section 4 in a many-country world, and look for beneficial gradual reform of all trade policies on a cooperative basis. An example of this is in Hatta and Fukushima (1979). They show that similar rules, e.g., a proportional reduction in all tariffs or a reduction in the largest tariff alone, yield potential benefit to the world. To be precise, the utility possibility frontier for the world shifts outward. International transfers of purchasing power may be necessary if these benefits are to be distributed into a Pareto improvement for the countries.

A case where one country uses trade policy as a second-best response to international externalities is examined by Markusen (1975). The first-best would require coordinated Pigovian taxation, and questions of distribution of gains among countries would arise.

5.2. *Customs unions*

Here we consider a group of countries, with disparate initial trade and tax regimes, getting together to coordinate policies to their mutual benefit. The cooperation may occur in different dimensions. A free-trade area abolishes tariffs among member countries, but allows each to set its own trade policy with non-members. A customs union has free trade among members and common external tariffs against non-members. A common market or economic union will involve further coordination, e.g., in fiscal and monetary policies, migration, etc.

The case of a customs union has been the one most extensively studied. As neither the pre-union nor the post-union outcome is one of complete free trade, the change is subject to the general problem of the second-best. This is the form in which it was first studied. The comparative statics of the move from an arbitrary initial regime to a set of common tariffs at arbitrary rates was examined, and yielded categories of trade-creation which was beneficial, and trade-diversion which could be harmful. The net effect was ambiguous. This literature is surveyed by Lipsey (1970) and Corden (1982).

However, from a normative or policy standpoint, we want to know whether it is possible to *choose* a common tariff to ensure benefit, even though some other level of it may be harmful. This should in principle present no difficulty. It is always possible to arrange the common external tariffs so that non-member countries face the same trading prices as they did before the union. The internal free trade leads to equalization of producer prices in member countries, which is a clear gain in efficiency. The only question is whether the gain can be distributed to consumers. Ohyama (1972) showed how this could be done using lump sum transfers. Dixit and Norman (1980a) extended the proposition to the case where there are no lump sum transfers across or within countries, but commodity taxation can be suitably arranged. These tax or subsidy rates can differ across member countries, but a configuration can be cooperatively implemented to the benefit of all members. An added advantage is that the composition of trade with non-members is exactly the same as before the union, so they are not hurt by the change either. Thus a customs union, with some coordination of the member countries' tax policies, can be arranged to ensure a Pareto improvement over the status quo. The proofs, and the conditions, are the same as those for similar exercises in Section 2, and there are therefore left to the readers.

5.3. Tax harmonization

International conflicts of interest are not confined to trade policies. In general equilibrium, any domestic policy measure by any country can affect all of them. In particular, consider a country's domestic production and consumption taxes or subsidies. We know that a combination of a production subsidy and a consumption tax at equal rates is tantamount to a tariff if the commodity is being imported, and an export subsidy if it is being exported. Thus one might regard a consumption tax on its own, or a production subsidy on its own, as partial substitutes for import restrictions, or export promotion, as the case may be. Import restrictions can harm other countries; export subsidies are regarded as "unfair" trade practices; GATT codes attempt to limit both. Consumption and production taxation has a legitimate domestic policy role for correcting externalities, raising revenues, etc. Ambiguities and conflicts arise when the legitimate policies are used in pursuit of the "harmful" or "unfair" trade aims. The issues involve political and strategic aspects that cannot be resolved here. But simple economic analysis helps correct some misconceptions and establish the economic facts concerning the damage that is alleged.

A case in point arises as follows. The theory speaks of taxing production and consumption *activities*; in practice taxes are collected at points of *transactions*, primarily sales. In any open economy, a production tax can be implemented by taxing sales of commodities which originate in the home country; this is the "origin principle". A consumption tax should similarly be implemented using the "destination principle", i.e., sales would be subject to tax when the buyer was home-based. An alternative is to use the origin method and then apply a "border tax adjustment", i.e., refund the tax for exports, and levy it on imports as if they were produced when brought into the country. This is the method commonly used for the E.E.C.'s Value Added Tax. The import-restricting or export-promoting aspect of a consumption tax is most visible in this border tax adjustment. The United States which rely mostly on direct taxes for which there is no border tax adjustment, have at times regarded such adjustments applied by other countries as unfair trade practices. This has led to calls for international tax harmonization using the origin principle.

Theoretical analyses of the problem generally consider uniform ad valorem taxes on all goods. Since only relative prices matter, such systems are neutral in their effects on trade. The clearest recent statement of this for our purpose is in Grossman (1980). First consider the case where there are no intermediate goods. Let r_k be the prices in the rest of the world, t_0 the origin-based tax rate in ad valorem form, and t_D the similar destination-based rate. Under origin-basing, home producers will receive $r_k/(1+t_0)$, so the relative prices they face will be, for goods 1 and 2, $[r_1/(1+t_0)]/[r_2/(1+t_0)]=r_1/r_2$. Consumers face prices r_k directly. Thus there is no distortion; the tax is effectively a pure rent tax on the incomes of the (inelastically supplied) primary factors. Under destination-basing, home producers face prices r_k and consumers, $r_k(1+t_D)$. Again there is no distortion, and the tax acts like a lump sum tax on the consumers' incomes (rents to the primary factors they supply).

If there are intermediate goods, the neutrality result persists so long as the tax applies to the value added at the processing stage just prior to the taxed transaction. Grossman demonstrates this, and shows how distortions can arise under other systems. In particular, he argues that a change to origin-basing, given the way the value added tax in the E.E.C. is administered, can work against U.S. interests.

Non-uniform tax systems will not be neutral with regard to trade. Theory alone can say little about the likely effects. Hamilton and Whalley (1983) have solved a numerical model of world trade to study the border tax adjustment issue mentioned above. They find that the welfare effects are small in comparison with wider issues of trade liberalization. But the U.S. gets some aggregate net benefit from the existing systems in Europe and Japan. This is because the U.S. is a net importer of manufactured goods from these regions, and such goods have higher rates of taxation there. A border tax adjustment would act like an export tax and worsen the U.S. terms of trade. Of course import-competing producers in the U.S. may gain at the expense of the rest of the economy.

6. Some further topics

The subject of the normative theory of international trade is too large to permit an exhaustive treatment here. In Section 1, I explained the limitations, some imposed by the state of the subject, others self-imposed. In the same way, I have selected three topics for brief treatment in this section. The first is that of quotas, whose practical relevance is running ahead of their theoretical analysis. The second is effective protection, which has been thoroughly analyzed, but is not so centrally placed in the public economics aspects which are my focus here. Finally, there is political economy, or the "positive" study of the effects of conflicting interest groups on the conduct of trade policy.

6.1. Quotas and non-tariff barriers

The traditional instruments of trade policy are tariffs, and the bulk of the theory of the subject is concerned with their effects. However, in recent years, various multilateral agreements have greatly reduced tariff levels, while quotas and other non-tariff barriers to trade have become much more prominent. Theory is beginning to catch up with these developments. Here I shall briefly review some work on quotas.

At the level of Walrasian general equilibrium, no new theory is needed. Each quota or other quantitative restriction has its rent or shadow price. The restriction could be replaced by a tariff at this rate, and the same equilibrium allocation would result, expect perhaps for differential income effects if the tariff revenues and the quota rents are differently distributed. A particularly important practical difference is that significant portions of quota rents go to foreign suppliers, especially if they own distribution channels for imports in the home country. The transfer of rents may be total if the quotas are implemented as "voluntary" export restrictions by other countries. In practice, if the policy bureaucracy allocates the quotas inefficiently, and re-sales cannot occur to restore efficiency, there will be further dead-weight losses which the "equivalent" tariff would have avoided.

Tariffs and quotas can differ in their allocative effects once we step outside the Walrasian model. The case of monoply is discussed, among others, by Bhagwati (1965) and McCulloch (1973), and I shall not repeat those issues here. Even within the Walrasian context, differences arise when the alternative policies are used in a "second-best" context. The equivalence noted above arises when it is possible to choose the rates of tariffs or quotas independently on all economically distinguishable commodities. When it is necessary to choose a common tariff rate for a group of commodities, or a quota applicable to the total of quantities of imports over such a group, we have in each case a second-best policy, and it is not possible to say in general how they will compare with each other.

A case in point is where trade takes place at several dates, with different technologies and preferences at each. The fully optimal policy will select appropriately time-varying tariffs or their equivalent time-varying quotas. Now suppose policy must be fixed in advance, in common for all periods. A uniform quota of this kind will have a shadow price that changes over time, while a uniform tariff will give rise to a changing trade pattern. Which second-best policy will come closer to the full optimum in the sense of producing a smaller welfare loss? The answer depends on the exact nature of the time dependence of the underlying conditions. A similar problem arises when some parameters of the model change. Comparative statics of a tariff regime will differ from those of a quota regime.

Another setting that has been studied a great deal is that of uncertainty. If the policy instruments must be set in advance, i.e., apply at a common rate across all states of the world, similar problems arise. Following the technique developed by Weitzman (1974), such comparisons have been made by Fishelson and Flatters (1975), Pelcovitz (1976) and others. The answers depend on the nature of the uncertainty, and on the slopes of demand and supply curves, as well as on other constraints or targets in the optimization problem. A special case of some interest is where a policy constrained in this way happens to yield the full optimum. This occurs in Young and Anderson (1980). Consider a partial equilibrium setting in which imports m of the good in question yield benefit $B(m)$, so the domestic price is $B'(m)=p$. The foreign price in state s of the world is $p^*(s)$, and the probability of this state occurring is $\theta(s)$. It is desired to maximize expected net benefit

$$\sum_s \theta(s)\{B(m(s))-p^*(s)m(s)\},$$

subject to a constraint on expected import cost

$$\sum_s \theta(s)p^*(s)m(s)\leq \overline{M}.$$

Introducing a multiplier μ for the constraint, the first-order conditions when imports can be varied across states of the world are

$$\theta(s)\{B'(m(s))-p^*(s)\}-\mu\theta(s)p^*(s)=0,$$

i.e.,

$$p(s)=(1+\mu)p^*(s).$$

This policy can be implemented by an ad valorem tariff at rate μ common to all states. If the constraint were on the expected quantity of imports, a uniform specific tariff would be best. More generally, trade restrictions under uncertainty create potential arbitrage gains in shifting contingent quotas across states of nature, and can serve as second-best replacements for missing contingent markets.

A case of particular interest arises when financial markets exist as a partial substitute for complete contingent markets. Helpman and Razin (1980) consider tax and tariff policy in such an economy, and extend several of the targeting results.

Finally, consider a situation of even greater practical relevance. In practice, it is never possible to distinguish commodities as finely as the theoretical ideal, and tariffs or quotas must be levied on relatively broad commodity groups. Thus a country may have a choice between a tariff and a quota on the commodity group "automobiles". In fact there are different kinds of automobiles, less than perfectly substitutable for each other in production as well as consumption. A higher level optimum policy would choose a separate quota, or its equivalent tariff, for each kind. Which of the two coarser policies, a common tariff or a group quota, would come closer to the optimum?

In practice, such groups usually involve commodities that are quite good substitutes for one another. The presumption from optimum taxation theory would be that such commodities should be taxed at nearly equal ad valorem rates. Any departure from this would alter relative prices and cause large substitutions (quantity changes) with their associated dead-weight losses. In our context, this can be seen most easily from the optimum tariff formula (3.8). For simplicity of exposition, suppose the matrix R_m is symmetric, as is the case if preferences in the rest of the world are homothetic (a common assumption in trade theory) or income effects on the group of commodities in question are negligible. Then

$$\tau_k = \sum_l m_l(\partial r_k/\partial m_l),$$

and for $k = 1, 2$,

$$\tau_1/r_1 - \tau_2/r_2 = \sum_l \partial \log(r_1/r_2)/\partial \log m_l.$$

When these commodities are very good substitutes in the rest of the world's excess supply, (r_1/r_2) is nearly constant and (τ_1/r_1) should be close to (τ_2/r_2).

In such a case, a uniform ad valorem tariff for the group will closely approximate the full optimum policy. We can also see how a quota for the group will depart from optimality. The shadow price of the quota will provide the wedge between the domestic price and the world price for each commodity in the group, i.e., it will act like a uniform specific tariff. This will imply too low ad valorem tariffs on the commodities with higher world prices, and too high tariffs on ones with low world prices. The rest of the world's supply will accordingly substitute away from the latter and towards the former. Such "quality upgrading" of imports in response to quotas is often observed in practice. It can greatly reduce the effect on domestic employment or output that the trade restriction was designed to achieve. Baldwin (1982) discusses in greater detail this and related undesirable consequences of quantitative restrictions on trade.

6.2. *Effective protection*

Most of the above analysis is based on a very general model of production, which permits all kinds of final goods, intermediate goods and primary factors, tradeable or non-tradeable. All the results concerning welfare effects of policy changes, characterization of optimum policies, etc. are valid in correspondingly general circumstances. All that is needed is convexity of the set of feasible net outputs of each sector, and therefore of the economy as a whole.

It only remains to interpret the results in specific contexts. For pure intermediate goods, for example, consumption optimality conditions are irrelevant, and only the production and trade conditions like (3.6) and (3.7) matter. These imply equalization of marginal rates of transformation through domestic production and trade, which includes preservation of production efficiency.

The traditional theory of trade involving intermediate goods introduces the new concepts of effective tariffs and effective protection. The starting point is that the extent to which a productive activity is encouraged or discouraged depends on the protection available not only to its output but also to its inputs. Tariffs raise the home price of a commodity above the world price. Thus output tariffs should make an activity more profitable and encourage it, while input tariffs should make it more costly and discourage it. Intuition suggests that the net effect should depend on whether the value added per unit scale of this activity at domestic prices exceeds that at world prices. Measuring the scale by the gross output, and letting a_{kl} be the input of the kth good per unit gross output of the lth, the excess of value added at domestic prices above that at world prices is

$$\left\{(r_l+\tau_l)-\sum_k(r_k+\tau_k)a_{kl}\right\}-\left\{r_l-\sum_k r_k a_{kl}\right\}=\tau_l-\sum_k\tau_k a_{kl}. \tag{6.1}$$

This is called the *effective tariff* rate (in specific rather than ad valorem form) for the activity of producing good l. It is supposed to be a determinant of the gross output of this good in the same way that the *nominal tariff* rate τ_l relates to the net output. We now examine whether this works, and whether it can help us in our normative analysis.

In conventional welfare economics, gross outputs or sectoral activity levels are of no concern. What matters is the net production that is available to consumers. And, as Ethier (1977) puts the matter succinctly: "...regardless of the structure of intermediate goods, nominal rates measure the distortions in the terms at which the domestic economy can transform available quantities of goods into each other." This is the implicit content of the general results of Sections 2–4 when applied to models with intermediate goods; explicit derivations of these propositions can be found in Ray (1980).

Gross outputs may enter the analysis via non-economic constraints. As usual, dynamic considerations from a more complex model lie behind these. A typical case is where changes in the terms of trade dictate contraction of some industries, and adversely affect the employment or real incomes of primary factors specific to these. Then there is pressure to maintain the levels of such activities above some floor, and tariff protection is proposed. When such industries use intermediate inputs, is the relevant concept that of effective protection?

At one level, protection of any kind is irrelevant. The theory of Sections 3.1–3.2 continues to apply, and in particular the principle of targeting remains valid. The best way to compensate the losers is not tariff protection at all, whether nominal or effective. It is a subsidy which raises the incomes of the owners of the factors in question, and encourages their employment by firms, without creating any by-product distortions elsewhere. This is discussed in Dixit and Norman (1980a, pp. 184–185).

Now suppose these superior policies are not available, and tariff protection must be used. We can always express each gross output in terms of all nominal tariff rates, and proceed. What is gained by using certain combinations of nominal tariff rates in the manner of (6.1)? If gross outputs can be expressed as functions of just these combinations, there will be some economy of notation and information.

Matters are relatively simple if the input coefficients (a_{kl}) are constant, but otherwise, serious problems arise. It is not clear whether formula (6.1) should be used with the coefficients appropriate to world prices, domestic prices, or some "average". The coefficients are functions of the relative prices of all inputs, intermediate and primary. The domestic prices of the former involve the nominal tariff rates. If these re-enter the analysis in this way, the economy of information is lost. Suitable separability in production may help, but its exact nature and role are unclear. These matters are discussed by Ethier (1977) and Jones and Neary (1982, sec. 3.1).

In some cases the magnitude of interest is not the gross output but something else, e.g., the real return to a primary factor specific to this sector. In each such case, a different combination of nominal rates can be relevant.

Finally, implementation of the policy must be in the form of taxes on international movements of commodities, i.e., the setting of *nominal* tariffs. Therefore it might be better to conduct the analysis in these terms throughout.

To sum up, Samuelson's dictum about consumer surplus seems to apply equally well to effective protection: the concept can safely be used only by those who understand it sufficiently well to do without it.

6.3. Political economy

The mainstream theory of public finance has been normative. It postulates a social welfare function, embodying alternative desiderata of efficiency, equity, etc., and the trade-offs among them. It then assumes that the available policy instruments are chosen to maximize this function, subject to constraints of technology, resource availability, compatibility with individual behavior, etc. The results consist of characterizations of optimum policies. The analysis of trade policy that was reviewed above belongs squarely in this tradition.

In recent years, an alternative "positive" view of the process of economic policy making has emerged. Here the policy choices are assumed to result from political action by interested individuals or groups. This literature has been surveyed by Mueller (1979). The branch that is most pertinent to the concerns of this chapter comes from Tullock (1967), Posner (1975) and, most importantly, Krueger (1974). This article led to a large volume of research on the political economy of trade policy; a recent extension and synthesis can be found in Bhagwati (1982).

The underlying idea is as follows. Most of the government's economic policy measures involve the creation or destruction of revenues, profits or rents. Tariffs and taxes produce revenues, subsidies disburse them; quotas create rents; regulation and deregulation can increase or decrease profits depending on the circumstances. Individuals and groups have incentives to obtain these benefits for themselves, and therefore to expend some resources on activities that promote the appropriate policies. These activities can range from lobbying for a tariff to bribing an official to secure the allocation of a quota. Consumers might wish to lobby for less protection, in the interests of lower prices. The success of such activities, singly or in competition with each other, will depend on circumstances. Groups will have to solve an internal free-rider problem to mount such efforts; thus diffuse consumer groups may be at a disadvantage relative to concentrated producers' lobbies.

These profit-seeking activities (the term being understood to include all the kinds mentioned above) do not produce any commodities for consumption. Rather, they produce income transfers, and may also in the process affect some distortions in the economic equilibrium. To the extent that the activities require economic resources (factor inputs), less is available for production of consumable commodities. Even when the primary activity is a pure transfer, such as a bribe, incentives will arise to spend resources in an activity that will help some individual to attain the position where he can receive such bribes. So long as there is some stage at which the relevant profit-seeking activity requires factor inputs and "produces" the profits or rents at constant returns to scale, the entire profit will in equilibrium accure as payments to those factors. In general, there will be at least a partial transformation of the rent or profit into such real resource cost.

Now let us return to our normative viewpoint and assess the economic cost of the policy in question. When there is profit seeking, this comprises not merely the conventional dead-weight burden of the distortion caused by the policy, but also that part (or whole) of the profit that is transformed into factor payments in the seeking activity. The presumption is that the efficiency costs of distortionary policies can be much higher when they are instituted by the process of profit seeking. This is the conclusion of Posner (1975) with regard to monopoly profits, and Krueger (1974) for tariffs and quotas.

Needless to say, further analysis produces several arguments qualifying this presumption. First, not all such activities work toward increasing distortions. A consumer lobby, if it overcame the free-rider problem, might achieve removal of an existing tariff. The efficiency gain from this policy must then be set against the resource cost of the lobbying. Or there may be a pre-existing tariff, and the lobbying may be intended solely to obtain its revenue. Now the price wedge is unchanged, but the move of some resources from the production sectors to the lobbying sector alters the output and trade levels. Since this is a change that takes place in an already distorted economy, it may prove to be beneficial as an instance of the paradox of the second-best. More specifically, we may have a case where the withdrawal of some inputs from productive activities raises the value of the national product at the appropriate shadow prices, which is immiserizing growth run backwards. Bhagwati (1982) discusses and catalogues the various possibilities.

In an economy with rent seeking, the shadow prices appropriate for project evaluation are also affected. Foster (1981) examines this issue, and shows that in some circumstances market prices should be used despite the presence of distortions. The best-known example is the Harris–Todaro model of a developing economy, where migrants from the rural sector spend resources (their own labor time while unemployed in the urban-sector) seeking the institutionally fixed high urban wage. Let w_r, w_u be the wages and marginal products in the two sectors, L the urban labor force, and E the urban employment. Assuming equal probability of employment for all in the urban labor force, and risk neutrality, the expected-wage equalization condition for equilibrium is $w_r = w_u(E/L)$. Now an urban-sector project that employs one person induces additional migration to increase the urban labor force by L/E, and causes the loss of $w_r(L/E) = w_u$ in the form of rural output. This is the opportunity cost of hiring the person, and therefore the shadow wage.

7. Empirical work

Kenen (1975, preface) expressed concern that international trade had become "the last refuge of the speculative theorist". That could never be quite true so long as debates on capital flourished; rapid growth of applied work on trade issues has made it even less valid. Such research on welfare and policy issues was surveyed in the Kenen volume by Corden (1975) and Magee (1975, sec. 4). More recent work is discussed by Greenway (1983, chs. 6, 9, 11). Here I shall give a very selective review of the problems and the literature; a fuller treatment would require at least a chapter by itself.

7.1. General issues and problems

It must be recognized at the outset that empirical work in this area faces formidable problems. Data are at least as scarce and error-prone as in work involving one country, and in addition are often incompatible across countries in coverage and classification. Trade data may also be incompatible with the industrial statistics for each country. There have been some improvements; note for example the sources used by Baldwin (1979, p. 12). But empirical implementation of the theory in an ideal way is still not possible.

Consider the information requirements of the theory developed in Sections 2–4. We need functions representing preferences and technologies, whether in primal form or dual. We need the first-order derivatives of these functions (the demands and supplies), and in places the second-order derivatives (the income and price elasticities of demand and supplies). In principle, we might attempt to estimate flexible functional forms, e.g., trans-log, but reality is some way off. Demand estimates are usually for imports or exports as a whole, or at most a few major commodity categories. In each case, the right-hand side variables are usually confined to income, own price, and sometimes the price of one close substitute. On the production side, detailed input–output tables are available, but information on elasticities of substitution among inputs is very poor.

Even if better data were available, serious econometric problems would remain. In the absence of a carefully specified model of the whole world, estimation of any one demand or supply equation suffers from the usual simultaneity bias. Secondly, since we hope to use the estimation as the basis for calculating the effects of policy changes, the the whole exercise is subject to the Lucas critique: the estimated parameters need not be stable in face of the policy shift.

There are faults on the side of the theory, too. It is the traditional metastatic model of general equilibrium. Therefore it leaves out several important aspects of the real world: increasing returns and imperfect competition, disequilibrium dynamics including adjustment lags and unemployment, money, exchange rates, trade imbalance and a whole lot more. Applied work, both in estimation and in prediction, has to make ad hoc modifications to the model to handle these features where they are deemed important.

One other item that figured prominently in our normative theory was the social welfare function. Applied work has usually stayed well clear of this. Welfare effects are often measured in terms of real income, i.e., concentrating on efficiency and ignoring distribution. Sometimes the effects of a policy on common ad hoc criteria such as employment or the trade balance are computed, with no attempt to fit them into a welfare framework.

When measuring the effects of trade policies, it is important but difficult to pay attention to quantitative restrictions. As measured by their tariff equivalents, they are usually several times more important than explicit tariffs, and dead-weight losses increase faster than linearly with the distortion. However, calculation of the tariff equivalent is no easy matter.

7.2. Marshallian surplus calculations

The first group of actual empirical studies I shall outline is based on the Marshallian methodology, i.e., welfare effects are calculated from the areas of dead-weight loss triangles. Consumer demand functions for individual commodities or groups are either taken from other prior work, or estimated for the purpose. Supply curves are similarly estimated; sometimes they are assumed to be infinitely elastic. Demands for intermediate inputs are handled in some studies by using an input–output table, and neglected in others.

The article by Magee (1972) is clearly worthy of leadership in this list. He computes the welfare effects for the U.S. of various hypothetical policy changes assumed to be implemented in 1971. Some distinguishing features of the work are as follows: (1) It is recognized that changes in dead-weight losses are annual flows, and that the costs of a distortion (or benefits of removing one) will increase over time, because of economic growth, and also because demands and supplies become more elastic in the long run. Adjustment costs (primarily unemployment) of policy changes are also taken into account; these diminish over time. The net effect is calculated using discounted present values. (2) Imports are classified into those which compete directly with U.S. production and those which do not; the price and production effects of tariff changes are calculated separately for the two using different elasticities. (3) Quantitative restrictions are handled by estimating their equivalent tariffs. (4) Macroeconomic effects on the government's budget and monetary policy, exchange rates, etc. are ignored.

Some of the central results are summarized in Table 7.1, adapted from Magee's table 13. They show that the U.S. stands to gain significantly from free-trade policies of its own or its trading partners, and that most of the gains come from elimination of quantitative restrictions. One suspects that these figures are underestimates since they neglect economies of scale, reduction of domestic monopoly power due to increased competition from imports, etc. One also suspects that the conclusions hold even more strongly in 1982 than they did in 1972, given the increased importance of quantitative restrictions in the intervening period.

Several studies were motivated by the multilateral trade negotiations under the auspices of GATT. Those attempting to compute potential benefits from the

Table 7.1
Gains to the U.S. economy from relaxation of trade restrictions ($ billions in discounted present values at 8%, 1971 prices).

Removal of U.S. import restrictions	
Tariffs: Directly competitive imports	19.55
Other imports	13.57
Quantitative restrictions	88.25
Removal of other countries' restrictions on U.S. exports	
Manufactures	11.40
Agriculture (mostly QRs)	125.16

Tokyo Round were carried out while the negotiations were in progress. Thus they missed the actual outcome in all its glory: most tariffs were to be cut from their existing levels t to new levels t' according to the formula $t' = 16t/(16+t)$. I shall use assumptions about cuts that are roughly comparable across studies.

Cline et al. (1978) examine several tariff cut formulae, and calculate the effects on trade patterns, employment, and overall welfare for several countries. These are short-run or impact effects, expressed in annual terms. Equilibrating changes in exchange rates and terms of trade are allowed, but found to be small in practice for the uniform multilateral tariff cuts considered. The economies are assumed to operate with enough slack to ignore full-employment constraints, and macroeconomic policies are assumed to be passive. Cross-effects both in demand and of the input–output kind in production are ignored.

For a 60% cut in all tariffs in all countries, it is estimated that the U.S. static welfare gains would be $490 million/year. (The total for U.S., Canada, E.E.C. and Japan is $1.4 billion/year.) This would be doubled if quantitative restrictions on textiles were also reduced pro rata. Import-competing industries would lose 90,000 jobs, but export industries would gain 120,000, representing a small net effect (gain of 30,000). Similar results are found for other industrial countries. LDCs are seen to score impressive increases in exports, but overall welfare effects are not given. The effects of removal of quantitative restrictions on textiles are particularly impressive.

Baldwin et al. (1980) conduct a similar analysis. The added features are : (1) Domestic and imported goods are imperfect substitutes. (2) Detailed input–output tables are used for the calculation of indirect effects in production. (3) One-year impact effects are found and capitalized at 10%. The policy change is a uniform 50% tariff cut in all countries. Quantitative restrictions are not removed. The welfare and employment effects for the U.S. are calculated. The benefits at 1967 prices come to $1056 million, swamping the one-off costs of adjustments of

$37 million for labor and $5 million for capital. The employment effect is small (a net loss of 15,400 jobs) as is the terms of trade effect (a 0.003% improvement).

The welfare gains are smaller than those found by Cline et al., and much smaller than Magee's figures. Recall that his figures for the complete removal of tariffs on U.S. imports and exports amount to $40 billion. If demand curves are linear, a 50% cut will achieve 75% of this gain. Magee allows the gains to increase over time at 4% due to growth, and further due to increases in elasticities through time. He also discounts them at a smaller rate. However, it seems that a sizeable discrepancy would remain even if the calculations of Baldwin et al. were modified to do the same.

Baldwin and Murray (1977) examine the effect of the same 50% multilateral tariff reduction on the LDCs. They find substantial benefits (over $2 billion discounted present value) in trade creation, swamping by a factor of 10 the losses that arise as generally lower tariffs erode the special advantage the LDCs have under GSP (Generalized System of Preferences). But they do not compute terms of trade shifts and the consequent welfare changes.

7.3. Computable general equilibrium models

The next group of studies has a closely related methodology, but a tighter general equilibrium framework. Specific functional forms are assumed for preferences and production functions; these are usually CES or some variant. The model is not subjected to any systematic econometric estimation. Some parameters are given values estimated in other contexts; others are educated guesses. Sensitivity studies are often carried out to check how critical the choices are. Finally, some parameters, typically scaling factors, are selected so as to replicate the initial situation as an equilibrium; this is called calibration.

The new equilibrium following the policy change is then solved numerically, using Scarf's algorithm or some other method. The price and quantity changes are thus found; the welfare change is implicit in the preferences and is usually converted to monetary measures for ease of interpretation. Thus the method is purely comparative-static, and ignores any disequilibrium or dynamic adjustment following the policy change.

The methodology is explained in detail for the case of international trade by Shoven and Whalley (1974), and a survey of several applications is in Shoven and Whalley (1983).

To illustrate the approach and compare the results with the Marshallian one, let us consider two studies of the Tokyo Round, Deardorff and Stern (1981) and Whalley (1982). These were carried out after the negotiations were complete, and use the actual cuts agreed, unlike the Baldwin and Cline studies outlined before. The two also differ from each other. Deardorff and Stern (i) treat individual countries, (ii) have no production substitution in their main calculation, and (iii) neglect most proposed changes in quantitative restrictions on the grounds that they were only advisory, and not quantifiable. Whalley (i) considers four country blocks, (ii) allows production substitution, and (iii) deals separately with the effects of the tariff cuts, and of best guesses about how the changes in quantitative restrictions would operate.

The results are qualitatively similar. Tariff cuts give most industrial countries welfare gains. Depending on the method used, Deardorff and Stern obtain totals ranging from \$1.1 billion/year to \$4.3 billion/year. Whalley's U.S., E.E.C. and Japan blocks total gains of \$3.84 billion/year. These figures are in the same range as those of the other studies discussed above. The present authors describe gains as small, being under 0.1% of GNP, but it is not clear why that is a relevant comparison. Employment and exchange rate figures are again small.

The striking new feature is that LDCs can lose as a result of tariff cuts. Deardorff and Stern find welfare losses for most LDCs, with their total ranging from \$112 million/year to \$63 million/year. Whalley's block labelled "Rest of the World", which includes LDCs, loses a more substantial \$1.96 billion/year. Whalley attributes this to terms of trade shifts. The reason in Deardorff and Stern's case is less clear, but there are some countries that suffer substantial losses of trade volume and employment. This is in contrast to the gains found by Cline et al. and Baldwin and Murray.

The effect of quantitative restrictions (non-tariff barriers) is evident from Whalley's results. Table 7.2, adapted from Whalley's table 4, highlights the differences. The reversal of fortunes between the E.E.C. and the "Rest of the World" is remarkable.

I shall mention two more studies to illustrate different applications of the method. Goulder, Shoven and Whalley (1983) examine the issue of international capital mobility. For a small country in a perfect international capital market, the

Table 7.2
Welfare effects measured by Hicksian compensating variations, in \$ billions/year.

Policy change	E.E.C.	U.S.	Japan	Rest of the World	Total
Tariffs cut	2.47	0.43	0.97	−1.93	1.94
Non-tariff barriers lowered	−4.04	1.48	0.38	3.64	1.46
The two together	−2.26	2.26	0.97	2.26	3.23

domestic tax treatment of saving does not affect investment at home; only the net lending abroad is changed. Similarly, a tax distorting the return to investment does not affect saving. In a world without capital mobility, both policies affect the common equilibrium level of domestic saving and investment. Thus the considerations of relative merits of personal income and consumption taxes, and alternative methods of corporate profit taxation, hinge upon the degree of capital mobility. The results show that the empirical importance of this is substantial. Consider a shift from income to consumption basing in personal taxation. Without capital flows, the U.S. economy stands to gain more than $500 billion in discounted present value terms in the central case. With high capital mobility, there can be a welfare loss of almost the same magnitude, because there are large capital outflows which earn only the net-of-foreign-tax return.

Heady and Mitra (1982) introduce an optimization approach, in contrast to the comparisons of two particular policies that characterized the above studies. They use an explicit social welfare function incorporating interpersonal distribution judgments. They also consider cases where the tax instruments are so limited that production efficiency may not be desirable; a systematic theoretical treatment would be quite difficult. Examples based on data on Brazil and India are studied. In particular, they examine the third-best role of tariffs for redistribution when commodity taxation is limited. The answers depend very sensitively on the redistribution parameter and the elasticity of substitution in production.

8. Concluding comment

There is a story of an eminent economist who, when he was a mere lecturer and department chairmen were in a position to give him orders, was asked to teach a course in international trade, a subject in which he was not then an expert. After spending three weeks studying the literature, he announced his finding to his colleagues: "I have been reading all about international trade, and it is just like any other economics." I hope this brief survey will suffice to convince readers that trade policy is just like any other public economics. More importantly, I hope it will contribute to the acceleration of the recent and welcome trend towards the routine incorporation of international trade in public finance models.

References

Anderson, J.E. and L. Young, 1982, The optimality of tariff quotas under uncertainty, Journal of International Economics 13, 337–351.

Atkinson, A.B. and N.H. Stern, 1974, Pigou, taxation, and public goods, Review of Economic Studies 41, 119–128.

Atkinson, A.B. and J.E. Stiglitz, 1980, Lectures on public economics (McGraw-Hill, New York).

Baldwin, R.E., 1979, Measuring trade and employment effects of various trade policies, in: R. Baldwin, R. Stern and H. Kierzkowski, eds., Evaluating the effects of trade liberalization (A.W. Sijthoff, Leiden).
Baldwin, R.E., 1982, The inefficacy of trade policy, Essay in international finance no. 150 (Princeton University, Princeton, NJ).
Baldwin, R.E. and T. Murray, 1977, MFN tariff reductions and developing country trade benefits under the GSP, Economic Journal 87, 30–46.
Baldwin, R.E., J.H. Mutti and J.D. Richardson, 1980, Welfare effects on the United States of a significant multilateral tariff reduction, Journal of International Economics 10, 405–423.
Bertrand, T.J. and J. Vanek, 1971, The theory of tariffs, taxes and subsidies: Some aspects of the second best, American Economic Review 61, 925–931.
Bhagwati, J.N., 1958, Immiserizing growth: A geometric note, Review of Economic Studies 25, 201–205.
Bhagwati, J.N., 1964, The pure theory of international trade: A survey, Economic Journal 74, 1–84.
Bhagwati, J.N., 1965, On the equivalence of tariffs and quotas, in: R.E. Baldwin et al., eds., Trade, growth and the balance of payments: Essays in honor of Gottfried Haberler (North-Holland, Amsterdam).
Bhagwati, J.N., 1971, The generalized theory of distortions and welfare, in: J.N. Bhagwati et al., eds., Trade, balance of payments and growth (North-Holland, Amsterdam).
Bhagwati, J.N., 1982, Directly unproductive profit-seeking activities, Journal of Political Economy 90, 988–1002.
Bhagwati, J.N. and T.N. Srinivasaen, 1983, Lectures on international trade (M.I.T. Press, Cambridge, MA).
Bhagwati, J.N., T.N. Srinivasan and H.Y. Wan, Jr., 1978, Value subtracted, negative shadow prices of factors in project evaluation, and immiserizing growth: Three paradoxes in the presence of trade distortions, Economic Journal 88, 121–125.
Boadway, R., S. Maital and M. Prachowny, 1973, Optimal tariffs, optimal taxes and public goods, Journal of Public Economics 2, 391–403.
Brecher, R.A. and J.N. Bhagwati, 1981, Foreign ownership and the theory of trade and welfare, Journal of Political Economy 89, 497–511.
Bruno, M., 1972, Market distortions and gradual reform, Review of Economic Studies 39, 373–383.
Chipman, J.S. and J.C. Moore, 1980, Real national income with homothetic preferences and a fixed distribution of income, Econometrica 48, 401–422.
Cline, W.R., N. Kawanabe, T. Kronsjo and T. Williams, 1978, Trade negotiations in the Tokyo round: A quantitative assessment (Brookings, Washington, DC).
Corden, W.M., 1974, Trade policy and economic welfare (Clarendon Press, Oxford).
Corden, W.M., 1975, The costs and consequences of protection: A survey of empirical work, in: P.B. Kenen, ed., International trade and finance: Frontiers for research (Cambridge University Press, Cambridge).
Corden, W.M., 1982, The normative theory of international trade, in: R.W. Jones and P.B. Kenen, eds., Handbook of international economics (North-Holland, Amsterdam).
Dasgupta, P.S. and J.E. Stiglitz, 1974, Benefit–cost analysis and trade policies, Journal of Political Economy 82, 1–33.
Deardorff, A.V. and R.M. Stern, 1981, A disaggregated model of world production and trade: An estimate of the impact of the Tokyo round, Journal of Policy Modeling 3, 127–152.
Diamond, P.A., 1973, Consumption externalities and imperfect corrective pricing, Bell Journal of Economics and Management Science 4, 526–538.
Diamond, P.A., 1975, A many-person Ramsey tax rule, Journal of Public Economics 4, 335–342.
Diamond, P.A. and J.A. Mirrlees, 1971, Optimal taxation and public production, American Economic Review 61, 8–27 and 261–278.
Diamond, P.A. and J.A. Mirrlees, 1976, Private constant returns and public shadow prices, Review of Economic Studies 43, 41–47.
Dixit, A., 1975, Welfare effects of tax and price changes, Journal of Public Economics 4, 103–123.
Dixit, A., 1984, International trade policy for oligopolistic industries, Economic Journal 94 (supplement) 1–16.
Dixit, A. and V. Norman, 1980a, Theory of international trade (Nisbets, Welwyn).

Dixit, A. and V. Norman, 1980b, The gains from free trade, Economic research paper no. 173 (University of Warwick, Coventry).

Dornbusch, R., 1980, Open economy macroeconomics (Basic Books, New York).

Dreze, J.P., 1982, On the choice of shadow prices for project evaluation, Discussion paper no. 16 (Development Economics Research Centre, University of Warwick, Coventry).

Edgeworth, F.Y., 1894, The theory of international values, Economic Journal 4, 35–50.

Ethier, W., 1977, The theory of effective protection in general equilibrium: Effective rate analogues of nominal rates, Canadian Journal of Economics 10, 233–245.

Fishelson, G. and F. Flatters, 1975, The (non-)equivalence of optimal tariffs and quotas under uncertainty, Journal of International Economics 5, 385–393.

Foster, E., 1981, The treatment of rents in cost–benefit analysis, American Economic Review 71, 171–178.

Goulder, L.H., J.B. Shoven and J. Whalley, 1983, Domestic tax policy and the foreign sector, in: M. Feldstein, ed., Behavioral simulation methods in tax policy analysis (University of Chicago Press, Chicago, IL).

Greenway, D., 1983, International trade policy: From tariffs to the new protectionism (Macmillan, London).

Grossman, G.M., 1980, Border tax adjustments: Do they distort trade?, Journal of International Economics 10, 117–128.

Grossman, G.M., 1984, The gains from international factor movements, Journal of International Economics, forthcoming.

Guesnerie, R., 1975, Production of the public sector and taxation in a simple second best model, Journal of Economic Theory 10, 127–156.

Haberler, G., 1950, Some problems in the pure theory of international trade, Economic Journal 60, 223–240.

Hamilton, B. and J. Whalley, 1983, Border tax adjustments and U.S. trade, Working paper no. 8317 (Centre for the Study of International Economic Relations, University of Western Ontario, London).

Hammond, P.J., 1979, Straightforward individual incentive compatibility in large economies, Review of Economic Studies 46, 263–282.

Hatta, T., 1977, A theory of piecemeal policy recommendations, Review of Economic Studies 44, 1–21.

Hatta, T. and T. Fukushima, 1979, The welfare effects of tariff rate reductions in a many country world, Journal of International Economics 9, 503–511.

Heady, C.J. and P.K. Mitra, 1982, Restricted redistributive taxation, shadow prices and trade policy, Journal of Public Economics 17, 1–22.

Helpman, E., 1983, Increasing returns, imperfect markets, and trade theory, in: R.W. Jones and P.B. Kenen, eds., Handbook of international economics (North-Holland, Amsterdam).

Helpman, E. and A. Razin, 1978, Welfare aspects of international trade in goods and securities, Quarterly Journal of Economics 92, 489–508.

Helpman, E. and A. Razin, 1980, Efficient protection under uncertainty, American Economic Review 70, 716–731.

Johnson, H.G., 1953–54, Optimum tariffs and retaliation, Review of Economic Studies 21, 142–153.

Johnson, H.G., 1967, The possibility of income losses from increased efficiency or factor accumulation in the presence of tariffs, Economic Journal 77, 151–154.

Jones, R.W., 1965, The structure of simple general equilibrium models, Journal of Political Economy 73, 557–572.

Jones, R.W., 1967, International capital movements and the theory of tariffs and trade, Quarterly Journal of Economics 81, 1–38.

Jones, R.W. and J.P. Neary, 1983, The positive theory of international trade, in: R.W. Jones and P.B. Kenen, eds., Handbook of international economics (North-Holland, Amsterdam).

Kemp, M.C., 1962, The gain from international trade, Economic Journal 72, 803–819.

Kenen, P.B., ed., 1975, International trade and finance: Frontiers for research (Cambridge University Press, Cambridge).

Kierzkowski, H., ed., 1984, Monopolistic competition in international trade (Oxford University Press, Oxford).

Krueger, A.O., 1974, The political economy of the rent-seeking society, American Economic Review 64, 291–303.

Lerner, A.P., 1936, The symmetry between import and export taxes, Economica 11, 306–313.

Lipsey, R.G., 1970, The theory of customs unions: A general equilibrium analysis (Weidenfeld and Nicholson, London).

Little, I.M.D. and J.A. Mirrlees, 1969, Manual of industrial project analysis in developing countries (OECD, Paris).

Lloyd, P.J., 1974, A more general theory of price distortions in open economies, Journal of International Economics 4, 365–386.

McCulloch, R., 1973, When are a tariff and a quota equivalent?, Canadian Journal of Economics 6, 503–511.

McCulloch, R. and H.G. Johnson, 1973, A note on proportionately distributed quotas, American Economic Review 63, 726–732.

McKenzie, L.W., 1955, Competitive equilibrium with dependent consumer preferences, in: H.A. Antosiewicz, ed., Proceedings of the second symposium in linear programming, Vol. I (National Bureau of Standards, Washington, DC).

Magee, S.P., 1972, The welfare effects of restrictions on U.S. trade, Brookings Papers on Economic Activity 3, 645–701.

Magee, S.P., 1975, Prices, incomes and foreign trade, in: P.B. Kenen, ed., International trade and finance: Frontiers for research (Cambridge University Press, Cambridge).

Markusen, J.R., 1975, International externalities and optimal tax structures, Journal of International Economics 4, 15–29.

Mayer, W., 1981, Theoretical considerations on negotiated tariff adjustments, Oxford Economic Papers 33, 135–153.

Meade, J.E., 1955, Trade and welfare (Oxford University Press, London).

Mirrlees, J.A., 1969, The evaluation of national income in an imperfect economy, Pakistan Development Review 9, 1–13.

Mueller, D.C., 1979, Public choice (Cambridge University Press, Cambridge).

Mundell, R.A., 1968, International economics (MacMillan, New York).

Ohyama, M., 1972, Trade and welfare in general equilibrium, Keio Economic Studies 9, 37–73.

Pelcovitz, M.D., 1976, Quotas versus tariffs, Journal of International Economics 6, 363–370.

Posner, R., 1975, The social costs of monopoly and regulation, Journal of Political Economy 83, 807–827.

Ray, A., 1980, Welfare significance of nominal and effective rates of protection, Australian Economic Papers 19, 182–192.

Roberts, K.W.S., 1978, On producer prices as shadow prices, Working paper (M.I.T., Cambridge, MA).

Saidi, N. and P. Srinagesh, 1981, On non-linear tariff schedules, Journal of International Economics 11, 173–195.

Samuelson, P.A., 1939, The gains from international trade, Canadian Journal of Economics and Political Science 5, 195–205.

Samuelson, P.A., 1956, Social indifference curves, Quarterly Journal of Economics 70, 1–22.

Samuelson, P.A., 1962, The gains from international trade once again, Economic Journal 72, 820–829.

Sandmo, A., 1975, Optimal taxation in the presence of externalities, Swedish Journal of Economics 77, 86–98.

Schelling, T.C., 1960, The strategy of conflict (Harvard University Press, Cambridge, MA).

Shoven, J.B. and J. Whalley, 1974, On the computation of competitive equilibrium on international markets with tariffs, Journal of International Economics 4, 341–354.

Shoven, J.B. and J. Whalley, 1983, Applied general equilibrium models of taxation and international trade, Journal of Economic Literature, forthcoming.

Smith, M.A.M., 1979, Intertemporal gains from trade, Journal of International Economics 9, 239–248.

Smith, M.A.M., 1980, Optimal public policy in open economies, Economic research paper no. 176 (University of Warwick, Coventry).

Smith, M.A.M., 1982, Some simple results on the gains from trade, from growth, and from public production, Journal of International Economics 13, 215–230.

Tullock, G., 1967, The welfare costs of tariffs, monopolies and theft, Western Economic Journal 5, 224–232.

Venables, A.J., 1982, Optimal tariffs for trade in monopolistically competitive industries, Journal of International Economics 12, 225–241.

Warr, P.G., 1982, Shadow pricing rules for non-traded commodities, Oxford Economic Papers 34, 305–325.

Weitzman, M.L., 1974, Prices vs. quantities, Review of Economic Studies 41, 447–491.

Weymark, J.A., 1979, A reconciliation of recent results in optimal taxation theory, Journal of Public Economics 12, 171–189.

Whalley, J., 1982, An evaluation of the Tokyo round trade agreement using general equilibrium computation methods, Journal of Policy Modeling 4, 341–361.

Young, L. and J.E. Anderson, 1980, The optimal policies for restricting trade under uncertainty, Review of Economic Studies 47, 927–932.

Chapter 7

HOUSING SUBSIDIES

Effects on Housing Decisions, Efficiency, and Equity

HARVEY S. ROSEN*

Princeton University, Princeton, NJ

1. Introduction

1.1. The U.S. housing stock

From virtually every point of view, housing is an important commodity. In 1981, the value of the net stock of residential capital in the United States was over a trillion dollars, measured in 1972 dollars. (See Table 1.1.) Although it is difficult to summarize in a single measure the quality of this stock, most experts agree that in general it is very high.[1] In 1980, for example, only 2.7 of the housing units lacked some or all of their plumbing facilities. Similarly, overcrowded housing which is characteristic of many countries does not appear to be a widespread problem in the U.S. In 1978, the median number of persons per owner-occupied unit was 2.6; for renter-occupied units of the figure was 2.0.[2] In 1980, only 4.5 of housing units had more than 1.01 persons per room.[3]

The flow of resources into housing continues to be large. In 1983, about 43% of expenditures on fixed total investment went into the residential capital stock. (See Table 1.2.) For the past two decades, the total value of housing output has been between nine and ten percent of gross national product.[4] For purpose of comparison, Table 1.3 shows the ratio of residential investment to total fixed investment in a number of countries. The U.S. does not appear to be an outlier.

*Part of the research was completed while I was a Visiting Scholar at the Hoover Institution. I would like to thank Patric Hendershott, Michael Murray, Richard Muth, and John Quigley for useful suggestions.

[1] See, for example, Aaron (1972, p. 30).
[2] U.S. Bureau of the Census (1982, p. 751).
[3] U.S. Bureau of the Census (1982, p. 754).
[4] U.S. Bureau of the Census (1982, p. 750).

Handbook of Public Economics, vol. I, edited by A.J. Auerbach and M. Feldstein

Table 1.1
U.S. net private residential capital stock (selected years, measured in 1972 billions of dollars).[a]

1960	1965	1970	1975	1981
593	711	818	964	1107

[a]*Source*: U.S. Department of Commerce, Bureau of the Census, *Statistical Abstract of the United States 1982–83*, 1982, p. 750.

Table 1.2
U.S. net fixed total investment and residential investment (selected years, measured in 1972 billions of dollars).[a]

	1960	1965	1970	1975	1980	1983[b]
Net fixed total investment	37.9	65.4	58.7	40.8	63.1	51.7
Residential investment	20.3	26.0	21.0	17.8	18.7	22.2

[a]*Source*: *Economic Report of the President*, February 1984, p. 239.
[b]Preliminary.

Table 1.3
Ratio of residential investment to fixed total investment (selected countries, 1980).[a]

Australia	0.33
Canada	0.17
France	0.25
Sweden	0.24
United Kingdom	0.15
United States	0.26

[a]*Source*: Computed from figures in Organization for Economic Cooperation and Development, *Quarterly Accounts Bulletin, 1967–81*, 1981.

1.2. Government and housing

The American housing market is subject to a mind-boggling array of government interventions by various levels of government.[5] These include: housing codes,

[5]The best source for an overall view of government housing policy remains Aaron's (1972) classic work.

which set quality standards that must be met by builders; licensure of real estate brokers and sales people; exclusionary zoning, which stipulates that land in a given area can be used only for certain purposes; open housing laws, which prohibit discrimination in the selling of housing; rent control; interest rate and other regulations on mortgage lending institutions; urban renewal programs, under which communities use their powers of eminent domain to acquire urban land, destroy "slums", and sell the land to private developers; real estate taxation; and interventions in the credit market to increase the flow of credit to housing (e.g., the Federal Home Loan Bank Board).[6]

This essay focuses on what are probably the two most important federal policies toward housing, at least in terms of costs to the government.[7] The first is not even explicitly a housing program. It consists of certain provisions of the federal income tax code which have the effect of lowering the costs of owner-occupied housing.[8] The second is the provision of housing for low-income families at rents below cost. Both programs subsidize the consumption of housing, the first mostly for middle- and upper-income groups, the second mostly for the poor. We will examine how each affects economic behavior, efficiency, and the distribution of real income.

As will be seen below, a number of countries have similar policies. Although most of our attention will be devoted to the American experience, some international comparisons will also be made.

1.3. Rationalizations for government intervention

Despite the fact that housing markets tend to be fairly competitive [see Mills (undated)], it has been suggested that government action is required for reasons of efficiency as well as equity. Each of these is discussed in turn.

1.3.1. Efficiency arguments

The most frequently encountered efficiency argument concerns externalities in housing consumption. When an individual improves his property, it increases the value of this investment. Simultaneously, the improvement may increase neighbors' property values. However, an individual's calculation of whether or not to undertake an improvement takes into account only the effect on his investments,

[6]See Congressional Budget Office (1981) for a concise description of these mortgage programs.
[7]See Aaron (1972, p. 162).
[8]As noted below, there are also favorable provisions for owners of rental housing, but these are not very large in comparison to those of owner-occupiers.

not those of his neighbors. Thus, the marginal social benefits of the improvement exceed the private marginal costs, and the "rational" property owner is likely to invest less than a socially efficient amount.

As a theoretical matter, it is hard to doubt that within a neighborhood, some kind of property value interdependence exists. But it is equally doubtful that all housing investments generate such externalities. Presumably, some such as painting outside walls create spillover effects. Others, such as painting interior walls, do not. The usual Pigouvian analysis requires that subsidies be targeted specifically at those activities that produce the externalities. It is pretty certain that the federal subsidies for owner-occupied housing, which in effect lower the cost of housing in general, are inefficient.

The empirical evidence for the existence of quantitatively significant spillovers is weak. One would expect, for example, that if externalities were important anywhere, it would be in the slums, where housing density is very high. Mills (undated, p. 15) notes that the presence of substantial externalities should provide a strong incentive for single ownership of neighboring dwellings in such neighborhoods. No such tendency appears to exist. Similarly, the literature reviewed by Muth (1973, p. 35) indicates that the removal of slums and their replacement by public housing does not have much of an impact upon the values of surrounding properties. To the extent such effects are present, they are probably due to the community facilities associated with the public housing (e.g., playgrounds), rather than the removal of slum dwellings *per se*.

Another externality sometimes mentioned is the "social cost of slums". The notion is that poor housing does more than merely lower neighborhood property values. It breeds crime, delinquency, fires, disease, mental illness, etc. [Weicher (1979, p. 491)]. It seems reasonable to believe, however, that it is the poverty associated with poor housing, rather than the housing *per se*, that causes these costly social problems. [See Mills (undated) or Aaron (1972, p. 22).]

A quite different efficiency argument is that federal subsidies for housing merely offset biases against housing consumption which are induced by local property taxes. The soundness of this view depends upon one's view of the role of the property tax. To the extent that it is an excise tax on housing, the view has some merit. However, if the property tax is just a fee for services provided by the community, then it is really not a distortion. Such a notion is consistent with the "Tiebout model", in which households shop around for the community whose bundle of public services best suits their needs, and property taxes finance these services.

The Tiebout benefit-tax result holds exactly only under very restrictive assumptions. Mills (undated) has argued that suburbs are more likely to satisfy the conditions required for a Tiebout equilibrium than inner cities, in part because suburbanites have more mobility than their urban counterparts. Thus, the notion of a federal housing subsidy as an offset to a pre-existing distortion is probably more relevant to inner cities than suburbs. Again, it is hard to justify subsidies for owner-occupied housing on this basis.

1.3.2. Equity arguments

Housing subsidies can also be rationalized in terms of redistributional goals. By providing subsidized housing for the poor, a more egalitarian income distribution can perhaps be achieved. It is hard to see the relevance of this point for subsidization of owner-occupied housing, because the incidence of owner-occupation increases with income. (See Section 3 below.) Egalitarian arguments cannot so easily be dismissed in the case of subsidized housing for low-income individuals. But here a puzzle arises. It is well-known that if the government's sole objective is redistribution, and the recipients' preferences are paramount, then using cash to redistribute income is more efficient than a subsidy, in the sense that the same utility level for the recipient can be reached with a smaller cash outlay.[9]

If this is the case, how can one account for the prevalence of subsidies and in-kind transfers? If the donor cares not only about the beneficiary's utility level, but the composition of the latter's consumption bundles as well, then inducements for the beneficiary to consume certain commodities may be efficient. Alternatively, attitudes toward housing may be influenced by "commodity egalitarianism", the notion that "society" cares not only about the distribution of income *per se*, but also about the distribution of certain "necessary" commodities [see Tobin (1970)]. In 1949 the U.S. Congress set as a national goal "... a decent home and a suitable living environment for every American family" [Weicher (1979, p. 470)].

Nichols and Zeckhauser (1981) have suggested another possible rationalization for in-kind transfers. Suppose that it is difficult for the welfare authorities to determine who is qualified for a program and who is not. In other words, "welfare fraud" is a possibility. In the Nichols–Zeckhauser model, in-kind transfers of inferior goods may discourage some impostors from applying for welfare. By forcing the "truly needy" to consume a certain bundle, consumption efficiency is reduced. But program efficiency increases, because the money is better targeted. The optimal design of transfer packages requires taking both kinds of efficiency into account.

It is hard to know how important any of these considerations are in determining policy. Perhaps it is the high visibility of housing that leads people to view it

[9]This argument is discussed more formally in Section 4.2. As usual it applies strictly only in the absence of other distortions of competitive market price.

as a "problem" that must be dealt with publicly. In any event, many economists find public policies based upon such paternalistic principles to be quite unattractive from a philosophical viewpoint. Indeed, Mills (undated) has suggested that in the U.S., official paternalism toward low-income groups may be tinged with racism – the poor are disproportionately black, and there is an underlying expectation that they cannot be expected to manage their lives without help.

Another explanation for the existence of low-income housing subsidies is political. An in-kind subsidy tends to help not only the beneficiary, but also the producers of the favored commodity. Thus, a transfer program that increases the demand for housing will tend to benefit the building industry, which will then lend its support to a coalition in favor of the program. As indicated in Section 4.1 below, housing programs for the poor have focused on the construction of new units, thus benefitting the housing industry rather directly.

It is also important to note that unlike cash transfers, the administration of a public housing program requires substantial amounts of resources. (Contracts must be arranged, standards set and enforced, etc.) According to most theories of bureaucratic behavior [see, e.g., Niskanen (1971)], one would therefore expect public employees to put their political support behind low-income housing programs. In 1977, when welfare reformers proposed that subsidized housing be phased out and replaced with cash grants, the Department of Housing and Urban Development (H.U.D.) was in vigorous opposition [Weicher (1980, p. 51)].

1.3.3. Summary and evaluation[10]

The main efficiency argument for subsidizing housing is the existence of externalities. However, the mechanisms through which these externalities work are not well understood and there is little evidence that they are quantitatively important. The redistributive rationalization is equally weak. To the extent that society seeks to distribute income to the poor, the subsidies to owner-occupation are perverse, because as will be seen below, they benefit mainly the middle- and upper-income classes. The in-kind subsidies involved in low-income public housing are inefficient in the sense that the poor could be made better off if the transfers were made directly in cash. Paternalism and political considerations seem to be the sources of this policy.

[10] We have discussed housing policies in terms of the traditional goals of equity and efficiency. It has been argued that public housing can be an effective means of alleviating racial discrimination in housing. [See, e.g., Sumka and Stegman (1978, pp. 409–410).] Even if it does have some efficacy, however, the question is whether or not there are more efficient ways of achieving this end.

2. Methodological issues

The theoretical considerations of the last section left unanswered many important *empirical* questions that surround housing policy. It may be, for example, that even if the policy is inefficient on *a priori* grounds, the actual magnitude of the distortions is small. Similarly, without examination of the data, one cannot assess the distributional effects of the policy.

In order to investigate such issues, one must first understand how the consumers and producers of housing make their decisions. Some special aspects of housing as a commodity make it difficult to use the standard theoretical and econometric tools. Because these difficulties crop up in virtually every empirical study of housing, we discuss them now all together, rather than later on a piecemeal basis.

2.1. Specifying a model

In general, the effect of a housing policy is to change the price of housing services facing a household, and perhaps its disposal income as well. [For example, a subsidy at rate s would change the effective price of housing services from its initial value, say p_h^0, to $(1-s)p_h^0$).] Therefore, given price and income elasticities, one can predict individuals' responses to given policies. These considerations suggest the following strategy: Employ appropriate econometric techniques to estimate the demand and supply for housing services, using either cross-sectional or time series data. This yields a set of the relevant elasticities. Then, assuming that people would react to the price and income differences generated by the policy in the same way as those generated "naturally", use the elasticities to estimate the program's impact on behavior. We discuss problems in estimating demand and supply functions, and then turn to the influence of the market environment upon the results.

2.1.1. Demand[11]

Empirical investigators typically begin by specifying a model that relates the quantity of housing services demanded for the ith observation (Q_{hi}^{D}), to some function $f(\cdot)$ of price (p_{hi}), income (Y_i) and a vector of demographic variables Z_i that theoretical considerations suggest might be relevant,

$$Q_{hi}^{\mathrm{D}}=f(p_{hi},Y_i,Z_i). \tag{2.1}$$

[11] For a useful survey of the results of housing demand studies, see Mayo (1981).

In some cases $f(\cdot)$ is specified in an *ad hoc* but convenient form such as log linear [Polinsky and Ellwood (1979)], while other times it is derived from maximization of an explicit utility function [Abbot and Ashenfelter (1976)], which is also chosen on the basis of convenience.

Equation (2.1) is deterministic, so the next step is to posit some stochastic specification. Usually, an error term is appended additively. Given a set of observations on Q_{hi}, p_{hi}, Y_i and Z_i and the stochastic specification, the model's parameters can be estimated using a variety of econometric techniques. The behavioral elasticities implied by the parameter estimates can then be used to predict the effects of policy changes. Alternatively, one can obtain such predictions by substituting the new values for price and income directly into equation (2.1).

There are several problems with this standard approach:

(1) Economic theory puts very few constraints on the form of $f(\cdot)$, so the investigator must make an essentially *ad hoc* choice with respect to the specification of either the demand or utility function.

(2) It must be assumed that $f(\cdot)$ is identical across individuals.[12] [When time series data are used, the analogous assumption is that $f(\cdot)$ does not change over time.]

(3) Demand functions like (2.1) ignore the dynamic nature of housing decisions. Because these decisions are made in a life cycle context, expected future prices and incomes as well as those of the current period are relevant. [See Henderson and Ionnides (1983) or Weiss (1978).]

(4) Observations on p_{hi} are never directly observed. Only $p_{hi} \times Q_{hi}$ – the value of the dwelling – is observable.

(5) For many owner-occupiers, housing is not only a consumption item, but an investment as well. To the extent this is the case, the theory of portfolio behavior suggests that the demand for housing depends upon the joint distribution of the returns from housing and other assets. Even those econometric studies discussed below which explicitly recognize the investment nature of housing decisions have failed to take into account this consideration.

(6) It must be assumed that the fitted relationship will continue to apply when a right-hand side variable for a given observation changes. For example, if an investigator using cross-sectional data finds that $(\partial Q^{\mathrm{D}}/\partial Y_{hi})(Y_{hi}/Q^{\mathrm{D}}_{hi})$ is less than one, it does not imply that increasing a particular family's income ten percent will increase its housing consumption by a smaller percentage. All that one really

[12] Note that this need *not* imply that the elasticities be identical across individuals; such will be the case only for the very simple Cobb–Douglas specification. One can also specify a random coefficients model, which allows for a distribution of elasticities across people. See King (1980).

learns is that in the data, poorer families devote a larger fraction of their income to housing than richer families, *ceteris paribus*. Only by *assuming* that poorer families would act like the richer ones if their incomes were increased, and *vice versa*, can one give any behavioral significance to elasticity estimates from regressions.

Moreover, most of the studies using cross-sectional data to examine housing demand implicitly or explicitly assume that all agents are in equilibrium.[13] Were not this the case, then a regression of housing services on price, income, and demographic variables could not be interpreted as a demand equation. On the other hand, analyses of longitudinal and time series data often allow for the possibility that at a given point in time, households may not be at their long-run equilibrium positions, because adjustment costs make it prohibitively expensive to respond immediately to changes in economic environment.

It is usually assumed that such a disequilibrium is eliminated over time as households move gradually to their equilibrium positions [e.g., Rosen and Rosen (1980)]. Such models lack a strong choice theoretic foundation, but tractable alternatives are lacking. Venti and Wise (1982) measure transactions costs by including them as a random parameter in a model of moving decisions. Their results confirm earlier conjectures that these costs are large relative to income ($60 per month in a sample of low-income households whose median monthly income was $320.)

2.1.2. Supply

A popular approach for studying the supply of housing is to assume some housing production function, estimate its parameters, and use them to infer the shape of the supply function.[14] For example, Ingram and Oron (1977, p. 284) assume that housing services are a constant elasticity of substitution (C.E.S.) function of "quality capital" and "operation inputs". Polinsky and Ellwood (1979) also posit a C.E.S. production function, but assume that its arguments are land and capital. Follain (1979) and Poterba (1980) eschew selection of a specific form for the production function, and instead start by postulating supply functions that include the price of housing input costs as arguments. (Of course, duality considerations suggest that one can work backward from the supply curve to the underlying production function.)

The specification of the underlying technology can sometimes predetermine substantive results. For example, since Polinsky and Ellwood (1979, p. 210)

[13]An important exception is King (1980), which is discussed below.

[14]Given the production function and input prices, one can derive the marginal cost schedule which, under competition, is the supply curve.

assume constant returns to scale, the implied long-run supply curve of housing services is perfectly elastic, regardless of parameter estimates.[15] Postulating such a technology, then, guarantees the result that policies that affect housing demand will have no effect on the long-run producer's price of housing services, at least as long as input prices remain unchanged. The interesting questions then become how high do prices rise in the short run, and how much time is required to reach long-run equilibrium?

Various approaches have been used to model the process of adjustment to the new equilibrium. Ingram and Oron (1977, p. 292) assume that the most a landlord can invest each period is limited to the amount of cash generated by the existing investment, even if this is insufficient to close the gap between the desired and actual housing stock. Poterba (1980) argues that the supply of housing may be affected by conditions in the credit market, and summarizes these by the flow of savings deposits received by savings and loan associations. He also assumes a delayed supply response to changes in all right-hand side variables, which are entered in polynomial distributed lags [Poterba (1980, p. 10)].

2.1.3. Market environment

In microeconometric studies of demand or supply, the key question is how individual units react to exogenous changes in their budget constraints. No explicit consideration of the market environment is usually taken. To understand overall effects, however, the question of market structure is crucial – the impact of a given housing policy will depend upon its effect upon the market price of housing, which will in turn depend *mutatis mutandis* upon the degree of competitiveness in the market, the amount of slack existing when the program is initiated, the extent of housing market segmentation, etc.

The standard assumption is that competition prevails. As de Leeuw and Struyk (1975) and Poterba (1980) note, however, even given competition, complications arise because *two* markets have to be equilibrated by the price of housing services: the market for existing houses and the market for new construction. The situation increases in complexity when one takes into account the multiplicity of tenure modes. Each type of housing is traded in its own submarket, and each of these (interrelated) markets has its own clearing price. If the housing market is

[15]The assumption of a horizontal supply curve is quite common, e.g., see DeLeeuw and Struyk (1975, p. 15). Of course, to the extent that input prices change with the size of the housing industry, the long-run supply curve will have a non-zero slope.

non-competitive, the question of supply effects is even more difficult because of the absence of a generally accepted theory of price determination.[16]

In practice, most econometric investigations of the issues discussed in this essay ignore such considerations. As will be seen below, attention tends to be focused upon the estimation of demand curves. It is usually assumed that the housing market is perfectly competitive, and that the long supply curve of housing services is infinitely elastic.[17]

2.2. Measuring quantity and price

Our discussion of model specification suggests that accurate measurement of the quantity and price of housing services is crucial. This is a very difficult task, because housing is intrinsically a multi-dimensional commodity – a dwelling is characterized by its number of rooms, their size, the quality of construction and plumbing, etc. It is therefore not obvious how to summarize in a single number the quantity of housing services generated by a given dwelling. Usually it is assumed that the amount of housing services is proportional to the rent paid, or, in the case of an owner-occupied dwelling, to the value of the house. [See, e.g., Polinsky and Ellwood (1979).] A problem here is that the rental value of a dwelling at a given time may reflect characteristics of the market that have nothing to do with the quantity of housing services actually generated. As King (1980) points out, for example, the special income tax treatment of rental income will generally influence market values.[18]

An alternative tack would be to abandon the possibility of summarizing housing services in a single variable, and instead to estimate a series of demand functions for various housing attributes. An immediate problem is the absence of observable market prices for attributes. Recently, Witte et al. (1979) have implemented the suggestion of Rosen (1974) that attribute demand equations be estimated in a two-step process: (1) estimate the implicit attribute prices from an

[16]An example of the use of a non-competitive framework is Rydell (1979), who attempts to explain the insensitivity of housing prices to apparent variations in market tightness by recourse to a theory of monopolistic competition.

[17]An exception is Englund and Persson (1982). In their simulation model of the Swedish housing market, they assume that the supply of housing services is perfectly inelastic.

[18]Other problems with the concept of housing services are discussed by Diamond and Smith (1981).

hedonic price equation[19] for housing; and (2) use these prices as explanatory variables in regressions with attribute quantities as the dependent variables. However, Brown and Rosen (1982) have shown that major statistical pitfalls are present in this procedure, and that the validity of Witte et al.'s results is therefore in question. Although some progress is being made in dealing with these problems [see Quigley (1982)], the approach that continues to predominate is to measure the quantity of a dwelling's housing services by its market value (if it is owner-occupied) or otherwise by its rental value.

Because the price of housing services is housing expenditures divided by the quantity of housing services, the above noted difficulties in measuring the latter are bound to create problems in measuring price. Several possible solutions are found in the literature. A popular approach is to estimate hedonic price equations for different cities, and use them as the bases for a housing price index. However, Alexander (1975) has pointed out several problems with this approach. One of the most important is that the selection of a set of attributes to be included in the hedonic price index must be decided on *ad hoc* grounds, but the substantive implications of the estimates often depend upon the choice made.

Further difficulties in measuring price are caused by the fact that even within a given housing market, the price per unit of housing services may not be a constant. Struyk et al. (1978) have argued that one of the key characteristics of urban housing markets is the existence of submarkets, each of which has different prices per unit of housing services. (Such differences might exist because of residential segregation.) Most empirical studies, however, continue to assume that any given city is characterized by a single (pre-tax) price of housing.

2.3. Measuring "shift" variables

In order to obtain unbiased estimates of demand and supply parameters, one must also take into account variables other than price that might be affecting decisions. On the demand side, probably the most obvious candidate is income. Standard theoretical considerations suggest that for income a permanent rather than annual measure should be used. It is not obvious how to compute permanent income, and investigators have dealt with the problem in various ways. Carliner (1972) and Rosen (1979), analyzing longitudinal data, take an average of several year's worth of annual income. Struyk (1976) uses the fitted value of a regression

[19]A regression of the price of a commodity R on its characteristics (a vector X) is the basis of an hedonic price index for the commodity. The implicit price of the ith characteristic is $\partial R/\partial X_i$. See Rosen (1974).

of income on a set of personal characteristics as his permanent income measure.[20] In time series analyses, a distributed lag on income is often used. [See, e.g., Hendershott and Shilling (1980).]

With respect to the selection of other shift variables, investigators have to make arbitrary decisions with respect to which ones to chose, their measurement, and how they interact with the other variables. Typical candidates for inclusion are race, sex and head of household, age, number of children, etc.

On the supply side, theory suggests that input prices are important variables. There are serious problems involved in obtaining operational measures of housing input costs. For example, Poterba (1980) uses the Boeckh index of the price of inputs for a new one-family structure to measure construction costs. Although this is a commonly used index, it is well-known that it is deficient because fixed weights are used in its computation. Ingram and Oron (1977) use the fuel component of the consumer's price index to account for the price of all operating inputs, but as Rothenberg (1977) points out, it is not clear that this index captures all the needed information.

2.4. *Summary*

The quandries facing students of housing are similar to those who seek to explain other kinds of complicated economic behavior (e.g., the determinants of business investment). Although it is easy to carp about the simplifications made by econometric investigators, compromises are required in order to obtain tractable models. On the other hand, in light of the serious methodological problems, one must regard substantive conclusions regarding policy with a very critical eye.

3. Housing behavior and the federal income tax

In this section we discuss: (1) the key provisions of the income tax code that pertain to housing; (2) how the provisions change the effective cost of housing; (3) the impact of these cost changes upon individuals' housing decisions; (4) the implications of these changes for economic efficiency and equity; and (5) some proposals that have been made for reform.

[20] Neither the necessity of using a permanent income measure nor the types of solutions just mentioned are unique to the study of housing; they appear throughout the literature on the estimation of demand functions.

3.1. Housing related tax provisions

Exclusion of net imputed rental. The U.S. federal tax code does not require that the net value of the services received by owner-occupants from their homes be included as taxable income. If these same units were rented out, the income obtained *would* be taxed, after deductions for taxes, interest, maintenance, etc. In other words, because an investment in owner-occupied housing produces in-kind income rather than cash, that income is untaxed.[21]

Deduction of mortgage interest. Tax payers can deduct from taxable income the full value of all interest payments, including the interest on home mortgage loans.[22] The deduction of interest has been a part of the tax law since its inception. At that time (1913), however, consumer interest payments were minimal.

Deduction of local property taxes. Homeowners are allowed to deduct all state, local and foreign taxes paid on real property. This provision, which also dates from the beginning of the code, was based on the idea that such taxes represent a reduction in disposable income. To the extent that local taxes are user fees for locally provided services, this rationalization lacks validity.

Deferral of capital gains on home sales. Excluded from taxable income are any capital gains from the sale of a principal residence when another residence costing at least as much is purchased within two years of the sale of the former one. This provision, introduced in 1951, was a consequence of the view that individuals' decisions to change houses were due to personal reasons or uncontrollable circumstances, as opposed to a profit motive. Therefore, taxation of the capital gain would cause undue hardship.

One-time exclusion of $125,000 capital gains in home sales for taxpayers 55 years of age and older. Provisions to shield elderly taxpayers from potentially heavy tax burdens when they decide to become renters or move to less costly residences were first introduced in 1964. The cut-off age at that time was 65 years and the exemption was available only under special circumstances. In light of this provision and the one concerning deferral just discussed, most investigators have found it safe to assume that for all practical purposes, the tax rate on capital gains from owner-occupied housing is zero.

Exclusion of income from tax exempt mortgage bonds. In 1978 states and localities began to sell tax exempt bonds to private mortgage funds for owner-occupied and rental units at below market interest rates. However, in 1980,

[21] For more detail, see Congressional Budget Office (1981), upon which most of this section is based.

[22] There are certain limitations for interest payments on property held for investment income, but these are not important in the current context. For certain homeowners, it may be more advantageous to take the standard deduction than to itemize. See Hendershott and Slemrod (1983).

Table 3.1

Approximate revenue losses from the special tax treatment of owner-occupied housing (fiscal year 1981, millions of dollars).[a]

Exemption of net imputed rent	16,413
Deductibility of mortgage interest	19,805
Deductibility of property taxes	8.915
Deferral of capital gains	1,110
Exclusion of capital gain for "elderly"	590
Tax exempt bond finance	840

[a]*Source*: Except for the exemption of net imputed rent, the figures are from Congressional Budget Office (1981, p. 7). A study for the Department of Housing and Urban Development estimated that in fiscal year 1979 revenue loss due to the non-taxation of net imputed rent was between $14 and $17 billion. [See Congressional Budget Office (1981, p. 20).] The figure in the table is found by taking $15 billion, and multiplying by 177/163, the ratio of the implicit GNP price deflators for 1980 and 1979.

significant limits were imposed on the issuance of new tax exempt bonds, and issues to finance new single-family housing are now banned beginning in 1983.

Table 3.1 shows some estimates of the foregone tax revenues associated with the various exclusions discussed above. Note that these estimates are based on the assumption that even if the provisions were eliminated, people would continue to make the same housing decisions. As both common sense and the empirical evidence reported below indicate, this is an unrealistic assumption. Nevertheless, the figures in the table at least indicate the orders of magnitude involved. The Congressional Budget Office estimated that if all the tax preferences associated with housing (except exclusion of imputed rent) were eliminated, it would be possible to lower all personal marginal tax rates by 10% without sustaining any revenue loss [Congressional Budget Office (1981, p. 40)].

The main federal tax item concerning rental housing is accelerated depreciation. Owners of rental property may claim accelerated depreciation on their buildings, and amortize construction period interest and real estate taxes over a ten-year period, rather than the full economic life.[23] The Congressional Budget Office (1981, p. 33) estimated that the foregone tax revenues due to the tax treatment of rental housing were about $1.9 billion in 1981, considerably less than those associated with owner-occupation.

[23]For a discussion of other features of the tax treatment of rental housing – recapture provisions, capital gains rules and minimum tax rules – see Hendershott and Shilling (1982).

With respect to tax concessions for housing interest payments, the United Sates is roughly comparable to Western Europe. Fainstein (1980) estimates that the revenue loss as a percentage of gross domestic product in the early 1970's was about 0.3% for Germany, 0.9% for the Netherlands, 1.1% for Sweden, 0.7% for the United Kingdom, and 0.6% for the United States. England, like the United States, levies no tax on imputed rental income (since 1963). On the other hand, some form of imputed net rental is taxed in Belgium, Denmark, Luxembourg, Netherlands, Portugal, Spain, Sweden and West Germany.

3.2. *Effects on the cost of housing*

Following Aaron (1972),[24] denote R^{G} = gross imputed rent, R^{N} = net imputed rent, MA = maintenance, D = depreciation, T = state and local taxes, and MI = mortgage interest. Assume that no changes are expected in either house prices or the general price level. Then by definition

$$R^{\mathrm{N}} = R^{\mathrm{G}} - MA - D - T - MI. \tag{3.1}$$

If net imputed rental were subject to income taxation and a homeowner's marginal tax rate were τ_y, then the tax liability associated with homeownership would be $\tau_y \times R^{\mathrm{N}}$. Under the current regime, the main tax consequences of homeownership are to reduce taxable income by the sum of MI and T, or alternatively, to reduce tax liability by $\tau_y \times (MI + T)$. To find the difference between tax liabilities under the status quo and those which would occur if net imputed rent were taxed, we simply compute

$$\tau_y \times R^{\mathrm{N}} - (-\tau_y \times (MI + T)) = \tau_y (R^{\mathrm{N}} + MI + T). \tag{3.2}$$

To get a sense for the numerical values involved, assume for simplicity that the mortgage rate and the individual's opportunity cost of capital are the same rate, i; property taxes are a proportion τ_p of house value; and depreciation plus maintenance are a proportion of house value d. Then (3.2) can be written as $\tau_y(i + \tau_p)V$, where V is the value of the house. When the homeowner spends $(i + \tau_p + d)V$ on housing services, he therefore derives tax savings of $\tau_y(i + \tau_p)V$, so the after-tax imputed rent is

$$(i + \tau_p + d)V - \tau_y(i + \tau_p)V = [(1 - \tau_y)i + (1 - \tau_y)\tau_p + d]V. \tag{3.3}$$

Alternatively, the difference between the pre- and post-income tax costs of

[24] See also Laidler (1969).

housing, expressed as a proportion of the pre-tax cost, is

$$(\tau_y(i+\tau_p))/(i+\tau_p+d). \tag{3.4}$$

Suppose that $\tau_p = 0.025$, $i = 0.06$, $d = 0.03$, and the individual's marginal tax rate is 0.2. The substitution into (3.4) indicates that the federal income tax lowers the cost of owning by about 15%. For an individual with the same circumstances but a marginal income tax rate of 0.4, the difference would be about 30%. The amounts involved are substantial, and increase with the marginal tax rate, *ceteris paribus*.

Hendershott and Shilling (1982) provide a more detailed analysis of the costs of owner-occupation which is based on the analogy between the cost of housing services and the "user cost of capital" from the literature on the neoclassical theory of investment.[25] Their derivation makes clear exactly what assumptions are required to obtain a simple expression like (3.3). It begins with the notion that in equilibrium, one expects that the present value of the net cash flows from a house will equal the initial equity investment. The positive cash flows consist of the net imputed rent from the house, and a lump sum received at the selling date. The negative cash flows include the after-tax costs of mortgage and property taxes, the selling costs at the date of sale, and the outstanding mortgage debt due at the time of the sale. Hendershott and Shilling assume that

(i) inflation is expected to generate increases in net revenues at rate p, and in housing prices at rate q;
(ii) physical depreciation of the house occurs at rate d;
(iii) the proportion, α, of the purchase price is financed with a mortgage at rate i;
(iv) the house is expected to be sold after N periods, at which time a percentage realtor's fee, ρ, is paid.

Then the equilibrium condition is

$$(1-\alpha)V = \sum_{t=1}^{N}\frac{(1+p-\gamma d)^{t-1}R}{(1+e)^t} - \sum_{t=1}^{N}\frac{(1-\tau_y)\tau_p(1+q-\gamma d)^{t-1}V}{(1+e)^t}$$

$$-\sum_{t=1}^{N}\frac{\zeta_t}{(1+e)^t} + \sum_{t=1}^{N}\frac{\tau_y i L_{t-1}}{(1+e)^t} + \frac{(1-\rho)(1+q-\gamma_s d)^N V - L_N}{(1+e)^N}, \tag{3.5}$$

[25] See, e.g., Jorgenson (1971).

where

V = purchase price of the house, including land,
e = after-tax rate of return available on other investments,
γ = ratio of the value of the structure to the value of the structure plus land,
R = implicit rent during the first period,
τ_y = marginal income tax rate,
τ_p = property tax rate,
ζ_t = mortgage payment in period t,
L_t = mortgage loan outstanding at the end of period t.

Because α is the loan to value ratio, $(1-\alpha)V$ is the equity investment in the house. The sums on the right-hand side are the present values of the stream of imputed rents, the after-tax cost of property taxes, the mortgage payments, the tax savings from interest reductions, and the net "profit" from selling the house. Note that the income tax rate is not included in the last term. This reflects the realistic approximation that the rate on housing capital gains is zero.

Hendershott and Shilling go on to show that if: (i) the mortgage is a standard fixed rate, fixed payment mortgage or if the variable rate is expected to remain at the constant value i through period N; (ii) the holding period is "large" (N approaches infinity); (iii) there are no selling costs ($\rho = 0$); (iv) the net mortgage rate equals the net rate of return available on other investments $[e = (1-\tau_y)i]$; (v) the expected rate of increase in implicit rents equals the expected rate of increase in housing prices ($p = q$); and (vi) the structure to value ratio is 1.0; then

$$R/P = \left[(1-\tau_y)i - q + d + (1-\tau_y)\tau_p\right]V/P. \tag{3.6}$$

where P is the general price level.

The crucial difference between (3.6) and (3.3) is the presence of q, the expected rate of increase in housing prices. When homeowners expect capital gains, it lowers their effective cost of housing. This fact is often ignored in popular discussions of housing markets. The expectation of rising prices is an incentive to buy a house provided that households are not constrained in their ability to borrow in the capital markets.

The fact that housing capital gains are untaxed is reflected by the fact that q is not multiplied by $(1-\tau_y)$. As a result, the decrease in the cost of housing as inflation rises is greater for individuals with high values of τ_y. To see this, assume for simplicity that increases in the inflation rate are matched by increases in the nominal interest rate, i.e., $\partial i/\partial q = 1$. Then taking the derivative of (3.6) with

Table 3.2
User cost of housing (1955–1979).[a]

Year	Owner-occupied $\tau_y = 0.30$	Owner-occupied $\tau_y = 0.45$	Rental
1955	0.0563	0.0478	0.0873
56	0.0500	0.0410	0.0803
57	0.0539	0.0446	0.0827
58	0.0591	0.0502	0.0878
59	0.0627	0.0536	0.0921
1960	0.0666	0.0572	0.0989
61	0.0680	0.0589	0.1010
62	0.0666	0.0576	0.0992
63	0.0671	0.0584	0.0988
64	0.0650	0.0563	0.0975
65	0.0596	0.0508	0.0936
66	0.0552	0.0460	0.0907
67	0.0514	0.0418	0.0859
68	0.0455	0.0355	0.0801
69	0.0402	0.0291	0.0786
1970	0.0492	0.0378	0.0927
71	0.0419	0.0313	0.0809
72	0.0407	0.0299	0.0818
73	0.0369	0.0250	0.0866
74	0.0350	0.0223	0.0866
75	0.0241	0.0117	0.0681
76	0.0292	0.0165	0.0801
77	0.0227	0.0093	0.0807
78	0.0177	0.0040	0.0847
79	0.0231	0.0059	0.0867

[a]*Source*: Averages of quarterly figures presented by Hendershott and Shilling (1982).

respect to q yields

$$\partial R/\partial q = -\tau_y.$$

Clearly, even if nominal interest rates increase on less than a one-for-one basis with inflation, the tax advantages associated with the deduction of nominal interest payments will still be greater the higher the tax rate, though the magnitude will be less.

Hendershott and Shilling evaluate (3.5) on a quarterly basis from 1955 through 1979. As usual, some arbitrary decisions have to be made to estimate expected inflation rates. They compute the general expected inflation rate as a 16-quarter distributed lag on current and past rates of change in prices. In Table 3.2 we present annual averages of Hendershott and Shilling's quarterly figures. The first column is based upon a marginal income tax rate of 0.30; the second of 0.45. The figures make clear that the cost of owner-occupation fell dramatically in the 1970s, a phenomenon due largely to increases in the inflation rate.[26] Note also that the higher marginal tax rate is associated with a low user cost, as expected.

As Hendershott and Shilling note, even this relatively elaborate estimate of the user cost of capital suffers from inadequacies. For example, it does not take into account people's expectations on the future course of tax policy. Neither does it allow for the holding period or depreciation rate to vary with the tax structure. Similar problems, of course, have been encountered in attempts to estimate the after-tax costs of business capital.

Hendershott and Shilling use a similar framework to derive the user cost of rental occupation. (The equilibrium condition takes into account the federal tax provisions for rental housing.) Their calculations are reported in the third column of Table 3.2. Over time, renting has become expensive relative to owning. The implications of this phenomenon are discussed below.

It is common to refer to the tax induced lowering of the relative cost of owner-occupation as an "implicit subsidy" of owner-occupied housing. Alternatively, housing related deductions are viewed as "tax expenditures", items that are exempt from tax but which would be included under a comprehensive tax base. Although we follow this practice, it should be noted that some object to it strenuously. First of all, in order to characterize an item as being "exempt", one must first have some kind of criterion for deciding what "ought" to be included. As is well known, there exists no rigorous set of principles for determining what belongs in income [Musgrave (1959)].

In addition, the tax expenditure concept has been attacked on more philosophical grounds [Jones (1978, p. 53)]:

> "... The tax expenditure concept implies that all income belongs of right to the government, and that what government decides, by exemption on qualification, not to collect in taxes constitutes a subsidy. This... violates a widely held conviction, basic to the American polity... that the income earned by the people belongs to them, not the government."

Characterizing the tax provision discussed herein as a "subsidy" is not meant to carry these ideological implications, but merely to describe their impact on the cost of owner-occupation.

[26] Presumably, if Hendershott and Shilling had used each year's average value of τ_y, rather than keeping it constant over time, an even greater decline would have been evident, given that inflation was pushing people into higher personal income tax brackets. See Hendershott and Slemrod (1983) for a discussion of the problems involved in computing the marginal tax rate relevant for homeownership decisions.

3.3. Effects on behavior

3.3.1. Housing decisions

Laidler's (1969) early attempt to assess the impact of the federal tax treatment of housing upon housing decisions begins with an estimate of its effect upon the cost of housing for each of several income groups. This is done by evaluating expression (3.4) with reasonable values of the appropriate parameters. (All parameters except the marginal tax rate are constant across income goups.) To find the amount of housing demand generated by these tax induced price changes, Laidler assumes a price elasticity of demand of -1.5, a figure consistent with much of the econometric literature completed at the time of his study. He finds that in 1960, the housing stock of $355,369 million dollars would have been $60,699 million smaller had imputed rent been taxed.[27] This calculation assumes that the long-run supply of housing services is perfectly elastic, an assumption that is in line with some econometric evidence.

One problem with the Laidler estimates is that the price elasticity used is based upon econometric studies which ignore the impact of taxes upon the relative price of housing. In addition, attention is focused only upon the quantity of housing consumed by owner-occupiers, with no attempt made to incorporate the effect of taxes upon the tenure choice. Subsequent work has attempted to remedy these problems.

Rosen (1979) uses cross-sectional U.S. data from 1970 to estimate jointly equations for the quantity of housing services demanded and the tenure choice. He assumes that the demand for housing services by owners (conditional upon owning) is a translog function in the relative prices of owner-occupied housing and permanent income, with an intercept which depends upon the indiviual's personal characteristics.[28] The price of owner-occupied housing is based upon equation (3.3). A probit equation is used to model the choice between renting and owning. The choice depends upon the relative prices of both owner- and renter-occupied housing, permanent income, and the same set of demographic variables as in the demand function. The two equations are estimated using a statistical procedure which corrects for possible biases associated with the fact that the assortment of people into tenure modes is not random. [See Heckman (1979).]

The results indicate that the price elasticity of demand for owner-occupied housing services evaluated at the mean is -1.0; the income elasticity, about

[27] Laidler (1969, p. 60).

[28] These include age of head of household, number of dependents under age 17 in the family unit, and age and sex of head of household. Permanent income is a four-year average of annual income.

Table 3.3
The effects of taxing net imputed income upon housing decisions (1970).[a]

Gross income group	Status quo house value	Change in house value	Change in % owning
0– 4,000	10,991	−1,254	−2.6
4– 8,000	14,022	−2,549	−3.9
8–12,000	17,856	−3,107	−4.7
12–16,000	21,134	−3,756	−4.9
16–20,000	26,665	−4,343	−5.0
20–24,000	29,893	−4,879	−5.4
24–28,000	36,477	−4,379	−5.1
> 28000	48,031	−4,250	−4.8

[a]*Source*: Rosen (1979).

0.76.[29] The sign of the price–income interaction term is positive, implying that the price elasticity of demand falls with income. The effective price of owner-occupied housing also enters the tenure choice equation with a negative sign, while income affects the probability of owning positively.

The parameter estimates are used to predict how housing decisions would change if net imputed rent were taxable. Such a change would generate a new value of the price owning for each family.[30] (Assuming that the long-run supply curve of housing services is perfectly elastic, the possibility of changes in the pre-tax price of housing services can be ignored.) By substituting these new values into the probit equation, the expected proportion of homeowners under the new regime can be calculated. Similarly, by substituting into the demand equation, the expected amount of housing demanded conditional on owning can be predicted.

The results are shown in Table 3.3. Taxation of net imputed rent produces substantial reductions in the expected amount of owner-occupied housing demanded. Although families in the highest income brackets face greater increases in the price of housing, their demand is sufficiently less price-elastic that their demands actually fall by smaller amounts. The third column shows how the expected percentage of homeowners decreases due to the removal of the tax advantages. The average change in the incidence of owner-occupied housing for the entire sample is 4.4%. In another simulation, Rosen assumes that the removal of the housing tax subsidy is accompanied by a proportional reduction in marginal tax rates so as to keep tax revenues constant. Despite the income effects

[29]McRae and Turner (1981) argue that allowing for the impact of taxes upon factor input ratios in the production of owner-occupied housing would lead to a lower estimates of the income elasticity of demand. Unfortunately, they study only purchasers of homes with mortgages from the Federal Housing Administration (FHA), a rather unrepresentative sample.

[30]Specifically, the price of a unit of housing services would rise from $\$1-(\tau_y(i+\tau_p))/(i+\tau_p+d)$ to \$1. See equation (3.4).

so generated, there are still sizeable decreases in the quantity of housing demanded and in the percentage of homeowners in each income bracket.

King (1980) studies the impact of taxes on housing decision in the United Kingdom, where, as noted in Section 3.1, the tax treatment of housing is similar to that of the United States. Like Rosen (1979), he examines both the tenure choice and the quantity of services demanded conditional on that choice. In Rosen's analysis the two decisions are modelled in an *ad hoc* fashion, so that there is no guarantee that the estimates are consistent with a single underlying utility function. In contrast, King derives both equations from the same structure of preferences.

Another important feature of King's model is that it allows for the possibility that there is rationing in the choice of tenure modes. In the United Kingdom, essentially three types of dwellings are available: owner-occupied, government-subsidized rental, and unsubsidized furnished rental. Mortgages are not freely available in the U.K., and are rationed among applicants. In addition, admission to the subsidized rental sector is also rationed. King assumes that the household chooses the unsubsidized rental sector only if it is rationed out of the other two.

In King's model, preferences are represented by a homothetic translog indirect utility function,

$$\ln v_i = \ln\left(\frac{y}{p_{gi}}\right) - \beta_1 \ln\left(\frac{p_{hi}}{p_{gi}}\right) - \beta_2\left(\ln\left(\frac{p_{hi}}{p_{gi}}\right)\right)^2, \tag{3.7}$$

where v_i is the ith individual's utility, y_i is income, p_{hi} is the price of housing services [which is defined using an expression like (3.4)], p_{gi} is a price index for all other goods, and the β's are the utility function parameters. On the basis of a suitable stochastic specification, King computes the probability that each individual will be observed in a given tenure mode as a function of the utility function parameters, and hence is able to deduce the likelihood function. The β's are then estimated by maximum likelihood.

An unusual aspect of King's model is that he does not include any controls for the demographic situation of the family, as is common in most housing demand studies. Income and the relative price of housing are the only explanatory variables. King does assume a "random coefficients" model, i.e., that β_1 and β_2 are to be regarded as means of the relevant distributions.

King estimates the model with the cross-sectional data from 1973–74 for England and Wales. He finds $\beta_1 = 0.1022$ (*s.e.* = 0.0008) and $\beta_2 = 0.0238$ (*s.e.* = 0.0009). Perhaps more useful are the implied price elasticities of demand for housing. Evaluated at the means, the price elasticity of demand for owner-occupied housing is -0.532; for subsidized rental -0.498; and for furnished rental -0.645 [King (1980, p. 156)]. This elasticity for owner-occupation is somewhat less than Rosen's (1979) figure of about -1.0 for U.S. data. King's analysis does not provide an estimate of the income elasticity, because a value of 1 is imposed by the utility function (3.7).

A disturbing aspect of King's results is that a statistical test of the hypothesis that the utility functions for the discrete and continuous choices are identical is rejected at conventional significance levels. He suggests two explanations for this finding. One is that different spouses are responsible for different parts of the decision, and the two spouses may have different utility functions. The second is that the assumption that rationing probabilities are exogenous results in a serious model misspecification. Presumably, this latter deficiency could be corrected by making the rationing probability a function of some observable demographic characteristics. But it is hard to imagine how to specify a set of characteristics that would affect the probability of rationing but *not* affect the decisions themselves.

In another paper, King (1981) uses his estimates to predict the consequences of taxing the imputed income from owner-occupation.[31] Under the assumption that the increased tax revenues are distributed as a flat rate lump-sum amount to each family, he finds that the taxation of net imputed rent leads to an overall decline in the long-run consumption of housing services of 13.7%. This is not too different from Rosen's results for the U.S.

In the exercise just described, King makes the "standard" assumption of an infinitely elastic supply of housing services. He also does the simulation assuming a price elasticity of supply of 2.0, a value found by Poterba (1980) in U.S. data. In this case, the overall average percentage decrease in housing consumption is 12.2%. This is less than the result obtained in the perfectly elastic case, because part of the removal of the subsidy is offset by a lower pre-tax price. It is interesting to note that departing from the assumption of perfectly elastic supply does not have a dramatic impact on the substantive results.

The studies discussed so far have ignored the impact of (non-taxable) expected capital gains upon housing decisions. This omission is probably a consequence of the fact that cross-sectional data are not well-suited for dealing with such a phenomenon. Rosen and Rosen (1980) use U.S. time series data to study the determinants of the choice between renting and homeownership. In their model, it is assumed that the overall proportion of families who desire to be owners in a given year depends upon relative price of homeowning to renting, per capita permanent income, and a vector of shift variables. They posit a simple partial adjustment model to account for the fact that in a given year, the actual number of homeowners will not necessarily equal the number who desire to own.

The expression for the price of owner-occupied housing used by Rosen and Rosen is essentially expression (3.6). The expected capital gains component of the expression is calculated as the difference between the one-year forward prediction of house value, $\tilde{V}_{t+1}$, and the current value, $\dot{V}_t = \tilde{V}_{t+1} - V_t$. An ARIMA model with one autoregressive and one moving average parameter is used to generate

[31] In these calculations, the tenure choice is assumed to be exogenous to the model.

$\tilde{V}_{t+1}$. The price of renting is simply the rental component of the consumer price index.

The relative price of owning to renting is entered as a polynomial distributed lag, and permanent income is "proxied" by consumption. To take account of the possibility that credit rationing may affect people's abilities to become homeowners, a variable measuring the availability of deposits at thrift institutions is also included.

The model is estimated using annual U.S. data for the period 1949–74. The price term is negative and significant at conventional levels. The coefficient on income is positive and also significant. There is no strong theoretical presumption for a positive effect of real per capita permanent income on the incidence of homeownership, but it crops up in virtually every study. The availability of funds at credit institutions exerts a positive effect on the proportion of homeowners, but this coefficient is not estimated precisely.

To assess the quantitate implications of their results, Rosen and Rosen use them to predict the long-run consequences of changing the tax treatment of housing. More specifically, the price of owner-occupied housing that would prevail in the absence of tax preferences is substituted into the regression and the long-run proportion of homeowners calculated. The model predicts a change in the incidence of owning from 64% to 60% of all households in 1974. Because the income tax provisions related to homeownership only became important with the rise in marginal tax rates associated with World War II, this implies that about one-fourth of the 16% increase in homeownership between 1945 and 1974 can be attributed to these tax factors.

In another time series analysis of the tenure choice in the U.S., Hendershott and Shilling (1982) study quarterly changes in an "adjusted homeownership rate", i.e., an ownership rate adjusted for changes in the demographic structure of the population. The relative cost of owning to renting and real disposable income per capita are the key explanatory variables. The costs of the two housing modes are computed as discussed in Section 3.2 (see the text surrounding Table 3.2). Both variables are entered in third-degree polynomial lags.

Estimating the model with quarterly data for the period 1960.2 to 1978.4, Hendershott and Shilling find a statistically significant response to changes in the relative costs of owning and renting. Long lags appear to be present; the peak response takes place after 12 to 15 quarters. Income has a positive and statistically significant effect on homeownership only when the user cost is based upon a tax rate of 0.30.

The regression coefficients are used to predict what the long-run homeownership rate would have been in 1974 if property taxes and interest payments had not been deductible. Hendershott and Shilling estimate that the incidence of homeownership would have been 59% conditional on the average marginal income tax rate being 15%, and 57.5% conditional on a value of 30%. It is striking to note the similarity to the result of Rosen and Rosen, despite the differences in model specification and definition of the price of housing services.

3.3.2. Investment decisions

The models discussed above view housing primarily as a consumption good, albeit one whose analysis is particularly complicated because of its durable nature. In addition, housing is a form of investment, and as such, it competes with other assets for a place in people's portfolios. [See, e.g., Henderson and Ioannides (1983).] This aspect of housing has recently received considerable attention in discussions of whether investment in housing has crowded out investment in business capital, and hence contributed to the "productivity crisis".

Empirical resolution of this issue would require joint specification and estimation of housing and physical plant and equipment equations. Unfortunately, even after several decades of careful research on the determinants of business investment, not much consensus with respect to how the process should be modelled has developed. [See, e.g., Sunley (1981).] We discuss, then, a few theoretical and empirical studies whose results are indicative of what might be happening, but are certainly not demonstrative.

To begin, it is important to note the asymmetry in the tax treatment of owner-occupied housing and business investments during inflationary periods. It is sometimes argued that the key to the difference is the fact that owner-occupiers are allowed to deduct nominal rather than real mortgage interest. However, as Summers (1980) points out, this is somewhat misleading reasoning, because nominal interest payments are also deductible on loans taken out to finance other types of investment. Thus, deductibility *per se* does not increase the attractiveness of owner-occupied housing vis-a-vis other forms of investment.[32] The important sources of asymetry are that: (1) in the presence of inflation, depreciation of business investment based on historical costs lowers the real value of depreciation allowances,[33] and (2) owners of physical capital pay tax on nominal rather than real capital gains. Other things being the same, then, increases in inflation increase the effective tax rate on business capital. Thus, inflation raises the relative cost of an investment in business capital to one in owner-occupied housing. When this fact is built into theoretical models which determine the amounts of residential and business investment, the result is predictable – with reasonable parameter values, when inflation increases, the amount of owner-occupied housing relative to business investment goes up. [See Hendershott and Hu (1981), Feldstein (1981), or Muth (1982).]

Summers (1980) notes that an implication of such theories is that, in the short run, an increase in the permanent expected rate of inflation should increase the

[32]A possible exception occurs if ownership of housing relaxes capital market constraints that would otherwise be binding [Summers (1980, p. 2)].

[33]Note that the distorting effect of a *given* level of inflation can be offset by a suitable rate of accelerated depreciation.

market price of housing and reduce the value of the stock market. He regresses the "excess returns" of both the stock market and owner-occupied housing on changes in the permanent expected rate of inflation. The excess return on the stock market during a given period is defined as the ratio of capital gains plus dividends to the beginning of period market valuation, all minus the beginning of period treasury bill rate. The analogous measure for housing is the appreciation in the price deflator for one-family structures less the beginning of period treasury bill rate. (Imputed rent is ignored.) Finally, the expected inflation rate is estimated by assuming that expectations are formed on the basis of an autoregressive moving average process applied to the preceding 10 years of data on inflation.

Summers estimates the regressions with quarterly U.S. data from 1958–78. The results suggest a strong negative relationship of excess stock returns to increases in the expected inflation rate. A 1% increase in the expected inflation rate reduces the value of the stock market by 7.6%. In contrast, a similar increase in inflation increases the value of a house by 1.68%. As Summers (1980, p. 11) emphasizes, these results do not prove that the inflation–taxation interaction has increased residential capital at the expense of business capital. First of all, inflation rates and housing prices generally have moved together over time, while the stock market has moved in the opposite direction. It is therefore dangerous to ascribe a structural interpretation to such regressions. More importantly, the regressions do not even attempt to establish a link between the price changes induced by the inflation–taxation interaction and individuals' investment decisions.

3.3.3. Summary and evaluation

The federal income tax treatment of owner-occupied housing lowers the cost of owner-occupation relative to renting. Studies of housing demand and tenure choice in the United States as well as the United Kingdom (where the relevant tax provisions are similar) suggest that these provisions have had a substantial impact on housing decisions. They induce people to become homeowners and to consume more housing conditional on owning. The interaction of inflation with the tax system has exaggerated these effects. Although there is speculation that the expansion of the housing stock has come at the expense of business capital, not much in the way of econometric evidence is available.

Although considerable progress has been made in explaining housing behavior, much remains to be done. Consider the figures in Table 3.4.[34] Even without any elaborate calculation of the user cost of housing, it is clear from columns 2 and 3 that owner-occupied housing was a good deal in the middle 1970s. The nominal capital gains rates tended to exceed mortgage rates. As a very rough approximation, one could say that owner-occupiers were consuming "free housing" over this

[34] This discussion is based on Rosen (1981).

Table 3.4
Some data on housing for 1973–78.

Year	Median value of owner-occupied housing units (1)	Nominal capital gain rate (2)	New home mortgage yields (3)	Owner-occupancy rate (4)
1973	$24,100	—%	7.95%	0.645
1974	27,200	12.8	8.92	0.646
1975	29,500	8.4	9.01	0.646
1976	32,300	9.4	8.99	0.647
1977	36,900	14.2	9.01	0.648
1978	41,500	12.5	9.54	0.652

[a]*Source:* For years prior to 1977, figures are from Rosen (1981, p. 325). For 1978, columns 1 and 4 are from *Statistical Abstract of the United States, 1981* (pp. 794 and 793, respectively), and column 3 is from *Economic Report of the President 1981* (p. 308). Column 2 is calculated from column 1.

period. Yet column 4 indicates that there was hardly a rush into owner-occupation. The proportion of owner-occupiers moved from just under 0.65 to just above it.

It is not hard to come with explanations for this phenomenon. Transactions costs may inhibit the switch from renting to owning. Rationing in the credit market may prevent individuals from obtaining loans.[35] Jaffee and Rosen (1979) have emphasized the fact that households with different demographic characteristics have quite different homeownership rates, and the proportion of the population of those groups with low rates has been increasing.

Finally, the price figures in the table are *ex post*. *Ex ante*, individuals do not know for sure how much and in what direction prices will move. Presumably, housing decisions depend upon the subjective uncertainty concerning the future course of prices. [See Rosen, Rosen and Holtz-Eakin (1984).] The point is that such potentially important phenomena as these have either been ignored or treated peripherally in most empirical studies of the impact of taxes on housing. As progress on the theoretical and econometric issues in dealing with these problems is made, one can expect more reliable estimates to be produced.

3.4. *Efficiency and equity implications*

For purposes of estimating efficiency effects, the basic problem is to model the tax law in such a way that the usual techniques for measuring excess burden can be

[35] This possibility is discussed by Kearl (1979).

used. Laidler (1969) recognizes that the tax provisions related to housing introduce a wedge between the effective price of housing services and their marginal cost. Therefore, it can be analyzed like any other distortion. In particular, assuming there are no other imperfections in the system, and given estimates of: (a) individual i's marginal tax rate, τ_{yi}, (b) the proportion of his housing costs which are not subject to tax, δ_i, and (c) the compensated price elasticity of demand, η_i, then the size of the welfare loss 'triangle' is[36]

$$0.5(\tau_{yi}\delta_i)^2 V_i \eta_i. \tag{3.8}$$

Laidler assumes a value of -1.5 for η, and 0.68 for δ. He computes a value of τ_{yi} for each of ten income groups on the basis of Internal Revenue Service statistics. Substituting into equation (3.8), he calculates the excess burden for each group, and then aggregates to find a figure of \$500 million dollars for the year 1960.[37] This is equivalent to about \$50 per household in 1980 dollars.

Rosen (1979) uses the same basic framework for calculating the excess burden on the basis of his estimates, with a few differences: The excess burden is computed on a household basis; a different price elasticity of demand[38] is used for each household (the translog functional form does not constrain the elasticity to be constant); and the behavioral response includes tax-induced changes in the tenure choice. The average annual excess burden for the entire sample for the year 1970 is \$107. In terms of 1980 dollars, this is about \$192.

It is difficult to decide whether or not excess burden of this magnitude should be characterized as "large". Ultimately, the decision to eliminate the excess burden depends upon the social and political costs of doing so.

To assess the distributional effects of taxing imputed rent, Rosen estimates how the disposable income of each household in his sample would change, assuming that each would modify its housing behavior as predicted by his model. In Table 3.5, the first column shows average disposable income for each income group under the *status quo*. Column 2 shows disposable income if net imputed rent is taxed, and the government makes no other adjustments in the tax schedule. Column 3 is based on the assumption that marginal tax rates are adjusted proportionately so as to keep tax revenues the same as they were under the *status quo*. As is well-known, it is impossible to summarize the degree of inequality in any "objective" distributional measure [Atkinson (1970)]. In any case, it appears that the taxation of net imputed rent would tend to distribute income away from

[36] See Harberger (1964).

[37] Laidler (1969, p. 64). This is about \$1.3 billion in terms of 1980 dollars.

[38] The uncompensated price elasticity is converted to the theoretically required compensated version by using the Slutsky equation.

Table 3.5
Disposable income under alternative tax treatment of net imputed rent (1970).[a]

Income group	Status quo (1)	Tax net imputed rent (2)	Tax net imputed rent and maintain constant tax revenues (3)
$ 0–4,000	$ 2,686	$ 2,666	$ 2,675
4–8,000	6,024	5,953	6,018
8–12,000	9,452	9,317	9,478
12–16,000	12,715	12,465	12,736
16–20,000	15,829	15,396	15,795
20–24,000	19,088	18,521	19,086
24–28,000	22,248	21,482	22,208
> 28,000	30,306	28,800	30,186

[a]*Source:* Rosen (1979, p. 20).

high-income groups, although at the very bottom end of the scale disposable incomes would fall by small amounts.

King (1981) uses his estimates of housing demand parameters in the United Kingdom to assess the efficiency and distributional consequences of the tax treatment of housing in that country. Instead of relying upon the usual second-order approximation, he estimates the welfare effects directly using the utility function (3.7). Specifically, King (1981, pp. 8–9) computes each household's "equivalent gain" (EG), the sum of money which it would have accepted under the *status quo* as equivalent to the impact of taxing the imputed rental from owner-occupation. The equivalent gain for the ith individual can be defined algebraically in terms of the indirect utility function,

$$v_i\left(y_i^0 + EG_i, p_{h+i}^0, p_g\right) = v_i\left(y_i^1, p_{h+i}^1, p_g\right),$$

where the superscripts 0 and 1 denote values under the *status quo* and the new regime, respectively, and the other variables are as defined above. King observes that for a tax reform that holds tax revenues constant, the sum of the equivalent gains provides a measure of the efficiency gain to the economy. Given constant revenues, a positive average EG "... is equivalent to a Pareto-improvement combined with a set of lump-sum redistribution among households" [King (1981, p. 9)].

For the sake of contrast, King (1981, p. 7) also computes for each household a "cash gain" (CG), which is just the effect of the reform on the household's cash flow on the assumption that its behavior is exogenous. A comparison of EG and

Table 3.6
Gains and losses from taxing imputed rent in the United Kingdom (£ per week, 1973 prices).[a]

Decile	Mean income	Mean *CG*	Mean *EG*
1	10.77	0.52	0.76
2	17.13	0.34	0.67
3	24.34	0.28	0.58
4	31.39	0.24	0.48
5	37.64	0.13	0.36
6	43.65	0.05	0.24
7	49.43	−0.05	0.14
8	57.07	−0.24	−0.09
9	67.64	−0.40	−0.32
10	103.20	−0.87	−1.15
Overall	44.23	0	0.17

[a]*Source:* King (1981, p. 41).

CG indicates whether or not allowing for endogenous housing decisions has important substantive consequences.

Table 3.6 shows the distribution of gains and losses by income decile for both measures. The reduction in excess burden, which is given by the overall mean value of the equivalent gain, is £0.17 per week, about 0.4 of one percent of mean income. The overall value of the cash gain has to be zero given that it is computed under the assumptions of exogenous behavior and constant tax revenues. The figures indicate that just as in the U.S., non-taxation of net imputed rent has substantial distributional implications.[39] Those with higher incomes would tend to be made worse off by the taxation of net imputed rent, and vice versa.

Of course, the estimates of efficiency and equity effects described in this section can be only as good as the underlying behavioral estimates, so all the *caveats* of Section 2 should be recalled. In addition, several other qualifications deserve attention:

(1) The results all involve comparison of long-run equilibria. The short-run capital gains and losses in housing which might occur between equilibrium positions could have important distributional consequences.

(2) The studies focus on housing as a *use* of income. Presumably, if there were major decreases in the demand for housing, it would have a large effect on the *sources* side of the account as well. The owners of those factors used intensively in the production of housing services would suffer reductions in income. As of yet, such effects have not been integrated into studies of the distributive aspects of the tax treatment of housing.

[39]Patric Hendershott has pointed out to me that comparison of King's results with those of Rosen for the U.S. (Table 3.5) must take into account the fact that Rosen assumes tax revenues are held constant via proportional changes in marginal tax rates, while King assumes a lump-sum rebate.

3.5. Proposals for reform

In the absence of clearly articulated goals for U.S. housing policy, it is bound to be difficult to determine how the tax treatment of housing should be changed. If we discount the externality arguments of Section 2, then it would appear that subsidizing owner-occupation is inefficient. Moreover, if we take the evidence on the distributional implications from Section 3.4 seriously, this inefficiency cannot be viewed as "buying" society more equality. Such considerations have lead a number of investigators to suggest that net imputed income should be taxed at the same rate as other sources of income. Thus, for example, Hughes (1980, p. 74) argues that "... the inclusion of imputed housing income in taxable income would be justified under almost any consistent income tax system". From this point of view, the only valid reason for not taxing imputed rent would be administrative difficulties involved in computing it.

This argument is in line with the famous Haig–Simons principle of tax design, which states that an individual should pay tax on his total income regardless of the source. It is often suggested that departures from the Haig–Simons criterion necessarily induce inefficiencies. Clearly, the excess burdens reported in the last section are non-trivial. But the excess burden computation is implicitly based upon a comparison with a lump-sum tax. In practice, such taxes are infeasible. The theory of optimal taxation shows that if lump-sum taxes are excluded, the efficiency maximizing set of tax rates is in general a complicated function of the elasticities of demand and supply for all commodities. [See Sandmo (1976).] It is only in very special cases that one would expect efficiency to require equal rates for all sources of income. On the other hand, it is also highly improbable that the efficient tax rate on imputed rental income is zero. Determination of the appropriate rate has received some attention [e.g., Atkinson (1977)], but remains an important topic for future research.

A number of reform suggestions have been made which maintain the basic structure of the *status quo*, but seek to ameliorate its inegalitarian income distributional consequences. Such a view might be consistent with the notion that there is some merit to the externality argument, but that the subsidy goes too far in helping high-income groups. Alternatively, one might believe that there is no valid externality argument, but that it is politically and administratively impossible to include imputed rent in the tax base. In any case, these reforms focus upon reducing the value of mortgage interest and property tax deductions to upper-income individuals. One possibility would be to put ceilings on the amounts of mortgage interest and property tax deductions, and/or capital gains exclusions. Other proposals would convert the deductions into credits – every homeowner would be allowed to subtract some proportion of interest and property tax payments from his tax liability. In this way, those with higher marginal tax rates would not enjoy an advantage, *ceteris paribus*.

Questions of administrative feasibility lessen the attractiveness of deduction limitations. Unless limitations in the deductibility of mortgage interest were accompanied by a ceiling on all interest deductions, taxpayers could simply secure mortgage loans to other assets. More generally, it is difficult to evaluate such proposals because it is not clear what their objectives are, and what other policy instruments are assumed to be available. If increased efficiency is the goal, why not tax imputed rent at the appropriate rate? If more income redistribution is sought, why not increase marginal tax rates at upper income levels?

So far, our discussion of the equity implications of the tax treatment of housing has focused on distribution of income between upper- and lower-income groups. A number of observers have urged reform because the *status quo* violates horizontal equity, the injunction that equals be treated equally for purposes of tax policy. If there are two identical people, but one owns and one rents, the renter does not obtain the tax advantages of owning.[40] A possible solution to this disparity would be to allow renters either a tax credit or a deduction for part or all of their rent payments.

Evaluation of this suggestion is complicated by the considerable controversy over the question of what horizontal equity really means. [See Feldstein (1976) or King (1983).] Feldstein, for example, has argued that given a fairly reasonable definition of horizontal equity, under certain conditions the tax treatment of owner-occupation is equitable. Specifically, define a horizontally equitable tax system as one that preserves the utility ordering: If two individuals would have the same utility level in the absence of taxation, they should also have the same utility level if there is a tax [Feldstein (1976, p. 94)]. Suppose that individuals' tastes are the same, and they are free to choose between renting and owning. Despite the fact that homeowners are not taxed on the net imputed income from their housing capital, there is no horizontal inequity in Feldstein's sense. As long as tastes are identical, everyone would choose ownership unless the price of houses adjusted to capitalize the tax advantage. Some individuals might choose to rent because (for example) the nature of their employment required a variety of temporary locations. In this case, however, one would expect their earnings to adjust enough to compensate them. Indeed, the surprising conclusion is that any attempts to change the *status quo* would probably *induce* horizontal inequities.

The fact that the opportunity to be a homeowner may be more available to those with high incomes is not *per se* a violation of horizontal equity. "If the opportunity is open to everyone with the high income, it is in effect a reduction in rate progressivity but not a source of horizontal inequity" [Feldstein (1976, p. 95)].

[40] Indeed, if increases in the demand for housing generated by the subsidy to owner-occupiers increases the price of rental housing, renters will be worse off. See White and White (1977).

This analysis relies heavily upon the assumption that tastes are identical. If this is not the case, then *any* tax treatment of housing will create horizontal inequities. It is therefore not clear *a priori* that moving to a system of credits for renters would result in less horizontal inequity.[41]

4. Housing assistance

As we have seen, housing subsidies for the middle- and upper-income groups are implicit in the federal income tax. In contrast, housing subsidies for the poor have tended to be more explicit, often taking the form of public housing provided at below market rents. In this section, we begin by describing briefly the structure of U.S. housing assistance programs, with most of the emphasis on public housing. This is followed by discussions of the program's equity and efficiency implications, and some possibilities for reform.

4.1. Provisions

In the United States, subsidies for the provision of housing to the poor began in 1937. Until very recently, the largest was public housing. Public housing units are developed, owned, and run by local authorities which operate within a municipality, county, or several counties as a group. Up to 1969, the federal government covered the capital cost of the housing, but did not subsidize operating costs, which were paid by the tenants. Since that time, a portion of the operating costs has been subsidized. To obtain finance, the authority sells its own tax exempt and federally guaranteed bonds; the interest and principal are paid by the federal government. By the end of fiscal year 1978, there were 1,173,000 public housing units [Straszheim (1980, p. 170)].[42]

The low-income housing program has been extended and modified many times. We discuss just a few of the key developments in its history.[43]

Section 235, authorized in 1968, provides subsidies for the annual mortgage payments made by low- and moderate-income persons who live in newly built or substantially rehabilitated homes. No new funds have been provided since fiscal year 1981 to finance additional Section 235 commitments.

[41] The difficult problems involved in quantifying the amounts of horizontal equity associated with various tax reforms are discussed by King (1983).

[42] As Murray (undated) has noted, it should not be assumed that this figure represents net additions to the housing stock. It may be the case that to some extent, subsidized housing displaces unsubsidized.

[43] More details can be found in Aaron (1972) or Congressional Budget Office (1982).

In 1969, Congress mandated an important change in the administration of public housing. The rent that could be paid by an eligible family in public housing was limited to 25% of its income, if this was less than the operating cost of the dwelling. This represented a fundamental change in the nature of the federal subsidy, making it income-conditioned as well as cost-conditioned. By 1976, 40% of operating costs were met by subsidies [Weicher (1979, p. 474)].

The turnkey program, also introduced in the 1960's, permitted the local authorities to purchase new, privately built projects. The idea was that by permitting the participation of more developers, construction costs could be reduced. Another attempt to reduce the authorities' participation in building itself was Section 23, the leased housing program (1968), under which local authorities could sign leases with private landlords for existing apartments, with the federal government making available the same subsidy it would for new units.

Section 8 of the Housing Act of 1974 included an important "existing housing and moderate rehabilitation program".[44] Under this program, which involved expenditures of about $1.9 billion in 1982,[45] eligible households search on the private market for housing units. If the dwelling meets certain quality standards and the rent is deemed to be "fair" by the government, then it subsidizes the rent with payments directly to the landlord. (The tenant's rent payment is a fixed proportion of his income, currently set at 25%, but due to rise to 30 percent by fiscal year 1986.) By the end of fiscal year 1978, there were 666,603 housing units covered under Section 8. [See Straszheim (1980, p. 170).]

European programs for low-income housing are qualitatively similar to those of the U.S. Great Britain, Sweden, Germany and the Netherlands also have rent subsidies, management of public housing by special authorities, etc. [Fainstein (1980, p. 216)]. The major difference between the United States and Western Europe concerns the extent of the subsidies. Table 4.1 shows estimates of direct public expenditure on housing and community development as a percentage of gross national product for a group of selected countries in the mid-1970s. Table 4.2 shows the percentage of dwellings completed by private persons. Both tables indicate that the U.S. has relied more heavily on the private market than its European counterparts.

On the other hand, while the amounts spent in the U.S. are relatively small, they are certainly not trivial. The Congressional Budget Office (1982, p. 17) estimated that in 1982 the federal government would spend nearly $10 billion on a variety of housing assistance programs for low- and moderate-income households. The various programs, and particularly public housing, have generated considerable political and academic controversy. The economic literature has

[44] Section 8 also includes a "new construction and substantial rehabilitation" section, which gives financial incentives for developers to house low income families. From the point of view of the inhabitants, this is the same as traditional low-income housing programs.

[45] Congressional Budget Office (1982, p. 17).

Table 4.1
Direct public expenditures on housing and community development as percent of GNP (selected countries, mid-1970s).[a]

United Kingdom (central government, local authorities, public corporations, 1976)	4.1%
Netherlands (central government, 1975)	2.5
Sweden (central government, 1976)	2.3
Germany, Fed. Republic (all governments, 1975)	1.9
United States (all governments, 1976)	0.5

[a]*Source:* Fainstein (1980, p. 218).

Table 4.2
Percent of dwellings completed by private persons (selected countries, 1979).[a]

Austria	45.9%
Denmark	81.5
France	50.4
Sweden	66.2
Switzerland	88.8
United Kingdom	54.0
United States[b]	99.9

[a]*Source:* Economic Commission for Europe, *Annual Bulletin of Housing and Building Statistics for Europe*, United Nations, New York, 1980, pp. 38–41.
[b]Figure for U.S. is for the year 1978.

focused on three allegations: Public housing is produced inefficiently; it is an inefficient method for distributing income to the poor; and it has anomalous distributional implications. Each of these is discussed in turn.

4.2. *Production inefficiency*

As noted above, for a considerable portion of its history, the federal government paid for the capital costs of public housing, but did not subsidize operating costs. To assess the efficiency implications of this practice, Muth (1973) assumes that housing services are produced with two inputs, "real estate inputs", which are used to build a structure, and "current inputs", which are used to maintain it. Presumably, there is some scope for substitution between them. For example, one can use relatively expensive aluminum siding which requires little maintenance, or wood siding, which is cheaper but needs more maintenance. The necessary condition for cost minimization is that the marginal rate of substitution between the inputs to be equal to the ratio of their marginal social costs. Because capital costs are paid by the federal government, local authorities in effect face a price of capital below its social marginal cost. This gives them an incentive to produce housing which uses too much capital and too little maintenance.

Muth's formal analysis focuses on the costs of this distortion in input ratios.[46] He postulates a constant elasticity of substitution unit cost function for housing services,

$$p_h = \left[\psi^{\xi} r^{(1-\xi)} + c^{(1-\xi)}\right]^{1/1-\xi}, \tag{4.1}$$

where p_h is the price per unit of housing services; r is the price per unit of real estate inputs; c is the price per unit of current inputs; ξ is the elasticity of substitution between real estate inputs and current inputs; and ψ is a parameter of the production function.

On the basis of earlier studies on production in housing, Muth assumes that $\xi = 0.2$ and $\psi = 0.243$. He normalizes prices such that in the private sector $r = 1$ and $c = 1$. To the extent the public housing authority pays for its operating expenses, it also faces a price of c equal to one. On the other hand, due to the federal subsidy, the authority's effective value of r is only about 0.05.

Substituting these figures into equations for input ratios derived from (4.1), Muth shows how the subsidy lowers the per unit price of housing produced by the housing authority, and induces it to use relatively less in the way of current inputs than the private sector. But the key question is what the resource cost of public housing is. This is found by pricing the inputs used by the local housing authorities at their *market* prices. Muth finds that the ratio of the market value of public housing to its resource cost is 0.82. Other studies using methodologies somewhat different than Muth's have found estimates of production inefficiencies similar in magnitude.[47] [See Weicher (1979, p. 497).]

[46] Muth (1973, p. 7) notes two other reasons why public housing tends to be more expensive than comparable private housing: (1) The Davis–Bacon Act forces contractors to use wage scales set by the Department of Labor. These tend to be higher than those prevailing in the labor market. (2) Cleared slum land is often used, and such land tends to be expensive due to proximity to downtown areas. Demolishing existing structures is also expensive.

[47] Of course, the validity of such estimates must be viewed in light of the methodological difficulties in studying housing supply discussed in Section 2.

In 1970, it was decided to reimburse local housing authorities for the excess of operating costs over revenues. As Olsen (forthcoming, p. 9) notes, in effect this reduces the price of marginal maintenance and rehabilitation facing the authorities to zero. Operating costs increased dramatically, and by 1976 federal operating subsidies mounted to 40 percent of the operating costs of public housing units. However, in many programs today, there are still mortgage subsidies which generate a bias toward capital intensive production techniques. There is also a persistent belief that publicly constructed housing is excessively expensive because public sector managers, unlike their counterparts in the private sector, have no incentive to give much weight to efficiency. Unfortunately, no systematic estimates of the importance of this effect are available. Similarly, despite the widespread publicity given to occurrences of outright corruption in the administration of public housing,[48] it is not clear what the impact of this has been on its cost.

4.3. Consumption inefficiency

An important motivation behind public housing appears to be income redistribution. Given the theoretical presumption that redistributing income via a price subsidy is inefficient relative to cash, the key empirical question is whether the inefficiency is large in dollar terms.

An early examination of this issue is due to Aaron and von Furstenberg (1971). They assume that a representative individual's utility, U, depends only upon his consumption of housing services, Q_h (which are defined so that the price of a unit equals one dollar), and all other goods, G,

$$U = U(Q_h, G).$$

Facing private market prices, the individual chooses some bundle (Q_h^0, G^0), with associated utility level U^0. Now suppose the government makes available to the individual the opportunity to purchase housing services at a price of $(1-s)$, where s is the subsidy rate. Geometrically this is equivalent to pivoting out the budget line. In general, the individual will change his consumption bundle to (Q_h^1, G^1), which gives utility $U^1 > U^0$.[49] The cost to the government of the program is sQ_h^1.

[48] In 1982, one member of the Chicago Housing Authority (CHA) opined that "the CHA is a political slop bucket, and everybody's drinking from it" (*Newsweek Magazine*, April 19, 1982).

[49] If the individual is not allowed to choose freely the quantity of subsidized housing he consumes, his utility may be less than U^1. In the extreme case where the housing authority offers a specific quantity–price bundle, the budget line does not pivot. The program simply adds one point to the family's budget set.

The problem is to find the amount of income that would be required for the recipient to attain, at market prices, the level of utility U^1 reached under the subsidy program. This is found simply by holding the price of housing at its original value, and giving the individual lump-sum income until his utility reaches U^1. (The geometrical analogue is a parallel shift outward of the budget line until it is just tangent to the indifference curve associated with U^1.) Call the amount of lump-sum income so required M. Then Aaron and von Furstenberg define the relative consumption inefficiency of the subsidy as

$$(sQ_h^1 - M)/sQ_h^1.$$

To implement this theoretical framework, one needs to choose a utility function and specific values for its parameters. Aaron and von Furstenberg assume a constant elasticity of substitution utility function. Parameters are selected so that they are consistent with a price elasticity of demand for housing of -1.0 and an income elasticity of 1.0. Assuming that the public housing subsidy rate is 50% (i.e., $s = 0.5$), they find that the relative consumption inefficiency is about 10%.

The price and income elasticities used by Aaron and von Furstenberg to compute the utility function parameters are from studies of the housing behavior of the general population. It might very well be the case, however, that the behavioral responses of the poor differ from those of the population at large. Moreover focusing on a representative individual does not allow one to address the important question of how benefits vary across individuals. Subsequent to the Aaron and von Furstenberg study, a number of others have been done which estimate utility function parameters with cross-sectional data on public housing recipients. This allows a more accurate depiction of the behavioral and distributional effects of the subsidy. We discuss here the analysis by Murray (1980), which is one of the most recent and careful.[50]

Murray assumes that preferences can be represented by the generalized constant elasticity of substitution form,

$$U = (\varepsilon_1 Q_h^{\varepsilon_2} + G^{\varepsilon_3})^{\varepsilon_4}, \tag{4.2}$$

where the ε's are parameters to be estimated, and the other variables are defined above.[51] The first-order conditions for utility maximization imply that

$$\ln \frac{p_h G}{p_g Q_h} = \ln \frac{\varepsilon_1 \varepsilon_2}{\varepsilon_3} + (\varepsilon_2 - 2)\ln Q_h + (2 - \varepsilon_3)\ln G. \tag{4.3}$$

[50] See also Kraft and Kraft (1979), Kraft and Olsen (1977), Sumka and Stegman (1978), and Olsen and Barton (1982).

[51] The version of this equation appearing in Murray (1980, p. 27) has a typographical error.

Murray partitions his sample into groups based on family size, and for each group estimates (4.3) using an instrumental variables technique.

The variable p_h is based upon the Bureau of Labor Statistics (BLS) estimate of the price of a "standard" unit in each city. The quantity of housing services provided by a given dwelling is its rent divided by the rental on the BLS standard unit. (Inter-city price indices are formed by taking the ratio of the prices of the BLS units in the different cities.)

Because market rents are unavailable for public housing units, it is not clear how to measure the quantity of housing services they provide. (Recall the discussion of Section 2 concerning the difficulties of measuring housing services in general.) To estimate the market value of each public housing unit, Murray uses an hedonic price equation produced by another study. By substituting into the hedonic equation the characteristics of a given public housing dwelling, he can obtain an estimate of what its rent would be in the private market.[52]

Equation (4.3) is estimated with 1971 data on nearly 1,400 successful public housing applicants across seven cities. The parameters imply that on average, the subsidy increased housing consumption by about 95% over what it would have been otherwise [Murray (1980, p. 33)]. If each household would have received instead an equivalent cash grant, housing consumption would have increased only 20% above the unsubsidized level.

To assess the efficiency of the program, Murray computes the subsidy cost associated with each public housing unit, defined as the resource cost of the unit[53] plus administrative costs minus the rent paid. He finds that in his sample, the average subsidy cost is $1,530, while the average nominal benefit is $948.[54] Thus, a shift to an equivalent cash grant would lower costs by 34%. Other studies have reached similar conclusions. [See Weicher (1979, p. 497).]

Although the results of such analyses have contributed considerably to our understanding of public housing, they suffer from several potentially important problems. The fact that the utility function parameters are estimated using only public housing inhabitants means that the estimates may be inconsistent due to selectivity bias.[55] The use of hedonic indices to value public housing units is also problematic because, as Aaron (1977, p. 69) has noted, public housing tenants may not value housing characteristics the same way that the market would.

Even if the parameter estimates were perfect, errors in measuring consumption inefficiency might arise due to the implicit assumption that the only distortion in the system is the subsidy on housing. For example, it is well-known that the welfare system tends to place high implicit marginal tax rates on the labor income

[52] The hedonic price equation is based on data from New York City.

[53] Building on research similar to that described in Section 4.1, Murray assumes that the resource cost exceeds the market value of the unit by 17 percent.

[54] There is considerable variation in these figures across families.

[55] For a discussion of this statistical problem, see Heckman (1979).

of the poor. Analyses of public housing subsidies should therefore also take work decisions into account. However, it is difficult to say *a priori* in what direction current estimates are biased by the failure to do so.

4.4. Distributional implications

The studies by Murray and others have shown that public housing confers a relatively large benefit upon the recipients. However, this benefit is available only to a small number of poor people. As noted above, there are a few million public housing units, but in 1981, there were about 32 million persons whose income fell below the U.S. government poverty line.[56] Hence, many more people desire entry into public housing than it is possible to accommodate. It turns out that although the incomes of the recipients are concentrated at the bottom of the income distribution, many people gain entry who are better off than those who do not. [See Aaron (1972, p. 115).]

A related issue is the distribution of benefits within the group of families who actually gain admittance. Murray (1980, p. 31) regressed his estimates of the actual benefit on annual income, holding constant various demographic characteristics of the families. He found that there is indeed a negative relation between income and benefits. But the R^2 of the equation is only 0.70, suggesting that there is quite a bit of randomness in the way the benefits are distributed across tenants.

Aaron (1972, p. 12) has pointed out that public housing may have general equilibrium effects with important distributional implications. Presumably, the availability of public housing decreases the demand for low-cost non-subsidized housing, lowering the rents in that sector. This would tend to increase the real incomes of the tenants and lower the real incomes of the landlords. These issues do not yet appear to have received econometric attention.

4.5. Possibilities for reform

The consensus from the literature is that public housing is inefficiently produced, distorts consumption patterns on the part of the beneficiaries, and redistributes income capriciously.[57] Most economists have been against the program for years. Muth's (1973, p. 43) sentiment is probably typical: "The only possible justifica-

[56] U.S. Bureau of The Census (1982, p. 440).

[57] We have not touched upon the administrative complexity of the program and the associated costs. Mills (undated, p. 26) notes that "... a cadre of specialized talent has sprung up to advise building landlords and tenants on procedures to find their way through or around the bureaucratic maze ...".

tion for housing programs I can see is that they are politically feasible whereas increased income maintenance is not."

It has been suggested that if subsidies have to be maintained, then their link to public provision of housing should be broken. If the subsidy could be applied to private sector housing, then it would no longer be necessary for the public sector to get involved in apartment construction and management. In addition, recipients of aid would no longer be geographically concentrated and marked publicly.

As noted above, under the Section 8 program, there are indeed subsidies for low-income individuals who rent on the private market. However, as of 1978, only about 1.3% of publicly subsidized dwellings for the poor were associated with demand side programs [Quigley (1980, p. 162)]. And even under Section 8, recipients are limited in their choice of dwellings, cannot spend more than 25% of their incomes on rent, and can only choose from landlords who participate in the program.

A demand-oriented subsidy program that has received a good deal of attention is "housing allowances".[58] Each qualified individual would receive from the government a payment equal to the difference between the cost of standard housing established by the program and some fraction of his income. The allowance could be spent on any housing on the private market, providing that it met certain quality standards. Recently, a large social experiment (the Experimental Housing Allowance Program) was conducted in several cities to determine how housing allowances would affect people's behavior.[59] Analyses of the data by Hanushek and Quigley (1981, p. 204) and Venti and Wise (1982) suggest a moderate effect upon housing consumption; the income elasticity of demand for housing services in the experiment was below 0.5. Interestingly, the increased demand generated by the housing allowances does not seem to have had much effect upon housing prices in the communities where the experiment was conducted. This is probably because the supply of housing services is fairly elastic and the response to the increased allowance takes place gradually over time.

The main problem with the housing allowances system examined in the experiment is the stipulation that the dwellings meet various quality standards. The purpose of this provision is presumably to protect the poor from unscrupulous landlords who would take their money and provide no services in return. The evidence from the experiment indicates that it would be very hard to set sensible standards and that enforcement would entail substantial administrative costs. In addition, the imposition of standards reduced participation in the program significantly [Allen et al. (1981, p. 26)].

Muth (1973) has proposed the introduction of "rent certificates", which could be used by the poor to pay for their rents in any public or private housing that

[58]A number of alternative policy approaches are discussed in Congressional Budget Office (1982).
[59]For details on the design of the experiment and its results, see Bradbury and Downs (1981).

they deemed reasonable. Such a program comes very close to being an unrestricted cash transfer. Clearly, there are powerful interest groups which, for one reason or another, wish to see income support for the poor closely linked to their consumption of housing. Whether or not a scheme like Muth's is perceived to be tied closely enough to housing to be politically acceptable is an open question.

5. Conclusions

Empirical investigation of the effects of government policies upon housing behavior presents researchers with difficult methodological problems. Given that there is no "best" way for dealing with these problems, investigators are bound to produce different answers. Nevertheless, there appears to be widespread agreement that in the United States, the income tax treatment of owner-occupied housing and the public provision of low-income housing have substantially increased the consumption of housing services. In the process, economic efficiency has decreased.

Moreover, the housing related provisions in the federal income tax have lead to a more unequal distribution of income. It is unlikely that the disequalizing effects of these provisions have been mitigated by the equalizing effects of the expenditure programs. Thus, judged by the standards of conventional welfare economics, reform seems appropriate, and we have discussed a number of possibilities. Of course, it might be that current programs are moving us toward important social and political goals that lie outside the scope of welfare economics. But given that these goals have never been carefully articulated, it is impossible to tell whether or not such is the case.

References

Aaron, Henry, 1972, Shelters and subsidies (Brookings Institution, Washington, DC).

Aaron, Henry, 1977, Comments, in: F. Thomas Juster, ed., The distribution of economic well-being (Ballinger, Cambridge, MA) 65–69.

Aaron, Henry J. and George M. von Furstenberg, 1971, The inefficiency of transfers in kind: The case of housing assistance, Western Economic Journal, 184–191.

Abbott, Michael and Orley Ashenfelter, 1976, Labor supply, commodity demand, and the allocation of time, Review of Economic Studies 43, 389–411.

Alexander, W.E., Comment, Annals of Economic and Social Measurement 4, 175–178.

Allen, Garland E., Jerry J. Fitts and Evelyn S. Glatt, 1981, The experimental housing allowance program, in: Katherine J. Bradbury and Anthony Downs, eds., Do housing allowances work? (Brookings Institution, Washington, DC) 1–32.

Atkinson, A.B., 1970, On the measurement of inequality, Journal of Economic Theory 2, 244–263.

Atkinson, A.B., 1977, Housing allowances, income maintenance and income taxation, in: M.S. Feldstein and R.P. Inman, eds., The economics of public services (Macmillan, London).

Bradbury, Katharine L. and Anthony Downs, eds., 1981, Do housing allowances work? (Brookings Institution, Washington, DC).

Brown, James N. and Harvey S. Rosen, 1982, On the estimation of structural hedonic price models, Econometrica 50, 765–768.

Carliner, Geoffrey, 1973, Income elasticity of housing demand, Review of Economics and Statistics 55, 528–532.

Congressional Budget Office, 1981, The tax treatment of homeownership: Issues and options (Congress of the United States, Washington, DC).

Congressional Budget Office, 1982, Federal housing assistance: Alternative approaches (Congress of the United States, Washington, DC).

de Leeuw, Frank and Raymond J. Struyk, 1975, The web of urban housing (The Urban Institute, Washington, DC).

Diamond, Douglas B. and Barton A. Smith, 1981, Housing as an explicit "good", Mimeo. (North Carolina State University, Raleigh, NC).

Englund, Peter and Mats Persson, 1982, Housing prices and tenure choice with asymmetric taxes and progressivity, Journal of Public Economics 19, 271–290.

Fainstain, Susan S., 1980, American policy for housing and community development: A comparative examination, in: Roger Montgomery and Dale Marshall, eds., Housing policy in the 1980's (Lexington Books, D.C. Heath and Co., Lexington, MA) 215–230.

Feldstein, Martin S., 1976, On the theory of tax reform, Journal of Public Economics 6, 77–104.

Feldstein, Martin S., 1981, Inflation, tax rules, and the accumulation of residential and nonresidential capital, National Bureau of Economic Research working paper no. 753.

Follain, James R., Jr., 1979, The price of elasticity of the long-run supply of new housing construction, Land Economics 55, 190–199.

Hanushek, Eric A. and John M. Quigley, 1981, Consumption aspects, in: Katharine L. Bradbury and Anthony Downs, eds., Do housing allowances work? (Brookings Institution, Washington, DC) 185–240.

Heckman, James, 1979, Sample bias as a specification error, Econometrica 47, 153–162.

Hendershott, Patric H. and Sheng Cheng Hu, 1981, The allocation of capital between residential and nonresidential uses: Taxes, inflation and capital market constraints, National Bureau of Economic Research working paper no. 718.

Hendershott, Patric H. and James D. Shilling, 1982, The economics of tenure choice, 1955–79, in: C. Sirmans, ed., Research in real estate, Vol. 1 (Jai Press, Greenwich, CT) 105–133.

Hendershott, Patric H. and Joel Slemrod, 1983, Taxes and the user cost of capital for owner-occupied housing, AREUEA Journal 10, 375–393.

Henderson, J.V. and Y. Ioannides, 1983, A model of housing tenure choice, American Economic Review 73, 98–113.

Hughes, G.A., 1980, Housing and the tax system, in: G.A. Hughes and G.M. Heal, eds., Public policy and the tax system (Allen and Unwin, Boston, MA) 67–105.

Ingram, Gregory K. and Yitzhak Oron, 1977, The production of housing services from existing dwelling units, in: Gregory K. Ingram, ed., Residential location and urban housing markets (Ballinger, Cambridge, MA) 273–314.

Jaffee, Dwight M. and Kenneth T. Rosen, 1979, Mortgage credit availability and residential construction, Brookings Papers in Economic Activity 2, 333–376.

Jones, Reginald H., 1978, Sunset legislation, Tax Review.

Jorgenson, Dale W., 1971, Econometric studies of investment behavior: A survey, Journal of Economic Literature, 1111–1147.

Kearl, J.R., 1979, Inflation, mortgages, and housing, Journal of Political Economy 5, 1115–1138.

King, Mervyn A., 1980, An econometric model of tenure choice and demand for housing as a joint decision, Journal of Public Economics, 137–160.

King, Mervyn A., 1981, The distribution of gains and losses from changes in the tax treatment of housing, Social Science Research Council Programme no. 20 (London).

King, Mervyn A., 1983, An index of inequality: With applications to horizontal equity and social mobility, Econometrica, January.

Kraft, John and Arthur Kraft, 1979, Benefits and costs of low rent public housing, Journal of Regional Science 19, 309–317.

Kraft, John and Edgar O. Olsen, 1977, The distribution of benefits from public housing, in: F. Thomas Juster, ed., The distribution of economic well-being (Ballinger, Cambridge, MA) 51–65.

Laidler, David, 1969, Income tax incentives for owner-occupied housing, in: Arnold C. Harberger and Martin J. Baily, eds., The taxation of income from capital (Brookings Institution, Washington, DC).
MacRae, C. Duncan and Margery Austin Turner, 1981, Estimating demand for owner-occupied housing subject to the income tax, Journal of Urban Economics 10, 338–356.
Mayo, Stephen K., 1981, Theory and estimation in the economics of housing demand, Journal of Urban Economics 10, 95–116.
Mills, Edwin S., undated, National housing policy: A critique and a proposal, Mimeo. (Princeton University, Princeton, NJ).
Murray, Michael P., 1980, Tenant benefits in alternative federal housing programs, Urban Studies 17, 25–34.
Murray, Michael P., undated, Subsidized and unsubsidized housing stocks: 1961–1977, Mimeo. (Claremont Graduate School, Claremont, CA).
Musgrave, Richard A., 1959, The theory of public finance (McGraw-Hill, New York).
Muth, Richard F., 1973, Public housing: An economic evaluation (American Enterprise Institute, Washington, DC).
Muth, Richard F., 1982, Effects of the U.S. tax system on housing prices and consumption, Hoover Institution working paper no. E-82-3.
Nichols, Albert L. and Richard J. Zeckhauser, 1982, Targeting transfers through restrictions on recipients, American Economic Review, Papers and Proceedings 72, 372–377.
Niskanen, W.A., Jr., 1971, Bureaucracy and representative government (Aldine, Chicago, IL).
Olsen, Edgar O., forthcoming, Implications of the experimental housing allowance program for housing policy, in: Joseph Friedman and Daniel Weinberg, eds., The great housing experiment.
Olsen, Edgar O. and David M. Barton, 1983, The benefits and costs of public housing in New York City, Journal of Public Economics 20, 299–332.
Polinsky, A. Mitchell and David T. Ellwood, 1979, An empirical reconciliation of micro and grouped estimates of the demand for housing, Review of Economics and Statistics 61, 199–205.
Poterba, James M., 1980, Inflation, income taxes and owner-occupied housing, National Bureau of Economic Research working paper no. 553.
Quigley, John M., 1980, Housing allowances and demand-oriented housing subsidies, in: Roger Montgomery and Dale Marshall, eds., Housing policy in the 1980's (Lexington Books, D.C. Heath and Co., Lexington, MA) 161–68.
Quigley, John M., 1982, Non-linear project constraints and consumer demand: An application to public programs to residential housing, Journal of Urban Economics.
Rosen, Harvey S., 1979, Housing decisions and the U.S. income tax: An econometric analysis, Journal of Public Economics 11, 1–23.
Rosen, Harvey S., 1981, Comments, in: H.J. Aaron and J.A. Pechman, eds., How taxes affect economic behavior (Brookings Institution, Washington, DC) 323–326.
Rosen, Harvey S. and Kenneth T. Rosen, 1980, Federal taxes and homeownership: Evidence from time series, Journal of Political Economy 88, 59–75.
Rosen, Harvey S., Kenneth T. Rosen and Douglas Holtz-Eakin, 1984, Housing tenure, uncertainty, and taxation, Review of Economics and Statistics.
Rosen, Sherwin, 1974, Hedonic prices and implicit markets: Product differentiation in pure competition, Journal of Political Economy 82, 34–55.
Rothenberg, Jerome, 1977, Comments on chapter 8, in: Gregory K. Ingram, ed., Residential location and urban housing markets (Ballinger, Cambridge, MA) 315–321.
Rydell, C. Peter, 1979, Shortrun response of housing markets to demand shifts, Rand Corporation working paper no. R-2453-HUD.
Sandmo, Agnar, 1976, Optimal taxation: An introduction to the literature, Journal of Public Economics 6, 37–54.
Straszheim, Mahlon R., 1980, The Section 8 rental-assistance program: Costs and policy options, in: Roger Montgomery and Dale Marshall, eds., Housing policy for the 1980's (Lexington Books, Lexington, MA) 169–184.
Struyk, Raymond J., 1976, Urban homeownership (Lexington Books, Lexington, MA).
Struyk, Raymond J., 1978, Sue A. Marshall and Larry J. Ozanne, Housing policies for the urban poor (The Urban Institute, Washington, DC).

Sumka, Howard J. and Michael A. Stegman, 1978, An economic analysis of public housing in small cities, Journal of Regional Science 18, 395–410.

Summers, Lawrence, 1980, Inflation, the stock market and owner-occupied housing, National Bureau of Economic Research working paper no. 606.

Sunley, Emil M., 1981, Comments, in: Henry J. Aaron and J.A. Pechman, eds., How taxes affect economic behavior (Brookings Institution, Washington, DC) 127–130.

Tobin, James, 1970, On limiting the domain of inequality, Journal of Law and Economics 13, 263–277.

U.S. Bureau of the Census, 1982, Statistical abstract of the United States: 1982–83, 103rd ed. (U.S. Government Printing Office, Washington, DC).

Venti, Steven F. and David A. Wise, 1982, Moving and housing expenditure: Transactions cost and disequilibrium, Mimeo. (Harvard University, Cambridge, MA).

Weicher, John C., 1979, Urban housing policy, in: Peter Mieszkowski and Mahlon Straszheim, eds., Current issues in urban economics (Johns Hopkins University Press, Baltimore, MD).

Weicher, John C., 1980, Housing: Federal policies and programs (American Enterprise Institute, Washington, DC).

Weiss, Yoram, 1978, Capital gains, discriminatory taxes, and the choice between renting and owning a house, Journal of Public Economics 10, 45–55.

White, Michelle J. and Lawrence White, The subsidy to owner-occupied housing: Who benefits?, Journal of Public Economics 7, 111–126.

Chapter 8

THE TAXATION OF NATURAL RESOURCES

TERRY HEAPS

Simon Fraser University, Burnaby, BC

JOHN F. HELLIWELL

University of British Columbia, Vancouver, BC

1. Introduction

The purpose of this chapter is to discuss the main issues that arise in the taxation and regulation of natural resources. Since natural resources are frequently owned or controlled by governments, as well as being subject to a variety of conventional taxes, the scope of the chapter must extend beyond conventional tax forms, since various royalties, rentals, bonus bids, direct government participation, and regulations are often used in combination with conventional taxes. Some attention must also be paid to overlapping jurisdictions, as natural resources are frequently the subject of taxation by more than one government, sometimes by different countries, since natural resource products are frequently traded goods.

After listing a fairly broad range of taxation issues and instruments, we shall restrict our more detailed theoretical and empirical analysis to a few example resources chosen to represent the main issues. To illustrate the issues relating to common property resources, we shall use the fishery. To cover the issues of optimal management and taxation of renewable resources subject to competing uses, but not to common property problems, we shall use forestry. For extractive resources, we shall use metal mining to expose some of the fundamental issues of optimal timing and the inevitable trade-offs between revenue collection and economic efficiency. For energy resources, which are the most important in terms of the size and variability of actual and potential tax revenues, we shall concentrate on crude oil and natural gas, with some references to hydro-electricity.

At all stages, we shall try to blend theoretical analysis and empirical results, although our main emphasis will be on exposing and quantifying the issues that are of the greatest importance in resource taxation.

After outlining the main issues in Section 2, we devote successive sections to fisheries, forests, mining, oil and natural gas, and hydro-electricity, followed by a short concluding section.

Handbook of Public Economics, vol. I, edited by A.J. Auerbach and M. Feldstein

2. Outline of issues and instruments

The essence of natural resources is that they are limited in total supply and varied in their quality or costliness. Intra-marginal resources offer the prospect of economic rents and hence the ability to pay taxes. From a public finance perspective, the taxable capacity possessed by economic rents from natural resources is especially attractive because such rents can in principle be collected without introducing inefficiency in the pattern of resource use. Indeed, we shall see that there are even some cases, for example in the open-access fishery or the collection of rents from hydro-electric sites, where the taxation of the resource can improve the efficiency of resource use. However, we shall also find that in general there is often, as in most other areas of taxation, a trade-off between revenue collection and efficiency. There is even more often a conflict between revenue collection and the other objectives of resource taxation as described in Section 2.2.

In this section we shall start by describing a number of the possible effects that resource taxation may have on the timing and scale of resource development, emphasizing the potential conflicts between revenue-raising and economic efficiency. We shall then list some of the other objectives and effects of resource taxation, and conclude with an introduction to the main types of taxes, subsidies, and regulations used to tax and distribute natural resource revenues.

2.1. Efficiency effects

(i) *The cut-off grade problem.* If a natural resource is subjected to a per-unit-of-output tax that does not make allowance for the higher costs of marginal deposits, then some of these resources will not be developed even though their value exceeds the costs (excluding taxes) of their recovery. This is known as the "cut-off grade" problem by reference to metal mining, where it is frequently argued that a gross royalty raises the cut-off grade and thereby leaves a substantial amount of otherwise economic ore undeveloped, and hence a proportion of the metal unrecovered. A royalty based on tons of ore processed creates more cut-off grade problems than a royalty based on the amount of metal recovered. As we shall explain in Section 5, the relative effects on ore and on metal recovered, and hence the overall efficiency effects, depend to an important extent on how easy it is to select the deposits in order of increasing costs and to eliminate only the most costly deposits from production.

The same issue naturally arises with other resources. A volume charge on timber harvested or fish landed tends to leave unharvested the species that have lower market values or are more costly to harvest. A per-barrel charge on crude oil also tends to leave undeveloped the deposits of lower value or higher cost oil, and to limit investment designed to increase the proportion of the oil that can be recovered.

Taxes or royalties based on the value rather than the volume of output remove the effect on the quality of output, but still limit the development of higher cost resources. In many jurisdictions, and for many resources, gross royalties have been adjusted to permit deduction of some operating and other costs, thus modifying the cut-off grade effects. Since taxes based on either the volume or value of output are often simple to administer and certain in application, they are often preferred by taxing authorities. Thus the assessment of their efficiency costs, acting through the cut-off grade effect, is an important research problem in resource taxation.

(ii) *Tilting of output.* The impact of resource taxation on the timing of output from an individual deposit of an extractive resource of constant quality [Dasgupta and Heal (1979, ch. 12)] has been an active topic for theoretical consideration. There has been less attention paid to measuring the efficiency consequences of these output-tilting effects. In general, taxes on the volume or value of output tend to tilt the output path by reducing initial output, although much depends on the role of the productive factors in resource production. Analogous issues arise with other resources, and at the industry level. For example, as we show in Section 4, different types of taxation influence the rotation period for a sustained yield forest. At the industry level, the tilting effect is less closely related to the effects of the tax system on the firm's choice of output rate from a single deposit, and much more closely linked to world market conditions and the extent to which governments encourage rapid exploitation of natural resources under their control. In making this decision, governments are often concerned to ensure fairly stable supplies of timber, fish or minerals to communities and enterprises that live by harvesting or processing the resource.

(iii) *Exhaustion effects.* We show in Sections 3 and 4 how in some circumstances taxation can either induce or prevent harvest rates for forestry or fishing being so rapid as to extinguish the resource, an extreme form of tilting production towards the present. We use the fishery to explain the common property problem and the use of taxation to raise and preserve the value of resources that can be dissipated by competitive open access. Similar issues arise in the case of oil and natural gas if adjacent surface rights have access to a common underground pool of oil or gas. Because it has proven relatively easy to find production-sharing solutions that minimize the common property problem in oil and gas production, we shall base our discussion on fishing. In the case of forestry the issue of dissipation or extinction of the resource has been due in part to competition from other uses and in part to insecurity of tenure that encourages early harvesting and discourages reforestation.

(iv) *Exploration effects.* The issue arises chiefly in the case of underground or undersea deposits of extractive resources. Any taxation of discovered deposits reduces the private value of such deposits, and hence reduces the profitability and scale of exploration activity aimed at finding new deposits. There may also be external effects that influence the pace of exploration activity and are in turn influenced by the tax system. One is the fact that one explorer's activity and results, if known, can help others to direct their activity in more profitable directions. The second is the "gold-rush effect" that accelerates the pace of exploration, or whatever other activity is required to acquire future development rights, in any situation where rights are acquired on a first-come first-served basis. These two external effects have opposite effects on the pace of exploration activity. Finally, uncertainty about the results of exploration activity may lead to a sufficient amount of non-diversifiable risk that private firms, facing risk-averse capital markets, may therefore do less than the socially optimal amount of exploration. Tax subsidies to exploration are sometimes advocated on this ground.

(v) *Factor mix.* Many types of resource taxation have direct or indirect effects on the ratio of resource to non-resource inputs used in the production of a natural resource and on the relative use of labour, capital, energy, and other materials in the mix of non-resource inputs. For example, a royalty that is levied on oil sold may cause it to be undervalued and overused in the energy-producing industry. Another frequently cited example is the corporation income tax, which is often levied equally on the equity-financed portion of the capital stock and on quasi-rents and resource rents accruing to the enterprise. A tax rate high enough to collect a large proportion of the resource rents then also acts to reduce the use of capital relative to other non-resource inputs. To circumvent this problem there are many jurisdictions that use only the normal rate of corporation income tax but impose an additional resource-based profits tax (e.g., the U.K. Petroleum Revenue Tax discussed in Section 6) that makes allowance for all current and capital costs.

(vi) *Efficiency of factor utilization.* With the aim of avoiding the various efficiency effects described above, many writers and tax authorities have advocated or adopted taxes based on net revenues, after deducting all costs of development. Since the tax base then approximates economic rents, the tax rate is set very high. However, these high rates may sharply reduce the pay-off to entrepreneurial efforts designed to control the overall efficiency of factor use. When cost reductions produce savings of "five-cent dollars" (as they would if the rate of rent tax were 95%), there is clearly less incentive to reduce costs in general and more incentive to incur certain costs (e.g., executive jets and company hunting lodges) that have a consumption component. As we shall describe later, there are ways of minimizing these effects. One is to use best-practice costs (as is sometimes done to determine forestry stumpage payments) rather than actual costs in defining the tax base. Another is to collect a substantial part of the rent by other means (e.g., some combination of competitive bids and gross royalties) to permit the marginal rent tax rate to be reduced without proportionate reduction in the amount of rent collected.

2.2. Other objectives of resource taxation

Although the effects of taxation on the efficiency of resource development, and on the pace of resource use relative to some competitive norm, have been the chief concern of academic studies of resource taxation, there are many other issues that have on occasion had more important influence on taxation policy. We shall list only a few of the more important of these factors.

(i) *Local employment.* In setting tax rates and subsidies for resource developments, governments are frequently influenced by the number of jobs directly or indirectly created by the project. This sometimes leads to the inclusion of training and local employment provisions in the licensing arrangements between host governments [especially in LDCs; see Mikesell (1980, p. 202)] and foreign developers. In principle, this influence is more likely to come into play where there is a supply of under-employed labour sufficiently great to produce a large gap between the market wage and the wage rate reflecting the next best alternative use of labour. It is also thought to be sometimes necessary to counter the tendency for foreign firms to employ their own nationals, especially when some training would be required to enable local labour to be used. In practice, the size and growth of employment are frequently given additional weight [as suggested, for example, by Church (1981, pp. 19–27)] in the choice of tax policies and subsidies. A low level of rent collection from natural resource projects offers a method of subsidizing employment and investment that is less likely to be critically evaluated than would be the case with direct tax or expenditure subsidies. Local employment objectives often underlie, to some extent, the encouragement of downstream processing, as described in (iv) below.

(ii) *Boom-town problems.* Resource development projects, especially mining projects, are often far from existing centres of population and offer a temporary (sometimes extending over scores of years) rather than permanent new centres for economic activity. The construction phase of a resource project creates one type of boom-town problem, as workers and equipment are drawn in for the construction phase and then idled or relocated when the project comes on stream. Tax policy can mitigate these costs by encouraging a co-ordinated sequence of projects in the region. The second type of boom-town problem occurs when the operation comes to an end and the mine closes down. The adjustment costs caused by the closure frequently fall on the government, which is called upon either to support the continuing mining of substandard ore or to support the costs of maintaining or relocating the unemployed workers. Since these costs are less in total for smaller longer-lived projects, tax policies are sometimes used to encourage the attenuation [Scott and Campbell (1979)] of mining projects.

(iii) *Macroeconomic issues.* For countries that specialize in natural resource exploitation, sharp changes in the pace of resource development or export may create macroeconomic issues ranging from regional or national inflationary pressures during the construction phase to structural adjustment problems [sometimes referred to as the Dutch disease; see, e.g., Ellman (1981) and other chapters in Barker and Brailovsky, eds. (1981)] caused by changes in the international competitiveness of the non-resource sector. Since the costs of these macroeconomic adjustments are usually less if there is a moderately paced exploitation of resources, these considerations usually incline tax authorities to use their tax and regulatory powers to achieve that result. On the other hand, chronic balance of payment deficits tend to encourage countries, especially developing countries, to accelerate the development of export-oriented natural resources.

(iv) *Downstream processing.* One of the frequent objectives of resource taxation is to achieve a greater degree of further processing of the resource before export from the producing region. This is generally done either by differential resource tax treatment based on the degree of processing or by the imposition of regulated prices or export taxes that favour domestic use. One reason for offering these subsidies is to offset the "reverse preferences" created by the tariff systems of resource importing countries, which frequently have tariffs that are lower for raw materials than for processed commodities, thus imposing a high effective tax burden on processing activity in the resource-exporting country. However, as noted by Beals et al. (1980, pp. 269–272), the use of tax allowances to encourage further processing can involve an effective rate of subsidy, and a corresponding loss of potential revenues, that far outweighs any possible economic gain conferred by the processing activity.

(v) *Distribution of benefits.* The distribution of the benefits from natural resources is at the heart of many resource taxation policies. The key margins of distribution are between producers and consumers, between government revenues and producer profits, between producing firms and their workers, between resource companies and their host communities, between domestic and foreign shareholders of producing firms, and between generations. Many of the policy instruments we shall describe below, especially regulated energy prices, have been adopted almost entirely on distributional grounds, often in preference to more efficient tax and transfer mechanisms that would make the redistribution more explicit and more subject to political objections.

(vi) *Competition and industrial structure.* Most of the theoretically efficient resource taxation systems rely for their efficiency on energetic competition among resource development firms and among the suppliers of factors to resource projects. The reliance on industry competition is especially great for countries or jurisdictions that do not have the technical knowledge required to supervise and closely monitor their own resource projects. Yet is it a feature of many natural resource industries that the degree of concentration is so high and the scale of many projects so great, that there are very few firms in competition for each project, even where some firm has not already achieved exclusive exploration or development rights. As a practical matter, this lack of potential competition, combined with a lack of monitoring skills, has encouraged many tax authorities to rely on gross royalties or other easy-to-administer tax forms in preference to more sophisticated systems. In some jurisdictions, the potential lack of competition has made the fostering of competition one of the goals of tax policy, although the operation of many of the complicated tax and regulation systems has often had the reverse effect [e.g., Bertrand (1981)] by forcing or encouraging the firms to collaborate in administering the regulations.

(vii) *Security of supply.* The adequacy of resource supply to meet future domestic needs is an important determinant of resource taxation and trade regulations, especially in the case of energy and exhaustible resources.

2.3. *Taxes and other policy instruments*

Most of our discussion of particular taxes will be found in subsequent sections. In this introductory section we shall just list the main types of tax and subsidy instruments used for natural resources.

(i) *Gross royalties or taxes based on the gross volume or value of output.* Landings taxes for fish, forestry yield taxes, and mineral severance taxes are generally of this type. Where resource deposits are privately owned, a percentage royalty or share of gross output is a typical form of payment to the owner, especially in the case of crude oil and natural gas. Royalties are also used for state-owned resources, with royalty-like taxes used to achieve comparable tax burdens for privately-owned deposits. As described earlier in the section, a gross royalty based on the quantity of output tends to restrict the production of lower-quality grades and higher-cost resources (relative to a no-tax situation), while a gross royalty based on value avoids the discrimination against lower-value output but still discriminates against higher-cost deposits. Many gross royalties have sliding scales based on the price of output (this is common for oil and gas) or on the costs of output, thus blurring the distinction between gross and net royalties.

(ii) *Net royalties or profits taxes allowing for actual costs.* For this class of tax, which comprises a continuum ranging from a gross royalty to a pure rent tax, the tax base is gross revenue minus certain costs. The tax naturally discriminates in favour of the use of factors whose expense is deductible, and against the use of other factors. If all costs are deductible, including exploration costs and a normal return on capital, then the tax base approximates pure rent. If the rate approaches 100% on this tax base, then the arrangement approaches a cost-plus contract with the taxing authority as the residual claimant.

(iii) *Net royalties or taxes based on hypothetical costs.* This form of tax is an attempt to combine a high degree of rent collection with maximum incentive for efficient management and factor use. Once the rate is set for each production unit (usually, as in the case of forestry stumpage payments, a per-volume charge for timber of given quality and cost classification), the enterprise keeps 100% of any cost savings. The payments are aligned with production and revenues. The biggest administrative problem with this type of tax lies in the definition and application of cost and quality classifications.

(iv) *Corporation income tax and related exemptions.* The corporation income tax, with a variety of special exemptions and provisions, has played an important role in resource taxation in many countries. The basic corporation income tax in most countries allows current expenses, interest expense, and historic cost depreciation as deductions. It is therefore roughly equal to a tax on economic rent plus the normal return on equity capital. Capital expenditures are deductible, subject only to a lag and to real diminution by subsequent inflation.

The extractive industries in North America have traditionally received favoured treatment under the corporation income tax.[1] For oil and natural gas, there has been a deduction called "percentage depletion", which had earlier been a means of writing off the original cost of a deposit, but eventually became a percentage reduction in gross income and has since been largely phased out for oil and natural gas. Exploration and development expenditures also receive favoured treatment relative to other forms of capital expenditure.

(v) *Direct government participation.* Equity participation by governments, whether in the form of joint ventures, partnerships, or carried interests (the latter

[1]See Brannon (1974, pp. 25–45) and Millsap, Spann and Erickson (1974, pp. 99–123) for the United States provisions and Helliwell (1968, ch. 9) for those in Canada.

is a form of option that permits the government to opt in at a later stage on favourable terms), is increasingly common, especially in developing countries. It is also common in off-shore oil [see Dam (1976)].

(vi) *Bidding for exploration or development rights.* Where the state owns the mineral rights, a bidding mechanism is sometimes used for rent collection, usually in conjunction with an established (but not unchangeable) royalty structure. Usually the bid is in the form of a cash payment or "bonus bid", but it can also be linked to the timing and value of subsequent production, in which case it is known as "royalty bidding". The advantage of the bonus-bidding method is that it leaves maximum incentive for efficient subsequent development; the disadvantage is that it will not collect the expected value of economic rents if the bidding is not competitive or if the bidder's discount rates are higher than the social opportunity cost of capital for investments of comparable risk.

(vii) *Property taxes.* Depending on the base used for valuation and the rates applied, the property tax can approximate a resource wealth tax, a license fee, or a fixed charge unrelated to the scale or value of resource production.

(viii) *Regulated prices.* These are generally used to transfer economic rents from producing firms or governments to consumers. For open economies, regulated domestic prices usually need to be supplemented by export and import taxes or subsidies. In some jurisdictions resource prices (e.g., natural gas in the United Kingdom and in British Columbia) are regulated by a government agency acting as the sole buyer. Differential export prices or taxes depending on the degree of processing are another way of encouraging or forcing further processing.

(ix) *Quantitative control of development rights.* In the major new oil-producing countries, for example Norway and the United Kingdom, the national government makes a broad decision about the desired rate and scale of development and releases development permits accordingly. The United Kingdom has chosen a fairly rapid pace of development, while Norway [see Dam (1976, pp. 63–69)], with its much smaller population, has chosen a production level that it expects to be able to sustain for more than a century.

(x) *Quantitative control of exports.* These controls are sometimes used to restrict the overall pace of development when development is less directly controllable by government, but where macroeconomic or conservation reasons suggest a slower pace of development. Restrictions on the export of unprocessed resources can provide, intentionally or unintentionally, a high effective rate of subsidy for sufficient subsequent processing to avoid the export restrictions. For example, restrictions on exports of raw logs from British Columbia led producers to square them off for sale as "squared timbers" before shipment to Japanese sawmills.

3. Fisheries

3.1. The common property problem

Many fisheries around the world have been exploited on a common property or open-access basis. This means that there has been no restriction or regulation of enterprises participating in the fishery. Gordon (1954) developed the economic theory of common property resources. Under open access conditions, firms will continue to enter the fishery as long as they believe they can catch enough fish to generate revenues in excess of their opportunity costs. "Bionomic" equilibrium occurs then when the least efficient fishing units are just earning revenues equal to these opportunity costs or when there is no longer any incentive for new fishing units to enter the fishery. Associated with this equilibrium should be a population of fish (stock size) which generates a sustainable yield equal to the catch of these vessels. Gordon pointed out that this open-access equilibrium dissipates the wealth (or rent) that the fishery could potentially generate. This is because individual vessels do not take account of the cost their presence in the fishery imposes on the rest of the fleet in terms of increased competition for the available catch. The result has been that excessive effort is used in the fishery, fish stocks may be dramatically reduced and fishermen tend to remain poor with incomes little more than their opportunity incomes.[2]

An example taken from Henderson and Tugwell (1979) of a Nova Scotia lobster fishery is instructive.[3] They estimate biological growth functions and a harvesting production function for this fishery. Then, using 1961 data, they indicate that current earnings in the fishery are close to average earnings in alternative occupations. They estimate that under open access, gross revenue from the fishery would be \$645,000 (= opportunity cost of fishing effort). If the effort level were reduced to 25% of the open-access level of effort, the value of effort savings minus the value of the reduced catch would be approximately \$200,000.

The important issue for fisheries economists is thus to devise institutions that will regulate the fishery in a more efficient manner. Currently, fisheries manage-

[2]Accounts of examples of this process are Crutchfield and Zellner (1962) for the Pacific halibut fisheries and Copes (1978) for Canada's Atlantic coast fisheries.

[3]The paucity of both biological and economic data in most fisheries has meant that few examples of the potential rent in particular fisheries have been worked out. Two other examples can be found in Clark (1976, pp. 45–50).

ment tends to concentrate on biological objectives such as maintaining stock sizes at levels which allow the largest possible catch (MSY = maximum sustainable yield). This is unsatisfactory from the economic point of view because it does not take account of the costs of catching fish. Moreover, the tools that are often used in fisheries management – closed seasons, closed areas, gear restrictions – are also unsatisfactory because they have the effect of raising the cost of catching the allowable harvest.

Among the suggestions for increasing the wealth generated in fisheries have been landing taxes and transferable quotas. It can be demonstrated that landing taxes and transferable quotas, in the context of simplified fisheries models, can be set at levels which will result in efficient operation of the fishery. The next part of this section sets out such a demonstration. The section then concludes with a discussion of a number of subsidiary considerations bearing on the choice of landing taxes or transferable quotas as a management tool.

The biology of a fish population is extremely complex and in general poorly understood. Nevertheless, to illustrate the general principles involved it will be assumed that the biology can be represented by the logistic growth curve represented in Figure 3.1. Let x_t denote the stock of fish at time t, often called the biomass. The growth of the stock will be assumed to depend on the stock level according to $x_{t+1} - x_t = F(x_t)$ in the absence of fishing. This growth is 0 when x reaches K, the carrying capacity of the environment, and is at a maximum when $x = x_{MSY}$. If h_t is the aggregate catch at time t, then the growth in the stock will be $x_{t+1} - x_t = F(x_t) - h_t$. In the subsequent analysis, it will be assumed that the fishery operates in a sustained yield equilibrium so that a stock level of x is maintained by an annual catch of $h = F(x)$.

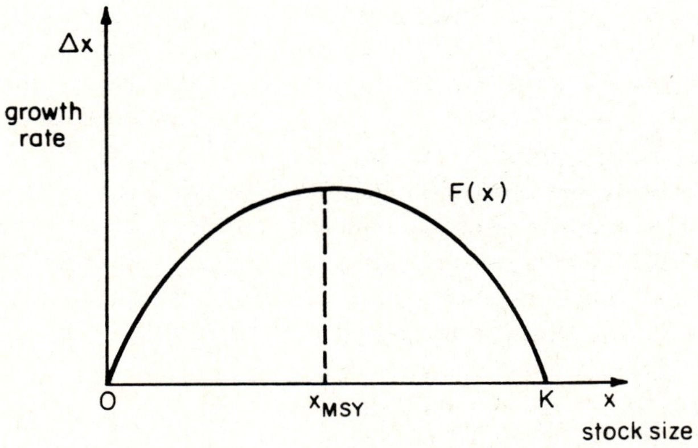

Figure 3.1. Growth rate of biomass.

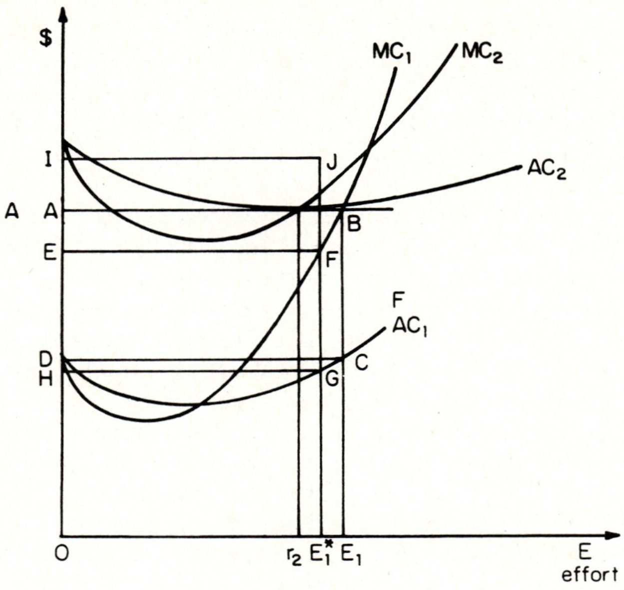

Figure 3.2. Comparison of two-vessel sustained yield equilibria. *Open access equilibrium*: Marginal cost $= pqx = OA$; vessel 1 exerts E_1 effort, vessel 2 exerts r_2 effort; fleet profits = area $ABCD$. *Fleet profit-maximizing equilibrium*: Marginal cost $= (p - \lambda)qx^* = OE$; vessel 1 exerts E_1^* effort, vessel 2 does not fish; fleet profits = area $IJGH$ where $OI = pqx^*$.

On the economic side, it will be assumed that there are a large number of vessels (indexed by $i = 1, 2, \ldots$) which could participate in the fishery. Each vessel's participation will be measured by the amount of fishing effort E_i it uses to obtain its catch.[4] Vessel fishing costs will then be modelled as $c_i(E_i)$ where the vessel's average cost curve is assumed to have the traditional U-shape with minimum average costs r_i occurring at $E_i = \underline{E}_i$. Two such average cost curves are illustrated in Figure 3.2. Vessels will be indexed so that $r_1 < r_2 < r_3$ and so on. The catch of each vessel depends on the amount of effort used and on the catchability of the fish – in particular on the density of the stock in the fishing grounds. A simple representation of the harvesting production function which captures these

[4] Fishing effort is taken here to be an index representing the intensity of fishing. It is a difficult concept to quantify, involving things like the time spent fishing, the skill of the crew, the size of the vessel, etc. For some discussion, see Hannesson (1978). The multi-vessel fishery model laid out here is due to Clark (1980) and Maloney and Pearse (1979).

effects is $h_i = qxE_i$ where q is called the catchability coefficient. This representation will be used here for convenience although in practice the relationship between h_i, x and E_i is undoubtedly more complex.[5] Vessel profits are then given by $\Pi_i = pqxE_i - c_i(E_i)$, and it is now possible to describe the various types of economic equilibrium in this fishery.

3.2. Open access equilibrium

Vessels will be assumed to choose an effort level which maximizes their profits given the stock of fish. Thus, if there are N vessels in the fishery,

$$pqx - c_i'(E_i) = 0, \qquad i = 1, 2, \dots, N. \tag{3.1}$$

Of course, non-negative profits must be obtained at this effort level so $pqx \geq c_i(E_i)/E_i$, and vessels must be operating at an effort level above that which minimizes their average cost. As well, in an open-access equilibrium, no other vessel can find it profitable to enter the fishery. The number of vessels is thus determined by the condition

$$r_N \leq pqx < r_{N+1}. \tag{3.2}$$

Thirdly, we have the sustained yield requirement

$$F(x) = \sum_{i=1}^{N} h_i = qx \sum_{i=1}^{N} E_i. \tag{3.3}$$

These conditions determine the open-access effort levels and equilibrium stock size simultaneously. The comparative statics of this equilibrium are derived in an appendix. As one might expect, an increase in the price of fish will raise vessel effort levels, increase vessel profits, and reduce the equilibrium stock level. A two-vessel open-access equilibrium is illustrated in Figure 3.2 for a case where $r_2 = pqx$.

[5] Henderson and Tugwell (1979) estimate the relationship $h = qx^{0.44}E^{0.48}$ in their empirical work on Nova Scotia lobster fisheries.

3.3. *Fleet profit maximizing equilibrium*[6]

A sole owner of the fleet would choose effort levels to maximize the sum of vessel profits

$$\sum_{i=1}^{N} pqxE_i - c_i(E_i),$$

subject to the sustained yield constraint

$$F(x) = qx \sum_{i=1}^{N} E_i.$$

Given N, the Lagrangian is

$$L = \sum_{i=1}^{N} [(p-\lambda)qxE_i - c_i(E_i)] + \lambda F(x),$$

and the necessary conditions for a maximum are

$$(p-\lambda)qx - c_i'(E_i) = 0 \quad \text{if} \quad E_i > 0, \tag{3.4}$$
$$(p-\lambda)qx \geq r_i \qquad\qquad \text{if} \quad E_i > 0, \tag{3.5}$$

$$(p-\lambda)q \sum_{i=1}^{N} E_i - \lambda F'(x) = 0, \tag{3.6}$$

$$F(x) = qx \sum_{i=1}^{N} E_i. \tag{3.7}$$

To determine the optimal number of vessels, suppose all N boats have $E_i > 0$ and then re-allocate ΔE_i effort from each boat to the $(N+1)$th boat (so total catch is

[6]A rational sole owner would choose effort levels to maximize the present value of the sum of vessel profits over the future. The solution to this dynamic optimization problem is discussed in Clark (1980). To simplify the mathematical analysis, we present here only the static profit-maximization case. The static case results in a different equilibrium stock size than the dynamic case. However, the management strategy that might be used to manage the fishery in an optimal manner is similar except in the period of adjustment towards the long-run equilibrium. The problems associated with the adjustment period are discussed later. The results of the analysis are also not altered if the price of fish depends on the quantity of fish offered for sale.

unchanged). Then

$$\Delta L \simeq \sum_{i=1}^{N} c_i'(E_i)\Delta E_i - c_{N+1}\left(\sum_{i=1}^{N}\Delta E_i\right)$$

$$= (p-\lambda)qx\sum_{i=1}^{N}\Delta E_i - c_{N+1}\left(\sum_{i=1}^{N}\Delta E_i\right).$$

This can only be done profitably if $(p-\lambda)qx \geq r_{N+1}$. Thus

$$r_N \leq (p-\lambda)qx < r_{N+1} \tag{3.8}$$

determines the optimal number of vessels. The sole-owner fishery is thus similar to the open-access fishery if the price of fish is $p-\lambda$. The multiplier λ may be interpreted as the shadow price of the stock of fish. Condition (3.6) says that the stock should be adjusted to a level where the landed value of a marginal stock reduction equals the marginal value of the lost sustainable yield. It is also clear from (3.6) that $F'(x)<0$, so a larger stock size than x_{MSY} is maintained. The comparative statics of the open-access fishery can be used to compare this profit-maximizing fishery with the open-access fishery. The lower landed value $p-\lambda$ means that fewer vessels will be used, effort levels on remaining vessels will be reduced, and the equilibrium stock size will be higher.[7] The two-vessel case is illustrated in Figure 3.2 where x^* denotes the profit-maximizing optimal stock size.

3.4. *A landings tax*

It is clear from the above that if a landings tax $\tau=\lambda$ is charged on all fish caught, then the open-access fishery will behave like the profit-maximizing fishery. From (3.6) and (3.7) it may be seen that $\lambda = pF(x^*)/(F(x^*)-x^*F'(x^*))$, so λ can be calculated easily if the optimal stock size x^* is known.[8] Calculation of the

[7] If the objective function was taken to be the present value of profits from the fishery with discount rate r, then (3.4) and (3.5) would still be necessary conditions. However, optimal stock size x and the shadow price of the stock would now vary over time, but would tend to equilibrium values where (3.4) to (3.7) held except that the RHS of (3.6) equals $r\lambda$. Thus the long-run optimal stock size is less than in the static profit-maximizing case. However, the general conclusions of the static analysis still hold in the dynamic case. The shadow price λ represents in this context the marginal user cost, so that (3.4) can be interpreted as marginal revenue equals marginal cost plus marginal user cost.

[8] A landings tax $\tau=\lambda_d$ can be used to make the fishery operate at any desired stock level x_d, above the bionomic stock level by choosing λ_d to satisfy (3.4), (3.5) and (3.7) with $x=x_d$. Thus a landings tax can also be used to get the fishery to operate at the long-run equilibrium for dynamic profit maximization. An additional problem is created if private costs incurred by vessel owners are higher than social opportunity costs. In this case, a different landings tax may be required on each vessel in order to get a social profit-maximizing result.

optimal stock size requires full knowledge of vessel production functions. However, a guess x at x^* could be made and λ set according to the above formula with x substituted for x^*. The open-access fishery with a landings tax will then result in an equilibrium stock size x_λ which will differ from x^* unless $x_\lambda = x^*$. Thus a process of trial and error could then be used to eventually calculate the optimal λ.

Another serious problem, which does not seem to have been emphasized in the literature, is that the vessels that remain in the fishery with the landings tax will make lower profits than they did in bionomic equilibrium[9] (this was shown in the comparative statics of open access). The main beneficiary of this system of managing the fishery will be the government, unless some form of compensation is offered to the fishermen to encourage the transition.

The size of the landings tax required is also of interest. In the example of the Nova Scotia lobster fishery the optimal tax is estimated at \$270 per thousand pounds given a price of \$485 per thousand pounds, i.e., the tax is more than 55% of the landed price.[10] This situation where the landings tax needs to be a large proportion of the landed price might be quite usual. A growth curve which is commonly used in fisheries economics is $F(x) = rx(1-(x/K))$. Maximum sustainable yield occurs at a stock size of $K/2$. If the optimal stock size was $(2K)/3$ (which reduces the sustained yield by a little more than a half), then the landings tax would need to be 50% of the landed price. It is of course difficult to obtain political approval for such large taxes, especially if the existing stock of vessels and crews is well above the size required to harvest the well-managed fishery.

3.5. *A quota system*

An alternative to a landings tax is the proposal that the authorities give, rent, or sell catch quotas to fishermen in amount $D = F(x^*)$. These quotas would be transferable, so market transactions would establish some price m for a unit of quota. A boat's participation in the fishery would then be determined by its ownership D_i of quotas according to $D_i = qx^*E_i$. Vessel profits would be

$$\Pi_i = (p-m)D_i - c_i(D_i/qx^*).$$

Profit-maximizing vessel owners would then purchase quotas to the point where

$$(p-m)qx^* - c_i'(D_i/qx^*) = 0, \tag{3.9}$$

[9] Total fleet pre-tax profits are increased by operating at x^* rather than at the bionomic equilibrium, but the tax share $\tau\sum_i qx^*E_i$ exceeds the amount of the increase.

[10] This is the landings tax for the dynamic profit-maximization case in Henderson and Tugwell (1979).

where $(p-m)qx^* \geq r_i$. Otherwise $D_i = 0$. This condition defines implicitly the vessel's demand curve $D_i(m)$ for quotas and it is clear that $D_i'(m) \leq 0$. When the quota market clears, the price m then satisfies

$$\sum_i D_i(m) = D = F(x^*). \tag{3.10}$$

It may be seen from (3.4) to (3.7) that the solution to the quota fishery is $m = \lambda$ and $D_i = qx^*E_i$, where λ and E_i are the solution of the profit-maximizing fishery. Thus the quota fishery is efficient.

One virtue of the quota system is that an indirect means, namely the market, is used to discover the shadow price of the stock. However, correct determination of the amount of quotas to issue requires, as for the landings tax, complete knowledge of vessel cost curves, and if this is not available, there is no trial and error method available for discovering the D.

The profits generated under a quota system can be allocated either to fishermen or to the governments, depending on whether the government allocates the quota free of charge or rents or sells the quota allocation at full market value. In case less than full market value is charged, a rationing problem results. However, this pricing strategy would allow the government to raise the incomes of some fishermen to ease the transition to the new system.

3.6. Subsidiary considerations[11]

The discussion above has been based on a model of the open-access fishery which is severly oversimplified (for the sake of tractability). The population dynamics of the stock really depend on the age, spatial and genetic characteristics of the population, all of which are ignored here. Interactions between different stocks are ignored. Uncertaintly about, and variability in, biological and economic factors have not been discussed. The timing of the catch affects costs in the processing sector, another factor which has been ignored. Here, a few comments are made concerning the desirability of a landings tax or a quota system in the light of these additional complications.

(i) *Adjustment*. If a management programme is instituted in a fishery, then the fish stock cannot change immediately to the new desired level, but will change continuously according to $x_{t+1} = x_t + F(x_t) - qx_t\Sigma_i E_i$. Consequently, the efforts will not adjust instantaneously to the desired levels either. For example, suppose a

[11] The reader is referred to Crutchfield (1979) and Scott (1979) for a more detailed discussion of these points.

landings tax is imposed when the fishery is initially in open-access equilibrium. Vessels will then reduce their effort levels so that $(p-\tau)qx_0 - c_i'(E_i) = 0$ or drop out of the fishery if $(p-\tau)qx_0 < r_i$. The reduction in aggregate fleet effort will reduce the catch below sustainable yield levels, and consequently the stock size will increase towards the desired level. As stock size grows, then vessel effort levels will also grow and vessels will re-enter the fishery. Thus this programme will force some vessels out of the fishery temporarily and potentially create hardship for their crews. This will be particularly true if these vessels cannot easily shift temporarily into and out of their best alternative occupations [see Clark (1980)].

The adjustment process for the quota system could involve a similar change for the fishing fleet. Initially a quota $D < F(x_0)$ could be used. Equations (3.8) and (3.9) then define the vessel demand functions for quotas $D_i(m, x)$, so the price of quotas is determined by $D = \Sigma_i D_i(m, x)$. Thus vessels would initially exit the fishery, effort levels on remaining vessels would fall, and the stock size would start to rise. It is easily seen that $\partial D_i/\partial x \geq 0$. Thus if the quota level was kept constant, then growth in the stock would cause the price of quotas to rise and some further reallocation of quotas might occur. Eventually, however, if the optimal catch exceeds the catch in bionomic equilibrium, an upwards adjustment of the quota would be required which would induce re-entry into the fishery. The advantage of the quota system then would be that boats exiting from the fishery could be given an initial quota allocation so that they would at least have the earnings from the sale of their quota rights.

(ii) *Uncertainty.* It is claimed that if fishermen are uncertain about the catch to be obtained from a given level of effort (either because of uncertainty about where the fish are or because they cannot predict their competitors' catches), then vessels will make investments in catching power (sonar, faster boats) which raise fishing costs beyond what is necessary for efficient fleet operation. These incentives to invest in excess catching power will be eliminated by a quota system but not by a landings tax. Since vessels are guaranteed some return from the quota holdings, even if they don't fish, uncertainty about financial returns is reduced under the quota system.

Another problem is that fluctuations in biological or economic conditions may alter the optimal landings tax and the optimal quota allocation. The authorities could intervene in quota markets to buy or sell quotas until the right number of quotas were outstanding. This would be a more complex procedure than altering the landings tax but would protect the financial return to fishermen.

(iii) *Crowding externalities.* In some fisheries, the operations of one vessel may interfere with the operations of other vessels. In this case, the vessel profit function should be modelled as $\Pi_i = pqxE_i - c_i(E_1, \ldots, E_N)$. In principle, landings taxes could be used to manage the fishery in a way that would maximize joint fleet profits. However, different taxes would be required for different boats making it difficult to implement such a system. A quota system cannot be used to manage this fishery optimally.

(iv) *Seasonality.* Another factor is that the timing of the catch of a fishery during a season may have an impact on profitability. Clark (1980) models such a fishery and shows that neither landings taxes or quotas can be used to manage such fisheries optimally, although if the intraseasonal variation in the stock size is small, then these management systems can give approximately optimal results.

(v) *Administration.* It has been demonstrated above that both landings tax and quota systems require complete knowledge of the biology and economics of the fishery for full implementation. This information would in general be extremely costly to obtain. The situation is complicated by the fact that the authorities need to deal with large numbers of species and fishing grounds. A final problem is enforcement. Under both systems, there is an incentive for new channels of distribution to open up which evade the reporting of the catch.

3.7. *Appendix: Comparative statics of open access*

Lemma.

$$\begin{vmatrix} a & -c_1 & & & \\ a & & & & 0 \\ \cdot & & & 0 & \\ \dot{a} & & & & -c_N \\ d & b & b & \dots & b \end{vmatrix} = \prod_{i=1}^{N} c_i \left[d + ab \sum_{i=1}^{N} \frac{1}{c_i} \right].$$

The lemma can be proven by induction.

Given N, open-access equilibrium is

$$pqx - c_i'(E_i) = 0, \qquad AF(x) - \sum_i qE_i = 0.$$

Total differentiation of these equations gives

$$\begin{bmatrix} pq & -c_1''(E_1) & 0 \\ \vdots & & \\ pq & 0 & -c_N''(E_N) \\ AF'(x) & -q & -q \end{bmatrix} \begin{bmatrix} \mathrm{d}x \\ \mathrm{d}E_1 \\ \vdots \\ \mathrm{d}E_N \end{bmatrix} = \begin{bmatrix} -qx \\ \vdots \\ -qx \\ -qx \\ 0 \end{bmatrix} \mathrm{d}p.$$

Using the lemma,

$$|D| = \prod_{i=1}^{N} c_i''(E_i)\left[AF'(x) - pq^2 \sum_{i=1}^{N} \frac{1}{c_i''(E_i)}\right] < 0,$$

$$|D_x| = \prod_{i=1}^{N} c_i''(E_i)\left[(q^2 x) \sum_{i=1}^{N} \frac{1}{c_i''(E_i)}\right] > 0,$$

$$|D_i| = AF'(x)(qx)\left[\prod_{i=1}^{N} c_i''(E_i)\right] / c_i''(E_i) < 0,$$

(since $AF'(x) < 0$ for all x).

Thus

$$\mathrm{d}x^*/\mathrm{d}p < 0 \quad \text{and} \quad \mathrm{d}E_i^*/\mathrm{d}p > 0.$$

A higher price will reduce stock size and raise effort levels.

Moreover,

$$\mathrm{d}(px^*)/\mathrm{d}p = \left(\prod_{i=1}^{N} c_i(E_i)[xAF'(x)]\right) \Big/ |D| > 0,$$

which implies

$$\mathrm{d}(\Pi_i^*)/\mathrm{d}p > 0.$$

4. Forestry

4.1. Forestry issues

Forests are a renewable resource having their own distinct management problems. The basic problem is to determine the age at which the trees will be cut so that the benefits society gets from the forest are maximized. This rotation period will typically be of the order of a number of decades, particularly in temperate climates. Thus private owners of forest lands face severe cash flow problems in that they must make outlays such as site management costs and taxes throughout the growing cycle but may not receive a cash return for many years. This would not be a problem if perfectly competitive markets in forest lands existed together with a complete set of future markets for lumber and other wood end products for several decades hence. The private owners would then be able to receive the full liquid value of their forest holdings at any time. The required markets do not exist, however, if only because of the uncertainties associated with planning and with tenure rights over such long time periods. The resulting pressure to obtain at least some financial return by harvesting trees has led to rates of exploitation of the forest which at one time or another most jurisdictions have considered excessive. Consequently, both in Europe and in North America, substantial amounts of forest land have been retained under state ownership in order to ensure that what were viewed as appropriate harvest rates and management practices were achieved. An important objective has been to ensure that new forests were started on cut over lands, as in the past much of the private sector may have believed that the returns to expenditure on regeneration were too far in the future to be worthwhile pursuing. Thus, the Scandinavian countries have imposed regulations on private owners of forest lands concerning when they can cut and what regeneration practices they must follow.[12]

A further problem with forest management is that forests provide multiple services to society, not merely the market value of the wood harvested. These services include recreation opportunities, aesthetic values, watershed protection, rangeland and wildlife services. Since many of these services are non-marketable, private owners will make cutting decisions which do not coincide with maximizing the social benefits from woodland exploitation. Private owners of forest land are usually subject to property taxes like owners of other types of land plus a yield tax when the trees are logged. In the interests of tax neutrality these taxes should be similar to those imposed on other owners of wealth-producing assets. However, the form in which these taxes are imposed influences the owner's decision on when to cut and hence the size of the social benefits obtainable from forestry. These issues are examined below in the context of a sustained yield model of the private owner's decision problem.

The public sector typically assigns the right to log particular stands of trees to private firms – the cutting date being decided by the state. The age at which trees should be cut on public lands continues to be a matter of controversy which will not be discussed here. What will be considered further here is the manner in which the state might ensure that it gets full value for the forest resource as it is harvested.

[12] See von Malmborg (1969), Helles (1969) and Svendsrud (1969) for practices in Sweden, Denmark and Norway, respectively.

4.2. Private sustained yield forestry

The growth profile of a stand of uniform-aged trees is usually supposed to have the logistic shape indicated in Figure 4.1. Some sample data for a good site of Douglas Fir are given in column 1 of Table 4.1. Let $F(T)$ be the yield (volume per hectare) of a T-year-old forest on a particular site. The net value of the crop will be denoted $R(F(T))$, i.e., the value of the logs minus the costs of cutting and transporting the logs. Normally the value of the wood per cubic meter increases with the size of the logs as more valuable products can be manufactured from them (large-dimension boards, veneer). Moreover, logging costs per cubic meter fall as fewer pieces need to be handled for the same volume of wood. Thus average revenue per cubic meter, i.e., $R(F(T))/F(T)$, should increase with the age of the trees. Column 3 of Table 4.1 allows for this effect. For simplicity, assume the private owner begins with bare land on which it costs $\$c$ to establish a crop of trees. Assume he plants a crop at time 0, lets it grow for T years, harvests the crop and then, since he is following sustained yield, plants another crop. Since the situation facing him at T is the same as he originally faced, a second crop of trees will be grown to age T, cut, the forest replanted and so on forever. Letting r denote his discount rate, the present value of this operation to him is then

$$PV(T) = \frac{[R(F(T)) - c](1+r)^{-T}}{1-(1+r)^{-T}} - c. \tag{4.1}$$

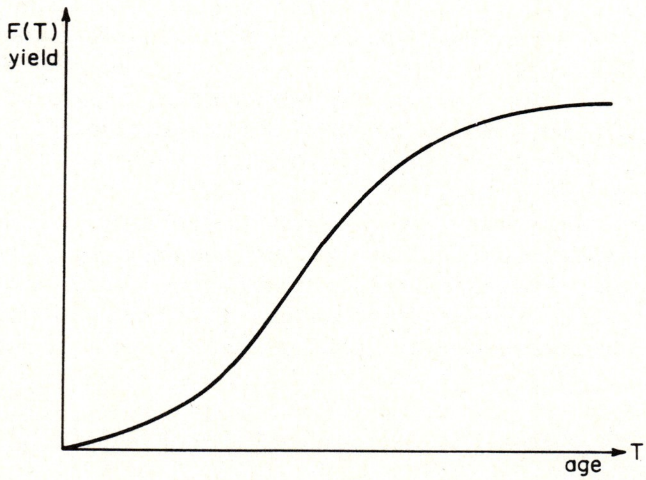

Figure 4.1. Typical volume–age curve.

Table 4.1
Data for Site 200 Douglas Fir.[a]

Rotation (years)	Yield (M.bd.ft.)[b]	Value per M ($/M)	Value of yield ($)	Present value of yield[c] ($)
20	4.9	10.00	49.00	29.64
30	24.4	14.00	341.60	102.83
40	47.0	17.20	808.40	133.84[d]
50	70.5	19.80	1,395.90	133.36
60	90.8	21.70	1,970.36	111.45
70	108.5	23.00	2,495.50	84.80
80	124.7	23.70	2,955.39	60.86
90	137.7	24.10	3,318.57	41.62
100	148.9	24.40	3,633.16	27.84

[a] *Source*: Duerr et al. (1979, p. 183).
[b] M.bd.ft. = one thousand board feet.
[c] $r = 5\%$.
[d] Faustmann rotation.

A wealth-maximizing owner would then choose his rotation period T to maximize this present value. The solution to this problem is commonly called the Faustmann formula and is given by

$$\frac{\mathrm{d}(R(F(T))/\mathrm{d}T}{R(F(T))-c}=\frac{\ln(1+r)}{1-(1+r)^{-T}}.^{13} \tag{4.2}$$

Let A^* be the maximum value of $PV(T)$. A^* is the value of this piece of bare forest land and is what this bare land should fetch when sold in the market place. The Faustmann formula can be rewritten as

$$\mathrm{d}[R(F(T))+A^*]/\mathrm{d}T=\ln(1+r)[R(F(T))+A^*]. \tag{4.3}$$

$R(F(T))+A^*$ is what the owner would receive if he harvested his forest at age T and then sold his land. Equation (4.3) says then that the optimal cutting date is when the growth rate of the value of his investment in trees and forest land is just equal to the rate of return on liquid capital. An alternative interpretation of (4.3) is that $\ln(1+r)[R+A^*]$ is the marginal user cost of cutting the forest at age T. Thus it is the opportunity return to using the forest land in the highest alternative use to its use for growing the current stock of trees. The trees should be cut when this marginal user cost is just equal to the marginal return to continuing to grow the current stock of trees.

[13] This formula for the optimal rotation period was originally proposed in 1849 by Martin Faustmann. His article is reprinted in Gane (1968).

Column 4 of Table 4.1 calculates the PV for various cutting dates and shows that $A^* = \$133.84$ when the rotation period is $T = 40$ years.

No imputation has been made for site preparation costs in these calculations, however, a feature which would lengthen the rotation period.

Property tax has been applied to private forest land as it has to other types of land and wealth-producing assets. It has the effect of reducing the timber supply by making it unprofitable to hold marginal timber land. However, if timber owners are to bear their share of the tax burden, this effect cannot be avoided. A serious problem has been deciding on a tax base for timber land which will result in equitable treatment for forest properties relative to other types of commercial property.[14] Some jurisdictions take the tax base to include only the value of the bare land, while others include the value of the current stock of trees as well. Including the value of the bare land in the tax base seems to be common and moreover will not alter the owner's decision about his rotation period.[15]

A property tax which is applied to the value of the trees will reduce the present value in (4.1) by

$$\left(\tau\sum_{t=1}^{T} R(F(t))(1+r)^{-t}\right)\Big/\left(1-(1+r)^{-T}\right).$$

Since the PV of this tax burden increases with T, the imposition of such a tax will cause the private owner to choose shorter rotation periods.[16] As well, some owners of marginal forest land will no longer be able to conduct sustained yield forestry in a profitable manner. These owners will simply cut the current stock of trees, probably at an earlier age than they would have under sustained yield forestry,

[14] Lindholm (1973) discusses the way property tax has been calculated in a number of different jurisdictions.

[15] The taxpayer pays τA^* annually forever, so his after-tax present value is $PV - (\tau/r)A^*$, which is maximized by the same rotation period as PV is maximized by. The after-tax value of the land is then $(1-(\tau/r))A^*$ and, so long as $\tau < r$, marginal timber land will still be profitable to hold. However, there will be less incentive to conduct the operations efficiently [see Section 2.1 (vi)].

[16] Some manipulation shows that the tax base after $(T+1)$ years exceeds the tax base after T years if

$$R(F(T+1))\left[1-(1+r)^{-T}\right] > r\sum_{t=1}^{T} R(F(t))(1+t)^{-t}.$$

This holds because

$$r\sum_{t=1}^{T} R(F(t))(1+r)^{-t} < rR(F(T))\sum_{t=1}^{T}(1+r)^{-t}$$

$$= R(F(T))\left[1-(1+r)^{-T}\right].$$

and then abandon their property. Column 1 of Table 4.2 calculates the after-tax present value for a tax of this type with $\tau = 0.01$. In this example, at least, the distortion does not appear to be serious. It must be noted as well that the tax on the value of the trees (if cut immediately) is far easier to calculate than the tax on the value of the bare land. A tax on the value of the trees (if cut immediately) requires current price and cost information and current information about stand volume and quality. A tax on the value of the bare land requires estimates of prices and costs far into the future. Information on sales of forest land may substitute for this to some extent. However, these sales may be few and they are for land plus the current crop of trees. Thus they are for properties differentiated by different growing conditions, different accessibility, and the state of the current crop of trees so that true competitive values of bare land of a particular quality may be very difficult to ascertain.

The market value of forest land containing a t-year-old forest is, of course, $A^*(1+r)^t$ rather than A^*, the value of bare land. Using the market value as the tax base can also be shown to lead to a reduction in rotation periods. Column 2 of Table 4.2 shows the after-tax present value when a tax rate of 1.5% is applied to the land's market value. The thinness of the market in forest land may make it difficult to estimate these market values.

A fourth type of tax base is now in use in Scandinavian countries. The base is taken to be $R(F(T))/T$, average sustainable value yield. The tax base is thus

Table 4.2
After-tax present value of bare forest land.

Rotation (years)	(1)[a]	(2)[b]	(3)[c]	(4)[d]
20	24.74	15.37	27.19	—
30	91.46	42.63[e]	91.45	29.38
40	111.68[e]	40.25	113.63[e]	56.03
50	92.29	23.87	105.84	66.51[e]
60	66.62	5.47	78.61	60.09
70	31.38	—	49.15	47.93
80	1.07	—	23.92	35.18
90	—	—	4.75	24.35
100	—	—	—	16.43

[a]A 1% tax per annum on the value of the trees. (Due to the nature of the data, the tax base in each decade was the average of the beginning and end of decade figures in the value of yield column in Table 4.1.)

[b]A 1.5% tax per annum on the market value of land containing a t-year-old crop of trees.

[c]A 5% tax on the annual sustainable value yield.

[d]A $10 yield tax per M board feet at the time of cutting.

[e]Faustmann rotation.

related to the average productivity of the site. This tax is easier to calculate than taxes based on land values. It can again be shown, however, that the use of a tax on this base shortens private rotation periods. Column 3 of Table 4.2 shows after-tax present value for a tax rate of $\tau = 0.05$. Again, in the example, the distortion is not serious.

Another type of tax applied to forest crops is a yield tax payable when the crop is harvested. The tax rate might apply to the volume of the cut or the value of the cut. This tax will not affect the choice of rotation period if it is based on the value of the harvest net of logging costs and there are no establishment costs for starting a new crop. Otherwise it lengthens the rotation period as this action defers payment of the tax for a longer period. This may be demonstrated formally for the case of a tax (at rate τ) on volume cut as follows. The after-tax present value of sustained yield forestry is then

$$PV(T) = \frac{[R(F(T)) - \tau F(T) - c](1+r)^{-T}}{1-(1+r)^{-T}} - c, \tag{4.4}$$

and this is maximized when

$$\frac{(R_F - \tau)(\mathrm{d}F(T)/\mathrm{d}T)}{R - \tau F - c} = \frac{\ln(1+r)}{1-(1+r)^{-T}}. \tag{4.5}$$

Economies of size with respect to net logging revenues imply $R(F(T))/F(T)$ is rising or $R_F(F(T)) > R(F(T))/F(T)$. It is easily checked that this implies $R_F/(R-c) < (R_F - \tau)/(R - \tau F - c)$. Hence, if the pre-tax optimal rotation period is inserted in the LHS of (4.5), the LHS of (4.5) will exceed the RHS of (4.5) and so the rotation period must be increased to get equality. In the example of column 4 in Table 4.2 a \$10 per M boardfeet yield tax is imposed on the volume harvested and the result is to increase the owner's optimal rotation period by ten years.

A yield tax thus has a number of desirable features. Due to the multiple-use nature of forests, the socially desirable rotation periods exceed those rotations chosen by private owners. Thus a yield tax, like a landings tax in fisheries, induces the private owner to choose rotation periods more in keeping with generating maximum social benefits from the forest. As well, it is relatively easily calculated and is paid when revenues are received by the operator of the forest, so that undue financial burdens on the owner are avoided. Moreover, it is not based on future forest product prices which may be extremely uncertain, so if the tax is on the value of the yield, gains due to unanticipated price increases are shared between forest owner and the taxing authority.

Yield taxes may eventually increase the annual fibre supply. This could be advantageous by providing employment opportunities for inhabitants of rural areas who had few alternatives to employment in forestry (particularly in the off-season for agriculture). The rotation age which maximizes the annual average cut $F(T)/T$ is usually substantially longer than the private owner's optimal rotation period. In the example here $F(T)/T$ is a maximum at $T=80$ years at 1.559 M boardfeet per year compared to 1.175 M boardfeet per year at $T=40$ years – an increase of 33%. This increase in average yield on stands which can still be operated profitably after the imposition of the tax, may be more than the loss of average yield from stands which are removed from production due to the imposition of the tax.

A few other aspects of the taxation of privately owned forests deserve mention. It may be desired to encourage forest owners to adopt better forestry practices, which might increase the external benefits produced by the forest for society. This might, for example, involve efforts to improve the regeneration of cutover lands and the maintenance of roads providing access to neighbouring properties. A possible way to encourage such expenditures is to allow owners to deduct all or part of these expenses from other taxable income.

Finally, governments are usually interested in having stable revenues from forestry and also stable employment in the industry. Private forestry will not lead to this result unless there are uniform age distributions of the various species. This particularly is not true in North America. The stability objective cannot be accomplished by taxation–subsidy methods alone, so some jurisdictions have deemed it necessary to directly regulate the cut on private forestry lands.

4.3. Public forest management

The issue of which rotation period should be used on public forest lands will not be discussed here. Public forests may be managed directly by a public forest service. In this case, the forest service assigns the right to cut particular stands at particular times to individual firms through a "timber sale".

The sale may be assigned in an auction to the bidder offering to pay the highest "stumpage" price for the timber. This system should result in the most efficient logger acquiring the timber. Moreover, if the bidding in timber sales is perfectly competitive, the highest bid should equal the value of the logs minus the best-practice costs of logging including the opportunity return to the logger, i.e., the full value of the resource. One problem is that there may not be enough logging firms capable of operating in the desired area to make the sale competitive. Forest services guard against this by appraising the timber before the sale. This is a complex, costly and imprecise process, involving estimation of the quantity and values of the logs cut in a stand and the costs of logging the stand (including a profit and risk allowance for the operator).[17] There are a large number of variables in this calculation, including such things as the size and quality of the trees, the accessibility of the stand, and the distance the logs must be transported. The appraised value is then the upset value for the auction and only bids in excess of the appraised value are accepted.

The experience of some jurisdictions (i.e., the United States Pacific North-West) is that bids may often exceed appraised values by large amounts indicating a strong degree of competition. Several reasons have been suggested for why this appraisal system fails to predict what operators will be willing to pay for timber. These include:

(i) The Forest Service's system of scaling substantially underpredicts the value of end products.
(ii) Operators count on inflation of end-product prices during the time (up to five years) between the sale and the actual harvesting.
(iii) Bid prices can be deducted for income tax purposes from other income during the year of the sale; however, the bid price is not paid until the time of harvest [see Haley (1980)].

In other jurisdictions, most public timber is sold at the appraised price. This may be because the government is pursuing objectives other than maximum rent collection, such as regional growth and stability. In British Columbia, for example, much of the allowable annual cut is pre-committed to particular firms under tenure arrangements such as "tree-farm licences" or "timber sale harvesting licences" [Pearse (1976)]. The justification seems to be that firms will not make investments in wood processing facilities unless guaranteed a long-term supply of fibre.[18]

The method by which timber prices are set in a non-competitive jurisdiction will naturally be the subject of much debate. The main disadvantage of an appraisal system is its expense, because each stand must be assessed separately as noted above. British Columbia prices are, however, adjusted every month for changes in product prices and are based on volumes actually harvested. Thus, this pricing system stabilizes operator net revenues by relating payments for the timber to actual values received. Where a pricing system is based on log prices, it

[17]See Juhasz (1976) for example. In many cases, the assessment is based on the value of end-products rather than log values as the log market is believed to be too narrow to generate prices reflecting the true value of logs. Estimated logging costs are supposed to be the costs of an operator of average efficiency. Lack of data on capital costs often leads to the profit and risk allowance being calculated as a percentage of estimated costs plus stumpage. This means that a general rise in costs results in reduced stumpage but not in reduced profits.

[18]American producers attempted in 1982 to get their government to impose a countervailing duty on imports of Canadian lumber, on the grounds that the Canadian stumpage system was equivalent to a subsidy paid to Canadian lumber producers.

might be improved by measures designed to get more accurate estimates of the competitive value of the logs. This might mean ensuring that more logs are sold in the marketplace, either by favouring independent loggers in the bidding for timber sales or by use of a log marketing agency which would pay firms to log particular stands. The agency would, however, retain ownership of the logs and be responsible for their sale to mills [see Mead (1976)].

An alternative to the appraisal system is a fixed rate or royalty system. Firms granted logging rights on public forest land would pay a charge which was in a fixed proportion either to the value or the volume of the cut. Clearly this system is much easier to administer and less subject to special pleading than is the appraisal system. Although rates can be set at levels that generate revenues at the same level as the appraisal system, the royalty system discriminates against the high-cost stands and many of these may cease to be profitable to log. This gives rise to the "cut-off grade" problem that we shall discuss in more detail when we deal with mining in Section 5. A royalty system based on the volume cut is also inflexible in that charges are not reduced when market conditions are poor. Thus more stands will become subeconomic in bad times, resulting in greater fluctuations in government revenues and forest-based employment.

Other alternatives that have been proposed to the appraisal systems are a land tax or rental and a profit-sharing scheme. These methods are subject to much the same advantages and problems as a royalty system. As well, the net profits of an integrated forest company operating in several jurisdictions may be difficult to identify.

5. Mining

5.1. Mining issues

The economic rents generated through the extraction of non-renewable resource deposits can be very substantial. For example, Mackenzie and Bilodeau (1979) investigate a sample of 124 metal deposits discovered in Canada in the period 1950–1974. They estimate that the potential net present value to society (e.g., the economic rent) of these deposits was \$2.75 billion (in 1974 Canadian dollars). However, rents in mining are in general much smaller than those in oil and natural gas. As we shall show in the next section, these mining rents are only 1% as large as those arising from Canadian oil and natural gas discovered over the same period.

Tax measures applied to the extractive industry usually act to reduce the rent generated by this industry.[19] The Mackenzie–Bilodeau study estimates that under

[19] The current tax laws for non-renewable resource industries are summarized for Canada in Boadway and Kitchen (1980) and Cairns (1982) and for the United States in Church (1981).

the 1974 Canadian tax laws only 82 of the deposits looked at could be exploited profitably and this reduced the economic rent potential to $2.65 billion. The taxation system may also cause firms to alter their extraction plans with respect to rates of extraction, cut-off grades and mine lives. The magnitude of this type of tax-induced inefficiency has been investigated in the context of open-pit copper mining in British Columbia by Bradley, Helliwell and Livernois (1981). It is shown there that taxes based on profits induce less inefficiency than taxes based on output. This latter type of tax can induce large inefficiencies if it is used to collect a large proportion of the economic rent.

The tax system also has an impact on the rate of exploration for and discovery of new deposits. Measures which decrease the profitability of discovered deposits naturally have a negative impact on the rate of exploration. However, most governments have attempted to escalate the rate of exploration, either by accepting reduced shares of the economic rent or, as in North America, giving mining corporations special concessions with respect to the corporation income tax such as immediate expensing of exploration and development costs and depletion allowances.

These issues are examined in further detail below, in the context of a simple model of the mine due essentially to Hotelling (1931).

A lengthy debate has been held on the issues of whether extractive industries receive unduly favourable tax treatment vis-a-vis other industries. This debate covers too much ground to be summarized here but the interested reader may refer to articles in Brannon (1975) and Erickson and Waverman (1974).

5.2. *Optimal non-renewable resource extraction*

Suppose a firm has discovered a resource deposit of size R. Let $\pi(q,t)$ denote the profits the firm can make at time t by extracting q of this resource and processing it into a standardized refined product. The variable profit function thus includes implicitly the price of the refined product and the costs of variable inputs used in the extraction process. Profits would normally also depend on the grade of the ore being mined, which will change as extraction proceeds and will depend on the sequence in which the different components of the ore body are extracted. We do not model these effects here, since they would complicate but not materially change the results [see Heaps (1985)].

Figure 5.1 illustrates the typical shape economic theory supposes the variable profit function to have. Thus the average profit curve is taken to be dome-shaped with a maximum occurring at $q=\underline{q}$.

The mine operator will choose a mine life T and an extraction plan $\langle q(t)\rangle$ that maximizes the present value V of profit obtained from the operation,

$$V=\int_0^T \pi(q,t)\,\mathrm{e}^{-rt}\,\mathrm{d}t.$$

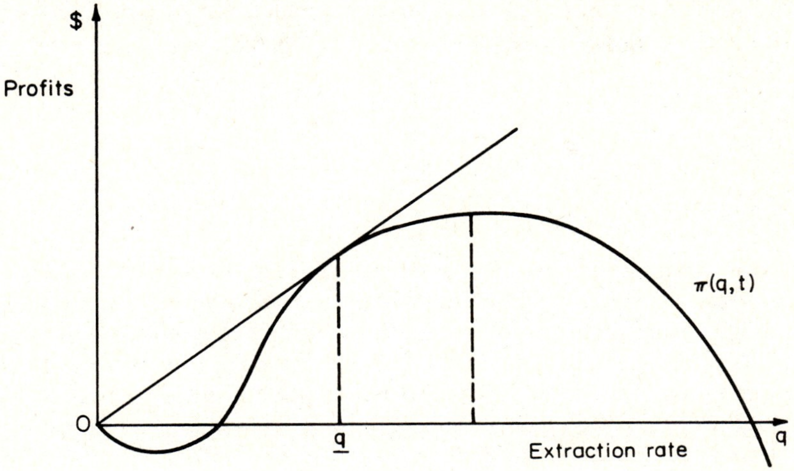

Figure 5.1. Typical variable profit function.

The following conditions characterize the operator's optimal strategy:

$$(\partial\pi/\partial q)\mathrm{e}^{-rt}=\lambda, \quad \text{a constant,} \tag{5.1}$$

$$q(T)=\underline{q}, \tag{5.2}$$

$$\int_0^T q\,\mathrm{d}t=R. \tag{5.3}$$

These conditions can easily be derived using optimal control theory, but an intuitive explanation can also be given.[20] Condition (5.1) says that discounted marginal profits should be the same at all points of time. Otherwise, ore extraction could be shifted from a time of low discounted $M\pi$ to a time of high discounted $M\pi$ resulting in an increase in V. Condition (5.2) is more difficult to understand, but suppose $q(T)>\underline{q}$ was the case. Note that for $q>\underline{q}$, average profits are falling so $M\pi<A\pi$ or $q\cdot M\pi<\pi(q)$. Now suppose extraction is reduced by a small amount Δq in every period from 0 to T. The loss in V from doing this is $\lambda\Delta qT$. The ore that is now left at time T $(\Delta R=\Delta qT)$ can be

[20]An elementary exposition of the optimal control approach is given in Lecomber (1979, pp. 58–63).

extracted over a period T to $T+\Delta T$ at a rate which keeps discounted marginal profit at λ. The gain in V from this is $\int_T^{T+\Delta T} \pi e^{-rt}\,dt$. Now if Δq is small enough, $q > \underline{q}$ during this period, so

$$\int_T^{T+\Delta T} \pi e^{-rt}\,dt > \int_T^{T+\Delta T} \lambda q\,dt = \lambda \Delta R,$$

and the gain from the transfer of extraction exceeds the loss. On the other hand, if $q(t) < \underline{q}$ were the case, V could be increased by shortening the extraction period. Incidentally, this calculation has shown that λ has an economic interpretation as the shadow price of ore in the ground. It is the marginal loss in present value of the ore remaining in the ground if the current extraction rate is increased. Thus λ is marginal user cost and optimal extraction rates are chosen to equate marginal profits to marginal user cost. This rule for dynamic profit maximization was previously encountered in the sole-owner fishery and the sustained-yield forestry model. Finally, condition (5.3) says that the entire ore body should be extracted. If not, the present value of profits could be increased by extending the life of the operation and extracting more ore.

Figure 5.2 illustrates the extraction profile the firm will choose according to conditions (5.1)–(5.3). Condition (5.3) says that the area under this curve is R, initial reserves. Differentiation of (5.1) gives

$$[\partial^2\pi/\partial q^2](dq/dt) = r(\partial\pi/\partial q) - [\partial^2\pi/\partial q\,\partial t]. \tag{5.4}$$

Since the profit function is concave in q over the operable range, the term $\partial^2\pi/\partial q^2 < 0$. As long as the price of the refined product is not rising too fast (i.e., $\partial^2\pi/\partial q\,\partial t$ small), then theory predicts that the extraction profile tilts with extraction rates falling over time. In reality, there may be capacity constraints imposed on the operation by the capital stock used in mining and milling which result in extraction rates being constant for long periods of time [see Campbell (1980)]. This complication would, however, make the analysis of taxation effects a great deal more difficult without substantially altering the qualitative results.

Taxation policy affects not only the choice of extraction rates $\langle q(t)\rangle$ but also the amount of resources employed in exploring for new deposits. This process is again very difficult to model, particularly if attention is paid to the uncertainty concerning the results of exploration. A simple extension of the above model may, however, give a few insights. Assume that initial reserves can be augmented by a certain exploration process at a cost of $C(R)$ (the present value of past exploration and development expenses at the moment extraction begins). Then the return

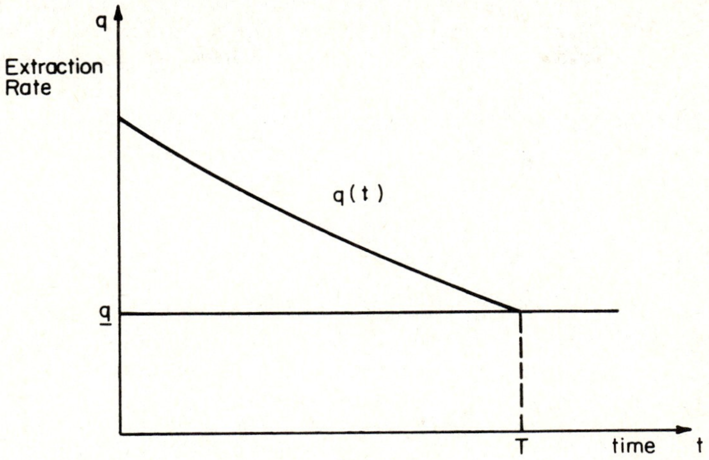

Figure 5.2. Typical extraction plan.

to the firm is

$$V=\int_0^T \pi(q)\,e^{-rt}\,dt - C(R),$$

and the optimal amount of exploration is determined by

$$\lambda - C'(R) = 0, \tag{5.5}$$

i.e., the shadow price of extra reserves should equal the marginal cost of finding them.

5.3. *Rent collecting taxes*

A number of taxes are applied to the extractive industries with the purpose of collecting a portion of the economic rent for the government. These taxes include severance taxes based on output or gross revenue (sometimes called royalties), net profit taxes, license fees, and property taxes. The impact of these taxes on the extraction plans of individual mines will be analyzed below in the context of the theoretical model of the mine developed above. In practice, firms are subject to a mixture of these taxes including corporation income tax, and taxes levied by lower jurisdictions may or may not be deductible for income tax purposes. However, for the sake of simplicity, the various types of taxes will be treated separately here.

A severance tax or royalty is usually a portion of gross output or of gross revenue. In either case it can be taken then to be $\sigma(t)q$, so the present value of a firm's extraction plan becomes

$$V = \int_0^T [\pi - \sigma q]\,\mathrm{e}^{-rt}\,\mathrm{d}t - C(R).$$

This is maximized when

$$[\partial\pi/\partial q - \sigma]\,\mathrm{e}^{-rt} = \lambda, \tag{5.6}$$

$$q(T) = \underline{q}, \tag{5.7}$$

$$\int_0^T q\,\mathrm{d}t = R, \tag{5.8}$$

$$[(\partial\pi/\partial q)(q(T),T) - \sigma(T)]\,\mathrm{e}^{-rT} = \lambda = C'(R). \tag{5.9}$$

The slope of the extraction path is now given by

$$[\partial^2\pi/\partial q^2](\mathrm{d}q/\mathrm{d}t) = r(\partial\pi/\partial q) - [\partial^2\pi/\partial q\,\partial t] + (\mathrm{d}\sigma/\mathrm{d}t) - r\sigma. \tag{5.10}$$

The slope of the extraction path is increased by the term $(\mathrm{d}\sigma/\mathrm{d}t - r\sigma)/(\partial^2\pi/\partial q^2)$ if $(\mathrm{d}\sigma/\mathrm{d}t - r\sigma) < 0$. In this case the extraction path under a severence tax is flatter than the no-tax extraction path. This result is reversed if $(\mathrm{d}\sigma/\mathrm{d}t - r\sigma) > 0$.

Figure 5.3 illustrates the three possible positions q_σ may have in relation to the no-tax extraction paths. Now (24) can be written as $(\partial\pi/\partial q)\mathrm{e}^{-rT} - C'(R) = \sigma(T)\mathrm{e}^{-rT} > 0$. The first term is a decreasing function of T since $(\mathrm{d}q/\mathrm{d}t) < 0$ at the end of the extraction period. Thus, if the severance tax increases T, it cannot at the same time raise R (assuming rising marginal exploration costs) so the highest path in Figure 5.3 cannot be optimal. Both of the other paths are possible however. Thus a severance tax reduces exploration effort and causes extraction rates to fall, at least initially.

The difference between the two cases seems to be in the rate at which marginal exploration costs are rising. If these costs are rising rapidly, the severance tax will not cause much change in exploration effort, so the reduced extraction rates will lead to a longer mine life (middle path). If marginal exploration costs are rising

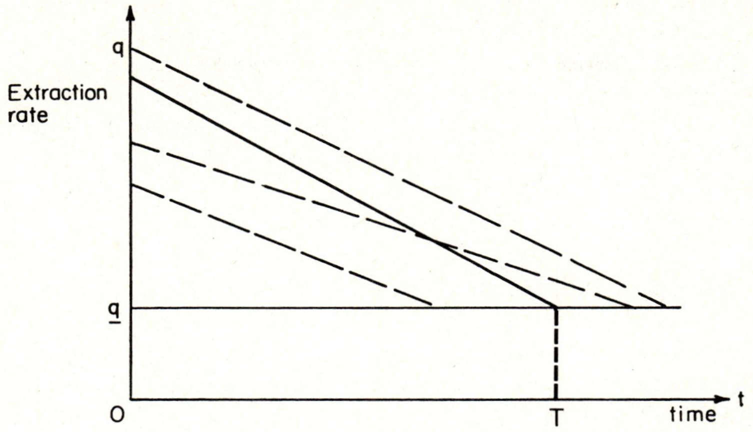

Figure 5.3. Possible effects of a severence tax. The solid line is the no-tax extraction path; the broken lines are the three possible extraction paths under a severence tax.

slowly, there will be larger adjustments of exploration effort and the mine life will be shortened (lower path).

An interesting claim sometimes made in the literature is that, if the severance tax rate rises at the rate of interest, then there will be no tax distortion.[21] In this case $(\mathrm{d}\sigma/\mathrm{d}t) = r\sigma$, so condition (5.10) is the same as condition (5.4). However, condition (5.9) now holds, so a different path satisfying (5.10) will be used. By the argument above, this path q_σ will lie completely below the no-tax extraction path so extraction rates will be reduced, less reserves will be discovered and the mine life will be shortened. Thus a severance tax which rises at the rate of interest is inefficient, although the degree of inefficiency will be small if marginal exploration costs are rising rapidly.

An alternative to a severance tax is to impose a special mining tax on the firm which is proportional to the firm's net profit. In some jurisdictions, the tax rate is itself made progressive in that it increases either with the firm's output or with the firm's profit. Thus the marginal deposit problem is avoided as a low or zero tax rate is charged on these deposits. The effect of a net profits tax will depend on the exact definition of net profits which tends to vary from jurisdiction to jurisdiction. Here it will be assumed that this type of tax is similar to the corporation income

[21] See Burness (1976) for example. Burness analyzes the effects of various taxes on mining firms in a manner similar to the manner used here, except that he has no exploration cost term.

tax. The corporation income taxes in both Canada and the U.S. contain special provisions allowing extractive firms to recover their exploration and development costs. One special provision allows immediate expensing of some or all of these costs against any taxable income the firm may have. If the tax rate is τ (constant) and the firm has enough taxable income from other sources to take full advantage of this provision, the after-tax return to the firm will then be

$$V_\tau = (1-\tau)\int_0^T \pi e^{-rt}\,dt - (1-\tau)C(R)$$

$$= (1-\tau)V.$$

Clearly this tax concession does not change the firm's extraction plans. However, it should be noted that this tax concession discriminates against small corporations who do not have enough other sources of income to take full advantage of the expensing concession.[22]

However, mining firms also benefit from a second special provision – the depletion allowance. In Canada, firms are allowed to deduct up to 25% of their net profits from taxable income. This allowance must be earned, however, in that it cannot exceed 33% of the firm's current expenditures on exploration and development. This concession, if the firm is able to take full advantage of it, changes the firm's after-tax earnings to

$$V_\tau = (1-0.75\tau)\int_0^T \pi e^{-rt}\,dt - (1-\tau)C(R).$$

The necessary conditions for maximizing V_τ are the same as those for maximizing V except that (5.5) is changed to

$$(\partial\pi/\partial q)e^{-rT} - C'(R) = -(0.25\tau/(1-0.75\tau))C'(R) < 0. \qquad (5.11)$$

The optimal extraction plan (q_τ) still satisfies the differential equation (5.4), so it lies completely below or completely above the no-tax extraction plan. A decrease of both T and R would increase the LHS of (5.11). Thus the opposite must be true. This type of depletion allowance raises extraction rates, increases exploration effort, and lengthens mine lives as illustrated in Figure 5.4.

The United States has a different method of calculating the depletion allowance. It is a percentage of gross revenue to a maximum of 50% of net income from the extraction operation. Thus, if the net income limitation is not binding, this allowance is equivalent to a negative severance tax proportional to the price

[22] The result that immediate expensing of capital expenditures makes the corporation income tax-neutral may be found in several places; e.g., Smith (1963).

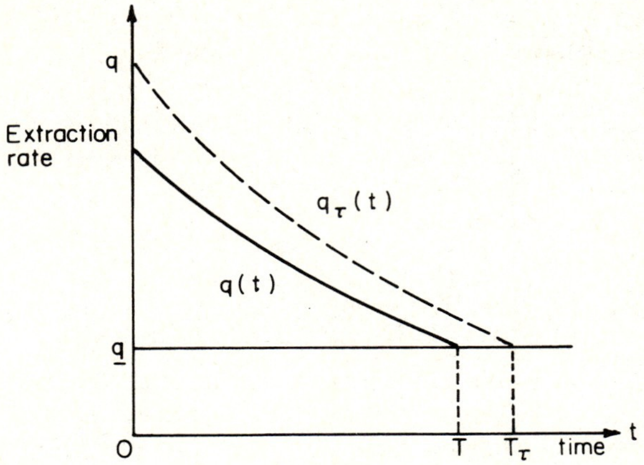

Figure 5.4. Effect of a depletion allowance.

of ore. If this price is not rising too quickly, then the case $(\mathrm{d}\sigma/\mathrm{d}t) - r\sigma > 0$ applies (since $\sigma < 0$), and this allowance also causes increases in exploration and extraction rates.

A profit tax rate which increases with the amount of profits made will also affect the firm's extraction plans. Intuitively, the firm will shift extraction away from times of high discounted profits (the present) to times of low discounted profits (the future). This is verified, at least in some circumstances, in Heaps (1985).

Another form of taxation which might be used is a license fee $\tau(t)$ paid at time t if the mine is still in operation at that time. In this form of taxation,

$$V = \int_0^T [\pi - \tau] \mathrm{e}^{-rt} \mathrm{d}t - C(R).$$

The necessary conditions for maximizing V are only altered in that $\pi - \tau$ is substituted for π in (5.1)–(5.5). The only change in these conditions is then that (5.2) is replaced by

$$\pi(q(T)) - q(T)(\partial\pi/\partial q)(q(T)) = \tau,$$

so that

$$q(T) > \underline{q}.$$

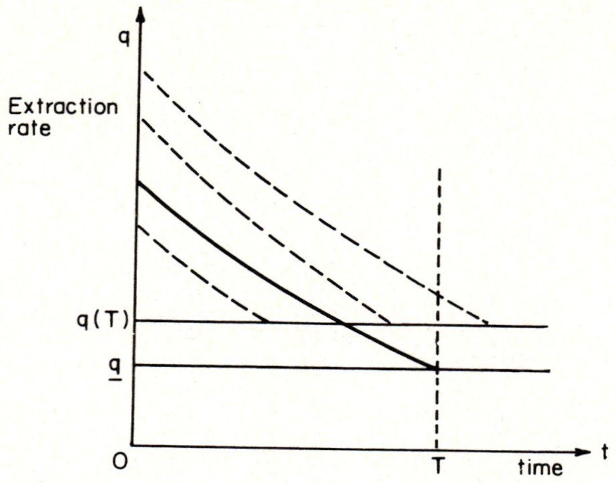

Figure 5.5. Possible effects of a license fee. The solid line is the no-tax extraction path; the broken lines are the three possible extraction paths under a license fee.

The post-tax extraction paths are themselves unchanged. Three possible cases are illustrated in Figure 5.5. Condition (5.5), $\lambda = C'(R)$, still applies. Since by (5.1) $\lambda = \pi_q(q(0))$ as well, R is changed by the franchise tax in the opposite direction to $q(0)$. This rules out both the upper and lower possibility in Figure 5.5. Thus the franchise tax raises extraction rates and reduces exploration effort and mine lives. As well, some high-cost mines might go out of operation completely when the present value of license fees exceeds the no-tax economic rents.

A property tax can be levied in a number of ways but properly it should depend on reserves remaining in the ground. As an example, assume it takes the form $\tau(t)R(t)$, where $R(t)$ are reserves remaining at the time t and $\tau(t)$ is the tax rate at time t. The present value of tax payments is then

$$PV_T = \int_0^T \tau(t)R(t)\mathrm{e}^{-rt}\,\mathrm{d}t.$$

Let $\sigma(t)$ be a function such that $\mathrm{d}\sigma/\mathrm{d}t - r\sigma = \tau(t)$ and $\sigma(0) = 0$ (so $\sigma \geq 0$ for all t). Then integrating by parts,

$$PV_T = \int_0^T \sigma q \mathrm{e}^{-rt}\,\mathrm{d}t,$$

and

$$V=\int_0^T[\pi-\sigma q]\mathrm{e}^{-rt}\mathrm{d}t-C(R).$$

Note that $\mathrm{d}\sigma/\mathrm{d}t-r\sigma>0$. Thus the situation is like a severance tax increasing at more than the rate of interest and the extraction paths are tilted up.

Figure 5.6 illustrates three possible relationships between the post-tax extraction paths and the no-tax extraction path. The upper path is ruled out by condition (5.9). $(\partial\pi/\partial q)\mathrm{e}^{-rt}-C'(R)>0$. Thus mine lives are shortened and extraction rates will eventually fall. It can additionally be shown that in either case total reserves discovered will fall.

One other type of tax called a resource rent tax (or rate of return tax) has been suggested in the literature [Garnaut and Clunies Ross (1975)]. This tax works as follows. The firm is not taxed until the present value of proceeds from extraction covers the firm's investment in the mine. Subsequently the firm is taxed on the excess of this present value over the value of investment, possibly at a rate which increases with the difference of these two values. This type of taxation is non-distortionary as may be seen as follows. Let

$$V(t)=\int_0^t\pi\mathrm{e}^{-rt}\mathrm{d}t-C(R)$$

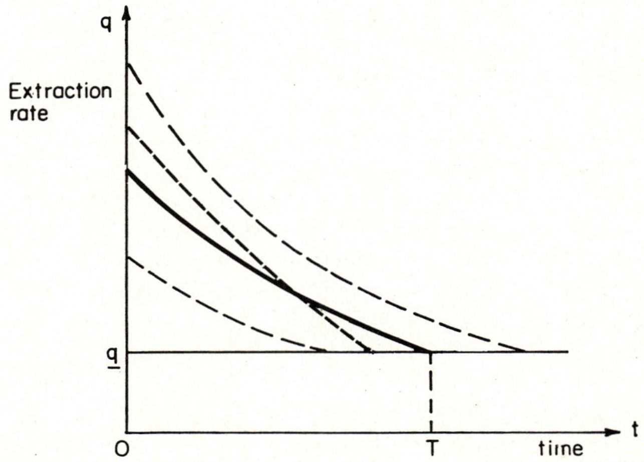

Figure 5.6. Possible effects of a property tax. The solid line is the no-tax extraction path; the broken lines are the three possible extraction paths under a property tax.

be the base on which the firm is taxed. Let $\tau(V)$ be the tax rate applied, where $\tau(V)=0$ if $V \leq 0$. Also let $\sigma(V)=\int_0^V \tau(U)\,dU$, so that $\sigma(V)=0$ for $V<0$ and $\sigma'=\tau(V)$, and note that $dV(t)/dt=\pi e^{-rt}$. The after-tax returns to the firm are then

$$W=\int_0^T [1-\tau(V)](dV/dt)\,dt - C(R)$$

$$= V(T)-\sigma(V(T))-V(0)+\sigma(V(0))-C(R)$$

$$= V(T)-\sigma(V(T)).$$

Now since $\sigma'(V)=\tau(V)<1$, $V-\sigma(V)$ is an increasing function of V. Thus $W=V-\sigma(V)$ is maximized by maximizing V, i.e., resource rent taxation is efficient. It has been pointed out, however, that this result depends on the rate at which the firm's profits are discounted for tax purposes being the same as the discount rate used by the firm. If the industry uses a discount rate containing a risk premium reflecting the particular economic, geological, and political risks of a project, it would be possible in principle, but very difficult in practice, to use an estimate of this discount rate for tax purposes. For further discussion, see Garnaut and Clunies Ross (1979).

6. Crude oil and natural gas

6.1. Economic rents in crude oil and natural gas

The taxation of crude-oil and natural-gas merits a separate section because of the enormous size and variability of oil revenues in the 1970's and 1980's. By any measure, crude oil is the most important resource commodity in world trade.[23] The sharp increase in its price in 1973–1974 and again in 1979–1980, followed in each case by much more gradual declines, relative to the prices of other goods, created enormous revenues that were very unevenly distributed. Even within the O.E.C.D. countries, which import more than 60% of their crude oil, the world

[23] Even in 1970, well before the four-fold increases in crude-oil prices of 1973–1974, crude petroleum and petroleum products amounted to almost 60% of world trade in extractive resources and 8% of all world merchandise trade. Net energy imports of the thirteen major O.E.C.D. countries grew from $12.6 billion in 1970 when they were 4% of world merchandise trade, to $225 billion in 1980 when they were 12% of world merchandise trade.

value of domestic oil production in 1980 was almost U.S. \$500 billion, or more than 6% of GNP. For Canada, which has an approximate trade balance in oil and natural gas, the foreign trade value of crude-oil and natural-gas production in 1980 was about U.S. \$30 billion, or 12% of GNP. These values far exceeded the direct costs of production. For example, economic rents in Canada from crude-oil and natural-gas production in 1980 have been estimated at about U.S. \$20 billion, which is about two-thirds of the gross value of production, or 8% of GNP. All past and currently foreseen Canadian non-frontier production of crude oil and natural gas (excluding potential Arctic and off-shore production) have been estimated to produce economic rents with a present value of about end-1983 U.S. \$450 billion, or one and one-half years of Canadian GNP.[24]

Faced with rising world oil prices, governments in the industrial countries have used their taxation and spending policies to restrain the domestic demand for imported energy, to encourage the production of domestic substitutes for imported energy, to obtain higher tax revenues from domestic production of low-cost energy sources, and to cushion their economies from the stagflationary macroeconomic effects of higher world oil prices. In this section, we shall bypass the macroeconomic issues and the use of downstream energy use taxes to reduce energy demand, focussing our attention instead upon the taxation of production income and the special tax treatment of exploration and development investment.

The taxation of oil and gas income has typically involved both some form of *ad valorem* tax on production income and some form of tax on net income. In jurisdictions where the government has ownership interests in oil and gas, and this includes all off-shore deposits and many on-shore ones, the two main types of tax may be supplemented by some bidding process for allocating production rights, or else a government equity interest in production revenues. Investment expenditures are usually given favoured treatment, relative to similar expenditures in other industries, by means of accelerated write-off of capital expenditures, depreciation allowances exceeding 100%, or some more direct form of investment. We shall first describe some of the particular forms that these taxes take in Canada, the United States, Norway, and the United Kingdom, and then make some general comparison of the main features of oil and gas taxation.

[24] These results are from Helliwell, MacGregor and Plourde (1983, table 1, case 4) and are calculated on the assumption that world oil prices are \$29 per barrel in 1983 and will grow at 2% in real terms for the rest of the 1980's. The real pre-tax opportunity cost of capital is taken to be 10%, with 7% used as the social and after-tax private real rate of time preference. The total rents include those going to energy users, producers and governments. The calculated economic rents to energy users are income-compensated consumer surpluses after allowing for waste from the use of energy priced at less than its opportunity cost. Over the 1981–1986 life of the current energy agreements between the federal and provincial governments, estimated rents have an end-1983 present value of 127 billion \$C, with 20% going to energy users, 17% to producing firms, 28% to the federal government and 35% to the provincial governments [Helliwell, MacGregor and Plourde (1983, table 1)].

6.2. *Oil and gas taxation in four countries* [25]

(i) *Canada.* In Canada, oil and natural gas in the provinces belongs in most instances to the provincial governments, and is subject to a provincial *ad valorem* royalty. The rate of royalty varies with the selling price and with the date of discovery, and thus has some of the features of a profits tax. The average royalty rate for new oil is about 36%, although there are numerous abatements and special provisions for new discoveries, low productivity wells, and oil obtained at higher cost by the use of enhanced recovery techniques. These royalty reductions for higher-cost sources also have the effect of making the gross royalty more like a profits tax. The provinces also have a tax on corporate profits, at rates ranging from 11% to 16% in the producing provinces. Prior to the introduction of the National Energy Program in October 1980, the federal government's main claim on oil and natural gas revenues in the provinces was the corporation income tax. Prior to 1974, provincial royalties were a deductible expense for the federal corporation income tax. In response to substantial increases in provincial mineral royalty rates in 1973 and 1974, the federal government acted to make provincial royalties a non-deductible expense and provided an alternative "resource allowance" deduction of 25% of net income before subtraction of exploration and development expenses. Before 1981, there was also an "earned depletion allowance", which is a slightly altered form of the depletion allowance described in Section 5. Under the earned depletion allowance, firms can deduct from taxable income an additional $1 for every $3 spent on exploration and development, up to a maximum of 25% of resource profits. Thus the earned depletion allowance could be regarded as an investment subsidy at the rate of 0.33τ, where τ is the corporation income tax rate, but available only when the corporation generates taxable income. Under the National Energy Program introduced in October 1980, the earned depletion allowance is being gradually phased out in provincial lands, to be replaced by taxable Petroleum Incentive Program (PIP) grants. These grants depend on location, on the type of expenditure, and on the degree of Canadian ownership. On provincial lands, there are no grants for firms with less than 50% Canadian ownership, and grants of 35% for exploration expenditure by firms with more than 75% Canadian ownership. For exploration expenditure on the "Canada Lands", which include all of the Arctic and off-shore areas, the earned depletion allowance remains at $1 for every $3 of investment, and there are also PIP grants ranging from 25% for foreign-owned firms to 80% for firms with more than 75% Canadian ownership. This pattern heavily favours investment in the Arctic and off-shore regions, continuing a bias established earlier in the 1970's when invest-

[25] This section is based on descriptions of the four tax systems in Helliwell (1982), Verleger (1982), Mitchell (1982) and Stauffer (1982), a group of four papers presented at the third annual conference of the I.A.E.E. and published in *The Energy Journal*, April 1982.

ment over \$5 million in Arctic and off-shore wells received the regular depletion allowance plus a "super-depletion" allowance of $66\frac{2}{3}\%$. The combination of depletion, super-depletion, and the immediate expensing of exploration, all of which were available to individuals as well as corporations, meant that 200% of expenditures over \$5 million (\$C) per well could be written off against resource income, putting their net cost below zero for those with marginal income tax rates above 50%.

The National Energy Program of 1980 introduced two new federal taxes: an 8% petroleum and gas revenue tax (PGRT) on net operating income and a specific tax on all natural gas sold to domestic or export customers. The government of Alberta, which controls 85% of Canada's oil and natural gas, responded to these measures by cutting the allowed production of conventional crude oil and deferring any approval of new plants for synthetic oil. It took until September of 1981 for the provincial and federal governments to reach agreements to cover the years 1981–1986. Under the agreements, the petroleum and gas revenue tax is set at an effective rate of 12%, world prices are to be paid for new oil and synthetic oil, the natural-gas tax is not levied on export sales, and a much higher schedule of prices was established for conventional "old oil", which were likely to reach a limit of 75% of the world price by mid-1983.[26]

To summarize (and over-simplify) the current Canadian tax treatment of new discoveries of conventional oil in Alberta, the net wellhead price is

$$P_n = (1-\tau_p)[P_w(1-0.29) - C_o] - 0.12(P_w - C_o) - \tau_f(P_w - C_o)(1-0.25), \tag{6.1}$$

where τ_f and τ_p are the federal and provincial rates of corporation income tax, currently 0.36 for τ_f and 11% for τ_p in Alberta; P_w is the world oil price; C_o is operating costs; 0.29 is the marginal new-oil royalty rate; 0.12 is the rate of federal PGRT; 0.25 is the rate of federal resource allowance. P_n is thus the net wellhead price after all taxes, royalties and operating costs, but before deduction of capital expenditures (the expression ignores the fact that interest expenses, which have recently become a very important component of oil industry financing, are deductible for both the federal and provincial corporation income taxes).

[26]Among the four countries surveyed, Canada is unusual in the extent to which it has relied, at least until the energy agreements of 1981, on low prices rather than high taxes to redistribute energy revenues from producing firms and regions. The likely reason for this, as described in Helliwell (1981), is that the federal price controls already in place at the time of the 1973 O.P.E.C. price shock gave rise to a policy of gradual adjustment towards the much higher world prices. By early 1979, this process was almost complete when the world price doubled again, creating vast potential economic rents and major adjustment costs. It took two years to reach federal–provincial agreements on a new set of pricing and taxing arrangements, and, in the meantime, prices were held down by federal regulation.

If we substitute in the current tax rates and ignore all of the tax deductions and subsidies related to capital expenditures, equation (6.1) can be simplified to

$$P_n = 0.24P_w - 0.50C_o. \tag{6.2}$$

Tax deductions and grants cover 65% of the related exploration investment (for a firm with more than 75% Canadian ownership).

(ii) *The United States.* Oil and natural-gas taxation in the United States, like that in Canada, shifted from a pre-1973 position of unusually favourable treatment (primarily because of the depletion allowance and the rapid expensing of exploration expenditure) to a post-OPEC position of higher than average tax rates (mainly through the application of the Windfall Profits Tax). There are state severance taxes on oil and gas; these are like the Canadian provincial royalties, but the rates are generally only one-third as high.

For new oil discovered after 1979, the approximate tax treatment is as follows, ignoring the depletion allowance still available for small producers:

$$P_n = (1-\tau)[(1-\tau_s)P_w - C_o - \tau_w[(P_w - P_b)(1-\tau_s)]], \tag{6.3}$$

where τ is the rate of corporation income tax, maximum 46%; τ_s is the rate of state severance tax, ranging from 7% to 12%; τ_w is the rate of windfall profits tax, ranging from 15% to 70% for post-1979 oil; P_b is the base price, equal to \$16/bbl for post-1979 oil.

Ignoring the tax treatment of capital expenditures, and using 12% for the rate of state severance tax, 47% for the corporation tax and 50% for the rate of windfall profits tax, this reduces to

$$P_n = 7.04 + 0.237P_w - 0.54C_o. \tag{6.4}$$

Capital expenses must, in general, be written off over the production period, although there are some accelerated depreciation provisions and in some cases an investment tax credit as in other U.S. industries. Tax deductions and investment tax credits would, in present value terms, cover substantially less than half of the cost of the investment.

(iii) *The United Kingdom.* Oil and gas taxation in the United Kingdom, like that in Canada and Norway, has involved a variety of complicated taxes and charges intended to obtain a high degree of rent collection with ample incentive for producers to minimize costs and adequate incentive for the development of smaller fields. With each sharp increase in world oil prices, the tax regime has been altered to raise government revenues, with adjustments made later in the face of rising costs or falling real oil prices.

Prior to 1981, there were three main components in the taxation of production of oil and natural gas from the U.K. continental shelf:

- a gross production royalty of 12.5%;
- Petroleum Revenue Tax (PRT) of 70%, based on revenues net of royalties, operating costs, and "uplifted" capital expenditures ("uplifting" permits more than 100% of capital expenditure to be charged against income, in lieu of any allowance for interest costs);
- corporation income tax at 52%, with royalties and PRT allowed as expenses.

Ignoring the treatment of capital expenditure and interest costs, the basic 1980 U.K. system could therefore be represented as follows:

$$P_{\mathrm{n}} = (1-\tau)(1-\tau_{\mathrm{p}})\left[P_{\mathrm{w}}(1-\tau_{\mathrm{r}}) - C_{\mathrm{o}}\right], \tag{6.5}$$

where τ is the rate of corporation income tax; τ_{r} is the rate of royalty; τ_{p} is the rate of petroleum revenue tax.

Using the 1980 tax rates, $P_{\mathrm{n}} = 0.125P_{\mathrm{w}} - 0.144C_{\mathrm{o}}$. In early 1981, the government proposed a new 20% Special Petroleum Duty, to be levied, like the royalty, on gross revenues and to be deductible for the corporation income tax. This had the effect of raising τ_{r} from 0.125 to 0.325 and making $P_{\mathrm{n}} = 0.097P_{\mathrm{w}} - 0.144C_{\mathrm{o}}$. In its March 1982 budget, the U.K. government announced that the Special Petroleum Duty would be removed at the end of 1982, to be replaced by an increase of the PRT rate from 70% to 75% and an advance payment of 20 points of the 75% PRT. The 1983 system therefore involves $\tau = 0.52$, $\tau_{\mathrm{r}} = 0.125$ and $\tau_{\mathrm{p}} = 0.75$. Once again ignoring the treatment of capital expenditures and interest expense, under these new tax rates equation (6.5) reduces to $P_{\mathrm{n}} = 0.105P_{\mathrm{w}} - 0.12C_{\mathrm{o}}$.

Capital expenditures are treated much more favourably than in the United States system, since they are "uplifted" before calculation of the tax base for the Petroleum Revenue Tax, and only the 20% "advance payment" portion of the PRT is paid before all capital expenditures have been recovered.

(iv) *Norway.* The Norwegian system relies more on direct participation and less on taxes than the systems described above. From the point of view of a private developer, state participation with matching contributions to capital expenditures is equivalent to a corporation income tax of the same rate, applicable to a tax base with full loss offsets and immediate expensing of capital expenditures. The other main elements of the system are a corporation income tax with a nominal rate of 50.8% (with dividends deductible against part of the tax), a sliding-scale royalty, a "Special Tax" somewhat akin to the U.K. Petroleum Revenue Tax, and a requirement that Norwegian sources be used for some expenditures. The system can be roughly represented as follows, from the point of view of the private participant:

$$P_n = (1 - P)(1 - \tau)(1 - \tau_s)[P_w(1 - \tau_r) - C_o], \tag{6.6}$$

where P is the STATOIL participation percentage; τ is the rate of corporation income tax; τ_s is the rate of Special Tax; τ_r is the royalty rate.

We do not have at hand the data to permit example calculations, but Stauffer (1982, p. 53) suggests that at the margin P_n is from 0.08 to 0.15 times as large as P_w. The tax treatment of capital expenditures is generous, like that in Canada and the U.K.; current deductions can exceed 125% of investment expenditures, and the Special Tax permits a 6.67% tax-free return on invested capital.

6.3. *Comparative summary*

In all of the countries whose systems we have surveyed, there have been periodic changes in the tax regimes in response to changes in world oil prices, coupled with the introduction of cost-related deductions and allowances to permit the development of higher-cost sources. These allowances have been most common in off-shore and frontier areas and for small-sized or other higher-cost sources. Under the current tax arrangements for new oil, the United Kingdom and Norway have the highest marginal rates of tax on changes in revenue brought about by changes in world oil prices, with rates in Canada and the United States being substantially less. The United Kingdom, Norway, and Canada all either subsidize oil and natural-gas investment directly or permit complete, or more than complete, write-off of capital expenditures before application of high rates of tax. In this way the three systems attempt to combine high rates of collection (or disbursement, when world oil prices fall) of economic rents caused by changes in world oil prices, while maintaining adequate economic incentive for the development of new sources whose costs are much higher than average yet nevertheless below current and expected world price levels.

In some countries, with Norway being the main example in the group of four examined in this section, the rate of development and production of oil reserves has been determined much less by the pattern of taxation than by the macroeconomic decision to limit the rate of oil production to a level that could be sustained for many decades and to limit the extent to which oil production dominates exports and the national economy. A strategy of extended development is implemented by the gradual release of new areas for exploration and development, coupled with tax rates high enough to restrict early development to the largest- and lowest-cost fields. In the United States and Canada, by contrast, the overall result of the interplay of market forces and the pattern of taxation has been to encourage the early development and use of the potential reserves of low-cost crude oil and natural gas. The United Kingdom has come on the scene as a producer much more recently, about the same time as Norway. The rate of U.K. production has risen fairly rapidly to a position of modest export surplus; this involves a much shorter producing horizon than in Norway. The difference between the U.K. and Norwegian development rates is due mainly to Norway's large resource base in relation to a much smaller population and not to any differences between the tax structures of the two countries.

Of the four countries, the United States (even with the full operation of the U.S. windfall profits tax) and Canada appear to offer the largest marginal return, on new oil with marginal returns, arising from increases in the world oil price, exceeding 0.2, compared to half as much for Norway and the United Kingdom. Thus we would expect to find drilling activity in North America to be more sharply responsive to changes in world oil prices (both up and down) than would be the case in the United Kingdom and Norway. The comparison cannot be carried too far, however, for the drilling programmes in the North Sea require in any event a longer lead time and a greater degree of commitment than is the case for exploration in the continental United States and Canada.

7. Hydro-electricity

7.1. The scope and value of hydro-electricity

For the O.E.C.D. countries as a whole, hydro-electricity provides about 15% of total energy production and 10% of total energy use. It is therefore substantially less important than fossil fuels as a current source of energy and as a source of potential current tax revenues. However, the prices of fossil fuels have risen so much in the decade since 1973 that the potential economic rents attributable to hydro-electric sites (using marginal cost to define potential revenues) are greater than from any other non-fuel natural resources.

Hydro-electric sites, like mineral deposits, are very unevenly distributed and development of the available sites has also proceeded at different rates. Potential annual hydro-electric rents per capita from existing installations range from $200 U.S. in Norway and $100 for Canada to $13 for the United States and almost nothing for Germany and the United Kingdom.

7.2. Electricity pricing and taxation

Hydro-electricity is unusual among energy resources, and even among natural resources as a whole, in being highly regulated but not highly taxed. In most countries the generation of electricity is either under government ownership or is regulated so that the electricity-producing utility earns only a normal return. In both cases, the potential rents from hydroelectricity have generally been distributed as lower average electricity prices rather than collected as taxes. Rising costs of alternative thermal and nuclear plants, rising fuel costs and increasing costs of developing new hydro sites have created in most countries a sharp wedge between the incremental cost of electricity from new plants and the average historic cost of pre-1970 hydro-electric installations. Electricity prices based on average historic cost can therefore create inefficiency in electricity use.

To attempt to correct the inefficiencies in electricity use, two-part tariffs have been advocated, with the trailing block or energy charge based on the marginal cost of electricity, with a lower-priced initial block, or a lump-sum credit, used to distribute the revenue surplus S,

$$S = (P_{\mathrm{m}} - P_{\mathrm{a}})Q, \tag{7.1}$$

where P_{m} is the marginal cost; P_{a} is the average historic cost; Q is the quantity of electricity sold. This use of the two-part tariff is a reversal of its original role in utility pricing, where it was intended to allocate fixed costs in a situation where average cost exceeded marginal cost.

In the light of the substantial post-OPEC increases in the economic rents attributable to hydro-electric sites, there have been increasing taxes on actual or potential hydro-electric revenues. Since most electric utilities are either government-owned or regulated, and since water rights are often also publicly-owned or at least subject to taxation, the establishment of a water-licence charge or other tax to collect the rents from hydro-electric sites seems a natural way of reducing the total excess burden of the tax system. In general, revenues from a hydro rent tax would serve to reduce marginal tax rates and excess burdens elsewhere in the tax system, while eliminating the inefficiencies, administrative costs and possible inequities of distributing the rents by means of low prices to electricity users.

It has been estimated that a full application of hydro-electricity rent taxes in Canada would have raised almost \$3 billion in 1979, equal to more than 1% of GNP or 3% of total government revenues. Some provinces (British Columbia and Quebec) have started moving in this direction, but only a small fraction of the potential rent is being collected. Hydro-electric resources are likely to become a more important natural resource tax base in many countries in the coming decades. As they do, questions of the tax design will become important, as it is clear that water licence charges or other taxes must be adjusted for the quality of the site, including the value of its alternative uses, if the "cut-off grade" problems we have described in earlier sections are not to emerge. This is particularly so for low-head and in-stream hydro units that are very capital-intensive and may involve little economic rent relative to alternative sources of electricity.

7.3. The impact of inflation on electricity pricing and taxation

High inflation rates, accompanied by high nominal interest rates, have served to exaggerate a long-standing defect in the intertemporal pricing of electricity. The problem lies in the allocation of capital charges and is especially important for hydro-electricity, which is highly capital-intensive.

The usual "rate base" method for allocating capital charges involves an annual payment of C_t,

$$C_t = (r + \delta) K_t, \tag{7.2}$$

where K_t is the rate base defined by

$$K_{t+1} = (1 - \delta) K_t + I_t, \tag{7.3}$$

and I_t is the capital cost (including interest during construction) of new projects brought on stream during the year. The rate of return r is usually a weighted average of the utility's actual nominal cost of capital. Depreciation is usually on a straight-line basis of 70 years or more for hydro-electric installations; we shall simplify by treating δ as a 0.02 annual rate of decay. Assuming that the real cost of capital is 7% and ignoring inflation for the moment, this method of allocating the capital cost of a hydro-electric project charges 9% (= 0.02 + 0.07) in the first year of the project, dropping to next to nothing in the last year when the rate base, K_t, is almost entirely written off. The initial charge is thus about twice as high as it would have to be if it were constant over the expected lifetime of the project.

Consider now what happens if the actual and expected inflation rate is 10%, raising the nominal interest rate to about 17%. The initial charge would then be 0.19, more than twice as high as in the no-inflation case, and four times as high as it would be if the capital charge were set constant in real terms over the life of the project.[27] This accounting method can have quite dramatic effects on the prices of an expanding hydro-electric or nuclear system. For example, in British Columbia, application of this pricing system has been forecast to almost double electricity prices from 1982 to 1986, even though the new projects being brought on stream are, in real terms, almost as cheap as any of the earlier projects. In fact, this method is expected to raise average historic costs above marginal costs by the end of the decade. This pricing system interacts with the potential for taxation by causing sharp changes in electricity prices, dropping potential tax revenues to zero whenever average historical cost approaches incremental cost.

[27] This alternative procedure is proposed and compared with conventional methods in Helliwell and Lester (1976).

Reform of the rate-base method to allow for inflation and to spread capital charges more evenly over time would do much to stabilize electric utility financing and taxable capacity. Electricity pricing based on inflation-adjusted measures of long-run marginal cost, coupled with either a two-part tariff or a hydro-electric rent tax to allocate the surplus, would reduce the effects of inflation on electricity pricing and use.

8. Conclusion

This chapter has been long and detailed and leaves us with little room or reason for concluding comments. Our aim has been to survey the main current issues in the taxation of natural resources, using particular examples chosen to represent topics of general interest and application. Our primary emphasis has been on the effects of taxation on the efficiency of resource development and use, although we have at all times tried to combine this with attention to the revenue-raising power, simplicity and ease of enforcement of the alternative types of taxes and regulation.

We have often concentrated on the impact that a particular set of tax rules has on decisions by private firms, but one of the main results of our survey is that any major change in world market conditions usually leads to major changes in the tax rules themselves. Thus each major jump in world oil prices has brought new taxes and new tax rates. We have documented some of these changes and dealt with them chiefly as changes in the relations between governments and firms. Yet there has also been competition for revenue shares between levels of government within a country (Canada provides the most striking example) and between countries. Indeed, one of the reasons advanced for the sharp increase in prices (and effective tax rates) by O.P.E.C. governments in 1973–1974 was to offset the increasing share of oil revenues accruing not only to the international oil companies but also to the governments of the consuming countries, both through their taxes on oil company profits and their taxes on oil consumption. At a slightly earlier stage, the U.S. tax on oil imports could also be regarded as increasing the U.S. government share of O.P.E.C. oil revenues, and similar reasoning is used now in the analysis of new proposals for oil import tariffs.

The consequence of the endogeneity of resource taxation systems and rates is that a full analysis of the effects of resource taxation depends more on actual and anticipated future changes in tax systems than on the details of a current system that is unlikely to be permanent. The impermanence of tax systems probably tends to accelerate resource developments when returns appear large, since anticipated future tax increases may act to depress the returns anticipated from delayed development. On the other hand, the combination of tax uncertainty and the large long-term investments required for resource projects may cause some otherwise profitable resource investments to be passed by. It is probably true that a stable but flexible tax system, that produces an acceptable distribution of costs and benefits under a variety of price and cost conditions, would be desirable from the points of view of governments as well as producers. In the absence of such taxes-for-all-seasons, it is perhaps not surprising that there is in many countries an increasing use of direct government participation and joint ventures that pass more of the development risk back to the government (or at least one of the governments) that sets the tax rules.

References

Barker, T. and V. Brailovsky, eds., 1981, Oil or industry? Energy, industrialization and economic policy in Canada, Mexico, the Netherlands, Norway and the United Kingdom (Academic Press, London).

Beals, R.E., M. Gillis, G. Jenkins and U. Peterson, 1980, Investment policy: Issues and analyses, in: M. Gillis and R.E. Beals, eds., Tax and investment policies for hard minerals (Ballinger, Cambridge, MA) 261–276.

Bertrand, R.J., 1981, The state of competition in the Canadian petroleum industry (Supply and Services, Ottawa).

Boadway, R.W. and H.M. Kitchen, 1980, Canadian tax policy, Canadian tax paper no. 63 (Canadian Tax Foundation, Toronto).

Bradley, P.G., J.F. Helliwell and J.R. Livernois, 1981, Efficient taxation of resource income: The case of copper mining in British Columbia, Resources Policy 7, 161–170.

Brannon, G.M., 1974, Energy, taxes and subsidies (Ballinger, Cambridge, MA).

Brannon, G.M., ed., 1975, Studies in energy tax policy (Ballinger, Cambridge, MA).

Burness, S., 1976, On the taxation of nonreplenishable natural resources, Journal of Environmental Economics and Management 3, 289–311.

Cairns, R.D., 1982, Extractive resource taxation in Canada, in: W.R. Thirsk and J. Whalley, eds., Tax policy options in the 1980s (Canadian Tax Foundation, Toronto).

Campbell, H.F., 1980, The effect of capital intensity on the optimal rate of extraction of a mineral deposit, Canadian Journal of Economics 13, 349–356.

Church, A.M., 1981, Taxation of nonrenewable resources (Lexington Books, Lexington, MA).

Clark, C.W., 1976, Mathematical bioeconomics (Wiley, New York).

Clark, C.W., 1980, Towards a predictive model for the economic regulation of fisheries, Canadian Journal of Fisheries and Aquatic Sciences 37, 1111–1129.

Copes, P., 1978, Canada's Atlantic coast fisheries: Policy development and the impact of extended jurisdiction, Canadian Public Policy 4, 155–171.

Crutchfield, J.A., 1979, Economic and social implications of the main policy alternatives for controlling fishing effort, Journal of the Fisheries Research Board of Canada 36, 742–752.

Crutchfield, J.A. and A. Zellner, 1962, Economic aspects of the Pacific halibut fishery, in: U.S. Department of the Interior, Fisheries industrial research 1-1 (U.S.G.P.O., Washington, DC).

Dam, K.W., 1976, Oil revenue: Who gets what how? (University of Chicago Press, Chicago, IL).

Dasgupta, P.S. and G.M. Heal, 1979, Economic theory and exhaustible resources (Cambridge University Press, Cambridge).

Duerr, W.A. et al., 1979, Forest resource management (W.B. Saunders, Philadelphia, PA).

Ellman, M., 1981, Natural gas, restructuring and reindustrialization: The Dutch experience of industrial policy, in: T. Barker and V. Brailovsky, eds., Oil or industry? Energy, industrialization and economic policy in Canada, Mexico, the Netherlands, Norway, and the United Kingdom (Academic Press, London).

Erickson, E.W. and L. Waverman, 1974, eds., The energy question: An international failure of policy, Vol. 2 (University of Toronto Press, Toronto).

Gane, M., ed., 1968, Martin Faustmann and the evolution of discounted cash flow, Oxford Institute paper no. 42.

Garnaut, R. and A. Clunies Ross, 1975, Uncertainty, risk aversion and the taxing of natural resource projects, Economic Journal 85, 271–287.

Garnaut, R. and A. Clunies Ross, 1979, The neutrality of the resource rent tax, Economic Record 55, 193–201.

Gordon, H.S., 1954, The economic theory of a common property resource: The fishery, Journal of Political Economy 62, 124–142.

Haley, D., 1980, A regional comparison of stumpage values in British Columbia and the United States Pacific North West, Forestry Chronicle 56, 225–230.

Hannesson, R., 1978, Economics of fisheries (Universitetsforlaget, Bergen).

Heaps, T., 1985, The taxation of nonreplenishable natural resources revisited, Journal of Environmental Economics and Management 11, 1–14.

Helles, F., 1969, Aims and means in Danish forest policy, in: A. Svendsrud, ed., Readings in forest economics (Universitetsforlaget, Oslo) 215–223.

Helliwell, J.F., 1968, Public policies and private investment (Clarendon Press, Oxford).

Helliwell, J.F., 1981, Canadian energy pricing, Canadian Journal of Economics 14, 577–595.

Helliwell, J.F., 1982, Taxation of oil and gas revenues: Canada, The Energy Journal 3, 20–31.

Helliwell, J.F. and John Lester, 1975, A new approach to price setting for regulated pipelines, Logistics and Transportation Review 11, 320–337.

Helliwell, J.F., M.E. MacGregor and A. Plourde, 1983, The national energy program meets falling world oil prices, Canadian Public Policy 9, 284–296.

Henderson, J.V. and M. Tugwell, 1979, Exploitation of the lobster fishery: Some empirical results, Journal of Environmental Economics and Management 6, 287–296.

Hotelling, H., 1931, The economics of exhaustible resources, Journal of Political Economy 39, 137–175.

Juhasz, J.J., 1976, Methods of Crown timber appraisal in British Columbia, in: W. McKillop and W.J. Mead, eds., Timber policy issues in British Columbia (University of British Columbia Press, Vancouver) 56–88.

Lecomber, R., 1979, The economics of natural resources (Macmillan, London).

Lindholm, R.W., 1973, Taxation of timber resources (Bureau of Business and Economic Research, College of Business Administration, University of Oregon, Eugene, OR).

Mackenzie, B.W. and M.L. Bilodeau, 1979, Effects of taxation on base metal mining in Canada (Centre for Resource Studies, Queen's University, Kingston).

Maloney, D.G. and P.H. Pearse, 1979, Quantitative rights as an instrument for regulating commercial fisheries, Journal of the Fisheries Research Board of Canada 36, 859–866.

Mead, W.J., 1976, Log sales versus timber sales policy, in: W. McKillop and W.J. Mead, eds., Timber policy issues in British Columbia (University of British Columbia Press, Vancouver) 94–100.

Mikesell, R.F., 1980, Mining agreement and conflict resolutions, in: S. Sideri and S. Johns, eds., Mining for development in the third world (Pergamon, New York).

Millsap, S.W., R.M. Spann and E.W. Erickson, 1974, Tax incentives in the US petroleum industry, in: E.W. Erickson and L. Waverman, eds., The energy question: An international failure of policy, Vol. 2 (University of Toronto Press, Toronto) 99–122.

Mitchell, J., 1982, Taxation of oil and gas revenues: The United Kingdom, The Energy Journal 3, 39–50.

Pearse, P.H., 1976, Timber rights and forest policy in British Columbia (Victoria).

Scott, A.D., 1979, Development of economic theory on fisheries regulation, Journal of the Fisheries Research Board of Canada 36, 725–741.

Scott, A.D. and H. Campbell, 1979, Policies towards proposals for large-scale natural resource projects: Attenuation versus postponement, Resources Policy 5, 113–140.

Smith, V.L., 1963, Tax depreciation policy and investment theory, International Economic Review 4, 80.

Stauffer, T.R., 1982, Taxation of oil and gas revenues: Norway, The Energy Journal 3, 51–54.

Svendsrud, A., 1969, Some features of Norwegian forest policy, in: A. Svendsrud, ed., Readings in forest economics (Universitetsforlaget, Oslo) 225–231.

Verleger, P.K., 1982, Taxation of oil and gas revenues: The United States, The Energy Journal 3, 32–38.

von Malmborg, G., 1969, Aims and means in Swedish forest policy, in: A. Svendsrud, ed., Readings in forest economics (Universitetsforlaget, Oslo) 201–213.

INDEX